THE
CHURCHILL
DOCUMENTS

THE CHURCHILL DOCUMENTS

RANDOLPH S. CHURCHILL

VOLUME 5
AT THE ADMIRALTY
1911–1914

Hillsdale College Press, Hillsdale, Michigan

Hillsdale College Press
33 East College Street
Hillsdale, Michigan 49242
www.hillsdale.edu

Originally published in 1969 by William Heinemann Ltd. in Great Britain
and by Houghton Mifflin in the United States.

Printed in the United States of America

Printed and bound by Edwards Brothers, Ann Arbor, Michigan

Cover design by Hesseltine & DeMason, Ann Arbor, Michigan

THE CHURCHILL DOCUMENTS
Volume 5: *At the Admiralty, 1911–1914*

Library of Congress Control Number: 2007902660

ISBN: 978-0-916308-15-5

First printing 2007

Contents

Note
to the New Edition

Winston Churchill's personal papers are among the most comprehensive ever assembled relating to the life and times of one man. They are so extensive that it was only possible to include in the narrative volumes of his biography a part of the relevant documents.

The Companion Volumes, now titled *The Churchill Documents*, were planned to run parallel with the narrative volumes, and with them to form a whole. When an extract or quotation appears in a narrative volume, the complete document appears in an accompanying volume of *The Churchill Documents*. Where space prevented the inclusion of a contemporary letter in the narrative volume, it is included in the document volume.

Here in these three volumes of *The Churchill Documents*—Volume 3: *Early Years in Politics, 1901–1907,* Volume 4: *Minister of the Crown, 1907–1911,* and Volume 5: *At the Admiralty, 1911–1914*— are set out all the documents relevant to *Winston S. Churchill*, Volume II: *Young Statesman, 1901–1914*. Mention in these texts of "Main Volume" refers to this second volume of the biography.

The chapter and page numbers for volumes 3, 4 and 5 of *The Churchill Documents* run consecutively through the volumes. The index to all three volumes appears in Volume 5.

18

Home Rule

(See Main Volume II, Chapter 12)

Stephen Gwynn[1] to WSC

29 July 1910

Irish Press Agency
2 Great Smith Street

Dear Mr Churchill,

Mr Redmond tells me you want to see books on Ireland. I send what we have here. Dubois is excellent.[2]

I believe Locker Lampson's[3] recent volume[4] is valuable, especially as from a Unionist.

You shd. certainly read Miss Murray's work on the Commercial and Financial Relations.[5] Also Mrs Green's two books *The Making of Ireland* and *Irish Nationality*.[6]

Lecky[7] doesn't need mention. I believe *Two Centuries of Irish History* is very useful for your purpose. I have marked a few on the accompanying list.

I have done a text book myself which will be out in a few days and will send you a copy as soon as I get one. But it is *ad populum*. I daresay Bryce's[8]

---

[1] Stephen Lucius Gwynn (1864–1950), Nationalist MP Galway City 1906–18; sometime Editor of Irish Press Agency; author of many books on Ireland; essayist, poet, biographer.
[2] *Contemporary Ireland*, by L. Paul-Dubois.
[3] Godfrey Lampson Tennyson Locker-Lampson (1875–1946), Unionist MP Salisbury 1910–18, Wood Green 1918–35; Under-Secretary of State Home Office 1923–4, for Foreign Affairs 1925–9; PC 1928.
[4] *A Consideration of the State of Ireland in the Nineteenth Century*, published in 1907.
[5] *Commercial Relations between England and Ireland* by A. E. Murray.
[6] Alice Sophia Amelia Green (d. 1929), authoress of many books on Ireland. *The Making of Ireland and Its Undoing* was published in 1908; *Irish Nationality* in 1911.
[7] William Edward Hartpole Lecky (1838–1903), Unionist MP for Dublin University 1896–1903; author of *Leaders of Public Opinion in Ireland*, and of the *History of England in the Eighteenth Century*.
[8] *Two Centuries of Irish History – 1691–1870* (2 vols). Introduction by James Bryce.

Two Centuries – which is by several very capable hands – will be the best for your purpose – that and Dubois.

Yours very truly
STEPHEN GWYNN

John Redmond to WSC
(*CSC Papers*)

15 February 1911

Private

My dear Mr Churchill,

I deeply regret my absence from the House during your speech & indeed I feel I owe you an apology. I was called away on a private affair & when I got back you had finished. I did not think you would speak so soon.

I have heard what you said and I feel most grateful. All of us count on *you* to put Home Rule through.

Very truly yrs
J. REDMOND

Viscount Morley to WSC
(*CSC Papers*)

16 February 1911   Flowermead
                                                     Wimbledon Park

My dear Winston,

Your speech has evidently made the impression that I earnestly hoped and confidently expected. It reads admirably, and its breadth and elevation make a magnificent opening for a grand, though a hazardous policy. Sincerely, and not conventionally, do I congratulate you.

Yrs
M

All grand policy has its hazards.

Cabinet Paper by WSC

24 February 1911

Confidential

It seems to me absolutely impossible that an English Parliament, and still more an English Executive, could exist side by side with an Imperial

Parliament and an Imperial Executive, whether based on separate or identical election. Imperial affairs could not in practice be separated from English party politics, which consist principally of domestic questions. The persons who are prominent in British party politics will be so mainly because of their following in England on internal questions; and it is not conceivable that such persons, having acquired mastery in the decisive field of home politics, would be willing, or would be able, to surrender the control of foreign, colonial, military, and naval affairs to another class of Ministers or politicians. The external sphere touches the internal at almost every point. The fortunes of the country abroad and at home are interdependent and indissoluble. Persons are trusted by the nation to manage the external affairs of the country because of the confidence and support accorded to their political action on great social, economic, and political issues at home; and the principles which are affirmed by the nation in domestic politics have always governed, and will always govern, the character and conduct of external affairs. No separation of the issues is possible in practice, and none is desirable. The strong positions of a British Foreign Minister, Chancellor of the Exchequer, or Ministers of Defence are based upon the support of vast organised party followings which come together for all purposes, but primarily for domestic purposes, and would be incompetent for action in either sphere alone.

These considerations appear to apply in varying degrees of unanswerable force in all the three possible contingencies of party distribution in the Imperial and English Parliaments: –

1. A Liberal majority, both in the Imperial and in the English Parliament (which is the least probable combination), would make it certain that the Leader of the English Parliament would have to be Prime Minister of the Imperial Parliament, and conversely. The same considerations would apply, with slightly lessened force, to his principal colleagues associated with him in the confidence of the party. We thus reach, on this hypothesis, the close Cabinet system of the present day united for all internal and external purposes.

2. A Conservative majority in the Imperial Parliament with a Liberal majority in the English Parliament: This would produce an immediate and violent collision between two organised bodies of almost equal strength. The Liberal majority in the English Parliament would never cease from its efforts to overthrow the Conservative Imperial administration, whose policy of armaments and foreign and colonial affairs would be the prime subject of their displeasure. There can be no doubt that this divergence would tear the State in half.

3. (The most probable contingency.) A Liberal majority in the Imperial

Parliament and a Conservative majority in the English Parliament: In this case the leader of the Liberal Opposition in the English Parliament will be the most powerful politician in the country. Though holding no office because his party is in a minority in the English Parliament, he will, nevers-less, be master of the whole party organisation upon which the Liberal Imperial Ministry itself will rest. Day after day he would be engaged in fighting the battle of democracy against heavy odds in the English Parlia-ment on all the great questions which now divide the country. Is it conceiv-able that these duties could be undertaken by any man except the Prime Minister of the Imperial Parliament or that he should be supported in these duties by any other persons than his principal colleagues in the party organis-ation? This, however, would be no solution of the difficulty; for the position of the Liberal Imperial Prime Minister in full control of one enormous sphere of action, and absolutely powerless in the other and more exciting sphere, could not be reconciled with any conception of reason or good government.

For these reasons, among others, I conclude that it is impossible for an English Parliament and an Imperial Parliament to exist together at the same time.

WSC

Cabinet Paper by WSC

1 March 1911

Confidential

I put the following outline forward as a basis for discussion: –

1. The Imperial Parliament to remain unaltered, except by a strict numerical redistribution between countries.

2. The United Kingdom to be divided into ten areas, having regard to geographical, racial, and historical considerations.

3. A legislative and administrative body, separately elected, to be created for each area.

4. In Ireland, Scotland, and Wales these bodies to be clothed with Parlia-mentary form so far as may be desirable in each case.

5. Women to vote and serve on all these bodies [except in Ireland, where the National Parliament will decide].

6. These bodies to assume –

(a) All the powers now exercised by County Councils;

(*b*) Certain powers now exercised by municipal bodies;

(*c*) Certain powers to be devolved upon them by the Imperial Parliament, including –

  (1.) Education.
  (2.) Licensing.
  (3.) Land.

   (All provision for compensation shall be on principles to be laid down by Imperial Parliament, and officials settling amount of compensation in individual cases shall be appointed and removed by Imperial authority.)

  (4.) Housing.
  (5.) Police.
  (6.) All local Judges and Magistrates.

   (After an interval of, say, five years, during which period all Judges shall be appointed as at present. These Judges to be removable on address by either local or Imperial Parliament.)

  (7.) Poor Law.
  (8.) Agriculture:
   Technical instruction.
   Experimental farms.
   Credit banks.
   Co-operation.
   Afforestation.
  (9.) Fisheries.
  (10.) Private Bill legislation.
  (11.) Roads.
  (12.) Boundary questions between counties, towns, and urban and rural areas.

(*d*) Such further powers as Parliament shall from time to time devolve on any or all of them.

7. The Imperial Parliament to retain all powers not specifically devolved.

8. The policy to be put forward in two separate Bills simultaneously announced but independently justified, one to deal with Ireland and the other with Great Britain. As the Bill dealing with Great Britain must involve a complete recasting of the methods of local taxation, the Irish Bill to be proceeded with in the first year, and the Bill affecting the larger island in the second year.

WSC

Lord Knollys to WSC

9 August 1911   Sandringham

My dear Churchill,

In *The Times* report of your speech in the House of Commons yesterday, you said that 'HM was fully acquainted in November with the true facts of the political situation and of all the matters at issue between the various parties in the State, among which Home Rule was unquestionably one of the most important.'

Now people will imply from these words that the Home Rule question formed part of the conversation which took place between the King and the PM and Lord Crewe. This however would be an entirely erroneous impression, as no reference to Home Rule was made either by HM to the PM and Lord Crewe, or by them to the King. But your words will lead people to suppose that his consent to the creation of Peers under hypothetical circumstances was given, not only for the purpose of enabling the Parliament Bill to be passed, but likewise for the Home Rule Bill.

In a great political crisis like that which is now going on, the King stands in a very helpless and peculiar position, as he is unable to defend himself; and the point in question is he thinks so important a one for him, that he would be glad if you would take steps to explain that nothing relating to Home Rule passed at the audience on 16th of November.

I return to London tomorrow morning,

Yours sincerely
KNOLLYS

Master of Elibank to WSC

11 December 1911   12 Downing Street

My dear Churchill,

It is really most kind of Mr Caird[1] to offer to assist the cause of Home Rule, and I need hardly say that the Organisation which you and I created,[2] and of which you are the Chairman, can turn this generous assistance to the most effective use. You might perhaps inform him that we have engaged the services of Mr Wallace Carter, who has done such admirable work for the Free Trade Union and who, under your guidance, turned to the best advantage Mr Caird's generous contributions to the Free Trade cause.

[1] James Caird (1864–1954), Scottish banker and shipowner whose wife, Henrietta, daughter of William Stephens, came from County Down; created Baronet 1928.
[2] The Home Rule Council, of which Elibank and WSC were each at times Chairman.

Will you be good enough to explain to Mr Caird that you and I have decided to keep full control over the activities of the Home Rule Council, because there are many unauthorised programmes on this subject, and it is essential that the government's plan should be adequately supported. Our decision entails, of course, a very heavy expenditure, and I would propose to ear-mark Mr Caird's gift solely for the purposes of this Home Rule campaign, which is to be conducted on an increasingly extended scale.

It would be of interest I think to Mr Caird if he were to read the accompanying letter which has been issued to the Party officials in the country giving particulars of our scheme of work for January to June 1912. It is, of course, obvious that, with Mr Caird's assistance, we shall be able very considerably to widen our scope of operations.

I would be glad if Mr Caird would send his contribution either to you or myself, and we will dole out grants as they are wanted. This enables us to keep a very close control over the expenditure and ensures economical working.

Please say to Mr Caird how much I appreciate his generous cooperation in the difficult campaign that is ahead of us.

Yours
ALEXANDER MURRAY

WSC to John Redmond

13 January 1912   Admiralty

Copy

I have been reflecting a good deal upon the meeting which has been arranged for us to address in Belfast on February 8th. As you well know it would be very agreeable to me to stand on the same platform in support of Home Rule with you and Mr Devlin wherever that combination may be found helpful to the cause in which we are engaged. It is a combination which I should welcome at Manchester, and to which I look forward at the Eighty Club when I preside at the dinner to be given to you on the 1st March. But I am extremely doubtful whether our joint appearance at Belfast will really conduce to the public advantage. The arrangements have been made without my being consulted, otherwise I should have expressed my view at an earlier date. What we want in Belfast are not demonstrations but discussions. Nothing will be of greater advantage to the violent Orange faction than a pretext, however unsubstantial, for creating a row, and they are no doubt on the look-out for all such pretexts. It is our duty, on the other hand, to make it clear to the British electorate who are the real audience, that we are reasonably forbearing and considerate, that we defer even to unjustifiable demands, that we are patient and conciliatory to the utmost limit which reasonable men can contemplate, and that they are seeking occasions for quarrel, and are unwilling even to embark on a fair and free discussion of the great question. It is no use my coming to Ireland to appeal to the Nationalists. They are already the partisans of the Home Rule cause. But there may be great use in a Minister endeavouring to reassure any genuine apprehensions or anxieties which the Protestants of Ulster feel. No doubt there is very little that words can do; but it will be a great gain even to give the appearance that a fair and reasonable discussion of the subject has begun in Ulster. I think I could do this better alone at this moment. Of course, so far as the meeting is concerned, the Nationalist Party must play the principal part in organising, sustaining and carrying it off. The Ulster Liberal Association, though of the greatest value as a figurehead, would never have the strength to stand by itself. The distribution of the tickets must be so arranged as to secure a thoroughly friendly and enthusiastic meeting, supported by favourable crowds outside while at the same time including every possible element in the Hall not absolutely irreconcilable. This should not be beyond the resources of civilisation. I would therefore advise that we should make a great virtue of meeting the objections to our joint meeting by your standing out as an act of consideration to Orange feeling, and by my going forward alone. Now that they have taken up this ground the fact that we defer to their claim, unreasonable though it be, will put those who wish to seek occasions for disturbance in a position of the greatest embarrassment, may produce effects which will be positively beneficial in Belfast, and will certainly have good results on English public opinion.

I would therefore suggest that you should write me a letter for publication, saying that you notice that there are complaints about our joint appearance, that you consider those complaints might well be thought to be only another instance of the excessive assertion of ascendancy which the Orange Party put forward, that, nevertheless, at the beginning of this long discussion you are so anxious that every possible consideration shall be shown, even to objections which are unreasonable in themselves, that you wish to defer to the one objection which has been taken, and desire, therefore, to withdraw your promise to support me on the platform. I am sure this is the wise course to take, but please write to me with the greatest frankness upon it. It is essential, however, that whether you come or not the Nationalists should make sure that the meeting is a thorough success.

I trust you are recovering from your accident, of which I heard with much regret, and it is especially unfortunate coming as it does at a time when so many serious tasks are imposed upon you.

Believe me, Yours sincerely
[WINSTON S. CHURCHILL]

WSC to Lord Londonderry

17 January 1912   33 Eccleston Square

Copy

Dear Lord Londonderry,

I read in this morning's papers that you have made yourself responsible for a resolution announcing the intention of the Ulster Unionist Council 'to take steps to prevent' my addressing the meeting in Belfast wh has been arranged for February 8th.[1] This is accompanied in the Conservative Press by various references to disturbance & bloodshed by wh it is suggested that the resolution will be enforced. No one knows better than you that it is perfectly easy for either the Orange or the Nationalist party to create a riot in Belfast in times of political excitement. It would certainly be possible for the Nationalists & Liberals to create a similar situation when Mr Bonar Law addresses his meeting in the city in April. Whatever happens on the occasion of my visit, I can assure you that every effort will be made by me through every channel open to me to make sure that no retaliatory tactics are adopted, & to secure him free speech & a fair hearing. If you & your friends choose at the outset of this great controversy to resort to riot, & to endeavour to prevent peaceable discussion, I shd be quite content in the interests of the Home Rule cause to leave the object lesson to the judgement of Great Britain & of the self-governing Colonies. No cruder assertion could be made of a claim to ascendancy than an open declaration by the Ulster Conservatives that they will not allow their fellow-countrymen from whom they differ the right of public meeting.

No more naked admission of argumentative embarrassment cd be afforded than that a British Minister cannot in the interests of Unionism be allowed to speak to those in Belfast who wish to hear him on the subject of Home Rule.

[1] Lord Londonderry was a member of the Standing Committee of the Ulster Unionist Council. It issued a statement observing 'with astonishment the deliberate challenge thrown down by Mr Winston Churchill, Mr John Redmond, Mr Joseph Devlin and Lord Pirrie in announcing their intention to hold a Home Rule meeting in the centre of the loyal city of Belfast, and resolves to take steps to prevent its being held.'

If the position wh you & your friends have adopted is that you will endeavour by force to deny the right of public meeting, & will prevent discussion if you can, then the responsibility for the consequences must rest with you; & it may be a very direct & personal responsibility. If however it is not against the right of public meeting that you wish to demonstrate, but only against the right of meeting in a particular hall, while I venture to think the country will consider such an objection not very reasonable, it shall if practically possible be met. We do not seek quarrels about trifles. We seek to debate matters serious to us and serious to you, wh will shortly become the subject of prolonged national & parliamentary examination. We have no wish to provoke unnecessary ill feeling. If therefore yr objections about public meeting are special & not general, it is I submit your duty to state them specifically, in order that everything possible may be done to avert disorder.

One thing however cannot be done. The right of public discussion cannot be abandoned; & in all circumstances I intend to keep my engagement with the Ulster Liberal Association.

[WINSTON S. CHURCHILL]

WSC to his wife
(*CSC Papers*)

EXTRACT

23 January 1912   [Admiralty]
11 pm

My Beloved darling,

Tis late, but I come in to this unusual spot to write you a line. The Belfast situation has developed. The Orangemen have obtained the hall the night before & will evidently attempt to hold it over the 8th. The W. Office is preparing 3 Brigades (2 from Ireland & 1 from England) to keep order. I don't like this, & am holding up the orders. I am quite ready to leave the Orange folk stewing in their hall, while we have a 4 miles triumphant procession through the Nationalist quarter & speak in security at the St Mary's.

This is the way that things will I think eventually solve themselves. Ld Pirrie[1] arrived to-day much perturbed. He wd advise the abandonment of

---

[1] William James Pirrie (1847–1924), Comptroller of the Household of the Lord Lieutenant of Ireland 1907–13; Lord Mayor of Belfast 1896–7; Member of Stormont Senate Northern Ireland 1921–4. PC (Great Britain) 1918; created Baron Pirrie of Belfast 1906; Viscount 1921.

the meeting. I told him that *coûte que coûte* I shall begin punctually at 8 o'clock on the 8th. of February to speak on Home Rule in Belfast. We are to have a conference tomorrow – Devlin, Alick (who comes with us) & the local people. I will let you know what happens.

Tell Freddie to come to Belfast.

I am pleased with the general developments.

Always your devoted husband –

WINSTON

WSC to his wife
(*CSC Papers*)

24 January 1912   Admiralty

My Beloved,

The plan on wh I have decided after full consultation is to hold the meeting in the Nationalist quarter & ostentatiously defer to Londonderry's demand. A whole block of old houses will be pulled down & a beautiful tent erected with sounding boards etc to hold 10,000. All the Protestant ticket holders who were coming to the Ulster Hall will be accommodated here, guarded not by troops but by thousands of Nationalists. We shall make a great torch-light procession down the Falls Road 3 miles long surrounded by the Nation-alist army, until we reach the Hall. The police will draw a cordon between the two parts of the city. The Orange faction will be left to brood morosely over their illegal & uncontested possession of the Ulster Hall. Dirty dogs 'chained like suffragettes to the railings'. These are the plans, & Alick wants Freddie to go over to make the arrangements. No expense will be spared.

I am entirely satisfied with the developments.

They are vy doubtful about your coming. But we will see how things shape. Do not be too venturesome hunting. Keep some of your luck unused.

I am hanging up my Paris plans for the moment, till I hear from Cassel. FE – vy unworthy of him.

Love to the babies,

Always your loving & devoted – the vy weary

WINSTON S C

Handwriting as slovenly as yours!! & not nearly as pretty
Many kisses

WSC to Lord Londonderry

25 January 1912   Admiralty

Copy

My Lord,

The very grave and direct personal responsibility which will fall upon you if serious rioting occurs in Belfast on the occasion of my visit, makes me sure that you will not lightly seek to widen the grounds of quarrel. For my part I only care about one thing. It is my duty to keep my promise to the Ulster Liberal Association, and to assert our right of free speech and public meeting. If, as I now gather from the newspapers, the main objections of yourself and your friends are directed against our holding our meeting in the Ulster Hall, then, although such claims are neither just nor reasonable, I will ask the Ulster Liberal Association to accede to your wish. There will thus be no necessity for your friends to endure the hardships of a vigil, or sustain the anxieties of a siege. Neither will it be necessary for you to break the law in an attempt to deprive us forcibly of the use of property to which we are lawfully entitled. It is not a point of any importance to me where I speak in Belfast. On the contrary, I desire to choose whatever hall or place is least likely to cause ill-feeling to the Orange Party.

It has, however, become of importance to the public liberties that the meeting should take place in Belfast on the 8th of February; & I intend to hold it there, in lawful exercise of the elementary rights of citizenship.

Yours faithfully

[WINSTON S. CHURCHILL]

Lord Londonderry to WSC

26 January 1912   Mountstewart
                                                       Co Down

Sir,

I have read in the Press your letter directed to me, but of which I have not yet received any copy.

In the interest of the peace and order of the great city of Belfast I note with satisfaction that you have abandoned the idea of holding a meeting in the Ulster Hall in that city.

I only regret that before you had announced your intention of holding such a meeting you did not consider how inevitable it was that such an intention could only intensify the feelings of bitter resentment and hostility to Home Rule which existed amongst the loyal citizens of our City.

By selecting the Ulster Hall with its historic traditions and the memories connected with your late Father's visit in 1886, and the advice he then gave to the people of Ulster, I have no doubt you intended directly to challenge the genuineness of the oft-expressed determination of those who have made up their minds never under any circumstances to allow themselves to be degraded from their present position under the Imperial Parliament; and so far as you could by a choice of the locality to falsely represent that those who are unalterably opposed to you were adherents of the policy you come to advocate.

Against such an attempt which was only the culmination of many acts of insult and arrogance towards the loyalists of Ulster, the Ulster Unionist Council felt bound in the most emphatic manner to protest with a full knowledge that peace and order could not be preserved if a meeting under such circumstances took place.

So far as the Council is concerned its main objection in the interests of law and order are removed, if you determine to hold your meeting outside the districts which passionately resent your action, and if you do so it certainly would be no party to and would strongly deprecate any attempt to interfere with your meeting.

At the same time having regard to the intense state of feeling that has been created by your proposed action, the Ulster Unionist Council cannot accept any responsibility with reference to your visit to Belfast and they do not desire to give any assurances that they might be unable to fulfil. With reference to the place where you propose to hold your meeting it is not for the Ulster Unionist Council to make any suggestion. As a Member of the Government you have access to all the information in the possession of the Executive Authorities in Belfast who, no doubt, thoroughly understand the situation and have already given you full particulars.

I only desire to add that as regards your references to the necessity of upholding 'the elementary rights of citizenship', (by which no doubt you mean the right of free speech) which appear almost cynical having regard to the action of your Government in repressing it in the House of Commons, I believe the citizens of Belfast and of the Province of Ulster are as jealous supporters of that principle as any of the inhabitants of the United Kingdom, and I repudiate the suggestion that their opposition to your provocative action was prompted by any desire to interfere with that precious heritage.

Yours faithfully
LONDONDERRY

WSC to Lord Londonderry

27 January 1912   Admiralty

My Lord,

You are wrong to think that the Ulster Hall was 'selected' by me as a 'challenge' to you or your friends. Beyond consenting, in fulfilment of an old promise, to make a speech for the Ulster Liberal Association before the meeting of Parliament, I had nothing to do with the local arrangements. I am told, and you no doubt are aware of it, that the Ulster Hall was only 'selected' by the Liberal party in Belfast, after other alternatives had fallen through, because it happened to be free on the date in question. You know quite well that it is a Hall by Act of Parliament open to all parties, and that many Home Rule meetings of importance – one of them as lately as last month – have been freely held there. It is therefore the Ulster Unionist Council who seek to fasten a quarrel, and search for grounds of offence where none are intended.

For my part I can truly say that I had no other idea or intention than to discuss in public, according to the long established custom of British politics, matters which are serious to us, and which we freely recognise are serious to you. The rightful interests of the Protestants of Ireland must be the deep concern of every British Government. They will be respected by all who faithfully strive to reconcile Ireland to the British Empire, and to see an end to hatreds which disturb the foundations of the State.

As to public order, I have invited no assurance from you. I rely upon the law of the land and upon the sense of justice of the citizens of Belfast. Unless a riot is covertly or openly organised and strangers are brought in for that purpose, I am confident that nothing will happen unworthy of the prosperity and honour of the city.

One word more. Your letter forces me to refer to a personal matter. Your Lordship has a claim, to which I bow, to remind me of the memory of Lord Randolph Churchill. You were his friend through evil as well as good days. The Unionist party, who within a few months of the very speech which is now on their lips pursued him with harsh ingratitude, have no such right.

Yours faithfully
WINSTON S. CHURCHILL

Augustine Birrell to WSC

28 January 1912   Chief Secretary's Office
                                                   Dublin Castle

Confidential

My dear Churchill,

I have now had the opportunity of going into the whole case about the Belfast Meeting with the Authorities here – civil and military – upon whom a great burden has been thrown – and I will cast my observations in a series of propositions which I hope you will place before the Master of Elibank.

First. As the Minister responsible to the Cabinet for Irish Affairs I think I ought to have been *consulted* before any arrangements whatever were made with either Devlin or the Ulster Liberals for the Meeting in Belfast. My advisers here and the Police Authorities in Belfast, if consulted, could and would have prevented all this agitation and trouble. I know you had really nothing whatever to do with the business – beyond loyally consenting to do whatever was demanded of you – however disagreeable.

Second. Upon being informed that the Meeting was to take place and in the *Ulster Hall* the Authorities here – civil and military – set to work to consider and prepare plans to maintain peace and repress disorder – and they are satisfied that if the Ulster Hall was on the evening of the 8th February *unoccupied* and *available,* they could have accomplished these ends. The idea that the Protestants of Belfast, however excited, would *begin* by fighting the soldiers is absurd. In Belfast *two Mobs* are necessary – a Catholic Mob and a Protestant Mob; it is they who fight, and it is the military who seek to prevent them murdering each other. In this case there would have been no Catholic Mob and consequently, though the excitement would have been *intense* and the risk of course not to be disregarded altogether, still peace could probably have been maintained. On the other hand, it is quite possible and even probable that, by trickery, the Ulster Hall would *beforehand* have been filled with Protestants, and in that case the Meeting could never have been held at all.

Third. The Ulster Hall being given up and (as I understand from Lord Pirrie) the *St Mary's Hall* being repugnant to the fine susceptibilities of the Ulster Liberals – it is (I am told) now suggested that no *evening Meeting* should be held, and that you should make your speech *somewhere* in the middle of the day. This abandonment of an evening Meeting is a proof how lightly and how inconsiderately the whole matter has been treated. I have no doubt there is much less chance of disorder in the middle of the day than at night, and personally I approve of the suggestion.

Fourth. The Belfast Police report to me this morning that the excitement is still *intense*, having been judiciously worked up, and that it would be rash to assume that the altered plans will greatly reduce it, and that consequently it is of much importance that I should be informed *as soon as possible* what is going to happen – *ie when* and *where* is the Meeting to be held? If in a building, in what building? If in a tent – where the tent is to be pitched? In Belfast all depends upon *locality* and the character of the surrounding streets.

Fifth. Both sides are in a *funk*. Lord Londonderry has been greatly perturbed. The Nationalists alone look on *amused:* they don't care much what happens.

Sixth. My own belief is that if you hold a mid-day Meeting in a tent, *no* blood will be shed. But the *moral* is (for the Master's consumption): Leave Ireland alone in future.

As to crowds coming in from outside – I am having this carefully looked after. Nothing so far has been done. If anything is done on a scale sufficiently large to create danger, I will consider what can be done to prevent it. It now all depends on what the final arrangements for the Meeting may prove to be & as to this I hope I may be fully advised without any delay.

Yours always
A. BIRRELL

Augustine Birrell to WSC

30 January 1912   Chief Secretary's Office
                                                      Dublin Castle

My dear Churchill,

I am coming over on Thursday and hope to see you on that night – I think we can manage to *hide* a good many of the soldiers from public view, and be content with a small *display* of Redcoats. The *interest* taken in the proceedings is *enormous* but I think it is *beginning* to wear a more peaceful aspect.

I have your telegram and will do my best.

Yrs in haste
A.B.

Master of Elibank to WSC

31 January 1912   Stafford Hotel
                                                   St James's Place

My dear Winston,

I am going to make a suggestion which I feel will be vy disagreeable to Mrs Churchill and yourself, but you and I are always vy frank with each other.

I think that the statement in today's press from the Belfast end – I have purposely kept it out of the papers here – that Mrs Churchill is to accompany you to Ireland, will have a bad effect, and I earnestly ask you to issue a contradiction today. It will be at once said by the enemy that we are all attempting to lessen *our* difficulties by her presence.

Her great courage and *spirit* naturally impel her to accompany you – but I assure you it is a mistake.

The police report that great quantities of bolts & rivets have been abstracted from the yards, and many revolvers have been taken out of pawn. My own feeling is that there will be no serious riot, but that isolated disturbance may take place is probable.

In any case I implore you not to bring Mrs Churchill with you: her presence might be a source of great embarrassment, and moreover you cannot satisfy yourself that she does not run considerable risk.

Forgive me for writing thus freely – but I know you well enough to do so.

And Mrs Churchill must also forgive me for interfering with a very natural impulse and in accordance with what all would expect of her.

A denial of the *rumour really* should be issued today.

Yrs always
ALICK

WSC spoke in Belfast on 8 February 1912 at a meeting organised by the Ulster Liberal Association. His remarks were printed by the Liberal Publication Department under the title *Irish Home Rule*.

Sir Bindon Blood to WSC

EXTRACT

9 February 1912   2 Queen Anne's Gate

My dear Churchill,

I congratulate you on your success at Belfast. I have heard quite a number of Unionist people praising your speech, and everyone is very glad that there was no row. . . .

Herbert Samuel to WSC

13 February 1912   Office of Post Master General

Dear Churchill,

Perhaps you may care to see the accompanying extract from an official Minute relating to the reporting by telephone of your speech at Belfast. It is the first instance in which newspapers at a distance have reported verbatim an important speech by telephone.

Yours sincerely
HERBERT SAMUEL

Report of transmission of WSC's Speech at Belfast

9 February 1912

Copy

The Postmaster General,

I submit an interesting report by Major O'Meara[1] on the arrangements made to transmit by telephone an account of the speech of Mr Winston Churchill at Belfast to a number of Northern newspapers. Owing to the interposition of the Submarine Cable between Stranraer and Larne, it would not have been possible to extend the service to London.

The arrangement arose from the discovery by Mr Lee,[2] one of the Telegraph Traffic Managers, that the *Liverpool Daily Post* proposed to get its report from Belfast by telephone. There are only two telephone circuits between Great Britain and Ireland; and it was evident that if rival newspapers endeavoured to monopolise the circuits for their reports, they would probably not only defeat each other's ends but would entirely prevent the use of the route by the ordinary public. The suggestion was therefore thrown out that a number of the most important Northern newspapers should combine to get a joint report; and the manager of the *Liverpool Post* quickly persuaded the *Manchester Guardian* and the *Yorkshire Post* to come into the arrangement, the Syndicate thus consisting of one Conservative and two Liberal papers. The scheme was that the main trunk telephone circuit between Belfast and Leeds should be used and that lines should be made up to the Leeds Trunk Exchange from the *Yorkshire Post* Office at Leeds and by use of other trunk lines from the newspaper offices at Liverpool and Manchester. Subsequently it was decided to endeavour to obtain the transmission of the actual words spoken by Mr Churchill by means of Electrophone apparatus; but provision was made, should the Electrophone fail, for a

[1] Walter Alfred John O'Meara (1863–1939), Engineer-in-Chief GPO 1907–12; served in the Royal Engineers and was Press Censor, Director of Telegraphs and Chief Officer at Kimberley during the siege; served on the General Staff 1915–18.

[2] John Lee (1867–1929), at this time the junior Post Office Telegraph and Telephone Traffic Manager; controller of the Central Telegraph Office 1919–27.

succession of reporters following at three minutes' intervals to dictate the speech from a Call Office just outside the tent where the Belfast meeting was held.

As one of the two telephone circuits between Great Britain and Ireland would thus be taken for newspaper purposes, the whole of the other traffic between the two countries would have had to be carried over a single line, had it not been for a further suggestion of the Engineers to superpose an additional circuit on the two metallic circuits in the cable, thus giving three circuits in all between the two countries, two of which would be available for the ordinary demands of the public.

The Electrophone Company of London willingly fell in with the suggested arrangement and provided the apparatus to transmit the speech from the platform at Belfast and to receive it in the newspaper offices.

The arrangements made by the Engineering Staff were very carefully thought out and supervised: and the fact that the whole programme was not realised appears to have been due chiefly to the unfortunate weather conditions, which were extremely unfavourable for telephonic transmission. The reporters in the newspaper offices at Liverpool, Manchester and Leeds heard distinctly the preliminary proceedings at Belfast and Lord Pirrie's speech. Mr Winston Churchill's voice was however pitched considerably lower, and it probably did not travel so well because he read from a manuscript. He was, moreover, subject to some interruption, and his voice thus failed to reach the reporters at the most distant point, namely, the Liverpool Office. It was therefore decided to abandon the idea of receiving the speech by Electrophone and fall back upon the alternative arrangement of having it transmitted by a series of reporters. The transmission under these conditions was exceedingly good, and the whole speech was taken down in the offices of the newspapers in question ten minutes after Mr Winston Churchill had sat down and considerably before the telegraphic reports of the speech arrived. It is understood that the newspapers were very well pleased; and I annex an article from the *Liverpool Post* commending the enterprise of the Post Office in Telephone matters.

J. L. Garvin to WSC

11 June 1912   *The Pall Mall Gazette*

Private

My dear Churchill,

I am astonished to learn this morning that the Home Rule Council of which you are president profess to issue a pamphlet, not only repeating all the grotesque misrepresentations with regard to my supposed attitude on Home Rule 'and dynamite' when I was 23, but endeavouring to connect all that with the 'Tory plot at the Veto Conference!' If you approved that, any honourable man would hold me free from all further obligation of secrecy in regard to the Conference negotiations. I can't think you do approve it, and hitherto I have been very silent as you know under attacks to which no other person in connection with the Conference has been exposed. Would you care to see me anywhere for ten minutes conversation on the whole subject?

Yours very truly
J. L. Garvin

PS As the Master of Elibank is the Chairman of the Home Rule Council I am writing to him on the same terms.

WSC to J. L. Garvin

10 August 1912 [Admiralty]

EXTRACT

Seriously, I am shocked at these threats of Ulster violence which are made by Conservative leaders. Do they think they will never come back to power? Have they no policy for Ireland except to make it ungovernable? They are the more inexcusable because no one that I know of has ever contemplated the application of force to Ulster. The principle and doctrine lately enunciated would dissolve the framework not only of the British Empire, but of civil society.

WSC to Lord Ashby St Ledgers

26 June 1912 Admiralty

Confidential

My dear Ivor,

You would in my opinion be unwise to accept any employment in Australia or New Zealand. You are not suited for it & wd not enjoy it. Bombay wd be a different matter.

You shd accept *with alacrity* the Nationalist invitation to go to Dublin, wh appears to me from every point of view a most useful & valuable idea. Make the best speech you can there and make *them* feel you are their friend.

I do not govern the course of these events but am most anxious you shd make no mistakes.

Yours affectly
WINSTON S. CHURCHILL

WSC to Sir George Ritchie[1]

14 August 1912

My dear Sir George Ritchie,

I did not expect to address you again so soon, but there are certain statements in a letter which the Leader of the Opposition has communicated to the newspapers, which deserve precise attention.

Mr Bonar Law now says: 'I do not anticipate civil war. . . . There would have been a real danger of civil war if the Government had been allowed to move blindly towards the precipice without a clear warning of the dangers in front of them.' The incitement to violence and the threats that armed force will be used, which have been so stridently reiterated by the Leader of the Opposition and his principal lieutenant, Sir Edward Carson, during the present year, are apparently now to be represented merely as solemn warnings which are not to be translated into action. This bears a strong resemblance to what is commonly called 'bluff'; and no doubt there is a good deal of bluff in these proceedings. If a man is firmly persuaded that a certain thing is not going to happen, it becomes rather a cheap business for him to utter bloodcurdling menaces of what he will do if it does happen; we pass into the region of hypothetical hyperbole – and there are shorter and less ceremonious expressions for that.

I am sorry that we cannot accept Mr Bonar Law's reassurances; although I fully admit that he has not intended – and does not intend – the extreme consequence of his words and actions, the position both local and general is far more serious than his present explanations imply; and his part in it and responsibility for it are in no way covered by what he now says. His colleague, Sir Edward Carson, is the moving spirit in an organization which has openly avowed its intention to set up a provisional Government, *ie*, a Government against the Crown and Parliament of these realms. There has been a large importation of arms into the Orange counties of Ulster: there is widespread drilling and training in the use of lethal weapons. Whatever Sir Edward Carson's merits as a military commander may be, no one is a better judge than he of how near you may actually go to the edge of a criminal conspiracy without actually crossing the frontiers which are guarded by the law. And for all that Sir Edward Carson may urge or organize under the impulse, as I readily recognize, of his own deep feelings, the Leader of the Conservative Party has, in advance and without limitation or condition, accepted responsibility and promised support: for he said: 'There is no length to which the people of Ulster may go in which I shall not support them.'

[1] George Ritchie (1849–1921), President of the Dundee Liberal Association; knighted 1910.

Surely these are very strange tactics for the leader of a great party: surely they are peculiarly inappropriate tactics for the leader of a Conservative and Constitutional Party: surely they are mad tactics for the leader of a party which hopes and believes that it will soon be called upon to govern the land, and vindicate without fear or favour the majesty of the laws?

The Leader of the Opposition occupies a situation of responsibility in the State second only to that of the Prime Minister. If from his place in Parliament he thought it necessary to utter a solemn warning as to the consequences of the Government pursuing a certain course, but carefully avoided associating himself with any lawless doctrine – still more with any revolutionary movement – no one could complain. He would do it to-morrow on the Navy or on foreign policy with the utmost care and circumspection, weighing every word. But these speeches which he and Sir Edward Carson have been making at large gatherings in the country, have not been warnings to the Government, but incitements to the Orangemen, and as the detestable incidents which have lately taken place in Belfast prove, they have been only too well interpreted by those to whom they were addressed. If warning at all he sought to give, was it necessary to give this brazen countenance to lawless doctrines? Was it necessary for the sake of warning the Government, to express approbation of the organized drilling and arming of a province intent to set up a provisional Government? Mr Bonar Law and those who have joined with him cannot escape from the responsibilities they have assumed, and from the censures which they have incurred by pretending that they meant no more than to warn the Government by telling us they have approved violence in order to prevent it, and that the only way to avert civil war was to organize it.

The extravagance and recklessness of his speech and conduct, and their disproportion to circumstances, their precipitancy, are all deeply antagonistic to the instincts of the Party which he leads. Had British statesmen and the Leaders of great Parties in the past allowed their thoughts so lightly to turn to projects of bloodshed within the bosom of the country, we should have shared the follies and the fate of Poland. What is this miserable quibble on which the Conservative Leader seeks to justify doctrines of rebellion? That Home Rule was not mentioned in the election addresses of certain Ministers; that the preamble to the Parliament Bill has not yet been carried into effect. Can such a slender fabric really span the gulf between constitutional action and civil war? Are they really grounds – put them at the highest rating of partisanship – which make killing no murder?

[WINSTON S. CHURCHILL]

WSC to David Lloyd George

EXTRACT

21 August 1912   HMS *Enchantress*

Copy

My dear David,

The time has come when action about Ulster must be settled. We ought to give any Irish county the option of remaining at Westminster for a period of 5 or 10 yrs, or some variant of this. This ought to be settled one way or the other with the Irish before Parlt meets, & announced at the vy beginning of the session, prior to or simultaneous with the guillotine motion. Time has in no way weakened the force of the arguments you used in January, & I am prepared to support you in pressing them. . . .

WSC to Sir George Ritchie

8 September 1912

Copy

I am very much obliged to you for your letter and look forward to hearing from you again more at length. The vital thing is to set up before the General Election the Irish Parliament in Dublin. Once set up it can never be cast down. As Pym[1] said 'None have gone about to break up Parliaments but that Parliaments have broken them up'. Anything short of that might easily be brushed away by a Tory administration with a subservient House of Lords.

It is my personal belief that with good management and determination this can be carried through, so long as the case of those three or four counties is met in some way or another. And, once an Irish Parliament is set up, the whole thing must ultimately come right. The economic pressure which the rest of Ireland could gradually bring to bear upon Belfast, and the feeling of confidence which would be created if the Irish Parliament was a dignified and successful body, would, I believe, overcome the misgivings of the Orangemen, or, at any rate, of a majority in the Orange Counties, in the course of a few years.

Of course it is possible and even probable that if this offer were made to them in all frankness and sincerity it would be refused. Even if that were the case I do not think that it is an argument against making the offer. The

[1] John Pym (1584–1643), Parliamentary firebrand in the opening stages of the English Civil War.

Orangemen would then be in a position to say that so long as any minority, however small, in any district of Ireland was opposed to Home Rule the measure could not be passed and that they would resist its passage by force. There are a good many misgivings felt at their proceedings in all but the most violent sections of the Tory Party, and I am distinctly of opinion that their refusal of such an offer would tend very greatly to isolate them and show very clearly to the English electorate what a 'dog in the manger' policy they were pursuing.

I would also, if I had my way, at an early stage in the proceedings take power to delay the operation of the Act in regard to certain counties where it was clear that the majority were opposed to it. In this way no excuse or opportunity would be given for any act of violence or organised resistance to the Law, and the Orange Party would be broken up and could be dealt with in detail.

So far their case has not made any impression in the English Constituencies, largely because of the violence of their language and their foolish conduct, and I am of opinion that they have a strong case so far as they themselves are concerned unless it is made clear, as it would be by the refusal of such an offer as I have indicated, that their attitude was purely obstructional and factious.

Again I say that these are my own opinions and that you must not read into them any more than what exactly appears on the surface. I am going to deal with Home Rule at length in my speech on Thursday at Dundee, but I shall only go so far and no farther than when I moved the Second Reading of the Bill.

I am not at all despondent about the political situation, and believe that with determination and good management we shall come through all right.

WSC to J. Bait

14 September 1912

Copy

Dear Sir,

There is not the slightest danger in my opinion of Protestants in Ulster being persecuted for their religion under a system of Home Rule. The danger is entirely the other way, *viz* – that the very strong and aggressive Protestant majority in parts of North East Ulster will maltreat and bully the Catholics in their midst. This has recently occurred on several occasions, and is in my opinion the direct result of the encouragement given to bigotry and lawlessness by the Leaders of the Conservative Party.

Yours faithfully
[WINSTON S. CHURCHILL]

J. L. Garvin to WSC

EXTRACT

24 September 1912

. . . But as for Ireland we are wide, wide apart. I heartily and wholly agree with Bonar Law. No man in his place could have said less and the whole mass of the Unionist party is behind him. Unanimity is not entire, but he has more of it than I have known in the Unionist party during the last ten years on any other question. Moderate, sympathetic, devoid of religious bigotry as my personal feelings towards Ireland are, no person can have a deeper conviction than mine with regard to Mr Redmond's position in Parliament and to the fact that the Parliament Bill in the eyes of Unionists like myself (and above all the Home Rule measure carried under the Parliament Bill by Nationalist votes) cannot possess that moral authority of law by which all citizens render willing obedience. The Ulstermen act spontaneously quite apart from us. What they have done they would have done in any case. We had only to say whether or not, in all the circumstances, we thought their movement was just as inevitable. We had to answer 'Yes'. Everything, in the Irish question is going to become far more difficult: as for federation apart from the present Home Rule Bill being in our view a real barrier to federation, my sense of the difficulties of adjustment increases the more I think. All we can do in these circumstances is to fight the Bill before the Country and to assume, unless or until it is withdrawn or modified, that it is meant to do what it professes to do. But I did not mean to say so much and have perhaps developed at indecent length what must probably seem to you a purely party argument. Never never have the Nationalists since Thomas Davis[1] nearly seventy years ago faced the Ulster question; never never can Ulster be dealt with by force without bringing infinite evil on Ireland & England too. If that principle is ever recognised I shall have renewed hope of the Irish question, but not before I fear. With many thanks and many apologies for the unintended length of this,

Yours sincerely
J. L. GARVIN

[1] Thomas Osborne Davis (1814–45), Irish poet and journalist who was active in Daniel O'Connell's repeal movement.

*   *   *   *   *

H. H. Asquith to WSC

12 September 1913   Hopeman Lodge
                                                     Morayshire

Secret

My dear Winston,

I understand that it is your turn to go to Balmoral next week: so I send a word of friendly warning.

You will find the Royal mind obsessed, and the Royal tongue exceptionally fluid and voluble.

I have just sent there a Memn, in which I have endeavoured, with all plainness and faithfulness, to make clear what are, *and what are not* the functions of a Constitutional Sovereign in regard to legislation.

The important thing is to emphasise the dangers of rejection, when the ship is just reaching port. An ungovernable Ireland is a much more serious prospect than rioting in 4 counties – serious (and, if possible, to be avoided) as the latter is.

As to a round table, I am all for it, provided the confabulations are to proceed upon some definite basis, and not to be mere talking at large.

Yours always
H.H.A.

Lord Stamfordham's Diary
(*Royal Archives*)

EXTRACT

17 September 1913   Balmoral

. . . The King saw Mr Churchill who had previously had a long & pleasant conversation with Mr Bonar Law who is staying here. They had spoken quite frankly & the latter consented to the substance of their conversation being reported to the Prime Minister. Mr Churchill is hopeful of a solution. History teaches us that in such cases British common sense generally triumphs. Up till now he had not been in favour of a conference & thought the right time for it had not arrived & that things must get worse. But he has changed his opinion & now believes that if the Opposition will come into Conference with reasonable proposals, the Govt, which has always been ready to consider any suggestions, would gladly treat with them. He has always admitted

C II—PT. III—B

that Ulster has a case. If Ireland has the right to claim separate government from England, Ulster cannot be refused similar exemption from Government by an Irish Parliament. But he strongly resents that Ulster should talk of 'Civil War' & do everything in her power to stir up rebellion before even the H.R. bill is [debated] let alone before the Irish Parliament is set up, from which rule they look for persecution & tyrannical injustice. Naturally the Opposition wish to turn out the Government.

But it is not 'playing the game' to try & do this by trying to raise a threat of civil war. Personally he would take a very strong line if the Navy or Army hesitated to put down any opposition to the responsible executive – Ireland has been earnestly waiting for the fulfilment of her dream for the past 30 years. Is it likely that she can now stand by & see the cup almost at her lips, dashed to the ground. If by chance the Bill is killed we shall be faced with similar difficulties in S & W Ireland. If only Sir E. Carson does not go too far arrangements will be arrived at. The Irish party will consider any scheme for securing their objects peacefully. Mr Churchill also had conversations with Mr Balfour, satisfactory to both. . . .

H. H. Asquith to WSC

19 September 1913   Hopeman Lodge

Secret

My dear Winston,

I was much interested in your report of your conversation with BL, and I will of course give it very serious consideration.

I always thought (and said) that, in the end, we should probably have to make some sort of bargain about Ulster as the price of Home Rule. But I have never doubted, that, as a matter of tactics and policy, we were right to launch our Bill on its present lines.

For the moment, the following points have to be carefully borne in mind: 1) the recent developments of Carsonism have much stiffened the backs of some moderate men against any seeming concession to bluff and blackmail. 2) Secrecy in these matters is nowadays impossible. What is going on always leaks out – generally in the shape of perverted and misleading gossip. 3) Consultations from which both Redmond and Carson were exluded – I do not mean corporeally, but in the sense of not being taken into counsel – would (apart from other difficulties) be only of provisional value.

I should add that the tactics wh BL threatens, of organised disorder in the H of Commons, and perhaps expulsion or secession, seem to me almost puerile in their crudity. The Tories got nothing but discredit out of their trial row last November, and a repetition of the same sort of thing on a large scale would be repellent to the best elements in their party, and be taken in the country as an admission that the game was up.

There is no folly, however, of which the present Tory leadership is incapable.

Yrs always
H.H.A.

I am keeping Hopwood for a day or two.

F. E. Smith to WSC

5 October 1913   4 Elm Court

Dear W,

I think you will agree that I have played up well. I hope you will do the same now.

Couldn't you ask – what does Sir Ed Carson mean by exclusion? Does he mean that he & his friends will abandon a factious opposition in that part of Ireland when they are in so small a minority? Does he mean that he & his friends will remember that they are Irishmen & apply their ability & influence to make the experiment a success in the South?

But you can do the thing much better than I can suggest. Only do play up. I have run no small risks & incurred considerable censure.

Yours ever
FE

Carson is most reasonable. I think he wd be glad to meet you.

T. P. O'Connor to WSC

7 October 1913   5 Morpeth Mansions

Private & Confidential

My dear Winston,

Carson, as you will see, has announced that he will address a meeting at Dundee on November 7th. I have told Allard, the Liberal agent there, that I am quite willing to address a meeting immediately after this in the course of a tour I am making in Scotland, and I have suggested Thursday, November 13th as the date. This will come, as you will see, within a few days of Carson's performance. I think it is as well to keep in touch with that gentleman, especially in Scotland, where, if in any place, his appeals to religious bigotry might produce some slight results among people not acquainted with the realities.

I am glad to tell you that all the soundings I have taken with regard to the feeling of the Liberal rank and file since my return to London have been most satisfactory. Carson, instead of frightening or weakening, has hardened their feeling.

I have been in touch with my friends in Ireland, and I find that they are irreconcilably hostile to any break-up of Ireland. I believe they would positively prefer a postponement of Home Rule for some years rather than consent to such a mutilation of the country. Indeed, even if they were willing to consent they would not be allowed by Irish public opinion to do so, and any surrender on their part would be followed by their displacement, possibly by William O'Brien as the leader of a revolt against such a policy. This feeling is due not merely to the intense sense of Ireland as a national unit, but also to the fact that we have in Ulster and even in the Four Counties some of the truest and best Nationalists in Ireland. Besides, as you know, the only minority in Ireland that suffers from religious persecution is the Catholic minority in the North.

The impression of our friends in Ireland, too, is that this is not the moment for a Conference. The Tories would lay down impossible terms. Their approaches for a Conference at the present moment are the best indication of the great breakup that 'Carsonism' is producing in their ranks. I find among rational Tories here, outside politics, the most profound disquiet with regard to Carson's performances. Besides, there is little doubt now that he is in a hole even in Ulster itself and that the business men in Belfast are more alarmed by his threats than are the Nationalist minority.

I enclose you a very valuable article written by John Clancy,[1] one of our most level-headed members, which I think will sufficiently reveal all the impossibilities of the Carson programme.

I hope you will give me the pleasure of letting me see you on your return to England. I shall be here all the Winter except when I am absent on the stump.

Yours very sincerely
T. P. O'CONNOR

PS I also enclose Devlin's speech and the leading article of yesterday's *Freeman's Journal.*

---

[1] John Joseph Clancy (1847–1928), Nationalist MP North Dublin 1885–1918.

WSC spoke to his constituents in Dundee on 8 October 1913 on the subject of Home Rule. He predicted that a Federal system of Government would soon be established that would give Wales and Scotland some measure of control over their own affairs. He felt that it would be the forerunner of an Imperial Federation.

James Maiendie[1] to WSC

9 October 1913   Hedingham Castle
                                                              Essex

My dear Winston Churchill,

I expect you have forgotten me entirely but we entered the House of Commons the same year 1900, you for Oldham, I for Portsmouth. You have got to the top practically of anyone's ambitions as a politician, anyhow in my opinion, for I always looked on being First Lord the very greatest of all attainments. Now for my real object in writing; I am a dying man and a useless man to any Party in any case, but may I say this, your speech of last night, October 8th is *quite* the *finest* I have ever read and I am proud to think we are both shoulder to shoulder in the House of Commons.

We have a great mutual friend in Jack Seely and I have always wired him on any success of his. Accept all my congratulations and forgive my bothering you with this effusion.

Yrs sincerely
JAMES H. A. MAJENDIE

Sir Frederick Milner[2] to WSC

12 October 1913   11 Hereford Gardens

My dear Winston Churchill,

I was very sorry to read what you said about the 'King's Prerogative' in your speech at Dundee. I think you were very unjust to your opponents in general & to Sir William Anson & Lord Hugh Cecil in particular.[3] I have

---

[1] James Henry Alexander Majendie (1871–1932), Conservative MP Portsmouth 1900–06.

[2] Frederick George Milner (1849–1931), Conservative MP York 1883–5, Bassetlaw Div, Notts 1890–1906; succeeded brother as 7th Baronet 1850; PE 1900. A close friend of Lord Randolph.

[3] In his speech at Dundee WSC had accused the Opposition of 'an attempt to involve the Crown in controversy and to induce the Sovereign of these realms to take sides with one of the great political organisations within his Dominion and lead him against the largest half of his faithful and loyal subjects . . .'

been a careful student of the speeches made by both sides, and I cannot think anybody can fairly assert, that any of our responsible politicians have urged interference by the King. On the contrary, when the subject has been alluded to, it has been to deprecate the introduction of the King's name into the controversy. It is true that Mr Cane KC[1] wrote a very temperate letter to *The Times,* suggesting that in view of the extreme gravity of the situation, it might be advisable for the King to take the opinion of his people: but *The Times* in its leading article described this as unthinkable. Sir William Anson & Lord Hugh Cecil wrote to *The Times* to point out that Mr Cane's suggestion was impracticable, inasmuch as the King could not act without the advice of his responsible ministers, & this view was endorsed by Professor Dicey;[2] so that you will see that so far from advocating the use of the King's Prerogative, they pointed out the impossibility of the King acting without the advice of his ministers. I am sure you would not wish to be unjust to your opponents, & that you will withdraw the aspersion you put on them.

I think you will agree with me that the less the King's name is introduced into Political speeches on either side the better. His position is difficult enough without making it the sport of Parties.

If Sir William Anson & Professor Dicey are right, the King apparently cannot constitutionally take any steps without the consent of his ministers. It should also be made quite plain that in that case no responsibility can attach to him for the action of his ministers. They & they alone must take full & complete responsibility. If the Government persist in their complete submission to Mr Redmond & force the Bill through as it stands, under the Parliament Act, & if Civil War results, they & they alone must bear all responsibility. Their Blood be on their heads.

I was very glad to see that you realise to the full the gravity of the situation in Ulster. It seems to me mere criminal folly to minimise it, & talk of it as bluff. Right or wrong they are in deadly earnest, & will not submit without a desperate struggle, that may convulse the United Kingdom.

I earnestly trust that you will press your views on your colleagues, and may succeed in persuading them to exclude Ulster from the Bill. It seems to me to be the one and only way to avoid civil war.

I remain, Very truly yrs
FRED MILNER

---

[1] Arthur Beresford Cane (1864–1939); Irish-born barrister.

[2] Albert Venn Dicey (1835–1922). Vinerian Professor of English Law Oxford 1882–1909; married in 1872 Elinor Mary, daughter of John Bonham Carter; author of *The Law of the Constitution, Law and Public Opinion in England during the Nineteenth Century,* and *England's Case Against Home Rule* (1886), one of the influencial works on the controversy.

T. P. O'Connor to WSC

22 October 1913   5 Morpeth Mansions

My dear Churchill,

Thanks for your letter. Of course I shall probably have to discuss the proposal of separating the Four Counties from the rest of Ireland, but I shall do it in a way I am sure which will respect your personal position.

As to Ulster, Carsonism is breaking up by the revolt from the business men and the more broad-minded Protestants. He has not 100,000 men drilled, perhaps not even 25,000. The covenant was not signed by 25 to 40 per cent of the Protestants of Ulster over 25 years of age.

There is no proposal which is more resented by the Liberal Protestants and Unionist Home Rulers, and, I am told, even by a considerable section of the Carsonites themselves, than the separation of Ulster from the rest of Ireland.

I am sorry you think Redmond closes a door which he had been careful to keep open. I don't think he ever kept it open, or intended to.

Yours very sincerely
T. P. O'CONNOR

Sir Edward Grey to WSC

28 October 1913   Foreign Office

Private

Dear Churchill,

I took so long about Ireland at my meeting yesterday [at Berwick] that I could not go on to broach the question of Naval Expenditure, but I will do it some time.

I see that I summed up more decidedly against exclusion of the four counties of Ulster than I intended though I think now that solution & agreement are not to be found in that particular way. I did not intend however to rule it out or shut the door as far as I was concerned. I had no opportunity of consulting with my colleague before I spoke but I don't think I can have done any harm to the prospect of agreement.

Yours sincerely
E. GREY

I am here till Friday afternoon. Will you lunch or dine any day?

Austen Chamberlain to WSC

29 November 1913   9 Egerton Place

Secret

My dear Winston,

'And what do you think of it all?' as Rosebery once said to a meeting. You told me that Asquith would say nothing at Leeds. I thought that dangerous, but he has done infinitely worse.

When he spoke at Ladybank we thought his offer was made in good faith & that he meant business. Selborne, Lansdowne & I, in the order named, all advanced to meet him, whereupon he withdraws. He may say what he likes, but he *has* slammed the door in our faces. It is difficult now to think that the Ladybank offer was made in good faith & impossible to believe that he means business. He has blown conciliation to the winds.

Could I have foreseen the terms of his speech (which I have only just been able to read in full) I would have talked navy shop with you – or the fashions or feminism or anything *except* the Irish question![1]

Well! He has chosen, but I would not have his responsibility on my hands. He would scarcely have spoken differently if he had deliberately set himself to provoke strife. I presume that he knew what he was doing.

Yrs sincerely

AUSTEN CHAMBERLAIN

P.S. We all three (*ie* my wife, Joe & myself) have the pleasantest memories of our trip & of your kindness.

Lord Lansdowne to Austen Chamberlain
(*Austen Chamberlain Papers*)

30 November 1913   Bowood
                                                         Wilts

Secret

My dear Austen,

I have to thank you for *two* extraordinarily interesting *letters,* and for the *memorandum* enclosed in the first of these. This I return herewith, and also the copy of your note to Winston. Your comments upon Asquith's Leeds speech were perfectly justified, but I am inclined to think that Asquith

[1] See *Main Volume II*, pp. 480–3.

probably believed himself to be doing exactly what Winston apparently thinks the leaders of both parties ought to do, *viz* 'to make speeches full of party claptrap and No Surrender, with a few sentences at the end for wise and discerning people to see and ponder.' He was, no doubt, bound to drag in a repudiation of the idea that he would make any surrender on questions of principle, but principles are not always capable of exact definition. I am glad however that you pointed out that, in our view, the grant of National Home Rule does involve a question of principle to which we attach the first importance.

I have no time to comment upon your conversation with WC. It leaves me under the impression that we have by no means done with overtures yet, and that we shall find Asquith ready to go pretty far. Meanwhile I hope we shall proceed upon the assumption that the position is unchanged, and that while we are justified in pressing for a general election, Ulster is also justified in continuing her preparations.

I should say that we were a long way from the realisation of Winston's fusionist aspirations.

It does not seem to me inconceivable that the moderates of both parties should some day or other combine, and I think Winston is right in holding that, if this were ever to happen, the country would expect a Government called into existence in such circumstances to deal with the greater controversies, *eg* the reconstruction of the Second Chamber and the adjustment of its relations with the House of Commons, and not merely with non-contentious measures, if there be such. If such a fusion ever took place, it would, I should think, probably be as the result of a general election ending in a 'stalemate'.

We ought really to make an effort to resuscitate Lloyd George's 15-page memorandum, of which both copies have, it appears, been so disastrously mislaid. . . .

Yours ever

L.

Austen Chamberlain to WSC

2 December 1913   Highbury

Secret

My dear Winston,

Many thanks for your letter of the 30th. Our fathers were friends in spite of political differences and I hope that you and I can preserve our friendship through like difficulties.

Your letter only reached me after my return from my meeting last night though I do not think that I could have spoken differently even if I had had the chance of reading your words first. I can only say that if the Prime Minister's position and mood are indeed unchanged, *his* words were singularly unhappy. He has managed to convey to everyone the opposite impression, whilst Lloyd George's outburst is beyond characterization.

You will see what I said – much interrupted by a defeated Socialist councillor and a little knot of opponents organised by him. And you will understand that though always delighted to see you and Morley on any pretext, I should prefer not to be asked to meet Lloyd George – at present at any rate.

Yrs sincerely

AUSTEN CHAMBERLAIN

PS I have just got your two letters of the 1st but this must go now if it is to catch the early post. I will return the prints this evening.

I am free on Monday and shall be delighted to dine with you and meet Morley. I think you spoke of asking FE and LlG also. Of course I should be glad to see FE but LlG and I can't meet just now.

A.C.

Samuel McFadzean to WSC

27 February 1914   Belfast

Dear Sir,

I take the liberty of enclosing a photograph of my son Winston aged 3 months, and I beg that you will accept it as a token of my esteem of your personal and political qualities.

Permit me to explain that as an Ulster Protestant taking an active interest in politics since my boyhood I was an ardent enthusiast in opposition to the Home Rule Bills of 1886 and 1893. The gradual progress of the cause of democracy so ably championed by you and by the Liberal Party generally has influenced men's minds in Ulster as elsewhere so that today the number of your admirers and supporters in Belfast and the north of Ireland is infinitely greater than any outward demonstration of political faith might convey. For the so-called tolerance of the Belfast Unionists does not recognise the free expression of political faith – least of all by their co-religionists. Thus it is that many Liberals who like myself are dependent for their livelihood on the maintenance of trade relations with the commercial community here are not at liberty to give outward manifestations of their political thought.

The reception you were accorded by your political opponents on the occasion of your visit to Belfast a few years ago will have left its own impression on your mind; it will also, I am sure, serve as an indication of the intolerance with which Protestant Liberals have to contend.

The valour and intrepedity which characterised your visit to Belfast appealed to the popular imagination; and it impelled me to give my son your name. In the years to come I hope that this name may serve him as a reminder of the object of your visit to Belfast, and your appeal to the people of Ulster as to the causes for which they would be justified in fighting.

Believe me, Your obedient humble Servant
SAMUEL McFADZEAN

WSC addressed a meeting in St George's Hall, Bradford, on 14 March 1914, on the subject of Irish Home Rule. Over 3,000 people were present. He outlined the Government's latest offer to the Ulster Protestants whereby any county could exclude themselves from the operation of a Home Rule Bill for six years by a majority vote in that county.

Sir John Fisher to WSC

EXTRACT

16 March 1914   Langham House
                                                   Ham Common

Monday night

My dear Winston,
    You asked me if I had read your Bradford Speech. I had not – but I have now. *I should say it's probably the very best speech you ever made!* . . .

John Redmond to WSC

20 March 1914   House of Commons

Private

My dear Mr Churchill,
    In consequence of our few words in conversation last night, I have taken the liberty to-day of discussing the Referendum question with my colleagues. I find they take exactly the view which I expressed to you yesterday.
    I send you herewith a copy of a letter which I have written to Mr Birrell

the substance of which I have asked him to communicate to the Prime Minister.

Very truly yours

J. E. REDMOND

John Redmond to Augustine Birrell

20 March 1914   House of Commons

Confidential

Copy

My dear Birrell,

As the Tories have renewed their proposal of a Referendum on the Home Rule Bill, I deem it necessary to state our views. This proposal, of course, is not new: it has been rejected already both by the Government and by us. It is also the fact that the Referendum was rejected when it came before us in a more favourable form, for it was rejected before the Government had offered their concessions, while now the proposal is that the Bill should be submitted to a Referendum with these concessions included. In other words, concessions offered as the price of peace are to be surrendered not only without peace but as a method of preventing peace.

I do not go into details as to the general merits of the Referendum: that it has, whenever tried, helped reaction: that it would be as costly as a General Election: that the very fact, which is now working so much in our favour, namely, that the question ought to be settled now when it is practically settled, would help towards our defeat by creating a small poll of our friends, and finally that the Referendum would practically be the destruction of the Parliament Act.

So far as we are concerned, we rejected the Referendum without these concessions: our rejection is even more emphatic now that it is proposed with the concessions embodied in the Bill; and our people would never permit us to consent to it.

Very Truly yrs

J. E. REDMOND

*   *   *   *   *

The celebrated Curragh incident, which is described in *Main Volume II*, Chapter 13, took place on March 20-1.

Memorandum by WSC
(*Asquith Papers*)

[No date]   Admiralty

It is necessary that a clear understanding should be reached on the following points:

(1) Sir Arthur Paget[1] received no orders or instructions for any movement of troops, beyond precautionary moves for guarding depots of ammunition and artillery at Dundalk. These movements were assented to in principle by Cabinet, and their details were approved at a conference, presided over by the Prime Minister, between members of the Cabinet, principal members of Army Council, and Sir Arthur Paget. No one believed that these precautionary moves were provocative or would lead to bloodshed. But it was necessary to take the possibility into consideration. As C in C in Ireland, and as a military officer carrying out those approved operations, Sir Arthur Paget had full discretionary power if new and totally different circumstances arose; if the depots were attacked or the columns marching to reinforce them were opposed, to make such dispositions of the force under his command as the emergency might require; and he was told that if necessary as the result of such events, large reinforcements would be sent to him from England. Six contingencies, separate or in combination, had to be borne in mind.

1st Armed opposition to the small bodies of troops moving to reinforce the depots.

2nd Attacks on those depots themselves, or on artillery at Dundalk.

3rd The blowing up or destruction of the railway lines.

4th The outbreak of a serious conflict in Belfast between the Protestant and Catholic elements following upon the proclamation of a Provisional Government, or arising from the general excitement.

5th Widespread sporadic disorders in the south and west of Ireland requiring use of large numbers of troops to protect scattered Protestants from reprisals made on them by the Catholic population.

6th (was added viz – as organised on Paget's suggestion) Warlike movement of the Ulster volunteers, under their responsible leaders, created the impression in their minds that active operations of an aggressive and offensive character, and on an extensive scale, were to be undertaken at once against Ulster; and they transmitted this impression in a still cruder form to their Brigades and Regiments.

All these contingencies were present in Sir Arthur Paget's mind; he was bound to be prepared for them, but none of them belong to the precautionary

[1] Arthur Henry Fitzroy Paget (1851–1925), General Officer Commanding in Ireland 1911–1917; knighted 1906.

movements alone authorised by the Government, or were a probable or
legitimate consequence of them.

When Sir Arthur Paget discussed the precautionary moves their contingent
possibility of disaffection among the officers had to be considered. The
Secretary of State gave him orally for his guidance in dealing with individual
cases of officers refusing to act, should they occur, the following two principles:

First, that officers ordered to act in support of the Civil Power should not
be permitted to resign their commissions, but must, if they refused to obey
orders, be dismissed from the army.

Secondly, indulgence might be shown, as asked, to officers who were
domiciled in or had special connection with Ulster.

There was no intention on the part of the Government or of the Secretary
of State, or of any other member of the Government, or of the Army Council,
that these two rules given for Sir Arthur Paget's guidance, in case of grave
emergencies arising, should be put as a test or a trial to the whole body of
officers in the Irish command; nor did Sir Arthur Paget intend to do so; nor
did he do so. When Sir Arthur Paget returned to Ireland, the grave anxiety
which he felt that the precautionary moves would be misinterpreted or
would be the signal for a violent counterstroke on the part of the Orange
army, made him feel that he must know what officers and units he could rely
upon if the worst came to the worst.

Upon his own initiative he summoned a conference of general officers and
told them, not only of the precautionary moves, but of his anxieties at what
might follow from them. These [anxieties] formed from Sir Arthur Paget's
statement created the impression in their minds that active operations of
an offensive and aggressive character, and on an extensive scale, were to be
undertaken at once against Ulster; and they transmitted their impression
in a still cruder form to their brigades and regiments. For this there was no
warrant in any instructions which had been given by the Secretary of State
or by the Government or any member of it to Sir Arthur Paget; nor was it
intended by Sir Arthur Paget in anything which he said to his generals.

It has been repeatedly stated that Sir Arthur Paget said that the provoca-
tion would come from Ulster, and on this has been founded the charge that
steps had been taken to arrange for or foment such provocative action on
their part. This imputation is an astonishing perversion of the truth. The
members of the Government who attended the conferences at which Sir
Arthur Paget was present in London, were deeply impressed by that officer's
strong sense of humanity and forbearance.

He repeatedly assured us that in no circumstances which could arise would he allow his troops to fire upon the Orangemen until the troops had themselves been fired at for some time and suffered effective loss from that fire. He impressed this point upon the Generals who met him in conference on Friday morning in order to make it clear to them that no aggressive action was contemplated by the orders on which he was acting and in order to make it clear to them the gulf which existed between the purely precautionary moves which he had been authorised to make, and the grave but improbable consequences which might follow from them. Indeed, on the Saturday when he visited the Cavalry Brigade at the Curragh in order to reassure the officers who had been thrown into such natural consternation and distress by the question put to them, Sir Arthur Paget went so far as to say that, not only would he never give the order for the troops to fire until they had first been attacked and had suffered loss, but that he intended himself to walk out in front and be shot down by the Orangemen before any firing in reply would be ordered of the troops. It is an extraordinary instance of the perversions of the truth which malice and rumour can effect, that these statements should have been twisted into a foundation for the vilest of calumnies.

To sum up:

1. While Sir Arthur Paget had discretionary power to take any action which a great and sudden emergency might require, he had received no directions from any quarter to take any action outside the precautionary moves for guarding the depots; and no orders were ever issued by him (except stand-by orders) for any purpose or plan outside these moves.

2. Sir Arthur Paget was never directed to subject the officers under his command to the test of whether they would declare themselves ready to take the offensive in military operations against Ulster, or be dismissed the service; nor did he intend at any time to force that alternative upon them.

3. So far from lending himself to any scheme intended to provoke wantonly a collision with the Ulster volunteers, Sir Arthur Paget resolved to observe every conceivable precaution which courage and humanity could suggest, to avoid a collision and to prevent bloodshed; and on this he was acting in the fullest harmony with what he knew were the wishes and hopes of the Government.

[WSC]

WSC to the Vice-Admiral Commanding 3rd Battle Squadron

TELEGRAM

19 March 1914   Admiralty

Secret

Proceed at once at ordinary speed to Lamlash, sending *Britannia* to Gibraltar. After clearing Ushant hand over command temporarily to Rear Admiral and proceed in your Flagship – to Plymouth, from where you are to proceed to London and report yourself at the Admiralty. Your Flagship should at once rejoin Squadron at Lamlash to which place you will proceed overland from London. Acknowledge and report dates of arrival.

[WSC]

WSC to HMS New Zealand

TELEGRAM

19 March 1914   Admiralty

Secret

Secret. Issue at once the following orders to Captain Johnson of *Attentive*. (begins) Proceed with *Attentive* and *Pathfinder* to Kingstown at such speed as to arrive by noon tomorrow. A staff officer will be sent from Dublin to communicate with you on arrival. You are to embark one Company Bedfordshire Regiment, one half in each ship and proceed to Belfast Lough so as to arrive off Carrickfergus at daybreak on Saturday 21st instant. The troops are to be landed at once. You should then take *Attentive* to Bangor, County Down, land yourself in plain clothes and proceed to Holywood Barracks and interview General Sir Nevil Macready as to co-operation with military in certain eventualities. You should comply with requests made so far as practicable without landing men. Captain of *Pathfinder* is to personally arrange with senior military officer in Carrickfergus for guarding the ammunition and other government stores there. This place is to be defended against attack by every means, and if co-operation of Navy is necessary, by guns and searchlights from the ship. You may if necessary exchange stations of the two ships provided one is kept at anchor off Bangor and one off Carrickfergus. Day leave may be given to reliable men during daylight hours, (ends). Acknowledge and report time of leaving.

[WSC]

WSC to HMS Gibraltar

TELEGRAM

19 March 1914   Admiralty

Secret

Gibraltar and *Royal Arthur* are to proceed at once to Kingstown Ireland to embark tomorrow 550 Infantry equally divided and proceed to Dundalk where ships should anchor not before daybreak on Saturday and at once disembark the troops. Report time of probable arrival at Kingstown.

[WSC]

The King to H. H. Asquith
(Asquith Papers)

EXTRACT

21 March 1914   Buckingham Palace

... I must further ask that I am kept fully informed of any proposed employment of the Navy in connection with Ulster, especially as I see in the press that some excitement has been caused already in Ireland by the movements of some ships & I have heard nothing from the First Lord of the Admiralty.

Augustine Birrell to WSC

20 April 1914

Secret

My dear Winston,

    This is a story I hear not only from the Kildare St Club, but on better authority.

    On board the *Pathfinder*, one of HM's ships sent to protect our Irish Coast at Belfast, an entertainment was given to some *Orangemen* (whose names I have) & whilst it was proceeding 5 tons of small arms ammunition – that will fit a mauser rifle – were removed from the ship & landed. The way this story is told is that 'an *Orange Lodge* was on board the *Pathfinder*'.

    It *may* be all a lie, but the truth is, the whole place is so completely in the hands of the Enemy that no *civilities* can take place without demonstrations.

I am glad the police of your ships are throwing their searchlights over the coast of Antrim & Down.

Yours in haste

AB

On the night of April 24–25, some 30,000 rifles and 3,000,000 cartridges were landed at Larne from a steamer temporarily bearing the historic name of *Mountjoy II*, after the famous ship which broke the boom which ended the siege of Londonderry in 1690. This material was distributed among the Ulster Protestants. Over 12,000 men were engaged in the operation and the scheme had been so admirably organized that the authorities in Dublin Castle heard nothing of it until noon of April 25.

WSC to his wife
(*CSC Papers*)

23 April 1914   Admiralty

My darling,

I have been hampered in my writing by the lag in time wh must necessarily intervene before the letter reaches you & by pressure here of all kinds.

The Madrid cold still hangs on to me & I croak like a frog. Gradually I am becoming vocal again, but Parkinson has had to prescribe some disagreeable mixture.

On my return I discovered as usual various symptoms of naughtiness among the Seals: & I have systematically laboured to reduce them to good order & discipline.

The 'Ulster Pogrom' is in full swing as you will read in the papers. We have now published everything and I am confident these wild charges will become gradually discredited. Bonar Law has excelled himself in rudeness to the PM! & feelings are on all sides bitter to a degree unknown hitherto.

Seely goes about like a disembodied spirit, trying to return from the wastes of the Infinite to the cosy world of man. He is terribly hard hit & losing poise. The world is pitiless to grief & failure.

The Federal & conciliation movements are going forward well, & there is a tremendous undercurrent on both sides towards a settlement.

I was all wrong about India.[1] It is not meant till December 1915: so there is no need to worry about it one way or t'other.

The kittens are extremely well and make continuous inquiries & complaints about your non-return. I do hope you are enjoying yourself and that

[1] This may refer to the move to make WSC Viceroy of India in succession to Hardinge. He had already been mooted as Viceroy in succession to Minto in 1910.

the sights & scenes repay the exile & exertion. I am vy glad to be back: & shall be gladder when you return. So far no answer has come to my telegrams.

I enclose you the 'Titus'[?] reincarnation joke. There is undoubtedly a resemblance.

Our finances are in a condition wh requires serious & prompt attention. The expense of the 1st quarter of 1914 with our holiday trip is astonishing. Money seems to flow away. I am seeing Cox today & propose to devote myself to this topic, unpleasant though it be, for some considerable time.

Fondest love my darling and many kisses from the babes & me,

Always your loving & devoted husband

W

WSC to his wife
(CSC Papers)

27 April 1914   In the train

My darling Clemmie,

I was delighted to get yr telegram advertising me of yr nearer approach to the domestic hearth. You shd have had a vy enjoyable tour & have seen things so well worth seeing, that my only regret is that we did not see them together.

I have been spending the weekend at Portsmouth, & am now returning to a busy week. Tomorrow I am to reply to Austen Chamberlain's vote of Censure on the Pogrom. The situation has from a Parliamentary point of view been altered much in our favour by the Gun Running escapade of the Ulstermen. They have put themselves entirely in the wrong, & justified to the full the modest precautions wh were taken. My line will be a vy stiff one.

Dearest – all is well at home. The kittens look forward to your return & much frequent inquiry. I think the nurse is vy good. My cold is better, but my voice is not wholly recovered. The weather is brilliant. If you don't return till the end of the week I shall go to the yacht again. I get away from my ordinary work and find much rest & refreshment on the sea.

E. Grey has been staying with me. He is much better and will make with time a complete recovery.

I had a long interview with Cox & in the result am preparing a scheme which will enable us to clear off our debts & bills and start on a clean ready money basis. We shall have to pull in our horns. The money simply drains away.

If you have anything left out of the £40, spend it on some little thing that you like in Paris.

Always your loving husband
W

WSC to his wife
(*CSC Papers*)

29 April 1914   Admiralty
8.15 p.m.

My darling & Precious one,

Your Alhambra letter has just reached me and warms & cheers my heart.

I am so glad you are coming back tomorrow – Let me know when I shall meet you.

I asked Randolph this morning whether he wanted you to come back & why & he said 'Becos I lurve her'. So now you must come my sweet pussy & return to the domestic basket.

I have just come back from the Pogrom debate. You must read all about it. We smashed the 'plot' altogether, but as you will see I yesterday at the end of my speech greatly daring & on my own account threw a sentence across the House to Carson wh has revolutionised the situation, & we are all back again in full conciliation. This is the biggest risk I have taken.

So far all is well – but the Irish are vy restive & there is danger everywhere. I took my political life in my hands. The PM comes along with the main body. Carson made a gt & cheering advance, & Balfour also shd be read.

Return my lovely one tomorrow night to your home where all who love you will salute your presence.

Give my love to your Mamma & tell her how much I hope she is progressing to good health – I am vy glad you went to see her.

Always my darling

Your loving husband
W

Robert Harcourt to WSC

28 April 1914   3 Chester Square

Private

My dear Churchill,

I hope you will not resent it as an impertinence if I write to you with the utmost frankness.

It is absolutely vital that you should realize the extent of the fury – for no milder term will fit the facts – which has been aroused in the Irish party and among large numbers of our liberal colleagues by the offer to Carson with which you concluded your speech. I do not deal with the merits of the proposal: I am concerned with the fact of its reception. Devlin is beside himself with rage and is openly telling everyone that you have betrayed the Irish cause. Radicals, and among them the most active and talented debaters in the party, are comparing your action with Seely's surrender to Gough.

A number of Liberals went to Illingworth[1] tonight and he is going to speak to the Prime Minister before the Cabinet tomorrow. They are afraid of an open row on the floor of the House which may shatter the whole basis of the Coalition.

Cave was of course put up to divert the issue from the gruelling they were getting for their conspiracy with the suggestion which they will sedulously propagate in the country that they have won a concession from our weakness by their daring determination.

I am acting the odious part of the candid friend out of a genuine admiration for your genius and your great service to the party.

Though I myself have had some part in the federal movement I felt so strongly that this was not the moment to parley with the enemy that I absolutely ignored the question in my speech.

I give my opinion for what it is worth and it is this: that unless the Prime Minister states unmistakeably that your offer was not the decision of the Cabinet there is a definite danger of an open rupture.

Please forgive me if you can for the frankness of this epistle.

Yrs sincerely
ROBERT HARCOURT

Rear-Admiral Archibald Moore[2] to WSC

29 April [1914]   Admiralty

First Lord,

I have shown this letter to the First Sea L & he does not think that the rumour referred to by Mr Birrell calls for an enquiry – certainly there is nothing in the official reports which suggests the possibility of any such landing having been attempted or made. It must be remembered that the CO of the *Pathfinder* had no instructions to take any action in regard to the

---

[1] Percy Holden Illingworth (1869–1915), Chief Liberal Whip 1912–15; Liberal MP for Shipley Division of W.R. of Yorks 1906–15; Junior Lord of the Treasury 1910–12.

[2] Archibald Gordon Henry Wilson Moore (1862–1934), Third Sea Lord 1912–14. Admiral 1919; knighted 1914.

prevention of the importation of arms, which was part of the police & customs duties, & if a landing did take place the CO would not have acted without orders. As to the idea that the *Pathfinder* actually assisted it seems to me an absurd hypothesis as the vessel did not know she was going to Bangor until she was sent & if any improper collusion had occurred while she was there it seems hardly likely that there would be no evidence of it. That Orangemen were entertained on board is probable, but the orders as to discretion in this respect were not given until the vessel had been there some time.

A.M.

If an enquiry is to be made I suggest that more precise data should be given.

A.M.

Note by WSC

30 April

Yes. The officer seems to have shown much less than usual naval dignity & self-restraint in circumstances of difficulty. But there is no use in pressing the matter further.

WSC

Augustine Birrell to WSC

17 May 1914

Confidential

My dear Winston,

    I have all kinds of *reports*, vague, but confirmatory one of another as to an impending *coup* of some sort in Ulster & I am *certain* that the Third Reading will not be allowed to pass without some theatricality. With the *Fanny* at Hamburg, & Major Crawford & Capt Agnew – the two heroes of the last escapade – still in foreign parts, something we may be confident is *brewing*.[1] I wish the Admiralty could send someone to Hamburg & Antwerp to look round. At Scotland Yard there is a capital man who looks like a German

---

[1] Major Fred Crawford was Director of Ordnance in the Ulster Volunteers. In 1894 he had conceived a plan to kidnap Mr Gladstone at Brighton, transport him to a Pacific island and leave him there, provided with an axe, writing-paper, a copy of *Homer* and the *Bible*, until a change of Government should avert the danger of Home Rule. The arms landed at Larne on April 24–25 had been bought by Crawford in Hamburg; he had also purchased the tramp steamer *Fanny* to convey the cargo. The vessel was navigated by Captain Andrew Agnew. The arms were transhipped from the *Fanny* to the *Mountjoy* off the Welsh coast.

trained engineer, & talks like a North German – Hugh [?] *Hester* – an In-spector, who knows these ports well. Sir E. Henry would lend him you I am sure. I shall feel very *chagrined* if we are *outwitted again.* Outnumbered we must be *always* until we have *soldiers.*

Yrs
A. BIRRELL

WSC to Sir Edward Grey

22 July 1914

Private

My dear Grey,
    The course you told me about last night can only be considered where everything else has failed. It is surely not the next step to the breakdown of the present negotiations.
    Failing an Irish agreement there ought to be a British decision. Carson & Redmond, whatever their wishes, may be unable to agree about Tyrone; they may think it worth a war, & from their point of view it may be worth a war. But that is hardly the position of the 40 millions who dwell in Great Britain; and their interests must when all is said & done be our chief & final care. In foreign affairs you wd proceed by two stages: First you wd labour to stop Austria & Russia going to war: second, if that failed, you wd try to prevent England, France, Germany & Italy being drawn in. Exactly what you wd do in Europe is right in this domestic danger, with the difference that in Europe the second step wd only hope to limit & localize the conflict; whereas at home the 2nd step, if practicable & adopted, wd prevent the local conflict.
    The Conference therefore shd labour to reduce the differences to the smallest definite limits possible. At that point if no agreement had been reached, the speaker shd be asked to propose a partition: & we shd offer the Unionist Leaders to accept it if *they* will.
    It is only when this or some such proposal has been made or refused that I shd be prepared to look for the no doubt good tactical positions you indicate. I do not want good tactical positions for war. I want peace by splitting the outstanding differences, if possible, with Irish acquiescence, but if necessary over the head of both Irish parties.

Yours ever
W

WSC to his wife
(CSC Papers)

22 July 1914   Admiralty

My darling,

This only a line to greet you with my love tomorrow morning.

Secretissimo

The conference is in extremis. We are preparing a partition of Tyrone with reluctant Nationalist acquiescence. Carson absolutely refuses although the Speaker strongly commended it. Carson & Redmond both just friendly and apparently not hopeless. But what about all of us – 40 millions!

On leaving the Palace Redmond & Dillon were followed by a cheering crowd and as they passed the barracks, the soldiers of the Irish Guards ran out waving & cheering in a vy remarkable demonstration. This will make Europe take unfavourable views of the British situation – wh serious though it is – they will greatly exaggerate.

Venetia asked me in a christian-like spirit to come to the Russian ballet tonight – but I had already engaged myself to F.E.

I am anxious about the political crisis: and what to do to help.

Tender love my dear one to you & the kittens from your devoted husband

W

John Redmond to WSC

4 August 1914   House of Commons

Private

My dear Mr Churchill,

I want to write you a purely informal letter & make an urgent appeal to you.

In making my speech yesterday I was quite aware that I was taking very great risks. My people are sincerely anxious to make friends with this country but, naturally enough, they are still full of suspicion & if the Home Rule Bill be postponed they will consider themselves sold & I will be simply unable to hold them. In that event deplorable things will be said & done in Ireland & the Home Rule cause may be lost for our time.

My suggestion is that the Royal Assent should be given to the Bill, that a pledge should be given that an Amending Bill would be introduced in the winter & that pending the disposal of the Amending Bill no step whatever would be taken to put the original Bill into operation.

I am convinced if this course be adopted that we will be able to agree with Carson on the terms of the Amending Bill. If it be not adopted, if we separate for 2 or 3 months with the Home Rule Bill still unpassed, bitterness will grow & settlement become more difficult. Besides, it is not fair play to subject us to all the risks & chances that may arise in the next 2 or 3 months.

The enactment of the Bill is, after all, in the circumstances, only the settlement of the principle & surety that we are entitled to. Furthermore in the *present* temper of the Unionist Party after my speech you can afford to take the course I suggest.

The Prime Minister knows my views & I think agrees with them. Now I urgently appeal to you to help me. Will you?

Very truly yrs

J. REDMOND

John Redmond to H. H. Asquith

5 August 1914   House of Commons

Copy

Confidential

Dear Mr Asquith,

I had an interview this afternoon with Sir Edward Carson in the Speaker's Library. The Speaker was also present. I found Sir Edward Carson in an absolutely irreconcilable mood about everything. So much so indeed, that it was impossible really to discuss matters calmly with him. The gist of our conversation was this – although, of course, I do not give you his words – that, if the Government dared to put the Home Rule Bill on the Statute Book, that he and the Tory Party would obstruct the Appropriation Bill and revive all the bitterness of the controversy. He would not listen to any suggested way out of the difficulty at all, and is evidently in the worst possible temper.

I can add very little to my letter of yesterday; but, if the Government allow themselves to be bullied in this way by Sir Edward Carson, a position of the most serious difficulty will arise with us. It will be quite impossible for us to abstain from raising a discussion on the Second Reading of the Appropriation Bill, which would have most unfortunate and disastrous results in Ireland, and really would put us and our country in an absolutely cruel position. It would make it quite impossible for me to go to Ireland, as I desire to do, and to translate into action the spirit of my speech the other day. It would revive all the suspicion and bitterness and controversy, all through the South and West of Ireland, and would exhibit us to the world as torn into a hundred fragments, and disaffected with the Government of the day.

For my part, I am not moved in the smallest degree by Sir Edward Carson's threats. In the present state of public opinion in England, and in the present state of opinion in the Tory Party in the House of Commons, I believe neither he nor any of the Unionist leaders dare take the extreme course which he threatened; and, if they did so, they would ruin themselves in the eyes of the public.

This undoubtedly is the greatest opportunity that has ever occurred in the history of Ireland to win the Irish people to loyalty to the Empire, and I do beg of you not to allow threats of the kind used to prevent you from taking the course which will enable me to preach the doctrines of peace, goodwill and loyalty in Ireland.

Very truly yours
J. E. REDMOND

Note by Redmond to WSC
I have sent this letter to Prime Minister. J E R

19

Votes for Women

(See Main Volume II, pp. 393–407)

———

IN 1897 Churchill had noted in a copy of the *Annual Register*: 'Once you give votes to the vast numbers of women who form the majority of the community, all power passes to their hands.'

Between 1910 and 1912 Churchill, as a Liberal minister, was under pressure, both peaceful and violent, from the supporters of female suffrage.

C. P. Scott to WSC

6 March 1910   The *Guardian* Office
                                                Manchester

Dear Churchill,

I want to send a line personally of thanks for your decision about the treatment of the suffragettes & similar persons. It strikes one as just common sense but it needed courage as well as sense. More & more one comes to think that courage is the first & the last of political virtues. I am deeply concerned as to the political outlook. So far as one can see we are going straight to a catastrophe & a quite unnecessary one. I expect to be in London tomorrow & Friday (15 Nottingham Place, W). I wonder if I could see you

Yours very sincerely
C. P. SCOTT

Miss Christabel Pankhurst[1] to A. J. Balfour
(Balfour Papers)

EXTRACT

10 April 1910   The Women's Social and Political Union[2]
4 Clements Inn

Dear Mr Balfour,

Mr Winston Churchill, last night, gave a list of measures which the Liberal Government are desirous of carrying and this list includes Electoral Reform.

You are speaking today at one o'clock, I notice, and no doubt you will have occasion to refer to Mr Churchill's statement. Will it be possible to ask in the course of your speech whether this scheme of Electoral Reform is to include woman suffrage? We shall be so grateful if you will do this!

Evidently Electoral Reform is to form part of the Liberal Election programme.

We shall of course protest against any attempt to alter the franchise for the exclusive benefit of men, but this point of view, (which you share, I know) will have if you give expression to it, a very much readier acceptance than if we are left to press it upon the country unaided.

For Mr Churchill to claim that the Government are 'fighting for equal rights for all whites', is really most audacious for as far as woman suffrage is concerned he and his colleagues have spent the past five years in opposing that principle.

I do hope you will help us by drawing attention to the fact.

Should your speech today contain a reference to our question this will give the greatest rejoicing to all of us. . . .

[CHRISTABEL PANKHURST]

[1] Christabel Pankhurst (1880–1958), eldest daughter of Emmeline Pankhurst; a founder of the Women's Social and Political Union; three times imprisoned by this date, she was to elude arrest in 1912 by escaping to Paris.

[2] The Women's Social and Political Union was founded in Manchester in October 1903 by Mrs Pankhurst and her daughters. Its motto was: 'Deeds, not words'.

H. N. Brailsford[1] to WSC

Conciliation Commitee for Woman Suffrage

13 April [1910]   32 Well Walk
                                             Hampstead

Private

Dear Mr Churchill,

You were good enough to say, when I talked to you about the new non-party suffrage committee, that you would give it a general support, provided you approved the documents which it proposes to publish.

I enclose (1) a letter which will be sent to all members of Parliament – not for publication. (2) a declaration which they will be asked to sign. It *may* be published, though it may be expedient not to do so. (3) a private memorandum (which you need not trouble to read) intended for Liberals only, which of course is not for publication and commits no one but myself.

What I venture to ask of you is that you should allow us to quote you in the covering letter (No 1) as one of the 'Rt Hon X.Y.Z.' who 'welcome the formation of the committee and would favour a solution on non-party lines.' The formula is vague & not I think at all compromising to you. It does not commit you either to the municipal basis, or to procedure by private Bill. But it would greatly help us if you would give us your blessing even in these very general terms. We are asking Sir Edward Grey, Lloyd George, Arthur Balfour, Alfred Lyttelton and Bonar Law to lend us their names in the same way. We are hopeful of getting Sir E. Grey & Alfred Lyttelton – nearly sure in fact. I don't yet know what success those of our friends who are approaching the others have had. Mr Balfour in private goes quite as far as this, and he is considering whether he ought to let us use his name.

Please note that the letter (No 1) will go to MPs but not to the press.

Sincerely yours
H. N. BRAILSFORD

H. N. Brailsford to WSC

15 April [1910]   32 Well Walk
Private

Dear Mr Churchill,

I am sorry to trouble you at a time when you must be busy and preoccupied. But I think you will understand the urgency of my business.

---

[1] Henry Noel Brailsford (1873–1958), author and journalist; Honorary Secretary of Conciliation Committee for Woman Suffrage 1910–12; Member of Independent Labour Party from 1907; Editor, *The New Leader* 1922–6.

I enclose, as you requested, a proof of the circular which we propose to send out to all MPs in about a week's time. The names are not yet complete. We still hope to [be] able to *quote* Mr Balfour as a supporter (he is friendly) but failing him, we can certainly get Mr Wyndham. The names will not be sent to the press. As you will see, we have now got the support of several adult suffragists *eg* Alden,[1] A. Williams,[2] Arthur Henderson and Shackleton, who would not support the old limited Bill. Our compromise will succeed if the Government will give us the two days or so which are all that so simple a Bill demands. The postponement for some weeks or months of the Veto issue ought to make this easy.

I should like to tell you a little of the history of this compromise. I tried twice last year, when the militant agitation was at its height to negotiate a truce – on my own initiative and not as the agent of the suffragettes. In one case I approached one of your colleagues; in the other case another colleague came to me. The attempt failed, because I was never able to say more to the WSPU than this – that several ministers *thought* a chance should be given to pass a private member's Bill early in 1910.

One could not bargain on so vague a basis as that. I then suggested to the WSPU that negotiations were a mistake, and that it would be wiser to declare a spontaneous truce, and trust to the Government's generosity. This they did a few weeks later, and the truce has now lasted four months. The next step was to build a bridge, a bridge of compromise, and this, I think, our committee has successfully done. We have got a Bill which practically all suffragists will accept. Nothing now is wanted but the time to pass it in.

I am sure you will realize what the refusal of facilities for this Bill must involve. It would mean, I am afraid, the end of the truce, and the renewal of the old bitter struggle. I feel so grave a responsibility, now that the moment has come to put our chances to the test, that I dread any false step which friendly advice might enable me to avoid.

Could you advise me as to how best our request for time could come before the Cabinet? Would you be so kind as to be our advocate? Or should a formal letter be written to the Prime Minister? Or should we wait until after the recess, when we could ask him to receive a deputation of MPs? My own preference, if it could be managed, would be that the decision should lie with the Cabinet as a whole.

We need not necessarily ask in the first instance for full facilities. All we need to begin with is an early day for the Second Reading, on the under-

[1] Percy Alden (1865-1944), Radical MP Tottenham 1906-18; Labour MP 1923-4; knighted 1933.
[2] Aneurin Williams (1859-1924), Liberal MP Plymouth 1910, NW Durham 1914, Consett 1918-22.

standing that our Bill would be sent upstairs for the Committee stage. That seems to me a very modest request.

With many thanks for the countenance you have already given us.

Believe me, Sincerely yours

H. N. BRAILSFORD

Circular sent to all MPs

CONCILIATION COMMITTEE FOR WOMAN SUFFRAGE

———————

Chairman – THE RT HON THE EARL OF LYTTON

PERCY ALDEN, MP

SIR THOMAS BARCLAY, MP[1]

G. J. BENTHAM, MP[2]

THE RT HON THOMAS BURT, MP[3]

NOEL BUXTON, MP[4]

H. G. CHANCELLOR, MP[5]

SIR WILLIAM CROSSLEY, MP[6]

J. A. DAWES, MP[7]

ELLIS G. GRIFFITH, MP[8]

C. A. McCURDY, MP[9]

E. A. GOULDING, MP

J. S. HARMOOD-BANNER, MP[10]

F. LEVERTON HARRIS, MP[11]

CHARLES McARTHUR, MP[12]

THE HON W. G. A. ORMSBY-GORE, MP

BASIL PETO, MP[13]

SIR J. S. RANDLES, MP[14]

SIR JOHN ROLLESTON, MP[15]

———

[1] Thomas Barclay (1853–1941), Liberal MP Blackburn 1910; knighted 1904.

[2] George Jackson Bentham (1863–1929). Liberal MP West Lindsey division of Lincolnshire 1910–18.

[3] Thomas Burt (1837–1922), Liberal MP Morpeth 1874–1918; PC 1906.

[4] Noel Edward Noel-Buxton (1869–1948), Liberal MP for Whitby 1905–6, N. Norfolk 1910–18; Labour MP 1922–30; PC 1924; created Baron Noel-Buxton of Aylsham 1930.

[5] Henry George Chancellor (1863–1945), Liberal MP Haggerston 1910–18.

[6] William John Crossley (1844–1911), Liberal MP Altrincham 1906–11; created Baronet 1909.

[7] James Arthur Dawes (1866–1921), Liberal MP Southwark 1910–21.

[8] Ellis Jones Ellis-Griffith (1860–1926); Liberal MP 1895–1918, 1923–4; Under-Secretary of State Home Department 1912–15; PC 1914; created Baronet 1918.

[9] Charles Albert McCurdy (1870–1941), Liberal MP Northampton 1910–23; Coalition Liberal Chief Whip 1921–2; PC 1921.

[10] John Sutherland Harmood-Banner (1847–1927), Conservative MP Liverpool Everton 1905–24; Lord Mayor of Liverpool 1913; knighted 1918; created Baronet 1924.

[11] Frederick Leverton Harris (1864–1926), Conservative MP Tynemouth 1900–6, Stepney 1907–11, E. Worcestershire 1914–18; PC 1916.

[12] Charles McArthur (1844–1910), 'Conservative MP 1897–1906, 1907–10 Kirkdale and Exchange Divisions of Liverpool.

[13] Basil Peto (1862–1945), Conservative MP Devizes 1910–18, Barnstaple 1922–3, 1924–35; created Baronet 1927.

[14] John Scurrah Randles (1857–1945), Conservative MP Cockermouth 1900–6, 1906–10, Exchange Div, Manchester 1912–22, knighted 1905.

[15] John Fowke Lancelot Rolleston (1848–1919), Conservative MP Leicester 1900–6, Hertford 1910–16; knighted 1897.

The Rt Hon Sir Chas
  McLaren, MP[1]
Walter S. McLaren, MP[2]
Max Muspratt, MP[3]
Sir George White, MP[4]
J. H. Whitehouse, MP[5]
Aneurin Williams, MP

G. A. Arbuthnot, MP[6]
Sir William Bull, MP[7]
H. S. Foster, MP[8]

Stephen L. Gwynn, MP
T. M. Kettle, MP[9]
J. C. Lardner, MP[10]
Hugh A. Law, MP[11]
Joseph P. Nannetti, MP[12]

J. Keir Hardie, MP
J. B. O'Grady, MP
David J. Shackleton, MP
Philip Snowden, MP

Hon Sec – H. N. Brailsford, 32 Well Walk, Hampstead, NW

The Conciliation Committee has been formed to press for an early solution of the Woman Suffrage question, on a plan which members of all parties may accept as a practicable minimum.

We have the permission of the following gentlemen –

The Rt Hon Augustine Birrell, KC, MP
The Rt Hon Winston S. Churchill, MP
The Rt Hon Sir Edward Grey, MP
The Rt Hon Alfred Lyttelton, KC, MP
G. N. Barnes, MP, and
Arthur Henderson, MP

to state that they welcome the formation of our Committee and would favour a solution on non-party lines.

[1] Charles Benjamin Bright McLaren (1850-1934), Liberal MP Stafford 1880-5, Leicestershire 1892-1910; created Baronet 1902; PC 1908; Baron Aberconway of Bodnant 1911.

[2] Francis Walter Stafford McLaren (1886-1917), Liberal MP Spalding 1910-17; youngest son of 1st Baron Aberconway; killed in action while flying 1917.

[3] Max Muspratt (1872-1934); Liberal MP Liverpool Exchange 1910; created Baronet 1922.

[4] George White (1840-1912), Liberal MP North-West Norfolk 1900-12; knighted 1907.

[5] John Howard Whitehouse (1873-1955), Liberal MP Mid-Lanark 1910-18.

[6] Gerald Archibald Arbuthnot (1872-1916), Unionist MP Burnley 1910; Vice-Chancellor Primrose League 1912; served in Agriculture, Local Government Board, and Irish Offices.

[7] William Bull (1863-1931), Conservative MP Hammersmith and Hammersmith South 1900-29; knighted 1905; PC 1918; created Baronet 1922.

[8] Harry Seymour Foster (1855-1938), Conservative MP Lowestoft 1892-1900, N. Suffolk 1910, Portsmouth Central 1924-9, Consul-General of Persia 1894-1923; knighted 1918.

[9] Thomas Michael Kettle (1880-1916), Nationalist MP East Tyrone 1906-10.

[10] James Carrige Rushe Lardner (1879-1925), Nationalist MP North Monaghan 1907-18.

[11] Hugh Alexander Law (d. 1943), Nationalist MP West Donegal 1902-18; served in Ministry of Munitions 1915-16; Foreign Office 1916-18; Member Irish Free State Parliament 1927-32.

[12] Joseph Patrick Nannetti (1851-1915), Nationalist MP College Division of Dublin 1900-15.

PROVISIONAL TEXT OF A BILL
TO EXTEND THE PARLIAMENTARY FRANCISE TO
WOMEN OCCUPIERS

Be it enacted, etc.:

1. Every woman possessed of a household qualification, or of a ten pound occupation qualification, within the meaning of The Representation of the People Act (1884), shall be entitled to be registered as a voter, and when registered to vote for the county or borough in which the qualifying premises are situate.
2. For the purposes of this Act, a woman shall not be disqualified by marriage for being registered as a voter, provided that a husband and wife shall not both be qualified in respect of the same property.
3. This Act may be cited as 'The Representation of the People Act, 1910.'[1]

EXPLANATORY MEMORANDUM

There is no doubt that the present House of Commons, like every House which has met since 1870, shows a majority for Woman Suffrage. Indeed, while over 400 Members are known to be favourable, not more than 70 have declared themselves hostile. But precisely because the question is now within the range of practical politics, the divergence of opinion regarding the actual method by which it should be solved has become acute. Under normal circumstances it would be left to the Government of the day to prescribe the solution and to overcome minor differences with regard to tactics. But neither this, nor any other Government in the near future, is likely to commit itself to Woman Suffrage. The initiative must be taken by Private Members. Failing a compromise between Suffragists of all schools and parties, a settlement may be indefinitely delayed.

[1] After this was inserted the following Amendment in holograph: – 'Amendment (mentioned in my second conversation) "provided that a husband and wife shall not both be qualified in respect of property situate in the same borough or county". – There could if it is really necessary be added: "a husband and wife or a father and an unmarried daughter".'

THE PRESENT DEADLOCK

The 'Conciliation Committee for Woman Suffrage' has set itself to enquire whether a basis of agreement can be found. Two solutions hold the field at present. There is the old Bill for the removal of the disability of sex, which was brought forward on the last occasion by Mr Stanger[1] in 1908. It admitted women on the same terms as men to all the existing franchises, and to all future extensions of them. Against this measure Liberal opinion has definitely hardened, on the ground that it would add to the property vote, and make facilities for 'faggot' or plural voting. The rival solution is Adult Suffrage, which claims 120 pledged supporters in the present House. Opposed as it would be by most Unionists – whether as a Private Member's Bill or as an Amendment to a Reform Bill – it certainly promises no early settlement; nor is it easy to believe that so large a revolution could ever be carried without the active support of a powerful Government.

A working compromise from a Parliamentary standpoint must (1) meet the objections of Liberals and Labour Members to any increase of the Ownership or Plural Vote; (2) satisfy Unionist opinion as a cautious and moderate advance; and (3) be capable of statement in a simple formula which can be debated without an undue demand on the time of the House. We claim for our Bill that it satisfies these three conditions.

THE MUNICIPAL BASIS

This Bill is far from inventing an arbitrary franchise. It enacts a measure of enfranchisement which practically reproduces the present Local Government Register for women as it exists in England and Wales. This register has worked satisfactorily for a quarter of a century, and neither party has ever proposed to alter it.

Our Bill meets Liberal critics by excluding the Ownership and Lodger Qualifications. It also provides against the enfranchisement of married women with their husbands under the £20 qualification for joint-occupiers – a qualification which would have included married women only in the middle and upper classes. It admits householders, even when they occupy only part of a house, without any limit of property. This basis is so democratic that the Independent Labour Party, after a careful inquiry, satisfied itself that of the women on the Municipal Register, 82 per cent belong to the working class. It should be noted that married women are not as such excluded, though few of them would, in fact, be qualified. Married men who can at present rarely vote themselves, eg, sailors and fishermen, would, under our Bill, be able, if they chose, to transfer their qualification to their wives.

[1] Henry Yorke Stanger (1849–1929), Liberal MP North Kensington 1906–10.

On the other hand the preference of Unionists for a cautious and experimental measure of enfranchisement is respected. There are some 870,000 women on the Local Government Register in England and Wales. Including the women of Scotland and Ireland, this Bill would confer the Parliamentary vote on about a million new electors. They would be in the main women who earn their own living – those, in short, who pay rates and taxes, and have, in consequence, a traditional claim to representation which public opinion readily concedes.

Finally, our Bill is so brief and simple that its discussion makes a minimum demand in regard to time upon the generosity of a Government. It cannot be said that Parliament is overburdened this Session with legislative work.

A WORKING COMPROMISE

We do not claim for our Bill that it is an ideal solution; it is a working compromise. Its single merit is that, in a way which no party can consider objectionable or unfair, it breaks down the barrier which at present excludes all women from citizen rights. It is against this insulting exclusion that women are protesting at present. For those women who care most about the Suffrage it is a secondary matter whether this or the other woman will be qualified under any given Bill. They are fighting for the status of their sex. Our basis has satisfied a Committee which includes both supporters and opponents of Adult Suffrage. It does not preclude a future advance towards Adult Suffrage; but neither does it render such an advance inevitable. It secures for women only those franchises which all parties regard as satisfactory. Failing Government action, we believe that it represents for many years to come the only practicable line of advance. The alternative is to wait, it may be for a generation, until one party or the other is strong enough and unanimous enough to force a contentious solution on party lines.

AN URGENT QUESTION

This question is as urgent as it is important. It is forty years since the first Suffrage Bill passed its second reading in the House of Commons. The patience and ability of the women of the older societies deserved an earlier reward. The failure of Parliaments to give effect to an opinion which they have repeatedly avowed, would, if continued, justify women in complaining that in regard to them the Constitution had broken down. The painful struggle of the past four years is an experience which no one would wish to see repeated. However opinions may differ as to the methods by which this cause has recently been advocated, everyone must deplore the fact that many women, whose high character gives them a commanding influence with their fellows, should be found in open hostility to the laws of the land,

and that their capacity for devotion and self-sacrifice should be called forth in opposition to public order. Such a situation is directly contrary to the best interests of the State. It is with the object of preventing the continuance of this evil and of forwarding an act of justice long overdue, that we ask for support for this Bill. The reform will be the more gracious if it comes by the united effort of men of all parties.

WSC to H. N. Brailsford

19 April 1910   Home Office

Copy

Dear Mr Brailsford,

Owing to great pressure of business I have not been able to study your papers, which I see you sent me on the 13th April, until this morning. Pray accept my expression of regret for the delay. I should be willing to allow myself to be quoted in the manner you suggest as 'welcoming the formation of a Committee and favouring its solution on non-party lines', provided that the others whom you mention, or most of them, are willing to come forward too. Perhaps you will write to me on this, and let me know what progress you have made.

I do not wish to be committed at the present juncture to any special form or basis in or upon which the franchise is to be granted to women. I have not sufficiently studied the bearings of the municipal franchise which you now favour. I am, however, anxious to see women relieved in principle from a disability which is injurious to them whilst it is based on grounds of sex.

Yours sincerely
WINSTON S. CHURCHILL

H. N. Brailsford to WSC

21 April [1910]   32 Well Walk

Dear Mr Churchill,

I am very much indebted to you for consenting to give the conciliation Committee your blessing. I will send you a proof of our letter some days before it goes out – which will not be before May 18 or 19. This I should in any case have done because we have a good deal altered its wording.

Sincerely yours
H. N. BRAILSFORD

Lord Lytton to WSC

6 June 1910   Knebworth House

Private

Dear Winston,

My talk with you today has made me very sad. I felt so incapable of conveying to you the depth of feeling which is behind this question. For me it has become so much more than a question of politics. It touches everything which I most value in my private life. It involves serious risk to my sister's life,[1] it has broken the health & spirits of my mother, and it is a cause of much sorrow and bitterness in my relations with Pamela.[2] For these reasons I have thrown myself heart and soul into the negotiations of the last 4 months, and I had hoped that this shadow was going to pass away at last. If we fail the disappointment will be hard to bear and the future will be difficult to face. I could not tell you this in our interview but I want you to know why I look upon the question as altogether different from such matters as plural voting or Welsh disestablishment and why I long to find a statesman who will treat the question apart from its relation to party matters.

The difficulty which I have experienced in getting the different sections to accept the basis of our Bill makes me realise that if the present moment is not utilised all the forces which we have been at such pains to concentrate will again be dissipated & the struggle will go on for another generation.

I did not see Pamela today but I left a message for her at North Audley Street asking her to communicate with you by telephone.

Yrs ever
LYTTON

H. N. Brailsford to WSC

8 July [1910]   32 Well Walk

Dear Mr Churchill,

I hope you will be able to speak, and as warmly as you honestly can, for our Bill on Monday or Tuesday. I am afraid we shall not fare well. I had

---

[1] Constance Georgina Lytton (1869–1923), daughter of the 1st Earl of Lytton. She belonged to the WSPU, was several times imprisoned, and underwent forcible feeding. She had been gaoled in February 1910 for agitating in Downing Street.
[2] Pamela Frances Audrey Lytton, Countess Lytton; she married the 2nd Earl in 1902.

hoped that Lloyd George would have consented to be neutral, but he is quite determined to do his best to smash us. On the other hand the Unionists cannot [do] away with their fear that the Bill means adult suffrage. It is a grotesque situation. George will smash us because it is not adult suffrage, and the Unionists will desert us because it will lead to adult suffrage. Our best hope is that men like yourself & Mr Birrell who really want a moderate solution should say so. I don't think much of the Liberal talk about adult suffrage is sincere. Adult suffrage means Greek Calends. That is why it is popular.

Then it is vital for us to get our Bill sent to a Grand Committee. If it stops short after an academic debate, we shall be no further forward than Jacob Bright,[1] who carried a second reading in 1870. That will be of course the signal for the revolt. We could do nothing further to check it. As long as the Bill is alive Lord Lytton & I have an argument.

The precedents are good and clear, Mr G. Hardy[2] moved in 1907 to except franchise Bills from the operation of the new rule about Grand Committees. C.B. opposed him in a very strong & definite speech (April 11) and the amendment was overwhelmingly defeated.

Then in 1909 the London Elections Bill, which the official opposition opposed, was sent up to a Grand Committee.

I enclose a reprint of an article of mine designed to answer the criticism that our Bill is not democratic.

Sincerely yours

H. N. BRAILSFORD

H. N. Brailsford to WSC

12 July 1910　　　　　　　　　　　　　　　　　　　　32 Well Walk

Sir,

I beg to inform you that in discussing your conduct in today's debate, I shall be obliged to describe it as treacherous. You knew when you 'welcomed the formation' of the Conciliation Committee the nature of the Bill which it was drafting.

I shall further state that you said what was false when you gave the House to understand that you are in favour of adult suffrage. You told me that you are strongly opposed to the duplicated vote of married women.

---

[1] Jacob Bright (1821–1899), brother of John Bright; Liberal MP for Manchester 1867–74, 1876–85; Manchester S.W. 1886–95; his suffrage bill of 1870 passed a second reading but was then defeated.

[2] George Alexander Hardy (1851–1920), Director London Missionary Society; Liberal MP Stowmarket 1906–10.

If you consider yourself insulted, I am at your service, and will study your convenience in making arrangements for a meeting.

I am Sir, Faithfully yours
H. N. BRAILSFORD

WSC to H. N. Brailsford

[12 July 1910]   Home Office

Copy

Sir,
   I was never consulted in any way as to the nature of the Bill. I never saw the Bill until after it was made public. As soon as I had examined it & had the opportunity of consulting others I wrote to Lord Lytton that it was 'one-sided' and 'undemocratic'. He has no doubt kept my letter. You are right in saying that I welcomed the formation of a Committee on non-party lines. You know perfectly well that you had no authority to use my name in connexion with the Bill – which I now learn you have done freely – but only in connexion with the formation of a Committee.
   With regard to the question of adult suffrage – you ought not to repeat for public purposes private conversation or such fragments of it as you can remember, or think you can remember. This is rather a well-known rule: but if your strong feelings lead you to break it, I can only say that I discussed with you quite freely at your request the objections & difficulties which attach to every solution of the woman's franchise question. Among other things I pointed out that adult suffrage would be largely a duplication of the existing franchise. That is quite true: & that is one reason why I should prefer the first solution I indicated to the House yesterday – if it were possible. If it is not possible, I am at the proper time & circumstances willing as I told my constituents in Dundee at the last election to vote for adult suffrage.
   Your accusation of 'treachery' is not well-grounded. Under what obligations had you or your friends ever placed me? For the last five years you have disturbed or tried to disturb almost every meeting I have addressed. During the last four elections that I have fought your organisations have opposed me with their utmost strength: & if I have been returned on three occasions it has been in spite of every effort on the part of the militant suffragists to prevent me.
   You personally have received from me nothing but courtesy, & the sympathy which I felt – and feel – for you in your earnestness & distress. You had no right or reason to suppose that I was not an entirely free agent

to give my vote & counsel in Parliament, agreeably with my public pledges, & according to my judgement.

Yours faithfully
WINSTON S. CHURCHILL

Edward Marsh to WSC

13 July 1910   Home Office

In *The Times* of October 20, 1909, appears a letter from Miss Christabel Pankhurst in which she professes to quote from a speech made by you on April 15, 1908:

'I will try my best as and when occasion offers, because I do sincerely think that the women always had a logical case, and that they have now got behind them a great and popular demand among women. It is no longer a movement of a few extravagant and excitable people, but a movement which is gradually spreading to all classes of women, and that being so, it assumes the same character as franchise movements have previously assumed.'

This is evidently meant to refer to your reply to Miss Clunas[1] at Dundee on the 19 October 1909.

H. N. Brailsford to WSC

13 July [1910]   32 Well Walk

Sir,

It is hardly accurate to say that you were 'not consulted in any way' as to the nature of our Bill. I outlined it in our first conversation, and its final form was exactly as I then sketched it. That you 'never saw it until it was published' I can only explain on the assumption that you did not receive the letter I sent you. At our first conversation you gave me provisionally your consent to my using your name as a supporter or rather patron of our Committee, in the formula that you 'welcome the formation of our Committee and would favour a solution on non-party lines.' You afterwards confirmed this in writing. I then sent you the proof [of] the memorandum which

---

[1] Lila Clunas was Secretary of the Dundee branch of the Women's Freedom League 1908–1912. In July 1909 she had been arrested in Downing Street.

I again enclose. I told you (as I had done in conversation) that this was going to all members. I added that unless you expressly authorised me I should not allow your name to be used in the press. To this I got no answer (nor was an answer necessary) – which in no way surprised me, for the King's Death disturbed everyone's normal business. But failing to get your reply, I assumed your consent (confirmed by letter) to what we had originally discussed *ie* the use of your name in the circular to members. By an accident for which I am not to blame – for I took every precaution against it – your name did get into one newspaper, the *Manchester Guardian*, & was then copied by others.

I should never have argued that you were committed to the details of our Bill, or even to our policy of forcing it on in this session. But I do not understand how a public man can say that he welcomes the formation of a Committee constituted to push a particular Bill, and then come forward as its most formidable opponent without treachery. If you had in your speech made your support contingent on the removal of the various opportunities for 'faggot' voting which you think you see in it, we should have made no complaint of your conduct. To that, as I told you in our second conversation, we have an answer. We have ourselves always been prepared to amend clause II as I indicate in the enclosed circular. But your opposition was more fundamental than this. You attacked us chiefly for omitting most married women. Both Lord Lytton & I gathered from you in conversation that this was the feature of our Bill which you specially approved. I will respect your reminder that even this part of our conversation was private – (the greater part of it I had of course regarded as highly confidential). But I can refer you to your statement in Dundee. When you said that something should be done for women who were 'at a loose end', the phrase, not a very lucid one, conveyed to me two things (1) that not all women in your view should have the vote and (2) that the class which ought to have it is in some way outside the usual social ties. I took this to mean single women or widows. At all events, as a declaration of faith in adult suffrage, it seems to lack your usual trenchancy of expression.

I have up to the present made no statement in public or to the press about your attitude. In conversation I have always stated that you made reserves on the details of the Bill. If I do make any public statement, I will take care that this is clear. To my main point I adhere. You did support the Committee. You then tried in a singularly bitter and vehement attack to destroy its work on the threshold. You have every right to point out that you owe nothing to the militants. That very fact would have made them the more grateful for the magnanimity of your support, had it been continued. I have spent a great deal of time in my talks with them in trying to persuade them that they take an unduly cynical view of politicians. You have made me a convert to their bitter reading of human nature.

Faithfully yours
H. N. BRAILSFORD

PS Allow me to add that I am fully sensible of the courtesy you have shown to myself personally. No personal factor enters into the resentment which I feel – and have thought it honest to express – on public grounds.

H.N.B.

The Times

14 July 1910

Speaking at a woman suffrage meeting at Welwyn, Herts, yesterday, Lord Lytton said the time had gone by for mere colourless generalities of the question.

He had listened to the speeches of the Home Secretary in the House of Commons with disgust. The Home Secretary's name was on the back of the manifesto of the committee responsible for the Bill, which from the first received his sanction not only in principle but in detail. He had told Lord Lytton that he was not only in favour of the principle but thought the committee had found the right way to carry the first instalment. Three months later Mr Churchill came to the House of Commons and voted against the Bill. He was not surprised that women were disgusted at statesmen who trifled with their liberties.

WSC to Lord Lytton

14 July 1910　　　　　　　　　　　　　　　　　Home Office

Copy

My Lord,

I am very sorry to read your statements as reported in *The Times* to-day. They do not maintain that standard of candour and good faith which I have always associated with you.

I was never consulted in any way upon the framing of the Woman's Suffrage Bill. I never saw the Bill or knew anything about its scope, charac-ter or provisions, until after it had been made public in its final form. No one knows this better than you; for you were the first person to show me the Bill for the first time when you asked me to receive you at the Home Office about five weeks ago in order to seek my help in obtaining facilities for its progress. I told you at once that I was quite certain there was no chance at all of any Bill on this subject being carried through the House of Commons this year. I also told you that it would in my opinion be an abuse to send a franchise bill upstairs to a Grand Committee. I then asked you to tell me about the new bill, and you described it to me. It is true to say that at first sight I was favourably impressed by the plan and by your accounts of it and of its effect on our electoral system. Our conversation was private, as you several times assured me, and I tried to soothe you for your disappointment at hearing my views against facilities for passing the measure, by congratulations on your having at last brought so many conflicting sections of opinion together upon a definite proposal. You understood perfectly that these opinions were provisional. I asked you to leave a copy of the Bill in my possession in order that I might have it examined, and I told you I would write to you in a few days about it. I sent the Bill at once to various authorities on whom I should rely in questions of electoral reform. Within three days of our interview I wrote to you that the Bill was 'one-sided and undemocratic', and that I saw no prospect of its obtaining facilities for discussion this year. I have kept no copy of this letter. It never occurred to me that such a precaution was necessary with you. I have, however, kept your long and indignant answer in which you repeat the very expressions 'one-sided and undemocratic' which I had used, and scold me terribly for my state of mind.

Reviewing the facts – that you first showed me the Bill yourself, that you knew I had no knowledge of its provisions till you explained them to me, that I asked you to leave me a copy of the Bill in order that I might have it examined, and that, having examined it, I wrote immediately to you that it was 'one-sided and undemocratic', – I am sure that your statements, as reported to-day, do you no credit, and will do me no harm.

There is only one other point. You say that my name was 'on the back of the manifesto of the Committee responsible for the Bill'. Four months ago, before any Bill had been framed, at Mr Brailsford's request I gave my consent to his using my name as 'welcoming the formation of the Conciliation Committee and favouring a solution on non-party lines'. I gave this consent in writing. I enclose the letter by which I did so. I have given no other sanction or authority of any kind, written or verbal. If you and your friends have made an improper use of this authority, and have tried to connect it with this Suffrage bill, or to lead others to believe that it was so connected, you have only yourselves to blame for any misunderstanding that has arisen.

Yours faithfully

WINSTON S. CHURCHILL

Lord Lytton to WSC

15 July 1910   Knebworth House

Sir,

I only received late last night the letter which you have addressed to me
and which in your anxiety to appeal to the public you sent to the Press
before giving me an opportunity of replying to it.

You impugn my candour and good faith in criticising the speech which
you made in the House of Commons on Tuesday. I am quite content that
with all the facts before them, the public, to whom you have appealed, shall
decide whether you or I have departed furthest from that standard of candour and good faith which is to be looked for between friends. You say that
you were never consulted in any way upon the framing of the Woman's
Suffrage Bill, that you never saw the Bill, or knew anything about its scope,
character, or provisions until after it had been made public; that you learnt
of the Bill for the first time from me about 5 weeks ago, that within 3 days of
our interview you wrote to me that the Bill was one-sided and undemocratic,
and that to assume that you favoured the Bill in any way was altogether
improper.

My answer to you is to recall the following facts: –

1. In March last Mr Brailsford, the Secretary of our Conciliation Committee, had an interview with you and described to you the outlines of the
Bill which we intended to produce. You discussed together briefly the nature
of the present Municipal franchise and its suitability for our purpose. Mr
Brailsford, who understood you to approve the plan subject to further reflection, asked for permission to cite you as a patron of our Committee, and
you accepted the formula that you 'welcomed the formation of our Committee and favoured a solution of the question on non-party lines.' This
sanction was subject to confirmation in writing.

2. In April Mr Brailsford sent you a further memorandum detailing our
plan more exactly. To this you replied in the letter which you sent to the
press yesterday.

3. During the Spring recess Mr Brailsford again sent you a proof of the
memorandum of the Conciliation Committee which was shortly afterwards
published. This document which is now familiar to everyone, contained a list
of the Committee at that date, a list of the supporters of the Committee, including your own name, the text of our Bill, and an explanatory memorandum of its provisions. In a covering letter Mr Brailsford called attention to the
list of supporters, hoping that it satisfied the conditions contained in your
letter of April 19th, and asking that if you had any comment or criticisms to
make, you would reply within a week as the memorandum would then be

sent out to Members of the House of Commons. No answer was received to this letter and we naturally assumed that this implied your consent to its publication. The memorandum was published and widely commented upon, but you gave no indication of your dissatisfaction with the course which we had taken.

4. At the beginning of June I sought an interview with you at the Home Office with the object of asking you to help us to secure facilities for the discussion of the Bill. You expressed the opinion that no time could be spared out of the present session but that something might be done in a subsequent session. I replied that all the arguments which you used against granting facilities at the present time would apply with even greater force to every session in the future, that the present moment was singularly opportune, and that we had become rather impatient of vague promises in some indefinite future. You then used these words 'I am offering you something much more definite than you have ever got before. I am not merely expressing approval of the general principle, but I think the actual solution which you propose is a good one. I should like to look into the matter more carefully but so far as I can judge your Bill seems to be the best proposal which has ever yet been made.' I expressed regret that you could not hold out more hope of the subject being dealt with in the present session, and wrote to you in the same sense the next day, explaining my reasons for feeling more strongly on this matter than on other political questions of the day.

5. On June 11th you replied to my letter that the results of your further enquiries were unfavourable to action at the present time. 'I cannot think it possible' your letter continued 'that this question can be settled in the present Parliament unless a longer life opens out to the House of Commons than is now probable. . . . I am also told that the Bill itself is open to many objections on the score of being partial and undemocratic.' This letter dealt, as did our interview which preceded it, almost exclusively with the question of facilities for the passage of the Bill, it being understood between us that the Bill itself was acceptable. It never occurred to me that you would have expressed to me decided approval of a Bill if its contents were entirely unknown to you or that having done so you would accept without any reference to those who had consulted you the statements of others that the Bill was entirely objectionable, and I replied to your letter that what you had been told about the 'partial and undemocratic' character of the Bill was untrue.

6. On July 2nd (only a week before the 2nd reading debate) Mr Brailsford had another interview with you in which the Bill was discussed at some length. You made no complaint of the use which we had made of your name in our manifesto, but you expressed some doubts as to the effect of the Bill. You referred in particular to the possibility of faggot voting (which figured

so largely in your speech last Tuesday). Mr Brailsford replied that we had foreseen this criticism, but thought such cases would be very rare. He added however, that if there were thought to be any serious danger of such a thing happening on a large scale, the matter could easily be remedied by an amendment in Committee to the effect that a husband and wife should not both be qualified in respect of premises situated in the same constituency.

7. On July 12th, you come down to the House of Commons and make a violent but altogether unsuccessful attack upon the Bill, knowing well while you are speaking that your criticisms are not only far-fetched, but are capable of being met by an amendment in Committee to which the promoters of the Bill would not be opposed.

Such is the history of the relations between the Conciliation Committee and yourself. The public will judge how far we were justified in counting on your support, or at least on your friendly criticism, and whether you have given cause for the resentment which I expressed on Wednesday. Of all the gentlemen on both sides of the House whose names appeared on our manifesto and with whom we had had communications of a similar character, you alone turned against us at the last moment and delivered a treacherous attack on those whom you had allowed to regard you as a friend. Your colleagues in the Cabinet who had given us encouragement had also 'been told that the Bill was open to many objections': they, too, had heard it criticised as undemocratic and had acquainted us frankly with these criticisms, but they did not serve them up in the House of Commons with rhetorical relish of their own, nor did they at the instigation of others deliberately parody our proposals for the sake of appearing to score an advantage in debate. The Members of the Conciliation Committee and the advocates of Woman's Suffrage throughout the country, are deeply grateful to the friends who upheld their cause in the recent debate, and they respect as worthy antagonists those who honestly opposed them, but I do not know in what quarter the part which you have played in the controversy will meet with either gratitude or respect.

I enclose a letter from Mr Brailsford on which my information of your communications with him is based.

I am, Yours faithfully
LYTTON

H. N. Brailsford to Lord Lytton

15 July 1910   32 Well Walk

Copy

Dear Lytton,

In view of Mr Churchill's letter in to-day's Press you may find it useful to have from me a statement of my communications as Honorary Secretary of the Conciliation Committee with him.

At my first conversation with him in March I explained to him the lines of the Bill which we intended to promote. It was not yet drafted in a technical shape, but we discussed briefly the nature of the present Municipal franchise, and its suitability for our purpose. I understood him to say that subject to further reflection he approved our plan. I asked for his authority to cite him as a patron of our Committee, and he accepted the formula that he 'welcomed the formation of our Committee and favoured a solution on non-party lines'. This sanction was subject to confirmation in writing.

In April I sent him a further memorandum detailing our plan more exactly. To this he replied, again stating that I might use his name, provided I got others. He reserved his opinion on the details of the Municipal franchise with which, he said, he was not well acquainted.

My next step was to send him a proof of the explanatory memorandum which we afterwards published. It contained a list of the supporters of our Committee including himself, and the text of our Bill. In my covering letter I drew his attention to the other names we had secured, presumed that they met the conditions we had made, and asked him if he had any comments or criticisms to make, and let me have them within a week, as we proposed then to send our circular to Members of the House of Commons. A reply was not necessary, and receiving no reply, I assumed his consent to publication.

On July 2nd, Mr Churchill again received me and we talked at some length. He made no complaint of the use we had made of his name in our manifesto. He told me, however, that he had some doubts as to the details of our Bill, and mentioned rather casually the possibilities of faggot voting which figures so largely in his speech. I replied that we had foreseen this criticism, but thought such cases would be rare. I said, however, that this difficulty could with ease be met and added that we should probably be prepared, if necessary, to table an amendment which I explained to him. I left him under the impression that he was satisfied with this solution of the difficulties which he had raised. I must refrain from any further account of a conversation most of which was clearly private. I cannot, however, refrain from expressing my surprise at the rapidity of his conversion to some of the views which he publicly expressed a fortnight later. Complete silence is impossible in view of his statement to you that he was 'never consulted in any way upon the framing of the Woman Suffrage Bill'. We consulted him at every step. I have already told Mr Churchill that his conduct in my opinion has been treacherous. I cannot admit that a public man who has given his name as one of its patrons to a Committee formed to promote a particular Bill, can honourably come forward, not merely as the friendly critic, but as the jubilant and malignant adversary of that Bill.

Sincerely yours

H. N. BRAILSFORD

WSC to Lord Lytton

15 July 1910   Home Office

Draft

My Lord,

The communication which you have sent me today is lengthy: but it does not conceal the facts. Those facts are: – first: that on the 19th of April in consenting to allow my name to be quoted as favouring the formation of your committee, I expressly & explicitly declined to be committed to any Bill which that Committee might prepare, or to the municipal franchise basis.

Secondly: that in the face of this letter you thought it proper without further authority from me to 'assume' that you had my consent not only to the form of your memorandum to members of the House of Commons, but to the actual text of the Bill itself: and that, as I now learn, you proceeded to use my name freely as being in favour of that measure (which at this time I had never read) 'not only in principle, but in its details'.

Thirdly: That for the purposes of public controversy you repeat your recollections of private conversation at an interview only granted on grounds of friendship. Fourthly: that although more than a month ago you had received & bitterly complained of my letter describing your Bill as 'partial & undemocratic' you continued to represent me for the purposes of your propaganda as being still in favour of it. Lastly: that on the materials aforesaid you are so bold as to accuse me of treachery & bad-faith.

These facts require no comment & I am glad that there is at any rate no dispute about them.

I am sure that on no other subject in the world would you have behaved in such a fashion.

Yours faithfully

WINSTON S. CHURCHILL

[*The following was added as a Footnote and then crossed out by WSC*]
Whatever the Suffrage agitation may do for women, there can be no doubt of its evil effects upon some men.

Edward Marsh to WSC

July 1910   Home Office

Dear Winston,
    I couldn't help writing to Victor – and I think I ought to show you what I have written. I am broken hearted abt this quarrel.
                                                                  Yr
                                                                  E

Note by WSC
You are a good little boy; & I am vy fond of you.

                                                                  W

Memorandum by WSC

Not for publication.

19 July 1910

    Mr Churchill has no wish to carry public controversy on this matter any further, but he thinks it right to place on record a full account of the circumstances as to his action upon the recent Woman's Suffrage Bill and Lord Lytton's charges.
    It must be borne in mind throughout that Mr Churchill and Lord Lytton regarded the whole question of Women's Votes from very different points of view. Lord Lytton's attitude has always assumed that it was Mr Churchill's duty, without delay, to remedy the great injustice under which women suffer by being excluded from the franchise, and to atone for his neglect to do so in the past. Mr Churchill's view has been that although in principle the absolute sex barrier is illogical, yet that there is no great practical grievance; and, further, that in any case the militant suffragists have less claim on him than on any other public man. For the last five years, these people have attempted in the course of their agitation to break up every meeting he has addressed in any part of the country. They have opposed him with the whole strength of their organisations at four successive elections. If Mr Churchill has been returned three times out of four, it has been in spite of the utmost opposition which the Women Suffragists could offer. They

have at all times treated him with the vilest discourtesy and unfairness. They have attacked him repeatedly in the most insulting terms. They have assaulted him physically. Shortly before the last election at Dundee he informed a deputation of his women constituents that he would give them no pledge whatever of any assistance in the immediate future. In consequence of this he was again opposed by the suffragist organisations throughout the campaign, and his return by a majority of six thousand clearly left him with the fullest liberty of action. There could be no question of his being under any obligation or of any claim of any sort being urged against him.

After the election was over and Mr Churchill became Home Secretary, Mr Brailsford asked to see him. Mr Churchill would not have received Mr Brailsford in ordinary circumstances; but, first, because complaints had been made that women suffragists and their friends could not get a fair hearing from members of the Government, and, secondly, because he knew that Mr Brailsford had sacrificed to his opinions his position on the *Daily News* at heavy cost to himself, Mr Churchill decided to accord him an interview.

3. Mr Brailsford then put forward the proposal for a non-party committee to be formed to see if it were not possible to arrive at a settlement by conciliation. Mr Brailsford's ideas of conciliation, it now turns out, was that a bargain should be struck between the different sections of the supporters of women's suffrage, and the resulting compromise embodied in a bill which should be immediately carried by the House of Commons in preference to all other business and all other controversies under threats of lawless violence, if not of murder.

4. Mr Churchill's idea of a Conciliation Committee was that it should endeavour to remove the whole question of female suffrage from the sphere of violence and rowdyism into which it had sunk, should try to seek by patient and peaceful methods for the line of least resistance, not merely among suffragists but among opponents of the principle, and that a spirit of forbearance on the part of suffragists, and of sympathy on the part of the Government and the public, should develop as the wounds of previous ill-usage and bad behaviour were gradually healed by time. At this interview, however, Mr Churchill made it clear to Mr Brailsford that he would not be committed to any particular form of Suffrage Bill. The formula agreed upon was carefully drawn up with a view to safeguarding Mr Churchill in this respect. All he was asked to do was to allow his name to be mentioned as being 'in favour of the formation of a Conciliation Committee, and to a settlement on non-party lines.' Other Ministers and ex-Ministers were no doubt similarly approached.

5. On the 13th April, Mr Brailsford forwarded Mr Churchill his proposals in writing, and asked for a confirmation of the permission aforesaid. Mr

Churchill merely glanced at the statement of the proposals, saw that he was asked to do no more than he had expressed himself as willing to do some weeks before, and wrote the letter of the 19th April. But he expressly stipulated in this letter that he was not to be held to any particular form of Suffrage Bill, and he even went so far as to mention the Municipal Franchise as a basis about which he was not sufficiently informed. The letter is appended.

6. Having taken up this attitude and limited himself thus carefully, he thought no more about the matter for some time.

In May Mr Brailsford forwarded to Mr Churchill a proof of the circular which had been drawn up by the Conciliation Committee, and which is appended. Mr Churchill had taken no part in the deliberations of this Committee, and had never given five minutes to the merits of their Bill. He had never expressed any opinion upon it. He was entirely occupied with many other matters of great consequence connected with the political and constitutional situation, with the administrative work of his Department and with the death of the King. He remembers to have received the draft circular. He looked only at the first page and saw that his name was quoted there in strict conformity with the conditions which he had dictated, never supposed for a moment that his assent to the Bill would be claimed or could be implied, pushed aside the circular with numbers of others which reach him every day, and continued to be absorbed in matters which, in his judgment, were of greater public importance.

7. When the circular was published Mr Churchill noticed references to it in the newspapers in which his name was mentioned. He never noticed any reference which went beyond saying that he and some other Ministers and ex-Ministers had expressed themselves as 'favourable to the formation of a Conciliation Committee and for a settlement on non-party lines.' He had no knowledge at any time that he had been represented as going at all beyond this, and he is strongly of opinion that any attempt to use his name beyond these limits was most improper.

8. Early in June Lord Lytton asked to see Mr Churchill at the Home Office. He was received at once because he was a close personal friend. Mr Churchill then, for the first time, heard from him the character of the Bill and a very enthusiastic account of its many advantages. He fully admits that he thought at first sight the municipal franchise was a practical proposal; he was impressed with the fact that all sections of the suffragists had come together upon it. He was, however, principally occupied in explaining to Lord Lytton that there was no possible chance of any facilities being given for any women's suffrage measure this session. He explained this very clearly to Lord Lytton with many reasons drawn from the general political

situation, and when told that Lord Lytton was greatly disappointed at this view, Mr Churchill dwelt on the good value of the work done by the Conciliation Committee as a civil and friendly way of consoling him. Mr Churchill regarded this interview as strictly private and confidential, thoroughly informal, and between old friends. He even impressed this upon Lord Lytton at its conclusion. He never would have expressed himself about that which he had not examined or studied in any way in such unguarded and incautious language, unless he had felt quite sure that he could trust the man he was talking to never to take the slightest advantage of any obviously unpremeditated utterances. If Mr Churchill was to blame for not practising all the reserve and precautions of public speech on this occasion, all he can say is that having for five years transacted important ministerial business, having talked in confidence and on the dead-level with hundreds of men, he has never had any previous experience of a breach of an honourable confidence.

9. There was, however, no misconception at the interview. Lord Lytton knew perfectly well that Mr Churchill was entirely opposed to the idea of any progress being made in order that any women's suffrage bill might be passed this year. He knew, further, that any opinions Mr Churchill had expressed upon the merits of the bill were purely provisional. Mr Churchill asked him to leave a copy of the Bill behind him when he went away, and in Lord Lytton's presence he gave it to Mr Marsh and asked him to have it examined and enquired into. After Lord Lytton had gone, Mr Churchill gave directions for the bill to be sent to the Whips of the party, and thereafter to certain other authorities who were asked to express an opinion upon its effect from an electoral point of view. It may be observed here that only experts can judge of the effect of these various franchises, and a mere scrutiny of the measure by one unacquainted with these matters would convey no true idea of its scope and character.

10. Such was the interview, and Lord Lytton was far from satisfied with it. Within a few hours he wrote to Mr Churchill a long and pathetic letter setting forth the keenness of his feelings upon the subject of women being given votes, the great trouble which their not having votes and their agitation to gain them, was causing in his family, his anxiety lest his sister's conduct in the agitation should endanger her life, and he expressed himself as deeply grieved that he had not obtained a clear promise that full facilities should be granted at once.

11. Mr Churchill did not reply to this letter until three days had passed, partly owing to pressure of work and partly because he had yet received the reports upon the bill which he had asked for from the various expert authorities. As soon as opportunity served and information was at hand,

however, he wrote to Lord Lytton a letter of which he has not kept a copy but which he recollects very clearly. The letter stated that as the result of Mr Churchill's inquiries he was bound to tell Lord Lytton, with many regrets for the pain it would cause him, that there was no chance whatever of this bill, or any other suffrage bill, being proceeded with in the present session and perhaps in the present Parliament. It stated, further, that Mr Churchill had now learned that the bill itself was 'open to many objections on the grounds of being partial and undemocratic.' If Mr Churchill did not express himself more strongly on these points and enter into them with more detail and elaboration, it was because he was conscious of how much pain such arguments would cause Lord Lytton, and he was, while informing him of the truth, trying to do it in the least painful and offensive manner possible.

12. Lord Lytton's reply to this letter was a long four-page letter of bitter and scornful reproaches and upbraidings. Mr Churchill regrets that he cannot find the letter but he thinks there is no dispute about its contents. It began by saying that Lord Lytton would rather have had no letter from Mr Churchill than to have received one like that. It proceeded to speak with contempt of statesmen who permitted their views on this subject to be coloured by mere considerations of party or electoral advantage, and it protested vehemently against 'trifling'. Mr Churchill found this letter awaiting him when he came home very late one night after a hard day's work. He was indignant at its tone and contents. He thought that, considering Lord Lytton as a suffragist had no claims whatever upon him (in view of the attitude of the suffragist organisations during the election) and considering that Mr Churchill had only consulted with him on a basis of pure friendship, it was hard that he should be assailed with such wearisome recriminations on a subject with which he was, after all, only indirectly concerned. It was, in fact, to the Prime Minister and not to Mr Churchill, that all representation on the subject of facilities should have been addressed. In his anger at receiving this letter Mr Churchill wrote a very sharp rejoinder. He did not send it off the same night however, and in the morning simply tore it up and wrote to Lord Lytton a short note saying 'You put a strain on friendship when you make a letter written you in friendly courtesy an excuse for so many reproaches.'

13. Reviewing these facts, Mr Churchill is utterly unable to understand how Lord Lytton can affect to have been under the impression that he and Mr Churchill were working together in close amity and co-operation. The correspondence had come to an abrupt conclusion with total divergence and disagreement between the parties. It should have been clear to Lord Lytton that the conversation which he had had with Mr Churchill some days previously was completely cancelled and superseded by the written communi-

cations which had passed. These communications had ended almost in a quarrel, and they were perfectly definite and precise in themselves. It should be remembered that Mr Churchill also took it for granted that Mr Brailsford had shown Lord Lytton Mr Churchill's letter of 19th April, and that taking this letter in conjunction with the later correspondence Lord Lytton could have been under no misapprehension as to Mr Churchill's views or as to his complete detachment from Lord Lytton's movement. Yet Mr Churchill now learns from many quarters that in spite of this Lord Lytton and Mr Brailsford freely used his name with Members of Parliament whose support they were anxious to obtain, not only as being favourable to the formation of the Committee, which was true; not only as approving the form of the memorandum to Members of Parliament, which was, to say the least of it, an assumption; but as being actively favourable to the principle and the details of the particular measure they were proposing.

Mr Churchill has searched in vain for any possible explanation of this.

14. The only other occasions when Mr Churchill has discussed in any way the question of the Women's Suffrage Bill were when Mr Brailsford visited him twice at the Home Office. On both occasions Mr Brailsford did not come up to talk over the details of the Bill as he and Lord Lytton have stated in their published statements, nor would he have been received for that purpose. He came in order to express to the Home Secretary his anxiety at the dangerous and murderous violence which he thought would follow if no facilities were accorded for the passage of the Suffrage Bill through this Parliament. It was Mr Churchill's duty to listen to anything Mr Brailsford might say on these grave matters, and to receive from him any warnings he might be in a position to give. It was with this aspect of the agitation that Mr Churchill's mind was occupied at these interviews and any conversation with Mr Brailsford on the subject of the Bill was purely incidental and accidental.

15. Mr Churchill does not think this subject was mentioned at all at their first interview. He remembers, however, to have told Mr Brailsford plainly at the outset of the second interview, 10 days before the second reading of the Bill, that he could not vote for the measure, and that he had never seen it until he had had it examined a few days previously. Mr Brailsford seemed surprised at this and said 'We sent you the text of the Bill some weeks ago.' Mr Churchill proceeded to say that he had been informed by those who had examined the measure with knowledge, that it was undemocratic, would favour the property vote unduly, would give great opportunities for creating faggot voters. It is true, however, also to say that Mr Churchill expressed his intention of not voting against the Bill. The interview was private and informal, Mr Churchill's mind was not fully made up, he never considered

himself as under the slightest obligation to Mr Brailsford, he thought he was perfectly free to explain frankly that his judgment was still balancing be-tween the different courses which were open to him as a Member of Parliament to take, and he is quite sure that Mr Brailsford fully understood the position.

16. Mr Churchill did not finally decide as to what action he should take on the second reading until two days before. His first inclination was neither to speak nor vote, and this is the course that would usually be taken by a Member of Parliament who disapproved of the method of a bill while not opposed to the general object at which it aims. Two considerations induced Mr Churchill to take a more decided line: First, that being now forced by the imminence of the debate and division to study the Bill for the first time with thoroughness, he perceived a long succession of vices and faults of which he had had no previous knowledge, and he became convinced that the bill was not only absurd and indefensible in itself, but deeply injurious to the Liberal cause by reason of its partiality. The second consideration was more serious. It was well-known that the Prime Minister intended to speak and vote against the Bill. Mr Churchill was also opposed to it. In view of the threats of personal violence which had been used, and of the information which Mr Brailsford had imparted to him, Mr Churchill felt that the Prime Minister's position after the debate and division would become one not unattended with danger. He thought it would be very cowardly if in face of such threats he allowed the Prime Minister and the Chancellor of the Exchequer (who had by this time made up his mind to vote and speak against the Bill) to take the whole burden of this upon their shoulders, while all the time he agreed with them, and was known to agree with them, that the Bill was a bad bill and ought not to pass; and he could not purchase an ignoble immunity by silence and abstention. He therefore decided on the Monday morning to vote and speak against the measure. He did not feel that any communication with Lord Lytton was necessary. All correspondence between them had been broken off in total disagreement five or six weeks before. He regarded his relations with Mr Brailsford as governed throughout by his former communication to that gentleman on April 19th, on which he had made no further advance than to say at their last interview that he could not support the Bill. He therefore set himself to work on the Monday afternoon and the Tuesday morning to put his objections to the measure into a definite and effective form.

17. On the morrow of the Division, the *Daily Telegraph* announced that 'the Conciliation Committee have stated that they hold Mr Churchill's promise in writing to vote for the Bill.' This lie Mr Churchill treated with contempt as it was not stated by any reputable authority. He thought it well,

however, to ask Mr Marsh to write a line to Lord Lytton and put on record the outlines of their last conversation and their subsequent correspondence, and ask (though this Mr Marsh forgot to do) for copies of his letters. Lord Lytton took no notice of this except to write to Mr Marsh and say that Mr Churchill 'would get no help from him in defending himself against charges of treachery and hypocrisy.' The next morning Mr Churchill read in *The Times* Lord Lytton's speech at Welwyn in which Lord Lytton stated that Mr Churchill had given his sanction from the beginning not only to the principle of the bill, but to the details of the bill – an absolute untruth; that his name was on the back of the Manifesto of the Committee – it had been put there without his authority, but, even so, in a form which clearly disconnected him from any responsibility for the text of the measure; and, thirdly, that Mr Churchill had told Lord Lytton that he thoroughly approved of the measure – a clear breach of private confidence, and a breach which became disingenuous because it suppressed all reference to the subsequent correspondence. The rest is upon record.

18. Had Lord Lytton chosen to write to Mr Churchill expressing his disappointment and surprise at the character of his speech, or had he called for an explanation on any particular point, Mr Churchill would have taken pains and trouble for the sake of old friendship, *but for no other reason*, to place all the facts as he knew them and all his reasons from his point of view at his Lordship's disposal. Instead of this Lord Lytton at once proceeded to make grievous and insulting charges publicly, to hold Mr Churchill up to execration and hatred to his excited followers, thereby not only impugning his honour, but possibly exposing him to outrage. Mr Churchill has taken the trouble to place these facts on record in order that it may be clear that he does not break the chain of old and valued friendship without reasons which are adequate.

[WSC]

Memorandum by Sir Edward Troup

17 July 1910   [Home Office]

No system of franchise can be unqualified: if every other limit were removed, there must still be a limit of age.

Our present franchise is limited by

(*a*) Age

(*b*) Sex

(*c*) either permanent residence (occupation vote) or property (ownership vote).

(*d*) exclusion of criminals, lunatics, and paupers.

There might be other modes of selection without affecting its democratic character. A franchise is undemocratic only if so limited as to favour one class.

If we were establishing a new democratic franchise, the individual voters might be selected on other and different principles e.g. education, or service to the state, the only essential being to make the standard such as to give the *people* its full proportion of voters.

It ought to be possible to frame a franchise for women which would not add enormously to the mass of voters, & yet be as democratic as the male franchise in the sense of giving a fair proportion to all classes.

The following is suggested, subject to necessary condition that no woman is to be registered except on application: –

(a) All women having a certain educational qualification, e.g. graduates of Universities and (in the case of Universities which do not admit women to degrees) those who have passed the equivalent examination.

(b) Women who have served at least three years as members of local authorities (Borough, County, & District Councils, Education Committees, Boards of Guardians &c).

(c) Women who (being qualified on having husbands qualified by residence) have brought up to adult life at least two [? three] legitimate children who are neither mentally defective, criminal, nor pauper.

The last class introduces the principle of qualification by service to the state. The primary service which the state demands of men is ability to bear arms and its defence – of women the birth and upbringing of citizens. If this principle is introduced for women, it might be applied also for men in a modified degree, e.g. by giving votes to men under 25 (? 30) only if they are serving, or have served 3 years in the Navy, Army, or Territorials.

The classes (a) & (b) add only a small number of votes (say 20,000) but would satisfy the strongest claims. It is quite impossible to calculate & almost impossible to guess at the number who would come in under (c) but probably the number of women registered on *claim* would be less than a million, very likely less than half a million.

[E. TROUP]

C. F. G. Masterman to WSC

[No date]

I have consulted Mr Baines, the Legal Adviser to the LGB about the occupation question. He says the question is difficult, but his personal opinion is that a husband could create votes for his wife or daughters by *letting* to them any property of the value of £10. Thus he might let his wife the stables or any separate building: it is even possible that different parts of the same house could be treated as separate tenements & votes conferred on daughters in respect of the rooms they occupied. But this last point is more doubtful: it depends on the difficult question what is a separate tenement, so far as regards any separate building, such as stables or outhouses. Mr Baines thought it pretty clear that by the device of letting, votes could be given to wives & daughters. There would need to be some evidence of the letting, such as a formal agreement, – but it would not be necessary that any rent should pass. 'Occupation' never depends on payment of rent: 'beneficial uses' is sufficient to create 'occupation'.

C. F. G. MASTERMAN

The LGB are not responsible for Parliamentary Franchise questions, – only local franchise questions – so that Mr Baines' opinion is only a *personal* one.

Notes in Cabinet

[undated]   10 Downing Street

Note by WSC: –
  1. Any woman over 25 who is at once an occupier & a wage earner.
  2. Any widow over 25
  3. Any woman over 25 who possesses certain educational or professional qualifications
Note by D. Lloyd George: –
  Honestly I think you are on the wrong track here. There is a much more practical solution – short of adult suffrage.
Note by WSC: –
  I think I would like to pursue the idea further. Help me to do the best I can for it. If it breaks down in construction & development – no harm is done. It *does* meet the real grievance.
Note by D. Lloyd George: –
  It is too much like the Disraeli 'fancy' Franchise Bill which was laughed out by Bright.
Note by Sir E. Grey: –
  I agree with the C of E as at present advised.

WSC to Sir Edward Henry

22 November 1910   Home Office

Copy

Dear Sir E. Henry,

I am hearing from every quarter that my strongly expressed wishes conveyed to you on Wed evening & repeated on Fri morning that the suffragettes were not to be allowed to exhaust themselves but were to be arrested forthwith upon any defiance of the law, were not observed by the police on Friday last, with the result that vy regrettable scenes occurred.[1] It was my desire to avoid this even at some risk; to arrest large numbers & then subsequently to prosecute only where serious grounds were shown & I am sorry that, no doubt through a misunderstanding, another course has been adopted. In future I must ask for a strict adherence to the policy outlined herein.

Yrs v. sincly
WSC

H. H. Asquith to WSC

23 November 1910

My dear Winston,

The assault on Birrell[2] seems to have been a serious one, and I think that case should be proceeded with: also all cases of *serious* assault on the police.

Yrs
H.H.A.

Notes of Evidence

Copy

Taken on oath the 28th day of November 1910 at the Bow Street Police Court, in the County of London, and within the Metropolitan Police District, before Sir Albert de Rutzen,[3] Knight, one of the Magistrates of the Police

[1] The 'regrettable scenes' were to be remembered in the suffragette movement as taking place on 'Black Friday', November 18. Angered by the Government's failure to make any pledge on their behalf, a deputation of 300 women besieged Parliament during the afternoon. At the end of the day 117 women and 2 men had been arrested.

[2] In a suffragette demonstration on 22 November 1910 Birrell was temporarily lamed.

[3] Albert de Rutzen (1831–1913), Chief Magistrate of Metropolitan Police Courts 1901–13; Metropolitan Police Magistrate Marylebone 1876–91, Westminster 1891–97; knighted 1901.

Courts of the Metropolis sitting at the Police Court aforesaid, in the presence and hearing of

Hugh Arthur Franklin[1]

who was charged for that on the 26th day of November 1910 in a certain carriage of a railway train then employed in a journey between Bradford in the County of York and King's Cross Station of the Great Northern Railway in the said County of London and in the District aforesaid and passing in the course of such journey through the jurisdiction of the said Court did unlawfully assault one Winston Leonard Spencer Churchill against the Peace.

Joseph Sandercock,[2] Sergt New Scotland Yard on oath saith as follows: On Saturday the 26th of November I was on the train leaving Bradford at 5.10 pm, Inspector Parker[3] being with me. I went through the train with him and in a third class compartment saw prisoner sitting – I knew him before. With him there was a lady, Miss Laura Ainsworth, whom I recognised. It was a corridor train.

About 7 pm, as the train was going through Newark, dinner was about to be served in the dining car.

Mr Churchill was at Bradford on the 26th and addressed a meeting. I was present and I saw prisoner there, he was ejected as he interrupted Mr Churchill by making references to 'Votes for women' or words to that effect. That was between 4 and 4–30 pm. I knew Miss Ainsworth by sight, she is connected with the suffragette movement, I didn't notice her at the meeting.

Mr Churchill joined the 5.10 train at Bradford, and at about 7 left his compartment and was proceeding in the direction of the dining car. Inspr Parker had given me instructions before Mr Churchill left his compartment, and in consequence I took a seat opposite prisoner. To get to the dining car Mr Churchill had to pass through that third class compartment in the centre, as there were seats on either side of the passage. As soon as the door opened through which Mr Churchill was going prisoner jumped up, drew a dog whip from his pocket and shouted 'Winston Churchill, take that, you dirty cur'. I immediately seized him by the throat and forced him back on to the corner of the seat, Inspr Parker forcibly dragged the whip from prisoner's right hand which whip prisoner was flourishing at the time; the whip is now produced. I kept prisoner in the compartment, he struggled violently with me trying to get at Mr Churchill.

I had been sitting by the side of the lady and opposite prisoner for about ten minutes before Mr Churchill came. I saw nothing of the whip till

---

[1] Hugh Arthur Franklin, an undergraduate at Cambridge until June 1910, was sentenced to six weeks' imprisonment. He was a nephew of Sir Herbert Samuel.

[2] Joseph Sandercock (1874–1932), retired 1922.

[3] Edward John Parker (b. 1871), Police Inspector; retired 1931.

prisoner drew it out, that was the first time I saw it and Mr Churchill was then close to him. Before that I had no reason to believe prisoner was in possession of the whip.

Mr Churchill passed on, and returned the same way. I kept in the same compartment with prisoner. At King's Cross he went to Somers Town police station with me and a PC, and he was charged there by Inspr Parker with assaulting Mr Churchill. The charge was read to him and he said nothing. He asked for bail and at ½ past 12 he was bailed out to attend here.

On previous occasions I have seen prisoner at meetings which I have attended as a police officer; Mr Churchill has been present to my knowledge at one prior to Saturday, and on that occasion prisoner was ejected, he having shouted out 'Votes for women' while Mr Churchill was speaking.
Cross-examined.

You were forcibly ejected.
I heard you say 'Winston Churchill, take that you dirty cur', I am sure you said 'dirty'. You were perfectly quiet after the arrest, in the train and going to the station. I am positive you used the word 'cur'.

Joseph Sandercock, recalled on oath saith as follows:
Cross-examined.

I was present at Bradford when Mr Churchill delivered his speech, I was on the platform within 5 or 6 yards of Mr Churchill, I couldn't see over the whole of the hall. I am not sure if prisoner was the first or second person ejected. I saw him ejected, I was too far away to see if he was struck. He had cried out 'and that's women's suffrage' or words to that effect. I saw several persons ejected, I don't know their names. I have heard that one man fell down, but not that his leg was broken. It was impossible for me to see exactly how persons were ejected.

The words used by the prisoner were 'dirty cur', I pledge my oath the word 'dirty' was used. I didn't take a note of it at the time. It is a question of certainty, I was in the compartment where prisoner and the lady were, I was by the side of the lady and opposite prisoner. I didn't ask the lady to remove her bag to let me sit by her, there was plenty of room. I wasn't in uniform.
Re-examined.

I told prisoner when at King's Cross that he would be taken to the police station. I remained in the compartment till we got there, and Inspr Parker a part of the time was in the compartment.

Edward Parker, Inspector, on oath saith as follows:
I was one of the officers of the police travelling with and in attendance on the Home Secretary. I was at the meeting at Bradford and saw prisoner there. I hadn't seen him before on that day but I knew him previous to the

26th November. I can't say if Miss Ainsworth was at the meeting. I saw prisoner ejected – between 4 and ½ past 4. I was at the meeting till Mr Churchill left and I accompanied him to the station and got in the 5.10 train; I didn't then know prisoner was in the train, later I heard that. About 7, dinner time in the dining car, I gave directions to Sergt Sandercock, I had seen prisoner before this in the train.

A few minutes after 7 Mr Churchill left his compartment and went towards the dining car. I followed close behind him. To go to the dining car he had to pass through a door opening into the compartment where was defendant. When Mr Churchill opened that door defendant jumped up and shouted 'Winston Churchill, take that you dirty cur'. He was about to strike Mr Churchill with a whip when Sandercock seized him and forced him back on his seat. Defendant struggled violently and it was with some force that I wrenched this whip (produced) from his hand. He was then put back in his seat and restrained, and I went on in attendance with Mr Churchill leaving Sandercock with defendant. I didn't see where defendant got the whip from, the whip was raised above defendant's head when I first saw it and he was not more than a yard from Mr Churchill.

He was taken to Somers Town police station and there charged with assault, he made no reply on the charge being read over.
Cross-examined.

When defendant was ejected I was on the balcony of the hall. Defendant was brought past me, he was struggling violently with the stewards. I saw no one strike or kick him. I was looking in his direction. They were running him out from behind, having hold of his arms. 3 I think had hold of him, I didn't see that they were putting their knees in his back. I saw others ejected; I saw Hawkins[1] being taken out, there was a commotion at the time. I afterwards heard that he met with an accident, not that his leg was broken. I wasn't in a position to say if unnecessary force was used to those who were ejected.

I am sure defendant used the words 'dirty cur'. I didn't hear him say anything about the treatment of suffragettes when he called Mr Churchill a dirty cur.
Re-examined.

Hawkins was ejected after defendant. The stewards ejected defendant, Mr Churchill was then speaking. As to the words defendant's Counsel asked me about, if defendant, said 'Take this you cur for treatment of suffragettes', I know defendant is connected with that meeting. I think the meeting consisted entirely of men.

Leonard Winston Spencer Churchill on oath saith as follows:

[1] Alfred Hawkins (b. 1857), a member of the Men's Political Union for Women's Suffrage and of the ILP; he was thrown out of the meeting at St George's Hall, Bradford.

I am Secretary of State for the Home Department. On 26 November I was at Bradford, I went there from Manchester. Inspr Parker and Sergt Sandercock accompanied me from Manchester to Bradford.

At the meeting at Bradford which I addressed I noticed 4 or 5 people were ejected but I didn't distinguish who they were. After the meeting I went direct to the station and left by the 5.10 train, I had not seen defendant before. A little after 7 I was going to the dining car and as I opened the door of a third class compartment the door pushed itself open as I came and I saw a man sitting towards my right front spring up and rush at me, lifting his arm. I didn't hear what he said, I saw he was drawing something as if to strike me but I couldn't say what it was. I thought he was going to close with me, but before he could do so Sergt Sandercock – who, unknown to me was sitting near him – intervened. I prepared to defend myself, but when I saw he was secured I went on to the car.

Cross-examined.

Prisoner was in the first section of the side of the compartment where I entered. He sprang up and advanced towards me 4 or 5 feet I should say. I was in the corridor and the length of the seat is about 6 feet.

So far as I know prisoner has no cause of personal grievance against me. One hardly ever gets interruptions at public meetings, such as would bring them to a conclusion, but there are hostile interruptions. For the last 5 years there have been interruptions by persons who support the suffragette movement at nearly every meeting I have addressed. Persons present have shown annoyance at such interruptions, particularly those interruptions in favour of the suffrage movement. Persons get ejected with great roughness. I couldn't see how these particular persons were treated, I only saw that persons rushed at them and put them out at the door. At this meeting I didn't suggest that those ejected should be treated gently. I used at the meeting the words now read to me by Counsel. I suggest that this militant movement is supported with money and that persons have that advantage in coming to these meetings, and I make the same suggestion as to persons engaged in this movement now as I've done at public meetings.

Edward Howard Marsh on oath saith as follows:

I am private secretary to Mr Churchill. I was with him at this meeting and in the train, and I went with him (behind him) to the dining car. When I got on the scene defendant was in the hands of the police, I didn't see what constituted the assault or hear the words.

The defendant on oath saith as follows:

I live at 29 Pembridge Gardens. I am 21 years old. Since 1908 I have been interested in the suffragette movement and in February last I joined the 'Men's political union', and since then I have worked and spoken for it.

I agree in the main with the evidence as to the incidents in the train, but I did not say 'dirty'. I don't personally know Mr Churchill and have no grievance against him except as to the suffrage movement. My motives in what I did were only political. Several incidents led up to what I did: –

On 18 November I was in Parliament Square when a woman's deputation was sent to the House of Commons. It was resisted by the police, the women were subjected to a good deal of violence before they were arrested, and on seeing one particular woman being maltreated by police I approached a constable and said 'You can arrest this woman if you want to, but you ought not to ill-treat her'. I was consequently arrested by two other constables on a charge of obstructing the police and brought up here and discharged without any evidence being given against me, I was given no opportunity of justifying my conduct or proving my innocence by the direct orders of the Home Secretary.

On the 22nd there was a deputation of women to the premier's house in Downing Street which also was met with resistance by the police. I was present and noticed some brutality to the women. After Downing St was cleared I was at the St James's Park end, when Mrs Cobden Sanderson[1] came out of Downing St and came up to me. I was with another lady and Mrs Sanderson made some remarks to me. Later on I saw Mr Churchill, not in Downing St.

At the Bradford meeting I made an interjection and I was turned out with violence. I heard no protest. The words that have been read out I heard Mr Churchill utter. I didn't see Hawkins ejected, I received information as to that. I went home by the 5.10 train, not till I got to the station did I know Mr Churchill was going by the same train.

Cross-examined.

I am in the employ of no one. The union of which I am a member is at 13 Buckingham St. I have no profession. I do other things than attend these meetings; in October and November at various dates I travelled about in connection with this union, I received my railway expenses only. I always travelled alone, save once with a lady. On 12 November I was at a meeting at Liverpool; I believe that a question I asked caused a disturbance. Mr Burns addressed that meeting. My grievance against Mr Churchill is that he gave direct orders that evidence against me was not to be given when I was arrested on the 22nd. On the 21st November I was ejected from the Paragon, Whitechapel. On the 22nd I am informed that 2 Ministers were hustled in

---

[1] Mrs Anne Cobden-Sanderson was the daughter of Richard Cobden. A member of the Women's Freedom League, she served a month's imprisonment in October 1906 for demonstrating in the lobby of the House of Commons.

Downing St – I didn't see it, I was in the crowd. I went there as a person interested in this movement, but not as knowing that HM's Ministers would be there. The same evening, on the 22nd, I was ejected from a meeting where Mr Churchill was. That afternoon Mrs Sanderson spoke to me and I went to ask a question, and from experience I knew I should be ejected when I did so. On the 25th I went to Hull, I met other members of my union there, I saw 2. So far as I know there were no other members of the union there, their railway fares were paid. I went to ask Mr Asquith a question and I was ejected as usual. On the 26th at ½ past 9 am. I got in the train for Bradford, I didn't know the premier was in the train till I got in. I wasn't stopped from going to the premier by Inspr Stephenson, I remained in my carriage all the time, Miss Ainsworth was with me. It is untrue that near Doncaster I approached the premier's carriage and was stopped by Inspr Stephenson. At Doncaster I got out and Miss Ainsworth went up to the premier's window to ask a question. She knocked at the window several times to attract the premier's attention.

The Inspr removed Miss Ainsworth; I interfered but he didn't remove me as the train was just going. I got out at Doncaster as I had to change. Miss Ainsworth didn't go to the meeting at Bradford; we parted, she to go to see some friends. We had made no arrangements to see one another again in the train, I met her outside the hall. When I was ejected she was speaking in the street. It was about ¾ of an hour after I was ejected that I saw her, about ¼ to 5; we went then straight to the station. After deciding to go by that train I found that Mr Churchill was travelling by the same train. I guessed where Mr Churchill was, and correctly. We sat in the same carriage as Mr Churchill and as near as possible to him, as I intended to whip him. I had intended to do so from the 22nd, I intended that immediately I was spoken to by Mrs Sanderson – I then said to my friend Miss Vera Wentworth[1] 'I'll whip him for that'. Mrs Sanderson must have heard me say that, I don't remember her saying I shouldn't do it. I afterwards said I might be trying to whip him, but I don't know to whom. I know some people who knew of it, but I don't think I told them. I told Miss Ainsworth, I'm not going to give the names of any others, I can't recollect telling any definite persons. Miss Ainsworth knew I was going to whip Mr Churchill before this happened, but she knew (sic). I expect we discussed as to what I was going to do, very probably I did. As soon as we knew Mr Churchill was going by that train we discussed it, that was 5 past 5. I got the whip from the Strand or Fleet St for this purpose on the 22nd after seeing Mrs Sanderson. I took the whip with me to Mr Churchill's meeting on the 22nd at Highbury, I intended to

---

[1] Vera Wentworth (b. 1890), official organizer of the Women's Social and Political Union for three years; seven times imprisoned by 1913.

use it then but couldn't get near enough to Mr Churchill. I went by myself. I didn't carry the whip about with me on the intervening days.
Re-examined.

Mrs Sanderson said to me 'I've just come from Downing St', Mr Churchill appeared on the scene and said to an Inspr 'Turn that woman away, allow no one to loiter here'. That is as far as I can remember. I think she said that had just happened. She didn't look very well, I think anyone could have observed that. She looked rather pale.

Apart from receiving railway fares I receive nothing from this union for my work. The other members are not paid, save fares, our services are voluntary. I give money to the movement.

In June I left the University, not through my connection with this movement. I had employment for about 7 weeks, but gave it up as its nature didn't give me enough scope for this movement. I have no desire to go to Ministers' meetings save to ask questions.
By the Court:

One of my grievances against the Home Secretary was that he ordered me to be discharged without any evidence being given. I was prepared to prove my innocence, but was quite satisfied with being charged. I didn't think of taking out a summons against the police as I thought the Home Secretary was responsible.

Sir Charles Mathews to WSC

1 December 1910   Director of Public Prosecutions Department

Dear Mr Churchill,

I found the report of the Suffragette Meeting at the Queen's Hall on Monday, in Tuesday's *Daily Telegraph,* and violent, and, it may well be, criminally punishable, as was the language used at it by Mrs Pethick Lawrence,[1] I venture to submit to you that no criminal proceeding should be founded upon her speech, as there seem to me to be valid objections to all of the three courses which lead to prosecution. The first might be by indictment, with trial before a Jury, which, however, has the disadvantages we have already discussed. The second might be by Summons, under section 54 of the Metropolitan Police Act of 1839, which makes it an offence for anyone

[1] Mrs Emmeline Pethick Lawrence (d. 1954), with her husband F. W. Pethick Lawrence, aided and sustained the WSPU. She and her husband broke with Christabel Pankhurst and left the Union in 1912.

within the limits of the Metropolitan Police district to use in a public place any threatening, abusive, or insulting, words, with intent to provoke a breach of the peace, or whereby a breach of the peace might be occasioned, but the penalty attached to this is only 40s, and for so insignificant a penalty, it would scarcely be worth while invoking the criminal law. The third might be by exhibiting articles of the peace, and calling for recognizances, with sureties, to keep it, but this would involve an Information sworn by you personally, containing a statement that you went in fear, and this I feel quite certain you would not make. In these circumstances, I hope you may agree with me that criminal action will not be advantageous.

You will have seen by the newspapers that Franklin renewed his application for bail to Sir Albert de Rutzen yesterday, who refused it, and referred him to a Judge at Chambers, and today Mr Justice Lush,[1] after taking a little time to consider his decision, confirmed the Magistrate, and refused bail.

I am, Dear Mr Churchill, Very faithfully yours
CHARLES MATHEWS

Note by WSC:
Answered, agreeing.

Dundee Advertiser

EXTRACT

Thursday

2 December 1910

In reply to a deputation from the Women's Liberal Association, Mr Churchill said it was a great advantage to be able to discuss these matters with ladies who he knew were sincere adherents of the true principles of Liberalism, and who had no part in or sympathy with the abominable methods which had now, he was sorry to say, become more and more identified with the cause of women's suffrage. The Premier's pledge regarding the Bill in next Parliament was a very important pledge, and the astonishing thing was that it had not been accepted in a fair spirit by what he might call the rowdy section of the movement. It was quite impossible for the Government to promise that the first session in the new Parliament could be devoted to these matters, because in the first session they were very much more likely to have to deal with the Lords than with the ladies. In any case, the franchise could not be operative till the close of Parliament. So that between a pledge

---

[1] Charles Montague Lush (1853–1930), Judge of King's Bench Division of High Court 1910–25; knighted 1910; PC 1925.

for facilities next session and a pledge for facilities in the next Parliament there was no real practical difference.

*   *   *

At the deputation of the Women's Freedom League, consisting of Miss Husband,[1] Miss Grant and Miss Clunas, Miss Clunas said Mr Asquith had given a sort of a pledge to the effect that in the next Parliament facilities would be given the Bill.

Mr Churchill – Why do you call it a sort of a pledge?

Miss Clunas – I do not think it is a pledge. What we want is a pledge for the first session of 1911.

Mr Churchill – You will not get that.

After further conversation Mr Churchill said the Prime Minister had given a pledge – not a sort of pledge – that in the next Parliament, if a bill was introduced which the House of Commons approved of, and was capable of free amendment – facilities would be given for that bill being carried through the Commons. There was no chance of that pledge being altered to a pledge that facilities would be given in the first session of Parliament. So far as he himself was concerned he was still of opinion that the sex disqualification was not a true or a logical disqualification, and he was therefore in favour of the principle of women being enfranchised. But he declined utterly to pledge himself to any particular Bill at the present time. He would not vote for any Bill which he considered would have the effect of unfairly altering the balance between parties by giving an undoubted preponderance to the property vote; and he would not vote for any Bill unless he was convinced that it had behind it the genuine majority of the electors. That was his position, and it was very desirable that they should not build any undue hopes on any words he might say. He had no desire to extend to them any encouragement which might afterwards afford ground for their reproaches. Whatever he had admitted in friendly discussion on this subject, he had always found it was only the excuse for renewed abuse and insult, and every step taken in friendship towards their bodies had only met grosser insults and more outrageous action. He was confident that while these tactics were employed the opinion of this country would be rendered less favourable and not more favourable to the cause which they keenly had at heart.

Miss Husband – You referred to hostility.

Mr Churchill – I call it hostility when meeting after meeting is disturbed, when people who come miles and miles to hear a speaker find the proceedings

[1] Agnes Husband had been a militant since 1906, and was also a prominent member of the Dundee Labour Party.

interrupted by senseless and deliberately-planned interruption. I call it hostility when threats of violence are used and personal violence is offered.

Miss Clunas – The Liberals are hostile to us.

Mr Churchill – But you are working your utmost to defeat me.

Miss Clunas – Yes.

Mr Churchill – What right have you to come here at all? If a body has definitely taken a part against a man, it is not usual for that body to come and examine the candidate. A neutral body free, free to take action in any way, and ready to be conciliated by the answer it receives – such a body may come, but I know you will do your best, as you have done on every occasion, to prevent my return. I make an exception for you, but if you were men I would not have received you on these conditions. I don't think that any body which has continued an active campaign has a right to be received.

Miss Clunas – Any one working actively against you would not be allowed to your meetings to ask questions.

Mr Churchill – If you find difficulty in getting into meetings it is because you have gone to wreck them.

Sir John Simon to WSC

EXTRACT

14 December 1910

My dear Churchill,

    I return the *Votes for Women* cutting which Marsh sent me.[1] It is of course scurrilous to a degree, & I am sure will be generally resented by decent people. But I would strongly urge you *not* to take proceedings on it. The cases are very rare in which a Minister ought to defend himself by himself taking action in the Courts for injurious statements, and it seems to me that for the Home Secretary personally to pursue a creature who has already been sentenced for an assault on him would be most unwise. The violence and hysteria of these people prevent what they say having any importance.

    I think it is probable that you will have arrived at the same conclusion as I. I feel quite clear about it.

Yours very truly
JOHN SIMON

PS To my deep regret I have got into a nasty personal controversy with FE. I'm afraid he's very much worn out with over-speaking. I think I may have to ask you to be conciliator between two old friends.

---

[1] In an article in *Votes for Women* Hugh Franklin wrote 'When Mr Churchill as the chief policeman orders his thousands of trained entrants to become a set of real hooligans, no one is left to act as protectors of law and order.'

Augustine Birrell to WSC

21 February 1911
Irish Office
Old Queen Street

My dear Churchill,

Sir Charles Mathews called here the other day & saw me about two women, one a Bristol lady whom I know by sight, and another an Irish woman whom I do not know, and he said that it was in contemplation prosecuting them for having taken part in the attack upon me last November.

I am perfectly satisfied that this would be a great mistake. I am sure the Bristol lady did not commit even a technical assault upon me, and the Irish woman I could not identify.

In these circumstances and having regard to the lapse of time it is plain to me that the most that would happen to these women would be that they would be bound over to keep the peace, and in order to accomplish this futile end they would have the opportunities of a public trial, photographs, & all the rest of it.

I should not make at all a good witness because, beastly as the whole thing was, there would have been very little in it but for the fact that whilst struggling to rid myself of their odious attentions I slipped the cartilage of my knee and should not be at all disposed in my evidence to make much of the occurrence; and having regard to that fact it may be they would not even be bound over.

Please therefore let the matter drop but keep your eye on the hags in question.

Yours
A. BIRRELL

Sir Edward Troup to Sir Charles Mathews

4 March 1911
Home Office

Dear Mathews,

Mr Churchill would be glad to know whether you think Miss Christabel Pankhurst or *The Times* could be prosecuted criminally for libel in connection with the enclosed.

The instructions to the police were to use every possible moderation in dealing with the women.

Yours sincerely
EDWARD TROUP

Enclosures

The Times

2 March 1911

Miss Christabel Pankhurst, presiding at a meeting of the Women's Social and Political Union at Steinway Hall last night, referred to the statement made by Mr Winston Churchill in the House of Commons on Wednesday in regard to the police and woman suffragists.

It was quite notorious, a matter of everyday and universal knowledge, she said, that the women who went to Westminster in November, 1910, were brutally and in many cases indecently ill-treated by the police acting under the orders of the Home Secretary. (Hisses.) They knew perfectly well that had the police been left to their own devices, they would have behaved as men and gentlemen.

Mrs Saul Solomon to the editor of The Times

3 March 1911   Les Lunes
                                                West Hampstead

Sir,

With regard to the memorandum forwarded to the Home Office on the above subject by the Conciliation Committee, Mr Winston Churchill is reported in your columns to have stated in the House of Commons yesterday that, if there were any truth in the charges made against the police, these charges should have been made at the time and not afterwards.

My name and evidence are referred to in the memorandum of the Conciliation Committee, and as a member of one of the deputations on the occasion referred to, November 18, 1910, my personal honour is implicated. I should like to state that I was not only assaulted myself by uniformed members of the police force at Westminster, but saw others assaulted. In consequence of the shameful brutality which I experienced at their hands, I was confined to bed, and was too ill to deal with the matter at once. But as soon as I was able to write – namely, on December 17, 1910, I addressed a letter to Mr Winston Churchill as Secretary of State for the Home Office laying the facts before him of what I had personally experienced and had seen others suffer. I received a formal acknowledgment of this letter and nothing more.

As the Home Secretary from his place in the House of Commons has led the House to believe that the said charges are now made for the first time, may I give you the following brief quotations from my letter, which perhaps you will kindly publish? At the same time I enclose a copy of the letter in full for reference: –

'Whatever I may have to say about the police in this letter or statement refers to them merely as the irresponsible obedient tools of the Government; and I do not mention their actions in any respect or instance whatsoever as actions for which I deem them to be individually responsible. The entire responsibility lies upon the shoulders of those who hold this national force at their disposal.'

'I was unable to write sooner, having been wholly invalided in consequence of the ill-treatment to which I was then subjected.'

'And, assuredly, the methods applied to us were those used by the police to conquer the pugilistic antagonist, to fell the burglar, to maim the hooligan, or to reduce to inanity the semi-barbaric and dangerous rough. If further personal evidence be required, I may add that I was gripped by the breast – by no means an exceptional act, for heart-breaking to relate, I am medically informed that younger women, women of an age to be my own daughters, were also assaulted in this and other repellent and equally cruel ways.'

'When walking along the road I found myself in danger of being knocked down, and endeavoured to regain a place on the pavement, but had scarcely secured a footing when a policeman made a rush at me. . . . He held and violently shook me while his helpers twirled round my arms as if to drag them from their sockets. Still worse, another caught me by the shoulders and mercilessly pressed his heavy weight upon my back, crushing me down, while he propelled me along the line, uniformed men assisting.'

I think it is not unreasonable on my part to urge that, if Mr Winston Churchill wished to investigate the entire matter at a much earlier date, the opportunity was certainly given for him to do so. Naturally it has taken a considerable time for the Conciliation Committee to obtain the different statements of 135 women, all of whom have been suffering from grievous violence at the hands of those whom I designate as 'the irresponsible obedient tools of the Government.'

I am, Sir, yours, &c
GEORGINA M. SOLOMON[1]

---

[1] Mrs Saul Solomon (b. 1844), a life-long Sunday school teacher who married a South African politician; she took part in several deputations for the WSPU.

John Burns to WSC

28 March 1911   Local Government Board

Dear Churchill,

No doubt you have noticed that the militant suffragists are endeavouring to defeat the Census which is to be taken on Sunday evening next. It appears that in London the Scala Theatre, the Gardenia Restaurant and some large private houses are to be occupied for the night by women who wish to be omitted from the count and who would refuse to give the full information required for the purpose of the Census schedule.

The Registrar-General who is responsible for the Census does not propose to force matters unduly and will be satisfied if he can obtain an estimate of the number of persons who congregate in the buildings referred to, but he is very anxious that the enumerators should receive all possible assistance in their task from the Metropolitan Police.

Another plan proposed by the suffragists is that their male supporters should masquerade as enumerators and should call at dwelling-houses for the Census papers and should destroy the same after they have been handed to them by unsuspecting occupiers.

Seeing that the organisers of the movement are engaged in a deliberate attempt to set the law at defiance, I think that you will agree with me that the police in London should render every assistance to the Registrar-General and to his enumerators and I should be obliged if you could arrange that this should be done. A rough enumeration of the persons gathering in the selected buildings is all that is desired.

I may add that if this plan of countering the movement can be made a success, the necessity of prosecuting any large number of persons in default may be obviated and the main object of the suffragists may thus be defeated.

Yours sincerely
JOHN BURNS

Lady Constance Lytton to WSC

16 May 1911   15 Somerset Terrace

Dear Mr Winston Churchill,

I write to appeal to you most earnestly on behalf of the Conciliation (W's franchise) Bill.

Any attempt to combine the Women's claim with other franchise reforms introduces party differences which it is unfair to awaken in connection with the removal of sex disability. That is a wide human question on which a majority of all parties are agreed on the lines of the Conciliation Bill. Alterations of the franchise basis, for women as for men, can be effected afterwards by the lovers of a wider democracy, according to their powers of persuading the electorate.

The present Bill is without the characteristics you chiefly objected to – if I remember right – in last year's Bill. At a crisis such as the present, when the Government is once more faced with the alternative of assisting or strangling the chances of our Bill, the women of the country – & indeed of the whole world – turn with hope & longing to those members of the Cabinet, such as yourself, who have frequently upheld their cause in public.

If you could know, as I do, the practical effect on women's lives of their present position of outlawry, I am convinced you would not hesitate to do your part in defending their claim.

In the name of the many thousands of women who make this same appeal, I thank you in advance for your support. May I take this opportunity of telling you how extremely sorry I am that this cause to which I give my life has stood in the way of your friendship with brother Vic. I valued that friendship ever since the happy day when you helped to guide his steps from the Diplomatic service into politics.

Yours sincerely
CONSTANCE LYTTON

Sir Edward Henry to Edward Marsh

24 May 1911   New Scotland Yard

Dear Marsh,

If Mr Asquith's reply to the Deputation about the Conciliation Bill is not deemed satisfactory, both women & men intend to resort again to militant tactics. It would be well therefore if Ministers would cause to be sent here a statement of their public engagements. Nash has promised to send me the Prime Minister's.

Yrs sincerely
E. R. HENRY

WSC to the Master of Elibank

18 December 1911   Admiralty

Copy

My dear Alick,

We are getting into vy gt peril over Female Suffrage.

Be quite sure of this: – the Franchise Bill will not get through without a dissolution if it contains a clause adding 8,000,000 women to the electorate. Nor ought it to get through.

How can the PM honourably use the Parlt Act to force it upon the King, when he has himself declared it to be a 'disastrous mistake'? In the second year of passage of this and the Home Rule Bill the Tories will demand a dissolution. Votes for women is so unpopular that by-elections will be un-favourable. The King will be entitled obviously to say to his Prime Minister, 'You cannot conscientiously advise me to assent to this vast change. The Constituencies have never been consulted. No responsible Govt is behind it. You do not believe in it yourself.' The King will dismiss the Ministry & Parliament will be dissolved on the old Plural voting register. We shall be in confusion ourselves. With us will go down the Irish cause.

The situation wh is developing is vy like the Trade split in the Tory party in 1903. I do not understand LG at all. Their one hope was the referendum wh alone gave a reasonable & honourable outlet. He knew my view. And yet he has gone out of his way to rule it out at the vy beginning. He is exactly like Joe in 1903. It is with most profound regret that I watch these develop-ments. I have been through it before. Do not I beseech you my friend underrate the danger.

What a ridiculous tragedy it will be if this strong Government & party which has made its mark in history were to go down on Petticoat politics! And the last chance of Ireland – our loyal friends – squandered too! It is damnable.

No doubt you have made some deep calculations as to voting in H of C. Please let me know what they are. But I do not think there is any safety there. If LG & Grey go on working themselves up, they will have to go, if female suffrage is knocked out. And the PM's position will become impossible if it is put in.

The only safe & honest course is to have a referendum – first to the women to know if they want it: & then to the men to know if they will give it. I am quite willing to abide by the result.

What I cannot stand is making this prodigious change in the teeth of public opinion, & out of pure weakness.

Alexander the Great (your forerunner) said that the peoples of Asia were slaves because they were not able to pronounce the word 'No'. Let you & me avoid their pusillanimity & their fate.

Your sincere friend
W

WSC to Sir E. Grey

20 December 1911   Admiralty

Copy

My dear Grey,

I am getting increasingly anxious about the woman's suffrage situation. If you and George are going to make a strong campaign in favour of adding 6,000,000 voters to the franchise, it will become increasingly difficult for those who do not think such a change at this juncture likely to be good for the country, not to participate actively in some counter movement. I do not think the Prime Minister's position is tenable except on the basis that the question is regarded as an unimportant one. But it cannot remain unimportant and as it approaches the domain of decisive action, it will not improbably dominate other issues. How can he possibly use the provisions of the Parliament Act to force through a measure which he has stated publicly he would regard as a disastrous political mistake? This strong Government on whose continuance so much depends may easily come in two and be utterly discredited by proceeding on the present course. With every wish to respect other people's feelings I could not remain silent on such a topic indefinitely. I see with great apprehension you and George working yourselves up into enthusiastic champions of the cause. I know how sincere natures gather force and conviction from motion and activity. After a point you may well persuade yourselves that women's suffrage is not merely the most important but the *only* question in politics. If so you will find it very difficult to regard me as anything but an opponent. It is because I am so deeply disturbed at the prospect I see ahead that I write to urge that an effort should be made to see whether we cannot come together on a referendum – men or women or both – I do not care. Your own honesty and candour will I am sure lead you to admit that the opinion of the country has never yet been tested on this subject.

Yours very sincerely
WINSTON S. CHURCHILL

These are the three questions on the answer to which the issue will be decided:

1. Do the women really want it?
2. Would it be for the good of the country to give it now?
3. Have the electors ever expressed any conscious opinion?

WSC

WSC to H. H. Asquith

EXTRACT

21 December 1911

[Copy]

Private & personal

My dear Prime Minister,

I apprehend great danger to the Govt over women's suffrage. There are 3 main questions wh must be answered satisfactorily.

1. Is there a real desire on the part of great numbers of women to assume political responsibilities? 2. Wd this addition to the Electorate be for the good of the country now? 3. Has the country ever been effectively consulted?

Your own position appears to me to be likely to become extraordinarily difficult from the moment that a female suffrage amendment is included in the Govt Bill; for you will then be accused of using the machinery of the Parliament Act to force upon the Sovereign & upon the constituencies a vast change for wh no organised Govt or party will become responsible, on wh the Electors have never pronounced, & wh you yrself have characterized as a 'disastrous political mistake.' Further, if yr colleagues are going to take the field & work themselves up into a keen enthusiasm for Female Suffrage, then members of the Govt who do not agree with them will be forced to express themselves in a contrary sense. You yrself may even be drawn into the fray. This anomalous condition may possibly be tolerated so long as the question is academic or of small importance; but if it became imminent & important & real, the Govt wd be utterly discredited. It is certain that as the issue became more real passion will rise in regard to it & make it a subject of overwhelming importance. What a ridiculous tragedy it wd be if this strong Govt from wh so much is hoped were to come to grief in this ignominious way, & perish like Sisera[1] at a woman's hand.[2]

[1] Sisera was the captain of the Army of Canaan. When he was defeated by the Israelites he fled for refuge to the tent of Jael, an Israelite woman. She killed him by driving a nail into his head while he slept. (Judges 4, verse 21.)

[2] Such a fate never befell a critic of woman's suffrage, but an attempt was made to kidnap the author.

What about the King: will he not be pressed to use the prerogative of dissolution in 1913 in the same way as he was pressed to use the prerogative of creating peers in 1911? I cannot help thinking that in all the circs wh I foresee he might be justified. He wd certainly not be disinclined. If we had to fight an election, in confusion ourselves, with Home Rule on our shoulders & with the Plural Voter still active, we shd be beaten decisively; & with us wd fall the Irish cause, with all the hopes wh are centred upon it. I am quite sure that the adding of 8,000,000 women to the register will never be achieved without some form of appeal to the nation. Nor ought it to be. I have written since their speeches both to Grey & to Lloyd George pointing out these dangers & explaining that I cd not indefinitely remain silent; & last night by arrangement we all three dined together to discuss the difficulty. We had a vy valuable talk, & both were vy much inclined to adopt a suggestion wh I put forward, & wh LG developed, that is, that if the women's clause were carried, the adult suffrage register shd be forthwith constructed, & as soon as this was complete the whole mass of the women to be enfranchised shd, either by referendum or initiative, decide whether they wd take up their responsibilities or not. In order to get them (Grey & LG) to adopt this position, I shd have to go with them on the democratic amendment, so that we cd all work together; & I am bound to say that any objections to the change wd be greatly diminished if 3 or 4,000,000 women, representing as they wd every household in the country, had specifically asked for it. Also, it wd probably get smashed wh again wd be a solution. The conciliabule[1] refrained from coming to any fixed agreement, but we parted with a feeling that unity on these lines was not impossible.

If the Tories were to say, why don't you have a referendum on Home Rule as well as abt the women, our answer (debating) is clear. We have no obiection at all to applying the same principle to Ireland & having a referendum on the Irish question to the Irish people.

I hope whatever happens nothing will be said to close up this loophole of escape, wh is the only one I can see. . . .

H. H. Asquith to WSC

23 December 1911　　　　　　　　　　　　　　　　Archerfield House
Private

My dear Winston,

Hopwood, as he told you, has felt obliged to decline my offer. I will write further as to your designs upon him in a day or two.

---

[1] A small or secret assembly.

There is much force in what you write about the women. London &
others are organising a great 'Anti' demonstration at the Albert Hall on
Feb 28th, and tho' I have not yet come to a final decision, I may feel it my
duty to go there.

I am clear that the Govt as a Govt, could not take any other course than
we have taken. The only alternative was for the minority among us to resign.

I reserve my judgement as to the practicability of your referendum until
I have further considered it. As I understand, you propose that only the
women should be referees? Why?

I am much more disquieted by the general political situation. These
Scotch bye-elections[1] were a great error of judgement on the part of the
Master [of Elibank], and would not have happened if I had insisted on my
own view. But they have their uses, as a fairly clear indication that, even
here in Scotland, Insurance is for the time costing us heavily. A man writes
to me to-day, from my own constituency, that he believes 80 per cent of
the ploughmen there would at this moment go against us: no doubt a great
exaggeration, but by no means a pure invention. All this means that we
open 1912 with a lack of cohesion & driving part in the forces behind us. I
am more & more convinced that if we are to escape ridicule & ultimate
disaster, we must, *coûte que coûte*, lighten our commitments for the year.
We cannot get through them except in a session of 10 or 11 months, with two
& probably three drastic guillotines. Even if the House of Commons does
not mutiny (which is more than likely) the members of the Government will
be reduced by the end of the year to physical & mental decrepitude.

The legal life of this Parliament does not terminate until Dec 1915, and a
session in that year would be available as the third session under the Parliament Act.

It is, of course, the natural (& not unnatural) jealousies of rival groups &
causes which have made it necessary to announce what I may call a *pari
passu* programme.

But their respective adherents may be brought to a more reasonable view
when they realise that to attempt the whole is to endanger every one of its
parts.

These are matters which seem to me to call, not for hasty decision, but
for the most serious consideration by all of us during the next few weeks.

Yrs vy sincerely
H. H. ASQUITH

---

[1] The by-election in Ayrshire North on 20 December and Govan on 22 December.

F. E. Smith to Andrew Bonar Law
(*Bonar Law Papers*)

27 December 1911   Blenheim

My dear Bonar,

Many thanks for your kind letter which I greatly valued. I really think I did good. I spoke four nights running averaging $1\frac{1}{4}$ hours to 20,000 people altogether and as I was reported verbatim to the extent of 5 columns a day in the *Western Morning News* I couldn't repeat a word which was rather a bore.

I want you to give your most serious attention to the question of female suffrage in the near future. Asquith is drifting into an absolutely impossible position and one that may upset the apple cart. We have now got (my idea and arrangement) Harcourt, McKenna, Hobhouse and perhaps the Lord Chancellor at an Albert Hall meeting in February at which Austen, myself, Long, Curzon (if in England) and Carson are also to speak. It is not yet certain that Asquith will not come. The position may easily become critical to them. Observe (*inter alia*) how it smashes the Parliament Bill. Grey says (Horticultural Hall meeting) if the female suffrage amendment is carried the proposal will become a Government proposal. Asquith says take off your coats and fight it during the two years so as to use them for the purpose of agitating effectively against a proposal which according to Grey 'will have the Government behind it'.

Privately I know there is the greatest bitterness among the Cabinet and they are not unconscious that the situation may undergo developments very sinister to them. Under these circumstances I write with a practical object. Asquith, Harcourt, McKenna and Hobhouse are sincere opponents in principle. Churchill (this is most private) greatly resents LG's statement that *under any risk and in any event* it will be carried forward. He has told LG not to rely upon him in any such quarrel. The position then in a word of all these opponents (among whom in effect Ch may be numbered) is that if the Tory party fights straight they will all take their lives in their hands and resist the policy *coûte que coûte* – and the price may well be their very existence for LG will bitterly resent it. But if the Tory party carries with Liberal help the 'Conciliation' amendment to the Franchise Bill all these men will vote for the extreme amendment on the pretext that if the vote is given against their wishes to women at all it shall at least not be given under circumstances which will load the dice against the Liberal party. It is therefore vital that we should no longer fool about with the Conciliation Bill. Recent events have made it clear that those of us were right who said its proposals were simply a leaping-off board for the larger policy. And make no mistake the whole thing is monstrously unpopular with the electorate. They stood up and cheered the roof off when I said at Barnstaple that I would not give the vote if every woman in England asked for it.

But I want you to consider your own position. I do not think you can simply repeat a half-hearted allegiance to the cause given under wholly different circumstances. Each member who hates it but has a vague commitment of the same origin will look to you for a dialectical escape and if he doesn't get it will travel down the road of sentimentalism to disaster. And surely you are bound in elementary consistency to give such a lead for quite other (and more overwhelming) reasons. How can you possibly run in double harness your 'indignant' campaign against using the Parliament Act to pass Home Rule with connivance in the attempt (far more gross, scandalous and revolutionary) to use the PA to pass Female Suffrage. You will not retain a rag of consistency or persuasiveness for your HR complaints. Surely the obvious line is that (1) the Constitution is in suspense (2) the question is of immense novelty and importance (3) it has never been as a specific subject before the people (4) that therefore whatever your own views you could under these circumstances no more be a party to carrying either the Conciliation or the more extreme proposals by means of the PA than you could be a party to carrying HR.

Forgive this long, hurried and dogmatic scrawl but I write quickly as I talk. Take it from me there is a real chance of a split among the Cabinet if we play our cards properly.

Yours ever
FE

Master of Elibank to WSC

EXTRACT

3 January 1912   Grand Hotel de Genes
                                                 Genoa

My dear Winston,

I have purposely delayed replying to your suffrage letter.

It is certainly a most delicate situation, and the most difficult problem I have come up against since I have been Chief Whip.

I mean from the point of view of the 'Cabinet from within': I join LG today and I shall write you again in 2 or 3 days after I have talked the unclean thing over with him. On this question I have no declared views and no principles. I am only concerned as to whether our party will gain by the inclusion or exclusion of women, & therefore the causes with which we are identified. I feel pretty certain that the suffrage will come; we can of course delay it.

Whenever I have been in a real difficulty, and it occurred on two vital occasions in the course of the last two years, my last card has been the personal friendships in the Cabinet. It looks rather like a similar situation again arising.

In any case, as soon as possible, I am going to suggest that the principal actors in this drama should meet: you: LG: Grey: the PM: Haldane: and I think Harcourt: and your humble servant with some electoral statistics in his pouch! . . . .

WSC to Lord Curzon

7 January 1912

Copy

My dear Curzon,

    I am strongly inclined to think that woman's suffrage ought not to pass into law without any appeal in some form or other to the households of the country. At the last Election I stated publicly that I regarded a Referendum as a vy suitable method for determining such a question, wh from the vy fact of its being non-party in its character was outside the scope of ordinary political machinery & of the usual tests whereby public opinion can be ascertained. I gather from the newspapers that you & yr friends of the Anti [Female] Suffrage League are also in favour of a Referendum; & I shd feel vy much disposed to advocate such a course, cd I be assured that the argument wd not be immediately applied to Home Rule & other measures of a party character for wh the Govt takes responsibility & by wh they must stand or fall. I think there are a good many Liberals who wd find such an assurance a great encouragement to them in supporting Referendum proposals for Woman's Suffrage. I believe it to be a right course, & one wh is fair to the Suffragists themselves. But I cannot compromise other issues wh I regard as of greater importance, & I say frankly that if WS is to be treated on the one side with an eye to party interest, a similar attitude will no doubt be assumed by the other.

I recognize that individuals cannot bind parties on a non party question. But that is not necessary. If the prominent Conservative Anti Suffragists wd make it clear that there are great distinctions between a referendum on a non-party question & one on party questions & that advocacy of the one is no ground for a charge of illogicality or inconsistency in regard to the other, then the party score wd be effectively sterilized, & personally I shd feel free to take a strong line in favour of a referendum. What do you think? F. E. Smith wd certainly make a public statement. But he dislikes V. for W. almost more than any other question. What will you do? What will A. Chamberlain do? I have kept quiet on this subject in order to be of use & I think the PM wd not be unwilling to come along. If you & A. Chambn wd indicate the sort of thing you cd say by way of 'sterilising' the party argument, I shd be willing to make a vy clear declaration. And these cd be mutually agreed upon. A little frankness now between us may save a deal of trouble later on.

With good wishes for the N.Y. Believe me, Yrs vy sin

WSC

Lord Curzon to WSC

20 January 1912   Hackwood
                                                       Basingstoke

Private and Confidential

My dear Churchill,

I have consulted with some of my friends who feel with me about Women's Suffrage, and we shall personally be quite prepared to argue on the lines that are suggested and to refrain from pressing a charge of inconsistency or illogicality for which I see no sufficient foundation.

We cannot of course pledge others, who do not share our views, or the party at large, which will always use party weapons that lie at hand.

I am not sure, however, that the basis of the distinction which you draw between the two classes of measures is altogether sound; for you place on the one side Woman's Suffrage, and on the other 'Home Rule and other measures of a party character for which the Government take responsibility and by which they must stand or fall.'

But is it not the case of the Prime Minister, that when and in whatever form the vote for women has been introduced into the Male Suffrage Bill, it does then become a part of a measure to which the above language exactly applies? For instance if the Bill so amended were thrown out on the 3rd reading the Government must resign.

Again when you speak of 'an appeal in some form or other to the households of the country' – what exactly have you in view? If you mean the existing male electors, that is what I understand by a Referendum. But if you mean a women's vote, whether of female municipal voters or others, it is clear that that means the introduction of an entirely new issue, which would divide people and parties on different lines, and would be interpreted by many as conceding the very point which the Anti-suffragists at any rate are resolved to resist.

There is a further difficulty about a Referendum which we all see, but which appears to be inseparable from it in the present state of affairs. If the result were unfavourable, so far from being accepted by the women, it would apparently lead to a revival of the agitation in a more acute form.

Yours v. sincerely
CURZON OF KEDLESTON

Miss Lila Clunas to WSC

19 February 1912   Votes for Women
                                    Women's Freedom League
                                           Dundee

Dear Sir,

I am desired by my Committee to remind you of your letter to me of 5th October 1911, in which you said that you 'realised that we would be entitled to a further statement of your intentions before any Bill dealing with the question of women's franchise comes up for Second Reading in the House of Commons.' As the Conciliation Bill has secured the third place in the ballot we should be greatly obliged if you will now let us have this statement. We wish to know if you will vote for the Conciliation Bill in all its stages and oppose any amendments likely to prevent its passing into law. As regards the Reform Bill – will you do all in your power to get Women Suffrage made an integral part of the Bill?

Will you move or vote for an amendment to include women in the bill either (a) on the same terms as men (b) on the lines of the Conciliation plus married women (c) on the lines of the Conciliation Bill.

Will you vote against the Third Reading of the Bill, if women are not included in it?

I am, Yours faithfully
LILA CLUNAS

WSC to Miss Lila Clunas

20 February 1912   Admiralty

Copy

Dear Madam,

In reply to your letter of the 19th instant, I have in the first instance to refer you to my statements made before the last Election on the subject of Woman's Suffrage to a deputation of my Dundee constituents. From this extract, which I enclose, you will apprehend the answers which I shall give to your questions.

I shall vote against the second reading of the Conciliation Bill and shall oppose its passing into law.

With regard to the Government Reform Bill, I prefer to wait until that measure is introduced before pronouncing upon hypothetical amendments to it. I may say generally, however, that I believe that the giving of the parliamentary vote to 7 or 8 millions of women is a step which the country is not prepared to take at the present time.

Lastly, the fact that Women's Suffrage was not included in any form in the Government Reform Bill would not prevent me from supporting it on the third reading.

H. H. Asquith to WSC
(*CSC Papers*)

1 April 1912   10 Downing Street

Private

My dear Winston,

I was delighted to get your very kind letter. Thank you very much.

Much the best thing that I have read for a long time on the Woman question is a short but very pointed letter in *The Times* today, signed CSC.[1]

Have you any clue to the identity of the writer?

Yrs always
H.H.A.

[1] Mrs Churchill had written a letter in reply to one from Sir Almroth Wright (1861–1947), who challenged, as a distinguished pathologist, women's 'fitness' to vote. Mrs Churchill commented: '. . . the question seems no longer to be "should women have votes" but "ought women not to be abolished altogether? . . . Cannot science give us some assurance, or at least some ground for hope, that we are on the eve of the greatest discovery of all – i.e. how to maintain a race of males by purely scientific means." '

20

Admiralty 1912–Part 1

(See Main Volume II, pp. 559–74)

(See Main Volume II, pp. 559–74)

WSC to H. H. Asquith

1 January 1912   Admiralty

[Copy]

Private

My dear Prime Minister,

The King has telegraphed approving both the constitution and composition of the War Staff and the appointment of Sir Francis Hopwood as Additional Civil Lord. I want very much to make the changes during the present week, or on Monday next at latest. The First Sea Lord is very anxious to be aided by the War Staff, and its principal Members who all know they are going to be appointed are, of course, impatient to be gazetted and come together regularly. Hopwood also would be most useful now. At present Admiral Troubridge is doing both his regular work as Private Secretary and, unofficially, his War Staff duties. He will be succeeded in the Private Office by Admiral David Beatty. I do not like, however, to bring Beatty up to London because of the deductions which would immediately be drawn. I am arranging the finance of the War Staff and Hopwood's appointment satisfactorily with the Treasury. I propose to consult my Board formally on the new appointments on Wednesday next, when I have every reason to expect unanimous concurrence. I have drafted myself two minutes dealing with the proposals, which would be published simultaneously with the publication of the appointments, and I enclose them herewith. That relating to the War Staff is largely the result of two long conferences with Haldane. I believe it will be found to remove all his doubts. It has also been discussed with Ottley. I am sending Haldane a copy simultaneously with this, and I shall go ahead as soon as I hear that you and he are satisfied.

It is not necessary at this first step to prescribe in minute detail the exact distribution and redistribution of Admiralty business which will follow from these changes. Before I can do that satisfactorily I must have the principal men in their places. You cannot build a Staff as you build a house, from the bottom upwards, and then when it is all finished put the Chief of the Staff on top of it like the chimney. One has to go the other way round and organise a good group of men at the top and let them work out the details in accordance with principles which have been clearly prescribed. We shall not be committed further than the Memorandum, which is general in its terms, and there will be plenty of time to make adjustments afterwards should they be found necessary. You will see that I have conceived the Memorandum with a view to soothing the sensitive nerves of our sailor-men.

I had a preliminary conversation with the Chancellor on Friday about the Estimates. They are pretty bad now, and the future prospect most gloomy. Although the New Construction Vote will diminish through the passing away of the contingent four Dreadnoughts, yet there is a steady automatic rise in pay, [incomplete]

WSC to Viscount Haldane
(R. B. Haldane Papers)

1 January 1912   Admiralty

Secret

My dear Haldane,

I send you herewith a draft Memorandum on the War Staff which it is proposed to issue simultaneously with the publication of the appointments. You will see that it is in general terms and that details can be adjusted afterwards. The principles, however, are I think those with which you concur. Without departing from the traditional form and custom of the Admiralty, I have placed the Staff directly under the First Sea Lord; and the War Staff circle with its attendant dignitaries has volatilised into unpretentious Staff meetings and a general admonition to the Chief of the Staff to keep in touch with other Departments. I shall be very grateful for any emendations or excisions which you may care to suggest. But time is pressing, and if you are in general agreement I shall be very glad if you will let me know at once. I want to publish on Monday next at the latest. All the parties concerned are red-hot to take up their appointments, and though the secret has been very well kept I expect something will leak out if delay is prolonged.

Yours vy sincerely
WINSTON S. CHURCHILL

Memorandum by WSC

8 January 1912   [Admiralty]

In establishing a War Staff for the Navy it is necessary to observe the broad differences of character and circumstances which distinguish naval from military problems. War on land varies in every country according to numberless local conditions, and each new theatre, like each separate battle-field, requires a special study. A whole series of intricate arrangements must be thought out and got ready for each particular case; and these are expanded and refined continuously by every increase in the size of armies, and by every step towards the perfection of military science. The means by which superior forces can be brought to decisive points in good condition and at the right time are no whit less vital, and involve far more elaborate processes than the strategic choice of those points, or the actual conduct of the fighting. The sea, on the other hand, is all one, and, though ever changing, always the same. Every ship is self-contained and self-propelled. The problems of transport and supply, the infinite peculiarities of topography which are the increasing study of the general staffs of Europe, do not affect the naval service except in an occasional and limited degree. The main part of the British Fleet, in sufficient strength to seek a general battle, is always ready to proceed to sea without any mobilisation of reserves as soon as steam is raised. Ships or fleets of ships are capable of free and continuous movement for many days and nights together, and travel at least as far in an hour as an army can march in a day. Every vessel is in instant communication with its fleet and with the Admiralty, and all can be directed from the ports where they are stationed on any sea points chosen for massing by a short and simple order. Unit efficiency, that is to say the individual fighting power of each vessel, is in the sea service for considerable periods entirely independent of all external arrangements, and unit efficiency at sea, far more even than on land, is the prime and final factor, without which the combinations of strategy and tactics are only the preliminaries of defeat, but with which even faulty dispositions can be swiftly and decisively retrieved. For these and other similar reasons a Naval War Staff does not require to be designed on the same scale or in the same form as the General Staff of the Army.

2. Naval war is at once more simple and more intense than war on land. The executive action and control of fleet and squadron Commanders is direct and personal in a far stronger degree than that of Generals in the field, especially under modern conditions. The art of handling a great fleet on important occasions with deft and sure judgment is the supreme gift of the Admiral, and practical seamanship must never be displaced from its position as the first qualification of every sailor. The formation of a War Staff does not mean the setting up of new standards of professional merit or the opening

of a road of advancement to a different class of officers. The War Staff is to be the means of preparing and training those officers who arrive, or are likely to arrive, by the excellence of their sea service, at stations of high responsibility, for dealing with the more extended problems which await them there. It is to be the means of sifting, developing, and applying the results of history and experience, and of preserving them as a general stock of reasoned opinion available as an aid and as a guide for all who are called upon to determine, in peace or war, the naval policy of the country. It is to be a brain far more comprehensive than that of any single man, however gifted, and tireless and unceasing in its action, applied continuously to the scientific and speculative study of naval strategy and preparation. It is to be an instrument capable of formulating any decision which has been taken or may be taken, by the Executive, in terms of precise and exhaustive detail.

3. It should not be supposed that these functions find no place in Admiralty organisation at the present time. On the contrary, during the course of years, all or nearly all the elements of a War Staff at the Admiralty have been successively evolved in the practical working of everyday affairs, and have been developing since the organisation of the Foreign Intelligence Branch in 1883. The time has now come to combine these elements into an harmonious and effective organisation, to invest that new body with a significance and influence which it has not hitherto possessed, and to place it in its proper relation to existing powers.

4. The government of the Navy has by long usage been exercised by the Board of Admiralty representing the office of Lord High Admiral in commission. There is no need to alter this constitution, which has been respected through centuries of naval supremacy by all ranks in the fleets. The War Staff will, like all other persons in the Admiralty or the Navy, be under the general authority of the Board of Admiralty. It will not interpose any barrier between the Board and the Navy. All the orders which emanate from the Board will continue to be transmitted in the regular manner by the Secretary to those whom they concern.

5. Each of the Sea Lords on the Board of Admiralty has a special sphere of superintendence assigned to him by the First Lord in pursuance of the Order in Council. The First Sea Lord is charged with preparations for war and the distribution of the Fleet. The Second Sea Lord, who is to be kept in close relation to the First Sea Lord, mans the Fleet and trains the men. The Third Sea Lord directs the military construction of the Fleet; and the Fourth Sea Lord is responsible for furnishing it with adequate and suitable stores and ammunition. All these Heads of large departments will have occasion, in the discharge of their respective duties, to recur to the War Staff or its various branches for general information or for working out special inquiries.

6. Since, however, under the distribution of Admiralty business on the Board, the First Sea Lord occupies for certain purposes, especially the daily distribution of the Fleet, on which the safety of the country depends, the position of a Commander-in-Chief of the Navy, with the First Lord immediately over him as the delegate of the Crown in exercising supreme executive power, it follows that the War Staff must work at all times directly under the First Sea Lord. His position is different in important respects from that of the senior member of the Army Council as constituted. The First Sea Lord is an executive officer in active control of daily Fleet movements who requires, like a general in the field, to have at his disposal a Chief of the Staff, but who is not the Chief of the Staff himself.

7. A proper Staff, whether naval or military, should comprise three main branches, namely, a branch to acquire the information on which action may be taken; a branch to deliberate on the facts so obtained in relation to the policy of the State, and to report thereupon; and thirdly, a branch to enable the final decision of superior authority to be put into actual effect. The War Staff at the Admiralty will, in pursuance of this principle, be organised from the existing elements, in three Divisions: the Intelligence Division, the Operations Division, and the Mobilisation Division. These may be shortly described as dealing with War Information, War Plans, and War Arrangements respectively. The Divisions will be equal in status, and each will be under a Director who will usually be a Captain of standing. The three Divisions will be combined together under a Chief of the Staff.

8. The Chief of the Staff will be a Flag Officer. He will be primarily responsible to the First Sea Lord, and will work under him as his principal assistant and agent. He will not, however, be the sole channel of communication between the First Sea Lord and the Staff; and the First Lord and the First Sea Lord will whenever convenient consult the Directors of the various Divisions or other officers if necessary. This direction is essential to prevent that group of evils which have always arisen from the 'narrow neck of the bottle' system. The Chief of the War Staff will guide and co-ordinate the work of the Staff in all its branches. He will, when desired, accompany the First Lord and the First Sea Lord to the Committee of Imperial Defence.

9. Although the methodical treatment of the vast number of subjects to be dealt with by the Staff requires that there should be divisions and subdivisions, yet it is imperative that these should never be permitted to develop into 'water-tight' compartments. It will be found that there is so much overlapping between divisions, that a constant, free, and informal intercourse between them is indispensable. To promote this, the Chief of the Staff will be enjoined to hold frequent meetings—to be called 'Staff meetings'—with the Heads of the three Divisions, and each of the Directors will be kept fully

acquainted with the work of their two colleagues. Each one of the Directors will be ready at any moment to act for the Chief of the Staff in the latter's absence from whatever cause. In times of profound peace, action has often to be taken immediately on the receipt of some telegraphic report, or a request from one of the other Departments of State; one of the three Directors will therefore always remain within prompt call by messenger, night and day.

10. The functions of the War Staff will be advisory. The Chief of the Staff, when decision has been taken upon any proposal, will be jointly responsible with the Secretary for the precise form in which the necessary orders to the Fleet are issued, but the Staff will possess no executive authority. It will discharge no administrative duties. Its responsibilities will end with the tendering of advice and with the accuracy of the facts on which that advice is based.

11. Decision as to accepting or rejecting the advice of the Staff wholly or in part rests with the First Sea Lord, who, in the name of the Board of Admiralty, discharges the duties assigned to him by the Minister. In the absence of the First Sea Lord for any cause the Second Sea Lord would act for him.

12. It is necessary that there should be a close and whole-hearted co-operation between the War Staff at the Admiralty and the General Staff of the Army. A proper connection will also be maintained between the War Staff and the various Departments of State which are involved in the different aspects of its work. It is not necessary to specify further in this memorandum the distribution of duties which will be made between the various branches of the Staff.

13. The personnel of the War Staff must be considerable in numbers, and will consist of naval officers, representing most grades and every specialist branch, fresh from the sea and returning to the sea fairly frequently. Nothing in the constitution of the Staff will be designed to arrest the free play of professional opinion in all its members from top to bottom. Fresh ideas, new suggestions bred by independent study and reflection, may find their proper expression in all ranks. Disciplined co-operation in working out schemes which have been prescribed will not exclude reasoned criticism and original conceptions, the central objects being to form at once a convenient and flexible machine for the elaboration of plans and a school of sound and progressive thought on naval science.

14. The selection and training of the officers to compose a Staff of the nature described is important. Hitherto no special qualifications have been regarded as essential for the officers employed in the Intelligence and Mobilising Departments, because the ordinary sea training of naval officers was supposed to supply all that was required. This training, however, although admirable on its practical side, affords no instruction in the broader questions

of strategy and policy, which become increasingly important year by year. A change in this respect is therefore considered advisable, and a special course of training at the War College will form an essential part of the new arrangements. The President of the College will be entrusted with this important duty, and, in order that it may be carried out to the best effect, he will at all times be in close touch and association with the Chief of the Staff. In course of time the appointment will be held by a Flag Officer who has been a Staff Officer himself. Candidates for the Staff will be selected from volunteers among Lieutenants of suitable seniority as well as officers of other branches throughout the service, irrespective of their previous qualifications as specialist officers or otherwise, and those who pass the necessary examinations at the end of or during the War College course will be eligible to receive appointments either at the Admiralty or on the Staff of Flag Officers afloat as they fall vacant. In all cases, however, regular periods of sea-going executive duty will alternate with the other duties of Staff Officers of all ranks, in order that they may be kept up to the necessary standard as practical sea officers. All appointments on sea-going staffs will in the course of time be filled by these officers, and form the proper avenue to eventual employment in the highest Staff positions at the Admiralty.

15. The personnel of the Staff as at first established will necessarily consist of officers who will not have received the new Staff training. A certain number of officers with suitable qualifications will therefore be appointed to the Staff at once. These officers, and in the future those who, having successfully graduated in the Staff course at the War College, may be selected for employment, will be constituted as a specialist branch as 'Staff Officers', with, in certain cases, special allowances, in the same manner as the officers who have specialised in gunnery, torpedo, and other branches. The organisation to which they belong while serving at the Admiralty will be officially known as the 'Admiralty War Staff'. The selection and appointment of the officers who will form the Staff on its first establishment will be promulgated at an early date, and their actual work will commence very shortly after.

16. It is hoped that the result of these arrangements will be to secure for the Navy a body of officers afloat and ashore whose aptitudes for staff duties have been systematically trained and developed; and secondly to place the First Sea Lord in a position whence he can decide and advise on the grand issues without being burdened with undue detail, and with every assurance that no detail has been neglected.

[W S C]

Viscount Haldane to WSC
(*CSC Papers*)

3 January 1912

Cloan
Auchterarder

My dear Winston,

Your letter and Memorandum have arrived tonight, & have given me the greatest pleasure. I have been through the latter. I should not have liked to suggest alterations in it in any case. But after reading it with close interest I can truthfully say that there is not a word I should have wished to change had I wanted to. In spirit and in substance it is an admirable document, and will mark a new and great departure in the history of the Navy. Nothing could be better phrased than the form in which these vital principles are stated.

I think it very important that you should send a copy beforehand to Repington (Maryon Hall, Frognal Lane, Hampstead, NW). I will write him a line. For this reform ought to have the greatest recognition. I am very happy about the Navy now. I could not have accomplished myself what you have done in so short a time, and the energy you have thrown into the general work is beyond praise. I am going to write tonight to Asquith to tell him so. It is worth your while considering whether, a little later on when your staff is in working order, you should not start a *Naval Review* like our *Army Review*. Of this I am sending you a copy, in case you have not seen this number. Every officer has the chance of studying it, & it is already stimulating thought in a marked degree.

Now about the dinner at the Savoy on the 12th. I propose to sit opposite you, placing Nicholson & French on each side of you, & having Bridgeman & Prince Louis beside myself. Of course the proceedings will be private. But I should like – after giving the toast of the King – to say a few words in support of one other toast, the new Board of Admiralty, to which you might reply emphasising cooperation in our great problems. If this is agreeable to you I will arrange it.

Yours most sincerely
HALDANE

WSC to Sir Ernest Casse

7 January 1912

Admiralty

Private

My dear Cassel,

It will not be wise for me at this juncture to have any parley with your august friend. If the King were to visit Germany & I went with him, both hypothetical conditions, I shd be honoured by being permitted to discuss the great matters wh hang in the balance. But the occasion wd have to arise naturally & I shd have to be empowered by Grey & the Prime Minister. Even then all that cd be said on our part wd be that till Germany dropped the Naval challenge her policy wd be continually viewed here with deepening suspicion & apprehension; but that any slackening on her part wd produce an immediate *détente* with much good will from all England. Failing that I see little in prospect but politeness & preparation.[1]

I deeply deplore the situation for as you know I have never had any but friendly feelings towards that great nation & her illustrious Sovereign & I regard the antagonism wh has developed as insensate. Anything in my power to terminate it, I wd gladly do. But the only way I see open is one which I fear Germany will be reluctant to take.

Will you then as you think best disengage me with the greatest respect from the suggestion using, so far as your judgement inclines you, what is written here. Always my dear Cassel your vy sincere friend

WINSTON S. CHURCHILL

I will try & come to see you one day this week

Viscount Esher to WSC
(*CSC Papers*)

8 January 1912   The Roman Camp
                                                             Callander

My dear Winston,

I cannot refrain from congratulating you warmly upon the most pregnant reform which has been carried out at the Admiralty since the days of Lord St Vincent. All other changes sink into insignificance compared with this one, which *you* have inaugurated. It is bound to have far reaching results not only as regards the Navy but as regards our whole national and imperial methods of preparing for war, and should the necessity ever arise, of striking the first blow in a great campaign.

There must follow from this step an entirely new manner of approaching the consideration of a great war. It has never hitherto been possible to get the minds of those who could control the initial stages of a continental struggle fixed upon the subject from the single standpoint of united effort.

That the creation of your War Staff will bring this about, everyone who has thought about the matter must feel confident.

Of course I am delighted with the details of your scheme. They appear to

[1] Sentence deleted: "What is mere imperialism to them is life & death to us."

me as perfect as they could possibly be on grounds which must at this stage be more or less *a priori*. Later on experience may lead you or others to make more modifications but the principles you have laid down so admirably in your memorandum will never I feel sure in the lifetime of anyone now living suffer any material change.

Wishing you all good fortune, believe me,

Yours very sincerely
ESHER

I cannot tell you how *first rate* I think it all.

A. J. Balfour to WSC

9 January 1912   Whittinghame
                                                  Prestonkirk
Private

My dear Winston Churchill,

Many thanks for the Paper you have been good enough to send me. It marks, I believe, a great advance in our War organisation.

Yours sincerely
ARTHUR JAMES BALFOUR

PS A propos of your letter, I entirely agree – indeed, I have long been strongly of opinion – that submarines modify the whole question of Home Defence. The old naval theory which rejected *in toto* the policy of separate flotillas for the purpose of defending our shores (in the shape of gunboats etc) was doubtless right at the time: but I do not believe that we can, or ought, now to avoid some differentiation in the type of ships allocated respectively to independent operations on the high seas and those tied closely to a base.

The Germans at one time built even their battle fleet to fight us in the North Sea, and were able thereby to use some of their displacement for carrying armaments instead of coal. I do not know whether they still continue a policy which, on the whole, seems of very doubtful wisdom: but it certainly gave them some advantage at the moment.

I am deeply interested in what you say of the new torpedoes and their tactical consequences.

AJB

H. H. Asquith to WSC

9 January 1912   10 Downing Street

My dear Winston,

The enclosed is a highly confidential Memn by Esher, which has much good sense in it. Please, when you have read it, send it on to Haldane, who in due course can return it to me.

Yours always
H.H.A.

Note by WSC

It shd not be supposed that mastery on the seas depends on the simultaneous occupation of every sea. On the contrary it depends upon ability to defeat the strongest battlefleet or combination wh can be brought to bear. This ability cannot be maintained by a policy of dispersion. The sea is all one, and war is all one. The supreme strategic principle of concentration of superior force in the decisive theatre, and the supreme tactical principle described by Napoleon as *'frapper la masse'* must govern all naval dispositions. All the rest will come *'par surcroit'*. Dispersion of strength, frittering of money, empty parades of foolish little ships 'displaying the flag' in unfrequented seas, are the certain features of a policy leading through extravagance to defeat.

Some doubt seems to be thrown on these 'fundamentals' by Esher's examples and the tone in wh they are referred to. So far as the Cte of ID is concerned, it appears to me that if Admiralty contemplate an important change like the concentration in Home Waters, they wd of course consult the Prime Minister. It would then rest with him whether the CID shd be involved. Personally, I shd be glad of its support.

However the ultimate responsibility of the First Lord must not be impaired. He cannot be expected to be responsible for faulty dispositions, or what he thinks are such!

WSC

Viscount Haldane to WSC

24 January 1912   28 Queen Anne's Gate

My dear Winston,

I had seen the Esher Memn. I do not think it amounts to much from your or my point of view. Whenever we have a case it will decide our way and we should in consequence have the PM at our backs. You and I must always be responsible for policy, but if we secure the head of the Govt we shall be in a still stronger position. And Co-ordination Cttee of the CID will help to this end, besides giving other results.

But I should like to talk it and other things germane over with you. Could you dine here alone on Monday night? Or could we meet after dinner if you are engaged. I would come anywhere. Or 6 o'clock at the Admiralty on Monday evening would suit me. Just what is most convenient to yourself.

Ever Yours
HALDANE

WSC to Lord Fisher
(Lennoxlove Papers)

10 January 1912   Admiralty

Secret

My dear Fisher,

Many thanks for your letters which I greatly enjoy and over which I ponder much. As the man wrote about white leather hunting breeches to his tailor 'Keep continually sending.' The Prime Minister is coming to Naples: he will come and see you. Talk to him about the Mediterranean and about shifting the bases.

Aviation is going ahead. In a few months the Navy List will contain regular flights of aeroplanes attached to the battle squadrons.

The 'Coast Admiral' project is advancing. There is no doubt the *Lion* can do 32 instead of the 28 promised. The February cruiser will be a distinct advance on this—perhaps 2 more knots. Gaunt's[1] letter is interesting but he ignores the real argument. Armour forces the use of armour-punching as against high explosive shells with consequent tremendous diminution in destructive power: with high explosive shells even, the bulk of the explosion remains outside. Still I agree with your principles and, like you, I see no limit to size. After a bit we shall plug at each other from our own countries. But not during the administration of the present Board. I am still moving about with the extra submarines. There is no difficulty about money this year. An excellent committee is sitting daily on oil. Hopwood has just joined it. The drift appears to be favourable to our view. But we must own the supplies, otherwise with general adoption prices would become prohibitive.

The War Staff has been received with a paean.

Burn this.

Yours ever
WINSTON S. C.

Later

PS I have added the 4 extra submarines.

[1] Ernest Frederick Augustus Gaunt (1865–1940), Rear-Admiral 1914; Admiral 1924; knighted 1919.

WSC to Sir Edward Grey

Interchange of Naval Infn with Germany.

11 January 1912

[Copy]

My dear Grey,

I have read Goschen's letter of Jan 7, 1912 wh you kindly sent me. If we were making a proposal, I agree that the time wd be unsuitable. We are however only replying, tardily, to their communicn at present unanswered. The reply, tho' friendly & favourable in substance, has a sting in its tail. It is not a reply inconsistent with the existing atmosphere. The reasons for delay are natural & true; first the crisis of the autumn, 2nd the changes at the Admy, 3rd the German elections. My conclusion is therefore the same as Goschen's, *viz* that as soon as the elections are complete the German Govt shd be given the reply.

The only reason wh wd override the above is the development of some much larger negotiation or situation, in relation to wh this project of interchange of naval infn has not yet been judged.

Yrs v sly
WSC

WSC to Viscount Haldane

15 January 1912   Admiralty

[Copy]

My dear Haldane,

The evidence collected by Captain Kell about German espionage in England etc ought to be submitted to one or two legal authorities of eminence. It may be necessary shortly to make public statements concerning its prevalence, & also about the arming of merchantmen. As absolute confirmation may be lacking, altho moral certainty exists, it wd be well to fortify ourselves with some cool judicial opinion trained in judging evidence and capable of being cited, to show that we have made no charges in haste or without good reason.

The Public Prosecutor, Sir Ch Mathews and/or Lord Murray seem to me to be the men for this.

What do you think? I must be ready to declare a policy in regard to armed merchantmen shortly after Parliament meets.

Yours vy sincly
W

Lord Roberts to WSC

21 January 1912   Englemere
                                                           Ascot
                                                           Berks

Private

My dear Churchill,

It is some little time since I last wrote to you, it is indeed some little time since we have met and discussed matters in friendly conversation, but I am moved to write to you now for several reasons which I will state as briefly and as clearly as I can. I hope I may be able to induce you to weigh the subject of this letter carefully, I am even tempted to the belief that you may agree with what I have to say.

The months of July, August, and September of last year found us on the edge of war, and in the balance of a life and death struggle for our very existence. Three months of strain and anxiety revealed something else – something very deplorable. They revealed that we were unprepared to take our part in such a struggle in a manner befitting a great nation.

It is an open secret that the Regular Army was not ready for war. It was realized that the men were ill armed, that there was a serious deficiency in ammunition, that horses were not forthcoming, that there was a shortage in officers, that no steps had been taken to supply aeroplanes and trained aviators, and that many other important matters had been neglected or overlooked.

As regards the Territorial Force, it is not too much to say that, during those anxious days, it was seen to be quite unfitted to play the part assigned to it. I need scarcely enumerate its shortcomings, they must be quite apparent to you. Its officers and non-commissioned officers untrained and lamentably short in numbers; its thousands of boys who had never been in camp and never held a rifle; its very inferior armament both in small arms and in guns; its lack of horses, of personnel, of administrative services, and so forth. In short, those summer months showed us that our Regular Army, small as it is, was unprepared for war, whilst our Territorial Force was wholly unfit to take the field.

As regards the Navy, I cannot speak with the same authority, but as I look back and note what has happened since last summer, I am constrained to think that there too there was something seriously amiss.

And now comes my first reason for writing this letter. I know that I am but stating the bare truth when I say that you took a prominent part in directing the policy of the Government in those critical months. Gossip has it, and I believe truly has it, that you and two or three other members of the

Government came forward in a most admirable manner, and that you behaved like a Statesman realizing the gravity of the situation and prepared to do your utmost should war have broken out.

Rumour has it, and I am confident that rumour is right, that it was due to the manly part you then took that you were made First Lord of the Admiralty – an appointment which I, and all those who put country above people and party, were heartily glad to see.

Since last summer, many things have happened. Your appointment as First Lord, the great change in the Naval part of the Admiralty Board, the new War Staff. All these mean much for the future of the Navy and of the safety of the Empire.

The Army remains the same – a constant factor of weakness and of danger in the European situation. On the Continent, as a direct result of last year's crisis, we see every country arming to the teeth and preparing for instant war on land and sea. History records no such vast efforts and preparations. And what is the attitude of Great Britain? Great Britain appears to think that an Expeditionary Force of Six Divisions is the last word, the final and triumphant solution of this vast problem. No matter how many Army Corps Germany may add to her Armies, our six divisions are supposed by the people of this country to retain their dominating position, their power of decisive and victorious action. The people are taught to believe that a Force of 315,000 Territorials, called into being to crush raids of 5,000 to 10,000 foreigners, can, when it has only reached a total of 260,000, deal in an equally crushing and drastic manner with 70,000 highly trained German soldiers.

And now comes my second reason for writing this letter.

If I am not mistaken, you showed, during the crisis last summer, that you were possessed of a real sense and appreciation of the situation. Will you not carry on that work now and in the future? Will you, and those colleagues of yours who agreed with you then, will you not face the situation – I had almost said the desperate situation – which lies before us, and take such action as regards the armed forces of the Crown, – and especially the military forces – as that situation demands?

The events of the summer and the part you took then and are still taking inspire me – if I may say so – with a faith in your patriotism and a belief in your ability, which encourage me to hope that you will come to the decision, that the continued existence of our Empire cannot rest on the voluntary efforts of a few of the best of our citizens, and that, if we are to continue amongst the Great Powers of the world, we must adopt compulsion as the bedrock of our military system. And I believe further that, should you agree with me in this matter, and should you be prepared to go forward with it, you will receive whole hearted assistance from the opposition, and immense support from all the best elements in the country.

I am afraid I have inflicted a long letter on a very busy man. My excuse must be the fact that to my mind, at all events, the danger of further delay in facing our problem is great, and the very existence of our country demands instant action.

I cannot forget that I am writing to the son of the man who was responsible for my selection as Commander-in-Chief in India, and for that reason, if for no other, I would like to see you take the lead in serving our country.

Believe me, Yours sincerely
ROBERTS

WSC to his wife
CSC Papers)

18 January 1912   HMS *Enchantress*

My darling,

I am so glad you are coming up to London tomorrow. It will be vy nice in this dirty weather to be back in our own basket again. I will work all day & we will patronise the drama in the evenings. I have a cold attacking me agst wh I am feebly defending myself with cinnamon.

Oedipus was most impressive. I am not sure I wd like to go again; but you shd certainly see it. I am telegraphing to Freddie to express my regrets at not returning. The weather here has stopped all my mobilisation plans. What a row the Belfast Orangemen are making & what fools they are! I am going to let the newspapers talk for a day or two.

Of course I must go.

With fondest love to you & the P.Ks.

Always your loving husband
W

WSC to Lord Roberts

23 January 1912

[Copy]

Private & con.

My dear Ld Roberts,

I am honoured by the letter wh you have written me wh I have read with the greatest care & upon wh I shall often reflect.

I was when I first went into Parlt opposed to the principle of compulsory service. I am disposed somewhat differently now towards it. As to the right of the State & the duty of the citizen there can be no doubt. But I am far less certain that it is necessary or that it wd be convenient. Further even if I were satisfied on these points, I do not see at this moment what steps shd be taken or what combination of force wd be available to support them.

Where the Navy is concerned there is every reason for confidence. It is true that the late crisis disclosed an imperfect appreciation of the importance of Staff work, & a lack of imaginative foresight on the part of some of those in responsible positions. But the men are good; the machine is vy good; the margins of superiority are vy large; the detail has been most thoroughly attended to; the strategic advantages of our position are most formidable. On all these points except the last it is my earnest hope that progress may be made. The new German increases wh are now threatened will be emphatically countered by ample developments here. And the grave but simple problems of naval defence will be studied with unremitting attention.

No money will be grudged by the H of C for wh necessity is shown. A series of measures is in preparation wh will greatly increase our naval strength in the decision theatre, & wh will enable it to be even more swiftly realisable than it is at present. We cannot imagine how 70,000 men cd be landed in this country once the alarm had been given. And if they came 'out of the blue' the regular army wd be here to meet them. In any case 70,000 men cd not conquer Britain. I do not feel that we are in danger so far as the immediate security of this country is concerned, & I see no problem in the near future wh we shall not be able to approach with reasonable prospects of success.

Let me thank you in conclusion for yr reference to my father whose memory is so dear to me.

Yrs vy sincly
W S C

Lord Roberts to WSC

25 January 1912   Ascot

Private

My dear Churchill,

I am much obliged to you for replying so promptly to my letter, and for the assurance that you will bear in mind the vitally important and pressing question of our armed forces for land as well as for sea warfare.

I feel encouraged by your saying that your disposition towards compulsory service is different, and more sympathetic than it was when you entered Parliament, for I am convinced that, provided you retain this open mind, the intimate and constant grappling with the subject of Imperial defence in all its bearings, which is imposed upon you by the important and responsible office which you now hold, cannot fail to bring home to you the necessity for compulsion in some form or another. I am not going to inflict upon you another long letter of argument in favour of this principle, but you must allow me to refer to one portion of your letter in which you allude to the invasion of this country by 70,000 men. That 70,000 Germans should invade this country at a time when our Expeditionary Force is at home is unthinkable – they are not such fools. But I cannot admit that such an invasion, 'out of the blue', would necessarily find our Expeditionary Force at home. On the contrary, the 'bolt from the blue' to be most feared and anticipated is one despatched at a time when most of our trained troops are already engaged in some other part of the world.

If in 1900 the feeling in Germany against this country had been as universally bitter as it is now, and if the balance of Naval power between the two countries had been in that year similar to what now obtains, a 'bolt from the blue' of 70,000 Germans might well have been sprung upon us.

And please remember that the figure 70,000 is purely hypothetical. I believe it arose from my saying, in answer to a question put to me, at a meeting of the Committee of Imperial Defence, that I considered 70,000 the smallest number with which the Germans would dream of invading this country. Personally I hold that, if the Germans ever invade these islands, they will do so with a larger army than 70,000, and I have never subscribed to the argument concerning this figure so often reiterated by Lord Haldane and other ministers.

Moreover, we must remember that the victories which have successfully ended the various crises in the history of this country, have taken place, not within these shores nor on the seas, but beyond them; and the real reason for raising our Citizen Army on a compulsory basis is that we can never obtain from volunteers during peace the time required for a military training that will fit them to back the Expeditionary Force at the decisive point.

All I beg of you is to enquire very closely into our present preparations for war, and not to retard any movement of your reason towards compulsion, by the thought that 'the country will not have it'. I have not the slightest fear about 'the country' accepting it, once it is placed before them in an honest and serious way by Ministers who are themselves convinced of its necessity.

Believe me, yours sincerely

ROBERTS

WSC to Lord Roberts

27 January 1912   Admiralty

Private

Copy

My dear Lord Roberts,

As to the 70,000. Is it not arguable that less wd be futile, & more, much much more difficult!

But I agree that the general question must be decided one way or the other on broader and less technical grounds.

Yours sincerely
WSC

Prince Louis of Battenberg to WSC

25 January 1912   Admiralty

First Lord:

I rejoice to hear that you have been discussing with the First Sea Lord the question of putting an end to the present unsound organisation in Home Fleet, whereby the C in C is charged, over and above his legitimate work, with the direct command of one of the Divisions of the Fleet.

It is exactly the same as if the Lieut Genl commanding a Division composed of several Brigades, were to be at the same time the Brigadier in command of the 1st Brigade.

I have long held this to be unsound and objectionable and soon after I assumed command of the 3rd and 4th Divs. I was allowed by F.L. to make a change on the above basis. I found the big ships divided into 3 principal groups at the 3 Home Ports. The one at Plymouth was under a Rear-Admiral, and so was the one at Portsmouth, but the one at Chatham-Sheerness was supposed to be under my personal charge; consequently, as regarded this group, I was expected to do the work of a junior Rear-Admiral. Luckily I had at hand a spare Rear-Admiral, who was supposed to act as my deputy for the whole Command, whenever I was absent. I gave him charge of the Chatham-Sheerness group & the arrangement proved a great success.

I should urge a Vice-Admiral being placed in charge of 1st Div H.F. [Home Fleet].

L B

Lord Crewe to WSC
(*CSC Papers*)

[29 January 1912]   India Office

Private

My dear Winston,

I must just tell you how much I have been impressed in these critical discussions with the ready knowledge, the lucidity, and the excellent temper, with which your share in them has been conducted: you have every reason to congratulate yourself on the line of country on which the argument has travelled.

No. answer, of course,

                                                                    Yrs
                                                                    C

WSC to Sir Edward Grey

31 January 1912   [Admiralty]

Copy

My dear Grey,

Cassel returned last night having travelled continuously from Berlin. At 10 on Monday he saw Ballin[1] who went forthwith to the German Chancellor, & in the afternoon he saw Ballin, Bethmann Hollweg[2] & the Emperor together. They all appeared deeply pleased by the venture. B.H. earnest & cordial, the Emperor 'enchanted, almost childishly so'. The Emperor talked a gt deal on naval matters to Cassel, the details of wh he was unable to follow. After much consultn the E wrote out with B.H. paper A, wh Ballin transcribed. The 2nd paper B is B.H.'s statement of the impending naval increases, translated by Cassel. C says they do not seem to know what they wanted in regard to Colonies. They did not seem to be greatly concerned abt expansion. 'There were 10 large companies in Berlin importing labour into Germany:' Over populn was not their problem. They were delighted with M no 3 on Cassel's rough notes. They are most anxious to hear from us soon. C does not believe that the 'exception' is a final or irrevocable position.

Lloyd George & I breakfasted with C this morning. Ballin having telegraphed again to C for news, C sent the telm marked C.

Such is my report.

[1] Albert Ballin (1857–1918), German shipping magnate. The Kaiser's closest adviser on maritime questions. Played a leading role in developing German merchant marine. Committed suicide two days before Armistice, 1918.

[2] Theobald von Bethmann Hollweg (1856–1921), German Chancellor 1909–17.

Observations.

It seems certain that the new Navy Law will be presented to the *Reichstag* & that it will be agreed to, even the Socialists not resisting. The naval increases are serious & will require new & vigorous measures on our part. The spirit may be good, but the facts are grim. I had been thinking that if the old German programme had been adhered to we shd have built 4,3,4,3,4,3 against their 6 years programme of 2,2,2,2,2,2. If their new programme stands, as I fear it must, & they build 3,2,3,2,3,2, we cannot build less than 5,4,5,4,5,4. This maintains 60% superiority over Germany only in Dreadnoughts & Dreadnt Cruisers. It will also be 2 keels to 1 on their additional 3 ships.

The matter of a 3rd squadron in full commission is also a serious and formidable provision. At present, owing to the fact that in the 6 winter months the 1st & 2nd squadrons of the High Sea Fleet are congested with recruits, there is great relief to us from the strain to wh we are put by German naval power. The addn of the 3rd squadron will make that strain continual throughout the year. The maintenance in full comm of 25 battleships wh after the next 4 or 5 years will all be Dreadnts exposes us to constant danger only to be warded off by vigilance approximating to war conditions. A further assurance against attack is at present found in the fact that several of the German Dreadnts are vy often the wrong side of the Kiel Canal wh they can't pass through & must therefore make a long detour.

The deepening of the Canal by 1915 will extinguish this safety signal. The fact that the defenders are always liable to be attacked when not at their ordinary average strength by an enemy at his selected moment & consequent maximum strength means that our margins wd have to be vy large. Agst 25 battleships we cd not keep less than 40 available within 24 hrs. This will involve addnal expense.

The German increase in personnel must also be met. I had intended to ask Parlt for 2,000 more this yr and 2,000 next. I expect to have to double these quotas. On the whole the addn to our estimates consequent upon German increases will not be less than 3 million a year.

This is certainly not dropping the naval challenge.

I agree with you that caution is necessary. In order to meet the new German squadron we are contemplating bringing home the Meditn battleships. This means relying on France in the Meditn & certainly no exchange of system wd be possible, even if desired by you.

The only chance I see is roughly this. They will announce their new programme, & we will make an immediate & effective reply. Then if they care to slow down the '*tempo*' so that their Fleet Law is accomplished in 12 and not in 6 years, friendly relations wd ensue, & we, though I shd be reluctant to bargain about it, cd slow down too. All they wd have to do wd be to make their quotas biennial instead of annual. Nothing wd be deranged in their plan. 12 years of tranquillity wd be assured in naval policy. The attempt ought to be made.

Yrs vy sincly
WSC

Sir Francis Hopwood to WSC

31 January 1912   13 Hornton Street

My dear Churchill,

We are in for trouble as to making public announcement of an advance of half a million. Treasury is scared to death of it! – Chalmers quite prepared to bury it in a contract with Vickers or anybody else but funks publicity. Wants to consult Ch of Ex. We must devise something quickly.

Yrs sincly
FRANCIS HOPWOOD

I was very much interested in hearing your conversation as to holding a Levée – it was done in old days. Curious that you should have instanced old Admiral Dalrymple Hay[1] for his death happened almost at the minute! Do you carry on a correspondence with the officer Commanding-in-Chief as the Sec of State does with the Governors? It would be a great 'fag' for you altho' I take it they would in these late days be pleased with dictated letters. It seems to me that it is most important to keep in touch with the thought & opinion of the top man in each unit. You will then know the opinion of the world's Navy. It does not appear to me that you get full measure of wide & generous opinion out of yr Board. You ought to know what the great machine outside is thinking of as it works its course, to compare that knowledge with your inside advice. Then, as in this docking question, I think you should make your Sea Lords advise you – take the responsibility: you are quite strong enough to combat & make them recall their advice if it is unsound. Don't let them finally place themselves in the position of saying 'The First Lord is good enough to fix this difficult job up for himself, we are glad to escape' – great risks are in front & you should not take the whole responsibility for matters which they should endorse. Fisher was a great & jealous

---

[1] John Charles Dalrymple Hay (1821–1912), 3rd Baronet; Rear-Admiral 1866, Vice-Admiral 1872, Admiral 1878; MP Wakefield 1862–5, Stamford 1866–80, Wigtown Burghs 1880–5; Chairman of Reuters Telegram Co; he died on 28 January 1912.

personality – he gathered everything into his hands & hated outside communication with the First Lord. It seems to me that now you have the centralization in the First Lord without the Fisher willing to share the responsibility. I was going on but I recognize that like a woman I have made my postscript longer than the letter – so I shut up!

Yrs v sincly
FRANCIS HOPWOOD

WSC to Sir Francis Bridgeman

[January 1912]   Admiralty

Threatened Coal Strike[1]

You should ask Sir Francis Hopwood, who knows the Board of Trade thoroughly, to keep you constantly informed as to the likelihood of a strike. Meanwhile you should prepare a plan, with his assistance and that of the Fourth Sea Lord, for coaling the Fleet during a strike. The dispositions of the Fleet should be conceived to facilitate such a plan. It may be convenient to keep the Atlantic Fleet at Gibraltar, and the Mediterranean battleships, and possibly the Third Division, off Vigo, and coal them with foreign coal during the whole period. On the other hand the consumption of fuel involved in sending the Third Division to Vigo is a factor. The international situation must not be overlooked. It may be possible to accumulate a floating reserve of foreign coal off Vigo which would serve in an emergency the fleet in general and not merely the vessels concentrated there. From the moment that the strike becomes certain all movement in Home Waters must absolutely cease, and even now the utmost precautions must be taken to husband reserves. The Mediterranean battleships are very well situated where they are at Vigo, and it ought not to be necessary to send them back to the Mediterranean for a month or two.

I shall be glad to hear from you by Wednesday or Thursday next what arrangements you consider most judicious.

[1] A ballot among miners beginning on 10 January resulted in a decision to strike. Despite the intervention of the Government, and a prayer devised by the two archbishops ('O God ... allay all danger and bitterness') the strike began at the end of February and was not settled until 11 April.

29 January 1912   Admiralty

Draft

My dear Harcourt,

I should like to have a talk with you in the near future about the Colonial Navies. I do not think anyone can doubt that the arrangements made in 1909 with Australia were not very satisfactory so far as British Naval interests were concerned. The whole principle of local Navies is, of course, thoroughly vicious, and no responsible sailor can be found who has a word to say in favour of it. The demands which are now falling due upon us to alienate from the decisive theatre in the North Sea upwards of 2,000 of our highly trained officers and men, is causing a great deal of anxiety and concern to my Naval advisers. This is particularly the case where the provision of officers is concerned; and having regard to the manning requirements of the War Fleets in 1912–13 and 1913–14 it is probable that I shall have to make some new proposals. The difficulties connected with the different rates of pay are also embarrassing. We cannot ourselves concede the principle of a different rate of pay to Imperial seamen just because they are serving in Australian waters. If the Australians would like to pay the extra money themselves, not only to Australian but to British seamen, there would be no objection; and, having regard to the discontent which will undoubtedly be caused by men serving together at different rates of pay, the Admiralty would be quite willing to agree to such action on the part of the Australian Government even if it should ultimately become necessary for the Australians to reduce the last instalment of their annual contribution for the purpose. If, however, the matter is satisfactorily settled so far as the Australian unit is concerned, the difficulty immediately extends to the ships to be maintained in New Zealand waters. Here Sir Joseph Ward[1] has already proposed to pay New Zealanders serving in this Squadron the extra money out of the £100,000 a year New Zealand contribution. It seems to me that it will be impossible to differentiate between the treatment of British sailors serving in either the Australian or New Zealand Squadrons, and the proposal to which I am being drawn is that the Australian and New Zealand Governments should pay an additional bounty over and above ordinary British rates of pay to all men serving in the two Squadrons irrespective of their origin, and unless the Colonies are prepared to make an additional grant the necessary sums will have to be deducted from their contributions.

---

[1] Joseph George Ward (1856–1930), Prime Minister of New Zealand 1906–12, 1928–30; created Baronet 1911.

So far as ships are concerned I do not expect that there is any chance of inducing Australia to let us have battle cruiser *Australia* in Home waters during the next few years. I propose, therefore, to put the best face on this that we can and to aid the Australian Government to establish their complete Fleet unit as quickly as possible. The departure of these valuable modern ships, so important to our Fleet in Home waters, is, of course, very unpleasant. The cessation of the £200,000 a year contribution, and the need, so far as we can meet it, for manning the Australian Fleet unit, make it essential that we should reduce our force in Australian waters at the earliest possible moment to the minimum. The Australians have made proposals that all four ships should be withdrawn during the course of 1912–13, and that the two detached for service in China should not come back. These proposals we shall certainly accept. Indeed, I think it highly probable that two ships, or at the outside three, will be sufficient for training purposes during the transition stage. It is essential that we should effect a substantial saving in order to cover us for the loss of the contribution and for the alienation at a critical time of so many valuable officers and men.

New Zealand stands in a different position. She has given her battle cruiser to the Imperial Government for service wherever desired. The existing arrangement is that the vessel shall be employed on the China Station, and shall, if possible, touch at New Zealand ports on her way to the China Station. The employment of a ship like the *New Zealand* in China is not to be defended on any military grounds. She will not find her match on that side of the world unless we are to assume a rupture of the Japanese alliance and a war with that Power, in which case totally different dispositions would have to be made. On the other hand the *New Zealand* will be urgently required here at home to take part in maintaining British naval superiority in the North Sea. It is necessary for us to reinforce the China Station in any case at once, and the First Sea Lord proposes to send the *Defence,* a magnificent armoured cruiser, sister ship to the *Minotaur* (now serving in China) and like the *Minotaur* stronger than any other armoured ship in Eastern waters other than Japanese. The *Defence* will be sent to China as soon as she can be got ready, and when this reinforcement reaches the China Fleet ample margin of preponderance will be secured over Germany on the China Station. We desire, therefore, to propose to the New Zealand Government that the *Defence* should go to the China Station as a substitute for the *New Zealand*, and that it should go now instead of waiting until September when the latter vessel will be completed. We wish to ask the New Zealand Government to come to the assistance of the mother country by agreeing to the *New Zealand's* being employed in the Home Fleet during the next few years. The moment for making this request would be exceptionally well chosen if it followed upon the announcement of the German intention to make further increases in their Navy Law, which I fear will not now be long delayed. Unless some crisis arises, which is very unlikely, during the winter months of 1912–13, we would propose to send the *New Zealand*, as soon as she was completed, to the Dominion to spend three months, including Christmas, in New Zealand ports. She would then return in January or February, 1913, to join the Second Cruiser Squadron of the Home Fleet. It would be very desirable to know in advance how the New Zealand Government would view this proposal. My own impression is that they would be very ready to fall in with it.

I enclose a draft telegram which we should be glad if you would convey to the New Zealand Government.

I have had various visits from persons professing to be in the confidence of the new Canadian Government so far as their naval policy is concerned. The most important of these has been from Sir [blank space] who was brought here specially by Lord Strathcona,[1] and introduced to me by him as being charged with an informal and secret, but duly authorised, mission. Sir [blank space] told me that the Canadian Government propose to seek the advice of the British Admiralty in regard to their Navy policy; that they were earnestly desirous of doing something really effective to help the British Navy; that anything in the shape of a local Navy would fail to carry any enthusiasm in Canada; that even a Canadian Squadron would be abhorrent to the Government now in power. Their only interest was in the Imperial Navy to which they desired to contribute two or perhaps three of the finest vessels in the world. These vessels should be named after Canadian Provinces, built out of Canadian money in Great Britain, manned, maintained and controlled by the British Admiralty. They would not have 'little ships looking after the factory, but great ships to fight in the front line'. To safeguard the principle of Canadian autonomy it would be necessary that Canada should have the power to withdraw these vessels at any time on giving sufficient notice to enable them to be replaced. In practice this would never happen. Ultimately it was hoped enough ships might be added to enable each Province to be represented.

The above I gathered was the policy which the Canadian Government, when they ask for advice, would like to be told authoritatively by the Admiralty they could adopt, and on this they believe they could appeal to the country at a special general election with good prospects of success. I should add that Sir [blank space] hinted that the Canadians would desire

---

[1] Donald Alexander Smith (1820–1914). After a career in the Hudson's Bay Company, and several years in the Dominion House of Commons he became High Commissioner for Canada in London 1896–1911; knighted 1896; created Baron Strathcona and Mount Royal 1897.

some assurance that these vessels should be in addition to, and not complementary to, the bare minimum which we thought it necessary for our own safety to maintain. All this was represented as being extremely confidential, and quite informal. I hope therefore that this letter may not be registered as an official paper in the Colonial Office, but kept among your private documents.

Naturally, from the Admiralty point of view, we could wish for nothing better. We shall have to maintain a large number of battleships in full commission, and the sooner these battleships are of the Dreadnought type the better for us. We should get an addition to our building programme most disheartening to Germany, while at the same time, by putting inferior vessels into the reserve instead of placing them into commission, we should escape any serious addition to our establishment charges. I only hope it will all come true.

Perhaps you will let me know when we shall discuss these matters together.

Note at end of Letter:
    Seen. L.B. 29.1.12.

[WSC]

WSC to Sir Joseph Ward

TELEGRAM

[undated]   Admiralty

Secret and Personal. In the event of further increases to the German Naval Programme being announced as now seems imminent and likely the interests of British naval supremacy would make it desirable that the battle cruiser *New Zealand* should instead of serving in China be appointed to the Home Fleet for service in the North Sea where alone she could be matched against vessels of her strength and quality. If your Government approve of this arrangement the Admiralty will send at once the armoured cruiser *Defence* sister to the *Minotaur* to the China station thus effectively securing British preponderance in those seas and will arrange that the battle cruiser *New Zealand* should visit the Dominion in October to make a three months' stay, including Christmas 1912, in New Zealand ports before taking up her duties with the Home Fleet. The Admiralty feel that prompt action of this kind on the part of New Zealand might play an important part in retarding and certainly of balancing the growth of European naval armaments.

Lewis Harcourt to WSC

1 February 1912   Nuneham Park
                                                   Oxford

My dear Churchill,

I do not at all differ with your proposal as regards the New Zealand battleship and shall be willing to send the telegram as from the Admiralty, but I think it is a matter on which we ought to consult the Cabinet before taking action.

1. Because there is almost certain to be immediate leakage of your request.

2. We may have a blank refusal.

3. In case of New Zealand's assent there would have to be a publication there of the reasons for your request and they will probably wish to have our case *vis-à-vis* to Germany put rather high and this may not be convenient to you or Grey when the publication takes place, so I think we ought to be prepared for eventualities so that we should all realise what we are doing. Perhaps you may like to raise this at the Cabinet tomorrow if we have time.

Note by WSC at top of page:

Ansd. not worth while to start long Cabinet discn. If you agree will raise question as part of general discn on Naval Estimates. If Germany abandon increases we will try to do without the ship, unless, as is not impossible, N.Z. actually prefer arrangement suggested in my letter.

Memorandum by WSC

[undated]   [Admiralty]

Copy

The safety of New Zealand and Australia is secured by the naval power and the alliances based on the naval power of Great Britain. No European State would or could invade or conquer New Zealand unless the British Navy had been destroyed. The same naval power of Great Britain in European waters also protects New Zealand and Australia from any present danger from Japan. While Japan is allied to Great Britain, and while Great Britain possesses a sufficient margin of naval superiority, Japan is safe from attack by sea from the great Fleets of Europe. In no other way in the years that lie immediately before us can Japan protect herself from the danger of European interference. It would appear that the reasons which have led Japan to contract and renew the Alliance will grow stronger with time. The growth of German interests in China, the re-building of the Russian Fleets in the Baltic and the Black Sea, and the general development of European Navies on a scale far greater than Japan can afford to imitate, will require her increasingly to seek that sure protection which British naval supremacy can so easily afford. The obligations of Great Britain to Japan under the Alliance are not limited to preventing an armada being despatched from European waters to alter suddenly the balance of naval strength in the China Seas. We are bound to maintain in these waters a force superior to that of any other European Power, and consequently any danger to Japan arising from a gradual increase of European Squadrons in the Far East is also provided against. The Alliance has now been renewed up to the year 1921. It is not to be expected that even after that date Japan will have less need of that powerful friend at the other end of the world who guarantees her from all European molestation. Quite apart from the good sense and moderation which the Japanese have shown since they became a civilised Power, and quite apart from the great services mutually rendered and advantages derived by both Powers from the Alliance, there is a strong continuing bond of self-interest. It is this that is the true and effective protection for the safety of Australia and New Zealand.

If the British Fleet were defeated in the North Sea, all the dangers which it now wards off from the Australasian Dominion would be liberated. If the victorious European Powers desired any territorial expansion or naval stations in the Pacific, there would be no forces which Australia and New Zealand could command which could effectively prevent them. If Japan chose to indulge in ambitions of Empire or Colonisation in the South Pacific, she would be no loser so far as the European situation was concerned. We should have lost at a stroke the means both of making our friendship service-able and our hostility effective. There are no means by which in the next 10 or 15 years Australia and New Zealand can expect to maintain them-selves single-handed against the powerful navy of Japan. If the power of Great Britain were shattered upon the sea, the only course open to the 5,000,000 of white men in the Pacific would be to seek the protection of the United States.

From this point of view the profound wisdom of the policy hitherto adopted by New Zealand can be appreciated. In giving a splendid ship to strengthen the British Navy at the decisive point, wherever that point may be according to the best principles of naval strategy, the Dominion of New Zealand have provided in the most effectual way alike for their own and for the common security. No greater insight into political and strategic truths has ever been shown by a community hitherto unversed in military matters.

The situation in the Pacific will be absolutely regulated by the decision in the North Sea. 2 or 3 Australian and New Zealand Dreadnoughts if brought into the line in the North Sea might turn the scale and make victory not merely certain but complete. The same 2 or 3 Dreadnoughts in Australian waters would be useless the day after the defeat of the British Navy in Home Waters. Their existence could only serve to prolong the agony without altering the course of events. Their effectiveness would have been destroyed by events which had taken place at the other side of the globe as surely as if they had been sunk in the battle. These facts may not be palatable; but the Admiralty is bound to expose the peril and military unwisdom of divided organisation, of dispersion or dissipation of forces, and of partial engagements in detail, which have led to the squandering of so many powerful States and Empires, and to behold and proclaim in their place the principles of unity in command and in strategic conceptions, and concentration in the decisive theatres and for the decisive events. The Dominions are perfectly free to take or reject our advice. The matter rests entirely in their hands, and the Admiralty responsibility ceases when the facts have been placed plainly before the responsible Ministers.

It is recognised, however, that time will be required before the true principles of naval policy are comprehended in the Dominions, and that in the interval arrangements must be made to develop, so far as possible, their local naval establishments. The Dominions want to have their own ships under their own control, cruising in their own waters, based on their own Ports. They want to see continually the result of the money they have spent or may spend. They wish to enjoy the custom and advantage which the presence of their own ships in their own waters confers. They want to have something they can see and touch and take pride in with feelings of ownership and control. These feelings, although unrecognised by military truth, are natural. They are real facts which will govern events if the choice which is open to us in the immediate future is not one between having Australian vessels in the right strategic stations or the wrong, but between having them in the wrong or not having them at all. It is easily understood that the difficulties of enlisting the active co-operation of the Dominions in naval defence by means of ships they rarely saw, and which were absorbed in the great fleets of Britain at the other end of the world, are at present insuperable. Such a policy would require an effort of imagination and a gift of military intuition, which so far only New Zealand has been capable of. The Admiralty have therefore, on political grounds rather than on military or strategic grounds, co-operated to the best of their ability in the development of the Australian Fleet Unit. They admit that the question of whether the ships should or should not be built claims priority over questions connected with what is the best use to make of them when they are built. They realise the importance of creating a naval sentiment in the Dominions, and of creating the reserves of personnel which are so valuable and the local naval establishments which are essential to the full mobility and employment of the Imperial Fleet. It is with the object of combining sound military principles with local aspirations that the design of an Imperial Squadron has been conceived.

Memorandum by WSC

[undated] [Admiralty]

Copy

I have carefully examined with my colleagues on the Board of Admiralty the questions connected with South African Naval Defence which I discussed with you and Mr [?] on the occasion of your visit; and at your request I now send you our considered observations on the subject.

It is with the greatest satisfaction that the Members of HM Government, and indeed men of all parties in the State, have noted the growing sense of recognition on the part of the Over-Sea Dominions of their vital stake in the integrity of the Empire.

A complete harmony exists between Imperial interests and South African needs. South Africa is the principal strategic point on the most sure highway to the British Dominions and Possessions in the Far East and the Pacific. Its preservation as a safe and efficient base for British ships must always be an important object of Admiralty policy and affect the dispositions of the Fleet in peace and war. The South African interest in the maintenance of the communications with Europe is also vital and clear. The interruption of the trade route would arrest, its insecurity would hamper, the whole economic development of South Africa, and sensibly and immediately affect the fortunes, both as producers and consumers, of persons of every race and occupation in South Africa. The value of the trade coming from the Cape to the United Kingdom is estimated at over £90,000,000 a year, and the enormous and increasing quantities of bullion and diamonds carried in individual ships would make it peculiarly attractive to hostile operations. There is a real South African interest not less obvious than the general Imperial interest in the safety of the Cape to Southampton trade route.

Apart from the general protection afforded by British naval supremacy to the South African route, a special local protection has been provided and is now maintained by the forces comprised in the Cape Naval Station. Your suggestion that the Union Government should make itself responsible for the maintenance of the Cape Naval Station and the Simonstown establishment seems to the Board of Admiralty a very sound application of your desire to combine the defence of South Africa with the safeguarding of common Imperial interests. As far as can be estimated the undertaking of that obligation, together with a reasonable charge for the replacement of the ships on your station as time goes on by vessels completely capable of satisfying modern standards, would probably involve an annual outlay of from £500,000 to £600,000.

The assumption by the Union Government, in whole or in part, of this charge and their acceptance in principle of this important part of their own and the common defence of the Empire would be regarded by the Admiralty as a step of the highest practical value.

Sir Ernest Cassel to Herr Ballin
TELEGRAM[1]

3 February 1912

Copy

Spirit in wh statements of German Govt have been made is most cordially appreciated here. New German programme wd entail serious & immediate increase of Br naval expenditure wh was based on assumption that existing German naval programme wd be adhered to.

If the Br Govt are compelled to make such increase, it wd make negotiations difficult if not impossible.

If on the other hand G naval expendr can be adapted by an alteration of the *tempo* or otherwise so as to render any serious increase unnecessary to meet G programme B Govt will be prepared at once to pursue negotns on the understanding that the point of naval expendre. is open to discussion & that there is a fair prospect of settling it favourably.

If this understanding is acceptable, the Br Govt will forthwith suggest the next step, as they think that the visit of a Br minister to Berlin wd in the first instance be private & unofficial.

Sir Charles L. Ottley to WSC

5 February 1912   Committee of Imperial Defence

Most Secret

Dear Mr Churchill,

The Admiralty have referred the question of the protection of the coal supplies of the Fleet to the Home Ports Defence Committee.

[1] Drafted by WSC, Sir Ernest Cassel, Lord Haldane, and Sir Edward Grey.

At a meeting of the Committee last Wednesday it was decided that the co-operation of the mine-owners and miners was essential to ensure the safety of the power houses, winding machinery and electric plant at the mines, from attacks by ill-disposed persons in (1) peace, (2) strained relations, and (3) war.

The question is however complicated by the probability (amounting almost to a certainty) that – in the present circumstances of a threatened coal-strike – the miners will regard with extreme suspicion any measures we may propose to the Mining Industry for the protection of the plant at the mines.

On the other hand, if we do not take the mining interests (both masters and men) into our confidence, it is almost impossible to suggest any measures to satisfactorily cope with the difficult problem of defending the mines against a sudden and well organized attack, such as might be delivered in the course of a single night by means of half a dozen motor cars carrying determined individuals and a supply of gun-cotton.

The Home Ports Defence Committee wish to know the desires of the Government before proceeding to consult the mining interests in the matter.

The attached Memorandum by General Macready very clearly indicates the dilemma. An opportunity arises next Friday, (when the South Wales Miners Conciliation Board is to meet) for consulting the representatives of both masters and men on this very important question. But, is it wise to thus put this delicate matter before them? How far can we rely on the reticence of the miners, or the owners?

It is quite clear that we must take no such step without the express permission of the Government.

Time presses, if the matter is to be proceeded with we must tell Mr. Davis (the Chairman of the Conciliation Board) tomorrow – Tuesday.

Under these circumstances I write to beg you to give me an interview this afternoon, when I could lay the whole matter before you, and you could perhaps thereafter take the Prime Minister's instructions on the point.

Your very sincerely

C. L. OTTLEY

Viscount Haldane to WSC

5 February 1912   28 Queen Anne's Gate

Thanks for the papers sent on Saturday – which have been vy useful. Will you send me, to 28 Queen Anne's Gate,

1) A paper showing our present shipbuilding programme.

2) A note on it showing the additions in ships & money which will be necessary if the proposed new German Fleet law is adopted.

3) An answer to the question whether we can reasonably object to the new German Squadron in full commission. Is it not necessary for them if they are to have – what we have – an always ready fleet?

HALDANE

PS It is possible you have anticipated all this in your Memorandum which you promised to send me for my guidance.

I leave after 9 am on Wednesday. No telegram, however, so far has confirmed the proposed visit.

Later The message has now come from Berlin. I start on Wednesday morning.

Please send me the latest *Navy list* with the other papers.

Memorandum by WSC

14 February 1912   [Admiralty]

Secret

I circulate herewith to my colleagues a translation of the proposed new German Navy Law. Since it was communicated to us by courtesy, it must be kept absolutely secret.

The main feature in the new law is the extraordinary increase in the striking force, of ships of all classes, immediately available throughout the year. Whereas now we reckon against 17 battleships, 4 battle cruisers, and 12 small cruisers in the active battle fleet, demobilised to a great extent during the winter months, we must in future prepare against 25, 12, and 18, which are not to be subject to anything like the same degree of temporary demobilisation. The high proportion of battle or armoured cruisers to be kept in full commission probably indicates an intention to use these vessels as commerce destroyers. Full permanent crews are to be provided for all, or nearly all, torpedo-boat destroyers, now aggregating 115, and working up to an authorised total of 144, instead of for half the number as at present. There is to be an increase on the already large provision of 750,000*l*, in this year's Estimates for submarines. The numbers are not stated, but from the fact that 121 additional executive officers are required for this service alone by 1920, we may infer that between 50 and 60 submarines are to be added. We know nothing of the rate at which this construction is to be achieved. The increases in personnel are also important. Under their existing law, the Germans are working to a total of 86,500* in 1917 by annual increments of

* Including 8,000 seamen artillery for coast defences.

3,500. The new law adds 15,000 officers and men, and raises the total in 1920 to 101,500. This involves an average annual addition to the existing additions of about 1,650. In the three years 1912–14 there is to be a further anticipated addition of 500 per annum. Thus, the total additions in personnel to the German Navy in the next three years will be about 5,600 per annum.

The cost of these changes is estimated at between 2 and 2¾ millions a year after 1913; but the fact that *personnel* is cheaply obtained makes this money go much further than in this country.

2.   The new German Fleet will consist of 41 battleships, 20 battle cruisers, and 40 small cruisers, besides torpedo-boat destroyers and submarines. This is not on paper a great advance upon the present establishment of 38 battleships, 20 battle cruisers, and 48 small cruisers. In fact, however, there is a remarkable expansion. The great development of immediate war power is effected by building three new battleships, by fully manning five others, four of which hitherto only counted on paper, by bringing home three large cruisers from abroad, and providing crews for four others now in the material reserve. Thus the number of large armoured ships in full commission and immediately available will be increased from 21 to 36, or an addition of 15 ships. This new scale of the fleet organised in five battle squadrons, each attended by a battle cruiser squadron complete with small cruisers and auxiliaries, and attended by flotillas of destroyers and submarines, of which nearly four-fifths will be maintained in full permanent commission, is extremely formidable.

3.   The new fleet in the beginning comprises about twenty battleships and large cruisers of low fighting power, whose principal immediate use will be to train the personnel and develop the great naval service which Germany has in view. But gradually as new ships are built, the fighting power of the fleet will rise until it will consist completely of Dreadnoughts and modern cruisers. In April 1914, the first two squadrons will consist entirely of Dreadnoughts, and the third of good ships like the 'Deutschlands' and 'Braunschweigs,' together with five Dreadnought cruisers. The proposed modifications which Lord Haldane has discussed would make the completed fleet short of one ship for three years.

4.   I defer any statement of the measures which this programme will entail on our part for the present.

WSC

Memorandum by WSC

15 February 1912   [Admiralty]

[Copy]

Secret

1. The naval situation disclosed by the new German Navy Law renders the formation of an additional Battle Squadron in Home waters necessary. We cannot afford to keep fully commissioned battleships abroad during these years of tension. The first ten days and especially the first five days of war wd require the maximum immediate development of naval power in the North Sea and the Channel. Once our mobilisation has been effected and even before any naval decision has been obtained it shd be possible, if desired, to detach a Battle Squadron for the Mediterranean. But the greatly increased striking force wh Germany is organising, and against wh we must *always* maintain sufficient margins, makes it necessary that all fully commissioned battleships, whether eventually destined for the Mediterranean or not, shd be retained in the main theatre of operations until our mobilisation is complete, or the enemy's fleet beaten.

2. Proposals shd be made for carrying out this policy. As it is not now possible to reduce the total number of ships in full commission, but on the contrary some increase is necessary, there is no longer any financial saving to be looked for. The alternative of basing one of the battle squadrons on Gibraltar and [Berehaven] shd not be excluded from consideration. The Atlantic fleet wd thus be recalled, and the Mediterranean battle squadron moved into the Atlantic station. It wd not then be necessary to strengthen the Mediterranean cruiser squadron.

The number of vessels for wh we shall have to provide accommodation may make it necessary to use Gibraltar to the full. The diplomatic aspect wd be better also.

Both places shd therefore be examined by the staff in their strategic and administrative aspects. The question is urgent.

WSC

Sir Charles Ottley to WSC

17 February 1912   Committee of Imperial Defence

Most Private

Dear Mr Churchill,

Will you please read through this letter from Captain Hankey and give it your sympathetic attention. I will only add that he has read it to me and I am strongly of opinion that – in the sad eventuality postulated (of my having to go to Elswick) I am quite convinced that Hankey is the best successor imaginable.

I remember that when Bonaparte's merits were being discussed before his star showed above the horizon, some one objected that he was 'too young' for high command.

You will not employ that entirely futile argument. Napoleon retorted that service on the field of battle might fairly be an offset to his want of years, and Hankey has had similar years of service in the particular career he is following.

Yours very sincerely
C. L. OTTLEY

Captain M. P. A. Hankey to WSC

17 February 1912   Committee of Imperial Defence

Dear Mr Churchill,

I venture to write to you because Sir Charles Ottley tells me that he may be leaving the Defence Committee in the near future, and that the question of his successor may even now be under consideration. He tells me that Elswick's have made him a good offer to join their Board, and that he may feel reluctantly obliged to accept, unless the Treasury will accede to certain proposals regarding his tenure of appointment and pension, which appears to be very uncertain.

In writing to ask if you would bring my name before the Prime Minister as a possible successor to Sir Charles Ottley I wish to emphasise that I am most anxious to avoid any action which would tend to diminish the chance that his proposals may be granted by the Treasury, as I am well aware that his qualifications for continuing as Secretary of the Defence Committee are absolutely unique.

The principal ground on which I base this request to you is that I have had the most intimate service relations with several of the principal members of your Board and War Staff, and am therefore in a good position to interpret the present policy of the Admiralty. I served for some years under Prince Louis in the Naval Intelligence Department, and afterwards in the Mediterranean. Immediately before I came to the Defence Committee I was serving as Intelligence Officer on the Staff of the C in C Mediterranean, where Admiral Troubridge was Chief of the Staff. Under his direction I worked out all the War Arrangements of the Mediterranean Fleet, and of the Malta Dockyard.

I also served for years in the War Division of the NID under Captain

Ballard; in 1906 I went round the world with him as second naval representative on the Owen Committee on Armaments;[1] and in the following year I worked for several strenuous months as Secretary to a Committee, of which he was Chairman, which was appointed by Admiral Fisher to work out detailed plans of a War with Germany.

It is no exaggeration therefore to claim that I am saturated with the principles held by your War Staff. Like Sir Charles Ottley therefore, I ought to be well qualified to comprehend, and in a secretarial capacity to give effect to the views of the Admiralty, and to ensure that the proceedings of the Defence Committee reflect those views.

I will not lengthen this letter by attempting to explain my views as to the immense work which lies before the Defence Committee in concentrating and organising all the resources of the Empire in direct support of our Sea Power in time of war.

I am fully aware that I am very junior in rank to aspire to so high a post, but I believe there are few persons available who have had such unique opportunities to qualify for it, and I feel convinced that, if you believe me to be suitable on other grounds, you would not consider me ineligible for reasons of youth alone. I could, of course, retire from the service, if the fact that I am still only a Captain was considered a bar.

With apologies for the length of this letter

I am, Yours sincerely
M. P. A. HANKEY

Lord Esher to WSC

17 February 1912　　　　　　　　　　　　　　　　　2 Tilney Street

Private

My dear Winston,

If Ottley goes from the CID for heaven's sake try and get the PM to appoint Hankey – in spite of his youth etc. No one else can carry on precisely the work as it is being done. It is so difficult to get together the Public Depts and to keep them together.

[1] John Fletcher Owen (1839–1924), Major-General on the Staff commanding Artillery Brigade, Malta, 1895–9; Lieutenant-General 1899; President Ordnance Committee 1902–4; KCB 1906.

Besides, Hankey is a brilliant fellow, and absolutely at one with you and all your ideas.

Yours ever
E

Note by WSC: ack to E & F that I believe it is all right for Hankey.

But write a letter to Ottley of regret for me to sign.

WSC

Sir Charles Ottley to WSC

27 February 1912   Committee of Imperial Defence

Dear Mr Churchill,

I have read your charming message of farewell with heartfelt gratitude and appreciation. I do not think it is a hyperbole to say that I am inexpressibly grieved at this parting from the interests of half a life-time, but such letters as yours are all the more a consolation.

Yours very sincerely
C. L. OTTLEY

Lord Stamfordham to WSC

25 February 1912   Buckingham Palace

Confidential

My dear Churchill,

The King would be much obliged if you could let him have a confidential report with regard to the supposed failure of HMS *Lion*.

His Majesty has been told that she is defective in speed and that the position of her funnels is wrong with the result that flames fifty feet high issue from them when steaming at high speed etc etc.

It is rumoured that the trials as to speed were not successful.

What is the estimated cost to rectify her defects?

There is so much gossip about her that the King is anxious to know the truth.

Believe me, Yours very truly
STAMFORDHAM

The compasses are said to be affected by their proximity to the funnels.

S

WSC to Lord Stamfordham
(*Royal Archives*)

Report on the speed trials of HMS *Lion*.

Confidential

27 February 1912   [Admiralty]

My dear Stamfordham,

The estimated speed of the *Lion* was 28 knots, and 27.623 was obtained on trial; on the other hand the horsepower, estimated at 70,000 proved to be 76,121. The machinery & boilers worked well on trial, & might have been pressed further if desired. The deficiency in speed which was not very large – is believed to have been due to the propellers, and arrangements have been made to shift them & carry out further trials. I may add that the trial was in 24 fathoms, which for a ship of this length may not have been sufficient for giving the best results.

The defects owing to the relative position of mast and funnel were a more serious matter. The 'flames fifty feet high' are an invention – no excessive flaming was reported; but it is a fact that the gases from the foremost funnel rendered the control top untenable & quite unsuitable for accurate observation with the range finder. The funnel itself was greatly heated, & caused variation in the deviation of the compass, besides much inconvenience to the officers on the manoeuvering platform; & the signal halyards were damaged by the heat.

Of course this had to be remedied, and after much consideration it was found that the only plan by which all the difficulties could be met was to shift the funnel further aft, place the mast before it, & enlarge the conning tower so as to permit of its being used as the navigating & control position instead of the control top as originally intended. As the vessel had not been finally accepted it was decided to carry out these alterations at once. The work is now in hand, & is estimated to cost £34,000.

The original design was based on the precedent of the Dreadnought, where the funnel is before the mast, & gives satisfactory results. The arrangement failed in the *Lion* because she has ten boilers leading into the foremost funnel, as against six in the Dreadnought so that the *Lion's* funnel has nearly double the area of the Dreadnought's. Also the *Lion* has Yarrow type boilers, which have proved to give off funnel gases of considerably higher temperature than those produced by the Babcock & Wilcox type used in the Dreadnought.

The matter has given me much anxiety; but I have every confidence that the measures which have been taken will prove successful.

I am far from considering the episode creditable to those concerned, & a special enquiry is to be held in secret by the 1st & 2nd Sea Lords. The *Lion* will however be made thoroughly efficient.

Yours sincerely
WINSTON S. CHURCHILL

Lord Northcliffe to WSC

1 March 1912   *The Times*

Private

My dear Churchill,
    At the request of the British Embassy in Berlin I am holding back news about the German naval scheme.
    I do not like doing this sort of thing, and I consider that an Ambassador takes great responsibility upon himself in making such a request.
    I think that you ought to see the enclosed cables. Your shrewd brain will understand the gist of them; and perhaps you may know what the Ambassador is after. Kindly hand them back to Mr Russell Wakefield,[1] who brings this letter.
    These same Ambassadors and Foreign Ministers are the people who, while they make use of the Press as a sort of doormat, are always talking of its dangerous tendencies etc etc etc.
    By the way, your colleagues are not particularly able in their management of the newspapers. My *Times, Daily Mail, Mirror* and *Evening News* have been really helping them the last two or three days almost against their wish.

Sincerely
NORTHCLIFFE

Lord Stamfordham to WSC

7 March 1912   Buckingham Palace

My Dear Churchill,
    The King quite agrees with you that *Iron Duke* will be a more suitable name than *Duke of Wellington* and he gladly approves of the former for one of the new Dreadnoughts.
    But the King is sorry that he does not like giving up the *Delhi*. Indeed he holds strongly to it as an appropriate name for one of the others: and as the chief point in his choice was the fact that it would mark the year in which the

---

[1] Lord Northcliffe's private secretary since 1911.

change of capital in India was made, to bestow it upon a ship to be laid down later on would have little significance – nor does he care about so naming a *Cruiser*.

His Majesty was so pleased with his conversation with you on this subject and hopes that you will be able to adhere to what you and he then agreed upon, substituting *Delhi* for either *Warspite* or *Benbow* as you prefer.

Yours very truly
STAMFORDHAM

Lord Stamfordham to WSC

8 March 1912   Buckingham Palace

My dear Churchill,

    The King greatly appreciates your prompt acquiescence in his wish to secure *Delhi* as a name to one of the new battleships.

Yrs vy truly
STAMFORDHAM

WSC to the King

7 March 1912

    Mr Churchill with his humble duty begs to submit for your Majesty's information the accompanying translation of the proposed new German Navy Law together with Mr Churchill's covering minute. Mr Churchill hopes shortly to be able to inform your Majesty of the effective measures it is proposed to take to meet this great increase in German naval strength.

WINSTON S. CHURCHILL

Cabinet Memorandum by WSC

9 March 1912

Secret

    The fundamental proposition from the Admiralty point of view was that the existing German Naval Law should not be increased, but, if possible, reduced. To this the German Government replied that 'the naval estimates for the current year 1912 must be considered as included in the existing naval programme, because all preparatory work on them had been done.' This does not, however, mean merely that the additional expense incurred in the year 1912 should be included, but that the new law of 1912 should be included; and the new law of 1912 governs not only the year 1912 but the five following years, and effects large and progressive increases in each of them. The Admiralty have felt very great difficulties in regarding this as satisfactory from their point of view.

Until the Admiralty were by the great courtesy of the German Government enabled to study the actual text of the new law, they had no idea of its effect. From the general indications which they had previously received, they were inclined to think that the new construction would be its most serious feature. But on examining the text they found that while the new construction was limited to three, or it may be two, capital ships in six years, the increase of personnel and the increases in the vessels of all classes maintained in full commission constituted a new development of the very highest importance. It practically amounted to putting about four-fifths of the German Navy permanently on a war-footing. It would enable the German Government to have available at all seasons of the year twenty-five, or perhaps twenty-nine, fully commissioned battleships; whereas at the present time the British Government have in full commission in Home Waters only twenty-two, even counting the Atlantic Fleet. Compared to this predominant fact, any alteration in the *tempo* of the proposed additional new construction appeared comparatively a small thing, however desirable in itself.

It was quite impossible that Lord Haldane could express an opinion upon the 'Novelle,' because he had not seen it, nor had it been examined by the naval experts, who could alone appreciate its significance, and to whom its scale and character came as a complete surprise. The Admiralty cannot, of course, express an opinion upon the international aspects of the case. It is their part only to define the British naval measures which would be appropriate to whatever scale of German increase is prescribed. Those measures, on the basis of the 'Novelle' as they have received it, even with the alteration of the *tempo* to the extent of a single ship, must necessarily be of such a character as to concentrate public attention upon the increasing naval rivalry rather than upon the improved cordial relations of the two Powers.

WSC

WSC to Lord Fisher
(*Lennoxlove Papers*)

9 March 1912   Admiralty

My dear Fisher,

You should see this enclosed report by Jellicoe on Super-Actives which in view of your very high opinion of him greatly influenced me. The difficulties of discussing these questions by correspondence have prevented my giving you a just appreciation of the new type. These vessels are intended primarily for service with the battle-fleet as destroyer-destroyers as well as scouts and patrols. In the last character they have many points of superiority over the Super-Swift: they have better observation platforms, stronger batteries, larger radius of action, and are much less likely to lose their speed in a sea-way. There are many days in the year when they could cut the Super-Swift down. They are also cruisers and count as such: there is no flotilla they cannot break up, and no flotilla-cruiser they cannot go round.

It is perfectly possible, if desired, to add something to their speed. I am glad you like the rest of the plans. I am not touching education for the present: it requires to be considered as a whole, and I certainly do not exclude from the area of practical consideration any reasonable method of widening the basis from which the officer class is drawn. With a view to sustaining the common-entry system I propose to give publicly a clear preference to Engineer-Lieutenants in all selections for the submarine service – with all its prizes of pay and distinction.

The letter from *The Times*, which you enclose, was written by Custance!

The published (i.e. next Tuesday night) Estimates which I send you are framed solely on the basis of no German increase, and Supplementary Estimates both for men and money will be presented to meet all new developments. In view however of the situation as we know it I shall unfold the whole plan of Fleet re-organisation, and announce publicly the policy of two keels to one on all increases above the existing German Navy Law.

I will give the gunnery of the fleet my closest personal attention as soon as the Estimates are disposed of.

What do you think of 'hoisting' the electrical turrets out of the *Invincible* for £150,000?

The more I hear from you the better I shall be pleased.

Yours ever
WINSTON SC

Charles A'Court Repington to WSC

21 March 1912   Maryon Hall
Hampstead

My dear Churchill,

The opinion of an amateur looker-on regarding our naval affairs may not be of much interest, but I should like to offer you my warmest congratulations upon your masculine handling of our naval policy, and to tell you how completely I am in accord with the policy which you have announced. I suppose that there must be a little yapping from Berlin for a week or so, but if your speech[1] is read in its complete text I cannot help hoping that the Germans will see the point of it all.

From my point of view you have converted me from an attitude of suspicious mistrust of the Admiralty into one of complete confidence and I think that this is so because for the first time policy seems to be based on war considerations and not on any other. Of course it is all promise at present and not performance and I hope that you may some day explain our theory of battleship distribution at home in time of peace, and of commerce protection in war, but, assuming that I am what Palmerston used to call a fair foolometer – I suppose that most people in the street will share my views and that you will have the great merit of having stabilised a national policy which will prove enduring.

The point of your great speech on March 18 which appeals to me most is that in which you guarantee to meet at one average moment the naval force of an enemy at his selected moment. There is a whole world of difference between this and the past.

There is one point about our battle squadrons that has always caused me much anxiety, namely that they are scarcely ever complete except at our selected moment. It has always seemed to me that, allowing for normal absences for repair, they should always be complete, and consequently that your squadrons, instead of numbering 8 ships, should be 9 or 10 or that there should be a small 'pool' unallotted to enable you to make up each squadron whenever it puts to sea. I rejoice to see that we shall soon have some of the 'leopards among the cats' and I trust that you will go on producing those leopards which are badly needed.

Again offering you my warmest congratulations I am,

Yours very sincerely
C. A'C-REPINGTON

Lord Esher to WSC

26 March 1912   The Roman Camp
Private   Callander
My dear Winston,

I have been meaning for ages to write you a line of affectionate congratulation.

In my time – extending now over 30 years of public life – no such speeches have been made as yours – so straight and so daringly truthful.

Ever yours
ESHER

[1] On 18 March 1912, announcing the policy of 'two keels to one on all increases above the existing German Navy Law'.

WSC to his wife
(CSC Papers)

24 March [1912]   Portland

My Beloved Clemmie,

We have had a vy peaceful Sunday down here. Church on board the *Neptune*, & visits to ships during the afternoon: young officers come to luncheon etc.

Sunny has enjoyed himself but leaves me tomorrow. He is much impressed by the yacht & the show generally. Tomorrow the target practice will take place weather permitting. There is a certain amount of swell & I may have to trust my fortunes to your suffragette friend's 'plaister'. I hope indeed no evil consequences will befall me. We dine tomorrow with the Admiral. He had just left me after 1½ hours discussion about war plans. They are vy simple these sailors; but this one – Callaghan – is sensible. Greenley is here – but returns tomorrow night.

My darling I do hope that you are not fretting & that all is going on well. It is probably for the best. I felt so awfully guilty to have imposed such a heavy task upon you so soon after your recovery. No wonder you have not felt well for the last month. Poor lamb. Anyhow you will be able to have a jolly year & hunt again in the winter. And there is plenty of time.

The strike seems vy remote from Portland with its well-disciplined fleet & mountains of coal. It will be a great relief to learn that it is settled. We have so many difficulties to contend with. Still I think we shall surmount them. Governments are vy tough organisations. They stand wear & tear & are made to stand it.

I hope Diana is dutiful & that Randolph perseveres in growth & teeth cutting. Unless some crisis occurs I shall not return till Wednesday. I hope you will be well enough to come down to Portsmouth on Friday – we will lie in the Solent & it will do you a lot of good.

Goodnight my darling & sweetest Kat always your loving husband

W

WSC to his wife
(CSC Papers)

25 March 1912

My darling,

The misty weather prevents our firing except with little tubes put in the big guns to fire quite small shot: but we are going out tomorrow and the weather prospects are more promising. It was a pleasant cruise in the good sea air; but there was a certain amount of motion, & I fell back on Mothersill with advantage. Sunny left this morning. He had to get back to London to have his shoulder electrified. I think he was interested in what he saw.

I am expecting to hear from Eddie, the news from London wh will determine my plans. If possible I will return on Wed afternoon. Thursday the Conciliation Bill will require my attention: but I hope you will be well enough to come away on Friday to Portsmouth. Make Goonie come & we will stay till the Tuesday. It will do you a lot of good.

The War Plans put forward by the staff have several stupid features about them wh have caused me some worry. I am gradually purging them of foolishness. It is extraordinary how little some of these officers have really thought upon war on the largest scale.

We dine with the Admiral tonight. I have got on the track of a lot of waste of money in refitting & repairing ships unnecessarily – just in order to make work for the Dockyards. Probe, Prune, Prepare – one cannot do too much of it. We shall be much stronger in a year. I wish I had nine lives like a cat, so that I cd go into each branch thoroughly. As it is I have to trust so much to others – when I am pretty confident I cd do it better myself. There are some vy nice fellows here – good hard-working smart officers of quality & conduct. The Fleet is large – we have 11 Dreadnoughts and 7 or 8 other large ships & a Flotilla.

Unluckily there are no Germans to be found. Tiresome people – but their turn will come.

Your wire was repeated to me by wireless on to the *Neptune*.

Do write & tell me all about yourself. With my best love to you my darling Clemmie Kat.

Always your loving husband
W

A. J. Balfour to WSC

22 March 1912   4 Carlton Gardens

Dictated

Private & Confidential

My dear Winston,

I return you the documents you were so very kind as to send me. I have read them with the deepest misgiving.

A war entered upon for no other object than to restore the Germanic

Empire of Charlemagne in a modern form, appears to me at once so wicked and so stupid as to be almost incredible! And yet it is almost impossible to make sense of modern German policy without crediting it with this intention. I am told that many good observers in France regard a war in May as inevitable. Personally, I am more disposed to think that, if war comes, it will come when the disparity between our naval forces is less than it is at present. But imagine it being possible to talk about war as inevitable when there is no quarrel, and nothing to fight over! We live in strange times!

Yours sincerely
ARTHUR JAMES BALFOUR

Hugh Watson[1] to Edward Marsh

EXTRACT

22 March 1912   Bendler Strasse 16
Personal   [Berlin]

Dear Marsh,

I think the 1st Lord may like to know that as far as I can see at present the wind is very much taken out of the sails of the advocates of larger naval expansion here. I don't think for a moment that it will actually stop the present proposed increases, which by the way are published in official papers tonight, from being ultimately approved of but I am told by those who know, that the naval authorities will have a lot of trouble and criticism as a result of the 1st Lord's speech which coming on the top of the controversies raging as to who is to provide the money, will introduce a weapon of cleavage which the men of all parties, who are not in the hands of the Tirpitz-Krupp-Shipbuilding-Navy League Group, will lay hold of and use to prevent further Tirpitzian expansion beyond the present proposals. My experience of the last few days, including dinner last night with Admiral von Tirpitz goes to show that the large naval people know they are fronted with difficulties here as the result of expressed naval policy of England.

We have only to go on now saying as little as we can and I believe we settle this naval competition for many a long day.

---

[1] Hugh Dudley Richards Watson (1872–1954), Naval attaché at Berlin, The Hague and Copenhagen 1910–13; Naval Secretary to the First Lord of the Admiralty 1921–3; Second-in-command Mediterranean Fleet 1924–5; Vice-Admiral commanding Reserve Fleet 1926–8; retired 1930.

As to the rumours of Admiral von Tirpitz going as Chancellor I do not believe he will take the position if offered, and his wise friends will urge him to stay as head of the Navy, as the difficulties of a new man taking on the Naval Minister's work at present time, even under Admiral v Tirpitz as Chancellor, would be too great for the Navy to wish the change. . . .

Yours truly
HUGH WATSON

Charles A'Court-Repington to WSC

27 March 1912   Maryon Hall
Private   Hampstead

My dear Churchill,

I now send you my views upon the naval aspects of an Anglo-German war. They are entirely my personal opinions, and the note is not due to any advice or assistance from anyone. I have not signed the note, for I should like you to obtain for me, if possible, some good naval opinions on the paper. They would be of great assistance to me and I do not care how critical they are, but I think they will be more valuable if they disregard the personality of the author & only deal with his arguments.

The only man who knows that I am sending you this paper is Sir John French, to whom I am sending a copy privately, and I shall ask him to show it to no one except Haldane.

Yours very sincerely
C. A'C-REPINGTON

Note by Captain M. P. A. Hankey on Repington's Memorandum

1 April 1912

(1) Standard of Strength.

It would appear that the possibilities of our own successful diplomacy are not to be considered while the diplomacy of Germany is given the fullest value.

(2) The Initiative.

I agree.

(3) Strained Relations.

This is a question of judgment.

Unless I was fully aware of all the circumstances that were at Sir Edward Grey's command, I should not feel competent to give an opinion upon his action last summer in this matter.

(4) There are other means of injuring this country besides invasion. If the Navy were defeated I do not believe it would be necessary for them to land any soldiers to attain their objectives and compel us to the peace terms they offered.

The probability of Germany taking the offensive in every way is undoubtedly the greatest, and is, I think, so considered by all Naval Officers.

I do not think it wise to follow Colonel Repington into details of Naval Policy in the event of war.

He is a very clever journalist and lives by it. He also enjoys a privileged position at the War Office, and his distinguished military career gives him many opportunities of acquiring information denied to other journalists. Such information added to his own study and knowledge gives a certain danger to his writing that would be only magnified were his views to be criticised or argued with by Admiralty officials in such a way as to indicate clearly to him what is in the mind of the Admiralty as regards the preparation for and conduct of a war with Germany.

M. HANKEY

Note by Captain Ballard on Repington's Memorandum

20 April 1912

There does not appear to be anything very original in these notes, and in parts they are inaccurate, but some of the conclusions appear to be sound.

Standard of Strength.

We may have no Allies in the sense that we have no defensive Treaties with other European Powers, but it does not follow from that that we should be left altogether unsupported if attacked. If Germany overwhelmed Great Britain all the world would suffer to some extent. Germany is becoming a general menace to Europe owing to the never-ceasing expansion of her armaments, and it is not to the interest even of her Allies that her power should become too great.

The initiative.

This section appears to be written upon a sort of assumption that a war must take place and that we should cast about for the *casus belli* from which we should derive most advantage and then begin it. There are of course plenty of historical precedents for such a policy, but it is questionable whether the assumption is justified under existing conditions. For 25 years after we seized Egypt war with France was constantly apprehended as inevitable, and persistently taken as the basis of Admiralty preparation and expenditure, but no war took place, and nobody thinks of it now. If war does break out with Germany it will probably arise as the outcome of a series of unforeseen events over which we have little control, rather than as a result of a quarrel intentionally picked by us over some selected Colonial or foreign question. I agree, however, that the initiative is more likely to rest with Germany than with us unless we are acting in support of France.

Strained Relations.

Many of the statements in this section are of questionable accuracy.

German Action.

The arguments in this section are mainly based upon the invasion idea, and the necessity for a large army in the British Isles to give 'freedom of action' to the Navy. The 'freedom of action' argument is one of the commonest fallacies of military writers and amateur naval strategists. They fail to understand that the only freedom required is freedom to attack the enemy on the water and that as long as the Navy possesses it, no hostile expedition can cross the water without exceptional risk. If the Navy is not strong enough to threaten the enemy seriously it is no proper remedy to increase the land forces.

The writer is wide of the mark when he says that no German plan of campaign can be made out unless based upon initiative and surprise, although he would be right in saying that no *aggressive* campaign could be based otherwise. As a matter of fact there is evidence to show that it is quite possible that it is the intention of the Germans to act at first on the defensive, in the hope that we shall expose our ships in close blockading operations which will afford them opportunities for torpedo attacks, until they can reduce us to something approaching an equality. Their elaborate and expensive system of coast defence is a fairly clear indication of the ideas which find acceptance in responsible quarters, mistaken though they may be. And even their latest destroyers are of small displacement and radius of action as compared to our own and correspondingly less fitted for offensive operations. Still, if the Germans declare war upon Great Britain they *must* take the initiative if they want to effect any appreciable injury to our interests, and so far the writer is sound.

But he is in the wrong when he says that Germany has concentrated her attention upon battleships and destroyers, because as a matter of fact Germany is the only country which has steadily and consistently turned out cruisers in such considerable numbers since the beginning of the century that our own cruiser predominance is seriously threatened.

Flotilla Storm Area.

The remarks in this section call for no comment as they represent personal opinions based upon an imperfect acquaintance with facts.

Close or Open Blockade.

The remarks in this section are sound and well expressed. At the same time it would be very undesirable to inform an unofficial press correspondent that they coincide with Admiralty views. It is of the utmost importance not to let our general policy as regards blockade become generally known, or even known outside the War Staff.

Position of the Main Fleets.

Not concurred in. The writer seems to misunderstand the general policy underlying the disposition of our forces in the French wars.

Character of the War.

Quite sound and well-reasoned but not, in any respect an original view of the subject.

Garrisons.

Generally concurred in, but the reference to the Owen Committee is not correct, as that Committee had nothing to do with garrisons. The purport of the reference to the Panama Canal is not very obvious.

In the covering private letter the writer states plainly that he desires 'assistance' of Naval opinion, but he does not say to what end. If it is to enable him to get an insight into authoritative Admiralty views, the supply of the information or criticisms he seeks is open to objections. A knowledge of Admiralty policy on the major points of the subject is confined to a very few officers within the Admiralty, and to a small number of selected Admirals, and it is highly undesirable that it should be communicated to any irresponsible person.

G. A. BALLARD

WSC to Prince Louis of Battenberg

27 March 1912

It really is necessary to have an authoritative report on the mast & funnel question as it affects not only *Lion, Princess Royal* & *Queen Mary* but other vessels now completing, especially *Conqueror*, which is so late that she cd easily be altered without further delay. It wd be disastrous to bring her out & then have to put her back again.

I had hoped to receive a final conclusion before now.

WSC

WSC to the King
(*Royal Archives*)

28 March 1912   Admiralty

Mr Churchill with his humble duty. He has been very carefully considering the conversation which Your Majesty was graciously pleased to hold with him a few days ago on the subject of high commands in the Navy; he has taken occasion to interview the principal officers concerned and he has now the honour to submit for Your Majesty's approval the appointment of Sir Hedworth Meux[1] to succeed Sir Arthur Moore as Commander-in-Chief at Portsmouth, and that of Sir Berkeley Milne to succeed Sir Edmund Poe in the Mediterranean.

Mr Churchill is confident that both these appointments are the best that could be made and will greatly conduce to the advantage of the Service. It would perhaps be well to make them public at an early date in order to put an end to an uncertainty which might otherwise cause some inconvenience.

Sir George Egerton is now quite reconciled to waiting for Devonport although no doubt he would have preferred the Mediterranean. It was only fair however that Sir Berkeley Milne should have the first choice.

With regard to Admiral Colville[2] and Captain Stanley[3] Mr Churchill is keeping Your Majesty's wishes in mind.

The end of April or the beginning of May would afford very favourable opportunities for a visit of Your Majesty to the Fleets and if a date or dates were intimated, two or three days of interesting and important fleet-work could be arranged when Your Majesty's presence with the Squadrons would afford the liveliest satisfaction to the officers and men.

All of which is submitted by Your Majesty's faithful and devoted servant
WINSTON S. CHURCHILL

[1] Hedworth (Lambton) Meux (1856–1929), C-in-C Portsmouth 1912–16; China Station 1908–10; Unionist MP Portsmouth 1916–18; Third son of 2nd Earl of Durham; assumed the name of Meux by Royal Licence 1911; Admiral of the Fleet 1915; knighted 1906.

[2] Stanley Cecil James Colville (1861–1939), Vice-Admiral Commanding First Battle Squadron 1912–14; C-in-C Portsmouth 1916–19; Admiral 1914; knighted 1912; second son of 1st Viscount Colville of Culross; married in 1902 Adelaide Jane Meade, daughter of 4th Earl of Clanwilliam.

[3] Victor Albert Stanley (1867–1934), second son of 16th Earl of Derby; served in Navy 1880–1926; knighted 1925; Admiral 1926.

Sir Edward Grey to WSC

13 April 1912   Foreign Office

Dear Churchill,

You will see the report of my last conversation with Metternich.

Things have got on to an amicable footing in our negotiations with Germany, and I should be reluctant to publish any papers about naval things that might be likely to give rise to controversy. But I do not see why we should not endeavour to take the negotiations for the exchange of naval information further, if you desire it.

I shall be glad to talk this over at any time; I am going away for a short holiday at the end of this week, but shall be here till tomorrow.

Yrs sincerely
E. GREY

WSC to Sir Ernest Cassel

14 April 1912   Admiralty

Copy

My dear Cassel,

I am deeply impressed by the Emperor's great consideration. I only mentioned the incident to Ballin as an example to show the kind of anxieties & the strain to wh the naval situation gives rise. I am vy glad to know that it was free from all sinister significance: and I take this opportunity of saying again that we have been throughout equally innocent of any offensive design. I suppose it is difficult for either country to realise how formidable it appears to the eyes of the other. Certainly it must be almost impossible for Germany with her splendid armies and warlike population capable of holding their native soil against all comers, and situated inland with road & railway communications on every side, to appreciate the sentiments with which an island state like Britain views the steady & remorseless development of a rival naval power of the vy highest efficiency. The more we admire the wonderful work that has been done in the swift creation of German naval strength, the stronger, the deeper & the more preoccupying those sentiments become.

Patience, however, and good temper accomplish much: & as the years pass many difficulties & dangers seem to settle themselves peacefully. Meanwhile there is an anxious defile to be traversed, and what will help more perhaps than anything else to make the journey safe for us all is the sincere desire for goodwill & confidence of wh Ballin's letter & its enclosure are a powerful testimony.

WSC

WSC to H. H. Asquith

14 April 1912   [Admiralty]

Draft

My dear Asquith,

I have of course been casting about for a naval policy for the Dominions. Canada is soon coming to ask advice, & no one can be satisfied with the present arrangement with Austla and NZ except at the 1st stage.

Briefly what I am coming to is this: – Gt Britain will keep a Navy strong enough to deal with the strongest probable combination in the decisive theatres. This means concentration, & consequent abandonment of all seas except those in wh the supreme issue will be settled. After a decision by battle had been obtained we cd of course spread our fleets again & restore the situation in any waters however remote. But what is to happen before such a decision, or before war comes at all? We shall be increasingly held concentrated in Home Waters. The war may never come, & all the time Imperial & Colonial interests will lack the support of available naval force in many parts of the world. What we want in fact is a movable squadron or Fleet, not tied up by the main situation, cruising about the Empire giving each part a turn & going to any threatened point; its influence wd be felt everywhere, not only in its actual station where it was, but wherever it might if necessary go. Here then is the fundamental division of labour wh the Mother Country shd make with her Colonies: – 'We will cope with the strongest combin in the decisive theatre, you shall patrol the Empire.'

Local Navies may have been the only possible 1st step. Can we not now take the next – namely – a joint Dominion Squadron? Separately these Navies are weak & even ridiculous. One Dreadnought, *et praeteria nihil!* But combined they might make a force wh no European power cd force without dispersing its own home concentrn & consequently releasing ours.

The scale of the Squadron & the time taken to complete it cd be varied to suit moods & circs. Let us make the plan on sound principles of policy & strategy, & the spaces can be filled in later. The following is only my sketch: –

THE IMPERIAL SQUADRON

Battle Cruisers:	Australia	1
	New Zealand	1
	Canada	2
		4

Light armoured cruisers:	South Africa	2
	India	2
		4

Control & duties.

In times of peace to move constantly from station to station spending 3 or 4 months in rotation in the waters of each Dominion, the movement being regulated by subctee of the CID composed of one repve from each Dominion & one or two Imperial repves. Also to move to any threatened point or discharge any special duty.

Discipline, training, administration & war employment to rest with the Admy.

Observe – the Squadron is to be additional to the European force, so that we are not sponging upon them for our own needs. Service in this Squadron may be specially arduous & always away from home. Therefore it would be right to pay Colonial rates of pay to officers & men. As we shall have to find the bulk of the officers & men at any rate for some years I shd propose to let our people be selected for not more than 2 yrs at a time. The extra pay wd thus be operative over the whole service, & not localised to particular crews on special stations. This wd avoid many difficulties wh now beset us in Australasian waters. Each wd have his turn or at least his chance.

Beyond this moving squadron other necessities come into view. Suppose they are required to proceed to Australian waters, or to Vancouver for a time. They will want docks. They will want to complete their war organisation with a flotilla. Therefore each Dominion can develop its own coastal defence on a sound principle, namely of affording the means for the Imp Sq to operate from their own coasts with full effect whenever the need arises. All this will take time. But the path will be clearly visible on the arrival of the Imp Sq at Sydney or Vancouver or Simonstown, it will find docking facilities, stores, coal, & the destroyer & submarine flotilla wh make it a Fleet in integrity. We set up a design looking far ahead, into wh all Colonial naval activities can be fitted as they arise. We show them the way; & it is the only way, to provide for their own proper naval defence, we holding off the big dog meanwhile.

If you like this general idea, the way to give effect to it is to persuade the

Canadians to summon a conference *in Canada* of the Dominions. We will go over there, it being their show primarily, to give them the Admy view, & clinch the whole thing. We cd take the 1st Cruiser Sqn in Aug – (all being quiet here) to show them what their force wd look like when complete.

'Four when you want them instead of one all the time.' The argument is vy pliant to all the needs & prejudices that have to be met.

As for S. Africa we have only to ask Botha, I am sure. NZ & Australia have done their part already.

The cost both of construction & maintenance to be borne by the Dominions.

Maintenance not vy great. 4 Battle Cruisers at £120,000 p.a. & 4 small cruisers at £60,000 p.a. for the general purpose; & the rest, flotillas etc being local at discretion.

The stay of the Sqn on each station if necessary to be proportioned to amount of contribution. But this is detail.

Will you please talk to me abt this when opportunity offers & give me yr guidance?

Yours ever
W

WSC to Jack Seely

16 April 1912   Admiralty

Copy

My dear Seely,

You appear to be at cross purposes with some of your friends, and considerable disadvantages may arise therefrom, yet the realities of the situation are perfectly clear.

1. It is essential that the yeomanry should retain their cavalry characteristic. Only ignorant people have associated this with the sword. The cavalry characteristic, as the word 'cavalry' shows, depends not on the sword but on the horse. The yeoman is a horseman first of all, with all that that implies. He is a cavalryman who has learned to shoot, and not an infantryman who has learned to ride. He should therefore be organised in regiments, squadrons, and troops, and drill and manoeuvre in cavalry formations so far as they are necessary to his service. It is true that he requires to study cavalry formations for other purposes than those of shock tactics. He could never with the limited time at his disposal, fit himself for shock tactics. But a squadron or regiment of yeomanry requires to be a flexible, mobile body of well-drilled horsemen, capable of moving fast and far over broken ground, and showing front whenever necessary in any direction. The existing or-

ganisation is very good in this respect, and all that we want is a Yeomanry Drill Book giving us the simplest cavalry evolutions for our practical work, and perhaps including a few oblique movements for the purpose of handiness and variation in training. In this connection it may be noted that the formation which the French call *'Ligne de colonnes de quatres'* is specially convenient for yeomanry work, and makes it very easy to lay a line of dismounted rifles on to the side of a hill, or to occupy with a squadron two or three small tactical points at intervals with great rapidity.

2. The only gap which requires to be filled in the present instruction and equipment of the yeomanry, is their action if by accident a small party, never more than a squadron – probably not more than a troop or even a few men, should find itself suddenly at such a short distance from an enemy that there was no time to dismount and fire from behind a sufficient obstacle. In this case I am clearly of opinion, after nearly 14 years reflection on the subject, that the proper weapon is the sword-bayonet similar to those which used to be issued to rifle regiments in the days of the Snider, *ie* a weapon with a flame-shaped blade about 2 ft 6 ins long, which could be worn unostentatiously on the saddle; this would serve its purpose in an emergency without getting in the way when mounting and dismounting, and would give the sentiment of elan without seducing the yeomanry from their proper position to that of sham cavalry. It would also meet a very serious need, namely, night work, dismounted pickets and camp. It very often happens that when a camp is attacked at night, it is most important to prevent indiscriminate firing, and strict orders are often issued to that effect. The possession of a bayonet on these occasions would be of the utmost convenience.

I really do not know which of the two contending parties is the more wrong-headed and foolish in this matter. To abolish the cavalry system in the yeomanry would unquestionably be deeply injurious to the popularity of the force. To re-arm them with the sword would be fatal to their efficiency. As for the compromise that they should have a sword when they go to war, that is simply impossible: how *could* you defend deliberately neglecting in time of peace to train men to the weapons they would have to use in war?

I should like to see a copy of the new Yeomanry Drill Book before it is issued; and some time ago Sir William Nicholson promised me that I should have an opportunity of commenting upon it. I should be very glad if you will send me a copy of the proofs over here as soon as possible. But don't fail to ask the Secretary of State if his authority is necessary.

Yours ever

[Winston S. Churchill]

WSC to his wife
(*CSC Papers*)

18 April 1912   Admiralty

My darling,

I have just returned here after a flying surprise visit to see the P.K. put to bed at 6.30. Whom do you think I found nursing her? Eva! I greeted quite pleasantly but she fled greatly embarrassed. When I came down stairs she had vanished. Both the chicks are well and truculent. Diana & I went through one Peter Rabbit picture book together & Randolph gurgled. You must have his tongue cut when you come home. It hampers his speech. He looks vy strong & prosperous.

A vy busy day. Bill [Hozier] arrived yesterday, so I slept in your bed & accommodated him in my room. He has been gambling and has won a hundred pounds. You are not to know this. Apparently you inspire an awe which no one else can rival in the breast of the young officer. He has gone down to Portsmouth tonight.

Now as to plans. It wd not have been worth while for me to come over to Paris for 12 hours: and in addition the business wh I have in mind is not yet ripe for treatment. But I propose this. You stay in Paris over next week, & on Friday 26th I will come over & spend 3 or 4 days – arranging with Cassel for his flat. I shall then I think be ready for a secret pow-wow. I am dining out on Monday night with Moreton Frewen & it is impossible for me to get away till after the Division on the Welsh Rabbit Bill on Thursday. But if you are bored in Paris you can cross & recross. Anyhow I am clearing the 26th-30th for Paris.

The 2nd Reading of the HR Bill is not till the middle of May & I shall not have to speak till then.

What good letters you write! Your description of the metallic light of the eclipse is perfectly correct. I noticed it myself. It also got much colder.

The *Titanic* disaster[1] is the prevailing theme here. The story is a good one. The strict observance of the great traditions of the sea towards women & children reflects nothing but honour upon our civilization. Even I hope it may mollify some of the young unmarried lady teachers who are so bitter in their sex antagonism, and think men so base & vile. They are rather snuffy about Bruce Ismay[2] – Chairman of the line – who, it is thought – on the

---

[1] On 14 April 1912 the liner *Titanic*, making her maiden voyage to New York, struck an iceberg. Of 2206 passengers, only 703 were saved.

[2] Joseph Bruce Ismay (1862–1937), Shipowner and Director of the London, Midland and Scottish Railway.

facts available – shd have gone down with the ship & her crew. I cannot help feeling proud of our race & its traditions as proved by this event. Boat loads of women & children tossing on the sea – safe & sound – & the rest – Silence. Honour to their memory.

Sweet & beloved cat – wire your wishes. The yacht will be at Dover on Saturday and I am inspecting there. LG & Isaacs come for the Sunday.

Always your loving & devoted husband
W

PS Nanny now offers 13th July! Will you answer yes.

WSC to his wife
(*CSC Papers*)

20 April 1912

HMS *Enchantress*
Dover

My darling,

Your telegram reached me here in good time. I hope the doctor's report will come tonight. There is nothing for it but a vy careful month. Did you get the flowers I ordered from Solomons? I hope they were fresh & beautiful.

Here we have had a fine day & the view of the harbour from the batteries on the hills was splendid. The sea turquoise – and the moles & piers all mapped in like a plan. I have been walking round the whole place & have found out several things – one – that the boom defences wh they are supposed to have to close the entrances of the harbour simply do not exist! Tomorrow we shall go to Portsmouth & return thence to London on Monday.

I watched a diver for a long time fixing enormous blocks of concrete. One diver does as much work for the contractors as 4 in another part of the harbour for the Admiralty Work Department!

There is another good account of the *Titanic* besides Beesley's in the *D.T.* this morning. The whole episode fascinates me. It shows that in spite of all the inequalities and artificialities of our modern life, at the bottom – tested to its foundations, our civilisation is humane, Christian, & absolutely democratic. How differently Imperial Rome or Ancient Greece wd have settled the problem. The swells, and potentates would have gone off with their concubines & pet slaves & soldier guards, & then the sailors wd have had their chance headed by the captain; as for the rest – whoever cd bribe the crew the most wd have had the preference & the rest cd go to hell. But such ethics can neither build Titanics with science nor lose them with honour.

I feel vy selfish playing about here and you tied by the leg in town. My fondest love. Goodnight my dearest Clemmie.

Your devoted loving husband
W

H. H. Asquith to WSC

21 April 1912   Ewelme Down
                             Wallingford

My dear Winston,

I shall see you on Thursday, and we can then talk about the War plans.

Of course, I hope that you will speak on the Second Reading of the HR Bill. I imagine the Debate may begin in the week of May 6.

Yrs always
H.H.A.

Prince Louis of Battenberg to WSC

24 April 1912   Admiralty

First Lord,

In a note to me the other day you said you thought Sir Wm May shd be made Chief Umpire at the coming Manoeuvres, and that he shd be accommodated with a proper Flagship and Staff. Of course this can be arranged, but I expect if Sir William's wishes are consulted on the point of going afloat to act as Umpire in Chief he will say that he wd sooner do the work at the Admiralty or at Admiralty House Devonport! Naval Manoeuvres are things that one can't get a bird's eye view of and an Umpire's work commences generally when the reports come in and these reports all come to the Admiralty. However all that can be discussed with Sir William himself when you offer him the position, which it might be well to do soon. *Note by WSC: I agree.*

I see the press have already begun to suggest that their correspondents shd be represented at the Manoeuvres. I hope you will take a very determined line on that subject. We have had bitter experiences with them in the past and I hope never to see them allowed on board ship again! they are most mischievous.

L.B.

Note by WSC

Oh! Pray remember I was once one of these creatures.

WSC

Prince Louis of Battenberg to WSC

24 April 1912   Admiralty

First Lord,

Pray forgive me! I had quite forgotten for the moment. – It is most good of you, making so light of a blunder on my part.

I will say no more about correspondents. – I have already said too much! Weather here quite beautiful and am feeling better for the change. –

L.B.

Lord Fisher to WSC

22 April 1912   Hotel Excelsior
Private and Confidential   Naples

My dear Winston,

I have only just this moment received your letter of April 12th sent me by a special messenger by our Ambassador at Rome and he calls for the answer to go by a King's Messenger at 5 pm today so I have not much time for reflection – but no reflection is required as the whole matter of your letter is absolutely without difficulty and it is just astounding how all the arguments you use are precisely identical with those supplied by me with the support of Lord Kelvin[1] in the verbal and informal discussions that took place on the ever memorable meetings with that great man in regard to the Dreadnought Design. But let me first clear off what has to be said in reply to your remarks on Hankey, Sir Hedworth Meux and Sir Berkeley Milne & Ottley. I wrote to Ottley & told him he was a d——d fool so I need say no more about him. As to Hankey I made the same answer as in your letter under reply, so we are agreed there also – I regret that in regard to what you say and what you have done in the appointments of Sir Hedworth Meux, Sir Berkeley Milne and Sir Reginald Custance that I fear this must be my last communication with you in any matter at all. I am sorry for it but I consider you have betrayed the Navy in these three appointments and what the pressure could have been to induce you to betray your trust is beyond my comprehension. You are aware that Sir Berkeley Milne is unfitted to be the Senior Admiral afloat as you have now made him – you are aware that Sir E. Poe should have been Commander-in-Chief at Portsmouth failing your promise to Admiral Egerton – and you must have been as cognizant as I am of Custance's views and animus. Even supposing McKenna had any faults (and I do not admit that he had any) he steadfastly declined pressure to his own hurt to make Beresford an Admiral of the Fleet. It is the deepest disappointment to me that you have not been able to see your way to resist pressure. Anyhow all I can do is to avoid any further communication with the Admiralty. The mischief is done – *Vestigia nulla retrorsum!*[2] To resume about designs of new ships: –

[1] William Thomson Kelvin (1824–1907), scientist; Professor of Natural Philosophy at Glasgow 1846–99; electrical engineer for ocean telegraphs; invented a new form of mariner's compass and a deep-sea sounding machine; President of the Royal Society 1890–5; knighted 1866; created Baron Kelvin 1892.

[2] 'No steps backward.' Horace, *Epistles* Book I, epis. xx, v. 74.

I have plainly indicated in previous letters that the path is plain and clear:

    I There MUST be the 15 inch gun
    II There MUST be sacrifice of armour
    III There MUST be only a 4 inch armament for anti-torpedo purposes and unassociated with armour
    IV There must be further VERY GREAT INCREASE OF SPEED
    V The ONE thing to armour is the motive power of the ship D——N ALL THE REST!!! but your speed *must* vastly exceed your possible *enemy*!
    VI A LOW target. Look at the original Dreadnought – The silhouette is a minimum!
    VII SIZE and sub-division to an extent that will cause deep cursing by all on board but it will be WAR as opposed to comfort in Peace.

I am glad you appreciate Jellicoe – you have practically annihilated him by your appointments of Meux and Milne. I CAN'T BELIEVE THAT YOU FORE-SEE ALL THE CONSEQUENCES! There are splendid officers of superior rank in the Navy but alas! in a Naval disaster there is no time to send for a Roberts to retrieve the incompetency of a Buller[1] You have arranged a Colenso! I am going to transfer my body & my money to the United States – I can't mend what has been done – and it's no d——d use squealing!

A Naval Colenso is irreparable, irremediable – eternal.

Adieu
Yrs
FISHER

I have finally decided not to return to England – I shall be here some little time longer with Lady Fisher[2] and then to Lucerne. I note your incisive criticism of Custance in this letter of yours just received 'It is pathetic to see a clever man like Custance serenely plodding away with a roasted chestnut argument for slow ships and weak guns at a moment when the absolute victory of the heavy projectile over almost any armour now afloat, glares us in the face', but ask the Prime Minister if HE thinks Custance 'CLEVER' when he recalls his aimless memorandum read out at the Beresford enquiry! Also I ought to thank you for your words as to myself that 'the adoption on a great scale of the Big Gun in such good time is one of the finest acts of

---

[1] Redvers Henry Buller (1839–1908), Commander of British forces in the first stages of the South African war until he was superseded by General Roberts. He suffered a reverse at Colenso in Natal, December 1899, when his forces made an unsuccessful attempt to cross the Tugela.

[2] Frances Katherina Josepha (d. 1918), only daughter of Rev Thomas Delves Broughton; she and Fisher were married in 1866.

foresight and wisdom by which your naval administration has been distinguished.'

[FISHER]

WSC to Lord Fisher

27 April 1912   [Admiralty]

Priv & Conf

My dear Fisher,

Yr letter is incomprehensible to me.

The Meditn Fleet shorn down to a cruiser sqadn is the smallest command over wh an Admiral has ever hoisted his flag in recent times. That Milne shd take it shows the modesty of his claims. It does not affect in any way the command of the Home Fleets, wh will be determined without regard to seniority as a matter of high state policy. My confidence in Jellicoe has increased every time I have seen him. We have been working a gt deal together.

The Court agreed with you in wishing Poe to have Portsmouth. But I consider Meux will fill the position with greater advantage to the public. Of course it was a terrible blow to him to close his career afloat. That you should make these 2 appts, neither of wh touches vital matters, both of wh reward eminent service, a cause for such a letter as I have had the sorrow to read, surely argues some want of proportion. I leave it at that.

Custance I have already explained to you will not in any way upset the main principles of the new system of entry. Every step I have taken has been to sustain it & to perfect it. I have dealt with you always in candour & sincerity. I regard you as a man of genius. I have & I shall vindicate & uphold yr naval adminn. But I participate in no vendettas. I am resolved that the high patronage of the Admy shall be evenly, representatively & not unkindly administered.

If this is to make a breach in our friendly & important corrdce, it will leave me full of personal regret, but without a scrap of doubt or repentance. But I hope this will not be so.

Yrs vy sincly
WSC

Charles A'Court Repington to WSC

2 May 1912   Maryon Hall
                                                   Hampstead
Private

My dear Churchill

I think that *The Times* will support your proposals about the dominions and the Navy, but of course nothing will be said till after your speech is made.

The Times has wind of your proposals for what seems to be a naval National Reserve. I have asked them to hold it over till I have consulted you. I shall be at the WO tomorrow Friday if you care to tell me anything about it, or to hand me over to anyone for the same purpose. I want *The Times* to take the right point of view and not to commit itself to a policy which may not be in line with yours for we must all pull together over defence questions if we can.

It is possible that you may be able to give me some paper bearing on the subject in order to enable us to keep our place in the line.

Yours very sincerely
C. A'C-REPINGTON

WSC to Viscount Haldane
(*R. B. Haldane Papers*)

3 May 1912   Admiralty

My dear Haldane,

I have been on the lookout for a chance of telling you about a meeting which is planned to take place at Malta at the end of May between Asquith, Kitchener & myself to discuss the Mediterranean situation as affected by the new organisation of the fleet. I must have a talk with you about this later, and I write in the meantime to let you know what is on foot.

Yours very sincerely
WINSTON S. CHURCHILL

WSC to Viscount Haldane
(*R. B. Haldane Papers*)

6 May 1912   In the train

Secret

My dear Haldane,

The Malta Conference can settle nothing. I hope they will however have the advantage of concentrating the PM's attention upon important questions in a way that wd be impossible in the rush of business over here. The actual point has been settled long ago by the brute force of facts. We cannot possibly hold the Mediterranean or guarantee any of our interests there until we have obtained a decision in the North Sea.

The War-plans for the last 5 years have provided for the evacuation of the Meditern as the first step consequent on a war with Germany, & all we are doing is to make peace dispositions wh approximate to war necessities. It wd be vy foolish to lose England in safeguarding Egypt.

Of course if the Cabinet & the House of Commons like to build another fleet of Dreadnoughts for the Meditern the attitude of the Adm'y will be that of a cat to a nice fresh dish of cream. But I do not look upon this as practical politics. It wd cost you 3 or 4 millions a year extra to make head against Austria & Italy in the Meditern & still keep a 60% preponderance in the North Sea. All the above is true, independent of anything France may do. If she is our friend, we shall not suffer. If she is not, we shall suffer. But if we win the big battle in the decisive theatre, we can put everything else straight afterwards. If we lose it, there will not be any afterwards. London is the key of Egypt – don't lose that.

Considering you propose to send the whole Br Army abroad, you ought to help me to keep the whole Br Navy at home.

Whatever the French do, my counsel is the same, & is the first of all the laws of war – overpowering strength at the decisive point. I cd meet you & Grey on Thursday night after dinner, but shall not be back during the rest of this week.

Yours very sincerely
WINSTON S. CHURCHILL

Lord Rothschild to WSC

8 May 1912   Newcourt

Private

My dear Winston,

I trust you will excuse my writing to you on a very important subject, which we have much at heart. My primary excuse for addressing you is that we are the financial agents for the Chilean Government, but that is only a very secondary point.

Thanks partly to the great advantages which the Chilean Government have received from their association with English financiers, but more because they are anxious to remain on the best of terms with England and to avoid political entanglement with the United States or with Germany, the Chilean Government have always followed our advice and have given all their orders for battleships to English manufacturers: they have just ordered a second Super-Dreadnought. Quite apart from the advantage this large order is to the English Labour Market, it must be self-evident to all that should unfortunately war break out while ships of this calibre are being built or are near completion in English shipyards, the English Government would in such untoward circumstances be able to purchase these ships and thus replenish their Navy; that is, I believe, one of the chief reasons why both the American and German Governments are anxious to secure these contracts.

Having stated so much, I must now tell you of the object of this letter: hitherto five Chilean officers have been allowed to study and learn their business on board an English man-of-war; their time has now expired and the Chilean Government are most anxious that a similar privilege should be extended to five other Chilean officers on board one of the newest ships. The Chilean minister has informed us that he spoke to Sir Edward Grey on the subject, who told him that the matter of Foreign officers serving on board English ships was under the consideration of His Majesty's Government, from which he inferred that there was a doubt whether the privilege hitherto conceded would be granted on this occasion.

I hope and trust that, whatever regulations may be made for other powers, you and your colleagues will see your way to granting the request of the Chilean Government.

The Chilean minister seemed to think that it would make a very bad impression in his country if, after they have just ordered this large ship to be built in England, a privilege which they had enjoyed before should be withdrawn, and I am sure that you would be the first to regret anything of this kind.

With many excuses for troubling you
I remain yours very truly
ROTHSCHILD

Lord Rothschild to WSC

15 May 1912   London

My dear Winston,

Very many thanks for your kind letter. I feel convinced that the Chilean Govt will appreciate your making an exception in [their] favour.

Allow me to seize this opportunity of congratulating you upon the great effect produced on your guests at the Naval Review by everything they saw and their appreciation of your great activity.

Believe me, Yours very truly
ROTHSCHILD

WSC to his wife
(*CSC Papers*)

12 May 1912   HMS *Enchantress*

My dearest darling,

I shall return tomorrow, but whether in time for dinner or not depends on the weather here. 4 torpedo boat destroyers are to go out and fire at the gallop from the saddle and it may be misty early in the day. I will therefore telegraph as soon as I know. Either I shall come by the 4.15 or the 6.

I got your letter soon after my expostulatory telegram was despatched, & am indeed rejoiced to feel that you are better & that you are no longer conscious of discomfort.

Jack, Goonie, & the Beattys made a long expedition in a picket boat under a middy all the way across the bay to Lulworth Cove. It was rather stormy, but they have returned safe & satisfied.

I have done some important things today – sacked Briggs, appointed Moore in his stead, & a new Commodore of Destroyers, & a new Director of Naval Ordnance. Generally I have cleared off a lot of difficulty & serious matters wh were hanging & flapping week after week. The King talked more stupidly about the Navy than I have ever heard him before. Really it is disheartening to hear this cheap & silly drivel with wh he lets himself be filled up.

He is recalcitrant about the C.B.s & will not give me more naval honours. He wants to make a new Order! I am therefore going to go on strike so far as the K.C.B.s are concerned, & let the whole thing stand over till a settlement is effected.

I have bruised my hip getting into the ship's boat & it is vy sore. This afternoon I studied the Torpedo again under my young officer. It is a tangle of complications: & the 2nd lesson opens up all sorts of vistas of wh I never dreamed. I cd write 10 pages on the 'Valve group'.

Goonie & Mrs Beatty are vy happy & tame.

Good night my sweet pussy cat

Always your loving husband
W

Jack Churchill to WSC

16 May [1912]   10 Talbot Square

Dear Winston,

Ld R. tells me you have written him a very civil letter about Chilean officers. He also tells me that AJB sang your praises very loudly and gave a great description of his visit and of your energy etc. He, AJB, was very much impressed with Prince Louis and torpedoes.

I spoke to R about submarines and told him that officers could not at present insure their lives. He has called a meeting of the Alliance Life Committee and intends to press them to 'move with the times' and accept submarine lives.

In the course of conversation about the *Orion* he told me that the next ship would have 15″ guns – at which I expressed great surprise! Are many people supposed to know that?

I go yeomanizing tomorrow.

Yrs ever
JACK SC

H. H. Asquith to WSC

10 May 1912   10 Downing Street

My dear Winston,

The Cabinet today, at the instance of Morley, discussed the question ot the proposed meeting of the CID at Malta.

The opinion expressed was practically unanimous – both Ll George and Grey consenting – that such a meeting in present circumstances could not be kept secret, and would almost certainly give rise to awkward questions in Parliament, and to considerable perturbation in Europe.

I feel bound (tho' I do not altogether share their apprehensions) to give effect to their considered view.

I shall therefore countermand the meeting of the Committee, and tell Hankey to cancel the invitations to the non-naval members, including himself.

This will not prevent our taking Malta in the cruise, and meeting Kitchener there, for an informal discussion of Mediterranean problems.

I am inclined to agree with my colleagues that the quieter the thing is kept, and the less said about it beforehand in the Press, the better.

Yours always
H.H.A.

WSC to Lord Fisher
(*Lennoxlove Papers*)

15 May 1912   Admiralty

My dear Fisher,

The Prime Minister & I are coming to Naples on the 24th for a few days *en route* for Malta & Gibraltar in the *Enchantress*. I shall look forward to having a good talk with you & I therefore defer replying to your last letter, wh I was so glad to get. If the consequences of recent appointments were to be what you apprehend I shd feel your censures were not undeserved. But they will not be. The highest positions in the Admiralty & in the Fleet will not be governed by seniority; & the future of the Navy rests in the hands of men in whom your confidence is as strong as mine.

No change of Government will take place in the near future: & no change of Government would carry with it any change of policy in this respect. For the rest let us wait till we can talk freely. Writing is wearisome & unsatisfactory.

Yours vy sincerely
WINSTON S. CHURCHILL

WSC to Lord Fisher
(*Lennoxlove Papers*)

TELEGRAM

17 May 1912   London

I hope we shall meet at Naples 23rd/25th.

CHURCHILL

WSC to Lord Fisher
(*Lennoxlove Papers*)

TELEGRAM

18 May 1912   London

Please keep 24th to 28th absolutely free greatly looking forward to seeing you.

CHURCHILL[1]

[1] An amusing and valuable account of the meeting between WSC and Fisher will be found in Violet Bonham Carter, *Winston Churchill as I knew him*, pp. 253–4.

Memorandum by WSC on Naval Manoeuvres[1]

25 May 1912   HMS *Enchantress*
                                               Naples

The following should be taken as a *guide* in recasting the scheme: –
(1) The forces are too unequal to illustrate the situation – 'Our average moment at this selected moment.' The 7th & 4th battle squadrons are to change sides, and Red is further to be re-inforced by 2 battle-cruisers, the 4th & 9th flotillas, and the 8th submarine section ('Ds').
(2) Prince Louis of Battenberg, as senior Admiral, will command the largest Fleet – the Blue, having with him as second-in-command Sir John Jellicoe. Admiral Callaghan will command the Red Fleet, having with him as second-in-command Sir Henry Jackson who will command the 7th battle squadron. To facilitate these arrangements the *1st and 2nd* battle-squadrons should change places.
(3) The objectives of the Red Fleet are, subject to what follows, correctly stated, but the idea of convoying 50 transports is absurd and bears no relation to actual conditions. The Red commander may count any of his 16 battle-ships as transports, each capable of carrying 3000 men, cyclists and no horses. Each battleship is also to count as a convoying battleship as prescribed in the draft. The consequence of any 3 or more enemy's transports at any practicable landing-point counts as a successful raid provided that the prescribed conditions are observed, excepting that the time for effecting a landing is to be 1 hour's uninterrupted stay in superior force for every 500 men landed at any one point. All enemy's forces in bodies not less than 9000 strong may be considered capable of effecting a junction after landing at any point of concentration not more than 30 miles from their landing-places.
(4) The regular forces in Great Britain are assumed to be 20,000 of which 5000 cannot leave London.
(5) The front which Blue has to guard must be measured in reasonable proportion to his strength which is now reduced. Red-land will comprise the coast of England from Yarmouth to Dungeness, and Harwich, the Thames and Dover will be available for Red bases. Neutral territory extends from Yarmouth to Flamborough Head: therefore no landing south of Flamborough Head may be made by Red. No landing force may attempt a raid and no Red vessel may come into action which has not previously made a

---

[1] The naval historian Arthur J. Marder writes (*From Dreadnought to Scapa Flow*, p. 352):
   'The purpose of the large-scale manœuvres in the summer of 1912 was to investigate the problem of intercepting the German Fleet before it could cover a landing of troops on the East Coast.'

detour to pass East of the 4th Meridian: and no Red ships are to cross the line Yarmouth – The Naze before the declaration of war.

(6) Blue-land extends from Flamborough Head to the Shetlands, and Blue is to prevent Red from either making raids on his coast or entering the Atlantic as prescribed in the draft scheme to interrupt commerce communication without being brought to battle. From the declaration of war it is to be assumed that the Straits of Dover have silted up.

(7) After the Review at Spithead the Red Fleet will proceed to its own ports as follows –

7th Battle Squadron – Dover   ⎫
6th Flotilla   – Dover   ⎬
4th Flotilla   – Harwich   ⎭

2nd Battle Squadron   ⎫
Training Squadron |
Mediterranean   ⎬ The Nore
Cruisers |
2 Battle Cruisers |
9th Flotilla   ⎭

(8) The Blue Fleet will return to northern ports: –
1st, 3rd & 4th Battle Squadrons – Lamlash
1st Cruiser Squadron   ⎫ Oban
1st Flotilla   ⎭
5th, 7th & 8th Flotillas   ⎫
5th Battle Squadron   ⎬ Rosyth
5th & 6th Cruiser Squadron ⎭
2nd & 3rd Cruiser Squadrons – Cromarty
Submarines   6th & 7th Sections – The Tyne
                  3rd & 4th Sections – Rosyth
Minelayers   – The Tyne
Minesweepers – Rosyth

A mobile force of Marines and Marine artillery will be at the disposal of the Blue Commander. This will be the situation when the warning telegram is received.

(9) Battleships and Cruisers are to be assessed on some simple principle according to their value. It is not reasonable to treat them all as equal.

(10) The war will last 14 days continuously unless stopped by Admiralty instructions.

Jack Seely to WSC

11 June 1912   29 Chester Square

My dear Winston,

The Prime Minister sent for me at eleven o'clock tonight, and all is as you prophesied at half past eight this morning.[1] I have but a moment before the twelve o'clock post, not so much to apologize to you for having bothered you at dinner time, as to tell you that I am not likely to forget all you have done for me. Nothing is to be announced until Thursday morning, but we may meet tomorrow I hope when I can tell you more fully than I can write how grateful I am to you.

Yours ever

JS

Violet Asquith to WSC

12 June 1912   10 Downing Street

My dear Winston,

I send one line to thank you for my heavenly three weeks – I have never loved anything so much & the memory of it will be a possession for life.

I am so very distressed to hear about Clemmie – & pray things may not turn out as long & wearisome as they sound. I am coming to see her tomorrow – would you tell her I might be rather later than I said – perhaps towards 6 as the Board of Trade garden party happens that afternoon. I have just been listening to McKenna's vindication of himself – very good & courageous I thought. He seemed to have an unanswerable case, so this vote of censure is probably the best thing that cld have happened. Austen's data was very sloppy – I feel *terribly* land-sick & long to be back with you all – lizard-catching at Paestium or eating at Malta or gliding on that oily Bay. Goodbye – & thank you again a *million* times.

Yrs
VIOLET

Austen Chamberlain to WSC

13 June 1912   9 Egerton Place

My dear Winston,

My wife & I both sincerely regret that we cannot accept your kind invitation to the *Enchantress* for the 8th & 9th. We had most unfortunately

[1] Seely succeeded Haldane as Secretary for War on 12 June 1912.

accepted other invitations for both days before I knew of the proposed visit of MPs to the Fleet.

It was very kind of you to ask us.

Yrs very truly
AUSTEN CHAMBERLAIN

*   *   *   *   *

WSC to the King
(*Royal Archives*)

12 May 1912   HMS *Enchantress*

Mr Churchill with his humble duty to Your Majesty feels bound to recur to this question of naval honours. He is convinced that the enormous disparity which exists between the Navy and the Army is unfair and ought not to continue. It would be invidious to select two officers alone, which is all that is possible under present conditions, for KCBs and leave them to be the only representatives of the Navy in the Honours List at a time when the Service is increasing in severity every year and when the whole fortunes of the country depend upon it. Such a step would only tend to emphasize unduly the existing anomaly.

Mr Churchill therefore hopes that he may receive some further indication of Your Majesty's pleasure in regard to the submission he has made. He is still of opinion that the best course would be to revise the conditions of naval CBs so as to make them accord with the KCBs; but if Your Majesty feels a difficulty in this, he would be very glad to know what alternatives are in Your Majesty's mind.

The institution of a new order in addition to the many that are already in existence is fraught with considerable difficulty and would require very careful consideration, involving undesirable delay. Mr Churchill has however no hesitation in apprising Your Majesty of the importance of this question.

The minister responsible for the Navy ought to be provided with means by which the favour of the Crown can be extended to those who have rendered distinguished service, in the same manner as prevails in other Departments of State. It is not in the public interest that the Navy should be excluded from a proportionate share in the lists which annually accompany the celebration of Your Majesty's Birthday, and Mr Churchill hopes that he may continue to receive from Your Majesty the gracious favour and support which have hitherto so greatly sustained him in the discharge of his duties.

WINSTON S. CHURCHILL

WSC to the King
(*Royal Archives*)

16 May 1912   Admiralty

Mr Churchill presents his humble duty & is vy grateful to Your Majesty for the full & gracious communication wh he has had the honour to receive & upon wh he has carefully reflected.

He does not feel convinced that the creation of a new order would be a satisfactory way of meeting the difficulty wh Your Majesty so thoroughly appreciates. That question could only be judged after all the details had been settled and the scope & character of the new order precisely defined. He agrees with Your Majesty that a committee shd be appointed to frame the statutes of a suitable order, but not to go into the policy of whether there shd be one or not. They shd assume the principle & supply the details. The result of their labours wd be to place Your Majesty & Your Majesty's advisers in a position to decide on a definite and practical proposal, wh is much better than dealing with such a subject in general terms. He wd be glad to learn Your Majesty's views as to the composition of the committee & the terms of reference. The Admiralty case & interests cd not be better represented than by Prince Louis of Battenberg.

Mr Churchill feels that to make it worthwhile to call into existence a new order, the real & practical needs of the naval service shd be met – naval officers shd be able to obtain on the average the same proportion of decorations as their military comrades: ie the Bath as enjoyed by the Navy plus the new order should broadly speaking become equal to the Bath as enjoyed by the Army, making allowance of course for the relative numbers of officers in the services. This would be the *raison d'être* of the order & wd explain obviously why it was exclusively reserved for the Navy. It wd also keep a strict limit on its size, & if a naval war opened the CB much more widely to naval officers, the new order wd in following years be restricted accordingly. The distribution cd further be based upon the perfectly true principle that naval service even in times of peace is never free from danger, is in fact a kind of active service.

Then Mr Churchill thinks that there are two main practical needs to be met – first an encouragement to rising young officers – senior lieutenants & commanders, & secondly a final recognition of good service in officers of Flag rank whom it is not possible to employ.

It is vy painful to the First Lord of the Admiralty to have to dash so many hopes & ambitions wh are perfectly creditable & legitimate in good & worthy officers, & to see them retire from the service to wh they have given their lives without any solace to their dignity or recognition of their toils.

These are the two main needs, & if the character of the new order cd be kept at a high level by restricting its distribution within fixed limits, it is possible that they might be met.

Submitted with his humble duty by Your Majesty's faithful & devoted servant & subject

WINSTON S. CHURCHILL

WSC to the King
(Royal Archives)

16 May 1912   Admiralty

Mr Churchill with his humble duty to Your Majesty. On the 19th of this month the important post of Your Majesty's principal Naval Aide-de-Camp becomes vacant by the retirement of Admiral Sir Lewis Beaumont.[1] This is a matter in which Your Majesty's personal wishes apart even from the supreme authority of the Crown should prevail. But Mr Churchill would venture vy respectfully to represent the desirability of Your Majesty's attaching to your person a naval officer of real & modern competence who from a position independent to some extent of the Board of Admiralty could nevertheless afford your Majesty the additional support in service matters. Sir William May appears to Mr Churchill to be in many respects extremely well qualified for this high honour; & it is not easy to discern anyone else who would fill the position with equal advantage, apart from Your Majesty's personal inclination. Mr Churchill would however be glad to receive an expression of your Majesty's wishes as soon as may be found convenient. And with his humble duty remains Your Majesty's faithful & devoted servant,

WINSTON S. CHURCHILL

Lord Stamfordham to WSC
(Royal Archives)

22 May 1912   Buckingham Palace

Copy

In reply to your letter to the King of the 16th May, respecting the vacant post of His Majesty's First and Principal Aide-de-Camp, the King desires me to let you know that as Sir William May could only hold the appointment till next March His Majesty wishes to appoint Admiral Sir Edmund Poe,

[1] Lewis Anthony Beaumont (1847–1922), First and Principal Naval ADC to the King 1911–12; Director of Naval Intelligence 1894–9; knighted 1901.

whose command of the Mediterranean has come to an end, and who would be able to hold the post for three years.

The King does not like frequent changes of his personal staff, and does not wish to have an Admiral of the Fleet acting in the capacity of First and Principal Naval Aide-de-Camp, which would be the case if Sir William May were appointed, as, in the ordinary course, he will be promoted to the rank of Admiral of the Fleet on the retirement of Sir Charles Hotham[1] for age next year.

His Majesty considers that the appointment of First and Principal Aide-de-Camp should always be held by a Full Admiral.

Sir Edmund Poe will be in every way personally acceptable to the King.

STAMFORDHAM

H. H. Asquith to WSC

13 June 1912   10 Downing Street

My dear Winston,

I saw Stamfordham: the King is very anxious to be able to announce the two KCBs tomorrow. He is distressed at the idea of a blank sheet for the Navy on his birthday.

I spoke very strongly on the injustice of the existing arrangements so far as the Navy is concerned, and the invidious position in which you are placed with 40 CBs at your potential disposal, a number of able officers who deserve reward, and yet a legal disability to bring together supply and demand.

S assented to all this, and said that the King as a sailor was most sympathetic, and wished the matter to be at once inquired into by a small Committee, perhaps with Prince Louis in the chair.

I think you might be content with this, and submit the two KCBs. The matter is of course very urgent, as the list must appear tomorrow.

Ever Yours
H.H.A.

WSC to the King

13 June 1912   Admiralty

Copy

Mr Churchill with his humble duty to Your Majesty. He has received from PM an intimn of your wishes that 2 offrs of the Navy & Marines shd

---

[1] Charles Frederick Hotham (1843–1925), Commander in Chief Pacific Station 1890–2; Naval ADC to Queen Victoria; Admiral of the Fleet 1903; knighted 1895.

be advanced to the grade of KCB on the occasion of your Birthday. The
PM agrees with Mr C in recognising the injustice of the existing arrangements so far as the Navy is concerned & the inviduous position in wh the
1st Ld is placed with 40 CBs at his potential disposal, a number of able
officers who deserve reward & yet a legal disability to bring together supply
& demand. Mr C cannot feel that the appearance of 2 officers advanced to
the grade of KCB will in any way mitigate the force of the comparisons wh
will be drawn between the treatment of the 2 services, & he earnestly hopes
that he may not again be placed in a sitn wh is to him so disappointing &
unsatisfactory. Yr by yr the Navy is increasingly becoming accustd to avert
its attention from the lists of Honours wh constitute the rewards of merit &
mark the bestowal of the favours of the Crown. Only a sense of the disabilities under wh the 1st Lord lies as compared with the Ministers responsible for other gt services has prompted Mr Ch most respectfully but most
earnestly to submit the whole question to YM's attention. It is not in the
public interest that the present conditions shd continue, & Mr Ch feels the
vy greatest difficulty in making recomms wh tho extremely partial &
restricted in themselves seem to imply his acquiescence in the system which
remains uncorrected. He realizes however that you feel the unfairness wh
exists strongly & deeply. It is his sincere desire at all times to conform to YM
pleasure, & esp upon so auspicious an occasion on the celebn of YM Bthdy.
He therefore submits the names of VA the Hon Stanley C. J. Colville CVO,
CB & of Lt-Gen William C. Nicholls, RMA for the KCB counting upon YM
gracious favour to relieve him from a task of selection so narrowed and
embarrassing in the future.

WSC

Lord Stamfordham to WSC
(*Royal Archives*)

13 June 1912   Buckingham Palace

The King has approved of the submissions contained in your letter to
His Majesty of today's date, namely, Vice-Admiral the Honble Stanley
C. J. Colville and Lt-Gen C. S. Nicholls, Royal Marine Artillery for the
Knight Commandership of the Bath.

STAMFORDHAM

The King to WSC

24 June 1912 Windsor Castle

My dear Churchill,

With regard to your letter of the 13th inst: I quite recognise the force of what you wrote as to the unfairness of the existing arrangements for the bestowal of Honours upon Officers of the Navy; &, as I stated in my letter to you of 15 of May, I am prepared to agree to the appointment of a small Committee to consider whether the institution of a special decoration for the Navy would be advisable.

Before doing this, however, I am anxious to know whether you can assure me that there is a general desire among the Officers of the Navy, Senior as well as Junior, for such a decoration for services in peace time, & also whether the subject has been carefully considered by the Board of Admiralty.

I would repeat again the importance of moving with caution & deliberation in this difficult question.

Believe me, very sincerely yours
GEORGE R.I.

WSC to the King
(*Royal Archives*)

25 [June] 1912 Admiralty

Dictated

Mr Churchill with his humble duty to Your Majesty acknowledges the letter which he has had the honour to receive from Your Majesty on the subject of Naval Honours.

He has no means which it would be suitable to employ in ascertaining the desires of the senior & junior officers of the Navy, though he is well aware that it is a common saying among them that 'the Navy is always cut out' of the Honours List. The fact that on the occasion of Your Majesty's Birthday 21 officers of the Army were decorated with or advanced in the Order of the Bath, presumably for peace-time services (since there has been no war for ten years), while only one Naval Officer was so rewarded, is in itself sufficient to prove that the existing system is neither satisfactory nor fair.

Mr Churchill does not consider that this subject is one which should be brought formally before the Board of Admiralty as a whole, but rather one on which the Minister responsible to the Crown & to Parliament for the administration of the Navy should respectfully tender his advice.

Mr Churchill has however consulted with the First & Second Sea Lords as well as with the Secretary to the Board, whose knowledge & experience on these matters are very great; & they all agree with him that the best way to mend the breakdown of the present system is not to institute a new & special order, but to make the necessary alterations in the Statutes of the Bath which would make them apply to modern needs. Those alterations are very small, & consist only in applying to the CB the same principle which prevails in regard to the KCB. This was the advice which Mr Churchill had the honour to offer to Your Majesty two & a half months ago; from which, though he has willingly considered other alternatives, his convictions have never been moved; & which he now ventures finally to renew. The Committee which Your Majesty proposes to appoint would find no difficulty in suggesting the necessary alterations in the Statutes of the Order. Mr Churchill has consulted the Prime Minister upon the question, & finds him in full agreement both as to the existence of the grievance & the propriety of the remedy.

Mr Churchill earnestly trusts that he may receive from Your Majesty the gracious favour & support which are due to the heavy responsibilities with which he is charged, & which have been so abundantly bestowed on him in the other offices which he has had the honour to hold in this & the previous Reign.

And with his humble duty remains

Your Majesty's faithful & devoted servant
WINSTON S. CHURCHILL

Lord Stamfordham to WSC
(*Royal Archives*)

5 July 1912   Buckingham Palace

I reported to the King by last night's Messenger the result of our talk, and His Majesty has telegraphed his approval of the proposed arrangements, as explained in my letter to him, which were as follows: –

That every year ten Civil CBs should be placed at the disposal of the First Lord of the Admiralty, for which recommendations for Officers not below the rank of Commander should be made to the King until the number (about 40) of Military CBs now apportioned to the Officers of the Navy has been worked off. After such time the number would be reduced from ten, so as to maintain the correct proportion of CBs granted annually to the Navy and Army.

In the case of Officers becoming qualified for the Military CBs by war service the grant of Civil CBs would cease.

Although ten CBs are to be placed at the disposal of the First Lord, they will not all necessarily be bestowed each year, care being taken that they are only given for very special service.

That His Majesty should approve of recommendations being made at once and given as for the King's birthday.

As soon as I hear from you I will communicate with the Prime Minister with a view of arranging that the 10 CBs are made available at once.

STAMFORDHAM

* * * * *

Memorandum by WSC

15 June 1912 [Admiralty]

I circulate to my colleagues a memorandum which I have prepared upon the naval situation at home and in the Mediterranean, and also a note of an arrangement which was worked out in agreement with Lord Kitchener, and which would, if acted upon, be satisfactory to him. I would ask that these papers may be returned to me after use.

WSC

Secret

The new German Navy Law provides for keeping 25 battleships in full permanent commission. There will also be 4 battleships of the Reserve, which will have full crews on board, and may consequently be used at very short notice. Against this we cannot keep less than 33 battleships in full commission, and all of these must be either in home waters or constantly and easily available. We are straining our margins even by basing one squadron of 8 on Gibraltar. While that squadron is abroad we shall only have an equality with the Germans in numbers of fully commissioned ships. We have, in addition, 8 battleships with full nucleus crews (5th battle squadron), and these compare in readiness with the 4 German reserve battleships above mentioned. It will be nearly 2 years before we have the men to man the 6th battle squadron with full nucleus crews. It will be seen, therefore, that we have no great superiority in the numbers of vessels ready at short notice, even when the arrangements which we are making are complete. We have of course, substantial superiority in quality, particularly in the older ships, but we are all agreed that the proportion of 33 to 25 fully commissioned ships is the very least in numbers that will provide for the safety of Great Britain.

2. We cannot afford to keep 6 battleships in the Mediterranean in full commission. It is not so much the ships, but the men that are wanted. It is a waste of our limited resources to use full complements to man inferior ships. In order to keep old battleships in full commission in the Mediterranean, we have hitherto been laying up much stronger ships in nucleus crews at home. We have now created a third and powerful squadron of 8 'King Edwards' in full commission, and we should have to lay these up, ship by ship, in order to man the new vessels, 5 more of which are coming to hand in the next 12 months unless we bring home the Atlantic Fleet altogether (as we have done), move the Malta battleships into its place, and make certain adjustments which this renders possible. The gain in war power from bringing home the 6 old battleships from the Mediterranean is two-fold: we put all our best ships into the highest status of commission; and we concentrate them in the decisive theatre. The return of the Malta squadron is absolutely indispensable.

3. But, anyhow, its utility in the Mediterranean is almost exhausted. We have hitherto always been able to keep a fleet in the Mediterranean equal to that of our rivals for the time being, whoever they were. Formerly, it was France, now they may be said to be Italy and Austria, separately or together. Unless we can face Italy and Austria in the Mediterranean, it would be a faulty strategic disposition to keep a battle squadron there. Neither Austria nor Italy have any Dreadnoughts actually commissioned at present; but in a few months the first Italian Dreadnought will be ready, and thereafter both Powers will continue to be reinforced at short intervals by very powerful modern units, until by January 1915 Austria and Italy together will dispose of no less than 10 Dreadnought vessels. Against this, or half this force, the 4 'Duncans' and the 2 'Swiftsures,' hitherto stationed at Malta, could offer no effective resistance. They would only be a cheap and certain spoil. We should be simply leaving a weak division of old ships to be overwhelmed in a subsidiary theatre, while the crews might have manned much better ships in the decisive theatre. The Malta squadron can do great good at home, and no good where it is.

4. It would be both wrong and futile to leave the present battle squadron at Malta *to keep up appearances*. It would be a bluff which would deceive nobody. The influence and authority of the Mediterranean Fleet is going to cease, not because of the withdrawal of the Malta battleships, but because

of the completion of the Austrian and Italian Dreadnoughts. It will cease certainly and soon whether the Malta battleships are withdrawn or not, only in the latter case we shall have more to lose in a subsidiary theatre and less to win with in the decisive theatre. As soon as the first two Austrian Dreadnoughts are ready, one in October of the present year and the other in April next, they with the 3 'Radetzkys' will be stronger than the present 6 Malta battleships, quite apart from Italy. This fact is perfectly appreciated by every General Staff in Europe. The power will have passed automatically to others, and only the empty but expensive symbols will remain. The Malta battleships left in the Mediterranean will in time of peace be only a pretence of strength which everyone would see through; and in time of war, a loss serious in themselves – still more serious by their subtraction from the decisive sphere.

5. If it were decided to maintain a purely British local superiority in the Mediterranean as well as adequate margins in the North Sea, it would be necessary to build and man an entirely new and additional squadron of modern battleships for that purpose. This would be a very extravagant policy, and is not necessary to the fundamental safety of the British Empire or to our ultimate victory and supremacy at sea. It would commit us to a two-Power standard against Italy and Austria in the Mediterranean, plus a 60 per cent preponderance always ready against Germany in home waters. This could not be justified by our primary needs. But anyhow this alternative, extravagant though it would be, is not open to us. There is no time, even if Parliament voted the money, to build a special squadron of Dreadnoughts for the Mediterranean. We could not get them ready soon enough; and if they were ready we could not provide trained officers and seamen for them. We have therefore got to face the fact that the naval control of the Mediterranean is swiftly passing from our hands whatever we do, while we remain single-handed.

6. Arrangements can, however, be made which will enable us, without undue expense, to provide for the adequate protection of our special interests in the Mediterranean, pending such a decision in the North Sea as would enable us to re-enter the Mediterranean in full strength. It must be plainly recognised that we must adopt the *rôle* in this minor theatre appropriate to the weaker naval Power, and while in the North Sea we rely on the gun as our first weapon, we must in the Mediterranean fall back mainly on the torpedo. The Admiralty would propose to leave a sufficient force of armoured and protected cruisers based on Malta to discharge all the diplomatic functions which our responsibilities entail. For the defence of Malta it will be necessary to build and organise a strong flotilla of submarines and to reinforce the destroyer flotilla already there. If Malta and the Malta Channel obtain

the reputation of being a nest of submarines and torpedo craft, and is effectually so defended, it would not be worth the while of Austria or Italy to risk either battleships or transports in an attempt to capture it by a regular attack. Unless they were prepared to pay an altogether disproportionate price for the island, the only two dangers to be apprehended would be surprise or starvation. The place is provisioned to stand at least three months' isolation, and the garrison should be sufficient to make a regular military expedition necessary for its reduction.

7. A new submarine and torpedo station will have to be established at Alexandria. Another new flotilla of submarines, possessing sufficient radius of action to enable them to threaten the Dardanelles, or cover the approaches to the Suez Canal, will be required. This flotilla, supported by the cruiser squadron which it is proposed to leave in the Mediterranean, would be available among other things for the purpose of coercing the Turk in minor matters. Its presence would make the invasion of Egypt by sea, whether from Italy, Austria, or Turkey, a very hazardous enterprise, involving heavy losses at the outset, and with the strong probability of ultimate expulsion when the naval situation in the North Sea had been cleared up. But before such a flotilla can be based on Alexandria, a defended harbour must be provided on a scale capable of resisting an attack by armoured vessels. It seems to the Admiralty very probable that these arrangements may be made to fit conveniently into any scheme for strengthening the British force in Egypt. The actual strength of the flotillas, both at Malta and Alexandria, have been referred, together with other technical matters, to the War Staff, in order that precise estimates may be framed.

8. It should be noted that these arrangements stand by themselves, and are put forward as the best we can make in the present circumstances. The situation would, however, become entirely favourable if France is taken into account. The French fleet, supported by an adequate British naval force, and enjoying the use of our fortified and torpedo-defended bases as well as their own, would be superior to any Austro-Italian alliance. An Anglo-French combination in a war would be able to maintain full control of the Mediterranean, and afford all necessary protection to British and French interests, both territorial and commercial, without impairing British margins in the North Sea. A definite naval arrangement should be made with France without delay.

This arrangement would come into force only if the two Powers were at any time allies in a war. It would not decide the question of whether they should be allies or not. No sound or effective dispositions can be made without it, and many obvious contingencies must be left unsatisfied.

9. There are two further important objects in the Mediterranean which

our naval dispositions must and can safeguard. First, to make sure that France will, with our aid, be strong enough to overcome the combined fleets of Italy and Austria. While this condition prevails in the Mediterranean, and while we can at the same time keep adequate margins in the North Sea, it is unlikely that the whole Triple Alliance will act together in a war against England and France; and even in that eventuality the naval situation would be quite satisfactory. At the present moment France is herself single-handed slightly superior in strength to the Austro-Italian combination. During 1913 and 1914, however, as may be seen from the attached diagram, the strength of France in modern units drops to the same level as that of the other two Powers, not counting the 3 Austrian 'Radetzkys' which are as good, or a little better, than our Lord Nelsons, which we count as Dreadnoughts till 1917, and it is not until October 1915 that, in consequence of the efforts now being made by M. Delcassé,[1] the French superiority will be again restored. Even this result may be frustrated or delayed by further mutually provocative building on the part of Austria and Italy. We have, therefore, to leave a naval force in the Mediterranean which, added to that of France, would secure for the combination an effective superiority. It is no use leaving a number of old ships for this purpose; such vessels would not turn the scale in war, and might only become a prey. In peace, too, calculations of European Powers will no doubt continue to be made upon the basis of Dreadnoughts. The Admiralty have therefore to consider what ships of first quality we can spare from home waters to maintain the Anglo-French preponderance in the Mediterranean. We have come to the conclusion that we can best spare two of the Dreadnought battle cruisers. These ships have many great advantages. Two of them will assure the French at least an equality in Dreadnoughts during 1913 and 1914. There are no ships like them built, building, or projected in the Mediterranean. Their great speed and power combined makes them fully able to look after themselves in all eventualities, and to concentrate at home, if necessary, in the minimum of time. Their being based on Malta will also have the effect of achieving our second object – the maintenance of British influence in the Mediterranean, far more effectively than a larger number of equally expensive to keep up, but less powerful or less well-advertised ships. The First Sea Lord writes of these vessels: 'At present the British battle cruisers have an immense prestige in themselves; no one really knows their full value; it is undoubtedly great – it may be even more than we imagine. In the Mediterranean they could operate with great effect; their speed, their armour, their armament, are all great assets, even their appear-

[1] Théophile Delcassé (1852–1923), French statesman who was instrumental in bringing about the *Entente Cordiale*; Ambassador in St Peterburg 1913-14; Foreign Minister August 1914 to October 1915.

ance has a sobering effect.' We therefore propose concurrently with the withdrawal of the battle squadron to base two battle cruisers – probably the *Indomitable* and *Invincible* – on Malta. This should be announced at once. My naval advisers are of opinion that some compensation will be required in our new construction at home.

10. The foregoing argument is based upon nominal standards of strength, which are the only data available for peace calculations. But these paper situations will require a great deal of modification to make them correspond with reasonable probabilities. It seems unlikely that Italy and Austria should embark upon an aggressive war in concert against England and France, with whom they have no cause of quarrel. It is still more unlikely that if they did so, their allied fleets would act together with vigour and harmony. The Admiralty view is that France would have a good chance of beating the two opponents single-handed, even if at a slight numerical disadvantage.

11. The contingencies which we must bear in mind may be classed in their order of probability, as follows: –

(i.) *Great Britain* v. *Germany*. – In this case the Mediterranean would not be involved.

(ii.) *Great Britain and France* v. *Germany and Austria*. – In this case the position in the Mediterranean would be secure.

(iii.) *Great Britain and France* v. *the Triple Alliance;* or

England, France, and Russia v. *the Triple Alliance*. – The arrangements proposed above would in this case be adequate for the Mediterranean.

(iv.) *Great Britain alone* v. *Germany and Austria*. – It is probable that by good management we could maintain ourselves simultaneously in both theatres once our mobilisation was complete; but a great many risks would have to be run in the subsidiary theatre until a decision was obtained in the North Sea.

(v.) *Great Britain alone* v. *the Triple Alliance*. – The situation would then be grave, and we should certainly suffer heavy losses in the Mediterranean; but there would be very good hopes, so far as the next three or four years are concerned, that we should be able to prevent the hostile fleets in the Mediterranean and the North Sea from joining, and to attack them separately in superior strength.

It will be seen that all the above contingencies, even the most improbable, are comprehended in the Admiralty proposals, which are concurred in by my advisers.   WSC

A. J. Balfour to WSC

20 June 1912   4 Carlton Gardens

Dictated

Private

My dear Winston Churchill,

I have read with great interest your memorandum, which I now return.

The situation is in many respects very unsatisfactory, and though I quite recognise all the difficulties involved in an Alliance, I feel anxious over a condition of things which may leave us or the French, or both, without the assistance of the other during the first and most critical fortnight of the war – if war there is to be.

Yours very sincerely
ARTHUR JAMES BALFOUR

Memorandum by WSC

22 June 1912   [Admiralty]

I circulate herewith to my colleagues a Memorandum in amplification of my last on the Naval Situation. They should be read together. A decision is urgently required.

Secret

1. Dealing for simplicity in battleships and battle cruisers only, our margins against Germany depend on –

    a. numbers of Dreadnoughts completed, and

    b. numbers of ships kept instantly ready, *i.e.*, in full commission.

For *a.* we require to build so as to keep a 60 per cent preponderance. Our present programme, namely 4, 5, 4, 4, 4, 4, just does this. But we must have all these Dreadnoughts constantly available for service in the North Sea.

For *b.* we require to keep as an irreducible minimum 33 battleships as against 25 German battleships in full permanent commission.

The above takes into consideration all minor points of superiority in individual ships.

Of these 33 ships 8, some of which will soon be Dreadnoughts, will be based on Gibraltar ($3\frac{1}{2}$ days distant and coaling); but that is only because we have to use the docking and repairing facilities there. Whenever we want them or think we want them they must come home. In war with Germany they will be used at home. They can, however, show themselves in the Mediterranean from time to time when all is quiet and when we are in good strength at home. But these excursions will have to be very carefully planned and special precautions taken meanwhile.

2. Besides the battleships in full commission we have eight with full nucleus crews (5th Squadron Second Fleet). Against these must be set four of the German reserve ships which are also fully manned.

It is intended, as the German squadrons improve in quality through new ships joining, to raise this Second Fleet to 16 battleships, and arrange that 8 will always be available at their Home Ports for rapid mobilisation. Dearth of men will prevent this (6th Squadron) being begun until the end of 1914, or finished till end of 1915. And meanwhile there would be a delay in mobilising the first 8 if they were cruising away from the ports where the rest of their crews are quartered.

3. Remember that although 33 battleships are in full commission, some are always away refitting, under repair, or on special duty. On the average 5 or 6 would be absent from the flag, except at manoeuvres. The same proportion would apply to Germany. They can arrange to be all ready for any selected date without our having any warning. So could we. But our date may not be theirs. We have to meet their selected moment with our average moment.

For a battle at 48 hours' notice we could not, unless the Gibraltar ships were *actually at home,* make certain of putting more than 21 full commissioned battleships and 6 full nucleus crew battleships in the line: total 27. There is no reason why – choosing their moment – the Germans should not put an equal number. In fact, our only margin for a sudden emergency is any superiority in the quality of our individual ships.

And bad luck with mines, torpedoes, surprise, breakdowns or mistakes may easily cancel out that.

So that even upon the margins above prescribed, we may have to fight an equal battle. But for very unequal stakes.

4. At present we have not got and cannot get the 33 ships. The rate at which our margins can be realised depends entirely upon the number of trained officers and men available. We are already recruiting up to our full limit under existing conditions. We started the year 2,000 men short. Special measures will be needed to overtake this deficit and make our necessary increase. Even after bringing home the six Mediterranean battleships, we

shall not be able for want of men to complete the first four squadrons, *i.e.,* our 33 ships till the end of 1913. This is just soon enough –

(28 now, + 2 in November, + 1 April, 1913, + 2 in August, 1913, = 33.)

We cannot spare the complements necessary to man six battleships in the Mediterranean. We cannot afford to waste full crews on inferior ships, nor to alienate Dreadnoughts to the Mediterranean (apart from the two battle cruisers already promised).

The argument for sparing these is that the late Board of Admiralty had proposed to send *Indomitable* to China, and to let *New Zealand* go there too. We have stopped *Indomitable* and have been allowed to keep *New Zealand*. We are therefore two to the good on these. If a third battle cruiser is wanted for the Mediterranean, an extra ship must be laid down forthwith to replace her.

5. In the Mediterranean Austria and Italy will, according to the Intelligence Division, have Dreadnoughts as shown on the diagram already circulated.

We have no force capable of meeting them in 1913, 1914, 1915, or 1916.

But if steps are taken at once a Fleet could be constructed and manned by the end of 1916.

Taking all chances and circumstances into consideration it would be enough if we had 75 per cent of their combined strength.

This means six to eight Dreadnoughts to be built as fast as they can be placed, additional to all previous programmes, together with increased flotillas.

To hold the Mediterranean single-handed will cost from 15 to 20 millions capital expenditure, plus *personnel* and upkeep, and cannot be fully achieved till 1916.

6. There are therefore four courses: –

　　a. To reduce our margins in the North Sea, which my naval advisors state will imperil the country.

　　b. To abandon the Mediterranean, which would be very injurious.

　　c. To build a new fleet for the Mediterranean, which will cost 15 to 20 millions and cannot be ready before 1916; and,

　　d. To make an arrangement with France and leave enough ships in the Mediterranean to give her undoubted superiority, as proposed in my memorandum of 16th inst.

7. Quite apart from the foregoing – Trustworthy reports have now been received that Austria intends to proceed with the construction of four additional Dreadnoughts. Should this prove true we must build *pari passu*, four extra ships above the numbers quoted in para 1 at a cost of nine millions.

The First and Second Sea Lords desire me to express their concurrence.

WSC

Memorandum by WSC

25 June 1912 [Admiralty]

Secret

1. The Home Secretary's paper contemplates simultaneous operations in the North Sea and the Mediterranean against the fleets of the Triple Alliance in 1914. For this purpose he divides the fleet into two parts, leaving all the Dreadnoughts in the North Sea and sending two squadrons of King Edwards and Formidables to the Mediterranean.

2. Taking the Mediterranean first. We should have 16 battleships, mounting 64 – 12-in. and 32 – 9·2-in. guns against 24 Austro-Italian battleships mounting 115 – 12-in. and 53 – 10-in. or 9·4-in. guns. Included in the Austro-Italian fleets would be 10 vessels (7 Dreadnoughts and 3 Radetzkys), all of which would be superior in armament, armour, and speed to any British vessel in the Mediterranean. Such a disposition of forces would expose the Malta and Gibraltar squadrons, even if they were successful in uniting (a very dangerous operation in the face of a superior force), to a general action in circumstances of serious inferiority. How serious cannot be precisely measured, because no one knows what the effect would be of bringing Formidables and King Edwards, unsustained by any vessels of modern type, in contact with the most powerful foreign Dreadnoughts afloat.

3. The following Table is supplied: –

Mediterranean. *April* 1914. *Battleships.*

BRITISH

	Guns	Guns
8 King Edwards	32—12″ ..	32—9·2″
8 Formidables	32—12″ ..	..
Total 16	64—12″	32—9·2″

AUSTRIAN

	Guns	Guns
3 Dreadnoughts.. ..	36—12″ ..	..
3 Radetzkys	12—12″ ..	24—9·4″
3 Ferdinand Max ..	.. ..	12—9·4″
3 Babenberg	.. ..	9—9·4″
Total 12	48—12″	45—9·4″

ITALIAN

	Guns		Guns
4 Dreadnoughts.. ..	51—12″	..	..
(1 Dante, 3 Da Vincis)			
4 Romas	8—12″	..	..
2 Margheritas	8—12″	..	..
2 Filibertas	..	..	8—10″
Total 12	67—12″		8—10″
Com-bined total 24	115—12″		53—10″ and 9·4″

4. These proportions must be subjected to practical analysis: –

A fleet action in which the ten modern Austro-Italian ships used their speed to keep level with the head of the British line would compare broadsides with the British ships opposite to them as follows: –

10 best Austro-Italian battle-ships –
99 – 12″ guns
12 – 9·4″ guns

against

10 best British battle-ships –
40 – 12″ guns
16 – 9·2″ guns.

Pending the decision of the above, which could not be long delayed, there would be left –

14 Austro-Italian battle-ships

against

6 British (Formidables).

My advisers are therefore agreed that the balance of forces in the Mediterranean under the proposed dispositions would be such as to expose a British fleet, equal to nearly a third of our total battleship strength and manned by 12,000 of our best officers and seamen, to certain destruction.

The situation would become worse in 1915, when 1 more Austrian and 2 more Italian Dreadnoughts are due.

5. Turning now to the North Sea: If 16 battleships are employed in the Mediterranean, the Mobilisation Division state that it would only be in our power in 1914 to keep 17 battleships fully commissioned in home waters: total 33. We should have, under the proposed dispositions, 22 Dreadnoughts and 2 Lord Nelsons available, and these could be formed into 3 squadrons, of which 2 squadrons and a flagship would be in full commission, and the third in nucleus crews (Second Fleet basis). We should have nothing behind

this except the 5 Duncans and 3 of the 9 Majestics all manned on the Third Fleet scale, *i.e.*, with reduced nucleus crews made up by reserves, and 14 of the weakest or oldest battleships in the Material Reserve (2 Swiftsures, 6 Majestics, and 6 Canopuses) *for which no active service crews of any kind can be provided.*

6. We are now raising men as fast as we can, and it is not possible to make large and immediate additions to *personnel,* even if expense be altogether disregarded. It takes two and a-half years to train a seaman even to the 'ordinary' standard, and eight years to train up to a lieutenant. The additional numbers of men available in the spring of 1914 will be the 4,813 extra men actually recruited in 1910–11 and 1911–12, out of the 7,000 for which Parliamentary sanction was obtained. Thus the deficit at the beginning of this year was 2,200. The 1912–13 recruits will not have come to hand in 1914. The extra numbers therefore will be 4,800, and not 12,000 as stated. All these men, *and many more,* are required *(a)* to man the 5 extra battleships which are to raise us from 28 to 33 in full commission, and *(b)* to man 4 new battle cruisers, and *(c)* to man the new flotilla of destroyers (IXth) to be formed in 1913. Serious shortages are anticipated during 1912 and 1913.

7. It is not understood how the deficiency in men can be made good by reducing cruisers to the Third Fleet as the Home Secretary suggests. If 4 full commissioned armoured cruisers based on Gibraltar are, as proposed, to be detached for service in the Mediterranean, there would remain of full commissioned cruisers in home waters 4, and in nucleus crews in the Second Fleet 5; total, 9. My advisers are agreed in regarding these numbers as inadequate to the strategic needs which would arise on the outbreak of war. In order to keep in full commission the 40 battleships proposed by the Home Secretary, it would be necessary to reduce the whole of these 9 cruisers and 2 of the battle cruisers to a Third Fleet basis, and this would leave us without a single armoured cruiser in home waters capable of being used instantly upon the outbreak of war; and even when a complete mobilisation had rendered them available, they would be manned to the extent of three-fifths with reserve men, and would be totally wanting in all the elements of cruiser efficiency. We are therefore of opinion that it is impossible to increase the number of battleships in full commission by the reductions of cruisers as proposed.

8. We may now examine the relative battleship strengths, according to the proposed dispositions, of the opposing war fleets in the North Sea on the outbreak of war. There would be 17 British battleships in full commission against 25 German, and we should further have 7 battleships with nucleus crews, against which must be set the 4 German battleships of the Reserve Division. The numbers available on paper for battle at short notice would be

24 British to 29 German. The total numbers available after mobilization was complete would be – British: full commission 17, nucleus crews 7, reduced nucleus 8 (5 Duncans and 3 Majestics) – total 32; German: active fleet, 25, Reserve 11 – total 36.

9. A table is again furnished: –

North Sea. April 1914. Battleships

At short notice:

BRITISH		GERMAN	
Full Commission		*Full Commission*	
Dreadnoughts	17	Dreadnoughts	16
		Pre-Dreadnoughts	9
Nucleus crews			
Dreadnoughts	5	*Reserve* parent ships ..	4
Lord Nelsons	2		
Total	24	Total	29

ARMOURED CRUISERS

Abroad		*At Home*	
China and Australia ..	5	Home—	
Malta	4	First Fleet	4
Gibraltar	4	Second Fleet	5
Training Squadron	6	Third Fleet..	6
	19		15

Total .. 34

7 battleships at 750 require	..	..	..	..	5,250
9 armoured cruisers at 750 give	..	..	..	6,750	
Deducting two-fifths for nucleus crews		..	2,700	
Gives	..	..	..	4,050	
2 battle cruisers at 900 give	..	..	1,800		
Deducting two-fifths	..	..	720		
Gives	..	..	..	1,080	
Total	..	..	..	..	5,130

On regular mobilisation: –

Active Fleet

BRITISH		GERMAN	
Dreadnoughts	22	Dreadnoughts	16
Lord Nelsons	2	Deutschlands	9

Reserve

Duncans ..	..	..	5	Deutschland	.. ..	1
Majestics	..	..	3	Wittelsbachs	.. ..	5
				Kaisers ..	.. ..	5
Total	..	..	32	Total	.. ..	36

Material Reserve—Without any Active Service Crews in Peace or War				*Old and Small Battleships*		
Swiftsures	..	..	2	Brandenburgs	.. ..	2
Canopus ..	..	..	6	Odins	.. ..	3
Majestics	..	..	6			
Total	..	..	14	Total	.. ..	5

10. I would here apply the argument unfolded in my last paper, namely, the advantage which choosing the moment of attack gives to the Power which assumes the offensive. It is necessary to reduce the British ships immediately available by 4 or 5 ships which would on the average be absent from the squadrons, except during manoeuvres, repairing or refitting. This proportion of unavailable ships is no more than the average proportion absent from the flag during 1910–11. The British numbers therefore available for a sudden battle – say within 48 hours – would not exceed 20 battleships against 25 or (with the 4 reserve ships) 29 German battleships; and the relative Dreadnought strength (including 2 Lord Nelsons) would be 20 against 16. The strength in battle cruisers is correctly stated at 10 British to 5 German, but the *Australia* will be at the Antipodes, and on the scheme proposed 2 others would have to be manned only with reduced nucleus crews, *i.e.*, not efficient till after at least a month's training at sea. The effective numbers would be 7 British to 5 German. The value of these great vessels in enabling the stronger fleet to bring the weaker fleet to action is fully appreciated, but they are not capable of filling the places of battleships in the line.

11. My advisers are of opinion that, after making all allowances for the individual superiority of some of the British battleships, there would be the gravest doubts as to the result of a general engagement between the British and German fleets as disposed above. At any rate, the risk would be far greater than we should be justified in running. If our fleet were defeated or seriously crippled in the battle, we should have nothing to fall back upon in home waters to oppose the enemy's victorious fleet except *(a)* any Dreadnoughts which had arrived too late for the battle or which were under repair, and *(b)* the 5 Duncans and 3 Majestics (whose fighting value will by

then be very low). Against these must further be set the 11 German battle-ships, (not including the 2 Brandenburgs and the 3 Odins) in the 2 reserve divisions (less 4 already counted for an emergency in the sea-going fleet): total 7.

12. To sum up, the dispositions proposed would divide our forces between two theatres of war in such a manner as to make victory doubtful in the Northern and decisive theatre, and defeat certain in the Southern. It would keep in full commission 8 Formidables, which should be in reserve, and keep in reserve 8 Dreadnoughts, which should be in full commission. It would compel us to lay up in the Third Fleet with reduced nucleus crews not only all the armoured cruisers which would be left in home waters, but 2 of our latest battle cruisers. It would place us, even after mobilisation, at less than a bare equality in numbers with the Germans in the North Sea, and at only two-thirds of their permanent strength in full commissioned ships; and in the Mediterranean it would expose two squadrons of our older vessels, un-protected by any superior units, to the attack of most powerful modern ships.

13. A war in which Great Britain had to encounter single-handed the combined strength of the Triple Alliance in 1914 would in any case involve us in grave difficulties and losses. We do not think it likely that the Austro-Italian Fleets as they will be in 1914 would be so unwisely handled as to run the gauntlet of submarine and destroyer flotillas in the Straits of Gibraltar for the purpose of entering the Atlantic Ocean, where they would have neither harbours, coal, nor supplies. If they did, very satisfactory opportunities would be presented to the British Navy; and the Admiralty would feel no serious misgivings as to the ultimate issue, provided that in the naval movements strategic considerations were permitted to prevail.

I fully recognise the difficultes which the Home Secretary has had in en-deavouring to deal with such a problem without the assistance of expert advisers, and I am indebted to him for the trouble which he has taken in preparing so detailed a memorandum. But I am compelled to observe that the distribution of the British Fleets proposed by him would be at variance with the accepted principles of strategy, and would directly court disaster.

14. The arguments here adduced have the full concurrence of the First and Second Sea Lords, and all figures and statements of fact have been verified by the War Staff.

WSC

Memorandum by WSC

26 June 1912   [Admiralty]

Secret

In case it should be thought that our present difficulties of manning arise from any reversal by me of my predecessor's policy, I have prepared the following note: –

Vote A for the 1911–12 Estimates was fixed at 134,000 (average). This allowed for a bearing of 136,000 on the 31st March, 1912, and a report was submitted by the Department to the Board in February 1911, in which this bearing of 136,000 at the end of the financial year 1911–12 was assumed. The late First Lord minuted the paper on the 25th February, 1911, in these words: –

'Approve generally, except that I cannot agree to the assumption that numbers are to be worked up to 136,000 in March 1912. It would not be safe to go beyond 135,000 until an increase in Vote A is approved for 1912–13.'

In other words, Mr McKenna was not prepared at that date to commit the Cabinet to an increase of 2,000 men in 1912–13. I concur fully in this decision and adhered to it in my Minutes of the 6th and 20th November, 1911.

Subsequently the First Sea Lord put forward the following Minute to me on the 15th January, 1912: –

'The numbers required to man the War Fleet, proposed for the 31st March, 1913, are 137,460. Accordingly, I propose that Vote A for 1912–13 should be 136,230.'

I minuted this proposal on the 17th January as follows: –

'Proceed on the basis of 136,000 (*i.e.*, for 1912–13). This figure will be reconsidered if a further German increase is announced.'

On the 21st March last Parliament agreed to Vote A at 136,000, meaning that we could increase by 3,000 men during the year. As the German increase was then certain, I proceeded at once to recruit as for an increase of 5,000, thus using up in the first part of the year the whole increase allowed me, and trusting to the Supplementary Estimates to provide for the second part of the year.

No time was therefore lost, and recruiting has proceeded steadily at full speed throughout the year.

But we started 2,000 short, and it is uncertain whether we shall make this up in addition to our increase of 5,000.

WSC

*   *   *   *   *

HMS Enchantress *Log Book*
(*Admiralty Archives*)

EXTRACT

6th Visit

16 January 1912	1.35 *pm*	WSC arrived Chatham.
	2.30 *pm*	WSC inspected Chatham dockyard.
	4.45 *pm*	WSC returned to ship.
17 January 1912		Chatham. WSC inspected RN Barracks *am* and Naval Hospital and RMLI *pm*.
18 January 1912		WSC on board.
19 January 1912	10.35 *am*	WSC left ship.

7th Visit

5 February 1912		Portsmouth. Return of King and Queen in HMS *Medina*.
	9.55 *am*	Board of Admiralty visited HMS *Medina*.
	11.45 *am*	Board of Admiralty left ship.

8th Visit

17 February 1912		WSC and party arrived on board, Portland, afternoon.
18 February 1912		WSC on board. Fourth Sea Lord arrived.
19 February 1912		WSC on board. Transferred to *Rommion* to witness battle practice.
	5.24 *pm*	WSC left ship.

9th Visit

23 March 1912	Evening	Portland. WSC and party arrived.
24 March 1912	*am*	Portland. WSC attended Divine Service in *Neptune*.
25 March 1912		Portland. WSC went on board *Neptune* to witness firing. WSC returned on board, afternoon.
27 March 1912	9.45 *am*	WSC and party left ship, Portland.

10th Visit

3 April 1912	7 *pm*	Portsmouth. WSC and party arrived.
4 April 1912	*am*	Portsmouth. WSC visited submarine Depot.
	1.30 *pm*	WSC visited *Swiftsure*.
	3.8 *pm*	WSC sailed on *Enchantress* to Portland.
5 April 1912	4 *pm*	WSC visited *Active*, Portland.
6 April 1912		Portland. WSC visited *Active am*, returned aboard noon.
7 April 1912	*am*	Portland. WSC visited *Orion*.
	pm	sailed to Torbay.
	6 *pm*	WSC landed at Paignton.
8 April 1912	*am*	WSC sailed from Torbay to Plymouth, visited Plymouth dockyard.
	5 *pm*	Returned on board.
9 April 1912		WSC sailed from Plymouth to Portsmouth.
10 April 1912		Portsmouth. WSC left ship.

11th Visit

20 April 1912	10.50 *am*	Dover. WSC on board ship.
	evening	8 absentees joined ship from Portsmouth.
21 April 1912		WSC sailed Dover to Portsmouth.
	pm	WSC inspected *Victory* and Portsmouth Dockyard.
22 April 1912	2.45 *pm*	WSC disembarked. Portsmouth.

12th Visit

27 April 1912	afternoon	Portsmouth. WSC embarked.
28 April 1912		WSC on board, Portsmouth.
29 April 1912	afternoon	WSC disembarked, Portsmouth.

13th Visit

6 May 1912	4.35 *pm*	WSC embarked, Portsmouth. Sailed to Portland full speed with 4 boilers in use.
7 May 1912	morning	Portland, WSC visited *Orion*.
	afternoon	WSC visited submarine *D.3*.

8 May 1912	morning	Portland, WSC visited *Falmouth*.
	2 *pm*	WSC passed between lines of fleet.
	2.50 *pm*	WSC visited *Orion*.
	8 *pm*	First Lord and party dined with His Majesty.
9 May 1912		WSC visited *Orion* in morning and left ship for London in the afternoon.

14th Visit

10 May 1912	7.30 *pm*	WSC returned, Portland.
11 May 1912		WSC on board, Portland.
12 May 1912	*pm*	WSC visited *Invincible*, Portland.
13 May 1912	morning	WSC visited HMS *Zulu*.
	evening	WSC disembarked.

15th Visit

22 May 1912	6.45 *pm*	Genoa.
		WSC, Second Sea Lord, Prime Minister and party embarked.
	7.40 *pm*	left Genoa for Naples.
23 May 1912		At sea, past Elba.
24 May 1912	At noon	At sea, arrived Naples.
25 May 1912	10.40 *am*	WSC and party landed.
	late afternoon	WSC and party returned.
26 May 1912		At sea, Naples to Syracuse.
	2.10 *pm*	WSC landed.
		returned late afternoon.
27 May 1912		Through straights of Messina.
		At sea.
	11.20 *am*	steamed round Taormina Bay.
28 May 1912		At sea, Syracuse to Malta.
29 May 1912		At sea.
	9.21 *am*	Arrived Malta. WSC visited Governor, morning.
	noon	Governor returned visit.
	afternoon	WSC visited *Egmont*.
30 May 1912		Malta. WSC inspected dockyard.
31 May 1912	morning	WSC on board *Kennet*, to witness firing.
	afternoon	inspected *Duncan*.

1 June 1912	morning	Malta. WSC inspected Garrison.
	11.22 *pm*	Ship sailed for Bizerta.
2 June 1912	4.30 *pm*	arrived Bizerta.
	5.15 *pm*	French Admiral visited ship.
	5.45 *pm*	WSC & Asquith on board French Destroyer and proceeded round Lake Bizerta.
3 June 1912	morning	Bizerta. Asquith but not WSC landed to visit Tunis.
	afternoon	WSC visited *Suffolk.*
4 June 1912		At sea, Bizerta to Gibraltar.
5 June 1912		At sea, Bizerta to Gibraltar.
6 June 1912	*am*	Arrived Gibraltar. WSC inspected Dockyard.
		Night attack on harbour by TBs.
7 June 1912		At sea, Gibraltar to Portsmouth.
	2.18 *am*	Trafalgar.
	noon	Cape Saint Vincent.
	evening	Held concert on board.
8 June 1912		At sea, Gibraltar to Portsmouth.
9 June 1912		At sea, Gibraltar to Portsmouth.
10 June 1912	6.44 *am*	Arrived Portsmouth.
		Asquith left ship before 8 *am.*
		WSC and party left ship before noon.

16th Visit

15 June 1912	afternoon	Portsmouth. WSC and Private Secretary embarked.
16 June 1912	afternoon	WSC visited *Vernon.*
17 June 1912	morning	Portsmouth. WSC on board *Conqueror.*
	late afternoon	WSC left ship.

21
Admiralty 1912 – Part 2

(See Main Volume II Chapter 15)

Prince Louis of Battenberg to WSC

1 July 1912   Admiralty

Dear Mr Churchill,

After lunching with the King yesterday he kept me for a considerable time to discuss 2 questions.

(1) Naval Decorations
(2) The Mediterranean

His remarks as to (1) will keep till we meet. [*Note at bottom of page:* Quite satisfactory on the whole].

On the big question (2) I found HM in complete ignorance of the naval aspect. I think he found my statements fairly unanswerable, after I had at length laid before him all which you had stated in your admirable reply to McK's paper, which it seems the King had read with interest and approval. My chief object in writing now is to suggest that no time should be lost in putting your reply before the King.

It is sad to think that our Sailor King stands on McK's level as a naval strategist!

I shall be up here on Thursday by the night mail from Plymouth. I can therefore meet you at the Admiralty as early as you like – or at your house – (from 9.30 am, on) if you will send a message the evening before to my house (24 Queen's Gate).

I have just sent off my reply re Cruisers to be kept at Queenstown; a good idea, with inherent drawbacks of delay.

In haste

Yours truly
LOUIS BATTENBERG

WSC to the King
(*Royal Archives*)

2 July 1912   [HMS *Enchantress*]

Dictated

Mr Churchill with his humble duty to Your Majesty has the honour to state that he was not aware that the Home Secretary had submitted to Your Majesty a memorandum adversely criticizing the Admiralty dispositions in the Mediterranean & the North Sea. As he now learns from the Second Sea Lord that this somewhat unusual course has been followed, he thinks that Your Majesty might perhaps care to see the other papers in this series, & he encloses two memoranda dealing with the subject.[1] The first was circulated simultaneously with the Home Secretary's paper, & the second in reply to it.

WINSTON S. CHURCHILL

Memorandum by WSC

2 July 1912

Secret

I circulate herewith a translation of the new German Navy Law.

The main feature in the new law is the extraordinary increase in the striking force of ships of all classes, immediately available throughout the year. Whereas formerly we reckoned against 17 battleships, 4 battle cruisers, and 12 small cruisers in the Active Battle Fleet, demobilised to a great extent during the winter months, we must in future prepare against 25, 8, and 18, which are not to be subject to anything like the same degree of temporary demobilisation. Full permanent crews are to be provided for 99 torpedo-boat destroyers out of the total of 144. There is an increase of 244,619*l* on the already large provision of 733,855*l* in this year's Estimates for submarines. Seventy-two of these are to be supplied, of which 54 will be provided with full crews. On the average 6 submarines will be laid down annually. The increases in personnel are also important. Under the previous law, the Germans were working to a total of 86,500[2] in 1920 by annual increments of about 3,500. The new law adds 15,000 officers and men, and raises the total in 1920 to 101,500. This involves an average annual addition to the existing additions of about 1,680. In the three years 1912–14 there is to be a further

[1] See above: WSC's Memoranda of 22 June and 25 June 1912.
[2] Including 8,000 seamen artillery for coast defences.

anticipated addition of 500 per annum. Thus the total additions in personnel to the German Navy in the next three years will be about 5,600 per annum.

The cost of these changes is estimated at about 2 millions a-year after 1913; but the fact that *personnel* is cheaply obtained makes this money go much further than in this country.

2. The new German Fleet will consist of 41 battle-ships, 20 battle cruisers, and 40 small cruisers, besides torpedo-boat destroyers and submarines. This is not on paper a great advance upon the present establishment of 38 battle-ships, 20 battle cruisers, and 38 small cruisers. In fact, however, there is a remarkable expansion. The number of large armoured ships in the Active Battle Fleet will be increased from 21 to 33, or an addition of 12 ships; and the number of large armoured ships in full commission, including those in the Reserve Battle Fleet, immediately available in home waters will be increased from 32 to 38. This new scale of the fleet organised in five battle squadrons, each attended by a battle-cruiser squadron complete with small cruisers and auxiliaries, and attended by flotillas of destroyers and submarines, of which nearly four-fifths will be maintained in full permanent commission, is extremely formidable.

3. The new fleet will in the beginning include about twenty battle-ships and large cruisers of small fighting power. But gradually, as new ships are built, the fighting power of the fleet will rise until it will consist completely of Dreadnoughts and modern cruisers. In April 1914, the first two squadrons will consist entirely of Dreadnoughts, and the third of good ships like the 'Deutschlands' and 'Braunschweigs,' together with five Dreadnought cruisers.

WSC

Note of Draft Arrangement concerted with Lord Kitchener.

2 July 1912

The new arrangements for the naval forces in the Mediterranean in the time of peace will be: –

(a) 2 battle cruisers – preferably 3.

(b) A cruiser squadron of 4 armoured cruisers; 2 to be 'Devonshires,' the other 2 to be of the same class as soon as circumstances permit.

(c) The present smaller vessels on the station (less *Yarmouth*).

(d) The present torpedo craft and submarines stationed at Malta.

The Mediterranean (Fourth) Battle Squadron will be based on Gibraltar, the *Yarmouth* being the attached cruiser. The Squadron will be raised to an ultimate total of 8 ships, as follows: –

The 2 'Lord Nelsons' to join the 4 'Duncans' about January or February 1913

The *Dreadnought* and *Albemarle* towards the end of 1913, as crews become available.

This Squadron will cruise in the Mediterranean as much as possible, but will be available for service elsewhere if seriously required in peace, or in case of war.

The Malta Dockyard to be maintained on its existing scale.

The Submarine Flotilla and, if necessity should arise, the Destroyer Flotilla, at Malta to be increased so as to provide an adequate system of local defence.

A Flotilla of Submarines capable of overseas action, with a battleship of the Royal Sovereign class, manned by a suitable nucleus crew, as a parent ship, to be based on Alexandria. The land defences of the port, erected by the Egyptian Government, to be sufficient to ensure their safety, the Admiralty agreeing to provide the necessary guns and mountings.

Admiral Sir William May to WSC

4 July 1912   Admiralty House
                                    Devonport

Dear Mr Churchill,

Referring to our conversation about the Manoeuvres. I think the main object is to gain experience on points of strategy & tactics and also to exercise & teach the officers of the different units how to combine both for attack & defence, consequently the longer the Manoeuvres last the better these objects are attained.

I should like the Admiral of the Red Fleet to have definite orders that he should if possible avoid the meeting of the Battle Fleets for about a week & his first object should be to weaken the Blue Fleet & especially the Patrolling Force; probably the Admiral of the Red Fleet may be of the same opinion & a private letter from you would have the desired effect.

I will continue to make any suggestions I consider necessary. I have the orders about the Admiralty communicating with me in Code, it will be a great advantage if I can have the movements of Blue Fleet sent to me. I have decided to remain with the Red Fleet.

I am so glad you promoted Fisher [to be Chairman of the Royal Commission on Oil Fuel] & I feel sure you will never regret it.

Believe me, sincerely yours
W. H. MAY

Draft Note of Reply by WSC

The First Lord desires me to thank you for your letter of 4th & to say that after giving your proposals his very careful consideration he has arrived at the conclusion that it will be best not to transfer Sir G. Callaghan.

Memorandum by WSC

6 July 1912

Secret

[Not circulated]

1. In the spring of 1915 Italy will have 5 Dreadnoughts and 6 good pre-Dreadnoughts – total 11; Austria will have 4 Dreadnoughts, 3 Lord Nelsons (Radetzkys), and 3 good pre-Dreadnoughts – total 10. Taking all circumstances into consideration, and after a careful scrutiny of individual ships, it is proposed to match either of these forces with 4 Dreadnoughts, 2 battle-cruisers, and 2 Lord Nelsons – total 8. (I do not refer to minor vessels.) We thus employ the fewest units possible, and substitute quality for numbers. This is tactically sound, and tends to throw the long tails of older, slower, but still powerful vessels which both Austria and Italy possess, into the shade. It is also the only way in which the manning difficulties can be minimised. The policy in the Mediterranean therefore will be to have the fewest possible ships that will give us a fair fighting chance against the next strongest Power, excepting France.

It is not advisable to proclaim in public the one-Power standard for the Mediterranean, because on any mere computation of units, gun-power, tonnage, &c., the British provision of 8 would be found insufficient. We do not want to get nailed up to hard and fast standards in these waters at a time when we are threatened with so much new construction there. It is sufficient to say that the British force of 8 capital units to be provided will be such as to be able to give a good account of itself in 1915 against any single antagonist except France.

2. It is not possible to provide a Battle Squadron worthy of the name for the Mediterranean until the spring of 1915. We could, it is true, send out the two Lord Nelsons at an earlier date, but what good would they be against the forces to which they might be opposed? It is not considered advisable or worth while to send out a Battle Squadron of less than 6 modern ships. Until we can form a regular line of battle against the best ships of the rival Power, it is better to meet superior strength with a force of an entirely different character. The sure way to get beaten is to do exactly what your

enemy does, but not quite so well or quite so strongly. The only chance of the weaker Power lies in striking variations from the systems of its most probable opponents. We shall not be in a position after the next few months are past to confront either Italy or Austria in the Mediterranean with an adequate Battle Squadron until the new one is ready in the spring of 1915. It is proposed, meanwhile, to occupy the Mediterranean with a containing force of battle-cruisers. For this purpose 4 battle-cruisers – *Indomitable, Inflexible, Invincible* and *Indefatigable* – will be based on Malta in April 1913, and 2 of them will go out in November this year. These 4 vessels, steaming at a uniform speed of 25 knots, and mounting together 32—12″ guns on the broadside, will not be comparable to any other force that could be brought against them, cannot be made to fight unless they wish, and can always choose their time for attack. It is proposed, further, to replace 3 ships in the Armoured Cruiser Squadron in the Mediterranean by stronger vessels, so that it will consist of *Shannon, Duke of Edinburgh, Black Prince,* and *Hampshire.* This is as fine a cruiser force as there is in the world, and steams at such a speed that whatever may happen in the Mediterranean, and however unfavourable the combinations, it can take care of itself. These are the best arrangements for maintaining British interests in the Mediterranean that can be devised, pending the formation of the new Battle Squadron.

3. Although this force will be based on Malta, and will in time of peace be constantly in the Mediterranean, we cannot undertake to dispense with its presence in Home waters should a serious situation arise between the spring of 1913 and the spring of 1915.

Our margins in Home waters against Germany will, in April 1914, be only 27 Dreadnoughts (battleships and battle-cruisers) and the 2 Lord Nelsons to 21 Dreadnoughts. This must be regarded as the worst pinch we shall go through, and it is probable that during a large part of 1914 the Mediterranean battle-cruisers will have to be in the neighbourhood of Gibraltar.

4. I now return to the spring of 1915.

It is then proposed to re-form the Mediterranean Battle Squadron as follows: 4 of the best Dreadnought battleships that can use the Malta dock – probably *St Vincent, Superb, Vanguard, Collingwood,* the 2 Lord Nelsons, and 2 battle-cruisers, *Indomitable* and *Inflexible.* (The other two battle-cruisers will come home.) We shall thus have alienated from the British force in Home waters 8 Dreadnought units [as hitherto counted] in addition to the *Australia* – total, 9 Dreadnought units unavailable against Germany.

This, of course, sweeps away the 60 per cent standard. If the existing programmes 4, 5, 4, 4, 4 were carried out, we should have in the spring of 1915 29 Dreadnoughts (battleships and battle-cruisers) to 23 German

Dreadnoughts – a superiority in the decisive theatre of only 6 modern ships and a ratio of only 5 to 4. The minimum number which we ought to have to maintain a 60 per cent basis would be 37 – deficit, 8.

It has always been understood, however, that the 60 per cent. standard against Germany should, within limits which have never hitherto been defined, cover our obligations on foreign stations. For instance, it had been proposed to send out the *New Zealand* and *Indomitable* as well as the *Australia* to the Fleet in the Far East. We have retrieved 2 of these ships, but the special demands of the Mediterranean have created a new situation which is beyond our existing resources or proposed programme to meet.

Taking all circumstances into consideration, and making allowance for the undoubted advantage to the Navy of extra new ships wherever stationed, we should in 1915 possess the following Dreadnought units in Home waters compared to Germany, *viz.*,

34 against 23,

or just under 3 ships to 2. We shall therefore be in 1915 5 ships short. Owing, however, to the greatly increased power of the latter classes of ships, I am prepared to be responsible if only 4 new ships are added, but these 4 must be begun at once, and their first instalment of money must be taken in the Supplementary Estimates.

5. I cannot at present state what the requirements of the Mediterranean for minor vessels will involve in new construction. I am not without hopes of being able to meet them out of existing resources, actual and prospective. We shall require, however, to raise men for 5 small cruisers, 3 extra destroyers, and 9 submarines, approximately 2,000 for this purpose alone.

6. I now turn from the demands of new construction to the Battle Fleet which must be kept ready at short notice in Home waters. It had been proposed to maintain in the spring of 1915 33 battleships and 10 battle-cruisers in full commission. It is now proposed to alienate to the Mediterranean 6 battleships and 2 battle-cruisers, of which 4 battleships are to be replaced by new construction. The number of battleships and battle-cruisers to be maintained in full commission will be increased by 6 to a total of 50.

By certain economies and reductions which have been carried out in the lower classes of ships this requirement has been reduced to approximately 3,000. The total increase in manning is therefore 5,000, of which 2,500 additional must be obtained this year, making a total addition this year to the Navy personnel under the Ordinary, Supplementary, and Mediterranean Estimates of 7,500, besides the 2,000 deficit which we are trying to make up – total, 9,500.

It is, however, doubtful whether we shall succeed in obtaining these men in the year, although every possible method will be employed.

I shall shortly lay before my colleagues the necessary proposals for increasing the pay of the sailors.

WSC

Prince Louis of Battenberg to WSC

10 July 1912

1st Lord.

How would the following formula do – I mean the appendix:
'We intend to keep such a force of ships & vessels of all classes in the Mediterranean, based on Malta, as will be able to give a good account of any reasonably probable hostile force (excepting France), which it may encounter in that sea, and which will ensure our communications through the Mediterranean being kept open at all times.'

Public opinion was more disturbed at the prospect of our trade being held up there, than at the possible fate of Malta. The Prime Minister also told me that his colleagues were chiefly impressed by Repington's Chart of Grain thro' Meditern.

I feel quite happy at our arrangements as I feel certain that we shall in any case profit by the French Command of the Western Basin, which she is bound to ensure for her own ends.

L.B.

Earl Brassey[1] to WSC

8 July 1912
Sunbeam R.Y.S.
Spithead

Dear Mr Churchill,

Having lately spent a week at Kiel and seen much of the chief people I briefly report.

I have come away convinced that building ships to the full limit of our requirements gives no offence. The cry of the pessimists, the discussions and the comparisons are not pleasant to Germany: they fully accept the ships.

I am assured that they have reached the limit of possible expenditure on the Navy. If the Glasgow speech policy is steadily and quietly pursued, the party in Germany opposed to costly rivalry will gain.

---

[1] Thomas Brassey (1836–1918), Civil Lord of Admiralty 1880–4; Secretary to Admiralty 1884–5; President Institute of Naval Architects 1893–5; Governor of Victoria 1895–1900. Founder and first Editor of *Naval Annual*. Knighted 1881; created Baron Brassey 1886; Earl Brassey 1911.

C II—PT. III—H

I should add that Admiral Holtzendorff,[1] commander in chief of the High Sea fleet, is against further increase of dimensions.

The same lesson is impressed at Spithead when we take into view the danger to the large ships from the torpedo and mine in the dark hours.

Yours sincerely
BRASSEY

WSC to his wife
(CSC Papers)

9 July 1912   Spithead

My darling one,

It was good of you to send me your telegram; but I have been feeling your pain & discomfort all day by reflexion. It is so difficult for me to abandon the Canadian Ministers here, that if no serious need arises as I cannot think likely, I shall not come back till tomorrow. I talked to Cassel about you & he said that Anna Jenkins his niece had had exactly the same thing after an operation for curetting. It is not unusual, and she got perfectly right & is now as strong as a horse.

But my darling I am so sorry for you. How I wish you cd have been here. It has all gone off splendidly so far – Glorious weather & all the arrangements for the MPs have given them the greatest satisfaction. They have been treated *en prince* & have thoroughly enjoyed it.

The submarine attack was vy dangerous owing to the traffic & one submarine fouled a little yacht. Luckily she came to the surface all right – but how near a tragedy! The Fleet is just going to weigh & steam off to sea. I have been on the run since 7 o'clock this morning & I am tired out.

Margot has enjoyed herself. She wanted to stay tonight – but I have no room & discouraged her. How she talks – anything & everything that comes into her head slips off her indiscreet tongue. Such views – & such expression of them.

The PM is quite indefatigable & has been on his legs all day. He loves this sort of life & is well suited to it. He would have made a much better Admiral than most I have to get along with. Prince Louis looked vy imposing on his splendid *Thunderer*.

I am coming up in Cassel's special train tomorrow & arrive at a little after 10 tomorrow. Meanwhile Fondest love, & may God give you a quiet & restful life.

Ever your devoted
W

Henning von Holtzendorff (1853–1919), C-in-C High Sea Fleet 1909–12; Chief of Admiralty Staff 1915.

Lord Roberts to WSC

10 July 1912   Englemere
                                                     Ascot
Private

My dear Churchill,

I understand that you shortly are going to make a statement in the House of Commons on the subject of our position in the Mediterranean. The question no doubt is receiving the close attention of His Majesty's Government, but it is one of such overwhelming importance that I cannot help writing to beg of you to do all in your power to remedy what I can only describe as a most dangerous state of affairs.

It is no exaggeration to say that the security of the Empire lies to a great extent in our being able to maintain our position in the Mediterranean and Egypt, and that our present weakness at those points is a direct menace to that security.

Apparently in your opinion and in the opinion of other Naval Authorities it is absolutely necessary that our Fleets should be massed in the North Sea, and in consequence of the military weakness of these islands that opinion is undoubtedly correct. But, should trouble arise in Egypt, or an attack made on that country by Turkey, (which, owing to the unfortunate change in our relations with Turkey, is, I believe not an impossibility) we should be forced to send the greater part of, if not all, our small expeditionary Force to that country; for a hostile power dominating Egypt would mean destruction to our communications with India, and a serious blow to our prestige in that country.

The despatch, however, of our Expeditionary Force to Egypt would not only make us powerless to render any assistance to our friends on the Continent, but the necessity for ensuring the safe convoy of the troops would create precisely that situation in the North Sea which the Admiralty is now planning to avoid. That is to say, a Fleet which is not strong enough to cope with the German Navy, while at the same time this country would be denuded of the only Force which can be trusted to hold its own against highly trained soldiers.

Quite apart from the strategical considerations, the importance of showing that we are determined to maintain unimpaired our position in the Mediterranean and Egypt is an uncalculable advantage from the point of view of India, for were we once to become seriously embroiled with Turkey, a feeling of unrest would certainly spread to the Mahomedans in India, and this would complicate our defensive arrangements to a dangerous extent.

If you could announce that Great Britain is determined without delay, and no matter at what cost, to strengthen her position, naval and militarily, in the Mediterranean, it would be received with feelings of the greatest relief throughout the Empire, and the policy would be supported by all parties who have its safety at heart.

Believe me, Yours sincerely
ROBERTS

WSC to Lord Roberts

12 July 1912 [Admiralty]

[Copy]

My dear Lord Roberts,

There are several important points in your letter with which I am not quite sure that I find myself fully in agreement. The massing of our fleet in home waters does not arise out of the military weakness of these islands solely, but from their dependence on oceanic communication, a dependence wh no military strength could cure. Secondly, the need of being always ready without a mobilisation to meet a hostile attack requires larger margins in peace of ships of the first line than wd perhaps be necessary a fortnight after war had broken out. It does not follow from our present dispositions that considerable forces cd not be detached for service in the Mediterranean or beyond it, once our mobilisation is complete. Surprise, the only chance of the weaker naval power, is our bugbear, & to guard against it, not merely for a few weeks, but year after year indefinitely, is our burden.

It wd be possible under actual and prospective Admiralty arrangements, if it were necessary, to provide a substantial naval force for service in the Eastern Mediterranean; but we shd have to make civil arrangements in this country wh wd amount to a practical mobilisation.

I admit that to maintain a naval war singlehanded with the Triple Alliance, & a great land war for the protection of Egypt against Turkey simultaneously is beyond our powers. The circumstances are formidable but also unlikely. It seems probable however that a decisive naval victory wd open up a series of situations wh wd lead to the capitulation of any force landed in Egypt in the interim.

Many naval authorities think that under modern conditions the Meditn wd become so precarious to commerce, if it were the theatre of a naval war, as to be practically closed. No-one wd care, I think, to send transports laden with troops through it either to Egypt or to India. The only safe routes for the British Empire in time of war are the oceans; & the Cape must ever be regarded as the mainstay of our Indian communications.

I may add that I hope you will not conclude from this that the Govt have any intention of abandoning the Mediterranean.

Yours sincerely

[WINSTON S. CHURCHILL]

Minutes of the Committee of Imperial Defence: 118th meeting

EXTRACT

11 July 1912

MR ASQUITH: Perhaps it will be convenient, as Sir Edward Grey has dealt with that aspect of the general question, that Mr Churchill should now speak to it from the naval point of view.

MR CHURCHILL: The main factor in the naval situation is, of course, the growth and the development of the German navy, and it is necessary that I should say a word or two on that. For fifteen years Admiral von Tirpitz has been the Minister of Marine, and during the whole of that period one ruling idea has been perseveringly and unswervingly pursued step by step to a conclusion which clearly has not yet been reached. I should like to read to the Committee two passages from the German Fleet Law of 1900, which was the great Fleet Law which superseded the Fleet Law of 1897, and which laid out the full scope and extent of the great proportion of the German fleet as it was intended to produce it. In this law the Germans, with great frankness, simplicity, and candour, state exactly the purposes and intentions with which their navy is in existence; and there are two passages in it which are so significant and so revealing that I must read them. The first passage refers to the Law of 1897, and it says that in that law, the Fleet Law of 1897, it is expressly stated that, as against the more important naval Powers, the battle fleet has solely the significance of a fleet for surprise attack; and that Memorandum goes on to explain that the 1900 Law was intended to open wider possibilities, besides that of a surprise attack, to the German battle fleet, and this very significant sentence occurs: –

'In order to protect German trade and commerce under existing conditions only one thing will suffice, namely, Germany must possess a battle fleet of such a strength that even for the most powerful naval adversary a war would involve such risks as to make that Power's own supremacy doubtful. For this purpose it is not absolutely necessary that the German fleet should be as strong as that of the greatest naval Power, for, as a rule, a great naval Power will not be in a position to concentrate all its forces against us.'

We see nothing that has happened in the twelve years that have followed those words to lead us to think that the main central idea of the development of the German navy expressed in these premises has been in any way departed from. The Law of 1900 made a great increase in the Law of 1897, but the Law of 1900 did not long remain unamended. In 1906 a further considerable increase was made – an increase which took the form of replacing very small old ships, which were called battleships and cruisers, but which were old and weak, by the very best modern types of ships. This of course enormously increased the value and strength of the German fleet and the defence of the Germans without in any way affecting the total number.

MR BORDEN[1]: Did the Law of 1900 lay down a programme for a period of years?

MR CHURCHILL: Yes.

MR BORDEN: For how long?

MR CHURCHILL: The Law of 1900 covered the period up to 1920, so it laid down a twenty years' programme. This law has been repeatedly modified by subsequent amendments, some of them not appearing in form to be very large, but all of them making the original scope of the law much larger and the strength of the fleet much greater.

MR ASQUITH: I think 1920 is still the nominal term?

MR CHURCHILL: Yes, it is. I should like to point out – and it is due to ourselves to point out – that these repeated increases occurred quite irrespective of what we had done ourselves; in fact the most notable increase, that of 1906, occurred at a period when we deliberately decided to try and set an example of checking naval competition, not merely by making speeches about it, but by deliberately restricting our programme in that year. We reduced our naval construction of great battleships in that year, and in the year after; I think we built only three or four in the two years put together, and we did our very best to effect a slackening in this ruinous competition. That was followed immediately by increases of a very marked character on the part of the Germans, and not only did they increase their programme of capital ships, but even the small ones. Up to 1906 they only built six destroyers a year, but from 1906 on they built twelve. Therefore, it is quite clear that their progress and development has been independent of any decreases which we may have from time to time tried to make.

The ultimate scale of the German fleet is of the most formidable character.

[1] Robert Laird Borden (1854–1937), Prime Minister of Canada 1911–20; responsible for the offer of three Dreadnoughts to the United Kingdom; invited in 1915 to attend meetings of the British War Cabinet. One of Canada's representatives at Versailles; knighted 1914.

Sir Edward Grey has just spoken about the two-Power standard. Of course, in the choice of the two-Power standard we were considering the potential combination of two Powers of an approximately equal naval strength, or something like equal naval strength. Such a combination is vitiated by all the weaknesses which attach to coalitions, to alliances at sea, and to combined fleets serving under different flags. With regard to Germany we have to face a steady, remorseless development year by year of an immense naval force, created with the very latest science and all the efficiency of one of the most efficient peoples in the world, concentrated and kept concentrated within easy striking distance of our shores.

Of course it is quite true that according to the German Navy Law, as a great many German speakers on the subject have always said, the German fleet does not exist in order to be a menace to the British fleet, and it does not contemplate anything of that character – it only exists for the protection of German trade and of German Colonies. We are speaking here without the reserves which are necessary in public utterance, and I am bound to say, speaking on behalf of the Admiralty, that we find it very difficult to reconcile such statements with truth – very difficult indeed. The whole character of the German fleet shows that it is designed for aggressive and offensive action of the largest possible character in the North Sea or the North Atlantic – action, according to the Memorandum accompanying their first Bill, against the strongest naval Power at some moment when that Power will not be able, owing to some duty which it may have to discharge to its Colonies or to some other part of the Empire, to keep all its forces concentrated to meet the blow. The structure of the German battleships shows clearly that they are intended for attack and for fleet action. They are not a cruiser fleet designed to protect Colonies and commerce all over the world. They have been preparing for years, and are continuing to prepare, on an ever larger scale a fleet which, from its structure and character, can be proved by naval experts to have the central and supreme object of drawing out a line of battle for a great trial of strength in the North Sea or in the ocean. I will not go into technical details, but the position of the guns, the armament, the way the torpedo tubes are placed – all these things enable naval experts to say that this idea of sudden and aggressive action on the greatest scale against a great modern naval Power, is undoubtedly the guiding principle of German naval policy. When you go to the smaller types of vessels, the same principle can be traced. In their torpedo boat destroyers, which they call torpedo boats, speed has been the principle essentially that they have gone upon, and that they have developed. We on our part have developed gun power and strength to a greater extent, because our destroyers would play the more defensive rôle of protecting our battle fleet against the attack of the enemy's destroyers. Their torpedo boats are undoubtedly designed with a view to developing an attack upon the great ships of the navy that they may be opposed to, whereas ours have in view the object of destroying the torpedo craft of the enemy which would be trying to make an attack. That again is a very significant fact. Now we come to the submarine. If there ever was a vessel in the world whose services to the defensive will be great, and which is a characteristic weapon for the defence, it is the submarine. But the German development of that vessel, from all the information we can obtain, shows that it is intended to turn even this weapon of defence into one of offence, that is to say, they are building not the smaller classes which will be useful for the defence of their somewhat limited coast-line, but the large classes which would be capable of sudden operation at a great distance from their base across the sea. So I think I am justified in saying that the German fleet, whatever may be said about it, exists for the purpose of fighting a great battle in the North Sea, both with battleships and with all ancillary vessels, against some other great naval Power which is not referred to by them.

We are sometimes told that the Germans only think of fighting a battle which will leave that greater naval Power seriously weakened after the battle is over; they will have been destroyed themselves and the greater naval Power will be weakened. I do not think anyone who respects the German nation and knows to how high a degree they carry their study of the military art on sea and on land will be much impressed by that. Anything more foolish than to spend all these millions year after year and to make all these efforts and sacrifices and exertions for no other purpose than certainly to come off second best on the day of trial cannot well be imagined; and I think it is useless and foolish to shut one's eyes to the fact that whatever may be the intention of the German Government, and whatever may be the intention of the German people, which is quite a different thing, the spirit and purpose of the inception and of the prolonged development of the German navy is such as to lead only to one conclusion, and that is that it is intended for a great trial of strength with the navy of the greatest naval Power.

I was going to say, but of course that is a matter for the Foreign Office, that we have no quarrel with Germany. There are questions on small points of foreign policy, but there is no quarrel at all, and everybody has done their best to avoid anything which increases antagonism and so forth. But the fact remains, and it cannot be doubted, that if the British navy were out of the way, either beaten in battle or in some other way had disappeared as a factor, a far wider prospect and a far more brilliant prospect would be opened to German action in any quarter of the world, if, of course, it has any such ambition.

I do not pretend to make any suggestion that the Germans would deliver any surprise or sudden attack upon us. It is not for us to assume that another great nation will fall markedly below the standard of civilisation which we ourselves should be bound by; but we at the Admiralty have got to see, not that they will not do it, but that they cannot do it. That is the view we take of the duties which are placed upon us, and I should like to tell the Committee that that involves a very great strain indeed. The advantages of the initiative are self-evident. I have spoken in public about the contrast between the average moment of one Power and the selected moment of another. That makes a great difference; it may make as much as 20 to 25 per cent. difference in the number of ships that can be brought immediately into the line. There is this great distinction which should be drawn between naval war and land war. On the continent of Europe you have great armies living side by side across a purely political frontier, but there is a cushion, a pad, which is a great buffer between them and the actual development of great operations of war, that is, mobilisation. The whole male population has to be withdrawn from its ordinary employment, the whole life of the country has to be suspended, and a vast operation of mobilisation has to be begun, the very first signs of which would be immediately apparent to the other country, before anything of a decisive or critical character could take place. No such security stands in the way of a sea operation. The ships which were assembled the other day at Spithead, or which are now assembled at Kiel and at Wilhelmshaven, can begin fighting as soon as they bring the ammunition up from below to the gun, and absolutely no preliminary steps need be taken which would be noticeable by any foreign Power, however great the vigilance might be. That being so, I say that there is a great deal of truth in the statement which was made last night in the House of Commons by Mr Bonar Law, when he said that this great concentrated fleet, ever growing in efficiency and strength, within twelve or fourteen hours' steam of our shores, was almost a loaded cannon continually pointed at us. Of course they may say that our fleet is similarly pointed at them, but nothing that we can do on the sea can menace the freedom or security of Germany, nothing that we can do on the sea can make any difference to that which makes life worth living for them. For us the matter is very different. Any serious misfortune which happened to us at sea would produce immediately the ruin of the greatness of this country, and the disruption of the many parts of the Empire now united to us.

We have at present, I was going to say, two safety signals which we watch very carefully – I hope I am not doing wrong in speaking quite plainly about these things. First of all, we see that in the winter the German fleet is largely demobilised, owing to the fact that they are full up with their recruits; consequently, in the winter the strain is relaxed, we are able to send our fleet away to refresh itself on the coast of Spain, and, generally speaking, we get repairs done on a larger scale when the strain is abated. Another indication which we have of security is when we see some of their great vessels of the newer type, the *Oldenburg*, the *Moltke*, or the *Von der Tann*, on the Baltic side of the Kiel Canal, because they cannot come through the canal at present, and we know that if any great enterprise were on foot it would be very unlikely that units of the greatest consequence would be left on the wrong side of the canal, whence they would have to make a great detour to come round. Unfortunately both these safety signals are going to be extinguished in the immediate future; the deepening of the Kiel Canal, which is to be accomplished in two years' time, will enable the greatest vessels to pàss through it in the same way as other vessels can now pass through. In addition, as regards the immunity which so far we have enjoyed in the winter, that too will be destroyed by the development of the new German Navy Law, to which, with the permission of the Committee, I will now come. Until we saw the new Navy Law, we thought that its intention would be to develop the building on a large scale, but when we got it and began to study it, we saw that it was not so much the building on a large scale that was its feature, although there was considerable building, but that it was the development of an immediate striking power that they were aiming at. The effect of the law is to put slightly less than four-fifths of their fleet permanently into full commission, that is to say, in the category of ships instantly ready for action, with no reserves needed, no mobilisation required, nothing lacking. A great development of personnel is also a characteristic of the new law. They are training the men and the officers and the ratings which will be required for the development of their navy in the future. For the present, a good many of the ships which they will keep in commission will not be very good ships, but the crews on them will be trained and will be worked up for the period when, at some further step forward in their naval evolution, new vessels can be provided with crews already trained for the work.

I say that the aspect of that fleet as it will be in the near future, to say nothing of what it will be when the law is worked out in 1920, is extremely formidable. It will consist of forty-one battleships, which will ultimately all be Dreadnought battleships, twenty large battle-cruisers, and forty small cruisers, besides torpedo-boat destroyers and submarines, a fleet quite as large as there was at Spithead two days ago, and much more formidable when, ultimately, all its units will consist exclusively of the best ships. In April 1914 its development will have reached this point – they will have two complete squadrons of modern Dreadnoughts, a third squadron consisting of very good ships of the 'Deutschland' and the 'Braunschweig' type, all of which will be in full continuous commission, that is to say, ready to start at any moment. The Ambassador may go to the Foreign Minister and raise some question, the reply to which they may consider unsatisfactory, and the destroyers, which are the heralds of attack of the fleet, can start almost immediately. In addition to that, they will have behind these three battle squadrons two squadrons of reserves which, indeed, it may take some time to mobilise, but which will contain four large ships having on board sufficient active service men to enable them to proceed at once wherever required, without any order being given which would be at all noticeable outside the naval barrack gates or the dockyards of Germany.

MR BORDEN: You spoke of Germany having four-fifths of her ships in full commission, which she could at once employ if an attack was designed. What is to be our standard?

MR CHURCHILL: Hitherto, until the passing of this law, we have maintained in the waters of the United Kingdom sixteen fully-commissioned battleships; we had six more at Gibraltar, making twenty-two, and six more in the Mediterranean, making twenty-eight. The Mediterranean battleships are nine and a-half days distant from this country with another day for coaling, and the Gibraltar ships are three to four days distant with another day for coaling; so we only had in Home waters sixteen ships at the time the Germans passed their law which will give them in the course of next year twenty-five ships in full commission. To meet that emergency we have had to take special measures to increase the number of ships which we keep in full commission in Home waters, and to make a greater concentration of the fleet than has hitherto been thought necessary. We consider that we ought to have thirty-three battleships immediately ready, that is, four squadrons to their twenty-five battleships in three squadrons. Our ships also will have a certain superiority over theirs, because we are still leading the world in naval construction. We consider that is a sufficient margin for the first shock of war when it comes, and after the first shock we hope to be in a much better position for any further developments, because then we could mobilise a large number of vessels which, although not good enough to face the newest battleships, would be very serviceable ships indeed once the newest vessels had been disabled or destroyed in the course of the preliminary battles. So, as our standard of strength of ships in commission against their twenty-five, we propose to have thirty-three in full commission and eight more in a very advanced state in reserve.

MR BORDEN: Does that number, thirty-three, accord with your present standard for your constructional programme?

MR CHURCHILL: I am dealing not with the new vessels we are building, but with vessels which, having been built, are to be maintained in the highest condition of readiness.

MR BORDEN: Then you are not dealing at all with future construction?

MR CHURCHILL: No; I am coming to construction in a minute.

Now, to conclude my argument, I turn from this problem of the North Sea – if I am not detaining the Committee too long – to the Mediterranean. In 1909 Austria began to build Dreadnoughts in the Mediterranean. It was a very unexpected step for her to take, because she was not menaced in any way from the sea, and she had no oversea possessions to guard. Nobody contemplated making an attack upon Austria by sea, and she was not in any danger when she started to build these four ships. Two of them were begun secretly as a speculation by the contractors in the yards – evidently on a hint by the Government – and they were afterwards taken over by the Government when the money was finally voted by the Austrian Delegation. Of course, I go outside my province in speaking of foreign affairs, but the Admiralty view is that Austria was instigated to build these ships by Germany, and that she built them as a return service to Germany for having helped her over Bosnia and Herzegovina. Whether there is any truth in that I do not know, but that is the Admiralty view as to the cause of it. At any rate, there are the ships, and a more sinister stroke was never devised, because the consequences of these ships being built is to provoke building on the part of Italy on a similarly large scale. Although Italy and Austria are very much opposed from the point of view of policy, yet they are in alliance. Nothing but the fear of Austria forced Italy to join the alliance, and one never can be certain that at the vital moment the terror which forced Italy to join the alliance may not operate to force her to make good the pact which she has signed. These two Powers mutually and reciprocally provoking each other – both being potential factors with which we have to deal – make a most difficult and unsatisfactory position in the Mediterranean. There are rumours – and information, which we believe to be authentic, has been received by the Admiralty to the like effect – that the Austrians are now proposing to build another four battleships in the Mediterranean, though how long they will take to build them, or when the actual laying of the keels will begin, is not yet known. I only say that information has been given to us, both from private and from official sources. If this be a fact, that, of course, will add to the difficulties there.

MR ASQUITH: Perhaps you had better tell the Committee when the first of the Austrian ships will be ready.

MR CHURCHILL: The first Italian Dreadnought will, it is stated, be ready in July 1912.

MR ASQUITH: That is this month.

MR CHURCHILL: Yes; the second and third in April 1913, the fourth in October 1913, and the fifth and sixth in January 1915; but we are rather doubtful whether the last of them will be ready as quickly as that. The first Austrian Dreadnought will be ready in October of this year, the second in April 1913, the third in April 1914, and the fourth in January 1915. That is quite apart from any further building programme which may be developed.

MR ASQUITH: It might be interesting to some of the Committee to state what is the extent of the Austrian sea-coast – it is 300 miles. That is the total extent of the Austrian sea-coast, and they have no oversea possessions of any kind.

MR CHURCHILL: The Government considered very carefully what position they should take up in view of these developments, and after a very long consultation at Malta, and also in the Cabinet and in the Committee of Imperial Defence, the conclusion which the Cabinet have arrived at is that, in the face of these difficulties, we cannot recede from our position as a great Mediterranean naval Power, and that we must maintain our position there, relying on our diplomacy no doubt, but also on our own navy, and that, without being drawn into entanglements or complications which might prejudice our freedom of action in other parts of the world, we must be capable by our own strength of affording proper protection to those interests which have grown up over so many years in the Mediterranean. That has led to the Admiralty being directed to supply a force for the Mediterranean.

In all these naval matters you have to look three years ahead. The battle which will decide the fate of a naval war will probably have been prejudged at least three years earlier by the building and training of the men and the arrangements that have been made. It is no good when the crisis has actually arisen to turn round and ask for ships, because they cannot be created under from two and a-half to three years, and there may be delays. So we are now looking forward to the year 1915. We propose to make arrangements in the interval for holding the Mediterranean – military arrangements and naval arrangements which I think will be satisfactory, but which do not affect the immediate point that I am on. It is intended that in the year 1915 we should be able to put a battle squadron into the Mediterranean strong enough to give a good account of itself if brought into contact with any other Power except France. That means, so far as we can estimate these things, that we must then have eight good Dreadnought ships, either cruisers or battleships, available there.

MR BORDEN: In 1915?

MR CHURCHILL: Yes; we cannot do it before that. Meanwhile, we shall make an entirely different disposition, which will safeguard our interests sufficiently, but which will not give us a strong battle squadron there. We shall not be able to develop a strong battle squadron there till 1915, if we begin now, which we propose to do.

MR ASQUITH: But the programme of neither of these Powers will be completed till then.

MR CHURCHILL: That is so; they gradually mature to their strength then. We consider that if we are able to find eight Dreadnought units then for the Mediterranean we shall have a force which either of them would respect.

MR BORDEN: I do not want to interrupt your line of argument, but I would like to understand at some time just what the situation is now in view of the recent action, and what it is likely to be between this date and 1915.

MR CHURCHILL: We are not in a position between now and 1915 to put a satisfactory battle squadron of new ships there, that is, of ships good enough to meet the new ships that are coming. We want them at home. But if we take steps now we shall be able to put such a squadron there in 1915, that is, by the time the Austrian development is completed. In the interval, and whilst their development is proceeding, we propose to hold the Mediterranean with a force of those very large, very strong battle-cruisers which are a different kind of force altogether from any that will be found in the Mediterranean. They are units of the greatest value and strength, whose speed is so great that they need never fight unless they choose, and can always fight whenever they wish. We think this method of confronting an enemy's battle fleet by a cruiser force of the greatest strength is the best substitute for a stronger line of battle, and a far better force to have than a line of battle which is weaker than the enemy. The sure way of obtaining a defeat is to have exactly the same thing as your enemy, but not quite so good or in such large numbers. If you are not in a position to prevail by simple strength the best plan is to make an original variation from the system of your probable antagonist. That is what we propose to do in the meanwhile, and of course to develop our destroyers and submarines, so as to make good the defence both of Egypt and of Malta.

MR PELLETIER:[1] Meanwhile the French fleet has been concentrated in the Mediterranean.

MR CHURCHILL: The French fleet, of course, will be strong in the Mediterranean, and they are making efforts to increase it.

If we are to provide eight units in 1915 for the Mediterranean, we have

[1] Louis Philippe Pelletier (1857–1921), Attorney-General of Quebec 1906; Canadian Postmaster-General 1911–14. He was one of four Canadian ministers who accompanied Borden to the meeting of 11 July.

got to see what will be left at home. The Admiralty consider that we ought to have at home three Dreadnought ships to every two which the Germans have. That is perhaps not a very large margin, but then we must take into consideration the fact that we have one other good strong squadron of ships built before the Dreadnought era, and that in the second line we are at present much stronger. We think we should aim at producing three ships to two in the Home waters for the purposes, if necessary, of a fleet action against Germany. I do not say that we may not now and again be one or two ships more than that, or now and again one or two ships less than that, because we cannot quite tell how the ships finish up their building – there may be delays and so forth on each side of the water. But that is the principle which we are following – to maintain in Home waters three ships to two. In order to do that we are building four ships this year, five the next, and four in each of the four years after that, as against the German construction of two this year, three the next, then two, two, three, and two in the sixth year. That is the arrangement which we are making now.

MR ASQUITH: That concludes the term of construction under the new Navy Law.

MR CHURCHILL: That makes provision for laying down two ships for every extra ship they build above their Navy Law, and as their new law builds next year one ship above the two which they have always said was all they intended to build, we shall lay down two ships. That is the answer to that. Out of these vessels which are being constructed we shall maintain, and we ought to maintain and we are seeking to maintain, three ships to two in Home waters, irrespective of our foreign obligations.

I am sorry to say that that leaves us with a deficit on the numbers we shall have actually available when we have deducted the ships for the Mediterranean station. If we send out now four battle-cruisers and keep them out there until June 1915 – I need not say how very secret these observations are – we shall be approximately two ships short until 1914, and then we shall be one ship short. I think, taking it all round, we must put up with that for the time being; but when the eight ships go out that we intend to send out in June or in December 1915 we shall be three or four ships short – it depends on how some of the ships finish up – and we shall continue to be four ships short for the next few years, because, although eight ships in the Mediterranean will be sufficient in 1915, we should probably want ten there in 1916 or 1917. That is a fair assumption.

MR ASQUITH: You mean, if the Austrian and Italian naval programmes are fully developed?

MR CHURCHILL: Yes. At any rate, looking forward to the sequence of years, 1915-16-17-18, if we detach eight ships as we shall have to do to

maintain our position in the Mediterranean and to prevent a hostile combination there, we shall be three to four ships short of our proper quota here.
The ships we want to maintain in Home waters would be these: When
Germany has ten battleships and three battle-cruisers, we want to have
fifteen battleships and five battle-cruisers; when she has sixteen battleships
and five battle-cruisers, we want to have twenty-four battleships and eight
battle-cruisers; when she has nineteen battleships, which she will have in
June 1916, and seven battle-cruisers, we ought to have twenty-eight battleships and ten battle-cruisers; and when in June 1917 she has twenty battleships and eight battle-cruisers, we ought to have thirty battleships and twelve
battle-cruisers. We shall be obliged to do that and to maintain that, and yet
at the same time to provide a force for the Mediterranean, but the fact is
that we shall be during those years three to four ships short.

MR BORDEN: Is the entire German naval force concentrated in Home
waters?

MR CHURCHILL: The whole German naval force is always concentrated
there, except that they sometimes send a ship or two on a visit of ceremony.
It is always concentrated in Home waters, and that is the problem, that is
the essence of our difficulty.

MR ASQUITH: They have not got anywhere else to go to.

MR CHURCHILL: Whatever happens we shall do what is necessary to
maintain our naval position, but I am entitled to refer to the very heavy
burden which the Naval Estimates throw upon the people of this country.
The House of Commons have never refused to supply all the money that is
required for the navy, and never will, but the strain is a very heavy one.
Our Annual Estimates, which a few years ago were in the 30's, have jumped
up 12 millions in the last few years, and they stand to-day at 45 millions
sterling. We have had to make great efforts not to be overtaken. My predecessor, the present Home Secretary, took very energetic action two years
ago, and thanks to that we are getting a great crop of fine new ships coming
in just at the time they are wanted. The Estimates, which are 45,000,000*l*
to-day, will go up considerably next year; I cannot say how much because
the Chancellor of the Exchequer is here, and I should not like to give him
a shock for which I have not properly prepared him, but certainly they will
go up very considerably next year. It comes to this, that really we ought to
lay down now three more ships over and above the four we are building.
Of course, there is a great advantage in laying down new ships, because you
are able to have the best that naval science can give up to the moment, and
there is no doubt that we should be able to spare a rather larger number
of ships for the Mediterranean in consideration of the three extra which we
laid down now. But it is a difficult thing for us to lay down three new ships

now. Financially it is inconvenient, but that can be got over. Beyond that, it is a difficult thing for us to do it, because here are our numbers – four, five, four, four, four, which we have collated, and which we have made correspond to the German construction. If we come forward now all of a sudden and add three new ships, that may have the effect of stimulating the naval competition once more, and they would ask us what new factor had occurred which justified or which required this increase of building on our part. If we could say that the new fact was that Canada had decided to take part in the defence of the British Empire, that would be an answer which would involve no invidious comparisons, and which would absolve us from going into detailed calculations as to the number of Austrian or German vessels available at any particular moment. It would be an answer absolutely inoffensive to any of the Great Powers of Europe, and no answer could possibly contribute more effectively to the prestige and the security of the British Empire. The need, I say, is a serious one, and it is an immediate need. I hope during the visit of the Canadian Ministers to this country that we shall have long consultations upon the details of a permanent naval policy, but it has not been to a permanent naval policy that I have directed the remarks which I have offered to the Committee this morning. I do not think that a permanent naval policy ought to be decided in a hurry. If it is to be a permanent line of policy, it will require very long and careful consideration. There are many matters in connection with it which ought not to be hurried in any way, and which ought to be considered with great care. But the other need is urgent, and if it is the intention of Canada to render assistance to the naval forces of the British Empire, now is the time when that aid would be most welcome and most timely. That is all I have to say.

MR PELLETIER: Is there any indication that Germany will increase her naval forces and her coaling stations abroad in order to carry out the assumption that she is only protecting her colonies?

MR CHURCHILL: No, there is not. As a matter of fact, the Admiralty would not view with deep concern the development by Germany of oversea possessions. On the contrary, if they were acquired in a fair manner without trampling upon weaker Powers, we should be rather glad to see what is now concentrated dissipated. New oversea possessions are, to some extent, a hostage to the stronger naval Power, and might easily relieve the tension. It is no part, if I understand him aright, of Sir Edward Grey's policy to stand in the way of Germany acquiring legitimate possessions abroad. On the contrary, it would really relieve the naval situation.

SIR EDWARD GREY: We have been endeavouring to make that clear.

MR ASQUITH: We are not what they call 'keeping her out of her place in the sun'; on the contrary. . . .

Sir Frederick Milner to WSC

11 July 1912   91 Lancaster Gate

Dear Winston Churchill,

I was looking through some old letters, & came upon one from you written at the time you brought out your Father's life. In it you say you look upon me as one of the best of your Father's Friends, & that though you feared I could not approve of the step you had taken, you hoped to retain my respect, & would value any expression of my opinion. I think in some ways I was able to show my Friendship for your Father, & certainly he had no Friend more devoted to him, or who has more sincerely cherished his memory. For that reason alone I have always followed your career sympathetically, & have wished much I could have been a Friend to you too, but my hopeless inferiority, which your dear Father helped me so much to bear by his encouragement, makes me dread so being a bore, that I lead a very lonely life & see less & less of my Friends as times goes on. I have found too that there is little room for cripples in the life of rush & gaiety that is lived now.

For some time after you joined the Radicals, I confess I could follow you with no sympathy. The violence & bitterness of your language, and your extreme views against your own class filled me with sorrow and dismay. I could not help contrasting your conduct with Randolph's after he gave up office, and it was almost impossible to believe that you could so suddenly and completely have changed all your opinions, which you had so vigorously advocated but a short time before.

From the first I always recognised your great abilities; and I remember well imploring Arthur Balfour to try & conciliate you, as I considered you the greatest asset in our Party, but it seemed to me you were prostituting these abilities on the sordid altar of Party.

Gradually however your speeches became less bitter & more statesmanlike. At the Home Office I thought you did really useful work (though the episode of the 'Old Shepherd!' was perhaps unfortunate). Since your appointment to the Admiralty you have done admirable work, and have gained my respect and esteem. You have the opportunity of your life now. The future welfare of your country lies in your hands, and I believe you will rise to the position. I am now able to watch your career with sympathy and deep interest. You have a difficult job, and many diverse interests to satisfy, but you have abilities second to none, & I only hope your health may stand the strain, for it will be a severe one. I was in the *Sunbeam* for the Review, & was greatly impressed by all I saw. I hope you wont mind my writing to you, as for your dear Father's sake I shall always feel deeply interested in your welfare.

Yours ever
FRED MILNER

WSC to David Lloyd George

12 July 1912   [Admiralty]

Confidential

Not circulated

My dear Chancellor of the Exchequer,
   MY first forecast (20th January, 1912) was: –

1912–13	1913–14	1914–15	1915–16	1916–17
£ 43,885,400	£ 43,068,000	£ 42,429,000	£ 42,250,000	£ 42,676,000

To this was added Rosyth, &c –

975,000	1,124,000	938,000	860,000	396,000
Total 44,860,400	44,192,000	43,367,000	43,110,000	43,072,000

I expected relief of under-spendings as follows: –

1912–13	1913–14	1914–15	1915–16	1916–17
£ 700,000	£ 100,000	£ ..	£ ..	£ ..

all I got was

300,000	..	..	..	..

and 1,400,000*l* was expected to be surrendered to the Exchequer.
   We did not want our Estimates to go up before the German Navy Law was settled, so no money was taken for the odd 400,000*l* (which we had

planned to advance to the Thames Company). We further reduced the provision for new construction under Vote 8 by 595,000*l** – a net reduction, after allowing for a small adjustment, of 975,000*l*. The consequence of these changes was, without increasing expenditure, to carry forward 950,000*l*.

Between the times when the Estimates were settled and the end of the financial year the coal strike caused a further under-spending of 592,000*l*, which increases the surrender to 2,000,000*l*. The whole of this further under-spending of 592,000*l* is passed on to 1913–14. The added burden on 1913–14 through under-spendings and under-budgettings therefore amounts to 1,542,000*l*. The same causes operate to throw an additional burden of 238,000*l* on 1914–15. Some slight reduction has been made in the figures for later years, and my revised forecast becomes as follows: –

1912–13	1913–14	1914–15	1915–16	1916–17
£ 44,065,400	£ 45,734,000	£ 43,585,000	£ 43,090,000	£ 43,062,000

Up to this point it is a mere change of accounting, and the apparent increase does not arise from any new projects or expense.

The adoption by Germany, Japan, and the United States of America of heavier guns than ours has forced us to advance also. This adds the following sums to the forecast: –

1913–14	1914–15	1915–16	1916–17
£ 321,000	£ 297,000	£ 291,000	£ 292,000

The adoption of the scheme for an Immediate Reserve added 20,000*l* to 1912–13, and will require 74,000*l* per annum in subsequent years.

Various increases in the rates of wages of dockyard workmen make it necessary to add 35,000*l* per annum to the Estimates.

My totals for the main Estimates therefore become: –

1912–13	1913–14	1914–15	1915–16	1916–17
£ 44,085,400	£ 46,164,000	£ 43,991,000	£ 43,490,000	£ 43,463,000

* 200,000*l* less was also taken under Vote 9, but this is going to be made good by the coming Supplementary Estimate, and does not therefore affect the account.

The difference between this and the original figure of 1913–14 is accounted for by the 1,542,000*l* underspendings and under-budgettings, the 321,000*l* through heavier guns, 74,000*l* for the Immediate Reserve, and 35,000*l* for dockyard wages.

New German Navy Law

Now I come to the additional expenditure consequent upon the new German Navy Law, which is calculated as follows: –

1912–13	1913–14	1914–15	1915–16	1916–17
£	£	£	£	£
(say) 1,000,000	1,543,000	4,112,000	3,635,000	3,293,000

yielding totals approximately as follows: –

1912–13	1913–14	1914–15	1915–16	1916–17
45,085,400	47,707,000	48,103,000	47,125,000	46,756,000

Add (say) 700,000*l* per annum for improved pay and 500,000*l* per annum which will be needed to build up the oil reserve (apart from annual consumption), and my final forecast to date is: –

1912–13	1913–14	1914–15	1915–16	1916–17
£	£	£	£	£
45,085,000	48,907,000	49,303,000	48,325,000	47,956,000

These final totals compare with the original totals, main and supplementary together, which I gave to the Cabinet in February as follows: –

See Appendix (B) (red figures)

———	1912–13	1913–14	1914–15	1915–16	1916–17
	£	£	£	£	£
Present figures ..	45,085,400	48,907,000	49,303,000	48,325,000	47,956,000
February figures .. (including Rosyth)	45,160,000	45,445,000	47,151,000	46,531,000	46,278,000
Increase or Decrease	74,600	3,462,000	2,152,000	1,794,000	1,678,000

This may be checked backward as follows: –

——	February figures	Add Rosyth	Total	Present figures	Increase or Decrease
	£	£	£	£	£
1912–13	44,185,000	975,000	45,160,000	45,085,400	74,600
1913–14	44,321,000	1,124,000	45,445,000	48,907,000	3,462,000
1914–15	46,213,000	938,000	47,151,000	49,303,000	2,152,000
1915–16	45,671,000	860,000	46,531,000	48,325,000	1,794,000
1916–17	45,882,000	396,000	46,278,000	47,956,000	1,678,000
Total ..	226,272,000	4,293,000	230,565,000	239,576,400	9,011,400

The increase is explainable as follows: –

	£
Improved pay to men of the Fleet (4 years at 700,000*l*) ..	2,800,000
Oil Fuel Reserve (4 years at 500,000*l*)	2,000,000
Submarines (4 years at 330,000*l* + 1 year at 161,000*l*) ..	1,481,000
Air Craft (4 years at 50,000*l* + 1 year at 60,000*l*)	260,000
Dockyard wages (5 years at 35,000*l*)	175,000
Increase in cost of Capital Ships, including Armament ..	1,201,000
Under-spending in 1911–12	1,185,000
Increase in cost of Pay and Victualling – additional numbers ..	45,000
Repair Ship and Depôt Ship – 1912–13 and 1913–14	319,000
	9,466,000

Abate –

	£	
Over-provided for Immediate Reserve in February Sketch (4 years at 26,000*l*)	104,000	
Reduction in cost of maintenance of additional squadrons	351,000	
		455,000
		9,011,000

The apportionment between the years can be varied within considerable limits to suit your convenience, though the only result of under-budgetting is to inflate succeeding years.

If no adjustments of this kind are made, the figures present a fairly level sequence. You could subject the whole four years to a common financial treatment. Any provision which meets the first year can be made to cover the others. I think you should lighten your burden effectually by providing out of existing taxation no more than this year's original total, viz., 44,000,000*l*, which was above the utmost your 1909 finance was expected to sustain, and defray the balance arising from new causes by imposing new direct taxation to a total of 5,000,000*l* per annum.

You will then have the situation well in hand again.

Unless some great development by Germany or Austria takes place, and apart from the new decisions about the Mediterranean, you would be able to run out the Parliament without any fresh arrangements.

If there is a general slackening, you would have large surpluses.

Assenting to the foregoing figures as the basis of a financial arrangement will not relieve me of my duty to cut them down in all possible ways of detail nor prejudge the Treasury examination of each specific item. On the other hand, it is a work of immense difficulty to forecast the future, and I can only say I have done my best, and believe that the forecast will come true.

——	1912–13	1913–14	1914–15	1915–16	1916–17
Personnel— Additional numbers—	No.	No.	No.	No.	No.
Vote A	1,000	2,200	3,200	4,000	4,000
Pay, Victualling, &c.—	£	£	£	£	£
Votes 1, 2, 3, and 11	75,000	165,000	240,000	300,000	300,000
New construction— 3 Battleships { Vote 8	225,000	2,247,000	2,304,000	1,074,000	..
Vote 9	120,000	600,000	480,000	150,000	..
Maintenance of additional ships in full commission from April 1, 1915— 3 Iron Dukes 2 Formidables 2 City Class Cruisers { Vote 8	..	..	..	285,000	285,000
2 Super-Actives { Vote 9	..	..	..	35,000	35,000
3 Destroyers { Vote 8	..	..	..	..	19,000
Vote 9	..	..	..	..	1,000
	420,000*	3,012,000	3,024,000	1,844,000	640,000

* Provision for this has been included in the 1,000,000*l* to be taken in the Supplementary Estimate.

The additional cost of building and maintaining the ships required to carry out the Mediterranean decision may be estimated as follows: –
[*Table referred to appears at foot of previous page.*]

The expense, so far as men and maintenance are concerned, might be added to the total estimates without seriously aggravating the problem; but if the capital cost of the three additional battleships has to be borne by this country, it would appear to place an undue strain on the taxpayer to raise the money by annual finance.

Yours very sincerely
WINSTON S. CHURCHILL

WSC to Lord Beauchamp

13 July 1912   Admiralty

Copy

Dear Beauchamp,

There seems to be a complete misunderstanding about the status of the reception rooms at Admiralty House. The arrangement made, to which the Treasury were parties, was that the ground floor should be maintained and held at the disposal of the First Lord for official entertainments. Quite apart from any personal feelings I may have, I could not agree to allow this historic suite of rooms to pass into the possession of the Office of Works, except in the general sense that regulates the control of other public buildings. I hope that this invitation has been issued without your personal attention being called to it. It is of course impossible for me to accept it, as it would be very unsuitable for any First Lord to attend an entertainment at the Admiralty except as host.

In the present case there is an additional objection, for the Naval War Staff is incessantly at work in the building during the manoeuvres, and the Admiralty staff are mobilised for work throughout the night. I hope therefore that you will choose some other place to hold your dinner, and thus enable me to accept your invitation. An official communication of the views of this Department will reach you through the usual channel, but I hope that we may settle it in a friendly way as colleagues without the necessity of troubling the Prime Minister with differences on such a point.

Yours sincerely
WINSTON S. CHURCHILL

Lord Esher to WSC

[no date]   The Roman Camp

My dear Winston,

You have probably heard from Jackie [Fisher] and others that I am strongly and irreconcilably opposed to 'abandoning' the Mediterranean, but I don't want you to think that I am opposed to *You*. Because of your youth, zeal, assiduity and great powers of mind, you are the only member of the government for this vital post which you occupy. Your speeches, as I said to you, are the best and frankest, upon naval and kindred matters since Dizzy's.

First, as you know, I have liked you since, as a child, you sat on my knee; and have admired your brilliance ever since you became a man.

So much for the personal aspect of this affair.

I see your strategical aims and entirely sympathize with your wish to be overwhelmingly strong at this crucial moment and at this crucial point in War.

There are, however, other considerations. When I wrote to you about your great speech, you will remember that I took exception to that portion of it which related to the Mediterranean Fleet.

For years I have been associated, very intimately, with a Society now very numerous and powerful, whose *raison d'être* was to press for 'Two keels to one.'

The whole object of this scale of shipbuilding was (a) to fight with a margin of 60% in our favour, at a moment's notice (b) to keep our prestige unimpaired, in *Peace,* in the Mediterranean.

Holding so strongly these views, and adhering to these engagements, you can realise what a shock it has been to me to find the country on the verge of abandoning the principle which underlies them.

Good, however, is certain to come out of this controversy. You will find the nation *anxious to give you the ships and men* you require for the double purpose – perhaps all the more anxious as you have not pressed for either. Please do not reply. I *may* come up for the CID.

                                        Always your friend
                                        ESHER

Show this to your wife.

Admiral of the Fleet Sir Gerard Noel to WSC

4 July 1912   Fincham
                                                    Norfolk

Dear Mr Churchill,

I presume that it is the possibility of invasion that causes the withdrawal
of the battleships from the Medn to a position nearer home. If so, does it
not mean that the military measures taken for the defence of this country
are totally inadequate? Ten years ago Col Seely strongly advocated the
introduction of National Training, as proposed by the Natl Service League,
(how much more is it now necessary); and Lord Haldane equally considered
a home army of 700,000 to 900,000 necessary, when he first started the
Territorials.

Is it not time for the Govt to pass a bill making National Training compulsory? With the country secured against a successful invasion, the Fleet
would be free to do its legitimate duty to the Empire; and moreover need
never be tied to the North Sea, where it must necessarily be always more
or less open to a surprise attack, which, it is possible, might be most
disastrous.

                                          Yours very truly
                                          GERARD NOEL

R. L. Borden to WSC

27 July 1912   Hotel Meurice
                                                    Paris

My dear Mr Churchill,

I have already in recent conversation urged upon you and upon the
Prime Minister as well the very great importance from an Imperial as well
as from a Canadian standpoint that you both should visit Canada at no
distant date. On no occasion has a Prime Minister of the Home Government
visited Canada, and I think only on one occasion has a minister been in our
country while holding office. It is doubtless a little difficult to make Mr
Asquith realise the importance and significance of such a visit. I am confident he would return an even greater Imperial figure than he is at present,

and that apart from such considerations he would rejoice in the inspiration that must come to him from a visit to that wonderful country now in a most interesting and important stage of its development. No day will ever dawn more appropriate for such a purpose or more opportune for such a visit.

This informal letter I am sending in the hope that you will permit me to extend to Mr Asquith and yourself a formal invitation from the Canadian Government with a view to its formal acceptance.

Yours faithfully
R. L. BORDEN

Note by Lord Morley

[1911]

No – I am far from desiring to hinder your going to Canada; if you have *convinced* yourself that it would do good. I am virulently averse to the *PM* going. But you are a shrewd being – so do as you will. Only don't overstrain your physical resources.

Admiral Sir A. Berkeley Milne to WSC

14 July 1912   HMS *Good Hope*
                                                        Alexandria
[Copy]

Dear Mr Winston Churchill,

I have to thank you for your cable of the 12th, and I am glad to think that, so far, my efforts have met with your approval.

Pray forgive me for writing to you again – my letter requires no reply – but I think it better to do so, as official letters often take long to reach the various offices, owing to more important matters. I do not wish to trench on official secrets, but should it be your intention to increase the destroyer flotilla on the Mediterranean Station, I would respectfully and earnestly urge you to send out a complete flotilla, that is, making up the number of destroyers to 18, but with their scouts and parent ship with stores and workshops appertaining to a flotilla. I attach the greatest importance to this. At present I do not consider the destroyer system satisfactory: the boats are efficient, but there is only a Commander (D), there should be a Captain. Now the dual control of *Egmont-Orontes* is abolished, the destroyers become tenders to *Egmont. I have recommended* this, because it *was the only thing to be done* when *Orontes* was abolished: but at the same time I had not lost sight of the possibility that if the destroyers were increased, you would make the flotilla complete and self-supporting. There would of course be a corresponding *decrease* of clerical department in *Egmont*. The Mediterranean is not like the English coast, where there are many ports only a few miles apart into which destroyers could put in. Here there are only three bases upwards of 1,000 miles apart. It must be borne in mind that the destroyers belong to the active and seagoing fleet, and *not* for the defence of Malta. I believe that in any case the 30-knotters are to be relieved by the River class; so I earnestly hope that you will see your way to make the flotilla complete and self-supporting.

For the present Local Defence of Malta, there are 6 2nd class T.Bs; they are also for the training of stokers, and go out with the submarines. They are now too slow for the latter; they are small, slow, and unable to remain outside in anything approaching bad weather. Should the 30-knotter destroyers be relieved by the River class, I would strongly recommend you to leave 3 or 4 of the 30-knotters to take the place of the old 2nd class T.Bs, being manned with nucleus crews, the majority of stokers being Maltese. I would *very strongly* recommend this: it would well nigh double the Local Defence: enemy's ships would fear the destroyers by night and the submarines by day.

I have received the Admiralty orders regarding paying off of *Orontes*, and in consequence am sending home 35 various ratings by the first Government opportunity: this is only a first instalment. One has to move carefully regarding reductions, so as not to injure the efficiency of Local Mobilisation: it requires much thinking out: but my absence from Malta will not delay matters. I hope to be back there about 17th Aug, when the new Admiral Superintendent arrives. I had several conversations with the Governor of Malta before leaving, and I told him that a large number of naval ratings *must* go home, and therefore there would require to be a modification in Local Defence so far as the Navy was concerned. He quite sees this, and if he could get another infantry regiment, the present difficulties would be very small. The truth is, a war establishment has been kept up in peace time; perhaps this has been necessary owing to Malta being so far from England. Anyhow I hope to be able to employ more Maltese and send English ratings home.

The cutting down of boats was satisfactory, as it came off without friction. Scarcely any English ratings were released, but there should be a considerable saving in money: the return will come home shortly. I regret delay, but it had to be returned to the Adml Supt for revision.

There is no doubt that the work done in the dockyard is *splendid*. I never saw men work like the Maltese, and I have never seen a symptom of idleness.

The French Commander on the Commission sitting at Malta is in the French Intelligence Department in Paris. He told me that last October they had accurate information that on one night, at Hamburg, the Germans embarked 40 guns of sorts in several merchant steamers; and in reply to my question, said they had informed the Admiralty in London.

I regret I am unable to go to Port Said as intended, but a case of plague prevents my doing so.

The weather is very hot indeed.

Believe me, Yours very truly
A. BERKELEY MILNE

Cabinet Notes

16 July 1912   10 Downing Street

LL.G: Bankruptcy stares me in the face.

WSC: Your only chance is to get £5,000,000 next year – and put the blame on me. Then you will be in clover again for the rest of the Parliament.

WSC

WSC to Lord Beauchamp

17 July 1912   Admiralty

[Copy]

Dear Beauchamp,

I am vy much obli to you for yr letter and in the circs I do not press for an alteration in the arrangements wh have been made.

I shd like to see the regns wh govern the use of the FO before agreeing that they are suitable to the Admy. The Ady is much more personal in its character than the FO. It will prob be used as a residence by my successor; and altho' it doesn't matter vy much to me I have to think of the gen rights of the office.

The bd will be vy much upset at the idea of the 'Fish Drawing Room' passing away from the Admy. They were already shocked at my not living in the building.

Yrs vy s
WSC

Hugh Watson to Edward Marsh

EXTRACT

3 August 1912   British Embassy
Personal   Berlin

Dear Marsh,

Berlin has gone to the sea-side to wash, so I shall not hear any serious comment on the British supplementary est^es until late Septr or even October.

The press comments are in some quarters not very pleasant, and rather allude to the necessity of Germany going on, and also point to efforts being made to stir up Austria to anger with us on the naval question. An attempt to belittle our supplementary est^es as an inducement to the Germans to go on is noticeable in one press quarter.

Perhaps the worst part is the naval port and Hamburg press which at this season, owing to people being in large numbers at sea-side resorts near these ports, is more widely read than usually by the idle holiday-makers.

The tone of this press is always hostile to us.

But we shall see better in September which way opinion is going. Will the large Navy Party, with their Imperial Royal, & naval official backing, be strong enough to start a new campaign, or will they weaken their position if they do, is the question they have to decide, or will they wait hoping we shall forget? . . .

Yours sincerely
HUGH WATSON

Memorandum by WSC

8 August 1912　　　　　　　　　　　　　　　　　　　Admiralty

First Sea Lord

It is very desirable to accelerate the formation of the 6th Battle Squadron. It is proposed at present to put 3 'Duncans' into this Squadron by June 1913. It ought to be possible to add to these 3 'Duncans', 3 battleships employed as gunnery tenders. These gunnery ships contain a high proportion of active service ratings; the *Revenge* for instance has over 300 men permanently on board. The engines of the gunnery ships are kept in good order; the vessels are lived in, and constantly ready to proceed to sea. Their guns are always ready for service at the shortest notice. These vessels ought therefore to be available for war with the rest of the 2nd Fleet ships. No doubt a good many new arrangements would have to be made in regard to their ammunition, stores, &c. They would require far less active service ratings to bring them up to war strength than any vessels in the 3rd Fleet. DMD should prepare an analysis of the complements now on board the battleships and cruisers used for gunnery purposes, and an estimate of the extra active service ratings necessary beyond those we now provide to bring them up to war strength on mobilisation as 2nd Fleet ships.

It should be noted that it is specially desirable to raise the number of battleships now in the 2nd Fleet so as to provide for at least half of them always being at their Home Ports. This was the principle on which it has always been intended to organise this fleet. Even if no extra active service ratings are provided, the fact that the gunnery ships were always ready for mobilisation at their Home Ports would enable the balance nucleus crews of 2nd Fleet ships which happen to be cruising, to be put on board the gunnery ships in an emergency: or again, these ships might be partly manned from the Immediate Reserve. All these alternatives should be considered.

If on examination these proposals should prove practicable, the class of ships employed for gunnery purposes might be raised.

It is now proposed by First Sea Lord to replace *Revenge* by *Vengeance*, and it may be worth while to use two other 'Canopuses' for this purpose, or even if we like to look ahead, 3 Duncans. No doubt the use of their armaments for practice purposes will tend to wear them out, but on the other hand the numbers of new vessels joining the fleet are rapidly pushing even good vessels like 'Duncans' down into the 3rd Fleet, or even on towards the Matériel Reserve.

I should like a report on how much deterioration would be caused to these ships by three or four years service as gunnery ships. It should be remembered that great deterioration takes place anyhow if they are allowed to be in the 3rd Fleet or still worse Matériel Reserve. In 1915 all 5 'Duncans' will have reached the Third Fleet in the normal course, and 3 'Formidables' will have reached the 6th Squadron, 2nd Fleet.

The above also applies to the *Grafton* which may be replaced by a more valuable ship of the Cressy class, which would otherwise be only maintained on a 3rd Fleet basis.

It will probably be best to have a small Committee of officers concerned to frame a scheme, point out difficulties, and suggest methods for overcoming them. The DMD, DNO, and Capt Bartolomé would appear to be all that is necessary.

[WSC]

J. L. Garvin to WSC

8 August 1912   *Pall Mall Gazette*

My dear Churchill,

For many months I have taken no notice of Beresford and have found that to be infinitely the more effective course. Replies simply nourish a legend that otherwise will expire of itself. We shall make the important corrections required, but shall do it in another way. But no one takes the charge seriously. I still think I was right in urging McKenna and Fisher at the beginning of last year to make Beresford Admiral of the Fleet or anything non-executive no matter how honorific. A gallant man (with all his faults) has become hopelessly perverse and soured and will remain a serious source of public mischief do what we will. To ignore his wild speeches as far as possible is far the wiser way.

I have been unhappy not to be able to take a more favourable view of your recent policy though the speeches unfolding it were the best you ever made. My business is the political side, not the technical and especially the measurement of political effect. Public opinion is in my view deeply disturbed and explanations about the enormous technical superiority of our individual ships will never reassure it. We want again above all things a standard, intelligible to the nation, and steady adhesion to it. Otherwise you will never have quiet *confidence* again which is what you want for credit & everything else. If we had a British Navy Law, providing up to 1920, there would never be another German one.

Did you get my volume of Carlyle? If so don't reply and I shall know you did. My holiday starts on Saturday for six weeks, and I depart not much liking several things in the public prospect. If you could get the fleet for ever out of the party rut how great a man you would be. Let me remain still with best wishes

Yours very sincerely

J. L. GARVIN

WSC to J. L. Garvin

EXTRACT

10 August 1912   [Admiralty]

My dear Garvin,

No doubt you are right about the best way to treat B. He really does a great deal of mischief, not only in trying to spread discontent and want of confidence through the Navy, but in leading the Germans to think we are thoroughly inefficient and unable to find sailors. Like you, I regret that it was not possible to make him an Admiral of the Fleet: indeed, I hoped at one time I might have repaired this deprivation which he feels so keenly – but he has injured his profession and has disgraced himself too much.

I have nothing to complain of in the way in which you have dealt with my policy. There really is no need for anxiety so far as the relative strength of the British and German fleets is concerned. A steady overhauling process has now begun and will operate from 1915 onwards. In this and the next five programmes, Germany proposes to build 14 capital ships, and we 35: this is very little short of two keels to one. You must remember also that the power of the units is continually increasing and that the great fleet of Dreadnoughts which the Germans have already built, will soon be outclassed by the preponderance of later British ships over later German ships.

If we survey the squadrons in 1915, you will find much to reassure you. The Germans will have two squadrons of Dreadnoughts, and we shall have three. Our first squadron composed of 4 'Iron Dukes' and the 4 ships of this year which are still more powerful, will be far and away the strongest squadron in the world.

The second British squadron armed with 13.5" guns, will be the second strongest in the world, and will fire a broadside more than 40% heavier than the best German squadron. The third British Squadron will contain 6 Dreadnoughts firing 10 guns on the beam and 2 firing 8; and this squadron could fight the first German squadron on very even terms, and would be much superior to the second. In addition, we shall have 2 Dreadnoughts and 2 Lord Nelsons over, available perhaps for the Mediterranean.

Now coming down the list, we have two squadrons, the 4th of 'King Edwards' and the 5th of 'Formidables', to set against the German 3rd Squadron 'Braunschweigs' and 'Deutschlands'. The 'Formidables' would make an even fight of it: the 'King Edwards' would be far stronger: and we have the two together. We shall have in addition by then 5 'Duncans' in the 6th Squadron.

In the 3rd Fleet we shall have two battle squadrons of 8 battleships each, all possessing 4—12″ guns, and the 7th Squadron manned not only by 2/5ths active service ratings, but by Immediate Reserve men, who will have done a genuine 28 days training each year at sea, the bulk of whom will be available at 24 hours notice. Either of these two squadrons when mobilised would be markedly superior to the fourth and fifth German reserve squadrons, which will still contain some ships armed only with 9.4″ guns. All this is irrespective of anything that Canada may do.

In armoured cruisers our superiority is of course overwhelming: that is the reason why we can afford to keep 4 battle cruisers in the Mediterranean.

A very steady overhaul will be maintained in the small cruisers. This year I am building 8 to the German 2. I am also re-arming with 9—4″ guns apiece, the 8 Scouts which have hitherto been so weakly armed as to be practically useless, but which with this armament will be admirable light cruisers, steaming over 25 knots, for service with the battle fleets. We have not yet decided the light cruiser programme for next year, but it will effect a good overhaul both in numbers and in quality.

I am going ahead with the destroyers in advance of the regular programme, and at the rate of 20 a year. They will maintain all their superiority in gun power and seaworthiness, and attain a greatly increased speed at, I am sorry to say, a greatly increased cost.

We have an enormous lead in submarines, and, what is not less important, in the trained personnel that handle them. That lead will be fully maintained and even improved upon.

I am increasing the personnel of the Navy by every means possible without lowering the standard unduly, and I hope when this year closes to have added 7,000 over and above wastage. The reserves are also increasing by several thousands a year, and we now have more than 30,000 reservists for whom we could find no room on any ship fit to send them to sea. Our estimates are double the German estimates, and will be more than double next year. Our reserves of ammunition, in torpedoes, in guns, show almost at every point a considerable surplus over the prescribed amount, and all the provision for future needs has been greatly accelerated.

This letter is for your private eye *alone*, and I write it because you are a patriot and deserve to be reassured. As long as we do not relax our exertions, and proceed on the sober lines I have laid down, we shall – in the absence of any new development – break these fellows' hearts in peace, or their necks in war! . . .

I got your volume of Carlyle, and am going to send it you back.

[W S C]

WSC to Oliver Locker-Lampson

11 August 1912   Admiralty

My dear Oliver,

It is very kind indeed of you to send me such a delightful invitation to visit you at Cromer, and we certainly hope to come and see you there. I shall be going up the East Coast this month inspecting different naval establishments and harbours in the yacht. I could arrive on Friday or Sat 23rd or 24th, and anchor there till Monday, weather permitting. Perhaps you will all dine with us one of the nights and let us dine with you the others? On Monday the 26th I must leave for Hull and Elswick; and I would suggest to you to come in the yacht, see the big docks at Hull on Monday, and Elswick on the Tuesday and Wednesday. We leave for Rosyth on Thursday, and you could return from Newcastle to Cromer if you liked by the night train Wednesday.

Let me know how these plans strike you as soon as you can.

Yours very sincerely
WINSTON S. CHURCHILL

Lord Northcliffe to WSC

12 August 1912   *The Times*

My dear Churchill,

Ever since the time when Mr Chamberlain was to have gone to Canada, when I was a witness of the enthusiasm aroused there by the prospect of a visit (unfortunately, owing to his illness abandoned), I have been convinced that, sooner or later, that virile nation would expect, and be highly complimented by, a visit from some British statesman, preferably one holding high office.

I have been to Canada often, and, in my judgment, there are only five public men whose presence would arouse enthusiasm – the Prime Minister, yourself, Mr Lloyd George, Mr Balfour, and, chiefly by reason of his Canadian birth, the leader of the Opposition in the House of Commons [Bonar Law].

I can understand that it would be very difficult for the Prime Minister to be absent at the opening of Parliament, and he therefore cannot go. You seem to be singled out for this great Empire welding precedent because

(1) of the new and fortunate interest in naval affairs in Canada;

(2) you have shown the capacity for delivering carefully thought out speeches that will endure;

(3) your maternal parentage makes you very acceptable to hundreds of thousands similarly born, resident in those doubtful provinces, Alberta and Saskatchewan;

(4) in my judgment it is far better that a Liberal of known views in regard to the linking up of the Dominions with the Mother Country by affection and sentiment should go rather than a Tariff Reformer, who would be preaching to the converted, or a Unionist Free Trader, who would not be understood.

There would be no need for you to touch on Party questions. There is no more necessity for you to refer to such matters as Imperial Preference than there has been for Mr Borden to do so while here. There may be endeavours to press you into the Party game, as there have been, happily unsuccessfully, in Mr Borden's case.

If you went after the Canadian offer had been made there could be no suggestion that you were touting for support, and if, moreover, your mission were one of thanks and appreciation the atmosphere of your progress from the Atlantic to the Pacific would be happy and *gemütlich*. The season is the right one – the great Canadian harvest will have been gathered in, and the people will have leisure to read, listen, and think.

Man and things are so much larger seen through the cable, as we newsmongers well know, that I am convinced that such a visit would have a good effect on the standing and fortunes of your party here, and no offence could be given to the little Navyites and other queer specimens that follow your flag.

Great Britain has invested, directly and indirectly, untold millions in railways, municipal loans, land companies, trust companies, telephones, electric lighting and milling concerns, mortgages and individual estates. The business world here devotes more and more attention to Canada, and I feel sure that a visit would therefore be welcome to a good many of your own Party who, justly or unjustly, are not a little timorous of the regard the present Government has for commercial interests.

I can advance many other reasons why I consider the visit would be a most happy innovation, and can think of none why it should not be.

There are numerous little local details that such a Canadian as Hamar Greenwood[1] could easily arrange. So far as my own share in the Press is concerned, and it is sufficient to secure the emulation of other newspaper owners, I can assure you that I would leave no stone unturned to make the journey fruitful.

Yours very sincerely
NORTHCLIFFE

WSC to H. H. Asquith

12 August 1912   [Admiralty]

Draft

My dear Prime Minister,

Northcliffe has been here and we have had some very interesting talks. His views about Liberal journalists and their treatment by the Government deserve to be reported to you. He says that we have never treated our journalists with the same consideration as Tory journalists are treated by their Government. He instanced the peerages bestowed on Burnham, Glenesk,[2] and himself, and the knighthoods most freely scattered about the Conservative country newspapers. Whenever there were any Press functions in any part of the country, like the visits of foreign or colonial editors, or any matter of trade business had to be undertaken, the tendency was as a general rule to put someone who had been knighted in the Chair, and that this gradually gave the ascendency to Conservative newspaper men. It was, he said, a matter of comment in journalistic circles that the Liberal Party did not reward the profession in the same way as the Conservatives, and that he had in consequence the greater pick of the younger men. Then he said we

---

[1] Hamar Greenwood (1870–1948), a Canadian by birth; Liberal MP, York, 1906–10; Sunderland 1910–22; Conservative MP, East Walthamstow, 1924–9; Secretary of Overseas Trade Department 1919–20; Chief Secretary for Ireland 1920–2; Chairman, Dorman Long and Co.; created Baronet 1915; PC 1920; Baron 1929; Viscount Greenwood of Holbourne 1937.

[2] Algernon Borthwick (1830–1908), Proprietor of *Morning Post*; Conservative MP for South Kensington 1885–95; knighted 1880; created Baronet 1887; Baron Glenesk 1895.

had some of the very best journalists in the country - men who would be worthy recipients of almost any honour they would care to take. He mentioned Scott, Massingham, Spender, Donald,[1] and Drysdale (*Yorkshire Daily Observer*). I said I did not think the first three would care for knighthoods; I believe they could have had them any time they had chosen. He replied: 'Why should they not be Privy Councillors, and have the KCB'. Dalziel[2] was a Privy Councillor, and surely Spender with his unequalled services to the Liberal Party, whose articles were taken as a sort of standard guide for Liberal newspapers all over the country whenever the editors went on a holiday, was more worthy of such an honour. He said that so far as the newspaper world was concerned, they were not very much impressed with the journalistic reputations either of our friend Riddell[3] whom we have made a knight, or of Dalziel of *Reynolds* whom we have made a PC.

Altogether I thought he talked very wisely; and you know I have long had in my mind the hope that you would be able in some way to recognise these able men who serve us so well.

This is a time when we ought to consolidate and encourage all our forces, and when we have need of all the help we can get. There is a strong professional feeling among journalists, quite apart from politics, and I do not see why this profession should not be recognised with something of the generosity shown to the Army, the Civil Service, and the House of Commons. I therefore venture to suggest that on the next occasion you should consider Spender for a Privy Councillorship, Massingham and Scott for Civil CB's, and Donald and Drysdale for knighthoods. I am sure you will find that such an act would be beneficial to the general interests of journalism, and to the special interest of the Liberal Party.

Northcliffe also told me that Spender was in some danger of being turned out of the *Westminster* by the Mond-Henry combination: he declares – though I cannot say with what truth – that Mond has wished him to assume a more critical attitude towards you, on account of the dissatisfaction he felt at not being included in the Ministry, and that Spender in consequence ran a considerable risk of being unemployed. He said that of course he would have been. . .

[1] Robert Donald (1861–1933), Editor of *Daily Chronicle* 1902–18; Managing Director of United Newspapers Limited; knighted 1924.

[2] James Henry Dalziel (1868–1935), Proprietor of *Reynolds' Weekly Newspaper*; Chairman *Daily Chronicle*, had financial interest in *Pall Mall Gazette* and *Era*; Liberal MP for Kirkcaldy 1892–1921; knighted 1908; PC 1912; created Baron Dalziel of Kirkcaldy 1921.

[3] George Allardice Riddell (1865–1934) Chairman, News of the World, Limited; George Newnes Limited; C. Arthur Pearson Limited; Chairman Newspaper Proprietors'Association; knighted 1909; created Baronet 1918; Baron Riddell of Walton Heath 1920.

H. H. Asquith to WSC

16 August 1912   The Wharf

Private

My dear Winston,

Northcliffe, of course, magnifies the importance of the profession which he has done more than any other living man to degrade.

His 'facts' about Spender & the *Westminster* are totally wrong. He, S, has as large an interest (pecuniary) in the paper as Mond himself, or any other proprietor.

As regards the ennobling of journalists, in addition to those you name we have given titles to Bunting,[1] Lucy & Russell[2] (of the *Liverpool Post*) not to mention Harold Harmsworth. I have reason to believe that neither Scott nor Donald would accept any such recognition, and to Massingham I shall certainly not offer it.

Spender stands by himself, & in due time will have anything he cares to take.

No party was ever worse served than ours by its Press.

As to the Canadian visit, we must wait for Borden's report on his return. I saw him the day I left London, & I thought he was a shade less confident than before as to his ability to do what he wishes.

I was very pleased at the trouncing you gave to Bonar Law.

Yrs always
H.H.A.

WSC to J. A. Spender

13 August 1912   [Admiralty]

Copy

Why don't you come and have a little blow on the *Enchantress?* It would do you all the good in the world. I propose you should embark at Chatham

---

[1] Percy Bunting (1836–1911), Editor of *Contemporary Review* from 1882, of *Methodist Times* 1902–7; knighted 1908.

[2] Edward Richard Russell (1834–1920), Editor *Liverpool Daily Post* 1869–1919; Liberal MP, Bridgeton division of Glasgow, 1885–7; knighted 1893; created Baron 1919.

on Monday the 19th if you have written your leading article; spend Tuesday the 20th at Shoeburyness – see cannons let off at armour plates and things like that – most interesting. On the 21st we go to Sheerness and see the ships and dockyard there; and on Thursday the 22nd we go on to Harwich, where there are many submarines. You could leave Harwich Thursday evening or Friday morning and be back in London in plenty of time to regain control of the thought of the nation on Friday the 23rd.

Pray send me a telegram.

[WINSTON S. CHURCHILL]

Note at top of letter:
   Spender (he couldn't).

WSC to Sir Edward Grey

13 August 1912   [Admiralty]

Copy

Why not join the yacht at Newcastle on the 28th and come and see Rosyth on the 29th and 30th; and Dundee and St Andrews on the 31st and 1st September: go on on Monday the 2nd to see Cromarty, and how it may be defended, leaving, if you like, on Tuesday the 3rd or Wednesday the 4th? It would give us so much pleasure if you would come with us then. Failing that, is there any chance of crimping you between Wednesday the 18th September and Monday the 21st? We shall then be the other side of the island and can give you an easy rendezvous.

[WINSTON S. CHURCHILL]

WSC to Lord Morley

13 August 1912   [Admiralty]

Copy

Would it suit you to join us at Hull on Monday the 26th instant, and spend the 27th and 28th in the Tyne, seeing the great shipbuilding yards there or not as you please, and going on on Thursday the 29th to Rosyth?

on the 30th to Dundee and the 31st to St Andrews – leaving us perhaps there on the 1st or 2nd September, or, better still, go on to Cromarty and leave us at Aberdeen on Thursday the 5th – or any variance of the above, less good because not so long?

Or again, Thursday the 19th at Glasgow and the other side of the island and spend two days with the fleet, and then go to attend the opening of an Institute by the Chancellor of the Exchequer at Criccieth on Saturday the 21st, and then on the 23rd and 24th see the great shipbuilding yards at Barrow-in-Furness.

My wife and I would be so glad if any of these plans found favour in your eyes.

I saw the late Lord Chancellor yesterday, who is living near here, much restored in health, but somewhat cooled in his enthusiasm for HMG – so unlike others who have left Government.

WSC to Mahmoud Muktar

15 August 1912   [Admiralty]

Copy

Your Excellency,

I have received with very great pleasure your letter. I took the greatest personal trouble in selecting Admiral Limpus[1] for service with the Turkish Navy, as I was anxious that you should have at your disposal an officer who would do credit to the reputation of the British Navy, and would confer the greatest amount of benefit upon the Turkish Fleet. Admiral Limpus is a personal friend of mine, and I first made his acquaintance 12 years ago in the war in South Africa, where he played a distinguished part. He is a sincere and thoroughly competent officer; and if you trust him and give him a fair chance, he will greatly increase your naval efficiency.

Let me thank you for the kind message you have sent to Mrs Churchill, with which she is very much pleased, and believe me, with very good wishes to you personally.

Yours very truly
[WINSTON S. CHURCHILL]

[1] Arthur Henry Limpus (1863–1931), Naval Adviser to Turkish Government 1912–14; Senior Naval Officer Malta 1915–16; Admiral; knighted 1916.

WSC to Prince Louis of Battenberg

15 August 1912   [Admiralty]

Copy

I have already on several occasions expressed to you my misgivings about the quality of young men we are obtaining for commissions in the Navy. The fact that all are selected at such a very early age from a comparatively limited class, and have practically only one chance of going in or not, does not assure the Navy that fair proportion of the best talent of the country which is due to the importance of the service. If it were not for the admirable custom of so many naval officers sending their sons into the service, the results would be even less satisfactory than they are, as we have at the present time to compete with all sorts of means of living, and good living, under far easier conditions that did not exist 20 years ago. A gentleman is no longer ashamed of going into business to make money, and if a man who is not a gentleman makes money, he has no great difficulty in getting treated as if he were one. You are very short of officers at the present time, and you have an urgent need to fill your Lieutenants' List. I think, therefore, we are entitled to make a few experiments. I do not agree that the Merchant Service is the only source to which we should look for replenishing the Royal Navy, though that may be one of the springs from which we should now draw. I am strongly of opinion that the public schools ought to have a chance and not be ruled out absolutely from the naval service. You have now, by reopening direct entry of marine officers, and giving the young men so obtained full equivalent naval rank and seeking to fit them for general services, made a very great departure in principle from the existing system. I saw these young marine officers when I visited Walmer the other day; they are a very good lot, though I think that if the advantages offered to them were more widely known, we should have had a far wider selection.

I now propose to you, as an experiment and as an exceptional measure to meet the present emergency, and as a counterpoise to the new promotions from the Lower Deck, that we should offer 20 commissions during the present year, to be competed for by candidates now at the great public schools. I believe that the prospects of joining the Navy almost at once would secure us a good response from among the very best and smartest young men in those establishments. The system would of course be personal selection by an Interview Committee, followed by a standard examination. In the event of there being a large response, the examination would become competitive.

The methods by which these young men would be trained would have to be worked out carefully: but if they went for 6 months to Greenwich, then for a whole year to sea on a training cruiser, and then for another 6 months to Greenwich, and then for a year as Midshipmen on board ship, they would make very good Sub-Lieutenants at 20.

How they should fit in fairly with the main stream from Osborne and Dartmouth is another question that would have to be worked out, but is certainly not insoluble.

We should then have three separate channels of entry into the service: the main one through Osborne and Dartmouth – say 70% – the second from the Lower Deck, and the third from the public schools – 15% each.

[WINSTON S. CHURCHILL]

WSC to H. H. Asquith

15 August 1912　　　　　　　　　　　　　　　　　　　　[Admiralty]

Copy

My dear Prime Minister,

Admiral Troubridge, the present Chief of the War Staff, will shortly have to go to sea. This is his wish, and I shall not indefinitely oppose it. There is no immediate hurry, but I have to consider how to fill his place. I have now made the acquaintance of all the principal officers of the Navy serving at home, and I am sorry to say that I cannot find one who possesses fully the qualities necessary for this most important post. It is indeed extremely difficult to find naval officers who have the bent of mind which elaborate and continuous staff work requires. The War Staff has begun bravely, but it requires more brain and more organizing power at the top. The recent manoeuvres have shown many deficiencies in purely staff work, and there are an enormous number of most important details which require to be worked out exhaustively if we are to avoid a series of preventable misfortunes in the early days of a war.

In these circumstances, neither the tastes of the Navy nor the rules of the Treasury ought to stand in the way of my obtaining the best man. Sir Charles Ottley is clearly the best man, and I think the only man who can fill this post satisfactorily. He is not happy where he is nor very proud of himself for being there. I have had a long talk with him, as the result of which he has written me the enclosed very private letter. You will see that his terms are very high: he wants £2,500 a year, plus a house or house allowance, and £1,000 a year pension on the termination of his appointment, whenever that may be. Still I am sure he is worth it; and it is not right that we should be denied his services. The Treasury will of course make difficulties, but there are none that cannot be surmounted if you desire it. The Navy will be inclined a little to sniff at an officer from the retired list being appointed, but I feel quite strong enough to carry them with me, especially having regard to the various small improvements which are likely to be made in the near future in the officers' pay. (There ought to be a good Latin quotation which would come in here, but I cannot find one in my repertoire.)

The increased salary will not cause any expense, for I should propose to meet it, and more than meet it, by 'putting down' the DNE, a Professor who is now receiving £3,000 a year, and whose work, however useful at first when the new education scheme was started, is now done, and has indeed to some extent to be undone. We have in mind a Council of Naval Education, on which naval officers will have more, and schoolmasters less, influence and which will cost practically nothing.

If I did not think the matter of very real importance, I would not trouble you with it, or face the inconveniences which attend on any action outside the regular lines.

Jack Seely to WSC

11 August 1912   Prydown
                                                 Seaford

My dear Winston,

You must be the first to know that the King has approved of Botha being gazetted an Honorary General in the Army.

I received the telegram conveying this welcome news this morning. Your extra civil Lord, Hopwood was the *deus-ex-machina*; it occurred to me that he might produce a 'new fact' to reverse the previous decision, and he did it. It must be recorded too that Stamfordham was very helpful in the matter. I know how glad you will be, for it was your idea, and Botha in his letter to me said as much.

Immersed as you must be in naval affairs I know that you do not forget this South African settlement which you did so much to secure, and of which this appointment of Botha's is a striking symbol.

Yours ever
J.S.

WSC to Jack Seely

12 August 1912   [Admiralty]

Copy

Many thanks for your letter about General Botha. I am delighted that this honour has at last been conferred upon him.[1]

With regard to the widows' pensions, you must see that if you demand the £8,000 a year for Army war pensions, you will simply crush all possibility of dealing with naval widows in time of peace, without getting any advantage whatever for the Army. This is of course the Treasury game, which they will play at every stage, not with a view of giving *you* anything, but in order to prevent any increase in the pay or emoluments of either service.

In the present case I think the best thing is to deal with the peace question only: when a war comes, there are always very large additional funds raised, and no doubt the demand would be irresistible to equalise the pensions then. But war is a remote and speculative possibility, and I do not see why proper arrangements in time of peace should not be made independently of it.

WSC to Sir Francis Bridgeman

19 August 1912   [Admiralty]

Copy

Rear Admiral Mark Kerr should be warned against imparting to the Greek Government and to the Greek naval officers, naval information of a specially secret character. It is not intended that the instruction and assistance we are giving to the Greek Navy should place them on the same level of naval science as the British. The refinements of our gunnery, torpedo, and submarine courses should not be disclosed but only that general information such as would be appropriate to foreign officers allowed for instructional purposes to attend certain courses. It must be continually borne in mind that information imparted to the Greek Government or the Greek Navy may be transmitted to Germany, and that we have no corresponding method of obtaining information of German developments. Admiral Mark Kerr will

---

[1] Botha was made an Honorary General of the British Army on 15 August 1912, an honour usually reserved for foreign sovereigns.

be held responsible that due caution and restraint is observed by him and by the officers of the Mission generally: and he should be told to ask for precise instructions on any point on which he is in doubt.

WSC to David Lloyd George

EXTRACT

21 August 1912   HMS *Enchantress*

Copy

. . . The Land question has now reached a point when the movement must either be disavowed or guided. You ought to put the main heads of your policy down on paper at any rate for my benefit. I want vy much to work with you if possible.

Surely the alternative vote is vital to our position. What action do you propose on this? I expect you will find a general accommodation with Labour on policy & seats very difficult to carry out without splitting the party.

I see no reason why we shd not surmount the winter session. A breakdown now wd be absolutely fatal. Home Rule, the Welsh Church, the Franchise, the Insurance Act, the Parlt Act itself, we all founder together. On the other hand once our 3 bills have been sent to the Lds the corner will be turned. We can do this if we don't quarrel among ourselves, if we don't play the fool over the women, & if we don't come to bloodshed in Ulster.

So far as Admiralty business is concerned, I have completed my proposals by improving the pay, & will have them ready for you in detail on yr return. I am going to put them as low as I possibly can without courting an expensive failure. They will be less than I told you, but they are vital to me.

I am speaking at Dundee on the 11th or 12th. It is important that we shd meet before then. If we cannot I hope you will write to me. The yacht will be at Criccieth on the 21st & I hope you will be able to come for a cruise.

[WINSTON S. CHURCHILL]

WSC to Lord Fisher
(*Lennoxlove Papers*)

TELEGRAM

22 August 1912   [HMS *Enchantress*]
                                                  Harwich

Weather permitting must stay Cromer having made plans with Locker Lampson who lives there but please come anyhow for one night in your Rolls Royce. If weather unfavourable we may have to shelter at Yarmouth when will wire you again.

WINSTON

WSC to Lord Fisher
(*Lennoxlove Papers*)

TELEGRAM

23 August 1912   [HMS *Enchantress*]
                                                  Great Yarmouth

Arrive Cromer early tomorrow hope you will lunch and come as early as possible before luncheon wire time of arrival to Yarmouth.

WINSTON

WSC to Lord Fisher
(*Lennoxlove Papers*)

TELEGRAM

24 August 1912   HMS *Enchantress*
12.50 pm   Scarborough

I want particularly to see you and no other opportunity will occur for six weeks. If you really cannot come Sunday for lunch send your car to Cromer pier head eleven thirty Sunday morning and I will come over to you for lunch. I shall be hung up if the wind shifts.

WINSTON

WSC to Lord Fisher
(*Lennoxlove Papers*)

24 August 1912   HMS *Enchantress*
7.35 p.m.   Scarborough

Alas it is coming on to blow and we must leave for Hull tonight. All plans for tomorrow therefore cancelled. Could you come to Grimsby Monday and see Elswick and Tuesday and Wednesday. Should be so delighted.

WINSTON

WSC to Sir Edward Grey and H. H. Asquith

23 August 1912   [HMS *Enchantress*]

Secret

Copy

The point I am anxious to safeguard is our freedom of choice if the occasion arises, and consequent power to influence French policy beforehand. That freedom will be sensibly impaired if the French can say that they have denuded their Atlantic seaboard and concentrated in the Mediterranean on the faith of naval arrangements made with us. This would not be true. If we did not exist, the French could not make better dispositions than at present. They are not strong enough to face Germany alone, still less to maintain themselves in two theatres. They therefore rightly concentrate their Navy in the Mediterranean where it can be safe and superior, where it can assure their African communications, and overawe Italy. Neither is it true that we are relying on France to maintain our position in the Mediterranean. We have greatly strengthened our forces there and the Government have decided to strengthen them further as occasion may require. If France did not exist, we should make no other disposition of our forces.

Circumstances might arise which in my judgment would make it desirable and right for us to come to the aid of France with all our force by land and sea. But we ask nothing in return. If we were attacked by Germany we should not make it a charge of bad faith against the French that they left us to fight it out alone; and nothing in naval and military arrangements ought to have the effect of exposing us to such a charge if when the time comes we decide to stand out.

This is my view, and I am sure I am in line with you on the principle. I am not at all particular how it is to be given effect to; and I make no point about what document it is set forth in. But I don't think Bertie understands it a bit, nor how tremendous would be the weapon which France would possess to compel our intervention if she could say 'on the advice of and by arrangement with your naval authorities we have left our Northern Coasts defenceless. We cannot possibly come back in time'. Indeed it would probably be decisive whatever is written down now. Everyone must feel who knows the facts that we have the obligations of an alliance without its advantages and above all without its precise definitions.

Notes by Sir Edward Grey and the Prime Minister:
We must wait till Cambon returns. E.G.
Yes. H.H.A.

Memorandum by WSC

24 August 1912   [HMS *Enchantress*
                                    Yarmouth Roads]

Copy

It is clearly necessary to provide more satisfactorily for the landing and recreation on shore of the men of the flotillas stationed at Harwich. This place will acquire an increasing naval importance in the next few years, and it is probable that the number of torpedo crews based upon it will increase.

Football Grounds should be leased and a good institute provided with a canteen and reading rooms, billiard tables, bowling alley, etc. There should be a small jetty and a proper means of crossing the Great Eastern Railway lines: at present the men have to thread their way through the goods trains to their own danger and to the company's anxiety. A certain amount of sleeping accommodation in Harwich should also be taken up, so that the men have proper places to go to when spending the night ashore. The present lack of any suitable institutes or arrangements is moreover detrimental to morals, and, but for the good character of the flotilla crews, would be harmful to discipline.

The policy must be considered as a whole, but I am inclined to think that some provision is required both in Harwich and at Parkeston.

What is also important is that it should be ready soon: if possible we should try to draw the men away from Harwich, and give them facilities for amusing themselves in the neighbourhood of Parkeston.

The Great Eastern Railway Company should be consulted: I am told that the big hotel which they have just done up at such expense is probably causing them a loss of three or four thousand pounds a year.

Let a scheme, with alternatives, be prepared, together with estimates both of money and time. I should be willing to ask Parliament for a moderate sum of money.

[WINSTON S. CHURCHILL]

WSC to Prince Louis of Battenberg

27 August 1912   [HMS *Enchantress*]

Copy

What do you think of the Sea Scout movement? I am much attracted by it and impressed with the value of the work which is being done among very poor boys.

It has occurred to me that it might be made to popularise the Navy among the rising generation and increase our field of selection of boys and youths.

What can the Admiralty do to help the movement, and what can the Boy Scouts do to help the Admiralty? General Baden-Powell has now returned to England, and I think it would be a very good thing if you had a talk to him on the subject and told him of my interest, and asked him whether he would care to make suggestions. A summer camp in a very old ship at different points along the coast would be an immense attraction and would put us in touch with lots of good small boys who a little later in their lives could be recruited for HM Navy. I should be willing to spend a little money on a good plan.

[WINSTON S. CHURCHILL]

Memorandum by WSC

27 August 1912   [HMS *Enchantress*]

Copy

There is one epicycle of action which it is important to avoid, *viz* – recognition of an evil; resolve to deal with it; appointment of a Committee to examine it and discover the remedy; formulation of the remedy; decision to adopt the remedy; consultation with various persons who raise objections; decision to defer to their objections; decision to delay application of remedy; decision to forget all about the remedy and put up with the evil.

As it had been practically decided to make large changes in the general scheme of refits, I do not see what the use was of inviting the opinions of the Commanders-in-Chief on the question of quadrennial service and Form S.180 on the assumption that the system of refits would remain unchanged. It was not possible for these Officers, as is pointed out by the Director of Dockyards, to give a serviceable opinion on the points put to them without their also knowing the other changes which the Board had in contemplation.

I approve therefore of the suggestion of the Director of Dockyards of the 3rd August, 1912, 'that the Commanders-in-Chief should be asked to review their own objections in the light of the revised procedure about to be adopted as a result of the investigations of the Committee on refits.'

I cannot however agree that the revised instructions for Quadrennial and the revised Form S.180 should not come into operation until the new refit scheme has actually been proved a success. It has been decided that this scheme is to have a year's trial and surely it is not proposed to delay all action on these important proposals until after that period has elapsed.

I am prepared however to agree to a postponement until the further reports which are to be called for have been received from the Commanders-in-Chief.

[WINSTON S. CHURCHILL]

R. L. Borden to WSC

EXTRACT

28 August 1912

. . . At our early interviews, and especially at that of the 16th July, you were good enough to give me two assurances which were especially encouraging and satisfactory to both myself and my colleagues: –

1st. That an unanswerable case for an immediate emergency contribution by Canada could, and would, be made out by the Admiralty.

2nd. That this case would be made in twofold form; one confidential and in detail for the Cabinet, the other public and more general in character for Parliament and the people.

The first form is essential, but the second is vital. Such a case must come from the Admiralty, and it would not be useful or possible for us to undertake its preparation. In all our debates, and in all our pledges, we have definitely and positively based our "emergency" action upon information to be supplied by the Admiralty; and we must be in a position to lay it before Parliament as coming from them and bearing their authority. Such 'emergency' or immediate action will have to be abandoned for the present unless an unanswerable or at least a sufficient case is presented in such form as can be submitted to Parliament. Upon returning to Canada I shall be obliged to admit to my colleagues that up to the present no such case has been placed before me in that available form. This I sincerely regret, as I have at some inconvenience postponed my departure from the 23rd to the 30th in order that the case in its twofold form might be considered, discussed, and settled before I left England. However, I must consider that the result is attributable to unavoidable conditions; and I most sincerely and heartily thank the members of the Government, and especially yourself, for the kindness and courtesy with which we have been received and for the frankness with which matters of great moment have been discussed. . . .

R. L. Borden to WSC

29 August 1912

My dear Mr Churchill,

I am enclosing herewith the rough draft which you were good enough to submit for my consideration, and upon which I have made such notes and suggestions as have occurred to me.

The Memorandum seems to be very thorough, and covers the points which were brought up at our interviews, so far as I can recall them at the moment, except as suggested in my letter of yesterday.

The further Memorandum which can be submitted to our Parliament is, however, of the highest importance, and I trust that this also can be drafted without much delay, as it will be necessary to take it into consideration in connection with that already submitted.

I have your telegram of this morning, enquiring as to the exact date of our departure, to which I replied without a moment's delay.

With renewed remembrances and best wishes,

Believe me, Yours faithfully

R. L. BORDEN

WSC to H. H. Asquith

31 August 1912   [Admiralty]

Copy

My dear Prime Minister,

The enclosed letter from Mr Borden is more satisfactory. His comments on the confidential memorandum also throw some light on his mood. They will of course be dealt with, and I now see my way to strengthen the memorandum in one or two new directions.

I have now completed the Admiralty memorandum for publication. It follows very closely the statements already made by me to Parliament, and I am less dissatisfied with it than I thought I should be before I began. I hope you will be able to approve it and still more to improve it and let me have it back as soon as possible. It has to be checked by the War Staff, passed by the Board at a formal meeting, and should be sent off to Canada by the next mail.

Nothing has been done about giving Borden a cypher. I propose therefore to send him one at the same time as these other papers are dispatched.

I hope very much that I may have an opportunity of seeing you before I make my speeches at Dundee on the 11th and 13th, as there are one or two points apart from Admiralty business on which I should like to receive some guidance. I do hope there is some chance of your coming for a day or two to Invercauld. It will be very pleasant and comfortable.

[WINSTON S. CHURCHILL]

WSC to David Lloyd George

1 September 1912   [HMS *Enchantress*]

Copy

How would it suit you if we arrived off Criccieth on Saturday the 21st instant, are present at the opening of your Institute, and then take you, Mrs

Lloyd George, and your daughter,[1] away with us for a cruise on the Sunday? I should propose to go to Barrow for one day and see over the great Vickers' works there which would be most interesting to everybody, and then we could return to the coast of Wales and move down southwards towards Pembroke and, if I do not have to go to Canada, go round the Land's End to Portsmouth.

Please let me know as soon as you get this whether these plans commend themselves to you. It will give my wife and me so much pleasure if you are able to come.

I have asked Masterman to supply me with a good brief on the broad aspects of the Insurance Act and its working for my meetings at Dundee on the 11th and 12th. I propose to lead off on this and make it clear that we regard it with the greatest pride and confidence. Will you give instructions to your people to help me? I do not want details, but the general position. The doctors seem to be behaving very badly: what shall I say about them?

I have not had a single day's holiday so far, though it is very pleasant cruising along the coasts.

[WINSTON S. CHURCHILL]

WSC to Albert Illingworth[2]

1 September 1912   [HMS *Enchantress*]

Copy

My dear Illingworth,

I am afraid I cannot usefully at the present time make any political engagements in addition to those which I propose to keep at Dundee on the 11th and 12th instant. The possibilities of my going to Canada make the future too uncertain for me to commit myself. This must apply also to the request which has reached me from your office that I should address a meeting at Perth. If I do not go to Canada these questions can be reconsidered but I am very hard pressed with the work of this office, which is by far the most exacting I have ever filled, and I can probably help the

---

[1] Megan Lloyd George (1902–66), Liberal MP 1929–31, Independent Liberal 1931–45, Liberal 1945–51, Labour 1957–66.

[2] Albert Holden Illingworth (1865–1942), Liberal MP Heywood division of East Lancashire 1915–18, Coalition Liberal Radcliffe Division of Heywood 1918–21; Postmaster-General 1916–21; PC 1916; created Baron Illingworth of Denton, 1921.

Government just as much at the present time by making a success of that as by playing Aunt Sally to the Suffragettes on the public platform.

What are your plans about the representation of Portsmouth? Have we candidates in the field? An idea has crossed my mind that Mr Lionel Yexley,[1] the editor of the *Fleet*, a lower deck newspaper, might make a very powerful candidate. I have found him a very good man to work with, and I think he would make a useful Member of Parliament. It would be very refreshing to have a genuine representative of the lower deck in the House of Commons instead of that poor old played-out Beresford. I have no knowledge of what Mr Yexley's politics are, but, if the course is still open and you approve, I will take steps to have him sounded.

I have been thinking a great deal about the Autumn Session and your responsibilities in relation thereto. This Winter Session will be the turning point of the Government's labours: a great disaster awaits on failure, and good prospects of continued success will reward victory. You have a fine chance of making your reputation. The battle will be long and tempers short, and everyone is tired and the burden very heavy.

I think we ought to revive that system of dinners which old [blank space] introduced during the Budget of 1909. It would enable Ministers to get into personal touch with our supporters and promote a feeling of comradeship. If I do not go to Canada, I should be very glad to give a couple of Dinners of 15 or 20 myself, and I would attend 2 or 3 more if the Whips liked to get them up. Very probably other Ministers would do the same, and so we might have 2 or 3 every week during the Session. I make this suggestion and the offer for what it is worth.

I hope you have good reports of Midlothian, and with good wishes to you in your new and very arduous work.

Believe me, Yours sincerely
[Winston S. Churchill]

---

[1] Lionel Yexley (1861–1933), entered Navy 1877; took up journalism 1898; Founder-Editor of *The Fleet*, 1905. He wrote three books while WSC was First Lord – *Victualling the Fleet* (1912), *The Naval Pay System* (1912), and *The British Navy from Within* (1914). He was a lecturer at the Royal Naval Staff College, Greenwich, 1919–27.

H. H. Asquith to WSC

2 September 1912   Lympne Castle
                                                    Kent

My dear Winston,

Many thanks for your time table; so far as I can foresee it will work out admirably.

I think it would please the King if you were to go and see him (after Tuesday) and explain the object, and under present conditions the urgency, of our proposed visit, and of the meeting of the Committee at Malta. I presume that Haldane altogether approves.

I will speak to Grey about Kitchener.

Good luck to your speech!

                                                        Yrs ever
                                                        H.H.A.

I think we might find Fisher a little too overwhelming!

WSC to the Director of Osborne Naval College

16 September 1912   [HMS *Enchantress*
                                                      Lamlash]

Copy

I have been considering what should happen at Osborne on war mobilisation, and am inclined to think that, on the order to mobilise, the college should immediately stop all studies, and all cadets not forward enough or matured enough to go to sea should go home to their parents on a month's leave, which may be extended if necessary. The whole of the staff for which any use can be found in the Fighting Ships should be *at once, ie* – within 6 hours, drafted on vessels of the Second Fleet in Portsmouth Harbour.

During next year there will be 2 'Duncans' serving as Gunnery Ships at Portsmouth which are intended to be used for manoeuvres and on mobilisation with the Second Fleet. These would be specially appropriate for the staff at Osborne as far as they could be fitted in, and it should be possible for two surprise mobilisations to be carried out during the year for these ships in order that all ratings employed on shore may be well acquainted with the positions in which they will serve in time of war.

No doubt after the war had been in progress for some time the college would be re-opened, and it is possible that some of the training staff might return, but, in the first instance, when every ship has to be put into the line at the shortest possible notice all trained active service ratings in the neighbourhood of the naval ports must be available and allocated. I shall be glad to have your views.

Next, are there any of your cadets fit to serve afloat in war as acting-midshipmen? If so, about how many. How would you choose them? Some mature much earlier than others, and age is not always a certain guide. My idea is that you should make the best selection possible, and I see no reason why they should not know that they have been chosen. Would it not be a great cause of emulation for these boys to know that they had been or might be selected and were the holders of war appointments? Here again, let me know what you think.

As for the others who are not selected, how could they be sent to their parents at the shortest notice and by the route least likely to congest the military traffic.

Everything should be foreseen beforehand, even the smallest details, and the point I want you to consider and discuss is that we may want your whole staff, or such portions as are of any use to us, to be on board certain vessels in Portsmouth Harbour within at the outside 6 hours from the receipt of the order, and this will have to be rehearsed once or twice every year.

You may write to me about this privately before any final decision is taken.

[WINSTON S. CHURCHILL]

Viscount Haldane to WSC

21 September 1912   Cloan
Perthshire

My dear Churchill,

I have this enclosed letter from Captain Hankey.

It is very important that the Cromarty business should be sanctioned without delay. As to Scapa we shall hear from you what you wish done. I think the way of least friction with the Treasury would be to have a meeting of the CID Sub-Committee to push the matter.

Could preside on Friday 11th if that suited you – or on Thursday 10th. After that week shall be sitting judicially from 10.30 to 4 daily.

I thought your first speech at Dundee admirable – one of the best in form and substance alike which has been delivered for some time by anybody. As for the Heptarchy idea, I am not so sure.

There is one small point in your new financial arrangements about which I should like to talk to you.

I was deeply impressed while at the War Office with the desirability of placing on the heads of war departments more financial responsibility and giving them more financial assistance. I only succeeded partially in accomplishing this, and I think it remains to be done with both services.

But this will keep till we meet.

Yours v. sincerely
HALDANE

Captain M. P. A. Hankey to WSC

23 September 1912   Committee of Imperial Defence

Personal & Confidential

Dear Mr Churchill,

I have been in correspondence with Lord Haldane as to the defences of Cromarty, Scapa Flow, and the Humber, the present state of this question being very un-satisfactory.

You will remember that the defence of these ports was originally to have been dealt with by a sub-Committee of which Lord Haldane was Chairman, and of which you were a Member. The Sub-Committee met once and then adjourned for some conferences between the Technical Members. As agreement had been reached between the Admiralty and War Office representatives on the subject of Cromarty, and as it was found difficult to arrange a meeting of the Sub-Committee in July, the question of Cromarty was brought before the Committee of Imperial Defence at its last Meeting, without waiting for the Sub-Committee's Report. There the Treasury put up a most unexpected opposition, and the question was reserved for consideration by the Cabinet.

Lord Haldane now tells me that the Cabinet has not disposed of the question of Cromarty. He thinks it would be well if the Sub-Committee were to meet, and he says he could preside during the week ending the 12th October, and he suggests Friday 11th October (11.30 am) for the Meeting. First, however, he asks me to ascertain your view.

I should be much obliged if you would let me know whether you agree that the Sub-Committee should meet, and if Friday October 11th at 11.30 am would suit you for the Meeting. We have material for arriving at a decision on Cromarty and the Humber, and by then perhaps the Admiralty will have arrived at a final decision on Scapa Flow.

If you would like to see me perhaps you would give me a day's notice as I am working at home this week.

Yours sincerely
M. P. A. HANKEY

26 September 1912   [HMS *Enchantress*]
                                                              Cromarty
Copy

Many thanks for your letter. I am most anxious that the Cromarty Sub-Committee should meet again as you propose under your presidency, and 11.30 on Friday the 11th October will suit me excellently. Since we separated I have obtained the written opinions of the First and Second Sea Lords on the vital necessity of fortifying this harbour without delay. I have sent these to the Prime Minister, who expressed his concurrence in writing, and the hope that the matter might be adjusted without a Cabinet. I sent this paper to the Chancellor, but as usual no answer of any kind. However, I shall see him next week when I go up to London for a day or two, and I will then find out what his view is.

Meanwhile I have spent a week in this wonderful natural harbour, incomparably the finest on the East Coast of Great Britain. No one can doubt that it should have been preferred to Rosyth as the site of the main naval base. As it is I am having a scheme prepared for putting a floating dock and a floating workshop there, so that we shall not be utterly unprepared as we are now with any means of docking heavy ships injured in action in the North Sea. This is becoming absolutely necessary in view of the very long delay which will intervene before we can expect to get any practical use out of Rosyth. These arrangements will make the fortification all the more essential.

I am strongly inclined to think that the main battery on the South Soutar ought to carry two 9.2″ instead of two 6″ guns. I cannot believe that the cost will be much greater, and the difference between throwing a 380lbs and 100lbs shot is enormous from the point of view of its deterrent effect upon hostile vessels. The site for this battery is necessarily much exposed, and were it armed only with 6″ guns, it might easily be knocked out from a safe distance by a heavy ship. I am enquiring from my people whether we cannot find a brace of these desirable 9.2s among our older marks; indeed I think we ought to try to use up the older types of naval ordnance on these coast defences, and it is possible that when we meet on the 11th, I may be able to make proposals which will somewhat reduce the expense. I should suggest also that the garrison should be withdrawn from some Western or Southern battery. The strategic front has changed, and there is no sense in our maintaining the same precautions against France as we used to in the old days. Please observe 'although on pleasure bent I have a frugal mind.'

It is very kind of you to say such nice things about my first speech at Dundee. The second has done no harm, for Carson has on behalf of Ulster refused anything in the nature of separate treatment. I made it quite clear that these were my own views, and that I was speaking of future and not of present politics.

I shall look forward with great interest to hearing your views about financial control.

[WINSTON S. CHURCHILL]

R. L. Borden to WSC

3 October 1912   Ottawa

Confidential

My dear Mr Churchill,

As I explained to you in England the objection may be strongly urged in some parts of this country that any considerable sum to be provided by Canada for immediate aid towards increasing the naval strength of the Empire ought to be expended in this country. On the other hand it is sufficiently manifest to me that the construction of battleships of the largest and most powerful class cannot be undertaken in this country within a reasonable period, having regard to the grave conditions which we are called upon to confront. At our interviews in London I suggested to you a possible solution which you will doubtless recall. If the Canadian Parliament should vote a large sum of money sufficient for the construction of two or three battleships of the latest type and should authorize the expenditure of that money in the United Kingdom, it would seem not only practicable but reasonable that the great shipbuilding firms to which the contracts might be let should undertake the beginning of a shipbuilding industry in one or two parts of this country. The points to which our attention has been particularly directed are Halifax in the Maritime Provinces and Montreal or Quebec in the Province of Quebec. I do not suggest this in any spirit of bargaining; but you of course realize that conditions of a somewhat difficult character from a political standpoint will have to be encountered. It is of vital importance that any proposals which we make to Parliament shall be carried to a successful issue as otherwise the moral effect upon the whole Empire will be disastrous.

Thus it seems to be not only in Canadian but in Imperial interests as well, that everything should be done to overcome local prejudice or sentiment of the character suggested.

Moreover you will perhaps agree in the importance from an Imperial standpoint of the early establishment not only of dockyards but of naval bases provided with the necessary equipment both for building and for repairing war vessels of the smaller type at least.

I cannot too strongly emphasize the importance of the considerations which have been very briefly set forth in this letter. Possibly the particulars, the early arrival of which your recent cable announces, may cover this point.

Yours faithfully

R. L. BORDEN

WSC to R. L. Borden

October 1912   [Admiralty]

Copy

My dear Mr Borden,

I have given careful consideration to your two letters about the encouragement of the shipbuilding industry in Canada. I recognise the importance of such a policy on general grounds not less than from the immediate Canadian standpoint: and any practical scheme for Admiralty co-operation would command my support. The main difficulty to be surmounted is to obtain that high degree of expert knowledge and experience which modern warships require for their efficient construction.

We might however in the first instance agree upon certain classes of vessels with which it may be considered that competent Canadian shipyards would be able to deal. The most suitable classes of vessels with which to inaugurate the system would be light cruisers, oil tank vessels and small craft for auxiliary services. We should, if it would meet your views, be prepared to invite tenders from approved Canadian firms for the construction of some vessels of such classes in the near future.

It would be understood that progress with this policy would have to be dependent on the prices quoted being reasonable, having regard to all the circumstances (including the fact that Canada will be prepared to share any extra cost), and also on the time required for construction not being excessive as compared with the dates fixed for completion of similar ships in England. No fixed scale or proportion of orders could be guaranteed to Canadian firms. We would begin by giving some orders at once, and further progress would depend upon the development of the industry and the extent of our programme.

The Admiralty would, of course, remain wholly responsible for the design of all vessels, and for the supervision of the construction of those building in Canada. Arrangements for this could be worked out in detail later and should not present any difficulty.

[WINSTON S. CHURCHILL]

Memorandum by WSC

5 October 1912   [Admiralty]

Copy

I note the War Staff concur in the importance of establishing a temporary secondary base at Cromarty. I think the opinion should now be cast in a short form, not more than a page, setting forth in so many sentences the purposes which such a base would serve, (a) generally, and (b) especially before Rosyth is completed.

In this connection it is not necessary to dwell on the disadvantages set out on page 5, as these have already been weighed and discounted by the War Staff. Of these, however,

(a) British fleets using Cromarty will be responsible for their own security by proper patrolling, and must not contemplate being attacked at anchor, whether in the single line or in other formation.

(b) I am informed that it is not impossible to close the entrance to Cromarty Firth by means of wire hawsers against submarines, and floating torpedo nets of special construction against torpedoes: it would anyhow be a small undertaking to moor a certain length of floating net defence against long-running torpedoes at the head of a line of vessels.

Attention is also directed to the great advantage which Cromarty has over Rosyth in the fact that a fleet leaving Cromarty comes almost immediately into the open sea, instead of having to make its way down 17 or 18 miles of difficult channel, affording many opportunities to mines and submarines. The indent of the Moray Firth is specially useful to aircraft reconnaissance, as short flights could be constantly and easily made across the entrance. Attention is also directed to the serious consequences which would arise if a battle were fought before the completion of Rosyth off the Norwegian coast or in the Northern waters of the North Sea, when there would be no means whatever of giving wounded battleships the first-aid necessary to enable them to reach the Southern ports for repair. The docks and dredged channel at Rosyth cannot be counted upon for 4 years: the temporary base at Cromarty could be brought into existence in 6 months, and we could have the use of it throughout the greater part of the critical years of 1913, 1914, and 1915.

[WINSTON S. CHURCHILL]

J. S. Sandars to A. J. Balfour
(*Balfour Papers*)

EXTRACT

10 October 1912   14 Egerton Gardens

My dear Chief,
    You may like a little gossip – it is about Winston & his colleagues at the Admiralty.
    Bridgeman came to sit with me the other day. He is always very frank about his office, as he knows you are the only person to whom I pass on his views.
    Winston, although promising not to offend again, has nevertheless outraged official decorum by the language of his official minutes. It appears he has been sending through his office and round the office the most peremptory orders to the Sea Lords. Bridgeman and Prince Louis met & agreed that respect & authority could not be maintained if Winston were allowed to issue papers couched in these terms. Bridgeman therefore, met Winston on the latter's return to the Admiralty and plainly told him that he must mend his manners or his Board would have to take action. Bridgeman pointed out that as Winston could not give a single order outside the Admiralty building without the consent of the Board & that he was only *primus inter pares* the terms in which he had been addressing his colleagues was most improper. Winston at first contested this position; whereupon Bridgeman replied that in that event the Sea Lords would address themselves to Asquith & ultimately to the King. Winston then, capitulated: abjectly: broke into tears and talked in such a melancholy manner about himself that Bridgeman thinks he must be ill. I assured Bridgeman that I had never known the time when sympathy was not asked for Winston on grounds of health.
    He has behaved better since: but the other day at the Board he exhibited great irritability and bad temper.
    I asked Bridgeman how Winston was getting on in matters of Naval policy. Bridgeman replied that they had hoped that after the mess Winston made over the Mediterranean arrangement he would be more careful & less impulsive. However, he has recently had another fiasco. It appears that Borden requested the Board of Admiralty to furnish him with some information about our ships, armament etc in the North sea. Winston told his colleagues that he would write the papers himself & then show it to them. He did so: the Sea Lords begged & implored him not to send the paper. They pointed out that it dealt with policy and that it was most dictatorial in its tone to the Canadian Govt & that it did not answer Borden's requirements.
    However: Winston would send it. Borden promptly returned it, saying

that the paper did not give the information for which he asked. Winston then prepared another paper on different lines and sent it to the Board, observing that they might criticize it, but that they should not alter it. The Board were equally opposed to this new paper, and took it upon themselves to rewrite the whole thing on their own lines. Winston was furious and told them he should take the papers to Asquith & if as he expected, Asquith approved of his (Winston's) paper, he should send it. When the papers reached Asquith, Winston's paper was wholly disallowed: the Sea Lords' was adopted and that has gone to Canada. Winston is now denouncing Borden in the strongest language! . . .

Lord Morley to WSC

11 October 1912   Privy Council Office

Viscount Morley presents his compliments to the First Lord of the Admiralty and has the pleasure to announce to him that at a meeting of the P[rivy] Council this morning HM in C. was pleased to pass an order increasing the emoluments of the Cook of the *Enchantress*. Lord Morley ventures to hope if his own emoluments should ever be assailed, on the ground that his office is of the nature of a sinecure, Mr Churchill will defend Ld Morley in whatever of the various parliaments of the UK his salary may be grudged.

J. S. Sandars to A. J. Balfour
(Balfour Papers)

EXTRACT

16 October 1912   Moulton Paddocks
                                                        Newmarket

Copy

My dear Chief,

So many thanks for your letter. I never meant you to answer it. You know I like to tell you any bit of gossip I hear from time to time.

Well – my Admiralty friend came again to see me – I have been a prisoner on the sofa until Monday of this week, and so he was charitably disposed to come and talk to me.

In this last conversation he said that I shd remember that Winston in his speech in the spring in the H. of Commons had announced that if Germany added a ship to her programme he should reply by laying down 2 ships. This statement was made after discussion with, & with the approval, of the Sea Lords.

The other day Winston suddenly announced that he shd not fulfil his pledge but in lieu of it that he should ask for £1,000,000 for submarines. The Board said, or rather Fisher & Second Sea Lord observed that this startling change of policy wd [be] difficult to defend, and that they thought it ought seriously to be considered at a Board meeting. Winston's reply was 'Leave it to me. I will manage the H. of Commons.'

Bridgeman accordingly asked me what I thought of the position. My answer was that, of course, I could express no opinion upon the merits, as I did not know the case; but that I considered that inasmuch as the original statement was made upon the authority of the B. of Admiralty, it was only right & proper that any departure from it shd be discussed by the Board &, if put forward, should be defended on the authority of the First Sea Lord & his professional colleagues. I pointed out that it was quite likely the opposition would question this change of plans & would ask Winston if the Board of Admiralty concurred with him in recommending it. On so important a matter it was obviously right that the First Lord shd be able to announce the agreement of his Colleagues. . . .

Lewis Harcourt to WSC

19 October 1912   14 Berkeley Square

Private

My dear Winston,

I had some talk yesterday with Mr Foster,[1] the Canadian Minister. He said that the position of Borden and his Cabinet would be much easier if they made their emergency contribution in the terms of Dreadnoughts and not cash, so that the Canadians could see what was being done with their money and perhaps the ships might have some name which would associate them with the Dominion. He even went so far as to mention *three* Dreadnoughts as their possible contribution. He asked me whether it was possible for us to express a preference for Dreadnoughts over cash. I said that, up to now, we had taken the attitude of asking for nothing but that if they made

---

[1] George Eulas Foster (1847–1931), MP Kings, New Brunswick, 1882–96; North Toronto 1904–21; Minister of Marine 1885; Finance Minister 1888; Minister of Trade and Commerce 1911–21; Member of Dominions Royal Commission 1912–17; represented Canada at Peace Conference 1919.

an intimation to us of an approaching gift I did not think it would be difficult for us to say that Dreadnoughts would be the most appropriate form.

Yours very sincerely
L. HARCOURT

F. E. Smith to WSC

19 October 1912   4 Elm Court

My dear Winston,

I wasn't at the cottage for the week end & they most stupidly did not forward your telegram.

I had arranged my legal affairs in such a way as would have made it possible to come but my wife is very depressed and I have been going home to dine & so forth every night so as to be with her as much as possible. I ought not to leave her at this time.

Would you mind sending to me to King's Sutton GWR the head you promised me from E. Africa? I should like a fairly large one if you could spare it to balance a 10 point stag that I shot myself.

Yours ever
F E

Sir Francis Hopwood to WSC

24 October 1912

Confidential

My dear Churchill,

I was fairly disgusted with the attitude of my civilian colleagues at the Board. They disclosed no real grievance but their mumblings, grumblings and flatulence were aggressive & offensive. I have noticed before that both treat you with scant courtesy. To a great extent it is a want of good manners. But both think they have a grievance & they make it as applicable to McKenna's administration as to yours – they are not consulted. In practical administration the grievance is inadmissible and cannot be admitted. But it is a chronic grievance in the minds of all budding ministers. It is always more acute where the under-Secretary sits in the same House with his Chief. For 25 years I have witnessed the same thing. It is either 'not consulted,' 'no really important work to do' or both. A minister has no relief from the situation unless his underman accepts the situation & behaves well. In the

Admiralty the situation is liable to be worse than elsewhere. You have two of them! I am still of opinion that the A. does not want three men on the Treasury bench. Either the Civil Lord should not exist or he should always be in the Lords when the First Lord is in the Commons – as in nine cases out of ten he will be in future. Then the title 'Finance Secretary' is not the best because it gives the holder of the office the idea, which may quickly develop into a mania, that no financial obligations can be assumed by anybody without his assent & that he is entitled to 'object' to a policy where the policy involves expenditure. This claim by a Financial Secretary is of course wholly a delusion. His duty is to see that honest, adequate & careful financial arrangements are made to give effect to the policy of the Board, & to stand to be shot at in the House & elsewhere when financial muddling occurs. With a new appointment it would be better to have a Parliamentary Sec to the Admiralty & assign him such duties as the First Lord think fit.

It is because the estimates & expenditure are so enormous that the presence of the First Lord in the Commons is now a necessity. His presence there is a reason and qualification for a reconsideration of the status of his subordinates.

I am bound to say that I feel more than some anxiety about the new Financial Committee. There is evidence that it may readily be used as a means of contriving, overhauling, & readjusting decisions on policy & that in the potent name of finance.

For the rest, the Sea Lords are very staunch to you. I am aware of course that there was some controversy about a memo you sent to Bridgeman. They have talked to me about it. There is really no virus & very little substance. It is really no more than a question of language. When, in order to secure the application of a speedy remedy, you dictate a forcible indictment of something wrong, you are condemning the subject matter; they assume you are reflecting on the individuals who have grown up with the system & have not attempted to correct it.

No one alive is so well able as yourself to make the points of criticism against that which is wrong & at the same time to stir their Lordships' warmest blood by calling them to your aid to apply the remedy!

Forgive this screed. It is written because I like you to know that my thoughts are with you in these personal difficulties, trivial in themselves, but alas! often so much more trying and irritating to a Cabinet Minister than important affairs of State. No reply.

Yrs v. sincerely
FRANCIS S. HOPWOOD

WSC to David Lloyd George

29 October 1912   Admiralty

[Copy]

My dear Chancellor of the Exchequer,

The figures supplied to Sir Robert Chalmers by Sir Graham Greene,[1] without my being consulted, are in several respects inaccurate.

It had been proposed by the late Board to construct for 1912/13 3 battleships at £1,795,000 each and one battle cruiser at £1,980,000, making an average price for the four ships of £1,841,250. This figure, and not the £1,706,000 which was the price of the 1910/11 battleships, should be taken as a fair basis of comparison for any increases in the cost of capital ships due to decisions for which I am responsible. The adoption of larger guns and of greater speed, involving as it did the temporary elimination of the battle cruiser type, made the comparable figure for the average of the ships designed by the new Board (Vote 8) £1,950,000. The decisions of policy involved in the change therefore produced the financial effect of raising the average of the ships from £1,840,000, as designed by the previous Board, to £1,950,000, instead of as shown in the figures given to Sir Robert Chalmers from £1,690,000 to £2,160,000. This is quite a different thing. The increased cost was fully explained to you in my letter of the 12th July (see page 3). For all this I accept the fullest responsibility. What I cannot be responsible for is the general increase in prices which has taken place, and which is particularly marked in all forms of warship building. The figure £2,176,000 is not at present recognised by my professional officers; but I hasten to let you know that it does not in my opinion reveal the full consequences of the price movement as disclosed by the tenders which are coming in.

Shipbuilding material is up more than 5%, and gun machinery between 10% and 12%. An average rise over the whole field of 7% would work out at over £500,000 additional for the four ships. I can no more control this than I can the weather; but the Treasury shall have the earliest and fullest information of every fact which is known to me.

The torpedo boat destroyers of 1912/13 were also my predecessor's design, and average £105,000 apiece, an increase of £12,500 over those of the previous year. The decision upon this was taken before I assumed office, and I have made no alteration in it. So far as the destroyers of the 1913/14 programme are concerned, the necessity of having vessels equal in speed to the

---

[1] William Graham Greene (1857-1950), Principal Clerk Admiralty 1902-7, Assistant Secretary 1907-11, Permanent Secretary 1911-17; Secretary, Ministry of Munitions 1917-20; knighted 1911. Uncle of Graham, Carleton and Raymond.

latest German boats instead of about 3 or 4 knots slower, conjoined with the rise in prices above referred to, will raise the whole average by a further £20,000 to a total of £125,000 a boat. To this, however, you are not committed at present, nor will you be until the best estimates which we can make on the subject are placed before you, together with all the necessary reasons.

It is quite impossible to compare submarines, which are of many classes, some costing as little as £50,000, while others rise much above any figure mentioned to you.

These figures now supplied are concurred in by my advisers, and I hope you will agree that, however regrettable they may be, the Treasury has been kept duly informed.

The question of whether the cost of battleships and destroyers is excessive, must be considered in relation to the types building abroad and to their cost. As far as we know the cost of the German battle cruiser, battleship for the year 1910-11 is £2,000,000 and £2,115,000.

There is every reason to believe that a further increase in the cost and power of all types has accompanied the years 1911-1912 & 1912/13, and will be continued in the year 1913/14. The battle cruiser *Seydlitz*, the latest German ship of which we have full details, is superior in armour, only slightly inferior in gun power and at least equal in every other particular to our latest comparable vessel the *Tiger*.

WSC to David Lloyd George

3 November 1912   The Wharf

Private & Personal

[Not sent]

My dear David,

My naval advisers take a serious view of the decision of the Cabinet about the Pay of the Men: and I may at any time be confronted by the resignation of the Sea Lords in a body. This would of course make my position quite untenable: for I fully share their view that the scheme we had passed with so much care was an extremely moderate one. As I cannot yet believe that you wish to bring about a smash, & as I am determined to be guiltless shd that be the result, I am preparing new proposals to meet you & your friends as far as possible. It is not possible that these proposals shd be confined to the crude or arbitrary limit of £300,000 p.a. I have obtained from the Prime

Minister the assurance that the decision of Friday's cabinet does not preclude me from making a further proposal. In putting such a proposal forward I must make it clear (1) that it is without prejudice to the existing Admiralty Scheme, wh we regard as the only satisfactory treatment of the subject: & (2) that my putting it forward must be conditional upon my obtaining the support of my naval advisers wh I have not yet got.

If you wd like to discuss this with me before it is brought before the Cabinet I am at your service, & I shd be glad to hear from you when I shd come. I shall be ready any time after Thursday.

From what you said the other morning about my 'having looked out for opportunities to squander money', it has occurred to me that you may perhaps prefer that final decision on the Pay question shd be deferred until the Estimates can be surveyed as a whole.

In that event I could tell the House that the Pay scheme wd not be completely settled until the beginning of December. This wd cause murmuring but wd not be impracticable. In the meantime the main question could be determined.

All my present indications show that the rise in prices will affect the whole range of the estimates as provisionally forecast by me.

If we are to separate, it had much better be on the great issue of Retrenchment v. National Defence, than on a small matter of £170,000 a year for sailors' Pay. These large political issues ought not to affect personal friendships nor will they so far as I am concerned whatever the consequences. Little petty squabbles about matters wh do not affect gt issues are far more trying.

Yours ever
W

WSC to Sir Edward Grey

8 November 1912

[Copy]

The 4 battleships & two armoured cruisers at Malta are going at ordinary speeds to Nauplia a harmless bay off the E. Gk Coast, where their posn can have no signifce but is within effective supporting distance of the other 4 at Suda Bay. We do not propose to bring home any ships from the Medn at present, but it is necessary that the vessels in the E. Medn shd be capable of concentrating for mutual protection. The force when united will be largely superior to the Austrian fleet & capable of looking after itself in all probable contingencies. Our margins at home are considered sufficient in view of the steps of a precautionary character wh are being taken. Not a single vessel will be mobilized. No interruption of the schools or movement of Reserves will take place. The Press are being asked to make as little as poss of the other measures.

Yrs sinc
WSC

I am not at all displeased with the naval position.

Sir Edward Grey to WSC

9 November 1912

Dear Churchill,
    We think Nauplia won't do at all for the fleet – there is no danger to life or property there & the wildest political motives may be ascribed to us & there may be no end of a scare. So also as regards Suda Bay. If the Admiralty really think the ships must be moved from Malta to keep in touch with the others, I think Smyrna would be best. There are dangers of massacre there & in Asia Minor generally & this would be sufficient reason.

Yrs sincerely
E. GREY

Duke of Marlborough to WSC

9 November 1912

Hotel Bristol
Place Vendôme
Paris

My dear Winston,
    I fear my manners will not be quite so good as your own, and that I am not going to answer your letter in my own hand. It was nice of you with all the amount of work which you have to discharge to find time to write me such a long and interesting letter.
    I am getting on very well indeed; I now can walk out for a couple of hours every day. The weather being beautiful helps me to make a good recovery.
    I propose staying here for a few days longer and then journeying via Boulogne and Folkestone to London. If I find the sea in a tranquil condition at Boulogne I shall stay at Folkestone. If on the other hand, I find the sea turbulent, I shall have to be like Napoleon and remain at Boulogne and look at the Dover cliffs from a distance.

I have seen a certain number of French people, and I have enjoyed the society of as many visitors as I wanted.

I fear foreign affairs must have involved the Cabinet in some anxious moments. Judging only from that which I read in the press, it looks as if Ferdinand[1] did not mean to hold any communication with the rest of Europe until he has safely established himself in the seat of the Byzantine Emperors. He must be an astute and able diplomatist, but whether it will be an advantage to us as a nation to have him permanently at Constantinople is a problem which I do not feel sufficiently competent to solve.

The question of Egypt must be embarrassing. Grey must have his hands full, since a portion of the map of Europe has to be re-painted.

The Vienna Cabinet seems to be very disagreeable to those poor Servians, and I fail to understand why they should not be permitted to have a littoral.

FE has kept me well informed of events at Westminster. The power of the Government, as you say, is overwhelming, even though its emblem should be that of a green bay tree.

I purchased you to-day a Christmas present, which is somewhat premature! I have been shocked at the manner in which you display your person when travelling to and from the bathroom, and I am making an effort to find you an appropriate leaf.

My love to you and Clemmy and in the hopes of seeing you soon.

Believe me, Your aff cousin
MARLBOROUGH

Admiral Beatty to WSC

1 November 1912   Admiralty

First Lord,

With regard to the question you put to me last night as to the desirability of comparing 8 ships mounting *4* heavy guns with 4 ships mounting *8* heavy guns I think in the first place it w^d be desirable to send down to Sir H. Jackson the alternative ideas with the instructions to have worked out in the Tactical Branch the advantages & disadvantages comparatively of the two. I feel that this will throw some interesting & illuminating light upon the

---

[1] Ferdinand I (1861–1948), 1st Tsar of Bulgaria, a Saxe-Coburg who was elected King by the Bulgarian parliament in 1887. In 1908 he declared that Bulgaria was independent of Turkey and assumed the title of Tsar. Bulgaria was greatly enlarged in the first Balkan war of 1912; greatly reduced again in the second Balkan war of 1913. Ferdinand allied Bulgaria with the Central Powers in 1915, and abdicated in October 1918 in favour of his son Boris. He retired to Coburg.

question which would have distinct & considerable value. I assume that the 8 gun ship w^d have an excess of speed over the 4 gun ship of 4 to 5 knots which to my mind as a tactical unit w^d prove the superiority over the 4 gun ship to be very great.

DAVID BEATTY

WSC to Sir Henry Jackson

5 November 1912   Admiralty

Copy

Private & Confidential

Dear Sir Henry Jackson,
    It wd oblige me if you would have tested on the war board the manoeuvring & fighting capabilities of a squadron of 8 ships with 4 big guns each against a squadron of 4 ships with 8 big guns each: speeds (a) equal: (b) the 8 gun ships 4 knots faster: all ships to have 4 [torpedo] tubes on the beam: torpedo as well as gunfire to be assessed.

Yours vy trly
[WINSTON S. CHURCHILL]

Admiral Beatty to WSC

14 November 1912   Admiralty

Dear Mr Churchill,
    It is with great pleasure I accept your offer of the Command of the First Battle Cruiser Squadron. It is indeed a command to be proud of and I trust that I shall justify your selection of me by my administration of this very valuable and important unit.

Yours sincerely
DAVID BEATTY

Prince Louis of Battenberg to WSC

14 November 1912   Admiralty

First Lord,
    I propose to go home when through with my regular papers.
    After what you told me this morning[1] I find it difficult to concentrate

---

[1] WSC must have intimated to Prince Louis that he would soon succeed Sir Francis Bridgeman as First Sea Lord.

my thoughts on anything else. I am face to face with the last great turning point in my career & must be alone with my thoughts.

L.B.

*   *   *   *   *

WSC to the King

[? 28 October 1912]   Admiralty

Copy

Mr Churchill with his humble duty to your Majesty has the honour to submit the following names for the four capital ships of this year's programme. These vessels will be the most powerful ever built, & will from many points of view present features of the most formidable character. Mr Churchill thinks that the four ships should be identified with the names of the great warriors and Sovereigns of English History, & he proposes *King Richard the First, King Henry the Fifth, Queen Elizabeth,* & *Oliver Cromwell.* Mr Churchill has consulted with the Prime Minister about this last name, & finds him in full accord with the view that the almost unequalled services which the Lord Protector rendered to the British Navy should find recognition in Your Majesty's Fleet. The proposal involves no departure from the estd principle of naval nomenclature, for there has already been a Lord Protector since the Restoration of the Monarchy.

Lord Stamfordham to WSC
(Royal Archives)

29 October 1912   Buckingham Palace

My Dear Churchill,

The King wishes me to return the enclosed submission as he feels sure there must be some mistake in the name of *Oliver Cromwell* being suggested for one of the new battleships. For that name was proposed for one of the ships of last year's programme; His Majesty was unable to agree to it and on his return from India personally explained to you the reasons for his objection.

The King's opinion on the subject has in no way changed and in these circumstances he naturally regrets at having again to ask that some other name may be submitted.

Believe me, Yours very truly
STAMFORDHAM

WSC to Lord Stamfordham
(*Royal Archives*)

1 November 1912 Admiralty

My dear Stamfordham,

I thought very carefully over the question of naming a battleship *Oliver Cromwell* during the year that has passed since this subject was raised. I have also consulted with the Prime Minister & others of my colleagues & find that they fully concur that such a name is not inappropriate for one of His Majesty's Ships, & is desirable on general grounds. I have also discussed the matter with various people on the Conservative side who have a good knowledge of the history of the Navy, & I find a very general agreement.

Oliver Cromwell was one of the founders of the Navy, & scarcely any man did so much for it. I am quite sure that nothing in history will justify the view that the adoption of such a name would constitute any reflection, however vague, upon His Majesty's Royal House. On the contrary, the great movement in politics & in religion of which Cromwell was the instrument, was intimately connected with all those forces which, through a long succession of Princes, have brought His Majesty to the Throne of a Constitutional & a Protestant country. The bitterness of the rebellions and tyrannies of the past has long ceased to stir men's minds; but the achievements of the country & of its greatest men endure. His Majesty is the heir of all the glories of the nation, & there is no chapter of English history from which he should feel himself divided.

I am satisfied that the name would be extremely well received; & that it would mark in a way that little else could the permanent ascendancy in this country of monarchical over republican ideas.

I hope therefore that you will bring some of these considerations, which are put forward with the greatest respect, to His Majesty's attention.

Yours vy sincerely
WINSTON S. CHURCHILL

Lord Morley to WSC

1 November 1912 Flowermead

Dear Winston,

These scraps may serve you. The point about the statue is, I think, a good one.

It would be most injurious to popularity if this boycott of Oliver were to be known. Ld S. should be advised to press this point.

Rosebery, I believe, found the money for the statue.

Yrs

M.

'In the success of the English navy Cromwell could have no selfish interest. Its triumphs added nothing to his fame; its increase added nothing to his means of overcoming his enemies; its great leader [Blake] was not his friend. *Yet he took a peculiar pleasure in encouraging that noble service . . .*' Macaulay: Ess. on Hallam's Hist.

'Hardly yet possessed of power, the English Navy sprang *rapidly into a new life* and vigour under his stern rule. England's rights of reparation for her wrongs, were demanded *by her fleet throughout the world,* – in the Baltic, in the Mediterranean, against the Barbary States, in the West Indies; and *under him* the conquest of Jamaica began that extension of her Empire, by force of arms which has gone on to our own days.' *Mahan's* Sea Power, p. 60.

He resolutely insisted on right of search and resolutely opposed exemption of private property from seizure in maritime war.

It is surely a strange paradox to refuse his name to a battleship, when *his commanding effigy* stands conspicuous in the very spot where of all others in the realm historic reverence and honour for great rulers of every line are most naturally and irresistibly awakened in English hearts. [*nb* not Scotch nor Irish, for he drubbed them both]. You may remember that it fell to me to withstand that proposal of a statue to Oliver in 1893, because the Irish and the Tories wd not have it.

Lord Stamfordham to WSC
(*Royal Archives*)

4 November 1912   Buckingham Palace

My dear Churchill,

Your letter to me of the 1st instant has been laid before the King. I cannot conceal from you His Majesty's regret that you suggest that he should reconsider his objection to the name of *Oliver Cromwell* for one of the new Warships.

The arguments you adduce do not alter the King's views on the subject. You express your conviction that the name would be extremely well received; but may I remind you that when the Government of the day in 1895 proposed to erect out of public funds a Statue of Oliver Cromwell they were rigorously opposed by the Irish and the Opposition and defeated by a majority of 137.

In debate Mr Justin McCarthy stated that what the Duke of Alva was in the memories of the people of the Netherlands so was Oliver Cromwell in the minds of the Irish, and 'he could not understand how a Liberal Government and above all a Home Rule Government could propose what was an insult to the Irish People'.

Mr Redmond described Cromwell as 'a murderer and a canting hypocritical murderer' and said the Irish would be false to the tradition of their country and its history, false to their forefathers, their religion and nationality if they did not protest.

Colonel Nolan condemned Cromwell as a 'treacherous brute'.

Colonel Saunderson on the other hand said no proposal would be more dear to the hearts of the Nonconformists but that the Government had decided to give away their Nonconformist supporters in obedience to the orders of their masters in Ireland.

Mr Balfour as Leader of the Opposition disputed the point that Cromwell was the founder of the Naval Power of England: for the Navy was already before Cromwell's advent to power the greatest in the world. 'As to Parliamentary Government he absolutely succeeded in uprooting its whole system.'

Sr W. Harcourt as Leader of the House of Commons admitted Cromwell's character was one upon which many people held different opinions: even he himself might not regard him as a hero; nor could the House of Commons admire some parts of his career!

If the idea of a Statue aroused so much animosity it is reasonable to expect no less opposition to the association of Cromwell with a Warship costing millions of public money.

Whatever His Majesty's own personal feelings may be with regard to Cromwell he is satisfied that your proposal would revive similar feelings of antagonism and religious bitterness to those of 17 years ago, and especially now at a time when there are alas, and especially in Ireland, signs that 'the bitterness of the rebellions and tyrannies of the past' have by no means 'ceased to stir men's minds.'

STAMFORDHAM

Lord Morley to WSC

[? 6 November 1912]   Privy Council Office
Confidential
Cromwell

It is true that Mr Balfour denied that O.C. was the *founder* of the naval power of England. But then neither Macaulay nor Mahan, to whom I referred, put it so high as all this. I need not repeat my quotations from them, but I respect Mr Balfour too much not to be quite sure that he would never dream (apart from exigencies of debate), of setting up his judgement on a historic point of this kind against either Macaulay or Mahan.

As for Mr Justin McCarthy[1] & Mr Redmond and Colonel Nolan[2] who, as you say, called O.C. 'a murderous brute', surely Englishmen are not to be frightened from proposals to honour their own worthies by language of this sort used in the political temper of the moment by Irishmen strongly interested in any demonstration of the strength of Irish national feeling. There is no reason whatever why we should expect the same heat at a time when the whole sentiment of nationalist Ireland towards Gt Brit has been brought to so different a pitch as we witness today. Ulster, I need not say, is not likely to add this association of an ultra-protestant hero with a war-ship, as a new article of indictment and complaint.

Whatever may be said about O.C.'s share in the strength and greatness of the Navy, – and in the face of the accredited historians like Gardiner,[3] Firth,[4] & others, it is really impossible to deny this share, – there is the marked and indisputable fact that O.C. brought the name & power of Engld into a recognized prominence over the continent of Europe which has not many times been equalled, & has never been surpassed. This, to be sure, is no answer to those who dislike, or even detest, O.C.'s domestic policy, but it is a reason why we should give to a battle-ship a name that never failed to make the enemies of Engld tremble. To come down from historic heights, may I remind you that the monument to O.C. was *provided* by Lord Rosebery. Of him I would venture to say two things: 1. That in his historic sentiment and conviction he is the representative of many, many Englishmen & Scotsmen in both political camps; 2. But even when he does not fully share their sentiment, he has an extraordinarily acute *flair* for it.

[1] Justin Huntly McCarthy (1830–1912), dramatist, novelist and historian; author of *Ireland Since the Union*. Nationalist MP 1884–92.

[2] John Philip Nolan (d. 1912), Nationalist MP for North Galway 1900–6; Colonel Royal Artillery.

[3] Samuel Rawson Gardiner (1829–1902), Professor of Modern History King's College London; Author of *Cromwell's Place in History*, published in 1897.

[4] Charles Harding Firth (1857–1936), Regius Professor of Modern History Oxford 1904–1925; wrote a number of books on Cromwell and the Commonwealth.

WSC to Lord Stamfordham
(Royal Archives)

5 November 1912

My dear Stamfordham,

My attention has been drawn to some very large estimates wh have been presented for the refit of the *Victoria & Albert,* & I have also been looking into the expenditure of the last five years on this vessel. I am sure the King would be surprised to see the enormous charges wh are made for quite small things. I know His Majesty wd disapprove anything in the nature of wasteful or extravagant expenditure apart from what is properly required for the maintenance of the yacht in the highest condition. I am asking Sir Francis Hopwood & the Director of Dockyards to go down to Portsmouth this week & go through the new estimate for £13,000 with the Commodore; & after I am more fully informed His Majesty wd probably wish me to lay the result of the investigation before him.

Yours very sincerely
WINSTON S. CHURCHILL

Note by Stamfordham: –

5 November 1912

Am sure HM wd deprecate unnecessary expendre or extravagance & that he will be glad to know result of Sir F.H's investigations.

S.

Further note: –

Read by the King 6.11.12.

Prince Louis of Battenberg to WSC

6 November [1912]   Admiralty

Private

First Lord,

You told me the other day that on your second application to the King re *Oliver Cromwell* he had again raised objections.

All my experience at the Admiralty & close intercourse with three sovereigns leads me to this: from all times the Sovereign's decision as to names for HM Ships has been accepted as final by all First Lords.

I am inclined to think the Service as a whole would go against you in this choice.

L.B.

WSC to Lord Stamfordham
(Royal Archives)

16 November 1912 Admiralty

My dear Stamfordham,

In the face of the accredited historians like Gardiner, Firth, and others, it is really impossible to deny Oliver Cromwell's share in the strength and greatness of the Navy. There is besides the marked and indisputable fact that he brought the name and power of England into a recognised prominence over the Continent of Europe which has not many times been equalled and has never been surpassed. It certainly seems right that we should give to a battleship a name that never failed to make the enemies of England tremble.

It has been my duty to place before the King in this and my last letter to you the good and serious reasons which have led me to submit this name. If they do not weigh with His Majesty I shall not on such a subject press my advice further. Meanwhile, I enclose you two quotations, for which I am indebted to the erudition of Lord Morley.

Yours sincerely
WINSTON S. CHURCHILL

'In the success of the English Navy Cromwell could have no selfish interest. Its triumph added nothing to his fame: its increase added nothing to his means of overcoming his enemies; its great leader (Blake) was not his friend; yet *he took a peculiar* pleasure in encouraging that noble service.' (Macaulay: *Essay on Hallam's History*).

'Hardly yet possessed of power, the English Navy sprang rapidly into a new life and vigour under his stern rule. England's rights of reparation for her wrongs were demanded by her Fleet throughout the world – in the Baltic, in the Mediterranean, against the Barbary States, in the West Indies; and *under him* the conquest of Jamaica began that expansion of her Empire by force of arms which has gone on to our own day.' (Mahan: *Sea Power*, page 60).

Lord Stamfordham to WSC
(Royal Archives)

20 November 1912 Windsor Castle

Copy

My dear Churchill,

You will, I am sure, realise how very distasteful it is to the King not to approve of recommendations coming from any of his Ministers, and especially when that Minister is the First Lord of the Admiralty.

But nothing which has been said or written since His Majesty discussed the matter personally with you some months ago has induced him to alter his strong opinion as to the undesirability of including among the coming additions to the Royal Navy *His Majesty's Ship Oliver Cromwell*.

In these circumstances the King must ask you to consider and submit some other name.

Yours very sincerely
STAMFORDHAM

WSC to Lord Stamfordham
(*Royal Archives*)

EXTRACT

20 November 1912

. . . I bow to the King's wish about the battleship's name and will submit the name *Valiant* as a substitute . . .

[WINSTON S. CHURCHILL]

*   *   *   *   *

WSC to David Lloyd George
(*Lloyd George Papers*)

18 November 1912   Admiralty

Private

My dear David,

Look at this. Do you realise what it means if it is true?

It is no use being vexed with me and reproaching me. I can no more control these facts than you can.

Should the Austrians build 3 extra Dreadnoughts *beyond anything yet foreseen* or provided against, we shall have to take further measures. What measures I cannot now say: but an *equal* provision in some form or another will be necessary.

However, it may all prove to be rumour. But I don't think so; my information has for some time pointed in this direction.

Yours ever
WSC

WSC to Sir Robert Chalmers

19 November 1912   Admiralty

Confidential

Copy

My dear Chalmers,

There seems to be no doubt that a substantial underspending will occur on Navy Votes for 1912–13. The shipyards are gorged with work, especially foreign warship orders, and strikes and other difficulties have delayed the progress of works under Vote 10. The best estimate at present of the net underspending is 700,000*l*, but it is practically certain that this will be increased as the year advances. Whatever surplus is thus available will be returnable to the Treasury. It will effect no diminution of the contracted liabilities of the Admiralty. It will become a direct addition beyond any estimates at present presented, including the 12th July figure, to the expense of 1913–14 and 1914–15.

The estimates of both these years will also be inflated beyond anything foreseen in the 12th July Letter by the high prices prevailing over the whole area of Admiralty purchases, and especially where new construction is concerned. There is a very serious rise in the cost of oil fuel, which is largely due to the scarcity of freightage. It is to be hoped that this will correct itself in a few years' time by new forms of liquid fuel being discovered, by increased freightage becoming available, and by the adoption of internal combustion engines. But so far as the immediate future is concerned, no prospect of relief from the high prices can be discerned.

If the estimates of 1913–14 are to be satisfactorily coped with, it will be necessary to take every legitimate step to relieve them out of the underspending of 1912–13. I have given my officers directions to make proposals to that end where possible in each Department. No expenditure is to be proposed in relief of the underspending which does not –

(*a*.) Figure as a necessary service in the provision of the approved draft estimates for 1913–14; and

(*b*.) Which does not relieve the Votes of 1913–14 and 1914–15 directly to a corresponding extent.

Various proposals will shortly reach you, or are now before you, which fall within this category.

I must draw your attention to a point which I think the Chancellor of the Exchequer has not fully appreciated. In my talks with him he often speaks as if the surplus accruing through underspending in 1912–13 could be used to reduce the estimates of 1913–14. This is only true if it is borne in mind that those estimates for 1913-14 and those of succeeding years are increased *pro tanto* by the 1912-13 underspending; so that no real relief is obtainable by the Treasury through any underspending surrender however applied to the reduction of future estimates. On the other hand, if the underspent surplus is not applied in relief of estimates and is surrendered to the National Debt, there is a direct loss to the Treasury of the whole amount; and it simply means that the taxpayer is making a more generous provision than was contemplated by Parliament for the repayment of debt without obtaining any diminution in the aggregate amount of naval expenditure and liability.

To take an example. Suppose the 1912-13 estimates were 45 millions and 1913-14 were 50 millions; suppose that an underspending of 5 million occurs in 1912-13. If the whole of that 5 millions is made available to reduce the estimates of 1913-14 and 1914-15, the financial position will be un-changed; it will not be any better, it will not be any worse. If, on the other hand, the 5 millions is surrendered to the National Debt, the estimates of 1913-14 and 1914-15 will, without any means of relief, be increased by exactly that sum. It is, therefore, no use looking upon the underspending as a fund in hand for reducing the expense of 1913-14. The estimates of 1913-14 and 1914-15 rise automatically as each underspending becomes clear. You will quite understand that the above is an example intended only to make the point plain, and that the figures bear no special relation to actual fact.

It is still my hope to keep within the figures for 1913-14 supplied on the 12th July; and experience of past underspendings and the general state of the shipyards will undoubtedly justify a large cut in these estimates on the ground of estimated short earnings by contractors. This will afford relief to the finance of next year. But here again I must point out that the ultimate governing factor is the aggregate amount of Admiralty liabilities under all programmes, that nothing can diminish this except its being earned by the contractor and paid for by the Treasury, and that all delays, whether they occur through underspendings returned to the Treasury or through cuts made by the First Lord on a general survey of the earning powers of con-tractors, move automatically forward to swell the estimates of future years. It is only a very short form of rejoicing that can be indulged in as a conse-quence of an underspending or of a legitimate cut. The programmes of new vessels are calculated in relation to building by foreign Powers, and if delays occur continuously, the programmes will have to be undertaken at an earlier period in the year than would otherwise have been necessary, in order to ensure the ships being ready at the dates by which they are required.

I am bound to say that the more I learn about it the more deeply im-pressed I am with the present unsatisfactory nature of the system of Navy finance. It is really not applicable to modern conditions of Admiralty work.

It does not conduce to the highest economy or to the best kind of Treasury control, and it reduces Parliamentary control almost to a nullity. The proper course would be for the House, when agreeing to the construction of a battle-ship or other war vessel, or great constructive work, to vote the whole sum, and authorise the Treasury to supply the Admiralty continuously with the money as the instalments were earned by the contractors, irrespective of any surrender at a fixed period in the year. In this way an absurdly complicated system of finance would be put an end to, and hurry and waste would be avoided.

I write you this letter only for your general information, and not with a view to action of any kind.

Yours sincerely
WINSTON S. CHURCHILL

WSC to Lord Stamfordham
(*Royal Archives*)

EXTRACT

20 November 1912   Admiralty

My dear Stamfordham,

I am very glad to hear from you that the King is pleased with the general character of my submissions about flag appointments.

Sir Alexander Bethell is specially qualified for the presidency of the War College from the fact that he has filled for a considerable period the position of Director of Naval Intelligence, which under the old system corresponded as nearly as possible to that of Chief of the War Staff. It is proposed that a very close connection shall exist between the War College and the War Staff in London. We do not want unnecessarily to widen the circle of officers who are privy to Admiralty secrets. Sir A. Bethell knows everything and can therefore guide the College in the right directions in tactical & strategic teaching without disclosing anything that ought to be kept secret. It is desirable to know everything in order to understand what to conceal. It is also desirable that the heads of the War Staff and War College should be able mutually to help each other.

I was agreeably surprised by the readiness of Sir A. Bethell to give up his lucrative East Indian command and know that he is willing to do so, subject to the King's approval, only to get nearer the front line in case of trouble.

In spite of his unimpressive manner he is an officer of first-rate ability. I am quite sure no better appointment is within reach at the present time. . . .

Yours vy sincerely
WINSTON S. CHURCHILL

WSC to Sir Francis Bridgeman

28 November 1912   [Admiralty]

[Copy]

My dear Sir Francis,

I am very glad to hear from various sources that you have now somewhat recovered from the chill which so unkindly spoiled your holiday, and I trust you will continue to make good progress in spite of the drop in the temperature.

I have been meaning for some time to write to you about your health, which causes me concern both as a colleague and a friend. During the year that we have worked together I have seen how heavily the strain of your great office has told upon you, and I know that only your high sense of duty and your consideration for me have enabled you successfully to overcome your strong inclination to retire. That strain will not, I fear, diminish in the future; and if, by any misadventure, we were to be involved in war, I feel that the burden might be more than you could sustain.

If therefore you should feel disposed at this juncture to retire, I could not, whatever my personal regrets, oppose your wish, and I believe that such a step would be a relief to you.

It would be a cause of very great pleasure to me if I could feel that our association in so much important business had in no way been a cause of regret or dissatisfaction to you.

Believe me, Yours very sincerely
WINSTON S. CHURCHILL

Sir Francis Bridgeman to WSC

29 November 1912   Copgrove Hall
                                          Yorkshire

My dear Mr Churchill,

I am in receipt of your kindly-meant letter, and will give it careful consideration. I am much better, I am glad to say, and am coming to London as soon as the doctor will allow me.

Believe me, Yours very sincerely
F. B. BRIDGEMAN

WSC to the King
(*Royal Archives*)

29 November 1912   Admiralty

Dictated

Mr Churchill with his humble duty to Your Majesty: he expressed in audience with Your Majesty the other day his increasing anxiety about the state of Sir Francis Bridgeman's health. He can no longer feel satisfied that this officer would be capable of bearing the immense responsibility and strain which would be cast upon him if by any misfortune we were involved in a great naval war. This conclusion once having been reached makes action imperative. Mr Churchill has therefore suggested to Sir Francis Bridgeman in terms of high consideration the propriety of his retirement at an early date. He will on this retirement becoming effective submit to Your Majesty a proposal for promoting Sir Francis Bridgeman to be an Admiral of the Fleet additional to the regular list. This distinction is well merited by Sir Francis by the great command he has held and the high esteem which he enjoys throughout the Navy.

Mr Churchill would then propose with the concurrence of the Prime Minister to submit to Your Majesty the name of Prince Louis of Battenberg to fill the office of First Sea Lord, and that of Sir John Jellicoe to succeed him as Second Sea Lord.

Before making these submissions Mr Churchill would be deeply grateful if he could receive from Your Majesty an intimation that Your Majesty's pleasure would be in accord with arrangements which Mr Churchill is convinced are required in the interests of the Navy and of the State.

WINSTON S. CHURCHILL

Lord Stamfordham to WSC
(*Royal Archives*)

2 December 1912   York Cottage
                                                            Sandringham

Copy

My dear Churchill,

In reply to your letter of the 29th ult to the King: His Majesty is grieved to hear of Sir Francis Bridgeman's illness which will necessitate his retirement at an early date – a loss to the Navy which His Majesty much deplores.

The King is sorry you did not mention the appointments which you propose in consequence of Sir Francis' retirement, when you were at Windsor a week ago as he could have then personally discussed them with you, which His Majesty feels sure you will agree is much more satisfactory than a discussion by letter.

The King is very glad to approve your recommendation of Prince Louis of Battenberg to be First Sea Lord whom he considers to be in every way fitted for that very important and responsible post.

His Majesty equally approves of Sir John Jellicoe, whom he knows well, and feels sure will prove an excellent successor to Prince Louis as Second Sea Lord.

As to the promotion of Sir Francis Bridgeman to Admiral of the Fleet, the King fears that this would raise difficulties and not be understood in the Service. If promoted now, he would pass over Admiral Sir William May who, it is assumed, will succeed Sir Charles Hotham on 20th March 1913: also Admiral Sir Hedworth Meux who in the usual course of things will become an Admiral of the Fleet on the retirement of Sir Gerard Noel in March 1915. Moreover, when Lord Charles Beresford retired, the King suggested that he should be promoted to Admiral of the Fleet. This was opposed by the then First Lord, Mr McKenna, on the grounds that it was unusual to promote an Admiral to the highest grade unless there was a vacancy among the Admirals of the Fleet before he reached the age of 65.

The King acquiesced and it was then settled, and no doubt a record to this effect is at the Admiralty, that no Admiral should be promoted out of his turn unless for war services or for very exceptional services rendered in peace time to the Navy and State.

The King has known Sir Francis Bridgeman for a great number of years and has the highest possible regard for him and fully appreciates his professional abilities. But at the same time His Majesty does not feel that his services call for the specially marked recognition which you suggest.

Believe me, Yours very sincerely

STAMFORDHAM

WSC to Sir Francis Bridgeman

2 December 1912   HMS *Enchantress*

Private

[Copy]

My dear Sir Francis,

Before writing to you I consulted the Prime Minister and informed the King. The conclusion at which I have arrived must necessarily be final; and I am confident that it will command your assent. I hope you will let me know your wishes in regard to any member of your staff for whom employment should be provided at the Admiralty or at sea.

I am very glad, indeed, to hear you are better. A warm climate during these winter months and relief from office cares will restore your health, I trust, for many honoured years.

Believe me, Yours very sincerely
WINSTON S. CHURCHILL

Sir Francis Bridgeman to WSC

3 December 1912   Copgrove Hall

My dear Mr Churchill,

You will be anxiously expecting my reply to your very kind and sympathetic letter suggesting that if my health was not good enough to allow me to continue the duties of my office, I should apply to resign.

I have carefully thought the matter over, and as it seemed to be more a question for the doctors to give an opinion on, I have consulted them. Dr Wexley-Smith, whom I usually consult, is of opinion that having now diagnosed thoroughly the malady, feels himself able to put me quite right, there being nothing organically wrong, but that I have been run down.

The change to this place has done me a lot of good, and I am returning to London on Monday next. I don't think there is a necessity to resign, neither do I think I need go abroad. I shall remain in London for a week or ten days, and then come back for Christmas and return for good to the Admiralty at the new year. This plan is what I originally arranged for earlier in the year with the Second Sea Lord.

I wish I had taken your advice six or seven months ago and gone abroad. I should probably have avoided all this trouble.

Believe me, Yours very sincerely
F. B. BRIDGEMAN

Sir Francis Bridgeman to WSC

4 December 1912   Copgrove Hall

My dear Mr Churchill,
   I am in receipt of your letter dated the 2nd December, and written from the Admiralty yacht. I think our letters must have crossed.
   I had no idea that my leaving the Admiralty had already been settled, and that you had discussed it with the King and the Prime Minister; had I known this I should not have written my letter in answer to yours of the 28th November, in which you express anxiety as to my health and ask me what I am disposed to do.
   I now understand that you expect me to resign, and I am happy to be able to meet your wishes.

Believe me, Yours very sincerely
F. B. BRIDGEMAN

WSC to Sir Francis Bridgeman

6 December 1912

[Copy]

My dear Sir Francis,
   I am very sorry indeed that the time has come when we should close our year of important and successful work. The general state of your health and vigour made me feel that if a war suddenly broke out upon us you would not be able to stand the tremendous strain that would fall on the First Sea Lord. The times are too critical to brook delay, and once this conviction had formed in my mind I was bound in duty to tell you, just as you would have been bound to tell me had our situations been reversed, or to tell any officer serving under your command, or any colleague on the Board. I am sure that this course on my part is only what you would wish and approve. The time comes to us all when the wheels begin to slow down, and when the burden becomes too heavy and the pace too hot. If a man has worked as you have done for so many years from a sense of duty, in spite of many attractions to ease and diversion, and has filled so many great commands and offices with conspicuous success, there is absolutely nothing to regret.
   I have acted towards you with loyalty and sincerity. When I have been in the wrong I have admitted it. I feel no prick of conscience on account of our relations. I hope most sincerely that the warm personal regard which I

have acquired for you during our year of co-operation will not be wholly unreciprocated. No one knows better than I do the soundness of your judgment in great matters of naval administration, or the value which your personal and professional reputation has been to the Board of Admiralty over which I have presided. It would be a sorrow to me if I could not keep in touch with you in naval matters, and if I felt that you regretted the close association into which we have been brought by official duties.

I understand that the promotion to Admiral of the Fleet of which I wrote to you will not be acceptable to you, and I am therefore making other recommendations to His Majesty. But if there are any officers whose merit you desire to see recognised, you have only to bring their names to my notice to ensure the most prompt and favourable consideration of their claims.

With all good wishes,

Believe me, Yours very sincerely
WINSTON S. CHURCHILL

WSC to the King
(*Royal Archives*)

5 December 1912   Admiralty

Dictated

Mr Churchill with his humble duty to Your Majesty. When he last had the honour of an audience he had not arrived at a final decision about changes on the Admiralty Board, nor had he consulted, as he is bound to do in regard to Board appointments, with the Prime Minister. He did not therefore feel justified in opening the subject to Your Majesty, as he was not in a position to express a definite opinion.

Mr Churchill has received with great satisfaction the expression in Stamfordham's letter of the approval with which Your Majesty views the proposals which Mr Churchill had put forward for Your Majesty's consideration. He is confident that they are the best arrangements which could be made, and that they will constitute a great reinforcement to the Board of Admiralty at a time when so many important and even grave issues are being dealt with. He thought it right to tell Prince Louis of Battenberg of the favour with which Your Majesty views the appointment of that officer to the first and most important naval situation under the Crown.

Mr Churchill feels strongly that great and exceptional abilities should be consistently recognised in the Service, and it is an additional advantage that they should be associated with high rank and kinship with Your Majesty's Royal House. Sir John Jellicoe has accepted, subject of course to Your Majesty's approval, the suggestion which Mr Churchill made to him to succeed Prince Louis as Second Sea Lord. Mr Churchill thinks it important, owing to the European situation, that these changes should be made without delay: he therefore sends with this letter the regular submission. He has received from Sir Francis Bridgeman his letter of resignation, and he would propose to make the announcement of the appointments public as soon as the final intimation of Your Majesty's pleasure has been received. Mr Churchill would be glad to be able to make the announcement either on Saturday or at latest on Monday morning; and he would be grateful therefore if he might be favoured with a telegraphic expression of Your Majesty's wishes.

With regard to the proposal that Sir Francis Bridgeman should be promoted Admiral of the Fleet additional to the list, Mr Churchill does not fully share the views expressed in Lord Stamfordham's letter. He has had the records and precedents examined, he will at a later date submit to Your Majesty some further observations on the principles which should govern in the public interest appointments to the highest naval rank. But Mr Churchill has heard from an indirect source that Sir Francis is himself personally disinclined to this distinction. Mr Churchill would therefore propose that simultaneously with his retirement being announced he should be raised to the Grand Cross of the Bath as a special mark of Your Majesty's favour to so distinguished an Officer. There are as it conveniently happens two vacant Grand Crosses available for the Navy at the present time, so that no difficulty should present itself in this respect.

On hearing from Your Majesty that these new arrangements are approved the necessary steps will be taken in the regular course.

Mr Churchill hopes that Your Majesty is pleased with the new scheme of pay. He confesses that it is not all that he could have wished for, but the sum of money, nearly £400,000, is a very great one at a time when naval expenditure from every quarter is rising.

The scheme has been most carefully studied in its details as Your Majesty will perceive on examining it, and the claims of the various ratings have been balanced one against the other so as to meet the true interests and needs of the service which, as Your Majesty knows, are only very vaguely comprehended by the general public. Mr Churchill has every reason to believe that it will give a real measure of contentment. The increases of pay have been made to date from the 1st of December in order that the men may have a month of the increased rate available for their Christmas leave. Owing to the European situation, all the flotillas will have to spend Christmas on the

East Coast in or near their war stations, and special arrangements are being made to enable the men to get back to their Home Ports for their leave without moving the flotillas.

Mr Churchill once more expresses to Your Majesty his pleasure at feeling that Your Majesty's judgement and knowledge approve the new arrangements for the high personnel of the Navy, and with his humble duty remains Your Majesty's faithful servant and subject

WINSTON S. CHURCHILL

Lord Stamfordham to WSC
(*Royal Archives*)

6 December 1912

York Cottage
Sandringham

Copy

My dear Churchill,

The King desires me to thank you for your letter of yesterday. I return the submission for the appointments of the new 1st and 2nd Sea Lords approved by His Majesty.

As His Majesty telegraphed last evening, he will be delighted to confer the GCB on Sir Francis Bridgeman on his relinquishing the Office of 1st Sea Lord. He is not quite certain from your letter whether Sir Francis is about to retire from the Service, *now:* probably he will not do so until he attains the age of 65.[1]

As to the new Scheme of Pay for the Navy, His Majesty is much pleased with it and congratulates you upon having carried it through, though he knows that you would have done more if the necessary funds had been forthcoming.

The King recognises in studying the details how carefully the claims of the various ratings have been considered and as you say, balanced one against the other. Your arrangements by which the men will get a month of the increased pay by Christmas seems to His Majesty excellent.

He is very glad that you have been able to improve the Lieuts pay and the half pay of Captains.

Of course The King would have welcomed anything that could have been done for the married men in some way similar to the Army system.

It would be a great advantage if a certain number of married quarters

[1] Sir Francis Bridgeman was succeeded as First Sea Lord by Prince Louis of Battenberg on 7 December 1912. He reached the age of 65 on 7 December 1913.

could be built in the Naval Barracks and Schools established for the education of the children. But His Majesty knows that this is a very big question.

The King will be in London on the 13th inst until within a few days of
Xmas in case there are any matters upon which you may wish to see him.

Yours very truly
STAMFORDHAM

WSC to Lord Stamfordham
(*Royal Archives*)

8 December 1912　　　　　　　　　　　　　　　　　　　　Admiralty

My dear Stamfordham,

You are quite right in assuming that Sir Francis will not retire from the
Service until he attains the age of 65. Before that date I propose to submit
to the King certain considerations governing the appointment of Admirals
of the Fleet. The almost invariable rule has been in practice that First Sea
Lords have attained that rank.

I am in full agreement with what you write about the King's views in
regard to the need of making provision for the married men. We have, of
course, taken a notable step in that direction by the manner in which the
present increases are applied. By concentrating on the older men the whole
available benefit, we have exercised a deterrent on early marriages, *ie* –
before 24 years of age, and we provide after 24 years of age an increase of
pay which will certainly make a real difference. This was much better than
spreading the benefit thinly over the whole area. If the seamen and stokers
will wait till they have served 6 years as men before marrying, they will be
able to keep a decent home together thereafter. Still, I do not look upon the
matter as officially settled even for our time, and I shall hope as opportunity
serves to obtain some greater advantages for them. On many grounds the
scheme of providing married quarters, to which the King refers, is most
attractive. There is, however, one great disadvantage, viz. – the steady
growth of the non-effective Vote in the Naval Estimates. I have a horror of
bricks and mortar, and much prefer spending the money on steel and
cordite. It is possible that a good housing scheme on a commercial basis,
apart from Admiralty Votes, in some of the Dockyard towns would be a
great assistance, and I shall give my attention to this if I have the time and
opportunity.

Will you express to His Majesty my thanks for the gracious manner in
which he has received my proposals for the important changes on the
Board, and for the promptness with which his assent was given. I have

received a nice telegram from Sir Francis Bridgeman, who is evidently gratified by the GCB and who, I believe, will greatly appreciate his relief from office cares.

Yours sincerely
WINSTON S. CHURCHILL

Morning Post

EXTRACT

14 December 1912

We are enabled to publish some particulars regarding the resignation of Admiral Sir Francis Bridgeman, the correctness of which is vouched for on the very best authority. Some time ago the late First Sea Lord took the initiative in urging his colleagues on the Board of Admiralty to tender their resignations on the subject of Pay and Manning in the Navy. This resolution was conveyed to the Prime Minister by Mr Winston Churchill, and it is not unreasonable to suppose that the result was the recent statement by the First Lord providing a general increase of pay. It will be remembered that in the House of Commons on Wednesday last, Sir C. Kinloch-Cooke asked the First Lord whether it was a fact that the Sea Lords had threatened more than once to resign during the last month. In answer to this Mr Churchill said: 'There is absolutely no truth in the suggestion.' This statement is in obvious conflict with the facts which we put before our readers; but no doubt the explanation is that the wording of Sir C. Kinloch-Cooke's question left some opening for the First Lord's answer. When he acquiesced in Mr Churchill's suggestion that he should retire, Sir Francis Bridgeman was offered the honour of Admiral of the Fleet, which, however, he refused.

WSC to Sir Francis Bridgeman

14 December 1912

My dear Sir Francis,

The enclosed extract from the *Morning Post* of today raises several serious issues on which it is necessary that I should know exactly where you stand. For such a gross breach of official confidence I am certain you cannot be directly responsible. But it seems to me probable that the question of your resignation will now be the subject of acrimonious debate in Parliament, and I must be free, if necessary, to deal fully and plainly with the facts. I have done my best to guard and sustain your professional reputation and personal dignity, and if I am to continue to do so with success it is essential that I should have your concurrence in making certain statements.

First. That no difference existed between us on the question of manning, and that you were satisfied with the provision (5,000) proposed for next year's increase. On this point I hold, of course, your assent on the official papers; but it will be better if I can state it with your permission.

Secondly. That you concurred in and accepted the scale of improved pay now published. On this point I hold your signed acceptance of the proposals, subject of course to your desire to get more if the money could be found. It will again be very advantageous if I can make this statement with your concurrence. If the matter is disputed, I should be forced to state that during your whole tenure as Second Sea Lord you made no proposals for increasing the pay, and that no proposals for increasing the pay either of officers or of men emanated from you during your tenure as First Sea Lord. Those proposals were initiated solely by me, though I acknowledge the loyal support which I received from you and from the other Sea Lords in my negotiations with the Treasury. No difference of view existed between us on the subject. You were willing to resign if necessary to strengthen my hands during the discussion, but no resignation was tendered by you or any other members of the Board, and you and all the other Sea Lords concurred in the conclusion finally reached.

I hope that it may not be necessary to argue out all these details in public. I shall not in the least shrink from doing so.

Thirdly. I desire to state that I have your authority in saying that no other cause of difference or disagreement in policy or view existed between us which had led, or was about to lead, to your resignation.

Your agreement in the above plain statements of fact will, I believe, enable me to close the incident without further unpleasantness. But unless I have your authority to make such a statement on behalf of us both it may be necessary – though I should regret it from every point of view – for me to publish to Parliament my letter to you of the 28th November, together with your replies of the 29th and the 3rd December; my second letter to you of the 2nd December and your reply dated the 4th.

It may also be necessary for me, if the point of your ill-health is disputed, to state that you wrote on the 25th November to Prince Louis as follows: –

'I have been very depressed lately about my health: two attacks of bronchitis within a few months, and coming on top of appendicitis, seems to have weakened my constitution, and I sometimes feel inclined to give up my post. However, I am now up and about the house, and it will, I hope, pass off. The fact is, I really ought to go somewhere warmer than England to spend the winter – an impossibility so long as one remains at the Admiralty.'

It may also be necessary for me to refer to your letter to my Naval Secretary of November 26th, in which you say that you had actually taken up your pen to write out your resignation overnight, but that feeling better in the morning you had changed your mind.

It would be very painful to me to go into these details, or to have to prove to the House of Commons, inch by inch, the facts which led me to the conclusion that your physical strength and energy were no longer equal to the duties of your office. But if I am challenged by persons who the public may think (though some of them are no friends of yours) are acting on your behalf, I shall be forced to vindicate the action which I took, at this dangerous period in international affairs, in asking you to relinquish your post.

Let me, then, recapitulate the three statements which I desire to make upon our joint authority: –

1. That no difference existed between us on the question of manning, and that you were satisfied with the provision proposed for next year's increase.

2. That you concurred in, and accepted, the improved scale of pay as now published.

3. That no cause of difference or disagreement in policy or view existed between us which had led, or was about to lead, to your resignation.

As it is important that I should receive your answer before Monday, the messenger is instructed to await your convenience.

Yours very sincerely
WINSTON S. CHURCHILL

Sir Francis Bridgeman to WSC

TELEGRAM

15 December 1912   Burton Leonard

Absolutely agree to all you say. I don't know where *Morning Post* article came from, but it's untrue. Am coming London today; address Grosvenor Hotel; if you wish to see me will call tomorrow.

BRIDGEMAN

Sir Francis Bridgeman to WSC

[15 December 1912]   Grosvenor Hotel

Dear Mr Churchill,

I now have to amplify my telegram dispatched to you this morning, in which I authorised you in general terms to state there was no disagreement between us on the three points mentioned in your letter to-day, *viz*, as to manning, improved pay, and general policy. But with regard to your third question, as to whether we have had no other causes of difference or dis-- agreement in policy or view which might have led to my resignation, you will recollect that on more than one occasion such differences have arisen on matters of serious importance. For example, I need only refer to a recent question of an appointment which involved so grave a conflict of opinion that I felt obliged to suggest my resignation.

Let me add that if, as you seem to intimate, you should publish my private letters to yourself and to officers serving at the Board of Admiralty, I must ask you to be good enough to include this letter with the other correspondence.

Yours sincerely
F. B. BRIDGEMAN

Sir Francis Bridgeman to WSC

16 December 1912   Grosvenor Hotel

Dear Mr Churchill,

Since I have not received any reply to my telegram to you asking whether you desired to see me, I am returning to the country this morning.

Yours sincerely
F. B. BRIDGEMAN

WSC to Sir Francis Bridgeman

16 December 1912

Copy

Dear Sir Francis,

I am very glad to hear from you by telegram and letter that you authorize me to state in general terms that there was no disagreement between us on the three points mentioned in my letter of the 14th. The reservation which you make in regard to the third does not seem to me to be material. It is quite true that differences of view have from time to time arisen between us, as between all persons who work together in the difficult business of government; but none of these differences led to your tendering your resignation, and all were adjusted to our mutual satisfaction by the ordinary process of frank and friendly discussion. None were outstanding between us at the time of your departure for Copgrove. The question to which in particular you refer, of the appointment of Admiral Farquhar[1] to the Coastguard and Reserves, was one in which, though I could not admit your claim to be the sole channel of advice in naval appointments, I quite gladly met your wish. It is impossible for anyone to state or suggest that this was a matter on which you had tendered or threatened your resignation, or which was 'about to lead to' your resignation. Beatty, who was present throughout our talks, shares my recollection of what took place. Your letter to me of the 3rd December, in which you expressed your willingness to continue, in spite of your health, and my letter of the 28th, also makes it clear that no outstanding difference, either this or any other, rendered our official co-operation unsatisfactory to you. I see therefore nothing in your letter which should prevent my making, on our joint authority, the three statements I put to you on Saturday. If you disagree, you should let me know.

It occurs to me that it would be a very good thing for us both, and for the interests of the Service, if we could have a talk together; and as you kindly suggest it in your telegram, I would propose 4.30 in my room at the Admiralty.

WSC to Sir Francis Bridgeman

16 December 1912

Copy

Dear Sir Francis,

I am extremely sorry to have missed you. I was out of town yesterday, and only got your telegram very late. My letter posted to you today will explain the situation.

Yours sincerely
WINSTON S. CHURCHILL

[1] Arthur Murray Farquhar (1855–1937). Commanded Coast Guard and Reserves 1913–15; 4th Cruiser Squadron 1909–11; Admiral 1914; Knighted 1914.

Sir Francis Bridgeman to WSC

17 December 1912   Copgrove Hall

Dear Mr Churchill,

In reply to your letter dated the 16th instant, I desire to say that the answer to your request is contained in the first paragraph of my letter written to you from the Grosvenor Hotel last Sunday, and that I have nothing to add to it.

Believe me, Yours sincerely
F. B. BRIDGEMAN

Sir Francis Bridgeman to WSC

TELEGRAM

18 December 1912   Burton Leonard

If you quote me as being in agreement with you in matters of general policy as mentioned in your letter you must not omit the reference in my letters to the fact that on other matters we have differed to the extent that I suggested resignation.

BRIDGEMAN

WSC to Sir Francis Bridgeman

18 December 1912

Copy

Dear Sir Francis Bridgeman,

I cannot accept the statement contained in your telegram just received by me. You have never on any occasion tendered your resignation to me. No resignation by you was threatened or impending at the time of your retirement. My letter to you of the 28th November imparted to you the fact that I did not 'consider your health and strength sufficient to bear the strain of a war.' In spite of this, however, you still proposed in your reply to continue in office. This alone proves that there was, in the words of my question, 'no difference in general policy between us which had led, or was about to lead, to your resignation,' and it is unworthy of you not to accept an opportunity of dissociating yourself from statements which are unfounded, and known to be unfounded by those with whom you worked.

I shall certainly not place any reliance upon your authority in any statement I may have to make, or quote you in any way as agreeing with me.

Yours very truly
WINSTON S. CHURCHILL

On 20 December, during the debate on the Christmas adjournment, WSC was attacked in the House over the retirement of Sir Francis Bridgeman. In a detailed reply, WSC said that Sir Francis' retirement was due to reasons of health and that there were no differences between them in policy. He read some of the correspondence and admitted that he himself had suggested that the First Sea Lord retire.

WSC to the King
(*Royal Archives*)

21 December 1912

Dictated

Mr Churchill with his humble duty has the honour to submit the enclosed copy of correspondence with Sir Francis Bridgeman wh he thinks it desirable Your Majesty shd read before receiving that officer.

Mr Churchill has no reason to object so far as he is concerned, to the full publication which is now proposed by Sir Francis; but he thinks that it would be deeply injurious to Sir Francis Bridgeman, who is repeatedly shown to be taking small points & false points to lend colour to vague general insinuations, & has clearly allowed his mind to be poisoned by persons who wish to make party attacks in Parliament. If Sir Francis desires it, the publication will be made on Monday, & as Your Majesty has a great regard for that officer Your Majesty may desire to warn him of the deplorable folly of persisting further in disclosures damaging only to himself.

If the correspondence is published, it is proposed that all passages affecting the question of promotion to Admiral of the Fleet be excluded, as they concern Your Majesty's opinion.

WINSTON S. CHURCHILL

Lord Stamfordham to WSC
(Royal Archives)

21 December 1912   Buckingham Palace

Copy

My dear Churchill,

The King has read the correspondence which you sent him this afternoon respecting this lamentable business of Sir Francis Bridgeman's retirement: and also the copies of the letters which passed between you and the Admiral today. His Majesty deprecates more than I can say the manner in which this unhappy controversy has become not only public property but a party question – Sir Francis, whom the King has seen, evidently feels that his reputation is impugned and that as already certain letters have been published it will only be fair to him that the whole correspondence, so far as it affects the causes of his retirement, should at once be given to the public.

In these circumstances His Majesty would prefer to give no advice and to leave the matter in your hands to be dealt with as you deem best.

The King approves of the proposed omission from the published correspondence of all reference to the question of promotion to Admiral of the Fleet. I may mention that the King's seeing Sir Francis today was in accordance with the usual custom of receiving Flag Officers and high Officials on retirement from office and was settled on the 11th. inst. and had no connection with subsequent events which I again assure you, are deeply deplored by His Majesty.

Yours sincerely
STAMFORDHAM

Sir Francis Bridgeman to WSC

21 December 1912   Grosvenor Hotel

Dear Mr Churchill,

I observe that in the reports of yesterday's debate in the House of Commons, in the course of your speech you thought proper to quote passages from private letters written by me to Prince Louis of Battenberg and to Admiral Beatty.

I beg to remind you that in my letter to you, replying to your letter of the 15th December last, in which you stated that '*it may also be necessary*' for you to quote from my letters to Prince Louis and Admiral Beatty, I made it a condition of granting my permission to do as you proposed, '*that if, as you seem to intimate, you should publish my private letters to yourself and to officers serving at the Board of Admiralty, I must ask you to be good enough to include this letter with the other correspondence.*' I think you will agree with me that I had some right to expect that you would comply with my request. I see, however, that you have quoted the letters in question without fulfilling the condition expressly stated by me. I feel, therefore, that I have now no choice but to urge that you will forthwith publish the whole correspondence which has taken place between us, with regard to my resignation.

I desire also to reserve my right of sending this letter, together with your reply, to the press.

I am returning to Copgrove to-day, where all letters should be addressed.

Believe me, Yours truly
F. B. BRIDGEMAN

WSC to Sir Francis Bridgeman

21 December 1912

Copy

Dear Sir Francis Bridgeman,

I see no reason to object to a further publication of the correspondence between us, so far as I am concerned, and if you desire it I will make arrangements to send it to the press in time for Monday. The correspondence must, however, be sufficiently full to convey from the series of letters and telegrams a true impression to the public. I should propose, therefore, to begin with my letter of the 6th December and your answer to it of the 8th December, in which you first refer to the alleged occasion of your having threatened resignation. From this letter there should, however, be omitted the recommendations of particular officers which you made to me, as there is no need to bring them in. This letter concludes with your good wishes to the new Board and to myself, and it is essential that it should be included. I should propose to publish my letter of the 9th December, omitting irrelevant references to individuals. It will be necessary that my letter of the 14th December should be published, in which I ask you certain specific questions, and your telegram in answer, in which 'you absolutely agree to all I say.' Then in its proper place will come your letter written from the Grosvenor Hotel later in the same day, when under what influence I cannot determine you go back on your spontaneous first thoughts and allow yourself to become the tool of party attack. My letter of the 16th December must be published, as it deals with the alleged incident of your threatening resignation, and shows the proper proportions of the affair. In this connection I may remind you that it is the Naval Secretary, and not the First Sea Lord, who by long-established custom advises the First Lord on naval appointments, and that even if it were true that you threatened to resign, which I was certainly not aware of, it would have been a most unreasonable and improper occasion. Had your resignation been tendered on such a subject I should have been bound to accept it forthwith. I should propose further to publish your letter of the 17th December and your telegram of the 18th December, together with my answer of the same date. The correspondence could include, if you desire it, with yours of to-day's date and this answer to it.

You have no claim, and have never had any claim, to prevent my making use, if necessary for a public purpose, of information as to your state of health, and your view of your state of health, which had reached me through official channels. Admiral Beatty, as Naval Secretary, was bound in duty to acquaint me with what you had written, just as he would have done if any flag officer in high command afloat communicated to him that his health was so bad that he was on the verge of resignation. Your letter to Prince Louis was in no sense a privileged document, and it would have been improper in any officer serving on the Board of Admiralty to withhold such information from the responsible Minister. It was your duty, indeed, which I am at last reluctantly compelled to remind you of, to have written to me yourself of your misgivings as to your ability to discharge your office. I thought it would be more considerate to you to establish, as I was bound to do for the satisfaction of Parliament, your ill-health from your own words rather than to prove the fact by going into details. I could, of course, have pointed out instead that you have only been able to attend three out of six meetings of the Committee of Imperial Defence, and that on one of those three occasions you were forced to leave from sudden faintness. But it was hateful for me to dwell on such things in public.

If you desire that a further publication shall be made I shall not resist your wish. But I warn you most earnestly that it would be deeply injurious to your reputation. That is the last service which I can render you.

Yours very truly

WINSTON S. CHURCHILL

Sir Francis Bridgeman to WSC
(Royal Archives)

23 December 1912   Copgrove Hall

Copy

Most secret

Dear Mr Churchill,

Yr letter of Sat 21st reached me at 5 pm after my interview with His Majesty.

The threatening character of this letter is such that I should have desired to reply with emphasis. However after a conversation with a High Personage I had already been led to the conclusion that the publication of our correspondence wd not conduce to the interests of the Service.

I accordingly withdraw my claim that the complete & unedited correspondence which has passed between us shd be published.

I have to add that HM who adopted a wholly impartial attitude at my audience, desires that his influence in the matter should not be the subject of conversation.

I shall do my utmost to fulfil HM's wishes tho' you will readily appreciate the circumstances which impel me to communicate this fact to yourself.

y.v.t.
F. B. BRIDGEMAN

Prince Louis of Battenberg to WSC

EXTRACT

27 December 1912   Admiralty

. . . Bridgeman's 'friends' are evidently in a hole over this correspondence. Portsmouth Naval Club is almost unanimous against Beresford, but Meux thinks you had other reasons besides health for getting rid of F.B. (I quote a mutual friend). You may like to reassure him. I also feel that a talk with His Majesty on an early date would be advisable. Bridgeman is so inaccurate in his statements based on recollection, that he may have persuaded the King that he *did* threaten to resign & convey an altogether wrong impression.

When Austria begins to de-mobilise I suppose we can cancel the 48-hour rule for ships refitting, get 3rd B.Sq home & let 1st & 2nd, also 4th & 5th (in 2 groups) cruise to Vigo.

Yrs very sincly
LOUIS BATTENBERG

Memorandum by WSC

30 December 1912

Sir Francis Bridgeman having desired that the recent correspondence between the First Lord of the Admiralty and himself should be published in full, the enclosed print is circulated for publication by Mr Churchill's direction.

The correspondence is complete with the exception of a few irrelevant passages which are omitted with Sir Francis Bridgeman's concurrence.

*   *   *   *   *

Jack Seely to WSC

30 November 1912   Blatchington House
                                                          Seaford

My dear Winston,

Many happy returns of your birthday, and may all good fortune attend you and yours in the years to come.

It is only on his birthday that a man may have his merits extolled by his friends, so may I tell you today that every year that passes increases my admiration and affection for you.

Yours ever
JACK

*   *   *   *   *

Memorandum by WSC

8 December 1912

Secret

New Programme, 1913–14

Financial criticism of estimates always concentrates on the new programme and the numbers of vessels of each class proposed in that programme must therefore be strictly regulated according to foreign construction.

The great increase in the cost of capital ships makes it specially necessary for us to adopt the most moderate proportions compatible with safety, and the maintenance of the requisite standards of strength.

We need not at this stage complicate our proposals by any question of substituting for a battleship or battleships increased programmes of smaller vessels; nor by the alternative of purchasing the Turkish battleship; nor by the question of smaller battleships. All these alternatives for the application of money available can be considered after the main number has been established and agreed.

On this basis the main outlines of the programme are clear. We are pledged to 5 capital ships, which, I presume, should either be 8-gun 'Queen Elizabeths' or 10-gun ships of a slower speed, the cost being approximately the same in both cases. I do not think any reason has been shown at present to go back on the 15″ gun. I propose therefore for your consideration that the capital ships of the programme should be stated as 5 'Queen Elizabeths'. If this is done it will be necessary to prepare a brief but conclusive statement on the advantages of the type and the justification for the increase in cost which arises from the progress of naval science and from the comparative types and cost of vessels building for foreign countries. I should be glad if a paper on this subject could be prepared.

I understand the Germans propose to spend in 1913 £1,000,000 on submarines. If that be true, no one can dispute the necessity on our part to take an equal sum for this purpose. Only our great lead in these vessels justifies us in being content with an equal rate of progress for 1913–14.

About destroyers the question arises whether the great increase in cost and speed combined with power of the projected type does not justify some reduction in numbers. It must be remembered that in 1909–10 we built 23 destroyers, and my predecessor has frequently referred to these 3 extra vessels constructed for the Australian Government as a reason for reducing the destroyer programme in any year of special financial strain. The destroyer programme is also affected by the number of light cruisers built, projected, or re-armed. It is indeed arguable whether in the near future the destroyer and light cruiser programme should not be thrown into one and a single type evolved of fast small cruisers which would be a true destroyer and bear the same relation to the German destroyers of to-day that the British destroyers used to bear to the French torpedo boats against which they were designed. Towards this very important conclusion I have found myself increasingly drawn during the present year, and I hope it may receive your most careful consideration.

In regard to the small cruiser programme, it must be remembered that we are re-arming the Scouts at a cost of £250,000. This, in the words of the Navy League Annual virtually adds 8 effective light cruisers to the British strength. It appears to me that this fact should receive some recognition in the new programme. It must be remembered that the Germans built last year only 2 small cruisers to our 8, and that their programme for the present year is again 2 only. In these circumstances, 3, or at the outside 4, small cruisers would appear to be the limits of any conventional programme which we are justified in presenting. This subject must also be considered in relation to the fast and powerful destroyers which are now being built.

We have provisionally approved the estimates for aircraft, but a paper should be prepared giving good reasons for the scale decided upon.

In regard to miscellaneous vessels, every effort should be made to keep them at a minimum. Only a very moderate sum has been allowed in the sketch Estimates as at present presented.

The fortification of Cromarty and the decisions taken in regard thereto necessitate the immediate provision of another floating dock, and also a floating factory. The bearing of this upon the Third Dock at Rosyth must be considered. Unless the Third Dock is dropped we shall be asking for an additional expenditure of nearly £500,000 beyond anything in contemplation by our predecessors. Although perhaps the additions to the capital ships made by the Colonies may be a reason for increasing our docking facilities, I should find much difficulty in using this argument either with the Treasury or the House of Commons at the present juncture.

From the above you will see that it is my desire that the new programme should be stated in the most moderate terms possible so far as numbers of units are concerned, and that there should be an unshakable foundation for every item put forward.

It will always be possible at any time before the construction of the last two battleships in the programme is actually commenced to decide on a change of policy and to substitute for them greatly increased programmes of submarines and destroyers or small cruisers. It is most undesirable to raise such a question now while the Canadians and the Federated Malay States are committing themselves to the construction of great ships. The adumbration of such a new idea would only darken counsel and greatly embarrass those who are working on our behalf. We have nearly a year from the present time before we need make any final decision. On the other hand, the possibilities of that decision may be borne in mind in considering the minor vessels included in the conventional new programme.

All these matters are pressing and I should propose that we go over them together on Wednesday afternoon.

[WSC]

9 December 1912

Confidential   [Admiralty]

Copy

My dear Chancellor of the Exchequer,

I send you herewith the forecast to date of the Naval Estimates for 1913–14. It is possible there may be some slight alterations in the course of the next two months. Votes 8, 9, and 10 are still undergoing examination by the Finance Committee. I have been through them all myself, however, and am not hopeful that the Finance Committee will discover any sources of reduction which are likely sensibly to affect the problem as it presents itself to you. On the other hand, minor new needs may crop up; prices may harden against us still more, and unexpected underspendings on this year's Estimates may, though the indications are against it, add to the burden of 1913–14.

You will no doubt wish to deal in the main with round figures. The total net Estimate for 1913–14 is 49,600,000*l*. This Estimate is approximately 700,000*l* more than the figures of the forecast with which I furnished you in my letter of the 12th July.

That forecast was in itself a very serious and grave statement, and although I gave it with great reserve, I very much regret that it should have been exceeded. In that forecast 700,000*l* was allowed for the pay of the men, and the Cabinet decision has reduced this to 400,000*l*. You may therefore say that the figures I now present are 1,000,000*l* out on the figures of the 12th July. This 1,000,000*l* is almost entirely accounted for by increase in prices, which is so formidable a factor in naval finance.

I should be very glad to go with you or with the Cabinet Committee into the causes which have led and are leading to the general increase in naval expense. The increase is out of all proportion to the programme of new construction. The new programme for the year 1913–14 contains nothing abnormal: 5 capital ships, which have already been announced to Parliament, against 3 German; the usual annual programme of 20 destroyers against the German 12; 1,000,000*l* for submarines against the 1,000,000*l* they are spending; 4 or 5 small cruisers, according to the standard; and the usual proportion of yard craft and miscellaneous auxiliaries. All these subjects proceed on lines which are very clearly marked out, and are well known to you and to the public. The increased number of men proposed for the year (5,000) is no more than my predecessor has proposed, and has already been brought to your notice and to the notice of Parliament.

Where, then, lies the cause of the enormous expansion in naval expense which has advanced our estimates 4,500,000*l* above the heavy estimates and supplementary estimates of 1912–13, and threatens still to further advance in future years – and this at a time when one would have expected the abnormal programme of 1909–10 ('we want 8,' &c) to be passing away? I do not propose to enter in this letter into the answer to that question.

I am preparing a series of papers dealing in detail, but in a form which can be readily understood by laymen, with every aspect.

For the present I confine myself simply to the results and to the facts we have to face.

The 49,600,000*l* of the estimates now presented has already been subjected to a total reduction of about 1,000,000*l* imposed by me on personal investigation or guided by the Finance Committee. It has further been reduced by allowing for possible short earnings on Vote 8 of 500,000*l* or 600,000*l*; on Vote 9 of 200,000*l*; and on Vote 10 of 200,000*l*; a total of, say, 1,000,000*l*. This by no means exhausts the possibilities of reducing the estimates on this score, but it makes a serious inroad upon my power to do so justifiably. The total of 49,600,000*l* will probably be reduced by about 400,000*l* as a result of applying the underspendings of this year to the relief of next year's services, bringing it to say, 49,000,000*l*. It would, in my opinion, be quite justifiable to allow for another 1,000,000*l* of short earnings, bringing the figure to 48,000,000*l*. My advisers believe that any reduction beyond this on the score of short earnings would not be safe, and might lead to financial embarrassments of a very grave and not easily explainable character at the end of the year. *You would therefore be wise to take the figure of 48,000,000l as the one which you should face.* *

While I regard it as my duty to aid you in any way in my power in regard to the methods by which the necessary naval services are financed, and to fall in with your general policy so long as the interests of the country do not suffer, I must again state my opinion that the proper and courageous course is to

* According to the latest information this forecast will prove to be right within £50,000. But the 1913 Estimates were actually presented at £46,300,000; £1,400,000 of services beyond the original estimates were authorised by the Cabinet during the year for Air, Oil, Dockyard pay, and Accelerated Battleships. We are asking for £1,750,000 more, which has been earned.

			£
Total Supplementary Estimate, 1913–14	..	..	3,150,000
Deduct for authorised additional services	..	..	1,400,000
			1,750,000
Original Estimates, 1913–14 ..	..	..	46,300,000
Add Supplementary now earned	..	..	1,750,000
			48,050,000

take Parliament fully into your confidence and to meet the expense either by new taxation or by a substantial diminution during these years of strain of the Sinking Fund.

Any other course will expose you in 1914–15 to difficulties greater than those which now confront you without your having the strength which you now possess to carry your policy for the urgent reasons which justify the expenditure.

I am prepared to take the whole responsibility of the present and prospective naval expenditure upon myself. Everything that is not uncontrollable and automatic can be fully justified in detail to Parliament and the public, in consequence of naval developments elsewhere; and I am sure the Government have only to put their case plainly and boldly to the House of Commons to receive from one source or another, without any serious difficulty, the sums which are necessary for the safety of the State.

I enclose you the outline of the financial statement. The detailed explanations of the causes of increase which are being prepared in the Admiralty under my direction will be printed in the form of a small Blue Book for circulation to the Committee on Estimates and to the Cabinet.

It is very desirable that our discussions on the general subject should begin this week. It will not otherwise be possible to go into the vast amount of detail which awaits consideration in the time available.

Yours very sincerely
WINSTON S. CHURCHILL

WSC to H. H. Asquith

December 1912   [Admiralty]

Draft

My dear Prime Minister,

You are asked from time to time questions in regard to the contribution which India pays towards the Imperial Naval Defence and the special services rendered her by the Admiralty.

I hope that in replying nothing will be said which will appear to definitely close the question of an increased contribution.

The case is indeed a very strong one from many points of view.

The cost of the services specially rendered by the Admiralty in the Persian Gulf and Indian waters is calculated at £393,000 a year, towards which India pays only £167,000, leaving an unrelieved burden on British Naval Estimates of £225,000 a year, against which there is no corresponding charge in German Estimates.

The expense of British armaments as a whole by sea and land has immensely increased of late years in consequence of similar increases all over the world. The expense of Indian armaments has not increased to any considerable extent. On the other hand, the wealth of India and, above all, the value of her sea-borne trade have advanced with enormous strides. For the protection of the whole of her sea-borne trade India makes no provision at all. This argument was one on which you yourself very strongly dwelt in the memorandum furnished to Canada, and it is certainly not without its application here.

The action of all the great Dominions in greatly increasing their naval contributions or in making important new contributions constitutes a new fact of much significance. They have all revised and extended their contributions since the date when the Indian contribution was last fixed by Lord Rosebery's Arbitration.

Lastly, there is the Federated Malay States, from whom the Government have accepted a first class battleship, and whose geographical position and general characteristics relate very closely to the case of India.

I was speaking to you the other day on the Bench about the Indian Marine, which is at present maintained at a cost of no less than £ [blank] a year. I enclose you the pages in the Navy List which set out the number of officers employed in that service. From this you will see what a very large and important affair it has become. From an Admiralty point of view and for war purposes this service is of no value whatever. A report has been prepared by Sir Edmond Slade for the India Office in which the inefficiency, extravagance, and ineffectiveness, of this service has been clearly shown. I should have thought that it would be quite possible to devise a general scheme of reorganisation which, while providing for a proportionate contribution from India for Imperial Naval Defence, would secure substantial economies from this source in mitigation of the increased charge.

Papers are being prepared by the Admiralty on all these points, and I am also proposing to show to what extent relief might be afforded to British Estimates in the future if a satisfactory Naval Policy were adopted by the Indian Government.

You will realise that I am only asking that these questions may be fairly considered between Departments and by the Cabinet before they are prejudged by answers in the House.

Sir Francis Hopwood to WSC

16 December 1912   The Reform Club

First Lord,

I had a talk with the King about the Royal Yacht[1] and took him through items and estimates. He was very much impressed with the extravagance of many of the demands. Once in two years for most of them is his opinion.

He will also personally examine proposals, when general renewals become necessary, for materials and so forth which will be much less expensive and more seaworthy than those used now.

He is going to send for the Commodore and will tell him that next year he must consider and report how little is required and not how much. For this year we have cut the Estimate in half and when we take into consideration that a lot of items will be bi-annual and not annual it is better than that.

F.H.

Note:

Good. WSC 16 December 1912.

Memorandum by WSC

EXTRACT

December 1912   [Admiralty]

. . . Whatever may be the decision of Canada at the present juncture, Great Britain will not in any circumstances fail in her duty to the Oversea Dominions of the Crown.

She has before now successfully made head alone and unaided against the most formidable combinations, and she has not lost her capacity, by a wise policy and strenuous exertions, to watch over and preserve the vital interests of the Empire.

The Admiralty are assured that His Majesty's Government will not hesitate to ask the House of Commons for whatever provision the circumstances of each year may require. But the aid which Canada could give at the present time is not to be measured only in ships or money. Any action on the part of Canada to increase the power and mobility of the Imperial Navy, and thus widen the margin of our common safety, would be recognised everywhere as a most significant witness to the united strength of the Empire, and to the renewed resolve of the Oversea Dominions to take their part in maintaining its integrity.

[1] See above, WSC's letter to Lord Stamfordham, 5 November 1912 on p. 1669.

The Prime Minister of the Dominion having enquired in what form any immediate aid that Canada might give would be most effective, we have no hesitation in answering, after a prolonged consideration of all the circumstances, that it is desirable that such aid should include the provision of a certain number of the largest and strongest ships of war which science can build or money supply. . . .

WSC to H. H. Asquith
(*Asquith Papers*)

17 December 1912   Admiralty

My dear Prime Minister,

The pictures in the *Sphere* are obvious fabrications, which bear no resemblance to what occurred, and are of no scientific value. The ships are dressed as for a Royal Review, which is unusual at gunnery practice; and if the target had been injured in the way depicted, it could not possibly have held together. Sir Percy Scott[1] categorically denies having had anything to do with the *Sphere* article or pictures, and I fully accept his word on the subject. The actual details of the invention have been kept most secret during the 6 years he has been developing it.

The 1st Sea Lord does not consider that the honour in question would be inappropriate. The alternative would be a very considerable grant of money which the value of the invention to the Service would fully justify. I may add that we should propose to Sir Percy Scott that he should retire on promotion to full Admiral, which cannot be later than next March. This will clear the list, and there is no reason to suppose that the Navy would view his baronetcy with disfavour.

Yours vy sincerely
WINSTON S. CHURCHILL

Sir Edward Grey to David Lloyd George

21 December 1912   24 Sloane Gdns

Copy

Private

My dear Lloyd George,

I have had a desperate week of work and haven't been able to see any colleagues except those whom I met at various ceremonies. I am circulating

[1] Percy Scott (1853–1924), served on Ordnance Committee; inventor of night signalling apparatus and several appliances for improving Navy gun shooting; knighted 1906; Admiral 1913; created Baronet 1913.

all the records of the meetings of Ambassadors, and am trying to get away for a few days this evening. But I send you a line to say that the progress made is really good.

Diplomatically we are past the biggest rocks and with good will we ought to get just past the others.

It will need a little time for the European Governments to digest the meal that the Ambassadors have given them and we can do no more for the moment.

The important thing to watch is Austrian mobilisation.

It ought to slacken after the agreement come to – it will be a bad sign if it does not, but Germany and Italy are now satisfied and I do not believe the Austrian military party can hold out against the pressure for peace of all the five Powers.

Peace negotiations between Turkey and Balkan States will go slow: I have given advice to the Balkan delegates that should avoid difficulties between them and the Great Powers and have urged them to keep a united front, & we are doing what we can at Constantinople to urge the Turks to give way. But the Turks will be slow.

Yrs sincerely

E. GREY

You might send this on to Winston I haven't time to write more at the moment.

*   *   *   *   *

HMS Enchantress *Log Book*

EXTRACT

17th Visit

29 June 1912	6.20 *pm*	Portsmouth. WSC, 1st Sea Lord and 4th Sea Lord on board. Sailed to Penzance.
30 June 1912		Penzance to Queenstown.
	early afternoon	WSC landed Queenstown.
1 July 1912		Queenstown. WSC visited *Hood*.
2 July 1912		Queenstown to Cork.
	noon	WSC visited Cork.
3 July 1912	11.15 *am*	Queenstown to Milford. WSC inspected Pembroke Dockyard.
	1.40 *pm*	WSC left for London.

18th Visit

7 July 1912	8.40 *pm*	WSC and Admiral Troubridge embarked.
	evening	Sailed to Portland.
8 July 1912	noon	Spithead. WSC passed through lines of Review Fleet.
	4.45 *pm*	WSC visited ships.
	7.35 *pm*	H. H. Asquith embarked.
	10 *pm*	3rd Sea Lord embarked.
9 July 1912	noon	Spithead. WSC passed through lines of Fleet followed by *Armodale Castle*, with Canadian Ministers and Members of Parliament.
	1.25 *pm*	Waterplane Flights. Attacks on Fleet by submarines and destroyers.
	7 *pm*	Asquith left ship: Foreign attaches and press representatives left.
10 July 1912	morning	Portsmouth. WSC left ship.

19th Visit

23 July 1912	6.15 *pm*	Portsmouth. WSC, 1st Sea Lord and 2nd Sea Lord embarked.
	10.20 *pm*	Sailed to Portland. WSC and 2nd Sea Lord embarked in *Thunderer*.
24 July 1912	afternoon	Fleet anchored, Torbay.
25 July 1912	8 *am*	WSC arrived on board.
	11.40 *am*	WSC left for *Thunderer*.
	noon	WSC witnessed tactical exercises.
	5.50 *pm*	WSC returned from *Thunderer*.
26 July 1912	9.5 *am*	WSC went on board *Thunderer*, witnessed tactical exercises.
	10.45 *pm*	Returned on board *Enchantress*.
27 July 1912		Portsmouth. WSC inspected dockyard.
	afternoon	WSC left ship.

20th Visit

19 August 1912	*pm*	Chatham. WSC and party embark.
20 August 1912	morning	WSC left ship to inspect Chatham dockyard.

	noon	WSC left in TB 12 for Shoeburyness.
	afternoon	WSC returned on board.
21 August 1912	3.45 *pm*	Sheerness. WSC visited dockyard and Floating dock.
22 August 1912	morning	Sheerness to Harwich.
	afternoon	WSC visited Shotley and shore installations, Harwich.
23 August 1912	9.40 *am*	Harwich. WSC left ship to witness submarine exercises from *Hebe*.
	1.44 *pm*	WSC returned *Enchantress*, sailed to Yarmouth roads.
24 August 1912	afternoon	Yarmouth Roads, WSC landed.
	evening	returned to *Enchantress*.
25 August 1912		Sailed to Cromer and River Humber.
26 August 1912	morning	WSC visited Lummingham docks.
27 August 1912	6.50 *pm*	WSC landed on Spurn Pt.
28 August 1912		Sailed Grimsby to the Tyne.
	10 *am*	WSC visited Armstrong's Works at Elswick.
	late afternoon	WSC returned.
29 August 1912		Sailed the Tyne to Rosyth.
	11 *am*	WSC embarked.
		Inspected Rosyth dockyard.
	3 *pm*	returned.
30 August 1912		Sailed Rosyth to Dundee.
	11 *am*	WSC left ship.
31 August 1912		Sailing Dundee to Cromarty.
1 September 1912		Sailing Dundee to Cromarty.
2 September 1912		Cruising off Burghead.
3 September 1912		Cromarty.
	morning	WSC left ship and embarked on TBD *Scourge*.
	noon	WSC returned.
	afternoon	WSC visited *Vulcan* and submarines.
	late afternoon	WSC visited *Shannon*.
4 September 1912	morning	Cromarty. WSC embarked in *Natal*.
	afternoon	WSC returned.
5 September 1912	2.45 *pm*	Cromarty to Aberdeen. WSC left ship.

21st Visit

13 September 1912	4 *pm*	WSC embarked. Greenock.
14 September 1912	morning	WSC visited Clyde shipyards.
	1.15 *pm*	WSC returned.
		Sailed to Lamlash.
15 September 1912		At Lamlash.
16 September 1912		At Lamlash.
	afternoon	WSC visited *Neptune.*
	11.20 *pm*	returned.
17 September 1912		Lamlash to Colonsay.
18 September 1912		At Colonsay.
	morning	WSC visited *Hindustan.*
	7 *pm*	WSC went on board *King Edward VII* to witness night firing.
19 September 1912	1.30 *am*	WSC returned on board.
	evening	Held concert on board.
20 September 1912		Colonsay.
		WSC visited *Hibernia.*
	evening	WSC on board *King Edward VII.*
21 September 1912		Colonsay to Oban.
22 September 1912		At Oban.
23 September 1912		Oban.
	morning	5th Battle Squadron held regatta.
	afternoon	WSC visited *Queen* and landed Isle of Mull.
24 September 1912		Oban to Greenock.
	10.45 *am*	WSC visited Clyde shipyards on board TBD *Fury.*
	evening	WSC returned.
25 September 1912		Greenock to Barrow in Furness.
	10.30 *am*	WSC visited works of Vickers & Co.
	4 *pm*	WSC returned.
26 September 1912		Barrow to Birkenhead.
27 September 1912		Birkenhead.
	noon	WSC landed to visit Cammell and Laird works.
	1.40 *pm*	WSC returned.
	4 *pm*	WSC visited *Conway.*
28 September 1912		Birkenhead to Holyhead.
	afternoon	WSC landed Holyhead.

29 September 1912	morning	WSC landed Holyhead.
	afternoon	Holyhead to Devonport.
30 September 1912		Plymouth Sound.
	2.45 pm	WSC visited dockyard and returned evening.
1 October 1912	8.40 am	WSC visited Royal Naval College, Dartmouth.
2 October 1912		Portsmouth.
	morning	WSC visited *Vernon*.
	afternoon	WSC visited Dockyard.
3 October 1912		Portsmouth.
	8 am	WSC went aboard submarine.
	11 am	WSC visited War College.
	afternoon	WSC left ship for London.

22nd Visit

| 12 October 1912 | | Portsmouth. |
| | noon | WSC visited ship for twenty minutes. |

23rd Visit

23 October 1912	6.40 pm	Portsmouth. WSC embarked.
24 October 1912	3.15 pm	Devonport. WSC attended launching HMS *Marlborough*.
	5.30 pm	WSC returned.
25 October 1912		Portland.
	9.45 am	WSC aboard *Neptune*. Witnessed tactical exercises and firing.
	3.30 pm	WSC returned.
	5 pm	WSC visits *Imperieuse*.

24th Visit

16 November 1912	3 pm	WSC embarked Portsmouth.
17 November 1912		Spithead.
18 November 1912	9.25 am	WSC disembarked at Spithead.

25th Visit

| 30 November 1913 | 1.45 am | WSC embarked Portsmouth. |
| 1 December 1912 | am | Portsmouth. WSC on Board *King George V*. |

2 December 1912	8.15 *am*	Portland. WSC left ship and went around *Indomitable*.
	noon	Witnessed firing.
	5 *pm*	returned on board.
	10.20 *pm*	WSC went on board *Hermes* to witness night attack.
	11.45 *pm*	WSC returned to *Enchantress*.
3 December 1912		Spithead.
4 December 1912	8.35 *am*	WSC disembarked at Portsmouth.

26th Visit

30 January 1913	11.50 *am*	WSC embarked at Dundee.
31 January 1913		Dundee to Burntisland.
1 February 1913		Burntisland to Queensferry.
2 February 1913		Queensferry to Chatham.
3 February 1913		Chatham to Portsmouth.
4 February 1913		Spithead.
5 February 1913	1.35 *pm*	Portsmouth. George V inspected *Enchantress*.
	4.5 *pm*	George V and WSC disembark.

(LOG ENDS: 27 FEBRUARY 1913)

22

Admiralty 1913

(See Main Volume II Chapter 16)

━━━━━

Memorandum by WSC

7 January 1913   [Admiralty]

The War Office say that, under the law as it now stands, the number of British soldiers rank and file entitled to vote is approximately 10,250. This figure is arrived at by taking the married establishment at home 12,850, less 2,600 for removals. If the qualification became six months' residence for those of 25 years of age and upwards, and if barracks counted as a residence, the number entitled to vote would be approximately 75,000 rank and file.

2. It would be interesting to have a report from the War Office of the distribution of these votes in the various existing constituencies. There are a certain number of stations like York, Colchester, Pembroke, Edinburgh, Plymouth, Portsmouth, Chatham, and Newcastle, where the military vote could conceivably be an effective factor in deciding the representation. But the most peculiar consequences would occur in the great camps of Aldershot, Salisbury Plain, Shorncliffe, and the Curragh. So far as the first two are concerned, it would appear that any scheme of redistribution would give these camps a special Member of their own, and an election would take place in which practically none but soldiers would vote. The course of such a contest could not fail to present some very novel features. It is the business of soldiers to keep clear of politics – above all, party politics – and to do their duty whatever party is in power. It is especially undesirable that persons under armed discipline should be encouraged at any time to forget the grades and ranks which are so necessary to their good order and for the safety of the civil population among whom they live.

3. No one can possibly doubt that the extension of the vote to 75,000 men dwelling together in large masses under military discipline will produce the

immediate development of a class campaign for the improvement of the soldiers' conditions. We shall have, in fact, a tremendous trade union made, voting as a trade union, and able to enforce their will on any point they care about sufficiently by the use of lethal weapons.

4. In Ireland the soldiers would be able to turn the vote to deciding the representation of a good many small constituencies; and it is possible that the intrusion of the British garrison in purely local affairs will be resented by the Nationalist party, and will possibly render their presence in the district unpopular.

5. The Navy apparently will hardly vote at all. As the movements of sailors from the barracks to the ships is so rapid, no very great number would obtain the qualification. It will no doubt be noted as an anomaly by those who approve of the extension of the vote to the military forces, that, while the soldiers are given every opportunity of deciding party and political issues, and of advancing their class interests, 140,000 men of the Navy will be almost totally debarred, and it seems certain that, if the franchise is extended to the soldiers, it will have in an equal measure to be given to the sailors too.

6. In all the great countries of the world persons actually serving with the military forces are either explicitly or practically disfranchised. In *France* all officers and soldiers in regular service are forbidden to vote, unless they are on leave of absence for periods exceeding one month. In *Germany*, although the age is 25, the prohibition against officers and soldiers of the standing army is absolute, and is a direct exception to the manhood suffrage basis of the Reichstag. In the *United States*, Federal soldiers are not prohibited from voting, provided that they comply with the civil formalities, involving registration within a month of the election *in the States and districts where they have their homes*. This, in fact, however, amounts to practical disfranchisement, as the States are many and the Federal garrisons few. In some States, moreover, they are specifically disfranchised.

WSC

WSC to Herbert Samuel

22 January 1913   Admiralty

Copy

My dear Samuel,

Thank you for sending me the map of the main underground telegraph routes – but I must say it puts in a striking light the preference given to English districts over the more storm beaten regions of Scotland, and makes one ask why Penzance & Chelmsford should be so much more favoured than Dundee or Aberdeen!

Yours sincerely
[WINSTON S. CHURCHILL]

Herbert Samuel to WSC

23 January 1913   Postmaster General

Dear Winston,

The reason why places such as Penzance and Chelmsford were selected when the underground telegraph lines were being laid is explained in the answer which I gave to questions on the 20th instant, of which I enclose a copy.

Yours sincerely
HERBERT SAMUEL

The Postmaster General's Answer to the Questions put down for Monday

20 January 1913

EXTRACT

. . . The underground cables mentioned in these questions have been laid with a view to connecting with the submarine cables. The route by way of Marlborough, Exeter and Penzance to Weston and Porthcurno connects with the submarine cables to America, Africa, Australia, New Zealand, the East and the Far East. The cable to Romford and Chelmsford will be continued to Bacton and Lowestoft and will there connect with the submarine cables to Germany and Holland. The cable to St Margaret's Bay and Abbotscliff by way of Dover connects with the submarine cables to France and Belgium. The revenue and importance of the whole foreign and colonial Telegraph business of the United Kingdom must be taken into account in considering the necessity for these lines. The cost of the western underground including the spurs to Weston and Plymouth was £456,633 exclusive of Head Quarter charges. The cost of the extension from Bristol to Cardiff was £79,491. The London-Bristol section is common to both routes. . . .

Jack Seely to WSC

29 January 1913   War Office

Secret

My dear Winston,

French is sending you a brief précis of our Home Defence plans, together with a map – all very secret. I thought that it might interest you to consider the matter in connection with your naval plans, especially in view of the approaching invasion Committee.

French also told me of your idea of a monthly meeting between you and me and the heads of the War Staffs – a sort of high level bridge.

It would seem to me to be an admirable plan, and I hope it may be carried out.

Yours sincerely
J. SEELY

Minute by WSC

2 January 1913   Admiralty

Harwich Hospital Accommodation

The answers prepared on this subject are not helpful. A brief general statement should be prepared showing the true position there. The following may be taken as a guide: –

Harwich is one of those places on the East Coast which has only in recent years acquired a naval importance. The following arrangements are made for the treatment of sickness among the increasing numbers of sailors stationed there. All ordinary cases occurring in the flotillas are taken on board the [blank], where the hospital accommodation is good, and are transferred to Chatham Naval Hospital at convenient opportunities; urgent and serious cases would be accommodated at Shotley, opposite to Harwich and half a mile away, where there is a large and well appointed naval hospital belonging to the Shotley Training Establishment. In ordinary times there is ample room in this hospital for treating such naval cases, but if there were to be an epidemic among the boys at Shotley difficulties in providing accommodation might arise. I am therefore making provision in the Estimates for this year for certain extensions at Shotley Hospital which will effectually provide against such a contingency. I am not prepared as at present advised to ask Parliament to build a separate naval hospital on the Harwich side of the water as that would involve duplication of services and heavy expenditure.

Any further extension to the hospital accommodation which the increasing naval force maintained at Harwich should require will be made to the existing establishment at Shotley as they become necessary.

Let me see a draft prepared on these lines supplying what is necessary and checking or modifying as required.

[WINSTON S. CHURCHILL]

WSC to his wife
(*CSC Papers*)

30 January 1913   HMS *Enchantress*

Beloved Clemmie,

All has gone off admirably. The PM in gt form, the suffragettes foiled, & the Dundonians highly delighted. I made, with vy little trouble, an almost impromptu speech, which was well received & generally commended.

It is blowing outside, & there has been a heavy fall of the barometer, so that what I call 'an ebb to the tides of digestion' may be at hand!

Urquhart,[1] the Lord Provost, has a most attractive little daughter, who sat next to me, & has taken her Musical degree. I promised her that I wd introduce her to you when a chance occurred.

There were many inquiries about the Kat & her motor smash. They are good folk up here & soberly appreciate their friends.

I hope you will take the Admiralty furniture in hand this week & be in a position to tell me what you propose when I return.

I was stupid last night – but you know what a prey I am to nerves & prepossessions. It is a great comfort to me to feel *absolute* confidence in your love & cherishment for your poor P.D.

With many kisses & devoted love always your loving husband

W

PS I wish you were here; I shd like to kiss your dear face and stroke your baby cheeks and make you purr softly in my arms.

Don't be disloyal to me in thought. I have no one but you to break the loneliness of a bustling and bustled existence.

Write to me to Queensferry on receipt of this. It will reach me Satdy morning, & tell me how much you care about your poor

W

× × × Here are three kisses one for each of you. Don't waste them. They are good ones.

---

[1] James Urquhart (1864–1930), Lord Provost and Lord Lieutenant of Dundee 1908–11 and 1911–14; knighted 1914.

WSC to his wife
(*CSC Papers*)

HMS *Enchantress*
1 February 1913   Forth Bridge

My precious One,

Your dear letter gave me the greatest pleasure & comfort.

The wind has turned completely & is now off the shore, so that we hope to have a fairly prosperous passage to the South. The PM is all for a return by water – to Tilbury or Chatham. We start tonight & hope to arrive Monday early. I shall be with you for lunch.

We went round Rosyth this morning. They have made vy little progress since I was here in August. Strikes, frosts, & gales have sensibly curbed the contractors' earning powers.

At 4 o'clock the First Destroyer Flotilla arrived in gallant fashion, firing a salute to the Admiralty flag. Battenberg leaves us tonight for London by train.

Derry is a fine feather to put in our caps. Indeed the outlook promises fairly steady weather at present.

Be vy careful not to open suspicious parcels arriving by post without precautions. On the other hand do not leave them lying unopened in the House. They shd be dealt with carefully & promptly. These harpies are quite capable of trying to burn us out. Telephone to Scotland Yard if you are doubtful about any packet.

Since you have kept the 3 kisses for yourself, I send you 2 more for the PK & CB and out of a store that will never be exhausted send you an additional six × × × × × ×

Always your loving & devoted
W

Prince Louis of Battenberg to WSC

5 March 1913

Secret

Dear First Lord,

Glad to hear that you had an interesting time at Toulon & that we may expect you back by the end of the week.

Everything is now ready for my interview with the French Chief of the Naval Staff in Paris so I have arranged to cross over next Tuesday & have the meeting at the Admiral's private residence next morning (Wednesday

12th inst). Nothing can possibly get into the papers – Saint-Seine[1] preceding me by a day. I do not intend to go near our Embassy, & hope to settle everything in one day.

On Monday next I can go over the papers again with you if you like. We have reached perfect agreement on the Mediterranean arrangement, but there is one new suggestion from their side which requires a little discussion, as I do not think it workable.

Everything going well here.

3rd S.L. is anxious for a fortnight's leave as soon as possible.

I quite concurred in your reply to Mr Borden.

I am very grateful to you for defending me so efficiently in the House.

LB

Hugh Watson to Edward Marsh

EXTRACT

12 March 1913   British Embassy
                                                  Berlin
Private

My dear Marsh,

I have made some close study on the spot of the actors and factors in the drama of German Naval policy and politics; and I have from the beginning of my time as Naval attaché felt that the best thing the officer filling that appointment in Germany could do was to study Admiral von Tirpitz and the points which have conspired to give him and the large Navy Party power. It has been a hobby with me, and I have been at it three years. I venture therefore to put the following remarks on paper, and in doing so would ask that they may be considered as *private*. I forward them to you in the hope they may be of use in sizing up the present situation, and in elucidation of my official reports.

1. In the winter of 1911–12 criticism of the Naval expansionist policy began to grow in Germany, and really began to shew an effective head for the first time in recent years. Had it not been for the violent anti-English propaganda, which was commenced in Nov 1911 on the rumours of a project in the previous summer on the part of England to attack the German Fleet, the criticism above referred to would have made more effective headway.

People in Germany had begun dimly to see that they were treading an expensive Naval road, especially as the cost of the upkeep of the Fleet came home

---

[1] Comte Christian-Marie le Gouz de Saint-Seine (1869–?), French Naval Attaché in London.

to the Reichstag members; which uncomfortable consciousness of the cost of upkeep naturally had the greater effect as *new Ship-building* programmes, and their consequent excitements, became less possible; as opposed to the growth of criticism of the expansionist Party, the winter of 1911–12 was the first time that the idea of a 3 to 2 proportion was raised in Germany by the Naval Party.

2. A year has passed since that time, and reviewing the year I consider that the idea of a 2 to 3 Naval proportion with England has not really taken on in Germany, and that it is becoming harder to rouse interest for Naval increases. Though of course one cannot say what would happen if another wave of anglo-phobia were to be spread by the able Naval Section. I mix in practically every class of Society and I find now even amongst conservatives, Centre, and National Liberals a feeling growing against German Naval expansion.

One reason given to me for this is that their expansion is undesirable because it creates bad feeling with England; and Parties of all shades are beginning to see the hopelessness of success in such competition, and also to acknowledge the logical reasons in support of England's Naval policy. Another reason given is a very real one, and that is that Germans of the Parties indicated are finding the competition costs them much good gold. It is particularly interesting to find this view expressed by conservatives. Of course this growing feeling against the competition is doubly voiced amongst the Radical and Socialist Parties, specially when pinched by taxation.

It is certain that this feeling of antagonism to Naval demands is due to the demands of the German army. Whatever the reasons be, though I believe I give them fairly correctly, the consequence of such thoughts is that opinion is at present turning towards the army authorities and against the Naval.

But I feel sure that the pendulum of opinion has by no means at present turned irretrievably against the German Naval expansionist Party. But it is, I consider, turning slowly against them, and will continue to do so as the result of steady quiet Naval pressure by England.

The Naval authorities here have begun to make sacrifices to the Reichstag, and from what I hear it would appear that more rigid economy is being enforced in all branches of the Naval administration, both in Berlin & in the Fleet, as the direct result of the difficulty of obtaining money. But the time is not yet.

3. After a year's observation of the effects of the 1st Lord's speeches of last year I would say that there is not a shadow of doubt that they have been a big factor in bringing about a widespread feeling in Germany that Naval competition with England is hopeless, and that Germany must stick to her proper arm of defence, the army. Indeed it is true to say that Germans are

realising at present that the army is the Nation's life, and the Navy a subsidiary, if not a luxury. Views to this effect have been expressed to me quite recently by strong Conservative-agrarians. It is true that Adml von Tirpitz has a following in the Conservative camp, but it is mainly personal; his following is bigger in the Centre and National Liberal Parties; but even there discontent with the Admiral is noticeable.

In stating the above as to the effect of the 1st Lord's speeches I do not desire to flatter in the slightest, but I endeavour to put the present position to you as clearly as possible.

I hold that Admiral von Tirpitz is well worth studying, and that to do so is only to recognise the Admiral's patriotism and ability. That the 1st Lord's remarks of last year made it difficult for the German Large Navy Party is I think proved by the irritation of Admiral von Tirpitz towards them at the time they were made, on which I then reported.

It was an unfortunate fact that certain remarks of Mr Churchill's predecessor lent themselves to distortion by Admiral von Tirpitz's party in previous years, *vide* my reports of 1910–11. Had you been in my place in Berlin in the winter of 1910–11 you would have seen very clearly how the German Large Navy Party, disappointed by the British Naval increase of 1908–09, attempted to make capital out of Mr McKenna's words, by labelling them here in society as offensive mis-statements.

4. Reverting to the present time I feel sure that, with a steady British Naval pressure erring if anything slightly on the strong side of the programme foreshadowed by the 1st Lord, the opinions growing in Germany as to the undesirability of competition with England will spread and render it increasingly difficult for Adml von Tirpitz or the Large Navy Party to obtain money for the Navy; while the task of doing so for any successor of Adml von Tirpitz, unless of course the Admiral is then sitting on the throne of the Imperial Chancellorship, will I believe be superhuman under existing conditions in the Reichstag, which are so totally different to when Adl von Tirpitz came into power.

The Adml has behind him now the prestige of the Navy Law and its amendments, his successor will have [to] make his career and will have difficulty in convincing the Reichstag of the necessity of spending money on the Navy.

I have for the past 2 years always said that, in my opinion, a steady strong policy on the part of England would have the German Large Navy Party worn down and beat within 5 years. The progress of events during the past year, and recently, have confirmed me in my opinion. Such a policy, as the 1st Lord has inaugurated, will rob the arguments of the Large Navy Party here of their power, and will render their weapons of abuse and misconstruction innocuous. I know well the confused circle of their arguments, into which circle they only hope we shall be fools enough to be again enmeshed. It was our unlucky entering into such confused circle that gave Adml von Tirpitz half his power; the Large Navy Party are annoyed with Mr Churchill because he declines to be drawn into the circle.

A foreign friend of mine said to me lately, 'the present position is that Tirpitz is standing at the door of a wire entanglement of 16 to 10, inviting Mr Churchill to enter, if he does enter he is done because then Tirpitz will successfully pass the period of unpopularity of German Naval expense; but if Mr Churchill does not enter, then Tirpitz will have few weapons left to him to use in support of German Naval growth.' . . .

Yours sincerely
HUGH WATSON

Lord Stamfordham to WSC

12 March 1913   Buckingham Palace

My dear Churchill,

The King desires me to thank you for having dealt so promptly with the question of an Honorary Commission in the Navy for the Prince of Wales. His Majesty will let you have an answer in the course of a few days.

Very truly yours
STAMFORDHAM

Sir W. Graham Greene to WSC

15 March 1913   Admiralty

My dear First Lord,

I dined at the Palace last night & Lord Stamfordham then spoke to me about the promotion of the Prince of Wales to Lieutenant & it was arranged that a memorial to Council should be submitted to the King on Monday authorizing the promotion as supplementary to the List, it being understood that HRH would draw no pay. The King later spoke to me on the subject, approving of the action proposed & of the gazetting of the rank as from the 17th, the date of the Council [*note by WSC:* Yes.]

I have issued notices for a Board on Tuesday, & I enclose a list of the subjects which you may wish to include in the Agenda. I am not sure whether things are ripe for a further discussion as to Cromarty, but at the last meeting it was decided that a report should be brought up to the Board. [*Note by WSC:* No.]

With reference to the scheme of 'Group Meetings' the Third Sea Lord spoke to me yesterday, and said you had enquired whether he had seen your minute, I think in connection with the instructions to the DNG. I had not shown the minute to anyone, as I was awaiting further instructions from you. I find that he is very much averse to the scheme as suggested in your minute & he appears to be also supported by the First & Second Sea Lords. They consider it as reflecting on their position as Lords Commissioners, as they maintain that they can & do hold meetings now & no further authority is required. I showed them the form in which I had proposed to embody the scheme in the Office Procedure, but in light of your minute they did not like that either.

I have therefore not sent the form to be printed, as I think I had better explain the matter fully when you return. [*Note by WSC:* print as directed and submit proof. WSC]

With regard to the DNG I thought I had explained that I had consulted him before I sent you the papers relating to the revised instructions. They meet his views, with the exception that he still thought more discretionary authority to settle points might have been conceded to him. I have not yet completed the answer to your enquiries; the regulations as to the Captain of the Dockyard are rather obscure.

I am going into the country for the Sunday in the hope of curing my cold, which is obstinate.

Believe me, Yours sincly
W. GRAHAM GREENE

David Lloyd George to WSC

3 April 1913   House of Commons

Secret

My dear Winston,

We have had a very lengthy discussion this morning on the situation in the East. Grey's view was, that if France came in, we should send our ships, but if both France and Russia held aloof, then we could not very well join in the naval demonstration. In his view the absence of those Powers would deprive the demonstration of its international character. Should Russia and France decline to join the others, he was emphatically of opinion that we were in honour bound to give a free hand to Austria to deal with the situation single-handed, in any way she thought fit; and he insisted that he should be in a position to say so at once to the Russian and French ambassadors.

This represents the ultimate decision of the Cabinet. I read your letter to the Cabinet but although it dealt with the first proposition, it did not cover Grey's alternative.

You will see that the situation is a very serious one. If the naval demonstration does not come off, or if it fails, and Austria marches in, we might find ourselves in a very embarrassing position. In fact, it may mean the end of the Triple Entente. I shall support Grey, because of the enormous difficulties which he has had to encounter, and because, I think he has directed the negotiations with admirable skill; and because also I approve of the two main objects which his diplomacy has striven to attain – the emancipation of the Balkan populations, and the maintenance of the peace of Europe.

I cannot pretend to like this last development, although I cannot suggest any alternative which would be consistent with the honourable undertaking which Grey has already given to the Powers.

I should like to hear your views.

The Marconi business is going well. The bankers' evidence today was smashing.

Ever sincerely
D. LLOYD GEORGE

WSC to Sir Henry Jackson
(*Admiralty Papers*)

3 April [1913]   HMS *Enchantress*

[Copy]

While armoured cruisers will usually fight and manoeuvre in squadrons, battle cruisers by reason of their great strength are capable of isolated action. From this point of view they are particularly suited to reinforce a light cruiser observation line. The tactical combinations of battle cruisers and light cruisers require special study and practice. The 30-knot light cruiser has nothing to fear from any vessel afloat except the enemy's battle cruiser. She can beat off destroyers; she can escape the enemy's small cruisers. It is only the enemy's battle cruiser who can at once catch her and kill her and who can do that with very great ease. The natural support of the light cruiser against the enemy's battle cruiser is our own battle cruiser. When the 'Arethusas' are ready, it will be desirable to exercise them in groups with battle cruisers, there being 1 battle cruiser to every 4 light cruisers. It cannot be doubted that this formation will be a very convenient one. 4 light cruisers and a battle cruiser in line at 15 miles apart, battle cruiser in the centre, will watch with ease in clear weather a front of 90 miles, and will watch a front of 30 to 40 miles even in misty weather. There will be no light cruiser in the longest of these lines which the protecting battle cruiser in the centre could not reach to support before the attack of an overtaking hostile battle cruiser could be delivered. On the other hand, the light cruisers can collect information just as well as the battle cruiser and can move almost as quickly. They are therefore, in a certain sense, multiplications in miniature of the battle cruiser. What they really ought to mean, if well handled, is a battle cruiser at the right point, wherever that point may be. It is suggested that the light cruiser squadrons ('Arethusas') should work with the battle cruiser squadron, and that in observation or scouting the battle cruiser should be in the front line with the light cruisers of his group or perhaps 5 or 6 miles in rear of it. At any rate the battle cruiser would be an essential part of the very front line in the closest contact with the enemy; the armoured cruiser squadrons lying distinctly further back in support.

These principles apply, though less strongly, to the 'Town' and 'Active' classes of light cruisers which are shortly to be formed into squadrons, and these squadrons should be accustomed in the meanwhile to work with the battle cruisers on frequent occasions.

WSC

WSC to his wife
(*CSC Papers*)

6 April 1913   HMS *Enchantress*
                                                    Portsmouth

My darling,

We have got back here after a good passage from Devonport & remain in harbour till tomorrow evening, when we sail for Chatham. The naval members of the Board having had quite enough of the sea have taken themselves off till Monday, so I am alone with Graham Greene & Masterton.[1] I have asked Brab down for the Sunday, & he is just now due to arrive.

I hope you & the PM will be well looked after at the Wharf, now that three creatures are in their prey.

The penal sentence on Mrs P. will enable the Government to deal with her from time to time as they please. It is as good as the Cat & Mouse Bill itself.

[1] James Edward Masterton-Smith (1878–1938), Private Secretary to successive First Lords of the Admiralty, including WSC, 1910–17; Assistant Secretary to WSC at Ministry of Munitions 1917–19, and at War Office 1919–20; Permanent Under-Secretary of State for the Colonies 1921–4; knighted 1919.

There is no news here, but of ships & guns. I always like this port. I stay placidly in my nice cabin working all the morning, walk round the Dockyard in the afternoon & then home to tea & a couple of hours more work before dinner. The papers in files & bags & boxes come rolling in. One never seems to do more than keep abreast of them.

It will be nice coming back to the Admiralty. I like the idea of those spacious rooms. I am sure you will take to it when you get there. I am afraid it all means vy hard work for you – Poor lamb. But remember I am going to turn over a new leaf! That I promise – the only mystery is 'What is written on the other side?' It may be only 'ditto ditto'!

I do hope you will have an enjoyable weekend with the Asquiths. Do not commit yourself & the yacht unnecessarily to Margot, if you can help it. But I know how discreet you are.

Good night my sweet darling – Fondest love & kisses from your ever loving & devoted,

W

WSC to T. J. Macnamara

12 April 1913   [Admiralty]

Private

Copy

My dear Macnamara,

I have been meaning for some time to write & thank you for the vy great aid wh you have given me in this office. It has most markedly contributed to any measure of success our admin has obtained. Whether on the Bd, or at the head of the Finance Ctee or in yr conduct of labour questions, or in the H of C, yr services to the Admy are of the highest value. Yr presence on the Bd enables me to leave the management of H of C business increasingly in yr hands, & I do so without the slightest anxiety. I also feel able with perfect confidence to follow yr judgment & adopt yr conclusions on an ever widening category of important questions.

Quite apart from personal friendships, I have felt it my duty to write in this sense to you, & I have also thought it proper to write the same thing to the PM.

Once more accept my warmest thanks. Don't bother to answer.

Yrs v. sincly
WSC

*   *   *   *   *

WSC to Vice-Admiral Bayly[1]

11 April 1913   [Admiralty]

Copy

Dear Admiral Bayly,

Please assume that you are in full control of all the German resources, and that your object is to land as many men as possible in England either at one, two, or three places simultaneously or successively. How would you do it? Take particularly Harwich, the Humber, Blyth, Cromarty, the Shetlands. The problem must be examined on two footings: –

(a) A Bolt from the Blue, *ie,* profound peace and the British regular army in the country, but not of course mobilised or prepared. In this case the object of the descent would be to prevent the British army leaving for the Continent.

(b) A war in India or some distant Colony has been in progress for 4 or 5 months. Although we are at peace with every European nation, we are anxious – as we were during the South African War – for our own safety in case of a sudden strike. We have therefore made certain preparations. The territorial force is embodied and has its war stations. The First and Second Fleets and the Patrol Flotillas are all completed to full strength and at their war stations; but the Third Fleet has not been mobilised by calling out the reservists. This appears to me to be a reasonable account of what might happen. One is a Bolt from the Blue, and the other a Bolt from the Grey. In both cases for your first movements which open the war you must not make any preparations which would be *certain* to attract attention over here. It is thought that you might get 20,000 men on to the necessary shipping without exciting suspicion: but that is about the limit for the first plunge. Then, however, the question is whether more can be sent to reinforce those who have landed before the British fleet can get round to dominate the situation. Or, again, assuming the British fleet has been attracted to one point, could a second disembarkation be made somewhere else?

Let me put the question precisely.

Make plans for landing the largest number of men at Harwich, the Humber, Blyth, Cromarty, &c, on the assumption –

(a) that the British fleet is manoeuvring in profound peace off the South Coast of Ireland; or

(b) that the First and Second Fleets are completed and at their war stations.

---

[1] Lewis Bayly (1857–1938), commanded 3rd Battle Squadron 1913–14; 1st Battle Squadron 1914; C in C Western Approaches 1915–19; knighted 1914; Admiral 1917.

Your responsibility to cease once the troops have been brought to land under reasonable support from the escorting cruisers.

If there are any points in this which require discussion, will you come and see me this afternoon?

WSC to Sir Henry Jackson

18 April 1913   [Admiralty]

Copy

I am sorry you do not like the style of the paper called 'A Time Table of a Nightmare'.[1] It was written with the intention of raising certain very serious issues, and which I think will be apparent the more the facts and arguments are studied with attention. The title was chosen with the object of justly and accurately describing the character of the paper and of disarming and discounting the very criticisms which you make. Leaving, however, the question of style, on which opinions may easily differ, and which in any case is not of serious importance, and coming to the question of fact, I do not gather from your minute that there is much dispute. By all means substitute Saturday the 19th April (to-morrow) for the initial date which I have used. You should note in this case that the fleet will not only be in Southern and S.Wn ports, but will be very low indeed in coal, and would certainly be delayed from that cause before it could go into action. I should be interested to know if the argument is affected by the change. It is clear that a Saturday is a dangerous moment for a Bolt from the Blue; and it is quite open to an enemy to choose some Saturday when other circumstances are favourable.

The fact that the German fleet is in the Baltic does not appear to me to be relevant, unless it is contended that if the German fleet had been off Heligoland Sir George Callaghan would not have been allowed to have his manoeuvres this week or to remain with his ships along the Southern coast. In practice, however, in time of peace the fact of the German fleet being in the North Sea does not excite apprehension, nor in ordinary circumstances alter the regular exercises of the British fleet. These are prescribed for some time in advance, and their dates are no doubt very often known abroad.

Page 2 of your Minute – Paragraph 1.

I have assumed that the conclusion of the last enquiry by the Committee of Imperial Defence into the question of invasion may be taken as a starting point for my argument: that is, I think, a fair assumption. If you will consult

[1] For the full text of this memorandum see Main Volume II, pp. 613–27.

the Red Book which some time ago I sent to the Admiralty War Staff, you will see that one of the conclusions concurred in by all present was that we were to assume that if it made the difference between victory and defeat, Germany would begin operations of war without either warning or pretext. This conclusion was concurred in not only by the Ministers but by Mr Balfour in his evidence and by the Foreign Office; and I do not think we are entitled to depart from it.

Paragraph 2.

This is, however, a political fact of first consequence. The Cabinet has agreed after a period of discussion extending over several years, that the military and naval experts may consult with each other as to the actual steps which would be taken in a war in which Great Britain and France found themselves allies. On the other hand, it has been most strongly laid down, and I conceive with absolute propriety, that we should reserve our right of decision, whether we are or are not committed to aid France, until we know what are the actual circumstances of the quarrel. Any other arrangement would leave us at the mercy of French diplomacy, would prevent us from exercising a moderating effect upon it if necessary, and might lead to our being at any moment dragged into a war essentially non-British. If all the military and naval arrangements which are necessary have been made beforehand, and if these arrangements are well conceived, it does not appear to me that it would be dangerous to leave the decision of whether they shall be put into operation or not until the specific circumstances of the occasion can be judged.

I agree with the third paragraph; and if so unwise a policy were followed as to send away or promise to send away the whole regular army in the circumstances assumed in my memo., no censure or punishment would be too serious for the public officers and personages concerned. That is exactly the moral which I seek to draw.

I am of course in agreement with paragraph 4 of your note, but it will be found impossible as a matter of fact to know when Germany is ready to strike, and the fleet cannot always remain tied to its war stations: it must have some freedom for exercise and manoeuvres. Indeed it has been continuously impressed upon me since I came to the Admiralty that the autumn cruise to Spanish waters is one of the most important features in the training and discipline of the fleet. Some risks have to be run every year in this respect.

Page 3 – Paragraph 1.

I agree that it is arguable whether the subtraction from Germany's military forces might not be a serious deterrent. But that cannot be judged without knowing for certain what the attitude of Russia will be at any particular moment. It after all only needs a word between two Emperors to remove the whole of this great restraint on German military action. At any rate our arrangements for defence ought to be made on the foundation of our own strength and not on the shifting sands of diplomatic combination.

I should be very glad if you will have the specific points which affect the Admiralty checked by some trustworthy officer in the War Staff. Particularly I wish to know whether the facts as stated in the first five pages are in accordance with reasonable probability.

Whether there is shipping available in the German ports.

Whether the soldiers could be embarked in the time.

Whether the forts at Harwich could be silenced as suggested.

Whether destroyer flotillas making a daylight attack could be beaten off by cruisers.

Whether ships of the tonnage mentioned could enter Harwich harbour.

Whether the disembarkation within the limits prescribed could be effected.

Also whether the first paragraph on page 9 can be sustained.

What follows after the maximum invading force which can be got ashore has landed does not really concern the Admiralty; and the sensational sketch of the operations and events which followed was only intended to be illustrative of certain general propositions. It was intentionally cast in a satirical vein. But after all a *reductio ad absurdum* is not an unknown argumentative method.

I am interested to notice your opinion is less unfavourable in regard to the memorandum entitled 'A Bolt from the Grey'. It is clear to me on reflection that the outline as then presented could not be reconciled with possibility. The essence of the plan was to provoke a concentration of the British army in the neighbourhood of Harwich and of the British fleet between Harwich and Heligoland or thereabouts, and then, profiting by this concentration of the fleet, to make other descents in force in different parts of the Island. It is clear, however, that the very concentration of the fleet which has been provoked will bar all such places as Webbon Hook, the Humber, and Blyth. Everything that is to have any chance must go far to the Northward of this. I have therefore redrafted the paragraphs which outline these propositions, and should be glad if the new moves could be examined in detail in order to establish whether they or something like them is practicable or not.

[WINSTON S. CHURCHILL]

WSC to Vice-Admiral Bayly

19 April 1913   [Admiralty]

Copy

Admiral Bayly.

In your own paper about oversea attack, you seem to think it a disadvantage to land in the neighbourhood of a big town, and for that reason you reject Dundee. The question is of course largely military. I cannot myself believe that the streets of a town constitute any real obstacle to a landing from the quays. A street is after all only a road along which men can march; and where do you get so many roads as you do in the streets of a town? The more streets there are the more easy it is to advance through a town. No system of barricades can be improvised in a few hours which good troops cannot easily turn or pierce. Columns move forward quite easily along parallel roads; and if the civil population attempt to resist them, they are of course dealt with according to the rigours of war. In the case of Dundee there would only be a few hundred volunteers, and it is very doubtful whether in these circumstances the authorities would allow them to undertake a resistance to a landing in force, which would bring down on the town the horrors of street fighting. In any case no military officer would be in the least deterred by a little sporadic resistance of this kind.

Secondly, the great thing a landing force requires is supplies, which are to be found in great abundance in a large city. No doubt there are three weeks supplies for 25,000 men at present in the city of Dundee. This constitutes a base ready-made for the operations of a field force.

Thirdly, Dundee is particularly well suited for an advance on Glasgow. By breaking the bridges across the Tay, the march would be absolutely protected as far as Perth, and thereafter the line of communications between Perth and Dundee would be secured.

Again, in your paper you speak of throwing up entrenchments after landing at Blyth or Harwich. But why? On such an enterprise one does not want to entrench but to advance. In the Blyth case you cannot be too quick in getting into [blank space]. The only chance of the raid being successful is speed. Once you are in possession of the Elswick Works and the valuable warships completing in the Tyne, you have something to bargain for and something to strike for. It would be deplorable indeed to be hung up entrenched at Blyth. *En avant* on land as on sea! A vigorous offensive is often the sole chance of the weaker. Otherwise I very much like your paper.

In your corrections of 'A Time Table of a Nightmare' you on several occasions make the enemy get information by intercepted wireless. But how is this possible? Surely our wireless orders will be in cypher, and we ought not to assume that they can be instantly intercepted and decoded?

[WINSTON S. CHURCHILL]

Memorandum by WSC

18 April 1913   Admiralty

The problem of oversea attack requires to be examined under three heads: –

(1) Absolute surprise to-morrow (19 April): everything going on as usual – Bolt from the Blue.

Objectives of raiders – to prevent the Expeditionary Force being sent to help France, and incidentally, if possible, to damage naval arsenals and dockyards.

(2) The whole expeditionary army has gone to India or some other distant theatre of war. The war has been going on some time: the Territorials have been embodied, but great numbers have been allowed to proceed on leave. The Second Fleet has been completed to full strength by the closing of the schools. The Immediate Reserve has been called out; and the whole of the First and Second Fleets are in those harbours which enable them to reach their actual war stations as quickly as possible. The patrol flotillas are mobilised in their war stations. The forts are manned, and the coastal look-out is active. But this has been going on for several months while complete peace continues in Europe. The tension has begun to be somewhat relaxed, and we have settled down to our ordinary way of life, while at the same time taking special precautions and having our forces so disposed that they are easily and readily available on the slightest sign of danger. This may be called a Bolt from the Grey. The only adequate objective of the enemy in this case would be invasion in such force as to overcome the comparatively feeble military establishment on foot in the United Kingdom.

(3) War with Germany has begun. All the fleets are fully mobilised and in active operation against the enemy according to the war plans of the Admiralty. The objectives open to the enemy would be minor raids to destroy naval arsenals and dockyards: the seizure of bases for flotilla action (this last may occur also in 1 and 2), and threats or attempts to invade in force to distract or divide the British fleet simultaneously with bringing about a great fleet action.

All these three situations with their variants deserve patient examination.

2. The first condition governing the dimensions of oversea attack from Germany is the number of troops available –

(i.) Instantly;

(ii.) In twenty-four hours; and

(iii.) At any time after a general mobilisation is complete.

This condition varies in each of the three cases above described. In (i) we must consider the number of troops instantly available to seize a harbour for the purpose of landing a larger force, and subsequently the additional number of troops who could be carried into that harbour before the British fleet could get round from its unprepared and accidental station. But since the objective of the Bolt from the Blue is to prevent the dispatch of an army to France, it is clear that it would not be worth while making it, unless the number of troops employed by Germany was substantially less than the number of troops we were going to send to France; *e.g.*, it would perhaps be worth while sending 20,000 to dislocate and delay the whole of the arrangements for the transportation of the expeditionary army. It would perhaps be worth sending 40,000 to stop the army going altogether. Having regard to the great dangers of the naval passage, it would certainly not be worth while risking more. It would be cheaper and better policy to fight the British divisions when they got to the continent.

(The above numbers are illustrative, not arbitrary; the military authorities should supply authoritative estimates.)

This part of the problem is again complicated by the number of German units it would be necessary to break up in order to supply (i) instantly or (ii) at twenty-four hours' notice, the forces required. At present, to find 20,000 men *instantly* would practically gut the IXth and Xth German Army Corps, *i.e.*, 4 Divisions to stop 6 (or perhaps only 4). To obtain 40,000 instantly would mean deranging and spoiling 8 Divisions: that would clearly be a bad bargain. The number of troops which it would be worth while for Germany to allot in any war in which she may expect to be engaged with France, and perhaps with Russia too, is necessarily limited, first, by the total numbers given, and secondly – and this is a far more real check – by the actual number of Divisions or Brigades which it would be necessary to mutilate, by taking them at peace strength.

But then it may be possible to dodge this; to have a couple of Divisions not near enough to the coast to excite suspicion, not too far from the coast to involve a long delay, and not situated so as to interrupt by their western transportation the great transportations to the south which we may expect will be going on at the same time. Observing all these limitations, it would be possible to invent a variety of devices by which a couple of Divisions could be found mobilised and available for a Bolt from the Blue.

In any case after October next, when the new German Army Law is in operation, the number of troops instantly available in the IXth and Xth Army Corps will be nearly double the present figure, owing to the great increase in the permanent strength of battalions. This is important, because although 4 Divisions is a great price to pay to keep 6 out of the decisive battle, yet it must be remembered that the arrival of a British army on the French left has a moral value above the value of the troops employed; and to strike a heavy blow at interfering England at the very outset, also has a moral value which is not necessarily measured by the actual material stake.

3. The numbers that might be launched in Case II, 'A Bolt from the Grey,' are of course more limited than in a Bolt from the Blue. Although in this case we may assume that Germany is not at war with any other Power, and consequently can devote her practically inexhaustible army to an attack on Great Britain (if she can get there), yet the Navy being in its proper stations and the whole apparatus of defence keyed up to semi-war pitch, she will not be able to push through anything except the first batch (*i.e.,* the number instantly ready without noticeable preparation) before the naval grip closes.

4. Case III is war pure and simple, and it would develop out of either 1 or 2, and be additional to anything that had happened under 1 or 2. Here, however, it would appear that there are only two methods open to Germany of getting troops into England: –

(*a.*) 'Driblets,' which in single ships elude the vigilance of our squadrons and flotillas, and make their way at great peril to unfrequented landing places for purposes not apparent unless to reinforce troops already there; and

(*b.*) An attempt to run, in one, two, or three detachments, a large army across the sea in transports methodically prepared, at the same moment and as part of the same strategic combination which is intended to bring about a great battle on the sea. In this case the number of troops available is practically unlimited, since mobilisation in Germany will be completed, and great numbers can be provided without spoiling many units. Also the shipping will be adapted to the special purposes both of carrying and landing troops.

5. A second great limiting condition is the shipping available in German ports. For all phases after the war has become open, whether under 1, 2, or 3, ample shipping is available of every class required, and the matter need not be further considered. But in case 1, the invading force is limited by the amount of suitable shipping available instantly at the right ports, and secondly, by what is available after 24 hours: in case 2, by the amount of shipping available instantly. After that, when war has actually begun, there is no difficulty in finding the ships or the men; the only difficulty is to get them across.

6. The third condition is the time taken to embark, transport, and land the various forces at different points concurrently and alternatively. This requires separate calculations in every case. These are complicated by the hours of daylight and darkness, the tides, the weather, and other uncertain features. Each case must be worked out separately, and risked on its merits.

7. The last consideration is the distance of the practicable objective from the landing point. Here again each case must be considered individually: –

Harwich is invaluable because it threatens London, and is unquestionably the best place for so doing. In no other way could you react so instantaneously upon British public opinion. On the other hand, once the invaders were turned out, the actual damage done would be small.

Immingham is a purely local injury not worth touching before war breaks out, and afterwards belonging to the 'driblets' phase.

Blyth or the Tyne are striking places for Newcastle, involving considerable moral effect and immense permanent damage, not of a vital character.

The Tay (Dundee) is valuable as affording a good landing place and ample supplies for a large army (if it could get there), within effective striking distance of Glasgow and the Clyde.

Cromarty, as long as it is undefended by land and if undefended by ships, would be a good place of disembarkation for a large force, but they would be isolated in barren country with great natural difficulties between them and any real vulnerable point. Cromarty and the Invergordon oil tanks might, however, be the object of a minor raid in the 'driblets' phase, if undefended.

Balta Sound, in the Shetlands, and those islands generally would be of the greatest value as a flotilla base to the Germans. Until they were expelled from them, which would be costly both in ships and men, all attempts to blockade the North Sea would be rendered futile.

On the West Coast there are numerous undefended landing places in sheltered waters suitable for the disembarkation of a large force (if it could get there). Oban, 60 miles away from the Clyde, deserves special attention. The mouth of the Clyde itself, which is lightly defended by land and has only three submarines at Lamlash, is suitable both for the landing of a large force and also for a raid on an arsenal. The same may be said of Barrow.

This would seem to exhaust the principal serviceable landing places which should be considered, but there may be others.

Grouping them according to the three phases under which oversea attack should be considered, we may assign to I (Bolt from the Blue): –

Harwich.

Newcastle–Blyth.

Balta Sound in the Shetlands.

To II (Bolt from the Grey): –
Harwich.
Newcastle–Blyth.
Firth of Tay.
Balta Sounds in the Shetlands.
Oban.
Firth of Clyde.
To III: –
(*a*) 'Driblets': The accessible and lightly defended naval arsenals and
    dockyards, *viz:* –
Newcastle–Blyth,
The Clyde,
Barrow,
together with Balta Sound in the Shetlands at any time.
(*b*)   All or any of the above practicable landing places for an invasion,
    provided the British fleet can be drawn away for the purpose of
    fighting a great battle, and the road consequently opened.
Combinations of these attacks are also possible within the limiting con-
ditions of men, ships, and time above described.

                                                            WSC

WSC to Jack Seely

17 April 1913   [Admiralty]

Copy

I cannot help thinking that it is a great mistake to attempt to deal by
answers to questions with the subjects now under discussion in the CID.
You have not yet heard the Admiralty case in its entirety. I most carefully
stated that we would at a later stage in the enquiry give you definitely our
data as to the scale of oversea attack the War Office might have to meet. But
we have not done so yet, nor ought it to be assumed that the Admiralty are
prepared to abandon the concentrated invading army of 70,000 as the
standard to which our preparations should be addressed. Further, even if
you were right upon the Admiralty view of the scale of attack, the question
of whether the Territorials alone would be able to meet the raiders or
invaders is surely one now under discussion at the CID. It is not sufficient
for the General Staff, any more than it would be sufficient for the Admiralty,
to make an assertion that their preparations are adequate. The whole
subject of our enquiry is to examine and decide that question. You will I
fancy find it very difficult to persuade the Committee that the Territorial

force is capable of dealing with 70,000 irrespective of whether they are landed in a concentrated or non-concentrated form.

But anyhow the decision of the Committee should not pre-judged, nor on these far-reaching matters should one Department commit the other. You would not like it if I were to say in answer to a question that the Navy were not prepared to say that in no circumstances could a force of 70,000 be landed in a concentrated form. It is for the Committee to decide after hearing the Admiralty evidence on this point what is the reasonable view to take. The piecemeal discussion in Parliament of our investigation so far as it has proceeded is extremely inconvenient, and will hamper us all in thinking our way towards the truth. I cannot see why it is necessary, as you have a perfect answer that the whole matter is now *sub judice*.

Jack Seely to WSC

17 April 1913   War Office

Secret

My dear Winston,

Many thanks for your letter.

I quite agree that it is undesirable to prejudge the discussion in CID in any way, but it was impossible to avoid making certain definite statements in view of discussions which previously have taken place.

The whole of our military arrangements have been based for a long time on the assumption that the forces remaining in this country after the Expeditionary Force has left are adequate to safeguard the national security from vital injury. This fact is well known to all our critics and if we were to make any statement suggesting that our present plans rendered us liable to a blow at the heart, the position would be impossible. It was necessary for me therefore, when challenged on the subject, to state definitely the conclusions to which the General Staff had come.

This could not be done without some reference to the Admiralty, for it must be assumed that the two War Staffs are in constant communication, but you will observe that I have committed the Admiralty to nothing except to a statement which one could say with certainty you would not dispute, *viz,* that an organised invasion by a European Army, anywhere in the neighbourhood of 60,000 or 70,000 men with *all* its cavalry, artillery, and transport, could not possibly elude the Fleet and land, in the absence of the Expeditionary Force, so long as we retain our present naval predominance.

The absence of the Expeditionary Force of necessity rules out the possibility of complete surprise. If any such operation were possible, our whole military arrangements ought to have been completely altered and we ought to have done it long ago. We cannot admit such a possibility therefore without stultifying our entire known arrangements.

It does not follow that HMG will endorse the views of the General Staff. When the CID has concluded its deliberations we may decide to adopt other methods of organisation and distribution, but to admit for a moment that an invading army is in a position to land and to keep our military arrangements in their present condition – which are, so obviously, ill-designed to meet such a danger – is a policy which we cannot announce.

Put in other words, if we are reasonably safe from disaster we can afford to wait for the considered judgment of HMG; if we are not, we ought not to wait a moment.

I have stated that we adopt the former alternative, and having now made the point quite clear I do not propose to say anything more about it.

Yours sincerely
JOHN BERNARD SEELY

Memorandum by WSC

Undated   [Admiralty]

Copy

Harwich

The COS in forwarding this observes 'I think it would have failed.' It would be better if an explanation of this opinion were supplied. On the hypotheses assumed throughout the paper by the War Staff it is difficult to see how it could have failed. It is assumed that from 2.15 a.m. on the 17th to 4.45 a.m. on the 19th, a period of more than 46 hours, the secret not merely of the despatch of the expedition but of the general hostile intentions of Germany, is kept and kept so well that not a breath of suspicion has been aroused in England, and that the Coast Guards mistake the attacking German cruisers for British vessels, and that the batteries are totally unprepared till firing actually commences from the enemy's ships. In these circumstances it is not understood how the purpose of the raiders could be frustrated or what forces there are in the neighbourhood ready to act immediately which could oppose them. On the contrary the War Staff paper shows very clearly that no force could arrive in time either to prevent the disembarkation of the troops or to intercept the returning transports. As for the torpedo craft in harbour, they would not have the warheads on their torpedoes, and would be totally unprepared for attack: and it is not apparent that they could make any effective resistance to the large force of enemy cruisers which has arrived on the scene. The War Staff in their paper give the times of these events and the strength of all the forces involved. If the C.O.S. does not concur in these times or in these estimates of forces, I should be glad if the corrected figures were supplied. If he does not concur in them I should be glad to know what new facts not disclosed in the War Staff paper led him to the conclusion he expresses in his covering minute.

It is to my mind incredible that the despatch of a hostile expedition of this magnitude would not have become known in England before 4.45 a.m. on the 19th April. But if this condition is assumed, the rest appears to follow inevitably.

Judgments without reasons are of as little use in argument as opinions unsupported by actual effects are in war.

For the rest, I must repeat what I have several times pointed out, that 20,000 men would be a force much more nearly proportioned to the ulterior purpose of the raid on Harwich than the 10,000 men dealt with in this example.

The Humber

I have studied the War Staff paper on this operation. The same unreal assumption is made that the expedition could have accomplished the whole crossing of the sea without any word leaking out, and that nothing would be known in England until the enemy's warships actually opened fire on the unsuspecting battery which had just saluted the German flag. The operation itself seems devoid of purpose. What would be the use of landing 10,000 men variously at Immingham, Grimsby, and Hull? Would not a smaller number suffice to destroy the oil tanks at Immingham? What other purpose can they discharge? What are they to do after their escort has gone away? The whole business of disembarking these comparatively small forces appears to me to be unreal and purposeless in the highest degree.

The Firth of Tay

Here, again, the main assumption is unreal. Further, it is impossible to find any strategic object which could be furthered by the landing of a force of 10,000 men in Dundee. Unless 30,000 or 40,000 men could be landed there in the absence from these shores of the regular army, it would not be worth going there at all.

If attention had been paid to the principles and directions contained in my two papers of the 24th and 26th April, a great deal of useless labour could have been saved to the Staff.

WSC

Memorandum by WSC

Undated   [Admiralty]

Copy

It is important to arrive at a clear understanding about what is meant by
'the command of the sea'. The mere power to encounter the enemy in a
general battle with superior force does not carry with it necessarily, or even
usually, the command of the sea. Even though the relative strength of the
fleets is such that the result of the battle may be awaited with confidence,
the command of the sea does not exist until after the battle has been actually
fought. But this decision may be indefinitely delayed, and may perhaps
never be obtained in the whole course of the war. Naval superiority does
not mean the command of the sea, but only the power to obtain the command
of the sea by fighting for it. In the case of France, a battle fleet which could
not put to sea for fear of encountering superior force would soon have lost its
efficiency and morale cooped up in harbour. No such consideration would
force the German fleet to fight unless they chose. The possession of the Kiel
Canal throws the whole of the Baltic open to their evolutions and their
training could proceed with perfect security during the whole course of a
naval war with Great Britain. Until the battle has been fought, the North
Sea will be an uncommanded sea. Even after the battle had been fought and
the German battle fleet decisively beaten, the command of the sea would
not be absolute, and the enterprises of squadrons, flotillas, and still more of
individual vessels, could be continued with diminishing effect for an indefinite period. These considerations apply to both belligerents. The defeat
of the British battle fleet by the Germans would not immediately expose
Great Britain to a concentrated invasion. A prolonged period of naval
warfare would probably follow before a regular invasion would be effected
and sustained, and to the very end the passage of the North Sea by transports
and the operation of landing would be fraught with serious risks. Nor, on
the other hand, is it impossible to move individual transports over an uncommanded sea. Many considerable British expeditions have in former
times actually been made over uncommanded seas watched by large and
undefeated hostile fleets. The element of certainty is lacking throughout,
and the degree of risk can only be even approximately estimated at the
moment of launching any particular enterprise. All that can be said with
certainty is that no attempt to effect a concentrated invasion of upwards of
70,000 men could succeed or would indeed be attempted in the face of
substantial superior naval force.

                                                                    WSC

*   *   *   *   *

Memorandum by WSC

Undated [Admiralty]

Copy

In order to reduce as far as possible the expenditure falling upon next year, we have decided not to have Grand Manoeuvres and to substitute for them a general mobilisation of the Third Fleet. A short one-clause bill will be required to call out the reservists for a week at a period which is not a national emergency. The test is one of the most important that will be made, and it is surprising we should have continued for so many years without ever once making it. The cost of the mobilisation, including a bounty of £1 to the reserves called up, is estimated at about £50,000. On the other hand the saving by not holding Grand Manoeuvres is estimated at upwards of £230,000. There is therefore a net saving of £180,000 by the change.[1]

H. H. Asquith to WSC

8 April 1913 10 Downing Street

My dear Winston,

I am sorry to have to tell you that in my opinion the provision by the Admiralty of a ship to convey the Papal Legate from Sicily to Malta, on his way to the Eucharistic Congress, ought not to have been sanctioned without previous consultation with the Colonial Secretary and myself. Very serious questions both ideal and Imperial were involved, and I fear grave difficulties may ensue.

In a matter of this kind, the Admiralty should not act on its own initiative.

Yours always

H.H.A.

WSC to H. H. Asquith

29 April 1913 [Admiralty]

Copy

My dear PM,

Yr rebuke about Malta has been carefully nursed by me.

In spite of Rundle's[2] extravagant apprehensions, & Harcourt's eager

---

[1] As a result of this Memorandum, which WSC drew up in order to economize on naval expenditure for 1913, the Fleet was in the North Sea, and mobilized, in July 1914, instead of being on manoeuvres in the Atlantic. Thus the dictates of economy played a decisive part in the sequence of events leading to Britain's declaration of war.

[2] Henry Macleod Leslie Rundle (1856–1934), GOC-in-C Northern Command 1905-7; Governor and C-in-C, Malta, 1909-15; knighted 1898.

mischiefmaking, everything has passed off perfectly at Malta, as everyone acquainted with the Island knew it wd. One unstarred question was the extent of the Parlty embarrassment at home.

I readily admit that the CO shd have been consulted, & directions have been given to ensure such action in the future. My regret however at this error in procedure, into wh precedent led my advisers, is tempered by the knowledge that had Harcourt been given the chance he wd have arrived at a wrong conclusion upon the facts & situation both here & in Malta.

I always take the greatest pains with my work & consult you on any questions of importance. I cannot think however that this matter was one in wh it was necessary for either me or H to trouble you. At the highest, we wd have adjusted it satisfactorily together.

Yrs vy sincly
WSC

Note: 'All's well that ends well.' H.H.A.

WSC to Lady Randolph

24 April 1913   Admiralty

Dearest Mamma,

It wd do you a gt deal of good to get away from England, worry & expense for three weeks & to bask a little in Mediterranean & Adriatic sunshine. Why will you not come with us on the 8th & be delivered safely (DV) back on the 1st or 2nd of June. We start from Venice & go round by the Dalmatian coast to Malta, Sicily, Ajaccio & Marseilles (perhaps Athens). The Asquiths are coming; so that you wd have to make up your mind to get on with Margot & the PM. But again why not?

Otherwise we are only Admiralty and Admirable.

It wd be so nice if you cd come, & Clemmie and I wd so greatly enjoy it.

It wd cost nothing or next to nothing.

Answer please in the affirmative.

Always your loving son
W

*   *   *   *   *

Lord Northcliffe to WSC

11 April 1913   22 St James's Place

My dear Winston,

I shall be glad to go in a submarine at the end of the Whitsuntide recess, if that would be convenient, but please do not trouble to come yourself. I presume Portsmouth is the nearest? If anything goes wrong with the submarine with *both* of us in it I am sure it will be the cause of much satisfaction to many.

Your Marconi friends stage-manage their affairs most damnably. For a couple of really clever people, I cannot understand such muddling. Yesterday afternoon a rumour went round Fleet Street, which is a whispering gallery, that if the newspapers printed some lunatic's speech, they would make themselves liable to a prosecution for libel. I sent one of my secretaries, young Russell Wakefield, to you, and he wrote to me that you kindly passed him on to Messrs LG and I. He found that the rumour was only partly true, but the damage had been done, with the result that the morning newspapers are obliged to give a self-advertising nonentity prominence he would never otherwise have had.

Moreover, the system of making mysteries of pieces of evidence in the inquiry, and doling them out like a serial story, has a bad effect on the public, though, as a matter of fact, the whole Marconi business looms much larger in Downing Street than among the mass of the people.

The total number of letters received by my newspapers has been exactly three, one of which was printed – the other two were foolish.

The method of dragging the thing out really does make some people think that there is something behind it all, though I personally, as I had your word for it that there is not, know there is not. If they had only taken the trouble to refer to *The Prince* they would have issued a twenty line paragraph in the Political Notes of *The Times* giving all the facts, and little more would have been heard of the subject. My own belief is that both of them throughout the whole matter have greatly lacked sense of proportion and foresight.

I think you might care to have a copy of a photograph I recently had taken in Paris, so send one to you, with this.

Yrs sincerely
NORTHCLIFFE

Lord Northcliffe to WSC

Sunday   Sutton Place
[? 20 April 1913]   by Guildford
Private   Surrey

My dear Winston,

We must have been writing the same sort of thing at about the same time.

Do get the PM or Rufus & LG to make some simple plain statement, expressing regret for error; every day it is postponed makes things worse. The absent are always wrong of course, but Murray does appear to be about the limit of secretiveness.

Your nephew's letter is honest & manly. I knew something of similar worth with Americans in Newfoundland. You must either eventually beat them at their own work or they will make you quit & it must be doubly difficult for a boy in a non-English country.

Murray's absence is causing universal talk in London & Provinces we hear.

In haste

Yrs v. sincerely
N

The Times

29 April 1913

At this stage of the proceedings Mr Winston Churchill entered the room, and Mr Powell's evidence was interrupted so that he might make a statement. When he had taken his seat in the witness-chair the Chairman said: We have asked you here to-day because of statements made by Mr Powell, the Editor of the *Financial News*, in which he used these words: 'The rumours with regard to Ministerial dealings in Marconi shares first began to circulate in London about the end of April or the beginning of May. They were obviously designed to support the shares. Three names were mentioned, two being those of Ministers who are now known to have been actually dealing in the shares, and the third that of a Minister who has not been mentioned in the affair for many months past.' We thought it right to ask Mr Powell who was the Minister referred to. He said it was only a rumour, but on our pressing him he gave your name, and then I asked him 'In what form did the rumours come to you with regard to Mr Winston Churchill having investments in Marconis?' His answer was, 'Precisely the same effect as in relation to the other two Ministers – namely, that he had been operating very success-fully in the Marconi market.' We wish to ask whether you have had any dealings in Marconi shares?

Mr Churchill: Sir Albert Spicer,[1] I received at ten minutes to 2 to-day the following letter from the Committee:

'Sir, The Select Committee on the Marconi Agreement desire me to draw your attention to page 435 of the evidence, which I enclose, given by the editor of the *Financial News*. In evidence today, the witness when desired to give the third name, mentioned you. He did so declaring that he had no evidence and believed the rumour to be false. The Committee are of opinion that, having been referred to, you should have the opportunity of answering the rumour with the least possible delay. They direct me to say they would be glad to receive your evidence at 2 o'clock today or as soon after as it may be convenient to you to come.'

Mr Churchill, speaking with vehemence, continued: This is a very insulting charge that you have thought proper to ask me to come here to answer. I am bound to point out that it is a most insulting charge. The charge which your Committee, Sir Albert, have thought it proper to summon me at a moment's notice to answer is nothing less than that, having had dealings in Marconi shares, I sat silent while friends and colleagues came forward and voluntarily disclosed their exact position – that I sat silent while they were subjected to gross ill-usage and covered with every species of calumny and insult, that all the time I sulked in the background, keeping my guilty knowledge to myself and desiring to conceal it from your Committee. I say it is a very insulting charge, a most grave and insulting charge, and I do think that before I am asked to answer it I am entitled, in all the common fairness of English life, to ask what is the evidence and foundation upon which your Committee have summoned me before them this afternoon.

The Chairman: The Committee did it, as they believed, in your interests, and we asked you to come at once because we believed you would be able at once to contradict these rumours. We felt that such a statement, with your name mentioned in it, compelled us at once in honour and justice to yourself, to ask you to come and contradict it.

Mr Churchill: – Am I to understand that it is simply upon this statement of the editor of the *Financial News* – I did not catch his name – that he had heard my name mentioned by some person or persons undisclosed, and that

[1] Albert Spicer (1847–1934), Chairman of the Select Committee of Inquiry into the Marconi Scandal; Liberal MP, Monmouth Boroughs, 1892–1900, Central Hackney 1906–18; Director of Spicers Ltd; member of the Commercial Intelligence Advisory Committee of the Board of Trade 1907–17, of the Advisory Committee to Army Council on the Spiritual and Moral Welfare of the Army 1907–17; created Baronet 1906; PC 1912.

he did not believe the rumour to be true and that he had no evidence to prove it – that on that foundation you have thought it right to bring me here?

The Chairman: The Committee thought, in justice to you, it was only right. You know well enough the difficulties we have had in connexion with this enquiry; we thought that the Press naturally would have this information all over the country; and we therefore thought it only right and fair to yourself to ask you to come at once so that the two statements – the statement and, we hoped, the contradiction – would go out simultaneously.

Mr Churchill: And am I to understand that every person, Minister or Member of Parliament, whose name is mentioned by current rumour and brought forward by a witness who says he does not believe it, is to be summoned before you to give a categorical denial to charges which, as I have pointed out, have become grossly insulting by reason of the fact that the Minister in question, it is suggested, has concealed up to this moment what his position was? Are you going to summon anybody else?

The Chairman: A very difficult and delicate matter has been entrusted to this Committee, and the Committee will do their best to carry out their instructions and the trust committed to them as fairly as they can. In asking you here to-day we are doing it, as we believe, in justice to yourself.

Mr Churchill: I fully sympathize with you in the difficult position you are in, but I do think I am entitled to represent to the Committee and to the public outside the ill-usage to which individuals are subjected: to which members of the House of Commons are subjected, in a case like this, when a Committee of their own fellow-members, upon the merest unsupported tittle-tattle, think it necessary to summon urgently a Minister of the Crown before them to give an answer on a matter which obviously affects his honour – to give an answer as to whether or no he has sat still while his friends and colleagues came forward and voluntarily disclosed their position – sat still, skulking in the background. I am grieved beyond words that a Committee of my fellow-members in the House of Commons should have thought it right to lend their sanction to the putting of such a question. Having said so much, I will proceed to answer your question. I have never at any time, in any circumstances, directly or indirectly, had any investments or any interests of any kind – however vaguely it may be described – in Marconi telegraphic shares, or any other shares of that description, in this or any other country in the inhabited globe (laughter); and if anybody at any time has said so, that person is a liar and a slanderer; and if anybody has repeated this statement and said he had no evidence and he believed it to be false but that there it was, the only difference between that person and a liar and slanderer is that he is a coward in addition.

Mr Powell (rising from his seat): On that Mr Chairman – (cries of 'Order').

The Chairman: I thought you ought to have the opportunity of clearing yourself, and you have done so.

Lord R. Cecil: I think it only right to say that it was only with great reluctance that Mr Powell did mention your name at all, but the difficulty was this – the name of a Cabinet Minister was mentioned and the Committee thought it undesirable that there should be an undefined charge resting on the Cabinet as a whole. We have been entrusted with the difficult duty of trying to ascertain the foundation of these rumours, and we, therefore, thought it right to press Mr Powell to mention the name, and he did so with great reluctance, adding that he believed there was no foundation for the charge. We then felt, seeing your name had been mentioned, that the contradiction which we are glad to notice has been forthcoming should follow the mention of your name so rapidly that there would be no chance of one being distributed without the other.

Mr Churchill: My remarks are of a general character – they do not refer to any person in particular – but I am protesting, as I think I am entitled to, against flimsy gossip – and what public man is there about whom lies are not in circulation? If I tried to contradict every lie put forward about me, since I have been a Minister, I could not get through my daily work. One is entitled to protest against such statements unless the person making them has good reason or some *prima facie* evidence to justify them, and I should have thought a House of Commons Committee – well, it is not for me to make any comment upon it. I quite understand your object in summoning me here was not injurious to myself at all.

Sir R. W. Essex:[1] Might I put this to you, with all respect? When it was said that a Cabinet Minister was mentioned we were bound to ask the name. You will appreciate that, I think, and we felt that one who in the opinion of every member, I doubt not, of this Committee bears a name that stands for chivalry, high feeling, and courage, like yours, would be the first to come and defend not only his own name, but that of his colleagues in so far as it lay in his power.

The end of Sir R. W. Essex's remarks were not distinctly heard, but he was understood to suggest that Mr Churchill, in 'laying about him so lustily' might have regarded this as interest and belief in himself and his colleagues.

Mr Churchill said he had seen a great many things said about himself, but he had paid no attention to them, having a good conscience and knowing that this was the kind of method by which political warfare of a particular

[1] Richard Walter Essex (1857–1941), Liberal MP Cirencester 1906–10; Stafford 1910–18; knighted 1913.

kind was carried on nowadays. What has annoyed and grieved me so much, he continued, is that a Committee of my fellow members, instead of brushing this aside, should have asked me to come and should have thought that my character was in such jeopardy that I required to hurry over here at a moment's notice. I hope I have lived an honourable life. I am bound to say that I think a little more was required than the evidence of a witness who says he has no evidence and does not believe a rumour to be true.

The Chairman: I do not think we need go any further. I am glad you have come and been able to dissipate the rumour, and I cannot help thinking that on reflection and if you had read all we have had to listen to during the last five months, you would feel that we have done not injustice, but justice to you in asking you to come to refute what appeared to be an idle rumour.

Mr Churchill: May I assume that your examination of me is finished?

The Chairman nodded assent.

Wilfrid Scawen Blunt to WSC

29 April 1913   Newbuildings Place

Dear Winston,

I congratulate you on your anger in the Marconi Committee room. It has cleared the atmosphere in a violent way which puts you in the first rank of men of courage & honour. Not that you needed any repudiation personally, for I really do not think anyone held you to be mixed up with these things or even mentioned your name in connection with them. But because it was necessary that someone with the traditions of an honourable house should repudiate all possible suggestion of it as an intolerable insult. What had been the ugly part of the business all these months had been that nobody connected with the Govt had resented the gambling charge as a disgrace in plain unmistakable words. You have done this, and it will be counted to you for virtue in days to come. It is in affairs like these that breeding asserts itself.

Yrs ever

WILFRID SCAWEN BLUNT

Lord Esher to WSC

29 April 1913   2 Tilney Street
                                       Mayfair

My dear Winston,
    Hearty profound enthusiastic congratulations. You have knocked the last remaining worm-eaten plank out of that ludicrous Committee. I only wish you could have kicked an Editor.

                                     Yours ever
                                     ESHER

Baron de Forest to WSC

3 May 1913   Prof Dr C. Dapper's
                           Sanatorium Neues Kurhaus'
                               Bad Kissingen

My dear Winston,
    Allow me to send you my heartiest congratulations on your remarks to the Marconi Committee and on the dressing down you gave them. I hope you have marked them up. From what I hear you have. It was splendidly said and done. I am ever so much better and shall be back after Whitsuntide. I have had a very dull time but it has done me much good. I hope you are well and send you every good wish.

                                     Yours ever
                                     De F

Note by WSC:
Telegraph thanks.

WSC to Lord Northcliffe
(*Northcliffe Papers*)

5 June 1913   Admiralty

Private & Personal

My dear Northcliffe,
    You will remember our talk. The enclosed from my brother-in-law reached me unexpectedly on my voyage. Let me have it back.
    This newly revealed transaction of the Master of Elibank is a complete surprise to us all. Neither the Chancellor of the Exchequer nor the Attorney

General nor anyone else in the Government has the slightest knowledge of it. Though the investment is in itself unobjectionable, the concealment of it from colleagues & friends & from the Prime Minister is deplorable. I expect it will keep this disagreeable business alive for some time.

What about our submarine expedition!

Yours vy sincerely
WINSTON S. CHURCHILL

Lord Northcliffe to WSC

6 June 1913   *The Times*
Private

My dear Winston,

When you came to ask me to treat the Marconi matter on non-Party lines, I accepted your word that there was nothing more than what you told me about the Attorney General and [Lloyd] George.

Their transactions do not seem to me to be of any particular demerit, except for the way in which they have been slowly dragged out before the Public. This morning I read of an entirely fresh crop of developments, of which I know you were unaware. They do not appear to affect Sir Rufus or George, nor to be particularly noxious in themselves, apart from the fact that they have been ferreted out by newspapers. I kept my promise to you most gladly, but I must express my opinion that steps should be taken to ask Lord Murray to come back. His absence gives the impression, probably quite erroneous, that there is what newspapers call 'a big story' behind the whole of this matter, and I have no intention of letting my journals remain silent on his abstention.

Three or four weeks ago I thought the whole subject was practically dead, but I now consider that the Master of Elibank's absence is a grave injustice, not only to George and the Attorney General and to your Party, but to the reputation of our Parliament altogether. As you probably know, the wildest rumours are in circulation in London about the Master of Elibank.

I have made some bad bungles myself, but the stage-management of this business beats any record of mine.

I am hoping for our little submersion later in the month, if you are agreeable. Pray do not trouble to come, as I can run down from Sutton Place to Portsmouth in my motor, and put myself in the charge of any of your young people who look after submarines. A Monday would suit me best.

Yours very sincerely
N

*   *   *   *   *

Memorandum by WSC

A

1. The War Office do not wish to be tied down to fixed points on the coast. The Admiralty only wish on land to be tied down to the defence of fixed points. The interests of the two Departments are therefore identical in principle.

2. The Admiralty propose that they should take over altogether the East Coast batteries north of Sheerness and man them adequately both in peace and war. For this purpose the Admiralty would use active service marines and marine or naval reservists supplemented, if convenient both to the War Office and Admiralty in any particular case, by territorial gunners.

3. The Admiralty wish themselves to construct any new batteries on the East Coast which may be required, and to provide for their construction and armament as well as for the maintenance of existing works from Navy Votes.

B

4. The Admiralty are willing to provide on mobilisation as many naval and marine reservists as the War Office may think necessary for the local and immediate defence of the coast batteries and harbours. These naval forces would be available from the 4th day of mobilisation.

5. The Admiralty wish to take over the whole business of coast watching on the Sheerness-Shetlands line, and to organise under Admiralty control whatever means exist, whether on the sea by their patrol flotillas, or along the coasts by their Coast Guard and war wireless stations, or by territorial cyclists, or by the police, in order to report any hostile landing, as quickly as possible.

6. The Admiralty think it desirable that all the above services, including the immediate local defence of the coast batteries and the ports, should be placed under the command of the naval or marine officer in charge of each patrol centre. This officer would be responsible (a) for fighting the batteries, for giving the batteries local protection, for protecting locally the actual port, (b) for organising, calculating and distributing intelligence along the whole section of the coast assigned to each particular patrol centre, and (c) for moving under Admiralty authority such flotillas as are at his disposal at the patrol centre to any point in his section of the coast on which the enemy are attempting a landing. He would not be responsible for the conduct of field operations or any land operation other than the local defence of the ports

and batteries aforesaid: nor for repulsing a landing at any point intermediate between the patrol centres.

The Admiralty would propose to establish permanently the commands of these patrol centres and to organise therefrom the whole service of their defence and of coast intelligence generally. The paramount need of having the patrol flotillas permanently protected in their harbours at all times and of obtaining the earliest news showing where to direct them would appear to require complete unity of control throughout the aforesaid services.

C

7. The duty of defending the coast ports against a sustained attack, of resisting any landing at an intermediate point on the coast, and of dealing with any raiding or invading force which has landed, belongs, like all field operations, inalienably to the domain of the Army. The War Office should control absolutely at all times all mobile forces not specifically assigned to coast observation or to the purely local defence of coast batteries and patrol centres. Their commanders would, for this purpose, establish themselves either in the patrol centres or at any other points strategically convenient. The relations of the military commanders and the Admiralty officers in charge of the patrol centres would be exactly those which prevail between General Officers Commanding Field Units and Base Commandants on the line of communication. In any case of emergency where the mobile troops are employed for the immediate defence of any Port, the whole of the land forces in that Port, whether marines in the batteries or naval reservists assigned to their local protection, would pass automatically under the Authority of the military commander-in-chief, the Admiralty commander of the patrol centre retaining only the patrol flotillas and such portions of the service of observation as are necessary for their proper direction.

8. The Admiralty will, after providing for the local requirements above described, organise 4 naval and marine brigades out of their surplus re-servists, probably aggregating 12,000 men, each brigade being commanded by a general officer of marines. Until these men are required for naval service the Admiralty will hold them at the disposal of the military commander-in-chief for the general defence of the United Kingdom against over-sea attack. These brigades shall be assembled by the 4th day of mobilisation at such convenient strategic and administrative points as may be agreed upon be-tween the Departments, and shall thereafter be administered by the Ad-miralty and controlled in all military movements absolutely by the War Office.

WSC to Sir W. Graham Greene, Prince Louis of Battenberg, Sir Henry Jackson and
Captain Thomas Jackson[1]

19 May [1913]   [Admiralty]

Secret

Copy

The German land pressure on Holland would be irresistible in a war and would compel her either to join Germany as an ally or to remain neutral in form while helping Germany by every means to carry on her trade. The second of these alternatives would be the worst for us and we should probably take measures which would have the effect of driving Holland into actual hostility or enable us to treat her ports as though she were hostile. The effectiveness of our blockade would be more important than the disadvantage of any naval force which Holland could contribute to Germany in the next few years. I do not believe there is any practicable means of making Holland take our side in such a war. Whatever her views, she would be compelled to go with Germany openly or covertly.

On the other hand the localisation of warship-building must be an important aim of British policy, and I agree that we should use our influence so far as possible to assist the placing of these orders in England instead of in Germany. We need not, however, regard the matter as of first consequence nor should we let the contractors think that we attach too much weight to it.

I will decide on the tenders as soon as the paper comes to me. A conference should be held as suggested.

With regard to the last paragraph of the minute of COS, while everything should be done to promote good relations with Holland, no military reliance should be placed on her and schemes should certainly be prepared in the sense of the COS's minute. The CID is not the proper means of dealing with matters of such secrecy as war plans. A conference between the First Sea Lord and the Chief of the Imperial General Staff held with the sanction of the Ministerial heads of departments should be sufficient to enable the necessary staff work to proceed. The importance of secrecy in these matters arises from the fact that while it is the duty of Staffs to prepare plans for all sorts of contingencies, even the most unlikely, the mere fact of such plans being in existence becoming known is prejudicial to good relations and tends to provoke preparations on the part of the power affected.

---

[1] Thomas Jackson (1868–1945), Director of Intelligence Division of the War Staff 1912–13; Director of Operations Division 1915–17; Commanded Egypt and Red Sea Division of Mediterranean Squadron 1917–19; knighted 1923; Admiral 1925.

WSC to the Greek Minister of Marine

2 June 1913   [Admiralty]

Copy

We have received from the Foreign Office the request of the Greek Government for a new and reinforced British Naval Mission to Greece composed of officers of the active list of the Royal Navy.

Although at the present time the rapid expansion of the British naval forces imposes a considerable strain upon our own resources in personnel, Prince Louis of Battenberg and I are anxious on grounds of general naval policy to do our best to meet your wishes. The actual numbers and rank of the officers who would be employed should not be settled until after consultation with the head of the mission. Without however going into that or any other detail in this letter, I can assure you that we are prepared to place some of the best officers on the active list of the British Navy at your disposal. There is, however, one indispensable condition. We cannot ask officers who have the brightest prospects of advancement in the British Service to leave the great fleets in home waters for service under the Greek Navy unless it is certain that their professional duties in the Greek Navy will be of a real and responsible character, and that they will have effective authority to discharge those responsibilities to the advantage of the Greek Navy and their own reputation. If you feel able to put me in a position to give the necessary assurances, I should propose to invite Rear-Admiral Mark Kerr to head the Naval Mission to Greece. This is one of the most gifted and brilliant officers in our service, of whom we fully expect in the future that he will rise at an early age to the most important commands. I am confident that there is no man who could more effectively aid the development of Greek naval power up to the point where it will be fully equal to the emergencies of the future.

I write to you personally and privately because I am anxious that you should know that we are ready to deal with the question of a Greek Naval Mission not in any perfunctory spirit but with an earnest desire if a fair chance is given to assist in producing results equally honourable to the navies of both countries.

WSC to A. J. Balfour

3 June 1913   [Admiralty]

Copy

There will be a strong fleet at Portland on the 19th and 20th of this
month, and I am arranging to have some exercises of special interest carried
out quite privately. Among these will be some firing by a battle cruiser at
full speed, which has never been tried before. It would give me the greatest
pleasure if you would come and stay with me on the *Enchantress* from the
Wednesday night till the Saturday morning. Asquith is coming and I am
going to ask Morley. We shall be the smallest of parties but I think I can
guarantee that you will have a better opportunity of posting yourself in the
latest developments of the Navy than at any other time in the year. I am
arranging this plan almost entirely for you and the Prime Minister, and I
do hope you will be able to come. There will be no ceremonies of any kind,
and nothing but naval officers, naval exercises, and naval arguments.

WSC to Prince Louis of Battenberg

5 June [1913]   [Admiralty]

Copy

First Sea Lord

I should be glad if you would consider the desirability of having a thorough
overhaul of the mobilisation arrangements. Would not Sir Reginald Custance
be an officer well suited to conduct such an enquiry? He should go round
from port to port and examine there and in the Mobilisation Department
the whole of the existing plans *de novo* and report whether any, and, if so,
what improvements can be made. He should have a good staff officer
attached to him for this purpose, and D.M.D. [Director of Mobilisation
Division] should accompany him whenever the latter wants to. I anticipate
the enquiry will take 3 or 4 months. As you know, this has been in my mind
for a long time. I should hope next year to obtain a mobilisation of the whole
of the Royal Fleet Reserve and to take money in the Estimates for that
purpose. Such a step is urgently needed. The new questions which are
arising on the East Coast have also their bearing on the subject, particularly
in regard to the disposal of the surplus Naval Reservists.

WSC to Rear-Admiral D. R. S. de Chair[1]

14 June [1913]   [Admiralty]

Copy

I notice that you propose the Gunnery Lieutenant of the *Orion* for promotion to Commander. It is a very bad system by which the gunnery officers of our best ships should change so repeatedly. This officer has only been six months in the vessel, from which an experienced Gunnery Lieutenant was removed on promotion last time. If he is now promoted there will be another movement, and the whole gunnery of the vessel turned upside down. The Gunnery Lieutenants of the latest vessels should hold their positions for at least two years, and if they are promoted meanwhile they should continue as Commanders, a two years period being the irreducible minimum.

Please let me have your opinion on this.

Rear-Admiral H. G. King-Hall[2] *to WSC*

11 July 1913   Seychelles to Kilindini

Dear Mr Churchill,

I am sending in an official letter in regard to the defenceless state of St Helena. It really seems risky to have a strongly fortified base left with the front door open for anyone to walk in and possess it for the asking. If nothing else was done the inhabitants might be made to provide a militia force as is done in all our Dominions now. I was at the Admiralty when the War Office finally succeeded in withdrawing the garrison, and I know how strongly the Admiralty protested against its being done. My raising the question may have no effect, but as I fancy Colonel Seely carries less weight than Lord Haldane – it is possible that the scale may be tipped the other way if you take it up.

I am half way through my East Coast Cruise in company with my small squadron. Though small it gets through quite a lot of exercises at Sea in the most approved Home Fleet fashion.

Believe me

Yours very truly
HERBERT KING-HALL

[1] Dudley Rawson Stratford de Chair (1864–1958), Naval Secretary to WSC 1912–14; Commanded 10th Cruiser Squadron 1914–16; 3rd Battle Squadron 1917–18; Governor of New South Wales 1923–30; knighted 1916; Admiral 1920.

[2] Herbert Goodenough King-Hall (1862–1936), Rear-Admiral 1909; Director of Naval Mobilization 1909–11; Rear-Admiral Second Division Home Fleet 1911–12; C-in-C Cape of Good Hope 1912–15; retired 1922.

WSC to his wife
(CSC Papers)

23 July 1913
HMS *Enchantress*
S. Queensferry

Clemmie darling,

We did not sail for Scapa yesterday after all, because the C in C is coming south & all we have to do is to meet him off the Forth. The result of this waiting here was to bring me your nice letter this morning. By all means ask K to lunch next week. Tuesday wd be a good day. Let us be just à trois. I have some things to talk to him about.

The party has settled down quite happily & I think they have made up their minds to enjoy themselves. The weather too is bright & clear & there is every prospect of the manœuvres beginning at least in smooth water.

Tender love to you my sweet one & to both those little kittens & especially that radiant Randolph. Diana is a darling too: & I repent to have expressed a preference. But somehow he seems a more genial generous nature: while she is mysterious and self conscious. They are vy beautiful & will win us honour some day when everyone is admiring her & grumbling about him.

My dearest you are vy precious to me and I rejoice indeed to have won & kept your loving heart. May it never cool towards me is my prayer, & that I may deserve your love my resolve.

Write daily –

Always your loving husband
W

WSC to Sir George Callaghan

29 July 1913
[Admiralty]

Private & Personal

Copy

My dear Sir George Callaghan,

Altho manoeuvres are only a partial resemblance to war, they afford our sole means in time of peace of testing naval dispositions & commanders; & they must therefore have a real significance as regards both conduct & results.

The task entrusted to you cannot be called disproportionate to the forces at yr disposal, & it is for you to find, as you wd do in war, the best method of achieving it. It wd seem that vy favourable chances are offered to a general offensive. [*The following crossed out:* and that the position of the Red Fleet is one of great difficulty.] Of course there can be no certainty in such movements. He may slip through or round yr front or he may again raid some

East coast port. But he cannot do either without running the utmost risk of being either brought to battle or cut from his only base of coal & reinforcements. Neither the landing of 36,000 men nor the egress of the Red Fleet into the Atlantic to cruise there till its coal is exhausted are worth the certain sacrifice of that Fleet itself. Therefore it seems to me that you can approach yr problem with a vy good confidence & a strong sense of freedom. You may be able to bring him to action, & with yr great cruiser strength this is to be expected. You may be able to drive him into the Thames & shut him up there. But even if the worst comes to the worst & you miss him altogether, you can at least shut him out: & that is after all one of the decisive positions in the game,

I shd have liked to come with you this time in the *Neptune* but I felt that you wd wish to be unencumbered so I am going in the *Thunderer* instead.

But my hopes & belief are strong that you will show that there still remain resources in the Br Navy not unequal to the task of hunting down an inferior fleet wh attempts to keep the seas.

With good wishes for yr success.

Yours vy truly
WINSTON S. CHURCHILL

WSC to Edwin Montagu

8 August 1913   Admiralty

Copy

After 'compliments', which are very well deserved by you just now, let me draw your attention to the Admiralty letter of the 12th of March on the subject of an increased contribution by India towards the cost of the vessels maintained in Indian waters. Since that letter was written we have been compelled to send one of our newest light cruisers and the battleship *Swiftsure* to the East Indian Squadron. The Estimates next year are very formidable, and the question of an Indian contribution ought to be dealt with by the two Departments in a fair and friendly spirit before the November and December Cabinets have to deal with the expenditure of next year. Whatever doubts there may be about India contributing to Imperial Defence, surely there can be no moral justification in her throwing the burden of purely local Indian defence upon the British taxpayer and the British Admiralty? The upkeep and maintenance of the East Indian Station ought to be paid for by India; and this question should be considered as quite separate from that of any contribution to the maintenance of general sea-power.

You ought also to turn your attention to the Indian Marine, which is one of the greatest scandals now existing in British administration. Its present condition is one of the grossest abuses which I have ever come across in official life, and as soon as I am released from official ties, I intend to do my best to break it up. You have an enormous annual expenditure, large numbers of highly paid and inefficient officers, and no result of the smallest military value. I have no doubt also that there is very excessive expenditure on the maintenance of marine fortifications by the Indian Government. The defences of Bombay alone are practically equal to those of Portsmouth and out of all proportion to what is needed. I am certain that from these two sources economies might be made which would go a long way to supplying the necessary funds for the upkeep and maintenance of the East Indian Squadron. Now that you are at home, I hope you will give these matters your attention.

This letter is for your private eye alone.

Yours sincerely
WINSTON S. CHURCHILL

WSC to Colonel James Allen[1]

25 August 1913 [Admiralty]

Copy

Dear Colonel Allen,

Your letter of the 27th June has crossed a long one from me dated 31st July, which would have been sent off earlier but for my absence in the Mediterranean and some serious preoccupations since my return.

I hope the memorandum which I enclosed will give you all the information which you asked for in your letter of the 24th April written after your departure. Should you desire to have it supplemented in any way you have only to write or telegraph and I will do what I can to meet your wishes. I think you will agree with me that it will be desirable that you should have before you the full information now on its way to you before we discuss any particular points.

I notice that you revert to the question of the Bristol cruisers which we discussed when you were here. I then fully explained our position to you and I understood that you concurred in our view, and that the new arrangements which we are endeavouring to make to meet your wishes were to be taken as definitely superseding those which were outlined in 1909. We are preparing, in deference to your wishes, to maintain on the New Zealand station 3

[1] James Allen (1855–1942), New Zealand's Minister of Defence 1912–20; High Commissioner in London 1920–26; knighted 1917.

cruisers instead of 2 : and we are to assist you in the development and training of a New Zealand naval personnel, one of our cruisers being specially assigned for this duty. You, on the other hand, propose as I now learn to utilise the New Zealand contribution primarily for the purpose of developing the New Zealand naval force, and only to devote any surplus that may be available thereafter to the general maintenance of the Imperial Navy. Although I believe you have it in contemplation to increase the total of your contribution from £100,000 to £150,000 per annum, it seems to me very probable that the amounts available for general purposes will in the future be less than it has been hitherto. In any case it will be considerably less than the cost of maintaining the squadron (*Cambrian, Psyche, Philomel* and *Torch*) in New Zealand waters.

We have also most gratefully and publicly acknowledged the patriotic and far-seeing action of the New Zealand Government in confirming the free gift made by New Zealand of the battle cruiser of that name for the general service of Imperial defence. We hope that the visit of this vessel to New Zealand and her mission around the Empire may make every New Zealander feel how very effective has been the service which they have rendered to the British Navy. We are very proud and glad to man and maintain this fine ship at a cost of £125,000 a year so long as she is available for general Imperial service. We accept in the fullest sense our duties and responsibilities for the effective defence of New Zealand and for shielding that Dominion from all menace or danger to her interests. If we are to discharge this task, especially in times like these, it is essential that we should be left free to distribute and dispose of the naval forces at the disposal of the Admiralty in what is judged to be the most effectual manner according to military and strategic needs. If and when those needs require the presence of the *New Zealand* or of other vessels of her type in the Pacific, they will certainly be sent. But we are clear and understand that you fully agree with us that to send a vessel where it is not needed, and where it could play no part in decisive events, would not be a policy on which the Admiralty would be justified in making a heavy annual outlay.

The same considerations apply to the Bristol cruisers. The events which have occurred since 1909 have markedly altered the naval situation. In the work of defending the British Empire which falls almost entirely upon the British taxpayer, we cannot afford not to make the best use, for the common defence, of the naval resources which are available. There is no class of ship of which we are shorter at the present time than these light, fast, modern cruisers. Great efforts are being made by the Admiralty to increase the margin of these vessels at our disposal. No less than 16 are being constructed in the programmes of the last two years; and it is probable that a further large programme will be begun in 1914–15. None of these will, however, be completed for at least a year: meanwhile, until a very large proportion of them have been commissioned, we have actually not got any Bristol cruisers which can be spared from definite military duties of serious importance. We are at this present moment sending 2 Bristol cruisers, one to the East Indies and the other to the China Station, available immediately for service in the Pacific or Indian Oceans in order to cover specific German vessels in those waters. Neither of these requirements could be foreseen in 1909; and we cannot spare 2 more to cruise in New Zealand waters where no military need at present exists for vessels of this speed. There are apparently no foreign cruisers of an equal type which require to be met within thousands of miles of New Zealand. If there were, we should immediately match them by similar vessels. I am sure you will agree with me that it would not be justifiable from any point of view for us to remove 2 of these ships from stations where they are urgently and immediately needed, in order to proceed to New Zealand waters in relief of vessels which are from every point of view adequate and suitable for every existing military requirement. If, therefore, the New Zealand Government desire to have 2 Bristol cruisers immediately provided for the New Zealand station, it is important that they should realise that these vessels will have to be specially built additional to the existing British programme, at a cost of about £700,000. I propose, therefore, that the new proposals which you put before the Admiralty should be considered and decided in the first instance. The presence or absence of these cruisers will not affect the carrying out of any scheme of training such as that proposed by you, and the question is rather one of the distribution of the ships of the China Squadron, of which they would be a part, than of the organization of a New Zealand naval service.

With regard to the drafting of a Bill to give effect to such scheme as may be approved by the New Zealand Government, I will arrange that every assistance you may require shall be afforded. It will be perfectly easy to draft a measure for the consideration of your legal advisers, to whom the New Zealand Government will naturally look for the final opinion. Our Parliamentary Counsel are, of course, not closely acquainted with the statutory procedure obtaining in the Dominion. In this matter it is legal constitutional advice rather than naval which is required, especially as the proposed legislation will be, presumably, of the same general character as that passed by the Commonwealth Government.

[31 July 1913]   [Admiralty]

Copy

I am sending my letter to Colonel Allen today. During my absence it is important that he should be seen and kept in touch with, and I hope that both of you will invite him to come and see you in order to discuss the general questions outstanding with New Zealand and take every possible opportunity of inculcating sound principles into his mind. He is at present full of very foolish and retrogressive ideas. He is possessed with the idea that we want to shirk our duty of providing for our own defence and obtain help to which we are not entitled from the Colonies as a substitute for our efforts. A little plain and faithful discussion with naval officers who know all the facts could not fail to be beneficial.

I have told Colonel Allen that I hope he will come to the Admiralty in my absence when he feels inclined, but perhaps you would also write to him and give him appointments.

There are now 17,800 Marines, of whom 11,400 are afloat and 6,400 ashore, thus observing the proper proportion of two afloat to one ashore. In the 6,400 ashore are included 1,700 recruits, a considerable instructional staff, and all details. In war time all active service Marines go afloat except 1,600 men, of whom 800 are unqualified recruits. The other 800 have been lately saved for a special purpose by employing a larger proportion of reserve Marines in the complements of Third Fleet ships. The special object is the formation of a mobile brigade of Marines which could if necessary be sent to protect the Orkneys or any other minor detached oversea service required by the Admiralty. The Admiralty, however, attach so much importance and urgency to the proper defence of the East Coast batteries that they would be prepared if necessary to defer the formation of this mobile brigade, and to employ these 800 men in the first instance in manning the East Coast batteries.

There are also approximately 4,900 marine reservists (including the Immediate Reserve). Of these, 2,100 are employed afloat in war, and the remaining 2,800 are available on shore for various duties, making with the 800 recruits a total of 3,600. From this force it would certainly be possible to find on mobilisation the Marines required to raise to war strength the permanent peace complements of the East Coast batteries. Alternatively, there would be available for this limited purpose an ample supply of seamen gunners of the Royal Fleet Reserve.

*   *   *   *   *

Sir Frederick Ponsonby to WSC
(*Royal Archives*)

3 August 1913   HM Yacht *Victoria & Albert*
                                                                           Cowes

Copy

My dear Churchill,

With reference to the enclosed submission, The King desires me to tell you that he quite approves of the names *Hero, Agincourt* and *Raleigh* for the new Battleships.

His Majesty is however inclined to think that the name *Pitt* is neither euphonious nor dignified, although Battleships have formerly been so named. There is moreover always the danger of the men giving the Ship nicknames of ill-conditioned words rhyming with it.

The name *Ark Royal* The King does not quite like; although no doubt it is historically interesting, it has no particular meaning. It seems a misnomer to apply to a Ship of metal and it would eventually be known as the *Noah's Ark*.

The King hopes you will suggest some other names in the place of these two.

His Majesty when looking through the Navy List observed there was no *Caledonia* nor *Rodney* and desired me to suggest these names to you.

Yours very truly
F. E. G. PONSONBY

WSC to Sir Frederick Ponsonby
(*Royal Archives*)

4 August 1913   [Admiralty]

My dear Ponsonby,

I have given very careful consideration indeed to the names of the Battleships in this year's programme, and I am strongly of opinion that the Navy ought not to be without a *Pitt* and an *Ark Royal,* for both of which vessels precedents exist, and around which historical associations of the greatest moment are gathered. I enclose the past history of these vessels and trust that the explanation may be satisfactory to the King and that His Majesty will approve the names as submitted. With regard to the *Rodney,* it is thought better to include that with a regular Admiral Class such as the *Howe* and the *Anson.*

Yours very sincerely
WINSTON S. CHURCHILL

Sir Frederick Ponsonby to WSC
(*Royal Archives*)

5 August 1913   HM Yacht *Victoria & Albert*
Cowes

My dear Churchill,

Many thanks for your letter which I have submitted to The King.

His Majesty was well aware that both *Pitt* and *Ark Royal* were old names with historical traditions but sees nothing in the records of former vessels to render a revival of these names so essential.

The King agrees with you in thinking that it is well when possible to keep alive the old names but considers that certain exceptions should be made. French names should now be avoided in case they might wound the susceptibilities of the French people. Monosyllables are as a rule a mistake when applied to Battleships although they may well be used with smaller vessels.

The King knows how carefully all these questions are considered at the Admiralty and how well the old records are kept. His Majesty thinks you will, therefore, have no difficulty in selecting two other old names in the place of these two which he dislikes.

Yours sincerely
F. E. G. PONSONBY

WSC to Sir Frederick Ponsonby
(*Royal Archives*)

8 August 1913   Admiralty

My dear Ponsonby,

I am very sorry to learn from you that the King does not like the names *Pitt* and *Ark Royal* for two of the battleships of this year's programme. I am convinced that they are from many points of view the best choice that could be made. The name 'Pitt' recalls the two famous statesmen under whom the most martial exploits of our race have been achieved. It was suggested to me as a specially appropriate name for a British battleship by the Prime Minister. The *Ark Royal* which, as is shown in the accompanying memorandum, was the flagship at the defeat of the Armada, revives the glories of the Elizabethan period as the *Warspite* did in the programme of 1912–13. For both these names, were precedent indispensable, precedent exists. It is not desirable to confine the naming of battleships solely to vessels associated with the Nelsonic epoch though they assuredly should play a principal part.

With regard to the *Pitt* in particular, I cannot feel that the reasons to which you refer in your letter ought to weigh either with the Admiralty or with the King against doing honour to one of the greatest names in the history of this or any other European country. It would of course be possible if the King desired it to call the vessel the *William Pitt;* but there are great advantages in brevity, and I do not recommend this alternative.

I would venture to observe that in this field, as in others where opinions so easily differ, a definite responsibility for advice attaches to the Minister who for the time being is entrusted by His Majesty with the duty of presiding over the Admiralty Board. If public criticism through the Press or in Parliament is directed upon the naming of battleships, whether from the point of view of the exclusion or inclusion of certain names, it is essential that it should be borne solely by the First Lord of the Admiralty and that no one should have the right to suppose that His Majesty's personal act is in any way involved.

It has been a cause of regret to me that on several occasions in the past the names which it was my duty to submit to the King have not been favoured by His Majesty and that this subject has led to an extensive correspondence. I have therefore been led to examine the past history of this branch of naval administration. I find that the custom of bringing the names of battleships to the Sovereign's notice did not exist during the reign of Queen Victoria, except in cases where it was proposed to name a ship after the Sovereign or a member of the Royal Family, and was only introduced in the last reign in connection with the proposal to institute a 'King Edward the Seventh' class of battleships. In these circumstances it occurs to me that the King might prefer not to be troubled at all in the matter, and that I should revert to the practice invariably followed up to a quite recent date.

Perhaps you will kindly let me know whether the King would like me to renew my submission in its amended form or to proceed in accordance with the older usage.

Yours sincerely
WINSTON S. CHURCHILL

Lord Stamfordham to WSC
(*Royal Archives*)

20 August 1913   Balmoral

Having returned from leave I am desired by the King to write to you regarding the names of *Pitt* and *Ark Royal* suggested for two of the new Battleships, about which you and Ponsonby have been in correspondence.

In your letter of the 8th August you refer to 'ministerial responsibility.'

It would undoubtedly be the duty of the First Lord to point out any objections to giving effect to the wishes of the Sovereign if they involved questions of organisation, efficiency, or expenditure: but in the present instance no such questions arise.

Battleships have to be named so as to distinguish them: but for all practical purposes they might equally well be numbered and lettered, like submarines.

The actual names are a matter of fancy, sentiment, and suitability, though, as you say, this is a field where opinions easily differ.

The King assumes that in submitting the names for his approval you expected to have His Majesty's views upon your selection: and His Majesty cannot help thinking that the Officers and Men of the Royal Navy would like to feel that the Ships were named with the approval of the Sovereign, all the more so as the King was himself for many years in the Service.

You mention that you find the custom of bringing the names of Battleships to the Sovereign's notice practically did not exist during the reign of Queen Victoria. But, speaking with 20 years experience of Her Majesty's methods of business, I cannot imagine one of her Ministers submitting a question for approval except on the understanding that due regard, if not actual effect, would be given to any expression of Her Majesty's pleasure.

The King's objections to the above two names have already been stated in the previous letters. But His Majesty noticed from the records you sent that the two last vessels called *Pitt* were used as Coal Depots: two previous ships of that name being respectively a captured French Privateer, and a vessel brought from the East India Company and changed from *Pitt* to *Doris*.

Moreover, up till now there has been no case of a ship in the Royal Navy bearing the name of any of our great Statesmen.

The King quite recognises the interest and trouble which you have taken in this matter, and indeed in everything connected with the great Service over which you preside. But at the same time his Majesty yields to no one in his concern for all that affects the daily life of the Sailor, with which the name of the Ship, wherein he lives, and wherein he may have to fight, must always be closely associated.

Under these circumstances the King hopes that you will see your way to carry out his wishes and submit two other names, which, together with the three already agreed upon, would meet with His Majesty's approval.

Would it not avoid difficulties if in the future you were to ask to see the King and talk over such matters with his Majesty before sending in the formal submission? As you know, the King is only too glad to receive you at any time.

STAMFORDHAM

WSC to Lord Stamfordham
(Royal Archives)

30 August 1913

My dear Stamfordham,

I will follow the advice contained in the last paragraph of your letter & seek an opportunity of talking the question of the names over with His Majesty. As I am commanded to be in attendance at Balmoral from the 16th to the 22nd of September this opportunity may easily occur.

You know well that I am never backward in studying the King's wishes & that I have always endeavoured to profit from any guidance His Majesty has been gracious and pleased to give me.

Yours vy try
WINSTON S. CHURCHILL

*   *   *   *   *

Memorandum by WSC

28 August 1913   Admiralty

Secret

Before the question of increasing the executive lists can be profitably considered, it is necessary to determine the War Fleet of 1920. This fleet is set out in detail in Appendix II of the Report of the Committee. The Committee were not, however, sufficiently informed as to the policy on which the War Fleet is based.

The foundation of the War Fleet of 1920 is the number of Dreadnoughts resulting from our present scale of building. Under the present declared programmes we shall have, by the third quarter of 1920 (counting the *Malaya, New Zealand,* and the 2 Lord Nelsons, but excluding the *Australia*), 59 Dreadnoughts to a German 35. Of this total of 59 Dreadnoughts, 52 must be maintained in Home Waters to give a 50 per cent. superiority over the German 35, leaving 7 available for the Mediterranean. Moreover, of our total of 59 Dreadnoughts, 9 are battle cruisers. It is not to be expected that we shall build any more of these, further additions to the fast ships of Germany being met by vessels of equal speed possessing all the attributes of a battleship and counting as such. We may assume that 5 of the Dreadnoughts serving in the Mediterranean will be battle cruisers and 2 battleships. Therefore, among the 52 Dreadnoughts remaining at home there will be 4 battle cruisers. Deducting these, we have 48 Dreadnought battleships available for the formation of battle squadrons.

We propose to complete our organization of 8 battle squadrons by 1920, and for this we require 65 battleships in full, active, or reserve commission. We shall therefore require in 1920, 17 pre-Dreadnoughts to complete our organization, which will probably be: –

In full commission –
Fleet flagship 1
4 squadrons of 8 Dreadnoughts 32
In active commission –
2 squadrons, 1 of 8 Dreadnoughts and the other of 5
Dreadnoughts, 2 Lord Nelsons, and 1 Duncan.. .. 16
In reserve commission –
2 squadrons of 8, formed out of –
8 King Edwards
4 Duncans
4 Formidables.

To this total must be added the 3 Canadian Dreadnoughts built either by them or by us for the Mediterranean (or their equivalents).

I propose, therefore, that, as a working policy, we assume that the battleship and battle cruiser establishment of the 1920 War Fleet will be as follows: –

Dreadnought battleships (including *Malaya* and 2 Lord
Nelsons) 50
Dreadnought battle cruisers (including *New Zealand,* but
excluding *Australia*).. 9
Canadian Dreadnoughts or their equivalents 3
———
62
Older battleships 17
———
Total 79

Of this total, 63 must be maintained in full or active commission. This does not allow for any further ships we may have to build in consequence of new Austrian or Italian programmes.

It compares with the Committee's figures as follows: –

It includes the Canadians or their equivalents, and yet it is 3 ships less.

According to the Committee's figures, provision is made for keeping 133 cruisers and light cruisers in full, active, or reserve commission. But even DOD, in his figures on S. 14526, only gives 51 Germans available, and we certainly cannot go beyond 2 keels to 1 as a whole-world standard of cruiser strength against Germany.

Armoured Cruisers

In considering cruiser strength, regard must first of all be paid both to speed and modernity. Speed must be considered in relation not only to the more powerful cruisers, but in relation to the speed of modern battleships. Whatever arrangements may be appropriate to the intervening period, we may safely say that in 1920 no cruiser under 22 or 23 knots will be of any service, for the battle squadrons will steam nearly 21 knots, and many new battleships will go considerably above that. The Germans will only have 3 armoured cruisers that fulfil this condition, against which it will be sufficient for us to maintain 28. Of these, 15 should be maintained in full or active commission, and 13 in reserve commission.

First Cruiser Squadron (Mediterranean)				4
Second ,, ,, ⎰ Home Fleet ⎱ (North Sea) ..				4
Third ,, ,, (Atlantic)				4
Fourth ,, ,, (China)				3

The 6 Cressys should pass into the material reserve.

Reduction on Committee's figures, 10 armoured cruisers from full or active commission, and an increase of 5 in reserve commission.

Light Cruisers

If 28 armoured cruisers are kept in full or reserve commission, there would only need to be provided 74 light cruisers to maintain the standard.

It is worth while, however, to analyse the British and German cruiser fleets of 1920. No light cruiser that does not steam 22 knots can be of any use at that date, it being impossible for them to escape the majority of battleships of which the fleets will then be composed. Applying this test to the two fleets, and taking the old classes as set forth in the August 1912 'War Vessels of the Principal Naval Powers,' the Germans will have the following: –

Germany.		Great Britain.	
2nd Class Protected Cruisers –			
Built and building ..	27	Built and building ..	31
Add 5 new programmes		Add 5 new programmes,	
of 2 each	10	1 of 8 and 4 of 6 each..	32
	37	?	63

Germany		Great Britain		
3rd Class Protected Cruisers –				
Germany.. 2		Great Britain 4		
Unprotected Cruisers –				
Germany.. .. .. Nil.		Great Britain 15		
These, together with armoured cruisers –				
Germany.. 3		Great Britain 28		
gives a total of –				
Germany.. 42		Great Britain 110		
		(Not counting 3 Australian Chathams)		

The analysis becomes more remarkable if vessels of 25 knots and upwards are taken. Great Britain will have, in 1920, 76 vessels of this speed to 25 of Germany.

It would therefore appear that the British light cruiser fleet for 1920 should be as follows: –

4 future programmes not yet declared, say, 6 each ..	24
1914–15 programme	8
Programmes of 1912–13 and 1913–14	16
Chathams	6
Bristols	5
Weymouths	4
Boadiceas	7
Scouts	8
Total light cruisers	78

This does not include 4 Gem class and 2 Challengers, nor 3 Australian Chathams.

The above 78 light or new cruisers may require to be disposed of as follows: –

In attendance on the battle squadrons of the 1st and 2nd Fleets, 6 squadrons of 6 (including repeating ships) ..	36
Flotilla cruisers	10
Mediterranean..	4
China	3
East Indies	3
New Zealand	2
Cape of Good Hope	4
West Atlantic	2
South-East Coast of America	1
Total	65

All the above require to be maintained in full or active commission. The remaining 13 should be maintained in the 3rd Fleet in reserve commission.

Destroyers

Future destroyer programmes have to be considered in relation both to the light cruiser and submarine construction. Subject to the German light cruiser programme continuing at 2 a year, we may assume that our conventional programme of new construction should be on the scale of 4 Birminghams a year – say, 1,600,000*l*. If, therefore, we are to aim at cruiser programmes of 6 a year, it would appear prudent to count on programmes of destroyers not exceeding 12 a year. For this purpose a destroyer may be counted as costing 125,000*l*. The dropping of 8 destroyers a year would therefore release an extra million for cruiser construction; and an average programme of 2,600,000*l* a year should yield either 8 Arethusas or a smaller number of larger and more powerful vessels. As the light cruiser will increasingly replace the destroyer in its true function of destroyer of the enemy's torpedo craft by gunfire, it would appear that in the future increasing stress should be laid upon the torpedo armament of the reduced number of destroyers we shall be building.

The Committee's figures should be corrected to 16 destroyers instead of 20 for the 1913–14 programme, and 12 for each of the 5 following years, all of which programmes should have matured by June or July 1920. By that date it will not be worth while keeping in commission any destroyers outside the following classes: –

> 80 Dragons, Acastas, Acherons, and Acorns, 12 Tribals, 16 Beagles, and 36 Coastals;

to which should be added 1 Swift and the 3 extra Acherons (built for New Zealand, but retained here), making a total flotilla of 224 vessels.

We must expect that, unless exceptional circumstances intervene, all Rivers, 30-knotters, and 27-knotters will have passed away from the flotillas; we may assume that, in 1920, 4 flotillas will be maintained in full and 6 (patrol flotillas) in active commission, absorbing 200 destroyers and leaving 24 for foreign service. Only the 4 full commission flotillas will require sea-going depôt ships; all the other destroyer depôt ships will pass away and be replaced by shore establishments. Only 4 destroyer depôt ships should therefore be included in the war fleet of 1920. On the other hand, an addition should be made to the harbour establishments on account of the shore depôts; this will be much less than would be required for the ships.

Submarines

There is no part of the war fleet of 1920 which is more difficult to forecast than submarines. We have now available 69; building and ordered, 26; to which should be added 5 conventional programmes of, say, 10 a year – a total by July 1920 of 145. But all these cannot be kept in full commission, still less with an additional spare crew to every 3 boats. A regular scheme must be worked out by which the older boats and those employed on local defence shall be gradually relegated –

(*a.*) To material reserve;

(*b.*) To 3rd Fleet scale;

(*c.*) To local or coastal defence (no spare crews);

viz., 45 complements of oversea boats at 3 officers each, 135; 75 complements of coastals at 2 officers each, 150, and 15 additional; total, 300. Reduction in Committee's figures, 87.

All the submarine establishments should go on shore with the exception of *Maidstone, Adamant,* and *Alecto.*

Air Service

We cannot afford to divert so many trained naval lieutenants to this service, and it is necessary to limit the number employed in 1920 to 120. The balance necessary to maintain the proper strength of the Flying Wing will be provided partly by the employment of petty officers as pilots, but mainly by the direct appointment of civilians.

The remaining items in Appendix II require further examination in detail. The 8 Edgars will disappear unless required for the training service.

Eighteen torpedo gunboats require close examination.

The depôt ship establishment should be completely revised in the light of the foregoing paragraphs.

The small ships from *Seahorse* down to *Espiègle* require examination in detail. *Torch* and *Imogene* will, I trust, have perished without replacement.

The Retinues and Shore Establishments generally require scrutiny. The 5 per cent. margin appears unduly large.

Lastly, the increased complements of the latest battleships have not been approved by the Board, nor have I ever seen any report or papers containing the so-called decision.

The description of the 6-inch guns, Appendix II, page 25, as 'secondary armament of battleships,' is not in accordance with the approved policy of the Board, 'anti-torpedo armament' being the only term at present authorised.

On the other hand, I do not see what provision is made for the boys' training service afloat and ashore. The cadet training cruisers need not be considered, as if maintained in 1920 they should be found from the 4 armoured cruisers allotted to the North Atlantic Station.

Appendix II should now be revised by DMD in the light of this Memorandum, and new totals submitted for Board decision.

                                                                    WSC

WSC to H. H. Asquith[1]

8 September 1913   [Admiralty]

Copy

My dear PM,

I send you herewith a memorandum, which has taken me some time to prepare, on the general question of British trade protection in time of war. I have not been for some time entirely satisfied with the views put forward by the War Staff. I also attach notes by Custance and Jellicoe on my paper. It has not yet been seen by the First Sea Lord, who has been on leave, but I do not anticipate any sensible divergence of opinion.

The two points to which I wish particularly to draw your attention are – First: the most important thing for us to is make sure that the trade is not frightened out of putting to sea. Secondly, we must apprehend that the war will begin against us suddenly and by surprise, and the defensively armed merchantman plying to his regular business along the ordinary route is the only thing we can make certain of having always at hand to confront enemy converted merchant cruisers engaged in commerce raiding.

I should be grateful if you would turn these papers over in your mind and, if you have leisure, let me know your views upon them. I will then prepare an authoritative minute in conjunction with the First Sea Lord which will embody and govern the policy of the Admiralty.

I have also been thinking about the general question of the capture of private property at sea, and I would like to know your views on the following ideas which I have in mind. The one thing that really matters to the Admiralty is the power of effective blockade. We want to be able to cut off and arrest completely the sea-borne trade of Germany, and by this means so to injure and dislocate her economic system as to compel a peace. For this purpose it is necessary for us to be able to intercept and intern all enemy vessels going to or returning from German ports. But we do not require to alter the ownership of these vessels in any way. It is of small consequence to us, so long as they are not used to carry material in or out Germany, whether they remain the property of the individual German citizens who own them or not. I see no reason why sailors at sea should do what it has long been

[1] A copy of this letter was sent to the 1st Sea Lord, Prince Louis of Battenberg.

considered dishonourable for soldiers on land to do, viz. – enrich themselves by pillage. I do not believe the incentive is needed to procure an effective patrol or blockade, and since the bulk of the insurance is done by our own people we should be after all in a great measure only rewarding our own sailors out of our own pockets by a roundabout process. I am inclined to think therefore that our policy should be to give up altogether the right of capture at sea (except as a specific measure of retaliation) and to substitute for it a simple right to detain till the termination of the war all enemy vessels. The abolition of the right of capture would carry with it the abolition of prize money. It would be easy to deal with this by arranging that during war the pay of the sailors should be increased by a substantial quarterly bounty as a compensation for the prize money they would have received. The announcement of this would remove all grievance: and until a war came (when the expense would be insignificant) it would cost the Treasury nothing. Modern conditions are indeed so different that the most capricious results would follow any attempt to distribute prize money.

It would be a great advantage to this country and to the Government and place them in a very good position, if we were able to take some step of this character. I believe that so long as the power of blockade is effectually maintained, I should not find any difficulty in obtaining the assent of my naval advisers. The difficulty of protecting the numberless vessels which fly the British flag from reckless and predatory operations of enemy commerce destroyers is so great that we profit in a very practical way and in a far larger scale from any increased immunity which may be obtained. They can destroy, but where can they intern? The more formalities their raiders have to observe, the less harm they will do, and the sooner they will be caught. The safety and immunity of sea-borne trade is a vital interest to us.

Of course I am not versed in the legal aspect, and only give you the result of my own reflections.

[WINSTON S. CHURCHILL]

Memorandum by WSC

21 August 1913   Admiralty

1. The first security for British merchant ships must be the superiority of the British Navy which should enable us to cover in peace, and hunt

down and bring to battle in war, every enemy's warship which attempts to keep the seas. A policy of vigorous offence against the enemy's warships wherever stationed, will give immediately far greater protection to British traders than large numbers of vessels scattered sparsely about in an attitude of weak and defensive expectancy. This should be enjoined as the first duty of all British warships. Enemy's cruisers cannot live in the oceans for any length of time. They cannot coal at sea with any certainty. They cannot make many prizes without much steaming; and in these days of W.T. their whereabouts will be constantly reported. If British cruisers of superior speed are hunting them they cannot do much harm before they are brought to action. Very few German Town Class cruisers are assigned to foreign stations for this work. If others are detached from the North Sea, and get out safely, we shall be able to detach a larger proportion of the similar British cruisers which have been hitherto opposing them there. They cannot afford to send away many without crippling their battle fleet.

2. As for enemy's armed merchantmen or merchantmen converted into cruisers for commerce destruction, the only answer to that is to have an equal number of British merchant vessels plying on the trade routes armed and commissioned to engage them when met with. The whole of this threat is very shadowy. Whether the German vessels have their guns on board is extremely doubtful. Not a scrap of evidence has been forthcoming during the last year and a half in spite of every effort to procure it. How are they to be converted on the high seas? Where are they to get rid of their passengers? Are they to take hundreds of non-combatants with them on what the stronger naval Power may well treat as a piratical enterprise? Where are they to coal? To say that we have to maintain a large cruiser fleet to deal with this danger appears extravagant in the highest degree. All that is needed is to arm a similar number of British merchant vessels of the right speed and make arrangements to commission these for their own defence and that of other British ships in their neighbourhood and on their route. The presence of these vessels plying always in considerable numbers along the regular trade routes will from the very outset of the war, and however suddenly it may begin, provide a constant and immediate counter to enemy armed merchantmen, and probably deter them from any injurious action.

3. But the best safeguard for the maintenance of British trade in war is the large number of merchant ships engaged in trading, and the immense number of harbours in the United Kingdom they can approach by ocean routes. This makes any serious interruption by enemy's commerce destroyers impossible. We must rely on numbers and averages. Provided that we can induce all these ships to put to sea and carry on their business boldly, and provided that they are warned in time and encouraged to leave the regular

trade routes and travel wide of them, very few captures will be made even in the early days of the war.

4. It is no use distributing isolated cruisers about the vast ocean spaces. To produce any result from such a method would require hundreds of cruisers. The ocean is itself the best protection. We must recognize that we cannot specifically protect trade routes; we can only protect [areas] confluences. The only safe trade routes in war are those which the enemy has not discovered & those upon wh he has been exterminated. There are areas where the trade necessarily converges and narrow channels through which it must pass; and these defiles or terminals of the trade routes should be made too dangerous for enemy's commerce destroyers to approach, by employing our older cruisers in adequate force so as to create an effective sanctuary, control, or catchment for our trading ships. These areas should be judiciously selected so as to husband our resources, and not with a view to finding employment for as many old cruisers as possible. It may be taken for certain that no enemy's armed merchantman unless possessed of exceptional speed will dare to approach the area where he may encounter a British cruiser. Many of our old cruisers steam 19 knots. The number of German merchantment wh steam more is not large. As for the enemy's warships, his few exceptionally fast vessels, they must be marked down and hunted by fast modern vessels which are concerned with nothing else but to bring them to action.

5. British attacks on the German trade are a comparatively unimportant feature in our operations, and British cruisers should not engage in them to the prejudice of other duties. Economic pressure will be put on Germany by the distant blockade of her shores which will cut off her trade, both export and import, as a whole. If this is effectively done it is of very little consequence to us whether individual German vessels are captured as prizes, or whether they take refuge in neutral harbours till the end of the war. It is reasonable to suppose that German merchant ships other than those armed and commissioned for warlike purposes, will run for neutral harbours as soon as war breaks out, and that very few will attempt under the German flag to return home running the gauntlet of the numerous British fleets operating in the North Sea.

6. Protection will be afforded to British seaborne trade in time of war by the following measures: –

A. Hunting down of enemy's warships and armed vessels.

Every German cruiser stationed abroad should be covered in peace and brought to action in war by a superior vessel of superior speed, or alternatively by two equal vessels having speed advantage.

B. Organized warning of British merchant vessels.

All British armed merchantmen plying on the routes will, on receiving the warning telegram by wireless, open their secret instructions which direct them to steam along their regular route warning all unarmed British vessels met with to leave the trade route, and steam without lights at night, keeping well away from their usual course, avoiding company, and making their own way to their port of destination. [The armed British merchant ships will continue their voyage along the trade route, defending themselves from enemy's armed merchantmen, giving warning and affording whatever protection is in their power to other British vessels].

7. Similar warnings and directions adapted to each case and each route will be issued by British Consuls at all ports. These should be prepared beforehand in the fullest detail and according to a general scheme. For instance, the British Consul at Buenos Ayres should have separate instructions all ready prepared for every British ship leaving the port for the United Kingdom. These instructions will be regularly kept up to date by the Trade Division of the Admiralty War Staff. They will prescribe for each ship the general course she is to follow, the portions of the voyage she should endeavour to cover in darkness, and the areas within which she will find safety. A good wireless organisation can of course deal at once with all vessels so fitted. Thus the unarmed trade will in the first week of the war be effectively scattered over immense areas of ocean.

The control and guidance of merchant traffic must of course vary with circumstances. There are two quite different situations to consider. The first is that which occurs at the moment of a sudden outbreak of war. We must assume that hostilities begin by surprise, and that the enemy's commerce destroyers, whether warships or armed merchantmen, will begin their attacks within a very few hours of the first warning being given. None of our Third Fleet cruisers will be on their stations. The only vessels available will be the ordinary foreign squadrons and the fast cruisers shadowing individual German warships, and these will probably not be in positions which have any special relation to the trade routes. None of the British converted auxiliary merchant cruisers will be on the routes: the only thing that will be there and that can be there are the defensive armed merchantmen. In these circumstances it seems probable that the best course would be to scatter the trade; and it is in any case essential that we should have the power to do so and that all arrangements should be made to that end.

8. When, however, the war has been in progress for some time, and in proportion as our available force increases and we pass from a peace to a war organization, it may well be that the scattering of the trade will no longer be necessary or even desirable, except perhaps locally between special points. Trading vessels would then be told to return to their regular trade

routes; and this might easily lead to drawing such commerce destroyers as then remain into areas where they could be reported, located, and destroyed, by the British cruisers.

9. The organization for the control and guidance of the trade should therefore be of so complete a character that the trade may be either dispersed about the ocean or concentrated along particular routes; or in some places dispersed and in others concentrated; and that changes from one policy to the other can be made when necessary at any time.

[From the moment when, in response to the wireless message, the British armed merchantman opens his secret instructions, he is thereby commissioned for police duty on the trade route. He will hoist the Blue Ensign, and his owners will be indemnified by the Government for all loss or damage to ship or cargo arising from acts of the enemy. There will be no difficulty in arranging the scale of this indemnity, for the ships will be limited in number, carefully selected, of superior class, and belonging to the best owners. These British armed merchantmen stand in the same relation to British ships of war or British merchantmen converted into auxiliary cruisers, as the special constable sworn in in times of emergency bears to the regular members of the police or military forces.]

10. The British armed merchantman will only be employed on a strictly limited service, namely, that of carrying food supplies [along] to the United Kingdom [police duties on the trade routes on which they are ordinarily running]. They will be forbidden to engage enemy's warships and are to surrender if overtaken by them. They will not molest or pursue unarmed ships of the enemy. They will only fire on enemy's armed merchantmen [if they find them attacking or pursuing British unarmed merchant ships or] if they are themselves attacked or pursued by them. [On arrival at the first Home Port an additional party of reservists will be put on board, and they may then, if we think it desirable, continue to carry their ordinary cargoes at their owners' expense and profits along their regular routes. The legal aspect of this requires full and careful investigation; but the questions open are mainly those of form].

The result of these arrangements will be that the enemy's armed merchantmen will either have to scatter in haphazard search for prizes, or run into a succession of armed British vessels plying the usual route, finding prizes few and far between on the first course, and nothing but kicks on the other.

11. As soon as possible after the outbreak of war a sufficient number of British merchant ships or liners of high speed, selected and prepared beforehand, will be converted into auxiliary cruisers and commissioned for the further policing of the trade routes, and incidentally or if desired to prey on enemy's commerce. These vessels will be taken over on the same or similar

basis as the Cunarders. They will differ from the armed merchantmen in 'B' in that their duties will not be limited to self defence and warning: they will be directly employed in hunting down enemy's armed merchantmen; they may be used offensively against enemy's trade; they will not carry on their ordinary business; they will be wholly taken over by and maintained by the Admiralty; they will be officered and manned by the Royal Navy, will fly the White Ensign, and execute the orders of the Admiralty.

12. While we have a large supply of older cruisers, they may be employed in protecting the approaches to the principal trade terminals, and at certain special points. The following is typical of the arrangements for the Atlantic: –

4 cruisers will operate from Valentia Island to Cape Finisterre so as to secure and dominate all waters East of that line.

2 cruisers will cruise off Buenos Ayres and Rio respectively.

2 cruisers will operate from Halifax and Bermuda to protect the American trade terminals.

2 cruisers will operate in the West Indies to protect the eastern exit of The Panama Canal.

2 cruisers will operate around the Cape de Verde Islands.

2 cruisers will protect the Cape terminal.

These cruisers will be additional to any fast modern British vessels employed on the general service of hunting down individual German cruisers. They will neglect no opportunity of engaging enemy's warships or armed merchantmen. They may be at any time withdrawn from their areas by the Admiralty for such a purpose. Only the older ships will be employed on this service; and as they wear out, control will be maintained by a smaller number of new, fast vessels employed on the general and primary service of hunting down the enemy's warships.

13. The last but indispensable condition of maintaining British food supplies and British trade in time of war, is that British traders should send their ships to sea, and from the very beginning of the war press forward boldly on their regular business. The question of encouraging them to do this by means of a system of State Insurance under certain restrictions to guard against fraud, is now being considered by a Sub-Committee of the CID. We have expressed on behalf of the Board of Admiralty the strongest opinion in favour of the adoption of such a system, it being essential to all our arrangements that very large numbers of British vessels, undeterred by a small proportion of captures, should continue to traverse the seas under the British flag.[1]

---

[1] *Note by Sir John Jellicoe in margin:* Also perhaps the most difficult condition to ensure.

In exceptional cases convoys will, if necessary, be organized under escort of Third Fleet vessels. It is hoped, however, that this cumbrous and inconvenient measure will not be required.

WSC

H. H. Asquith to WSC

23 August 1913   Hopeman Lodge
Morayshire

My dear Winston,

I should like to have, when it is ready, a condensed account of the Umpire's judgements on the late Naval manoeuvres.

On another point, I think the 'Navy List' would be more handy & instructive, if, underneath the name of each ship, there were put not only (as now) Tonnage & i.h.p. [indicated horse-power] but also the character of her armament.

I hope you are having a good time.

Yrs always
H.H.A.

Lord Stamfordham to WSC

3 September 1913   Balmoral

My dear Churchill,

The King desires me to thank you for the copy of the Narrative of the recent manoeuvres with plans which you have sent for his perusal.

His Majesty hopes to discuss it with you when you are here.

Many thanks for your letter re the naming of ships which I shewed to the King.

Yours very truly
STAMFORDHAM

H. H. Asquith to WSC

16 September 1913   Hopeman Lodge

Confidential

My dear Winston,

Many thanks for your letter *re* the yacht. I will at any rate close with the first voyage – beginning September 29th and ending October 3. I hope the other may be feasible also, but perhaps you will allow me to keep it open.

You probably find yourself in a rather 'fuliginous' atmosphere. Between ourselves, I have already sent the first part, and tomorrow or next day hope to send the second, of a Memorandum which I have drawn up for the Royal Eye on the whole situation. But don't allude to this, unless the matter is opened by the King, as our communications are under the seal of strict confidence.

I shall be interested to know what Bonar Law and Curzon had to say.

I wrote to Loreburn begging him to tell me *precisely* what he means (I doubt whether he knows himself): and in particular, what practical overture, at this stage, any side or party could make. He writes that he is preparing a reasoned reply: which I shall be curious to see.

Yours always
H.H.A.

WSC to his wife
(*CSC Papers*)

EXTRACT

1 September 1913   Balmoral

I was in gt danger on this date in 1897[1]
Beloved Cat,

Most caressing reception after a successful journey. I shd have been done, if I had not abandoned the Greenock motor in favour of the 1.56 train. Steel[2] was a mug not to tell me about it.

They are rather perturbed, I think, at the stir & hum that is getting up around them. Anyhow Stamfordham & HM are entirely friendly in manner, & so far quite reasonable in argument. Bonar Law is here, & Curzon & H. Chaplin. Tomorrow comes Arthur Balfour.

I have obtained permission to leave Sunday night instead of Monday. I did not think it wise to suggest Saturday. The King only leaves *Monday for the manoeuvres*.

So I go to London Sunday night. (It appears your Scots can manage a train then) We will have our lunch at the Ritz on Monday instead of Sunday: & you can [?] the presence of the male P.K. [Randolph] at Admiralty House on that day. There must be good afternoon trains to Rugby. No operations of importance will take place till 23rd or even 24th.

I am going to play golf with Bonar Law tomorrow at 11. I have left it to his sense of decency to fix the handicap I am to receive. We shall see how he balances things mentally! . . .

[1] WSC described his near escape from death on the North West Frontier in 1897 in a graphic letter to his mother which is printed in Main Volume One, pp. 358–9.
[2] Gerald Arthur Steel (1883–   ), Assistant Private Secretary to WSC 1911–15; served also in Ministry of Transport and Scottish office; a governor of Rugby School. CB 1919.

WSC to Prince Louis of Battenberg

18 September 1913   [Balmoral]

Secret

Copy

Although I have concurred in the war orders to the 4th, 5th, and 9th Cruiser Squadrons employed on the service of trade protection, I cannot regard these arrangements as a satisfactory or final solution of the problem.

We have embarked upon the policy of arming merchant steamers, and are preparing to supply 4.7″ guns to 50 or 60 such vessels. To this course there are many serious objections: and I am not at all surprised that it has excited much adverse comment both in Parliament and in shipping circles. The whole reason for adopting it has been the allegation that the Germans have a large number, say 30 or 40, merchant ships and liners which they propose to convert into commerce destroyers on the high seas, and that these vessels have their armament and ammunition already on board. On this I was led with your full agreement to argue that the only answer to an enemy armed merchantman was a British merchantman similarly equipped: and to point out that the alternative to the arming of a certain number of British merchant ships would be a very large and costly multiplication of cruisers. Now that we are thoroughly committed to this policy, I am told that the defensive arming of all these merchantmen does not meet the problem in any way, except to the extent of the protection afforded to each individual ship, i.e. that in order to get any real relief from it, it will be necessary to arm the whole of the hundreds and thousands of vessels flying under the British flag; and that the menace of armed German merchantmen remains practically unmet and must be dealt with by the maintenance and distribution of cruisers on a very large scale.

This is not a position which I can accept. It could not be defended in the Committee of Imperial Defence or in Parliament with any prospect of success. I should never have assented to the arming of British merchant ships except as an answer to the menace of the alleged German armed merchant ships and the vessels which have already been armed must be made to play an effective part in protecting British commerce.

I question further the policy of dotting the British cruisers at regular intervals along the trade routes. It is a waste of force. The intervals of 800 miles and more are so numerous, and the withdrawals of cruisers for coaling will be so frequent, that practically no protection will be offered to the individual merchant ship. Only one of the vessels detailed for this work is fast enough to catch the German cruiser stationed in the Atlantic. The effect of establishing this thin and costly line of British cruisers will be to induce British trade to follow the usual routes without affording compensation protection, and so actually facilitate the enemy's commerce-destroying operations, whereas true safety at the outset is to encourage and direct the British trade to scatter widely and to follow unfrequented sea routes.

I attach a memorandum which I have prepared on the subject.

WSC to Admiral Limpus

19 September 1913   [Balmoral]

Copy

You must not think that because I do not answer I do not appreciate your letters. The situation in Turkey has been too unsettled and changing for me to attempt to give you any advice except to hold on from day to day as best you can and await developments. Now I think the wheel seems to have turned very decisively in favour of the Young Turks, and I should imagine you can see the prospect in the future of having a strong well-established Government to deal with.

The Government certainly wish the Mission to continue. I recognise very plainly the difficulties and discouragements of the task, but, even if very little positive progress is made, we at any rate keep one sphere of Turkish affairs from falling under German influence.

I sympathise with you very much in the difficulties and disappointments you have to face. Still, you have been at the centre of affairs during a very exciting time.

WSC to his wife
(CSC Papers)

20 September 1913   Balmoral

EXTRACT

My beloved,

I am writing in one of the Keeper's lodges to wh I have returned after stalking & where I am waiting for the Prince of Wales. Quite the best days sport I have had in this country – 4 good stags & home early! Three were running & one of these a really difficult shot – downhill, half covered, & running fast. Not a bad performance for I have not fired a shot since last year. I hope they won't think I shot too many: but the King complained to me bitterly about the few they have killed this year & the bad effect on the forest of so many being left; & the stalker urged me to go on – so I did – & redressed the balance a little. Shooting 3 in quick succession I cd have shot more – but refrained not wishing to become a butcher.

A silly spiteful paragraph has been copied into the London papers about my departure from Perth. It is an absolute invention – except that I took an ordinary taxi in mistake for the car reserved for me – & never found it out till I read the papers.

Last night I had a long talk with the young Prince and we went through all my Admiralty boxes together. He is so nice, & we have made rather friends. They are worried a little about him, as he has become very spartan – rising at 6 & eating hardly anything. He requires to fall in love with a pretty cat, who will prevent him from getting too strenuous.

The King has been extremely cordial & intimate in his conversations with me, and I am glad to think that I reassured him a good deal about the general position.

A. Balfour has not discussed politics at all with me, but at Bonar Law's suggestion I shall raise the topic – conference with King tonight or to-morrow. . . .

W

Memorandum by WSC

23 September 1913 [Admiralty]

If Germany does not lay down the extra battleship, we shall have under our existing programmes (including *New Zealand, Malaya, Lord Nelson,* and *Agamemnon,* but excluding *Australia*) 59 Dreadnoughts. If Germany builds the extra battleship, we shall build two against it, and our total Dreadnought strength on the above basis will be 61. The number of ships maintained in commission will not be increased by such a change. Two older ships will pass into Material Reserve, their places in the 2nd Fleet being taken by the 2 extra Dreadnoughts. The only difference in manning requirements which will be made if these 2 extra Dreadnoughts have to be built is the difference between the complements of such 2 Dreadnoughts and the complements of, say, 2 Duncans. To that extent, but no further, the manning requirements of 1920 would be increased if the Germans built the extra ship. The difference in complements of officers and men is not sufficiently large, and the contingency itself not sufficiently probable, to make necessary special provision against it in our manning preparations at the present time.

I note your opinion about the *Lord Nelson* and *Agamemnon*. For the purposes of the 50 and 60 per cent. standard, the 2 Lord Nelsons are counted as Dreadnoughts till April 1917. Standards of strength are necessarily arbitrary, and for the purpose of these standards of strength these 2 ships are defined as Dreadnoughts; or, to put it another way, 'we maintain a standard of 60 per cent. in new construction over Germany in Dreadnoughts including the Lord Nelsons till April 1917.' The reasons for this have been fully stated by me to Parliament with the concurrence both of the present and the late First Sea Lord. Whether they are used tactically with the Dreadnoughts or with the King Edwards is irrelevant to the present enquiry; but if your reference to them means that you consider they should be replaced in the 50 or 60 per cent. standards by new ships laid down additional to our programme, I do not agree.

It is not reasonable to count the complements of the group ships in the German reserve battle fleet as if they were available for maintaining these 5 vessels in full commission and were available a second time over for providing the nucleus crews of all the vessels in the reserve. Either they should be counted as fully commissioned, and the other vessels of the reserve as in the Material Reserve, for which no crews are provided, or alternatively these 5 group ships and the vessels of the reserve associated with them should all be counted as if they were ships maintained on a scale comparable to our 3rd Fleet ships. One or the other, but not both. It seems to me very unlikely that any Power, least of all one so methodical as Germany, would think it worth while to destroy the whole organisation of 2 reserve squadrons in order to bring the 5 group ships a few days earlier into the line. I therefore regard the Navy Law as maintaining not more than 33 capital vessels in full or active commission. I treat all effective ships in the reserve battle fleet as if they were maintained on our 3rd Fleet scale. The 5 Wittelsbachs, the old Kaisers, and all the armoured cruisers except 3, are now of very small fighting value, and I do not think it is necessary to take them into consideration at all in the War Fleets of 1920.

Proceeding on these assumptions, it appears that in 1920 Germany can have in Home waters the following effective battleships and battle cruisers: –
In full commission –
24 Dreadnought battleships.
1 pre-Dreadnought battleship.
8 Dreadnought battle cruisers.
In reserve commission –
9 pre-Dreadnought battleships.

1 battle cruiser.

Total in full commission　..　..　..　..　..　33
Total in reserve commission　　..　..　..　..　10
　　　　　　　　　　　　　　　　　　　　　　——
Grand total　..　..　..　..　..　..　43

This would leave 2 battle cruisers for foreign service.

To have a 50 per cent. superiority over this, Great Britain requires –

In full commission –

36 Dreadnought battleships.

2 pre-Dreadnought battleships.

12 battle cruisers or fast Dreadnought battleships.

In reserve commission –

15 pre-Dreadnought battleships.

2 battle cruisers or fast battleships.

Total in full commission　..　..　..　..　..　50
Total in reserve commission　　..　..　..　..　17
　　　　　　　　　　　　　　　　　　　　　　——
Grand total　..　..　..　..　..　..　67

Of these 67, 50 would be Dreadnought battleships, fast Dreadnought battleships, or battle cruisers.

This is a purely conventional interpretation of the standard, and I propose as a practical organisation the following: –

In full commission –

Fleet Flagship　　..　..　..　..　..　..　1

4 squadrons of 8 Dreadnoughts　..　..　..　..　32

In active commission –

2 squadrons (1 of 8 Dreadnoughts and the other of 7
Dreadnoughts and 1 Duncan) ..　..　..　..　16

In reserve commission –

2 squadrons of 8 pre-Dreadnoughts (formed of 8 King
Edwards, 4 Duncans, 4 Formidables) ..　..　..　16
　　　　　　　　　　　　　　　　　　　　　　　——
Total　..　..　..　..　..　..　..　65

Of the 4 squadrons of 8 Dreadnoughts kept in full commission, at least 1 would consist of fast battleships, some of which must be fast enough to match the fastest German battle cruisers ship for ship.

In addition to the above there is a squadron of 4 battle cruisers, making a total in Home waters of 69; of these, 52 will be Dreadnought battleships, fast Dreadnought battleships, or battle cruisers. Add 10 for the Mediterranean (including the 3 Canadians) and we get: –

Total Dreadnought battleships, fast Dreadnought battleships, or battle cruisers	62
Total capital ships in commission..	79

(See my first minute.)

Beyond this it is proposed to maintain in full commission in the Home fleets (leaving out for the moment the Mediterranean) 8 armoured cruisers, and in reserve commission 13 armoured cruisers; total 21. Against these the Germans have only 3 comparable armoured cruisers. It will be seen, therefore, that we provide 90 large armoured ships at Home against 43 German plus 3 effective armoured cruisers, equals 46; of which 61 are maintained in full or active commission against 33.

Beyond these respective organisations are the ships on each side of the Material Reserve. In this category the Germans have available 5 Wittelsbachs and 6 armoured cruisers. We have available 4 Formidables, 6 Canopuses, 9 Majestics, 6 Cressys; a total of 25 British ships against 11 German, every one of the British ships being markedly superior to the German.

It will be seen that the ships in Home waters – 52 to 33 – maintain to within half a ship the 50 per cent. Dreadnought margin, even if the 2 battle cruisers, which are in all probability intended for foreign service, should be kept at home. If they are sent abroad, then the *Australia* comes into our calculations, and raises our present strength in battle cruisers from 9 to 10. In any case, 2 Dreadnoughts could be found from the Home Fleet to follow and match them abroad, leaving 50 Dreadnoughts against 33, which is half a ship better than the 50 per cent. margin.

In all these calculations no account has been taken of the 10 Dreadnoughts we are providing for the Mediterranean, yet they bear powerfully on the situation as regards Germany. We have to regard it as extremely improbable that we shall be at war at once with Germany and Austria, or Germany and Italy, or still more Germany, Austria, and Italy, without having France as our friend. The French intend to maintain a superiority over the Austro-Italian fleets combined, and, in any case, this superiority could always be assured by a British addition of something much less than the 10 Dreadnoughts and 4 armoured cruisers we are providing. All the balance would be available, if necessary, to reinforce the Home Fleet; and in a war with Germany only the Mediterranean Fleet would come home. In this last contingency, as against Germany, only our organisation would provide 104 large armoured ships against a maximum 46 German comparable vessels, of which 75 would be maintained in full or active commission against 33. It must be further stated that the British Fleet is all along the line, ship for ship and squadron for squadron, markedly superior to the corresponding German units.

I have given very careful consideration to this subject during the last 5 years, and in the absence of new facts, such as a fresh German Navy Law, or other changes not now foreseeable, the provision I propose seems in every respect sufficient.

On the assumption that the Germans do not add the extra ship, my figure of 52 Dreadnoughts at Home stands, leaving, out of 59, 7 available for the Mediterranean. If the Germans add the extra ship, our total will become 61, of which 54 would be required to maintain the 50 per cent. standard at Home, again leaving 7 available for the Mediterranean. If the 3 Canadian Dreadnoughts or their equivalent are added to this, the 10 ships you consider necessary for the Mediterranean in 1920 will be provided.

From the above I see no reason to alter my total of 79 battleships and battle cruisers. Of these, 49 battleships and 4 battle cruisers will be required in full commission in Home waters, total 53; and 7, plus the 3 Canadians, will be maintained in the Mediterranean, total 63. My figure of 60 in full and active commission should therefore be increased by 3. I had omitted to count the Canadians. The remaining 16 battleships will be maintained in reserve commission.

Cruisers

For the purposes of a computation according to standards, no distinction is drawn between cruisers and light cruisers. A 100 per cent. general superiority is the only standard which has received any sanction from the Cabinet or the House of Commons. I do not say that this standard is absolutely rigid, and I have myself, for good reasons, allowed in my memorandum some slight increase upon it. But we are discussing at the moment arbitrary standards. We shall have in 1920, according to my memorandum, 28 armoured cruisers and 78 light cruisers; total cruiser fleet, 106. Even if you count the whole 9 armoured cruisers which Germany possesses as effective in 1920, which, considering their poor speed and character, seems an extravagant supposition, you will not get their total of effective ships built and building higher than 51. Your method ignores altogether our great preponderance in armoured cruisers, and seeks to establish a separate 100 per cent. preponderance in light cruisers. You would apparently keep all the existing 34 armoured cruisers in commission as against the German 9 armoured cruisers, and then have 100 per cent. on the light cruisers as well, making a total of 118. I regard this as excessive.

The same observations apply to what you say about 1916. In 1916 we shall have 34 armoured cruisers. I do not know how you reach your figure 65 light cruisers, nor why you credit us in 1916 with only 6 of this year's programme. But accepting your figure of 65 and increasing it by the 2 remaining vessels of this year's programme to a total of 67, we get a total cruiser fleet of 101; or, adding the 3 Australian Chathams, 104. Against this the Germans will have, on your own showing, 9 armoured cruisers and 42 light cruisers; total 51. There does not appear to be much reason for concern.

Further, I demur entirely to the method of calculation by which British vessels are struck off arbitrarily because they have passed the 20 years' limit, no matter how good and valuable they are, while German vessels are counted as effective for all purposes if they are under that limit, no matter how weak, slow, or generally inferior they are known to be. I do not admit that there is any shortage, actual or prospective, in the cruiser fleet according to a fair interpretation of any of the standards we have been following. On the contrary, it is clear that our existing enormous preponderance in good armoured cruisers, and the large prospective programmes of light cruisers which are contemplated in my memorandum, are much more in danger of being criticised on the ground of being excessive than of falling short of requirements.

The light cruisers built in substitution of a portion of the destroyer programme are, of course, additional to the ordinary cruiser programme, and the prospective programmes of our new construction have been calculated accordingly. When we leave new construction and come to maintenance in commission, this rule does not necessarily apply, and the whole position has to be re-surveyed. I have pointed out that our cruiser programmes, even excluding the 3 Australian Chathams, are already in excess of the 100 per cent. requirements. If thought necessary, however, we have always the 4 Gems and 1 Challenger to draw upon up to 1920. To man these on a 3rd Fleet scale is a very small affair.

Generally speaking, I see no reason to suppose that my cruiser calculations require revision.

Destroyers

My figures do not include torpedo-boats used for the purposes of port defence. I have enumerated the vessels we shall have on present and prospective programmes which can fairly be counted as effective ships in 1920. I do not know why you exclude the 1918–19 programme from the 1920 totals. You yourself specially included this 5th programme in light cruisers. I was only counting 4, and you convinced me that 5 should be counted. Having regard to our great superiority in submarines, which you do not seem to notice in your calculations, I am of opinion that the 224 destroyers enumerated by me are quite sufficient as against the 144 destroyers prescribed by the German Navy Law. In this connection see also my minute examining the organisation of German destroyers, which shows that even of the German vessels maintained in full commission one-third are always full of recruits in their first year of service, and another third only trained for 2 months in the year.

I shall be glad to see detailed proposals for the requirements in port defence torpedo boats. This is not a branch of naval construction which depends on the strength of another Power, but rather on our own requirements at the different ports. There is no question of the torpedo boats on either side 'meeting' each other. They both remain on opposite sides of the sea protecting their own harbours. Surely you do not expect that 6 patrol flotillas maintained in active commission along the East Coast will not count in any way for the defence of its ports, or for Rosyth and Cromarty. What are they for if not to protect the harbours on the East Coast?

With regard to the 70 German destroyers over twelve years old, I must point out that no crews are allowed for these under the Navy Law. They are therefore vessels maintained in what we should call the Material Reserve, and I agree that we should maintain a number of TBD's and TB's in Material Reserve. But this does not affect manning.

Submarines

I am satisfied from enquiries I have made that the provision of 300 officers for the submarine service in 1920 will, in the absence of submarines built in lieu of battleships, be quite sufficient, and a scheme should be worked out as prescribed in my memorandum to effect the gradual reduction of older boats to a lower status of commission.

Air Service

I cannot agree that more than 120 officers should be taken from the Navy for the Flying Corps. I regard a large increase in this Corps as necessary, but it must be made by the training of Warrant and Petty Officers as in France and Germany, or by the direct engagement under a new system of volunteers from civil life. It is a great waste to use officers who have had the 7 or 8 years' training of a Naval Lieutenant as chauffeurs of aeroplanes. The proportion of naval officers in the Naval Wing of the Flying Corps must be related to what is necessary to maintain a high naval tone and character. For that, the provision I propose is ample.

I am afraid I must ask that my remarks about the small ships, to which you refer in paragraph 7 of your paper, should not be dismissed in a single sentence, and that papers should be prepared examining in detail the duties for which each of these vessels will be required and the qualifications which they will possess in 1920 for the discharge of such duties. I certainly did not contemplate the 'Torch' being kept going 7 years from now.

I have always understood that the increase in the officer complements of German Dreadnoughts is due to their having retained a secondary armament for use in a general action, whereas the British Admiralty have definitely adopted the policy of a 'primary armament only' for the purposes of a fleet action, their smaller guns being reserved for anti-torpedo defence. The Germans attach the greatest importance to their secondary armaments, and believe, with many officers in the British Navy, that they have been right to retain them. It does not therefore seem to me very likely that they will cripple their ships and give up the advantage they believe they possess by withdrawing the officers required for the secondary armament in order to man in 1920 a number of vessels more ancient and more obsolete even than the Wittelsbachs. Another reason why German ships require larger complements of officers than British ships is that British ships are manned with trained long-service seamen and German ships are manned with 3 years' men, one third of whom are recruits. It is obvious that a larger number of officers is required to train in peace and handle in war *personnel* which has this very scanty acquaintance with the sea. I think, therefore, that the danger you apprehend in paragraph 8, that the Germans will cut down the officer complements of their best ships in order to bring a larger number of very old vessels into the line is not a real one. If you were to work out in detail the ships for 1920 which you consider they might by this means bring from the Material Reserve into the Active Fleet, you would see what a very worthless lot they are, and how great an advantage it would be to us to have the general sea-going efficiency of the German full commissioned squadrons reduced for the sake of getting a few of these obsolete vessels into the line.

Subject to any modifications in this minute, the DMD should be told to proceed to revise Appendix II of the Report in the light of my Memorandum of the 28th August, and to present new details, which can afterwards be the subject of Board discussion.

WSC

WSC to Sir W. Graham Greene

14 October 1913   [Admiralty]

[Copy]

It is very inconvenient that a mistake should have been made about the *Monmouth,* and I am of opinion that the despatch should be stopped and returned unopened by the Governor, a corrected version being sent by the next mail.

I think you had better see the Colonial Office yourself on the point. Such a mistake would have very injurious consequences and tend to destroy confidence in Admiralty statements.

2. I am of opinion that a general Naval Conference ought to meet in London in the summer of 1914. It is extremely probable that Mr Borden's naval policy will have been settled by then, and that the 3 ships will already be under construction. In any case, however, the loyalty of his intentions need not be doubted, and there is no reason to suppose that he will use the prospect of a conference as a reason for delay. I am anxious that the general questions relating to the Pacific should be raised at this conference, and that the fullest discussion should take place. The Australian Navy is now launched and the situation should be reviewed. The fleet unity policy of 1909 has been abandoned, and the Dominions have a right to have the whole situation arising out of that abandonment re-examined. The Canadian permanent policy will develop better after a general conference than without one. The New Zealand situation is extremely unsatisfactory, and can only be settled as a part of a general conference. It is probable that the present New Zealand Government will have disappeared and that we shall have seen the last of Mr Allen. The South African naval contribution also requires to be considered and discussed.

I am not at all afraid of the Admiralty being led into further expense as a result of such a conference. It is high time that the Dominions had the true strategic conception on which the Empire is conducted impressed upon them. On general grounds I do not think it is practicable without serious disadvantage to resist the widespread desire of the Dominions to confer on naval matters.

WSC to his wife
(CSC Papers)

19 October 1913   HMS *Enchantress*
                                                    Newcastle

My dearest one,

It was a wrench to leave you at that Club – I loved your coming so much – everyone was so delighted & I so proud. I do hope it was not a *corvée* to you.

We had a good journey here and are now spending a peaceful Sunday on board. I am going to play golf this afternoon. I was really *quite* tired & slept vy soundly. It is a strain to make a speech – like that – so many different things to consider & keep constantly in view. I expect one must make many mistakes.

If the Germans refuse I shall have made my case for action. If they accept it will be a big event in the world's affairs.

If they say 'we wd accept but for the Canadians' – I wd say – we will postpone them too for a year – if you agree!

This wd be a thunderbolt. But they won't accept – They will just butt on on the water as in the air!

Here is a letter from Cornelia. I want you to write & accept. I have a great regard for her – & we have not too many friends. If however you don't want to go – I will go alone. Don't come with all your hackles up & your fur brushed the wrong way – you naughty.

We are to go to the F. E. Smith's for the 8th & 9th Novr. I am writing to him, & presently will you write to Mrs F. E. when she writes. Anyhow mark the dates.

                                        Your ever loving husband
                                                    W

Sir Edward Grey to WSC

21 October 1913   Foreign Office

Private

Dear Churchill,

I think there was no choice but to say something to our own people about naval expenditure. The Continental response is very bad, but that cannot be helped: the question is a vital one to us & our people must know where they stand & why. It must be pretty clear to them now.

The French have deprecated our bringing them into the matter as you will see by the paper I am sending for you & the PM to see, but that is a minor point.

I have to speak to my constituents on Monday & think I shall put in a sentence or two about Naval expenditure generally.

The German comments seem to ignore or be unaware of the fact that you pointed out that it was not Germany alone who was forcing the pace, but that the question has become more serious generally & for Europe especially by the ship building of other nations besides Germany, though England & Germany are leading factors.

Yrs sincerely
E. GREY

WSC to Sir Edward Grey

21 October [1913]   HMS *Enchantress*

Copy

Sir Edward Goschen[1] is quite mistaken in speaking of the concentration of the British Fleet as a strategic mistake. All the best naval opinion which I have access to is unanimous in regarding the steps taken as necessary, though of course a good many officers would like to have the ships abroad as well as having them at home. We have met the great increases in the building of other Powers in the last 10 years partly by concentration and partly by increase of expenditure. If there had not been concentration there must have been a much greater increase in expenditure.

The German Emperor's remark about the Russian Fleet is, as you say, ludicrous. I presume you realise that we are maintaining consistently a 50% superiority in Home Waters during the absence of the Fleet that has gone to the Mediterranean. It is possible to send so great a Fleet there at the present time because of the lateness of some of the German ships and the fact that their increases have not fully matured. We cannot tell when it will be possible to send such a large force again without prejudice to the 50% preponderance.

Watson has done very well, and I agree entirely with Goschen's appreciation. Both he and Captain Kelly[2] (Naval Attaché in Paris) are deserving

---

[1] William Edward Goschen (1847–1924), Diplomat; Envoy Extraordinary and Minister Plenipotentiary at Belgrade 1898–1900, at Copenhagen 1900–5; Ambassador in Vienna 1905–8; Berlin 1908–14; knighted 1901; created Baronet 1916.

[2] William Archibald Howard Kelly (1873–1952), Naval Attaché in Paris 1911–14; Head of British Naval Mission to Greece 1919–21; Rear-Admiral First Battle Squadron Atlantic Fleet 1923–4; Commander, 2nd Cruiser Squadron, 1925–7; Second in Command, Mediterranean Fleet 1929–30; C-in-C China Station 1931–3; retired 1936; recalled to active list 1940 and British Naval Representative in Turkey 1940–4; retired 1944; CMG 1917.

of some recognition as both have discharged work of exceptional delicacy and difficulty. The Director of the Intelligence Division strongly recommends Captain Kelly for a CMG, and seems inclined to rate his services higher than those of Captain Watson. It would be a very good thing if you could recommend both these officers for that honour. It would tend to make senior officers of the Navy turn their attention more to foreign languages and foreign attachéships than they do at present.

Memorandum by WSC

22 October 1913   [HMS *Enchantress*]

We have now had manœuvres in the North Sea on the largest scale for two years running, and we have obtained a great deal of valuable data which requires to be studied. It does not therefore seem necessary to supplement the ordinary tactical exercises of the year 1914–15 by Grand Manœuvres. A saving of nearly £200,000 could apparently be effected in coal and oil consumption, and a certain measure of relief would be accorded to the Estimates in the exceptionally heavy year.

In these circumstances I am drawn to the conclusion that it would be better to have no Grand Manœuvres in 1914–15, but to substitute instead a mobilisation of the Third Fleet. The whole of the Royal Fleet Reserve, and the whole of the Reserve officers could be mobilised and trained together for a week or ten days. The Third Fleet ships would be given the exact complements they would have in war, and the whole mobilisation system would be subjected to a real test. The balance Fleet Reservists could be carefully tested as to quality, and trained either afloat or ashore. I should anticipate that this would not cost more than £100,000, in which case there would still be a saving on the fuel of the manœuvres. While the Third Fleet ships were mobilised the First Fleet ships would rest, and thus plenty of officers would be available for the training of the reservists on shore, and possibly, if need be, for their peace training afloat. This last would, of course, reveal what shortage exists. A very large staff would be employed at all the mobilising centres to report upon the whole workings of the mobilisation. The schools and training establishments would be closed temporarily according to the mobilisation orders, and the whole process of putting the Navy on a war footing, so far as the Third Fleet was concerned, would be carried out. I should not propose to complete the Second Fleet, as we know all about that.

At another time in the year I should desire to see mobilised the whole of the Royal Naval Volunteer Reserve, and put them afloat on First Fleet ships for a week as additional to complements.

Please put forward definite proposals, with estimates, for carrying out the above policy, and at the same time let me have your opinion upon it.

WSC to H. H. Asquith

30 October 1913   Portsmouth

Private & Confidential

My dear Prime Minister,

Rear-Admiral Pakenham, the Fourth Sea Lord, completes 2 years' service on the Board on the 5th of December. Although there is no fixed limit to these appointments, 2 years is a convenient changing point and there happens to be a suitable Cruiser Squadron, to which this officer could be appointed, vacant at the same time.

I hope I may have your concurrence in submitting to the King the name of Commodore Lambert[1] (he of the jowl!) I attach great importance to this officer's services because coming as he does fresh from the oil-burning flotillas, he will be able to assist me in enforcing a proper economy in the use of this most expensive fuel. I do not need to tell you that he is a very able man, for you have had your own opportunities of judging.

Winsloe has written to Prince Louis that he does not want to go to the Nore as Commander-in-Chief. What he would like is the Mediterranean. But Milne does not complete 3 years till June 1915 and I should regret to see an officer of Winsloe's standing and record out of employment for so long. I am therefore going to offer Milne the Nore command consequent on the termination of his Mediterranean appointment at 2 years instead of 3, and tell him that this will be his only chance in the next 3 or 4 years of succeeding to the command of a great Home port. I shall not leave him an option in the matter except to refuse altogether. He would be exchanging 1 year's additional employment in the Mediterranean for 3 years' employment at home, and he would have 5 years' continuous employment so that he has no reason to complain. It is necessary however that I should speak to the King on the subject as otherwise intrigues might be set on foot, and I thought that I would take the occasion to do this when I see him about the

[1] Cecil Foley Lambert (1864–1928), Fourth Sea Lord 1913–19; Director of Personnel Air Ministry 1919–21; KCB 1920; Admiral 1926.

new Board appointment. I hope to be able to announce Winsloe's appointment in the course of the next few weeks. Meanwhile it is important that Winsloe should not know what I have in mind.

The firings at the Empress of India have been postponed owing to bad weather. We hope to try again next week – say the 3rd, 4th, or 5th. Is there any chance of your being free?

Enclosed covers your & Margot's winnings last time we played bridge. I am horrified not to have remembered sooner.

Yours v. sincerely
WINSTON S. CHURCHILL

Note in Margin:
The Prime Minister agrees to the appointment of Commodore Lambert & thinks that Admiral Winsloe is much more suited to the Mediterranean command than to the Nore.

MBC [Maurice Bonham-Carter][1]

Admiral Meux to WSC

1 November 1913　　　　　　　　　　　　　　　　Admiralty House
Portsmouth

My dear Winston,

You must have a chatterbox amongst your entourage. Yesterday you told me in strict confidence that you were considering some alteration re promotion to Admiral of the Fleet. Today my wife hears from an officer in the Home Fleet that it is public gossip that two elderly officers Prince Louis of Battenberg & Sir George Callaghan are to be promoted Admirals of the Fleet over my head on the ridiculous pretext that I am too young.

I am 20 years older than the First Lord! The rumour alone is an affront & if there is any truth in it an unforgivable insult.[2]

Sincerely yrs
HEDWORTH MEUX

Do you expect me to go round with you tomorrow?

[1] Maurice Bonham-Carter (1880–1960), Private Secretary to H. H. Asquith 1910–16; Director of Blackburn and General Aircraft Ltd; married Violet Asquith 1915.

[2] Admiral Meux was promoted to Admiral of the Fleet in 1915, Admiral Callaghan in 1917, and Prince Louis (then 1st Marquess of Milford Haven) in 1921.

WSC to his wife
(*CSC Papers*)

2 November 1913   Portland

Catling dear,

I was vy ill to-day coming round but bore up with gt courage. Now we are here & the 'Board' is all embarked, it is blowing like the devil and everyone thinks nothing will take place! Such are the uncertainties of a naval life.

I had an extraordinary letter from Hedworth who had heard a rumour that Prince Louis & Callaghan were to be promoted Admirals of the Fleet over his head, & who put this rumour to my talk with him making a most disconcerting (to him) conclusion. I have pacified him – with considerable formality of style.

We are an enormous crowd on board, & every cabin chock full.

I mewed at the departure of the Catling, but I must admit it wd be but a poor show for her here. Wind rain & sea = crowds of men talking shop = cold & sleet = more shop.

But it amuses me – I am a fool who shd not have been born.

Still you dearest Clemmicat I have been vy happy in your love & in your sweet embrace. Do not cast away your poor – who loves & cherishes you always. Give my kisses to the chicks.

Prince L. wants us to dine with him next Friday. I have said a provisional 'Yes'.

Ever and always,   Your loving & devoted
                                                                    husband
                                                                        W

WSC to Lord Fisher

12 November 1913   Admiralty

My dear Fisher,

I am very much indebted to you for the epoch-making memo about submarines, and when I have thoroughly digested it I will communicate with you again.

There can be no question of abandoning Chatham, in which scores of millions have been sunk and which is the home of one-third of the Fleet and almost its best recruiting ground.

As for the dockyard workmen, it is socially just that men who work all their lives faithfully for the State should have permanency and pension guaranteed, just like Admirals!

                            Yours impenitently but with much love
                                                                        W

Sir Francis Hopwood to Lord Stamfordham
(*Royal Archives*)

9 November 1913   13 Hornton Street

My dear Stamfordham,

There is a fierce quarrel raging between Churchill and his Naval Lords. C very foolishly travels round the coast holding reviews and inspections & so forth without reference to Naval opinion and regulation. He is also much addicted to sending for junior officers & discussing with them the proceedings of their superiors; this naturally enrages the latter & is very mischievous to the former. It is on the score of breaches of discipline that the present trouble has been founded. The facts as described to me are as follows: Churchill interviewed a Lieutenant of the *Vernon* & encouraged him to put forward some scheme or other about torpedo working. The Captain of the *Vernon* refused to forward it to the Commander-in-Chief at the Nore *en route* to the Admiralty whereupon the Lieutenant said 'Then I shall send it direct to Mr Churchill wh invited (or ordered) me to do so . . .' Then the row began. The Captain of the *Vernon* wrote in strong terms of complaint to the Commander-in-Chief who wrote on in equally strong terms to Jellicoe criticising the First Lord's method. Now somehow Churchill had heard that this correspondence had begun. Perhaps the Lieutenant at the *Vernon* had written him to say he had got into trouble. But anyhow Churchill sent his Private Secretary to Jellicoe to say that if any despatch came from the C-in-C at the Nore on the subject he (Churchill) desired to see it immediately. It did come & Jellicoe finding it couched in strong terms determined, in order to keep the peace, to send it back for some amendment. Jellicoe accordingly returned the despatch with a private letter of his own enclosed. When a few hours later C found the despatch had been sent back he went dancing mad & on his own sent a telegram to the General Post Office asking that the letter should be found & returned at once to *him*. He also telegraphed to the C in C Nore to return the letter to him at the Admiralty unopened. He got it back from the GPO, & so came into possession of the correspondence & also Jellicoe's private letter with comments! To get out of the difficulty of the latter he professes not to have read it! Jellicoe has of course intimated that he will resign. Churchill has now announced that he will get rid of both the C in C Nore & the Captain of the *Vernon*. On that issue Moore & Pakenham both want to go. Prince Louis felt that way at first but Jellicoe tells me that Churchill has talked the First Sea Lord over. Churchill is reported to have told the 4 Naval Lords that if any one of them desired to criticise his methods he should expect him to resign as they could not work together.

C has not mentioned the subject to me, all this comes from the Admirals.

Of course it is very private but The King may be interested in the facts as unless differences are composed there may be a resignation & some publicity at any moment. It is deplorable.

Ever yrs
FRANCIS S. HOPWOOD

Sir Francis Hopwood to Lord Stamfordham
(Royal Archives)

10 November 1913

My dear Stamfordham,

There are evidences of saner mind. I think there will be a climb down if a way can be found. Perhaps it would be well to keep my letter back until to-morrow as one does not want to worry HM if the crisis is going to pass. If it blows over he can read what has happened with an equable mind.

The real difficulty will be to find a way of sufficiently scolding the C in C to satisfy Churchill without really affecting that officer unduly!

Ever yrs
FsDH

Prince Louis of Battenberg to WSC
(Mountbatten Papers)

12 November 1913   Admiralty

I beg to inform you that I have, as desired, discussed the matter again with my Naval colleagues and that we are unable to modify our views which I conveyed to you last night.

You have informed us that it is your intention, whether we agree or whether we do not, to issue an order to the C in C, Nore, to strike his flag forthwith.

According to the very clear terms of the Patent under which we act, the First Lord has not, in our opinion, the power to issue such an order.

We, therefore, cannot share the responsibility for such an act and we have no alternative but to resign our seats on the Board.

L B

Sir Francis Hopwood to Lord Stamfordham
(Royal Archives)

13 November 1913

My dear Stamfordham,

The crisis is over, no thanks to the First Lord. We got as far as all four Naval Lords signing their resignation. But we induced Poore[1] to withdraw

---

[1] Richard Poore (1853–1930), C-in-C the Nore 1911–15; Rear-Admiral 1903; Vice-Admiral 1907; C-in-C Australian station 1908–11; retired 1917; succeeded his father as 4th Baronet 1893.

his letter & express regret & under vast pressure he agreed not to resign. Winston would not be flattered if he knew the arguments used by the Naval Lords to keep the Commander-in-Chief from going. They were in short that he (Churchill) was so much off his head over the whole business that Poore need take no notice of it! We thought Poore would ask for a Court Martial in which case the whole business would have turned on the accusations of the Commander in Chief against the First Lord & the latter would really have been on his defence.

If Poore had gone Jellicoe & Pakenham would have resigned. I doubt whether the other two would have stuck to their guns. But if Poore had been dismissed or superseded (as Winston wished) all 4 Naval Lords would have resigned.

Laus Deo! it is over for the time but we shall have it again in some form. Jellicoe will not put up with it for long.

Yours ever
FRANCIS S. HOPWOOD

WSC to Austen Chamberlain
(Austen Chamberlain Papers)

12 November 1913   Admiralty

My dear Austen,

It will give us very great pleasure if you and Mrs Austen will join the *Enchantress* at Portsmouth on the afternoon of Tuesday the 25th and come with us to Devonport by sea for the launch next day. I should propose to give a dinner party in your honour on Wednesday evening, to take you to Portsmouth by Thursday morning, when if you would care for a trip in a submarine I should be very glad to arrange it for you.

Yours vy sincerely
WINSTON S. CHURCHILL

WSC to Austen Chamberlain
(Austen Chamberlain Papers)

13 November 1913   Admiralty

My dear Austen,

I am so sorry to hear that I was too late in inviting you to the *Enchantress* – but glad that you will dine with us on Wednesday. If Lord Mount Edgcumbe[1] will let you off dining with him on that evening, would he not let you stay

---

[1] William Henry Edgcumbe (1832–1917), Conservative MP, Plymouth, 1859–61; Lord Lieutenant of Cornwall 1877–1917; Keeper of Privy Seal to HRH Prince of Wales 1907–17: succeeded father as 4th Earl of Mount Edgcumbe 1861.

on board for the night? It would be much more convenient for you than going back to him late at night; and I think you might like to go round Portsmouth Dockyard with me on Thursday morning; besides which the journey back to London from Portsmouth would be much shorter than from Devonport.

I do hope you may be able to modify your plan to this extent.

There is heaps of room for your boy: & he wd like the adventure.

Yours vy sincerely
WINSTON S. CHURCHILL

WSC to Austen Chamberlain
(Austen Chamberlain Papers)

18 November 1913   Admiralty

My dear Austen,

Certainly bring man & maid. We are delighted you will come.

Let us then have one of those 'frank, free and unfettered' conversations wh are so much in fashion now.

Yours vy sincerely
WINSTON S. CHURCHILL

WSC to Lord Fisher
(Lennoxlove Papers)

18 November 1913   Admiralty

My dear Fisher,

I won't take 'No' for an answer without another try. Do come. Cassel is coming and Austen Chamberlain. It is a good thing for you & me to be seen together a little sometimes & teases the sweeps: also so jolly.

Yours ever
W

WSC to Lord Fisher
(Lennoxlove Papers)

19 November 1913   Parliament Street

TELEGRAM

How unkind you are. What can you have to do? Please reconsider

WINSTON

Admiral Limpus to WSC

Wednesday

3 December 1913

c/o British Embassy
Constantinople

Dear Mr Churchill,

It may fairly be said that something tangible has been done, and a success scored which should retain a predominant British interest here in naval affairs for many – probably 30 years.

Hard negotiating has been going on from the latter part of September until today. Often we are at it from 9.30 a.m. till 6.30 p.m. with a very brief lunch interval; but today the Directors have gone back to England with the matter settled. Twice the negotiations so nearly failed that I wrote for your help. But at the last moment the difficulty was surmounted and the letters were not sent.

If it interests you, you shall have the whole yarn when I return; just now there is no need to trouble you with more than the first two pages of the first letter. They follow this page: –

29 October 1913

c/o British Embassy
Constantinople

Dear Mr Churchill,

As regards influence in naval matters in Turkey we are now, in my opinion, face to face with the German Government. If I am correct, then it is not to be expected that the Armstrong Group can successfully compete, unless the British Government will accord to them its support. The situation is as follows: –

The Turks have built the *Rechadieh*. They need a dock for her. Their arsenals in the Golden Horn are crumbling – have nearly crumbled – to decay. They need capable management, workmen, and money. Then they could be used both for the navy and commercially. But in the future their main arsenal must be outside the Golden Horn. I have persuaded the Armstrong Group to take this business up. They have formulated in writing certain terms upon which they will do so. The Turk Govt has accepted these terms, in principle, in writing, and invited directors with full powers to come here & discuss & settle details. Sir Vincent Caillard[1] (Vickers) and Sir Charles Ottley (Armstrong) arrived on Wedn 22nd Oct. The Min of Mar Djavid Bey, and I have discussed the matter with them.

[*Note by WSC on a typed copy of this letter:* 'This seems to be the end of the old letter.']

[1] Vincent Harry Penalver Caillard (1856-1930), Director of Metropolitan Carriage, Wagon and Finance Co Ltd, of Southern Railway, etc; expert on the Balkans and the Near East; President of Federation of British Industries 1919; knighted 1896.

Djavid Bey left for Berlin Oct 29th and the Government gave us Haladjian Effendi (an ex-Minister of Public Works) in his place. The agreement was re-drafted 13 times! But now it is settled.

It may well be considered not only as the day of the renaissance of the Turkish Navy, though it may very well be that, but more important still, as a really vital nucleus for the building up of a large industry in Turkey.

The final scene was interesting to me because I was called upon to address all the Ministers in Council on the general bearing of the agreement. However, thank goodness it is *done*. Here it is in outline: –

3 parties to the agreement, Government, the public debt, and the Group (Armstrong Vickers). They form a *Compagnie Cointeressée*. Object: naval & commercial construction & repair works. Duration: 30 years. Existing docks & arsenals, and, aided by the public debt, guarantees the interest & sinking fund on the £1,300,000 capital and agree to have all its work done by the Société Impériale Ottomane des Docks &c, and, what the Société cannot do is to be done in England. The Group finds the capital, finds the management & direction & certain English workpeople, and engages to put the existing plant into order, install a floating dock near Ismidt with the necessary nucleus of workshops on shore & a model village. Engages to be in a position to execute certain classes of work in certain definite times, & to so train the Turkish personnel that at the end of the term it shall be handed back to the Governmt as a going Turkish concern.

That is a rough outline of the agreement.

Of course the unforeseen is always to be reckoned with, but barring the unforeseen a really useful work has been born. Its nationality is very distinctly British, and if I do not mistake, undesirable aliens are shut out for 30 years. If that is so, then quite apart from the other odds and ends of work that have been done, we have justified our mission both to the Turks & to those who sent us.

It is bad to shout too soon, but the appearance of the infant is so healthy that the temptation to cheer a little is strong.

Sincerely yours
ARTHUR H. LIMPUS

WSC to Admiral Limpus

10 December 1913   [Admiralty]

Copy

I have received your letter of the 3rd instant, and I am glad to hear from you and from other quarters of the agreement which has been reached between the Turkish Government and Messrs Vickers. I recognise that you have played a useful and effective part in the negotiations, and I congratulate you upon the result.

I find it necessary to criticise the general style and presentment of your letters. A flag officer writing to a member of the Board of Admiralty on service matters ought to observe a proper seriousness and formality. The letters should be well written or typed on good paper; the sentences should be complete and follow the regular British form. Mere jottings of passing impressions hurriedly put together without sequence, and very often with marked confusion, are calculated to give an impression the reverse of that which is desirable. You do not do yourself justice in these matters. No one can be so busy as not to be able to cast a letter to a superior in a proper form. You should make up your mind beforehand exactly what you mean to say, and study to say it in the clearest and shortest way, if necessary re-drafting your letter. In your latest communication three letters appear to be mixed up without beginning or end. Knowing the good work which you did in South Africa and your zeal in your Turkish mission, I am able to dispel from my mind the impression which the chaotic character of your correspondence would otherwise convey.

[WINSTON S. CHURCHILL]

WSC to the King
(Royal Archives)

6 December 1913   Admiralty

Mr Churchill with his humble duty has the honour to refer to Your Majesty's approval of his submission of July 1912 whereby officers of your Majesty's Navy were specially admitted to the Civil Division of the Third Class of the Order of the Bath, to which effect was given by a Statute of the Order dated 27 September 1912.

This Statute provides that a number not exceeding ten of the officers of your Majesty's Navy or Royal Marines holding at the time of nomination Commission in your Majesty's Navy of or above the rank of Commander, Engineer Commander, Fleet Surgeon, or Fleet Paymaster, or Commissions in your Majesty's Royal Marines of or above the rank of Lieutenant Colonel, may be appointed annually to the said Civil Division of the Third Class, provided nevertheless that the total number of officers in your Majesty's

Navy & Royal Marines, both in the Military and Civil Divisions of the said class, shall not exceed the number of a hundred and thirty.

The effect of this Statute is that the number of officers appointed to the Third Class of the Civil Division will be abated from the number of Companions allowed in the Military Division by Statute – while no surrender of the Companionship of the Civil Division will take place on the appointment of such Companions to the Second Class of the Military Division of the Order. It follows therefore that the number of Companions in the Military Division of the Order will be permanently reduced.

Mr Churchill would point out that this result was not contemplated when he made his submission of July 1912, & he would humbly submit that approval may be given to an arrangement whereby officers appointed to the Civil Division of the Order under the provisions of the Statute of 27 September 1912 shall be removed from the Third Class of the Civil Division on appointment to the Second Class of the Military Division of the Order, in the same manner as if the advancement took place in the same Division of the Order; the resulting vacancies in the number annually available being filled when desirable.

Mr Churchill would also humbly refer to your Majesty's approval of his submission of November last, in which he proposed that Admiral Randolph F. O. Foote[1] should be appointed in special circumstances to the Second Class of the Military Division of the Order of the Bath. He finds on enquiry that there is no vacancy in the Civil Division to which Admiral Foote could be appointed, & he therefore submits to Your Majesty that service as President of the Board of Ordnance may with your Majesty's approval be held to be equivalent to an appointment in which an officer might hoist his flag. In Mr Churchill's opinion good & efficient service in such an appointment of great Naval & Military importance should rank with service as Superintendent of one of your Majesty's Dockyards, which technically would come within the wording of the Statute of 28 May 1913, the officer flying his flag.

WINSTON S. CHURCHILL

Lord Stamfordham to WSC
(*Royal Archives*)
16 December 1913   Buckingham Palace

Your suggestion that officers possessing the Civil CB should relinquish it on appointment to the Military KCB has been thoroughly gone into with the Officials of the Order.

[1] Randolph Frank Ollive Foote (1853–1931), President of the Ordnance Board 1908–13; Admiral 1911. As requested by WSC he was knighted in 1914.

The King is very sorry that he cannot approve of this arrangement: but it is quite contrary to the Statutes of the Order.

The Civil and Military Divisions are absolutely distinct, as are their respective decorations. Moreover, no member of any Order is allowed to resign. Were an officer possessing the Civil CB to be called upon to give it up on his appointment to the Military KCB he would be right in refusing to do so: otherwise, he would be sending back a decoration which had been bestowed upon him by his Sovereign.

His receiving the Military KCB would not be a case of *promotion*: but of a new appointment just as much as if the KCMG had been conferred upon him. The following is a striking instance. Captain Fairfax, RN received the Civil CB as Captain of the *Britannia* when the King and his elder brother were there as Cadets. Later, for the bombardment of Alexandria he was given the *Military* CB and wore *both*.

His Majesty quite understands your views in proposing this new departure, but it would involve a radical change in the Statutes and an alteration in a use which has obtained for many years in both Services.

STAMFORDHAM

Throughout 1913 WSC and R. L. Borden, the Canadian Prime Minister, were in touch about the proposal that Canada should pay for the construction of three Dreadnoughts. Early in 1914 it became apparent that the Canadian Senate would prevent the plan from going through. See Main Volume II, pp. 665 and 667.

WSC to R. L. Borden
TELEGRAM

19 March 1913   [Admiralty]

Secret and Personal

In my naval speech introducing naval estimates on 26th instant, I propose to outline the following scheme for the employment by the Admiralty of any capital ships provided by Canada for general Imperial service. It is proposed to form them, with the *Malaya* and if possible the *New Zealand*, into a new squadron of five ships of high uniform speed to be called the Imperial Squadron. This squadron will be based on Gibraltar, and from that station will be able to reach Halifax in five days, Quebec in six, Jamaica in nine, South American coast in twelve, Capetown in thirteen, Alexandria in three, Sydney in twenty-eight, New Zealand in thirty-two, Hong Kong in twenty-two, Vancouver in twenty-three, that is, faster than any other equally strong European force. The intention is that the squadron shall, as opportunity serves, cruise freely about the British Empire visiting the various Dominions and ready to operate at any threatened point at home or abroad. The Dominions would be consulted by Admiralty on all movements not dominated by military considerations, and special facilities would be given for Canadians, Australians, South Africans, and New Zealanders to serve in the squadron. In this way a true idea will be given of a mobile Imperial Squadron of the greatest strength and speed patrolling the Empire, showing the Flag, and bringing effective aid where it is needed. Side by side with this the Dominions will be encouraged to develop naval bases, dockyards, local flotillas, or other ancillary craft which would be necessary to enable the Imperial Squadron to operate for a prolonged period in any particular threatened theatre. The squadron could be strengthened from time to time by the supply of light cruisers or ancillary vessels if the Dominions saw fit. This is the right and sound plan which ought eventually to eliminate the policy of tying up individual isolated Dreadnoughts to particular localities. The idea can of course only be broached in general terms for reflection and discussion. What do you think of it? I expect it would be helpful to you as raising the principle of combined inter-Dominion action as against purely local navies on the one hand or complete absorption in the British Navy on the other, and also as opening a large field for development of naval bases and other local resources. I shall be much obliged if you will cable me your private opinion, or alternatively say if you would rather not be consulted.

CHURCHILL

R. L. Borden to WSC
TELEGRAM

23 March 1913

Secret

Your telegram of 19th March. We thoroughly approve, subject to considerations mentioned below, of inspiring proposal to form three Canadian ships with other ships mentioned, all of unsurpassed strength and speed, into a great Imperial cruising squadron, based on Gibraltar. As Canada may eventually desire to establish and maintain one or more fleet units in co-operation with and close relation to Imperial Navy, I would suggest that you should allude to their possible recall upon reasonable notice, as three ships might be required to form part of such unit or units. Later on this Session we shall probably announce that, pending consideration of great and difficult problems attending the thorough co-operation of the Dominions in matters affecting Imperial defence and foreign policy, Canada proposes to undertake certain measures of defence which, while primarily designed for the protection of her own shores and her interests in contiguous waters, will nevertheless be of importance from an Imperial standpoint. It is anticipated that this will be upon following lines:—

1. Provision of dry docks, useful for commercial as well as Admiralty purposes.

2. Establishment of naval bases and fortification of ports and harbours, also defence of such ports and harbours by submarines, torpedo-boats, &c.

3. Establishment and gradual extension of shipbuilding and repair plants.

4. Training of officers in naval colleges and of men in training ships.

5. Subsidizing of fast and modern merchant vessels useful for scouting and other purposes, equipment of such ships with necessary guns and fittings, and manning by trained seamen.

6. Gradual extension of fishery protection service by addition of light cruisers manned by trained men and under naval discipline, which, while specially useful for primary purpose of protecting fisheries, will also be effective and available in time of war.

R. L. Borden to WSC

TELEGRAM

23 March 1913

Private and Confidential

As telegrams to the British Press may have exaggerated Liberal criticism of your letters of 23rd January and 24th January, I wish to assure you that no criticism of an important character has been put forward, and that certain vapourings have proceeded altogether from two or three men of minor importance in the House of Commons whose opinions count for little, and who will probably disappear from public life after the next general election. As is evident by the utterances of all independent newspapers, the vast majority of the people of Canada entirely approve view which you expressed in those letters.

Speech by WSC

EXTRACT

31 March 1913   House of Commons

. . . Having regard to the responsibilities of the British Empire both in the Pacific and in the Mediterranean, and having regard in particular to the new development of forces in the Mediterranean, it is clear that the margin of strength available for the whole world service of the British Empire will not be sufficient after the first quarter of 1916 unless further steps are taken either by the Dominions or by ourselves. From this point of view, the reality of the need of the three Canadian vessels can be well appreciated. . . . It is necessary, however, to make it clear that the three ships now under dis-cussion in Canada are absolutely required from 1916 onwards for the whole world defence of the British Empire, apart altogether from the needs of Great Britain in Home waters; that they will play a real part in the defence of the Empire; and that, if they fail, a gap will be opened to fill which further sacrifices will have to be made without undue delay by others.

With these facts in view, I ask the House seriously: Is it not unwise for some people on one side of the House to say that the Canadian ships are redundant, superfluous, and an unnecessary burden (Hon. Members, 'No'), and is it not equally unwise for other people on the other side to say that they ought to be redundant, superfluous, and an unnecessary burden? Both these views seem to me to be equally wrong and equally harmful to our interests, and I must repeat that the Canadian ships are absolutely necessary for the whole world defence of the British Empire from the end of 1915, or from the beginning of 1916 onwards. . . .

Note by WSC:

All these statements have been the subject of protracted debate in Canada, the Government, based on the Admiralty Memorandum, always contending that an 'emergency' existed which Canada should fill, the Opposition deny-ing this and arguing that there was no need for very special action. Pages of extracts could be cited to show how fiercely this point has been discussed, and how great a reliance the Canadian Government have placed upon our declaration.

WSC

WSC to Sir Francis Hopwood

EXTRACT

21 May 1913   [Admiralty]

You should write McBride[1] a nice soothing letter, but I really cannot see the use of a Royal Commission. If enquiry is wanted, the proper course is to have a conference either here or in Canada between members of one or both Canadian parties and representatives of the Admiralty.

[1] Richard McBride (1870–1917), Conservative Prime Minister British Columbia 1903–16; Member of Canadian Parliament 1898–1917; knighted 1912.

You should write to Fisher and cool him down with reminders of his own enthusiasms and comfortings upon the present position, and you may reassure him that we shall not hold him or his Commission responsible for anything but the advice which they have given.

I see snarls of the Dockyard men in the papers. I can quite believe that Macnamara will be very disappointed. Now I think we shall have to put the screws on both by increasing the establishment and by disciplinary action. You and he should consider this very carefully together. There will be many worse times to face a row in the Dockyards than the next two or three months. . . .

Sir Francis Hopwood to WSC

EXTRACT

29 May 1913

My dear Churchill,

Many thanks for your letter. I have written to McBride. The position in Canada is very unpleasant, and I feel it all the more acutely after reading what you say as to the European situation. My information is that the Naval Bill will certainly be thrown out and that after the manner of *our* 'Lords' the Senate may follow it up by throwing out the Supply Bill also, – in order to make quite certain that Borden shall go to the Country. If this is true then the Senate no doubt are advised that an election will favour the Liberals, and this is the opinion of friends including Percy Girouard who has just come back from Canada, and who has had conversations with French Canadian Senators. What do you think of a Liberal Upper House throwing out the money bills of the representative Chamber so recently elected by an overwhelming majority of the people! . . .

Memorandum by WSC

3 June 1913   [Admiralty]

Confidential

I desire to draw the attention of the Cabinet to my paper of the 29th November, 1912, appended. The rejection of the Canadian Naval Aid Bill prevents any Canadian ships from being available during 1915 or the first half of 1916. Even after that, the prospect of our getting any real use of those ships now appears very doubtful. On the other hand, the 4 battle cruisers which are now assigned to the Mediterranean will not be sufficient to maintain the independent one-Power standard prescribed by the Cabinet, when once the Dreadnought ships now building for Austria and Italy are complete. The deficit of 4 ships I mentioned in my paper of the 29th November has been reduced to 3 by the gift of the *Malaya*. This gap, however, remains to be filled.

Two courses are open. The first and more obvious which will be pressed upon us is that we should lay down 3 extra ships in place of the Canadians, and additional to our existing and prospective programmes. I am extremely reluctant to advise this step. It would mean an addition of $8\frac{1}{2}$ millions to the Navy Estimates of this and the two following years. It would spoil whatever chances there are of the 'Naval Holiday'; and it would commit us to a further great development of capital ships at a time when submarines are continually increasing in power.

The second course is to proceed not by increasing the programmes of capital ships, but by an acceleration in construction of those already sanctioned in such a way as to secure the requisite numbers in time. Nothing can now be done to affect the first and second quarters of 1915. We must try to carry on as well as we can with the 4 battle cruisers till the autumn of that year. Fortunately delays are taking place in the building of the later dreadnoughts, both of Austria and of Italy, and it now appears probable that the strengths as set out in my paper of the 29th November will not be realised until the middle instead of the beginning of 1915. If we accelerate 3 ships of this year's programme by inviting tenders for them at once (June), they can be ready in 27 months, *i.e.*, by the end of the third quarter of 1915 (September). We should then have 41 Dreadnoughts (including 2 Lord Nelsons and 1 New Zealand, and excluding the *Australia*, as usual). Of these, 35 will be required for the minimum of 50 per cent. over the German 23 leaving available for the Mediterranean the six Dreadnoughts (apart from older ships) required. By this means (so long as no new Austrian or Italian ships are begun beyond what are at present being built), the Cabinet standards can be maintained without an addition to total numbers or to total expense. The financial effect will be to increase the Estimates of this year by about half a million, to leave those of 1914–15 unchanged, and to diminish those of 1915–16 by whatever amount those of the present year are increased. There may be some opportunity for adjustment as to the amount which will fall upon this year. Whether an excess Vote will be needed or not depends upon the earning powers of contractors on this and on other parts of the programme. But this cannot be judged at present.

I see no other way by which the pledges given to Parliament, both in regard to our margin in Home waters and our position in the Mediterranean can be made good. Certainly it imposes the minimum of expense upon us, and gives the maximum support to the Canadian Government by proving the reality of the need they have failed to meet.

If the principles of this proposal are approved, the details will be worked out. It would appear, however, most desirable to make an early announcement in general terms and so forestall the demand which will otherwise certainly be made for a direct addition to our new construction.

Of course the relief given by a mere acceleration of ships can only be temporary. The difficulty will recur next year in relation to the second quarter of 1916. By next year, however, the Canadian situation will have defined itself and we shall be in a better position to judge whether a direct addition to our programmes will be forced upon us.

R. L. Borden to WSC

14 August 1913   Ottawa

Secret and Private

My dear Mr Churchill,

While undertaking a holiday at St Andrews during July I cabled you in reply to your letter of June 30th as follows: –

'Secret, private and personal. Letter received. Our Parliament will probably not meet before eighth January. We firmly adhere to our intention of providing three capital ships. I cannot at present definitely state method we shall pursue. My own opinion strongly inclines to insertion of substantial sum in estimates but there are political difficulties which I hope to overcome but which render consultation with colleagues imperative before final conclusion is reached.'

After the stress of the late session our Ministers rapidly dispersed for the summer vacation and for this reason and many others there was hardly any opportunity of considering future action beyond the general lines laid down in my observations on the day of prorogation. For this reason it was not possible for me to convey to you information of so precise and definite a character as I would have desired. However, in the meantime my colleagues Mr White[1] and Mr Burrell[2] have doubtless had an opportunity of discussing

---

[1] William Thomas White (1866–1955), MP for Leeds, Ontario, 1911–21; Minister of Finance 1911–19; knighted 1916; PC 1920.

[2] Martin Burrell (1858–1938), Mayor of Grand Forks, British Columbia, 1903; Minister of Agriculture 1911–17; Secretary of State for Canada and Minister of Mines 1917–19. His published work included: *Betwixt Heaven and Charing Cross* (1928) and *Crumbs are also Bread* (1934).

the subject with you; and I look forward with much interest to a consideration of the whole situation upon their return.

I observe that your Parliament is to be free from the labours of an autumn
session and I fully realise how much you will appreciate the opportunity
thus afforded for a much needed holiday and for the necessary attention to
matters of administration.

Sir Richard McBride is expected to arrive in Ottawa on the 17th inst *en
route* for England and naturally I shall discuss with him the questions of
naval defence from the standpoint of the Pacific seaboard.

Believe me, dear Mr Churchill,

Yours faithfully
R. L. BORDEN

P.S. Since dictating the above Sir Richard McBride has arrived and I have
conferred with him. I would be glad to have you discuss the situation with
him fully and frankly as I have done.

RLB

Note by WSC at top of page:
Prime Minister:
Mr Harcourt:
not vy promising!

Lewis Harcourt to WSC

5 September 1913   The Roman Camp
                                                Callander

My dear Winston,

The PM asks me to return the enclosed to you. It is not promising. I saw
Ian Hamilton here 2 days ago and he had derived the impression from
Ministers in Canada that they wd have a majority in the Senate in 12
months owing to the exceptional mortality amongst its members.

Yours
L. HARCOURT

Viscount Haldane to WSC

9 September 1913   28 Queen Anne's Gate

Private

My dear Winston,

I had a long talk with Borden about Naval matters. Hopwood will give you details of the situation, but I think it amounts to this: –

Borden means to bring in a satisfactory estimate in the latter part of October, & to get an assent of his cabinet to driving it through. But he thinks Laurier may advise the senate to throw out the entire Budget containing his estimate in order to force a dissolution. If he does Borden believes that he will beat him.

I pointed out the difficulties here that delay would cause. B. promises as little delay as possible & hopes that people over here will see that Canada is in real earnest & means to provide at least 2 great ships + the equivalent in smaller craft of a third, if not three ships. He is confident that Canada is going to do this. It may be January, however, before Laurier shows his hand.

The prospect is not wholly satisfactory, but Borden is very willing. I had the most agreeable conversations with him.

If you & Mrs Churchill are to be in the North do come to Cloan, Auchterarder.

Ever yours
HALDANE

Sir Richard McBride to WSC

19 November 1913   Victoria
British Columbia

Personal and confidential

Dear Mr Churchill,

Following my note to you from Ottawa it would be difficult to say with certainty that Mr Borden's plan to have Parliament vote by direct money grant part of his naval estimate will pass. That he has fully made up his mind to submit the matter to the House soon after it assembles and do everything possible to carry it through expeditiously there can be no question. I had several lengthy conferences with him and he gave me every assurance that this would be the case.

The amount of this Session's contribution might probably be placed at

$15,000,000, – a further sum would follow next year. Sir Wilfrid, to be consistent with his recent utterances, will likely oppose this policy in the Commons and later force the Senate to throw it out altogether. While it would be a most unusual thing for our Upper House to go so far as to refuse 'Supply' even if it covered the Navy contribution, – in its present frame of mind, with the domination of the Liberal Leader, nothing would surprise me.

Sir Wilfrid has been making some extraordinary speeches of late in the direction of what might be termed an independent Canada, but of course he is always careful to protect any position of this sort by strong and clever protestations of his affection for British institutions.

Here are two or three notes of interest:

The by-election at Châteauguay, Quebec, stimulated the Government to an appreciable extent because the contest was fought mostly on the Navy issue; since then there has been a seat in Ontario won over from the Government and this has offset the effect of this Châteauguay victory. In the Ontario campaign a direct appeal was made to German Canadians of whom there were scores on the Voters' List and enclosed is a circular over the signature of the Liberal candidate; this needs no explanation.

Sir Wilfrid is always dwelling on our National Autonomy as something that may be jeopardised by a policy of contribution and he invariably tries to appeal especially to Quebec.

If Mr Borden is successful I know with what appreciation his effort will be met in the Old Country: if he fails I see no alternative but a general election. It was a mistake not to have had one last year.

The indifference in some sections of the Dominion on Empire Defence is appalling. I have in my journey home from the East taken occasion in Montreal, Ottawa and Toronto to point out a few things relative to Canada's duty and have received scores of letters and messages of approval.

I am disappointed to have to tell you that as far as his permanent policy is concerned I am unable to report anything from our Prime Minister. He seems to approve now as he did a year ago of my proposal for an Expert Board of Advisors but still nothing has been done nor is there any promise that anything will be attempted.

If anything of interest arises within the next few months I shall take the liberty of again writing to you.

Believe me, Dear Mr Churchill, Sincerely yours

RICHARD MCBRIDE

R. L. Borden to WSC

TELEGRAM

31 December 1913

Secret, Private, Personal

Your letter 19th received.

During past four weeks we have carefully reviewed situation, and are gravely impressed by fear that Imperial interests will be materially prejudiced by renewed rejection of proposals in Senate. Another rejection would seriously emphasise very unfortunate impression created throughout world by Senate's action last session. Informal negotiations are pending with Liberal leader in Senate, who professes himself anxious to pass necessary Estimate. We greatly doubt his ability to enforce his apparent wish, as we are convinced that Opposition leader is absolutely determined to prevent effective assistance. Three courses must be considered. First, reintroduction of last year's measure, which is sure to be rejected by Senate. Second, introduction of Estimate for twelve or fifteen millions, coupled with statement that ships could not be completed and commissioned until after our next General Election, and that either party then returned to power could utilise them according to its declared policy. As at present advised, we believe this would also be rejected by Senate. Third, in absence of any assurance as to Senate's favourable action we could declare it undesirable on Imperial consideration to submit measure to irresponsible Senate for further rejection, but that we are firm in determination to provide ships as soon as Senate majority are in accord with popular will. We would adopt second course if absolutely assured that Senate will pass estimate, but not otherwise. As between first and third course we favour third for reasons above stated. In any case, we would be glad to add proviso as mentioned in your letter, that if cessation in naval armament is accomplished by mutual understanding ships will not be built, but otherwise Canadian Government and people esteem it their imperative duty to make provision by reason of urgent recognised needs. If you desire, we could introduce naval holiday resolution somewhat along the lines of that passed by Congress, with added declaration of Canada's determination to grant necessary aid in case rivalry in armaments continues. Please understand that we desire and intend to support you in every possible way, and that we firmly adhere to last year's proposals, recognising, however, grave danger of enabling Senate once more to exercise its temporary power to Empire's serious detriment.

WSC to H. H. Asquith

5 January 1914　　　　　　　　　　　　　　　　　　　Admiralty

My dear PM,

Do not I pray encourage – query? discourage – the King with the idea that a Borden visit will be a way out of our difficulties.

We had better next time address ourselves to other aspects of the Naval Estimates. If these are adjusted the smallness of the amt of money involved in the Canadian commitment may be a helpful consideration.

Yours always
W

R. L. Borden to WSC

TELEGRAM

11 January 1914

Secret

Private

Personal

We consider objections are most serious to introducing Bill with absolutely no hope of passing it. Our members and people generally would regard such course as useless, unwise, and insincere. Probably no reference to subject in Speech from Throne, but firm declaration by me in replying to Leader of Opposition in debate on Address, which will take place not later than Monday, the 19th. Carefully guarded statements as to effect of naval holiday will also be made, and door will be kept entirely open for subsequent estimate, introduction of which will depend on development that cannot presently be predicted with certainty. It is just possible that before end of Session we may secure majority in Senate.

Sir Francis Hopwood to Lord Stamfordham
(Royal Archives)

12 January 1914　　　　　　　　　　　　　　　　　　Admiralty

My dear Stamfordham,

Borden has telegraphed to say that in consequence of various difficulties he cannot proceed with his proposals to give us 3 battleships!! This is *secret* – except, of course, to His Majesty.

C II—PT. III—P

The reason is not far to seek. Borden has heard of the intrigue here & of the proposal to reduce the battleship programme. It was therefore necessary for Borden to take action at once. He could not go on with building battleships for us in the name of emergency when we were saying that we ourselves were building too many! Laurier would have crushed him.

Now what next?

Ever yrs
F. HOPWOOD

WSC to Prince Louis of Battenberg

14 January 1914   Admiralty

News having been received from Mr Borden that no effective progress will be made this year with the construction of the three Canadian Dreadnoughts, it would appear to be necessary for us to accelerate ships of the 1914–15 programme to secure a further period of delay to Canada without departure from our previous declaration. I have asked Third Sea Lord to make proposals for accelerating the construction of the two contract battleships of the 1914–15 programme so that they may be completed before the end of the second quarter of 1916. This would entail their being repeats of the 'Royal Sovereigns,' making seven out of the complete squadron of eight which we considered desirable. The additional expense necessitated by this change should be met in part by a re-adjustment between the items of first instalments of the 1914–15 new programme; in part by a slight reduction of that programme; and in part by a direct financial addition, either to the Supplementary Estimate of this year, or to the vote for next. The Third Sea Lord has been requested to make proposals accordingly.

2. It will be necessary for the board to consider whether, in view of the new burden which the Canadian failure will force upon us and of other circumstances now known to us all, we should not be justified for the purpose of effecting a general settlement in reducing the light cruiser programme from eight to six, and in dropping altogether the ten torpedo boats.

3. The effect of the acceleration of the two ships as proposed above would enable us to maintain six Dreadnoughts or 'Lord Nelsons' in the Mediterranean up to the end of the first quarter of 1917 without prejudice to the 50 per cent margin at home. It should be possible to select these six vessels so as to give an effective superiority over the four Austrian Dreadnoughts and the three 'Radetzkys,' which is all that Power can have by that

date. If necessary, however, as a makeweight, two 'King Edwards' could be added. It would be better not to break up the present Third Squadron.

I should be glad if you would take an opportunity of discussing these proposals with me verbally.

23

Naval Estimates Crisis

(See Main Volume II, pp. 655–86)

Memorandum by WSC

5 December 1913   Admiralty

Secret

Navy Estimates, 1914–15

It is proposed to present net Naval Estimates for 1914–15 of 50,694,800*l*. The Original Estimates of last year were 46,309,300*l*, and a Supplementary Estimate of not less than 1,400,000*l* will be required, making the total for 1913–14 47,709,300*l*. The increase over the Original and Supplementary Estimates of last year is therefore 2,985,500*l*.

As in the case of last year's Estimates, large reductions have been made on Vote 8, Section 3 – Contract Shipbuilding – and on Votes 9 and 10, and these Estimates again represent 'the minimum estimate of the possible earning powers of the contractors within the year, rather than the full provision which the approved services would require if the contractors had a clear run for their work.' The maximum possible liability which could fall due for payment in the currency of the year, if no delay of any kind occurred, would be about 4 millions in excess of these large figures. Past experience and a survey of the present conditions of the shipyards justify the belief that the provision now asked for should be sufficient. But if trade falls off, the contractors may concentrate their energies increasingly on the Government work now in their hands, and if they make better progress than is now anticipated, further funds may be required towards the end of the year. Care will, however, be taken wherever possible to control any tendency to acceleration by contractors, provided always that the ships are finished at such dates as the progress of foreign shipbuilding renders necessary. The possibility of a Supplementary Estimate of about 2 millions at the end of 1914–15 cannot, however, be excluded from consideration. If the contractors earned this extra sum in the currency of 1914–15 the Estimates of

1915–16 would be relieved accordingly, and in that case I should anticipate that they would be presented at a total lower than those of 1914–15.

New Programme

The new programme for the year 1914–15 contains nothing abnormal.

Four capital ships (one less than last year), which were announced to Parliament in 1912, as against two Germans;*

Instead of building the usual annual programme of 20 destroyers against the German 12 and 4 small 'Town Class' cruisers according to the standard, it is proposed to reduce the destroyers to 12 and to increase the cruisers to 8, of about the same size as the 'Arethusa' class now building. The aggregate total cost will not be altered by this substitution;

Ten small torpedo boats are also required for harbour defence;

A million and a quarter pounds for submarines against 1,000,000l the Germans are spending; and

Rather less than the usual proportion of yard craft and miscellaneous auxiliaries.

Power is taken in the new programme to construct, if necessary, 4 large airships in addition to those sanctioned by the Cabinet this year. It is, however, not intended to begin these airships until the end of the financial year, and only 20,000l is taken on account of them. The Chancellor of the Exchequer has expressed a wish that the whole policy of airships should be reviewed during next year by the Committee of Imperial Defence, and I have undertaken that until this or some similar discussion has taken place no new construction of airships beyond that already sanctioned shall be proceeded with.

The total cost of the 1914–15 new programme (Vote 8) is 13,930,000l as against 15,958,525l for the present year. The difference is explainable by the fact that we are building 4 capital ships instead of 5. The amount of money taken on account of the new programme 1914–15 is 2,040,000l as compared with 2,052,000l of last year.

The total sum of money actually taken in the Estimates on account of new construction on all programmes old and new (Votes 8 and 9) is 16,921,820l as against the corresponding German provision for the year of 10,463,035l.

The recruiting during the present year has been in every way satisfactory. Not only will the full maximum numbers (146,000) authorised by Parliament be attained, but the proper proportions of almost every rank and

	British	German		British	German
*1912–13	4	2	1915–16	4	2
1913–14	5	3	1916–17	4	3
1914–15	4	2	1917–18	4	2

rating, except officers, have been made good. The shortage of 2,000 which existed at the beginning of the year has been made good, as well as the increase of 5,000 sanctioned by Parliament. In order not to overrun the numbers authorised, the standards have been raised. A further increase of 5,000 men is required in the year 1914–15, and no doubt is entertained that this can be effected on the higher standards now established. The German increase as proposed in the estimates for 1914–15 is 6,210.

In order to reduce as far as possible the expenditure falling upon next year, we have decided not to have Grand Manœuvres and to substitute for them a general mobilisation of the Third Fleet. A short one-clause Bill will be required to call out the reservists for a week at a period which is not a national emergency. The test is one of the most important that can be made, and it is surprising we should have continued for so many years without ever once making it. The cost of the mobilisation, including a bounty of 1*l* to the reservists called up, is estimated at about 50,000*l*. On the other hand, the saving by not holding Grand Manœuvres is estimated at upwards of 230,000*l*. There is therefore a net saving of 180,000*l* by the change.

Causes of Increase

I repeat my statement made on this subject in the Cabinet Memorandum of last year.

The increases in the Estimates of 1912–13, 1913–14, and 1914–15 arise from four main causes: –

First: From the decisions of policy to increase the programmes of new construction and the number of ships maintained in full commission in consequence of the new German Navy Law, and the decision to increase the numbers and pay of the personnel.

Secondly: From the increase in the size, speed, armament, equipment, and cost of warships of all kinds necessary to keep pace with the similar vessels building all over the world.

Thirdly: From the introduction and development of new services, principally Oil Fuel, Air Service, and Wireless Telegraphy.

Fourthly: From the general increase in prices and wages, and particularly in the cost of coal, oil, steel, and all materials used in connection with shipbuilding.

Attention is drawn to the remarkable way in which Admiralty finance is governed by earlier decisions. During his tenure my predecessor took the following steps: –

1. He built or ordered 16 super-Dreadnoughts mounting between them 152 13·5 inch guns and aggregating 632,000 horse-power. Not one of

these vessels joined the fleet until I had succeeded. All have now to be maintained. Very little relief can be obtained by striking off old ships at the other end, because, first, of the increased establishments required by the German Navy Law, and, secondly, because it costs far more to maintain fast, complicated, modern ships mounting 10 13·5-inch guns apiece than old, simple, low-power vessels mounting 4 12-inch guns. My predecessor had to maintain in full commission a maximum of 16 Dreadnoughts: I have to provide in the present year for 33. His 4 latest battle cruisers require complements of over 1,000 each, and his 4 latest battleships complements of 900 each, compared with about 750 required for the earlier Dreadnoughts.

2. It was already decided, when I came to the Admiralty, to resume the 6-inch armaments of battleships, and to provide armoured protection. The addition to the cost of the armament (apart from the consequential addition to the cost of construction) of the ships built and building, affected by this decision, is 547,000*l*, of which 177,000*l* falls on the present year. (This excludes personnel.)

It had also been approved to leave the 18-inch torpedo and advance to the 21-inch, involving an increase in the cost of every torpedo of 217*l* and of each tube of 500*l*.

3. My predecessor, during his tenure, authorised the construction of 4 successive flotillas aggregating 79 destroyers, all using these more costly torpedoes, and 63 of them burning oil. Not one of these had come to hand in his time, but the whole crop will have matured in the currency of the present year. Out of a total oil fuel consumption in the year 1914–15 of 211,000 tons, 165,000 is required for flotillas and ships ordered before my time, and only 46,000 tons for those for which I am responsible. The reserves of oil which have to be built up are proportioned to the number of oil-using vessels available for service during the year. The total sum required for reserves in 1914–15 is 1,205,000*l*, of which 730,000*l* would have been required for the oil-burning ships laid down by my predecessor, leaving 475,000*l* on account of the oil ships for which I am responsible.

The present Board fully associate themselves with these decisions of Mr McKenna, which they regard as necessary to the efficiency of the Navy and wise and farseeing in every respect. But it must be recognized that their consequences involve large, increasing, and inevitable additions to the Estimates of future years.

It has been suggested that the rise in Naval Estimates is due to the increased power of the four capital ships designed under the 1912–13 programme. It is necessary to point out within what narrow limits this statement is true. Had no change taken place in the policy of the Board of

Admiralty, one battle-cruiser (a repeat of the *Tiger*) and 3 battleships (repeats of the *Iron Duke*), at a cost of 7,910,000*l*,* would have been constructed, mounting in all 38 13·5-inch guns. Instead of this, 4 fast battleships with 15-inch guns ('Queen Elizabeths') were designed at a total comparable charge of 2,080,000*l* each, aggregating a total of 8,320,000*l*. The substitution of 4 26-knot ships for 1 30-knot ship and 3 21½-knot ships, and certain minor structural improvements such as have been made each year since the 'Dreadnought' was designed, cost on the 4 ships 410,000*l*. These were the estimates which were presented to me by the Constructive Department, whose forecasts have proved in previous years to be very accurate guides to the prices at which the trade would tender. During the year 1912, however, the boom in the shipbuilding trade caused an advance in the prices of material of about 15 per cent. This involved an automatic and uncontrollable addition to the cost of these ships of 320,500*l* each, about half of which falls upon 1914–15. On new construction as a whole, apart from other votes, the additional burden thrown upon 1914–15 on account of the rise of prices since 1911–12 is about 1,200,000*l*.

The argument for the design of the 'Queen Elizabeths' was fully explained to the Cabinet last year, and no doubt can be entertained of the decisive military advantages inherent in the creation of a fast division of vessels of the maximum fighting power. The fact that oil-burning ships can refuel at sea, and thus avoid the growing submarine menace which will await them near their coaling bases, is a newly realised advantage of first importance.

A table is appended showing in detail the causes of increase of the 1914–15 Estimates over those of my predecessor in 1911–12. In considering this table with reference to new construction under Votes 8 and 9, it must be noted that the figure on which the Estimates for 1914–15 are presented on these heads does not represent the full potential liability, and is therefore not comparable to the sum taken in 1911–12, on which, indeed, it shows an actual decrease.

Reference must be made to the following large questions of naval policy: –

1. *The Canadian Ships*

It is believed that Mr Borden intends to take a Vote of 2 or 3 millions in supply for the immediate construction of the 3 Canadian Dreadnoughts, and that this will be announced in January when the Dominion Parliament meets (before the Imperial Parliament assembles). What the fate of this new effort will be cannot be forecast; but I consider that, provided a definite step has been taken by the Canadian Government and while the matter is

* These figures include ships and outfit of guns and mountings only, and are strictly comparable with the usual figures on this subject.

in suspense, we should resist any demands to take separate action. If, however, no provision is made by Canada in the Estimates of next year for these ships, or if, having been proposed, it is rejected, a decision will have to be taken by the Cabinet.

2. *The Mediterranean*

Although both Austria and Italy are contemplating new programmes of 4 capital ships each, no actual step has up to the present time been taken, and no consequential measures are included in our Estimates for 1914–15.

I must remind my colleagues that, on the recommendation of the Committee of Imperial Defence, the Cabinet decided in July 1912 that a one-Power standard should be maintained in the Mediterranean against the next strongest Power, excluding France. It will not be possible to carry out the Cabinet decision as regards the Mediterranean, in any case until the Canadian ships or their equivalents are built at the end of 1916 or the beginning of 1917. Until then no British line of battle can be formed in that sea, and even then further mutually provoked construction by Italy and Austria may involve more delay in conforming to the standard and require additional construction. In the meanwhile we propose to content ourselves with continuing to keep a containing force of battle cruisers and fast armoured cruisers in the Mediterranean, which will not, indeed, fulfil a one-Power standard against any of the three principal Powers there, but will make us a formidable factor for diplomatic purposes, and a decisive reinforcement if joined to the French Navy. As long as the speed of this fleet is maintained at a high and uniform superiority over any other equal force, there is no danger of its being cut off and destroyed in detail, even if we were confronted by the most improbable and unfavourable of combinations. During the coming year 4 battle cruisers, 4 armoured cruisers, 4 modern light cruisers, and a new flotilla of 16 good destroyers (Beagles) will be kept based on Malta. If the Germans continue to keep their battle cruiser *Goeben* in the Mediterranean, the British force there will be reinforced by the *New Zealand* as soon as the *Tiger* joins the 1st Battle Cruiser Squadron at the end of 1914. We have no other capital ship (except older battleships, which would ruin the speed of the fleet and add little to its effective strength) which can permanently reinforce the Mediterranean until the *Malaya* is ready in the autumn of 1915. Our force will then, however, be a good one for the limited purposes set out above. The arrival of the 3 Canadian fast battleships would enable us, if no further Austrian or Italian ships are completed, to form a line of battle in accordance with the Cabinet decision. So long as the understanding with France remains unimpaired the delay will not necessarily be injurious.

3. *Prize Money and Private Property at Sea*

The decision of the Cabinet to maintain the right of capture of private property at sea was taken by Sir Henry Campbell-Bannerman's Cabinet, of which I was not a member. I did not agree with that decision at the time, and am not now wholly convinced of its necessity. It is no doubt vital to us to maintain the effective power of blockade, which is our principal method of putting economic pressure on Germany or other hostile States in time of war, but the power to arrest the traffic on the seas does not appear to me necessarily to carry with it the need of capturing, in the sense of changing the ownership of, individual enemy vessels, and still less of transferring the private property of individual Germans or other enemy subjects to the private possession of individual British sailors. The institution of prize money is a barbarous survival, and is so regarded by many naval officers. My naval colleagues were unanimously of opinion that it might be abolished, subject to the payment of some bounty in time of war by way of compensation. I should be glad if these suggestions could be examined by a Committee of the Cabinet.

4. *Arming of Merchant Ships*

Much misconception has arisen on this subject, which is in danger of becoming a stumbling-block to many. 30 ships have at present been armed with two 4·7-inch guns each, and by the end of 1914–15, 70 will probably have been so equipped. These vessels are armed solely for defensive purposes. Their guns are mounted at the stern and can only be fired upon a pursuer. The vessels so armed have nothing in common with merchant ships taken over by the Government and converted into auxiliary cruisers. They are exclusively ships which carry food to this country. They are not allowed to fight with any ship of war, for these will be dealt with by the Navy, and their instructions will direct them to surrender at once if overtaken by one. They are, however, thoroughly capable of self-defence against an enemy's armed merchantman, and the fact of their being so armed would probably prove an effective protection for the vital supplies they carry. The sole reason for this policy is the need of maintaining the food supply of Great Britain against an enemy's armed merchant ships.

WSC

Jack Seely to WSC

12 December 1913   Blatchington House
                                                         Seaford

My dear Winston,

Simon was in most truculent mood yesterday about your estimates. He kept on muttering to me that it was scandalous and so on. I disagreed with

him and asked him what practical criticism he had to make. He said 'what
we want is a clear statement shewing what Germany was spending four
years ago and what she is spending this year, and the same figures for ourselves; you will then see that our advance in expenditure is out of all proportion to theirs.' Now, you can fight your corner better than anyone, so I
hesitate to make a suggestion to you but if, as I believe to be the case, Simon
is entirely wrong, and that comparing like with like including loans and
other charges in the German figures as in our own, our increase is pro-
portionately less, it seems to me it would be well worth your while to make
the point clear next Monday.

Yours ever

JACK

Memorandum by WSC

13 December 1913   Admiralty

Confidential

I circulate to my colleagues notes on the various suggestions for reduction
of the Naval Estimates made in the course of Thursday's discussion.

First, Mr Samuel has proposed that only two capital ships shall be built
next year. The attached Table[1] shows that the series of programmes announced by me in March 1912, namely, 4, 5, 4, 4, 4, 4, as compared with
the German 2, 3, 2, 2, 2, 2, only just maintains the 60 per cent standard. In
order to do this, it is necessary to count the *New Zealand,* against which the
Government of New Zealand have protested. The two 'Lord Nelsons,'
neither of which were counted as Dreadnoughts in my predecessor's time,
must be counted up to 1917. The *Malaya* is not included, as a specific pledge
has been given by the Colonial Secretary that she was to be additional;
neither is the *Australia,* which is not at our disposal.

Secondly, the proposal that the number of men should be reduced has
been already dealt with in Sir John Jellicoe's paper circulated on Saturday
last. I can only repeat that the number of men required for the Navy in a
given year is based upon the number of effective ships which have to be
manned with proper complements in war. Ships of the First and Second
Fleets receive full complements of active service ratings. Ships of the Third
Fleet receive complements of two-fifths active service ratings, the rest being
supplied from the reserves on mobilisation. The strength of the war fleets
for particular years is based on the duties which the different ships and

---

[1] Table A, printed on p. 1827.

squadrons have to discharge in home and foreign waters under the war plans.

The totals which are thus arrived at synthetically, may be checked by reference to the German increases of *personnel* in the Table which was circulated with my Memorandum[1] of the 3rd instant, and which, for the sake of convenience, I attach reprinted. The increase in the figures of *personnel* of other navies is also included.

Thirdly, Mr Samuel's proposal to reduce the provision for submarines.[2] I reprint the figures I read to the Cabinet of the respective amounts spent in the last six programmes, including the present one, by Great Britain and Germany on this class of vessel. The significance of these figures in relation to the relative strength in large modern submarines will be apparent.

Fourthly, the proposal to reduce the number of light cruisers. The programme of 8 light cruisers must be taken in conjunction with (a) size of these vessels; and (b) the programme of destroyers. I append a note showing that the expense of the 8 light cruisers[3] and 12 destroyers is almost exactly equal to that of 4 Town Class cruisers and 20 destroyers, which would be the conventional programme on the lines adopted by my predecessor.

Not less than 8 light cruisers, as will be seen from the note attached,[4] are required, apart from the reduction of the destroyer programme, to maintain the 100 per cent standard in cruiser strength which has long been followed by the Admiralty, and which I inherited from my predecessor.

I also circulate statements bearing on the 50 per cent margin of Dreadnoughts[5] which we regard as the minimum in Home waters. From these it will be seen that this is less than the margin we maintained against France in the first 5 years of the present century, and less than the margin maintained by my precedessor during his administration; and it is of course incomparably less than the margin we had at our disposal in the days of the Great War. The 50 per cent superiority in Dreadnoughts over Germany in Home waters includes the squadron at Gibraltar ($3\frac{1}{2}$ days away and 1 to coal), the two 'Lord Nelsons,' and allows for any vessels which may be unavailable through refits or other circumstances. It does not ensure more than 20 or 25 per cent superiority in Dreadnoughts for a decisive battle at the German selected *versus* our average moment, and it could not be accepted as sufficient but for the undoubted superiority of our ships unit for unit. In this connection the disproportionate consequences of a naval defeat to Germany and to Great Britain have to be considered.

WSC

[1] Paper B. [2] Paper C. [3] Paper D. [4] Paper E. [5] Paper F.

TABLE A

GREAT BRITAIN AND GERMANY
Comparative Table of Fleet Strength, showing the 60 per cent Margin.

—	Germany will have	Add 60 per cent	Standard Total	Great Britain will have	Deliveries Great Britain	Deliveries Germany
1913 31st Dec	17	10·2	27·2	28		
1914 31st March	17	10·2	27·2	30	{ Iron Duke / Marlborough	
30th June	18	10·8	28·8	30	—	König { Markgraf
30th Sept	21	12·6	33·6	32	{ Benbow / Emperor of India	{ Grosser Kurfürst / Derfflinger
31st Dec	21	12·6	33·6	35	{ Queen Elizabeth / Warspite / Tiger	
1915 31st March	21	12·6	33·6	35		
30th June	23	13·8	36·8	35	—	{ Ersatz Brandenburg / Lützow
30th Sept	23	13·8	36·8	37	{ Valiant† / Barham	
31st Dec	23	13·8	36·8	40	{ Ramillies / Revenge / Resolution	
1916 31st March	23	13·8	36·8	42	{ Royal Sovereign / Royal Oak	
30th June	26	15·6	41·6	42	—	{ Ersatz Wörth / T / Ersatz Hertha
30th Sept	26	15·6	41·6	42		
31st Dec	26	15·6	41·6	42	2 of 1914–15 Progr	
1917 31st March	26	15·6	41·6	44		
*30th June	28	16·8	44·8	42*	—	{ Ersatz K. Friedrich III / Ersatz Victoria Louise
30th Sept	28	16·8	44·8	44	—	
31st Dec	28	16·8	44·8	46	2 of 1915–16 Progr	
1918 31st March	28	16·8	44·8	48	2 of 1915–16 Progr	
30th June	30	18·0	48·0	48	—	{ Ersatz Freya / Ersatz K. Wilhelm II
30th Sept	30	18·0	48·0	48	—	
31st Dec	30	18·0	48·0	50	2 of 1916–17 Progr	
1919 31st March	30	18·0	48·0	52	2 of 1916–17 Progr	
30th June	33	19·8	52·8	52	—	{ Er K. Wilhelm d. Grosser / U. / Ersatz Vineta
30th Sept	33	19·8	52·8	52		
31st Dec	33	19·8	52·8	54	2 of 1917–18 Progr	
1920 31st March	33	19·8	52·8	56	2 of 1917–18 Progr	
30th June	35	21·0	56·0	56	—	{ Er Kaiser Barbarossa / Ersatz Hansa

* Two *Lord Nelsons* fall out in April 1917. † *Malaya* due for delivery, but is not counted.

One German battleship, whose date of laying down is reserved, has not been included.

New Zealand is included, but neither *Australia* nor *Malaya*.

FLEETS IN COMMISSION

Comparison of Ships maintained in Full or Active Commission at Home and Abroad in the Summer of 1911 and 1915.

—	June 1911		June 1915	
	Great Britain	Germany	Great Britain	Germany
In Full Commission : –				
Dreadnought Battleships	10	4	25	17
Dreadnought Battle Cruisers ..	4	1	9	6
Pre-Dreadnought Battleships ..	18	13	9	8
Armoured Cruisers	23	8	16	7
In Active Commission, including Gunnery Tenders : –				
Dreadnought Battleships	—	—	3	—
Pre-Dreadnought Battleships ..	15	9	13	12
Armoured Cruisers	8	—	10*	2

* Six of these Cruisers are included in the Immediate Reserve.

FLEET STRENGTHS ON CHINA STATION
December 1913

—	Great Britain	Germany
Battleship (in reserve)	1	—
Cruisers	2	2
Light Cruisers	2	3
Destroyers	5	2
For local defence at Hong Kong –		
Destroyers (in reserve)	3	—
Torpedo Boats (in reserve)	4	—
Submarine Depôt Ship	1	—
Submarines	3	—

Paper B

INCREASE OF PERSONNEL

Year	Great Britain		Germany	Austria-Hungary	Italy	United States
1900–01 ...	113,589		28,313	9,065	26,151	28,256
1901–02 ..	118,884		31,157	9,069	26,750	33,351
1902–03 ..	124,413		33,542	9,391	26,948	37,426
1903–04 ..	128,474		35,834	10,277	26,994	41,805
1904–05 ..	130,078		38,128	10,469	26,994	45,398
1905–06 ..	127,366		40,843	11,989	27,492	50,049
1906–07 ..	127,028		43,654	13,099	28,000	50,295
1907–08 ..	127,584		46,936	13,133	28,476	51,942
1908–09 ..	126,935		50,531	14,053	29,571	54,867
1909–10 ..	128,871		53,946	14,954	30,613	58,827
1910–11 ..	131,871		57,373	16,148	30,613	61,890
1911–12 ..	133,698		60,805	17,277	30,587	63,468
1912–13 ..	140,000		66,810	17,347	35,095	67,244
1913–14 ..	146,000		73,176	19,091	37,095	67,907
	Average	Maximum*				
1914–15 ..	148,500	151,000	79,386†			
1915–16 ..	153,500	156,000	85,000‡			
1916–17 ..	158,250	160,500	91,000			
1917–18 ..	162,500	164,500	95,000	No later figures available.		
1918–19 ..	166,250	168,000	99,000			
1919–20 ..	169,500	171,000	104,000			
1920–21 ..	172,000	173,000	108,000			

* These numbers represent the maximum to be reached by the end of the year.
† This figure shows a slight increase on the numbers which were forecast last year.
‡ From 1915–16, inclusive, the *estimated* numbers are given (to the nearest 1,000).

PAPER C

COST OF SUBMARINE CONSTRUCTION IN ENGLAND AND GERMANY

The following are the sums voted in the last five years for the construction of British and German submarines: –

—	British	German
	£	£
1909–10	537,552	489,236
1910–11	516,477	733,855
1911–12	709,580	733,855
1912–13	969,360	978,473
1913–14	1,020,484	978,473
1914–15 .. .. (Proposed)	1,115,000	929,550
	4,868,453	4,843,442

H. F. OLIVER,[1] *DID*

PAPER D

COST OF LIGHT CRUISERS

The minor German programme for 1914–15 is 2 small cruisers (improved Town Class) and 12 destroyers. Against this the conventional British programme would be: –

	£
4 Town Class Cruisers of comparable strength, at 360,000*l* a piece ..	1,440,000
20 Destroyers at 125,000*l*	2,500,000
	3,940,000

Instead of this, we propose to reduce the number of our destroyers from 20 to 12, 2 torpedo-boat destroyer leaders at 180,000*l* each, 10 torpedo-boat destroyers at 121,000*l* each, and the size of our 4 cruisers from about 5,800 tons to 3,700 tons; thus effecting a reduction in cost upon the destroyers of 930,000*l*, and upon the small cruisers of 240,000*l* – a total of 1,170,000*l*;

[1] Henry Francis Oliver (1865–1965), Director of Intelligence, Admiralty War Staff 1913–1914; Chief of War Staff 1914–17; Second Sea Lord 1920–4; Admiral of the Fleet 1928; knighted 1916.

and to build 4 additional light cruisers, making 8 in all, at 300,000*l* each. The actual substitution of 8 light cruisers and 12 destroyers for 4 Town Class cruisers and 20 destroyers involves an increase of 30,000*l* only on the aggregate.

	£			£
4 Town Class Cruisers	.. 1,440,000		8 Light Cruisers ..	.. 2,400,000
20 Torpedo-boat Destroyers	.. 2,500,000		2 Destroyer Leaders ..	.. 360,000
			10 Torpedo-boat Destroyers ..	1,210,000
Total ..	.. 3,940,000		Total ..	.. 3,970,000

PAPER E

REQUIREMENTS OF LIGHT CRUISERS

The ships built in 1914–15 year will come on the Effective List in the summer of 1916. At that date Germany will have a total of 9 large cruisers and 44 light cruisers under twenty years of age from the date of the launch. Leaving out the 1914–15 Programme, this country will have on the same date 34 large cruisers, 23 old type cruisers and light cruisers, and 38 new type light cruisers, a total of 95. This excludes the Australian cruisers, but includes such vessels as the *Hermes* and such of the 'Diadem' class as are not being converted into hulks. It includes also 5 vessels of the 'Pegasus' class which are well known to be a frequent source of trouble in connection with their machinery. The British total includes 18 vessels with a speed lower than 22 knots. The German total includes 13 such vessels. It will be seen, therefore, that even including the 3 Australian vessels, we shall have in 1916 98 vessels, which is considerably below the total (106) necessary to maintain a standard of 100 per cent superiority in cruisers over Germany alone. The inclusion of 8 vessels in the 1914–15 Programme will only just bring about the standard of 100 per cent superiority.

It should, however, be remembered that a proportion of the British cruisers which have been built in the current year, and which it is proposed to build next year, are in substitution of what might be called the normal destroyer programme, for in the current year only 16 British destroyers were built as against 12 German; and in 1914–15 it is proposed only to build the same number of destroyers (12) as Germany, whereas in previous years it has been considered necessary to build 20 British against 12 German destroyers.

Confidential

COST OF CERTAIN CAPITAL SHIPS

—	Cost as per Navy Estimates					Outfit	Reserves		Grand Total of Columns (a) to (g)
	Propelling Machinery (a.)	Armour (b.)	Hull and other Items (c.)	Outfit of Guns (d.)	Total	Ammunition Torpedoes (e.)	Guns and Transferable Mountings (f.)	Ammunition and Torpedoes (g.)	
	£	£	£	£	£	£	£	£	£
Hercules	235,087	354,288	940,233	131,700	1,661,308	83,200	48,650	83,800	1,876,958
Orion	254,570	448,150	1,009,346	144,300	1,856,366	87,200	49,270	91,800	2,084,636
Iron Duke	262,574	519,559	1,123,184	151,630	2,056,947	105,700	58,985	107,400	2,329,032
Queen Elizabeth ..	447,728	560,000	1,262,554	161,600	2,431,872*	122,100	64,055	142,300	2,760,337
Queen Elizabeth at Iron Duke prices	..	..	..	..	2,112,000	..	..	..	2,426,500
Queen Mary	510,394	379,470	1,078,519	118,500	2,086,883†	77,440	40,673	83,500	2,288,496
Tiger‡	556,271	442,000	1,034,880	126,350	2,159,507†	95,400	43,825	98,800	2,397,532
Tiger at Queen Elizabeth prices	..	..	..	..	2,450,000	..	..	..	2,625,250

* Queen Elizabeth at Iron Duke prices would be 2,112,000l.
† These amounts include 42,089l for Queen Mary and 22,058l for Tiger for extra payment for alterations.
‡ Trials will be run probably by contractor at a cost of 41,600l.

Cabinet Notes
(*Lloyd George Papers*)

WSC to Lloyd George

16 December 1913   10 Downing Street

I consider that you are going back on your word: in trying to drive me out after we had settled, & you promised to support the Estimates.

David Lloyd George to WSC

I agreed to the figure for this year & I have stood by it *& carried it* much to the disappointment of my economical friends. But I told you distinctly I would press for a reduction of a new programme with a view to 1915 & I think quite respectfully you are unnecessarily stubborn. It is only a question of a 6 months' postponement of laying down. That cannot endanger our safety.

D.LL.G.

WSC to David Lloyd George

No. You said you would *support the Estimates.*

Sir Francis Hopwood to Lord Stamfordham
(*Royal Archives*)

17 December 1913   Admiralty

Confidential

My Dear Stamfordham,

Following hard on the description of forthcoming finance I sent (the figures were agreed with the Chancellor of the Exchequer) another difficulty has cropped up. The Cabinet has become thoroughly scared by the Radicals who are for a smaller navy, and is putting pressure upon Churchill to reduce the *programme.* This he cannot do for the simple reason that he was fool enough to tell the world what his programme was going to be for about half a dozen years ahead. To this he is bound hand and foot. It is said that practically all the Cabinet is for a reduction in programme. What they mean by it I cannot imagine for the numbers are deeply committed. Not only did they not dissent when Churchill made his speech about building 4.5.4.4.4 battleships in each year but they made themselves a party to the despatch laid on the table of the Canadian Parliament in which the coming programme is set forth. To cut the programme hardly reduces the Estimates at all for next year. Building 2 battleships instead of 4 reduces the estimates in the second year, *viz* 1915–16. In the first year very little is spent upon them. The only way of largely reducing estimates is to knock off construction on ships already building which is of course absurd.

They are odd people indeed! Is it possible they are riding for a fall or do they merely want to shed Winston?

Yrs ever

FRANCIS S. HOPWOOD

WSC to H. H. Asquith

18 December 1913   [Admiralty]

Copy

My dear Prime Minister,

Your letter is vy kind & I appreciate *fully* all the difficulties of the situation. But there is no chance whatever of my being able to go on, if the quota of capital ships for 1914–15 is reduced below 4. Even the *Daily News* does not expect that. I base myself on 1) my public declarations in Parlt; 2) the 60% standard (see minute of the Sea Lords); 3) the Cabinet decision on the Meditn and 4) my obligations towards Mr Borden. You must in this last aspect consider broad effects. How cd I argue in the H of C that the 'emergency' was so far removed that our forecasted programme cd be halved, at the vy time that the unfortunate Borden was arguing in Canada that it was so real & serious that 3 ships must be built at once additional to the declared British programme? It wd destroy him.

If on a general *revirement* of Naval policy the Cabinet decide to reduce the quota, it wd be indispensable that a new exponent shd be chosen. I have no doubts at all abt my duty.

You know the repeated efforts I have made to meet Lloyd George, & now that the financial corner has been turned, it is too stupid of him to throw the car off the track.

As to the Meditn you surely wd have to consider whether the deliberate conclusions of the CID & the Cabinet can be discarded without good reasons, & new facts & renewed examination. The Meditn decision was the foundation of the Canadian policy. All the argument for Borden stands on that.

My own standards have never varied. As a matter of fact we have only to hold firm now to have good chances of a complete success.

The finance can be adjusted without fresh taxation. Borden will act. If he succeeds, the Cabinet policy in the Meditn can be carried out. If he fails – then 6 months from now I can develop an argument abt submarines in that sea wh will obviate a further constrn of battleships for this 2dary theatre. Either way we can get through.

Germany every month is more drawn to a naval understanding. The Dreadnought era will eventually pass away. A weakening, a reversal, an upset now, will ruin everything.

My loyalty to you, my conviction of yr superior judgment & superior record on naval matters, prompt me to go all possible lengths to prevent disagreement in the Cabinet. But no reduction or postponement beyond the year of the 4 ships is possible to me.

I gathered that the final decision was to stand over till we reassemble in Jany. But there is no hope of any alteration in my view on this cardinal point, or of the view of my naval advisers. Meanwhile I am having the details of the Estimates worked out on the basis reached with L.G.

Turning from these tiresome subjects, wh never cd and never shall affect in the slightest degree my gratitude and regard for you, is there any prospect of yr coming to dine tonight? Cassel is coming, & we shall just be 4 for bridge, not counting Nelly, who for this purpose takes rank as a 'Ld Nelson'.

Yrs sincly
WSC

WSC to David Lloyd George

18 December 1913   Admiralty

Confidential

Copy

Dear Chancellor of the Exchequer,

I have told the Accountant General to notify the Treasury officially that the expenditure on Navy votes for purposes sanctioned by Parliament and the Cabinet will require in the current year a supplementary estimate of about £3,000,000. I see no prospect of reducing this amount to the limits of £1,400,000 wh you mentioned to me. The contractors ought to be paid the money they have earned within the financial year and the estimates of the following year ought not to be artificially inflated by suspending payments wh have already fallen due. I regret that it is not possible for me to meet your wishes in this matter.

Yours vy try
WINSTON S. CHURCHILL

Viscountess Wimborne to WSC

18 December 1913   Templeton House
                                                 Roehampton

Dearest Winston,

I am going to write very frankly, and I know you won't take it amiss, because I love you and care so much for your career. I have an instinct you are going wrong. Even the ablest of men may wreck their political life, witness your dear Father, by an error of judgement and I who saw him eating out his heart in years of disappointment feel I can't keep silence. You are breaking with the traditions of Liberalism in your Naval expenditure, you are in danger of becoming purely a 'Navy man' and losing sight of the far greater job of a great leader of the Liberal party. Peace retrenchment and reform must ever be its policy and you are being carried away by the attraction of perfecting your machine for war and expenditure.

What will it lead to as regards yourself – the Tories are already counting on your return to them which is absolutely unthinkable, and would indeed break one's heart. But to lead the Liberal party you must respect its traditions, and I believe nothing is doing the present Govt so much harm as this naval expenditure. They will either have to drop you or suffer defeat.

I am sure this is the situation, and it is because I feel it is so critical as regards your own future that I beseech you to pause. If you are looking to some different combination of parties it is a delusion. Tories will always be Tories, a Tory democracy is a myth. Liberalism has the promise of the future, and will always attract all the talent and ideals of men.

I won't say any more and I don't want any answer if you will only read mark and digest the reflexions of one who has lived through a good bit of political life and cares for you a good deal.

                                                   Yrs affecy
                                            C. WIMBORNE

WSC to Sir Edward Grey
EXTRACT

25 December 1913   [Admiralty]

Private

Copy

My dear Grey,

So far as my personal position is concerned I do not seek help about the 4 battleships: for I see my duty quite plainly and am willing to pay any forfeit the fates may exact while on that path. But I hope in these weeks you will turn over in yr mind the effect which the abandonment of programmes, definitely matched against the series in the German Navy Law, would have upon the position of England in Europe. My statements on the subject were not made without consultation & agreement; and such as they were they were spoken in the name of Britain. We have offered the Germans to reduce or drop our quota if they will do the same. They have refused: and now it is suggested – seriously that we should do for nothing what only last October we said we would not do except they did the same. The country will be made ridiculous before the whole world. *I* can clear my reputation by immediate resignation. But what happens to an individual minister is of very small importance compared to the public interest. Then look at Borden. In response to our statements made in the CID and the House of Commons, and confirmed in the Admiralty Memorandum, he is coming forward with 3 extra Dreadnoughts and staking the fortunes of his Government & party thereon. At this very time a British First Lord is to argue in Parliament that what we want is not 3 more but 2 less! It would be a breach of faith. Thirdly, what about the Mediterranean? How can we all go back upon the resolution of the CID, arrived at after much prolonged examination of the whole subject, with no better reason for our refusal than lassitude.

I was amazed at the countenance given by the Cabinet to such reckless propositions. I could hardly believe the discussion was serious till the third day.

If the party has made up its mind to a complete *revirement* of naval policy, at least let them wait till the Canadian business is settled one way or the other. If Borden succeeds the whole policy of the cabinet can be carried through consistently & triumphantly. If he fails you will be free to review the situation and if you all think that I and my pledges are too expensive to keep, and that a new exponent is wanted, let the necessary changes be made. But to throw up the sponge *now* is purposeless indeed.

I am sure that to desert the programmes which have been set up (and never before criticised except for their moderation) while Germany goes on her path unmoved & unwavering would be to mar very seriously the high prestige and authority which the country has acquired abroad during the eight years of your work at the Foreign Office.

Believe me it is not for my own personal interest that I write. I am inflexible – thank God – on some things. It was good of you to intervene to postpone the decision when we last met. But unless a very serious disaster to national policy is to happen you will have to rouse yourself and exert the influence which you at the Foreign Office alone command.

If there be any point on which you have doubts – I mean as to the necessity of particular services or standards, or as to the thriftiness & prudence of Admiralty administration, let me have the opportunity of giving you the fullest information. . . .

Yrs vy sincerely

WSC

WSC to Prince Louis of Battenberg

26 December 1913   [Admiralty]

Copy

My dear Prince Louis,

The paper which the Chancellor of the Exchequer has circulated to the Cabinet must be regarded as a most serious challenge to the whole of our policy. I shall be glad if you and your Naval colleagues will devote your close attention not only to it but to the restatement of the case for the programmes and standards the Admiralty are pursuing.

I could not in any circumstances remain responsible if the declared programme of 4 ships were cut down. But my responsibility is greater than anyone else's and I hold my naval colleagues perfectly free to review the situation without regard to the action which I should take in the circumstances which may now be apprehended.

I am preparing a more general statement on the Naval position as a whole, and we can compare our separate productions later.

Yrs vy sincerely

WSC

WSC to J. Masterton-Smith

29 December 1913   [Admiralty]

Copy

My dear Masterton,

I send you herewith my reply to the Chancellor's memorandum. I have taken a deal of trouble with it and I think it is pretty good. I have tried to avoid undue detail or technicalities, and to use arguments which traverse rather than meet the Treasury contentions. Please have it printed at once as a Cabinet memorandum on white paper not blue (it is so hard to get these fellows to read anything) with half margin in the same style as the Canadian memorandum. Fill in the references and the blanks and check every statement carefully. Do not let the paper get out of your hands but go with it to the DID and the First and Second Sea Lords for anything that may be necessary. Take it also to Colonel Seely, telling him it is at my request, and ask him to check the military information which I have used. It is founded on what he told me when we were at Brook together this year. I think it will help him over his own affairs. Do not print any appendices actually in this white paper, but print separately the protest of the Imperial Maritime League lately received.

I send you also an explanation of the sort of diagrams I want prepared to show our relative position in Europe. They must ring all the changes on them over all the years of the present century, taking the 5 great Powers as against England, then all the States of Europe big and little, and then all the States of the world, including America and Japan and the South American Republics, and let us see how we stand and what combination is likely to be most edifying to those who so greatly need instruction.

Upon the whole I think this is the best case I have ever had anything to do with. I shall make no circulation before about the 15th though perhaps I will send one or two people an advance copy to ask for advice beforehand. If things go wrong, I should publish this almost word for word.

WSC to J. Masterton-Smith

3 January 1914   [Admiralty]
Copy

I am sure that there was some answer given in the House of Commons about the *Malaya*. If you will look up all the references to the *Malaya* battle-ship, you will find that either Mr Harcourt or myself on several occasions referred to it as being given under the specific condition of being additional.

WSC to J. Masterton-Smith and Sir Alfred Eyles[1]

3 January 1914   [Admiralty]

Please see this enclosed letter to Sir John Bradbury[2] on the question of the Supplementary Estimate and advise me as to the correctness, or indeed the correctitude, of the facts as quoted by me.

You can despatch the letter unless there is any objection to its facts.

---

[1] Alfred Eyles (1856–1945), Accountant-General of the Navy 1906–18; knighted 1913.
[2] John Swanwick Bradbury (1872–1950), Joint Permanent Secretary to the Treasury 1913–19; Principal Delegate to Reparation Commission, Paris 1919–25; Chairman National Food Council 1925–9; knighted 1913; created Baron Bradbury of Winsford 1925.

WSC to Sir John Bradbury

3 January 1914   [Admiralty]

Copy

Dear Sir John Bradbury,

The Accountant General has sent me your correspondence with him on the question of the Supplementary Estimate which will be needed this year. I am afraid I am not in a position to assume responsibility, without direct and formal Treasury sanction, for any exceptional measures to reduce the total of the Supplementary Estimate below the figure at which it is estimated by my professional advisers. If, for instance, a change occurred in the tenure of the Admiralty, my successor might raise objections to the procedure to which I should have no adequate answer. The excess expenditure is due, first, to additional expenditure specifically approved by the Treasury, secondly, to increases of an automatic character such as prices, and, thirdly, to the fact that the contractors are earning in the current year in the execution of projects which have already received Treasury, Cabinet, and Parliamentary sanction, larger sums than were provided for when the Estimates were presented. This last prospect was clearly foreshadowed by me in my memorandum to the Cabinet on the 1913–14 Estimates, and was explained to the House of Commons on the 26th March last (see Hansard, page 1741). It has always seemed to me a very questionable policy to claim credit from Parliament for making re-payments of the National Debt when these re-payments could in fact only be achieved by not paying contractors' bills for work actually done. Special accommodations of this character, when given to a Government by private firms, are bound in one way or the other to prove more costly to the State than actual borrowing by regular methods would be. It is of course my duty to endeavour by every legitimate means in my power to meet the wishes of the Chancellor of the Exchequer, but I must ask that, in regard to a procedure so unusual, I should receive full covering authority from the Treasury. I have therefore instructed the Accountant General to notify the Treasury in the regular manner of the excesses which will indubitably occur and a series of letters on this subject will reach you in due course. I agree with you, however, that a reply to them should be suspended pending the return of the Chancellor of the Exchequer from abroad.

WSC to J. Masterton-Smith

3 January 1914   [Admiralty]

Copy

My dear Masterton,
  Borden's telegram is a heavy blow, and I am surprised you did not appreciate its unpleasant significance. It will, in all probability, necessitate further alterations in the last memorandum I prepared. However, the argument can be turned either way. If Borden starts out on his 3 ships, we are bound in honour not to compromise his position. If he fails to make any effort for his 3 ships, all the more reason for our going forward with our 4. I am, however, all for trying to get him to keep the project alive even if it is certain that the Senate will reject the Bill, and I have therefore drafted the attached telegram which I am afraid you will have to cypher by the laborious method to which you have referred and despatch. Get Steel or Baddeley[1] to help you, if necessary.
  I am thinking of writing to Lambert and Macnamara asking them whether they wish to be kept informed of the serious questions which are now open between the Admiralty and the Treasury. I do not wish to involve them in what may easily be a disastrous struggle. On the other hand, would they not have a right to complain if, as Members of the Board, they were kept in ignorance until the last minute? Also what should be done about Hopwood? It seems to me that the position of the civil Members of the Board will be greatly impaired if only the Naval Lords are made acquainted with what is going forward. Perhaps you will discuss it with the Secretary and let me know whether there are any precedents on the subject.
  I return you the proofs of the 4 papers, revised and supplemented. 40 copies should be printed, of which you should send me 2, together with the proof of the Sea Lords' memorandum on the Treasury paper. It should be printed as No 3 of the series. I have made a few suggestions but the whole paper is admirable, and I wish it to be the spontaneous work of the Sea Lords. A covering sheet 'Table of Contents' should be printed as well.
  The Chancellor of the Exchequer's interview in the *Daily Chronicle* is a fine illustration of his methods, and I should imagine that it would deeply vex the Prime Minister.[2]

---

[1] Vincent Wilberforce Baddeley (1874–1961), Assistant Secretary for Finance Duties, Admiralty 1911–20; First Principal Assistant Secretary 1921–31; knighted 1921.
[2] In an interview published in the *Daily Chronicle* on 1 January 1914, David Lloyd George declared that had the present armament figures remained at the 1887 level – a level, he said, that Lord Randolph considered 'bloated and extravagant' – a 4s saving in the pound on local rates would have been effected. He went on to say that the amount of expenditure should be reconsidered in the light of a) his belief that Anglo-German relations

I return you various stuff that I do not want at present.

Pray let me have the discussions in the CID when the Canadian Ministers were present, and also on the Mediterranean, which I asked for before I left London. Send me also my memorandum to the Cabinet on the 1913–14 Estimates, and that which was prepared by me and, I think, circulated on the Senate's rejection of Mr Borden's proposal. Send me also that paper which I circulated to the Cabinet at the end of 1912, which I used to call my 'prose poem'.

Some of the figures supplied by the DID are very good and the only awkward thing is my second speech in March this year, when I was trying to state the Government case for what was being done at its highest.

Impress on all concerned the importance of secrecy at this juncture. That there is a row everyone will know after the Chancellor's interview, but whether it is about 2 ships or 4 ships or 7 ships should remain, for the present, in security.

I am looking forward to receiving proofs of my latest memorandum as soon as possible.

Sir Francis Hopwood to Lord Stamfordham
(*Royal Archives*)

5 January 1914   Hawkshead House
                                                              Herts

My dear Stamfordham,

Our affairs are very critical and Winston is returning in haste. The Cabinet being mad on general subjects now naturally descends to the particular – the Navy. I think that I pointed out in a previous letter to you & also in conversation that a reduction in the Programme could not really affect the Estimates for 1914–15. Cutting down battleships & so forth in this year brings in the heavy payments the following year, *viz* 15–16. So if Winston goes, the bills for 14–15 must be paid all the same. The fact is the Cabinet is sick of Churchill's perpetually undermining & exploiting its policy and are picking a quarrel with him. As a colleague he is a great trial to them. But their battleground is very ill chosen as in consequence of their indolence he has probably got chapter & verse for every item of the Naval Programme. For example; he has told the House of Commons how many ships he pro-

were more cordial than for years past, b) his belief that the continental countries were concentrating more on land forces, thus precluding Germany from challenging British sea power, and c) a general revolt against military supremacy.

posed to build each year & no member of the Cabinet objected. He sent Borden a paper to lay on the table of the Canadian House saying that after a *specified* programme over a series of years 3 additional battleships from Canada were necessary because of the 'emergency' in German shipbuilding.

The Cabinet did not dissent from this. As a matter of fact the Canadian memo was written by me as an amendment to Churchill's draft at the dictation of the Prime Minister on the billiard table at Balmoral in the autumn of 1912! If Winston goes in consequence of a quarrel on general subjects he will have all the [advantage] of the fight chosen by his colleagues on Naval Programmes. He will knock them about dreadfully in the country & this will have an effect on their general stability.

Then again a sad part of the quarrel is the effect it may have on Borden's Government. How is the Canadian Prime Minister to go on when he has staked his existence on giving us 3 battleships *in the name of emergency* when we say we can safely reduce the number of ships *without those three!* It ought to break him. Only one point remains and that is what should be the conduct of the Naval Lords in the crisis? If it comes to Winston's resignation he will press them fiercely to go with him. In my opinion they should not do so. The quarrel is political not administrative as it stands. I am sure that the true policy is for the Naval Lords to say that they will 'wait & see' what a new First Lord proposes in the way of a programme & then consider whether they can agree in it. Then if they don't think it good enough they should resign. You will observe the important effect of this. The Sea Lords ought not to waste themselves on Winston but on his successor. The results then would be more marked. I do not think that this Government could stand the double shock.

Prince Louis ought to be impressed with the importance of seeing what a successor to Winston would propose before he decided on a course. I have impressed this opinion on all four of the Naval Lords but they may be driven out of it.

The whole affair may blow over but it looks very ugly. Winston writes that he has his 'back against the wall'.

Sn yrs

FRANCIS S. HOPWOOD

I am off home again tonight. This requires no reply.

H. H. Asquith to Miss Venetia Stanley
(*Montagu Papers*)

EXTRACT

Tuesday   10 Downing Street
6 January 1914

. . . I have had quite a stream of visitors this morning, mostly of the official type: Illingworth, Edward Grey, the Arch Colonel,[1] and the Infant Samuel. They all mutter severe things about Ll George and the needless folly of his 'interview' which has set all Europe (not to mention the poor Liberal Party here at home) by the ears. I find that Winston does not return from his Paris fleshpots till Friday: meanwhile he preserves a dignified and moody silence. . . .

H. H. Asquith to Miss Venetia Stanley
(*Montagu Papers*)

EXTRACT

9 January 1914   10 Downing Street

He [WSC] has been hunting the boar in . . . [?], and has come back with his own tusks well whetted and all his bristles in good order. There will be wigs on the green, before his tussle with Ll G is over. A fallen wig *can* be readjusted, but the process of putting it on again and alooking as tho' nothing had happened, is as a rule neither easy nor dignified. You see I speak to you in allegories, but I know no one who is more skilled in reading between (and behind) the lines. . . .

Sir Francis Hopwood to Lord Stamfordham
(*Royal Archives*)

11 January 1914   13 Hornton St

My dear Stamfordham,
    I have been at home for a couple of days and have not seen Winston but on his arrival & after seeing the PM he wrote me 'The situation is serious and may prove fatal to the Government unless it should turn out that the Ch of Ex is only trying it on' . . . 'I don't want any of my Admiralty colleagues to get unnecessarily involved in what may easily become a disastrous conflict'.

[1] Colonel J. E. B. Seely, Secretary of State for War.

I think myself that the Ch of Ex was only trying it on but in his irresponsible way he may have created a position of so much aggravation that he cannot smooth it out again. In this connection it should be borne in mind that Lloyd George did not originate the row – he agreed to the estimates – it was McKenna, Samuel, Runciman & Harcourt – all anti-Churchill men – then others followed. Now the malcontents having got Lloyd George to commit himself to their side in an interview to a newspaper may very easily refuse to let him escape from the halter into which he has put his neck! Anyhow things are not getting easier for HMG. 'Patience' is the watchword! We may not want that state paper after all.

No reply.

Ever yrs
FRANCIS S. HOPWOOD

H. H. Asquith to Miss Venetia Stanley
(*Montagu Papers*)

EXTRACT

Monday   10 Downing Street
12 January 1914

I have had another long dose of Winston today and am rather late. I always think of you – with *joy and love*. . . .

WSC to the King
(*Royal Archives*)

13 January 1914   Admiralty

Mr Churchill with his humble duty to your Majesty has the honour to submit a series of Admiralty papers and a paper of his own upon the serious questions wh have arisen about the Naval estimates & Programme.

By the direction of the Prime Minister Mr Churchill also sends the Treasury memorandum & the covering minute of the Chancellor of the Exchequer, to which the Admiralty papers are in reply.

Some of the matters treated upon in Mr Churchill's paper are of peculiar secrecy – especially those which relate to Finance.

Mr Churchill is forced to regard the maintenance of the declared programme of 4 ships this year as a vital matter affecting the recovery strength of the Fleet. The advice wh he has received from his naval colleagues and the continuous study wh he has made of the whole naval situation during the last two years, leave him in no doubt as to what his duty wd be if the Cabinet decided to reduce the provision from 4 to 2 ships.

If this fundamental question were settled satisfactorily, Mr Churchill believes that the other difficult questions wd not be found incapable of solutions agreeable to the general interests of the Government & the special requirements of the Navy.

And with his humble duty remains your Majesty's faithful & devoted servant

WINSTON S. CHURCHILL

WSC to Sir Alfred Eyles

14 January 1914   [Admiralty]

Copy

Accountant General.

Please call upon all Departments as you did last year in strict confidence to produce a forecast of the Estimates of 1915–16 on the basis of the latest approved figures for the Supplementary of 1913–14 and the general Estimates for 1914–15.

Sir John Bradbury to WSC

15 January 1914   Treasury Chambers

Dear Mr Churchill,

I hear from Sir A. Eyles that now the Chancellor of the Exchequer has returned you are anxious to send in the letters about which we spoke on Saturday at once. I had hoped from the trend of our discussion on Saturday that you were prepared to let the matter stand over until after the Cabinets next week. But if you do not feel able to do this I hope you will see the Chancellor before taking any official action.

I do not think (so far as I am concerned) that I can add anything on the subject to what I said on Saturday except that I have told the Chancellor what happened & that I write this on his authority.

Yours sincerely
JOHN BRADBURY

Memorandum by WSC

EXTRACT

16 January 1914

I circulate to the Cabinet the report of the Finance Committee on the Naval Estimates for 1914–15 . . .

The zeal and industry of the Financial Secretary[1] have been beyond all praise, and every portion of the naval notes has been subjected item by item to detailed scrutiny. In consequence of this there is no part of naval expenditure upon which I should not welcome the fullest enquiry by a Parliamentary Committee, free to discuss not merely administration but policy. Such a committee, if composed, of serious and reputable members of the House of Commons, however selected, would arrive at no conclusion except that increases were desirable under many heads.

WSC to H. H. Asquith

16 January 1914   [Admiralty]

Secret

My dear PM,

I have now made some investigation of the 1915–16 position. It is almost impossible to deal with the Estimates of a year so far in advance, & none of my predecessors have ever attempted to do so.

The dominant adverse factor is the arrears of shipbuilding wh have accumulated, & wh mature in undue proportion in that year. In these circs it wd not be possible for me to give an assurance to Plt that the 1915–16 Estimates will not exceed those of 1914–15, tho' I wd of course use every legitimate means to reduce them.

I hope you have good weather.

                                                        Yours always
                                                        W

Note by WSC:
Not sent.

[1] T. J. Macnamara.
C II—PT. III—Q

The King to WSC

18 January 1914   York Cottage
Sandringham

My dear Churchill,

I was very glad to receive your letter of the 13th inst & its most interesting enclosures, but as Stamfordham explained to you, I wished to read these carefully before sending you my reply. This I have done & in my opinion your answer to the Treasury memorandum especially the able manner in which you sum up the general situation (page 16) establishes without a doubt the fact, that if the Government are to carry out the Naval policy which they have already sanctioned, this year's programme of 4 Battleships must be adhered to. I recognise the difficulties with which you are confronted, but it is you as the head of the Navy, with the assistance of your expert advisers, who are responsible to the Country that the Navy is maintained in such a condition as to be able to carry out whatever the policy of the Country may necessitate. Since you have been at the Admiralty you have by your zeal & ability done great work for the Navy & I sympathize with you in your present position. I hope the question may be satisfactorily settled & that a solution may be found to the financial problem.

I have kept the papers you sent me.

Believe me my dear Churchill, very sincerely yours
GEORGE R.I.

WSC to the King
(Royal Archives)

21 January 1914   Admiralty

Sir,

I am deeply grateful to Your Majesty for the kindness of a letter which will ever be valued by me. The difficulties though serious are not I believe insuperable, & whatever may be the result I shall always remember the gracious words of encouragement & approval wh Your Majesty has honoured me by writing.

I remain Sir, Your Majesty's faithful & devoted servant
WINSTON S. CHURCHILL

WSC to David Lloyd George

18 January 1914   [Admiralty

Draft

In our conversation on Friday, you asked me what were the prospects of a substantial reduction in the Estimates of 1915–16. No predecessor of mine has ever been asked or has ever attempted to forecast the Estimates of any but the coming year. I have several times endeavoured to make forecasts for my own information; but the departmental figures are always so inflated to guard against all possible contingencies, and the reductions made by the Ministers are always so speculative, that no trustworthy or useful result has been obtained. The vast mass of contract work which in the dockyards and the shipyards is in progress, subject to all the accidents and incidence of industry and weather, makes it impossible to form a certain estimate even for the coming year. In the fifteen months which such an estimate must cover, a long frost, a great strike, a decline or congestion in the activity of the shipyards, the failure of particular supplies of armour or projectiles, delays attendant on new inventions, have falsified year after year either in an upward or in a downward direction the best estimates which it has been possible to make.

You now ask me to attempt to forecast not merely the expenditure for 27 months ahead, but its distribution between the two financial years comprised in that period. I could not undertake such a task; the most I can do is to trace the main tendencies which are at work and show precisely the outstanding liabilities. It appears to me certain that the increase of personnel, the automatic maturing of existing pay and incremental scales, and of pensions, comprised in the series of Votes under the control of the Accountant General, will involve an increase of not less than £ [blank] in the Estimates of 1915–16 over those of 1914–15. The large additions to the horse-power of the fleet will entail an increase in the expenditure on oil and coal, for the same amount of movement, which cannot be estimated at less than £ [blank]. There will be an increase in the amount of practice ammunition proportionate to the larger number of guns mounted in the new vessels joining the fleet; and there are the usual minor augmentations, for all of which not less than £ [blank] should be allowed. It would not be prudent so far ahead to count on an increase in the Establishment and Maintenance Votes of less than £ [blank]. Against this there could only be set any relief due to a fall in prices, and the effects of any administrative economies during the year.

Now I turn to the new construction side of naval expenditure. The attached paper shows the whole series of new programmes, including that now proposed to the Cabinet, from 1903–06 onwards. It corresponds with

the years we have been in office, with the whole period in which Dreadnoughts have been built, and with the period of German naval expansion.

WSC to H. H. Asquith

19 January 1914   [Admiralty]

Private

Copy

My dear PM,

I have sent the enclosed letter to C. of E. as the result of a conversation
wh I had with him last Friday.

The relief cannot become effective until the arrears have been cleared
away. The arrears in 1915–16 will be of the most intractable description.
Ships however long delayed finish some time, & all expense in connection
with them must be met.

My relations with him are civil & sombre.

Yrs v. s.
WSC

WSC to David Lloyd George

19 January 1914   [Admiralty]

Chancellor of the Exchequer,

No predecessor of mine has ever been asked or has ever attempted to
forecast the Estimates of any but the coming year, and I cannot undertake
to do so now. The enclosed Table will show you the total amount of shipbuilding liabilities (Votes 8 and 9) which will be outstanding at the end of
the financial year 1914. It shows that, whereas Mr McKenna inherited $10\frac{1}{4}$
millions of liabilities from Lord Tweedmouth, I inherited 23 millions of
liabilities from Mr McKenna. The profound dislocations of the coal strike
of 1912 and the congestion of the shipyards during the trade activity of the
last two years, have caused the execution of the programmes authorised by
Parliament to fall seriously into arrear, and it is estimated that about
£4,800,000 worth of shipbuilding which ought to have been extinguished in
previous years, is steadily maturing for payment. In this connection may I
remind you of my letter to Chalmers of the 19th November 1912, the relevant
extract from which is attached.

So far, the contractors have been fully provided with every penny they have earned; and if either by Supplementary Estimate in 1913 or by the Estimates, general and supplementary, of 1914, the contractual liabilities of the State are defrayed as they accrue for payment, it is highly probable that $3\frac{1}{2}$ millions of these arrears will be worked off. All this would directly relieve the Estimates of 1915. Even so, that year would still be burdened with abnormal arrears which cannot be avoided. If, on the other hand, the contractors fail to earn their instalments, or if those instalments were not defrayed as and when they were earned, the whole amount of the short earnings or short payments would be transferred bodily to the Estimates of 1915, and would be a further direct addition to the expense of that year.

Increases in personnel, in the cost of pay and pensions, and in the expenditure on coal and oil proportionate to the growing horse-power of the fleet, are inevitable each year from causes which are either automatic or have been fully explained. Any relief from price movements would be gradual and uncertain. It is not therefore in my power to give you any guarantee about 1915 of the kind you desire, and I am sure there is no honest person acquainted with the facts who could or would do so. It should be recognised that the expenditure both of 1914 and of 1915 has, in the main, already been determined by past decisions of Parliament, and by the delay in working off approved programmes.

The new commitments both of this year and the next will, however, be substantially less than in 1913. The arrears of shipbuilding will almost certainly have to be cleared out of the way before the end of 1915. In these circumstances 1916 offers a far more hopeful prospect for a reduction in expense than 1915. Unhappily this distant oasis lies beyond the gulf of a General Election, and will more probably afford relief to another caravan.

David Lloyd George to WSC

20 January 1914   11 Downing Street

My dear Winston,

The Prime Minister thinks you and I ought to have another conference before he intervenes. I am free any time this afternoon and could see you either there or here.

Yours
D. LL. G.

WSC to the Prime Minister

23 January 1914

Secret

[Copy]

My dear Prime Minister,

It seems to me possible that the following series of estimates cd be maintained, subject to the Sea Lords agreeing *now* to several important steps affecting the estimates of 1915–16. Before I address myself to them I must know (1) that the 1913–14 supplementary + the 1914–15 estimates will be sufficient to discharge fully all liabilities wh may reasonably be expected to mature before 31st Mar 1915. (2) That the programme for 1914–15 will be 4 Battleships & (3) that an early laying down of 2 of these by readjustments not in excess of the original total first instalment of the 1914–15 new programme will be assented to, to cover for the time being the Canadian default. Armed on these points I shall be in a good position to present to the Sea Lords the very serious proposals I shall have to make for reductions. If I fail to convince them, or if upon further investigation the measures I propose are found in whole or in substantial part impracticable, the assent of the Chancellor of the Exchequer to the above 3 points could of course be withdrawn. It is conditional on the confirmation of the arrangement as a whole. That is fully understood by me. Here is the series of estimates: –

	1913–14	supplementary	£3,150,000	
total	1913–14		£49,450,000	
	1914–15		£52,850,000	
	1915–16		£48,150,000	
	1916–17		£47,000,000	or *less*.

This is the best plan.[1]

No allowance has been made for any alteration in prices beyond what is now evident. I propose that if prices rise my estimates shall be increased accordingly; & if they fall a further direct reduction will be made. The basis can be agreed between the Admiralty & the Treasury.

No allowance has been made for minor administrative savings, experience showing that unexpected charges of a minor character are certain. These shd balance subject to Treasury approval on details. In the event of underspending occurring in 1914–15 the surplus must be made available for 1915–16, as the charges wd also be transferred to that year.

---

[1] *Sentence deleted:* The undue inflation of 1914–15 exposes me to very unfair attack at a time already of great difficulty, and I press most strongly that at least the full 1913–14 obligations shall be discharged.

The whole of these figures and of the arrangement on both sides must be subject to confirmation in the course of the next fortnight. It may be found possible to present Parliament with definite estimates for 3 years or even 4: and I am inclined to think that, if this were so, the general defence of Naval expenditure could be more advantageously conducted than on the present annual basis.

If the Chancellor of the Exchequer finds it possible to accept in principle these arrangements I shd welcome an opportunity of entering more fully into them with him in your presence this morning.

Time is short now, & I have a task of the greatest difficulty to attempt with my naval colleagues after a provisional agreement has been reached with Chancellor. In this I may subsequently require your & his aid.

Yours always
WINSTON S. CHURCHILL

WSC to David Lloyd George

26 January 1914   Admiralty

Confidential

Draft

My dear Chancellor of the Exchequer,

The figure for 1914–15 in my letter to the Prime Minister, *viz*: £52,850,000, on the basis of a Supplementary Estimate of £3,150,000, and as now proposed to be modified by me, includes new construction (votes 8 & 9) £18,666,000. As the supplementary is reduced, this figure will be directly raised.

The establishment & maintenance votes have been for four months the subject of ceaseless scrutiny & pruning to reach the figures of the Estimates presented to the Cabinet when it was desired to work to a total of under 50 millions. There is no possibility of any further reduction in this sphere, unless the Sea Lords are able to agree to a reduction in men (this is improbable and the relief wd even so be small.) No additions of any kind have been made to these charges during the recent fundamental recasting of the Estimates. Only the sums of money for new construction wh had been arbitrarily cut from votes 8, 9 & 10 have been restored. There is no reason to doubt that these sums will be earned during the year. To take less would be to incur a supplementary Estimate in 1914–15, or directly to transfer the burden to 1915–16. If a great strike or some extraordinary event produced an under-spending in new construction, none of the saving could be transferred as your friends apprehended to Establishment & maintenance charges without Treasury sanction & covering Parliamentary confirmation.

Any one of the following series of estimates can be worked to; but I must know *which*:

1913–14 + Supplementary	1914–15	1915–16	Totals	1916–17
46300^m + 3150^m	52850^m	48500^m	150800^m	less than 1915–16, but
or 46300^m + 2000^m	54000^m	48500^m	150800^m	all forecasts of the esti-
or 46300^m + 2500^m	53500^m	48500^m	150800^m	mate of 1916–17 are
or 46300^m + 2500^m	52500^m	49500^m	150800^m	extremely speculative

The uncertainty about the amount of the supplementary estimates of 1913–14, & the many variations upon which the estimates have now been prepared, are causing a heavy strain upon the Admiralty departments concerned, & will if continued much longer lead to a serious delay in the presentation of the estimates.

[WINSTON S. CHURCHILL]

WSC to David Lloyd George

26 January 1914   Admiralty

Draft

My dear David,

In Cabinet tomorrow it will be my duty to state that while I will do my best to work to the figures mentioned in my letter, I cannot be bound to them in any extraordinary or improper sense. While I am responsible, what is necessary will have to be provided. The estimates of 1914–15 have been prepared with the strictest economy. For all expenditure incurred or proposed there is full warrant & good reason. There is no act of Admiralty administration for which I am responsible wh cannot be vindicated to the House of Commons. I cannot buy a year of office by a bargain under duress about estimates of 1915–16. No forecasts beyond the year have ever been made by my predecessors; & I have no power – even if I were willing – to bind the Board of Admiralty of 1915 to any exact decision.

I recognise your friendship, but I ask no favours & I shall enter into no irregular obligations.[1]

I am now approaching the end of my resources, & I can only await the decision of my colleagues & of the Prime Minister.

Yours sincerely
WINSTON S. CHURCHILL

David Lloyd George to H. H. Asquith
(*Asquith Papers*)

EXTRACT

27 January 1914

My dear Prime Minister,

I have laboured in vain to effect an arrangement between Churchill & the critics of his Estimates which would save you and the Cabinet the necessity for entering upon an unpleasant & maybe a disastrous controversy.

I have utterly failed . . . The economists have always contended that Winston's latest figures were not real & that he meant to take his £54,000,000 this year without honouring his promise of reduction for 1915–16. Winston's letter to me confirms this suspicion.

You promised on Friday to see Bradbury. Could you manage it today?

Ever sincerely
D. LLOYD GEORGE

McKenna, Beauchamp & Samuel entirely agree with Simon & Hobhouse.

WSC to David Lloyd George
(*Lloyd George Papers*)

27 January 1914   Admiralty

My dear David,

Only a line to thank you for the warmth and kindness of your letter.[2] It is a comfort to me that if the worst happens, personal ill-will between us will not be added to the many other causes for regret.

You put a wrong construction on my letter – but about that I will not argue now.

Yours ever
WSC

---

[1] *Sentence deleted:* Tomorrow you must make up your mind & strike without $\frac{\text{compromise}}{\text{remorse}}$ where your duty points.

[2] No copy of Lloyd George's letter can be found in the Chartwell or Lloyd George papers.

David Lloyd George to WSC
(*Lloyd George Papers*)

27 January 1914   Treasury Chambers

My dear Winston,

I have striven hard for a friendly and honourable settlement without the slightest regard for the effect upon my personal position, but your letter has driven me to despair, and I must now decline further negotiations, leaving the issue to be decided by the Prime Minister and the Cabinet.

Your letter warns me – in time – that you can no more be held bound by your latest figures than you were by your original figure of £49,966,000. This intimation completely alters the situation. I now thoroughly appreciate your idea of a bargain: it is an argument which binds the Treasury not even to attempt any further economies in the interest of the taxpayer, whilst it does not in the least impose any obligation on the Admiralty not to incur fresh liabilities. Such understandings are surely not worth all the time and anxiety you and I have devoted to arriving at them.

In one vital respect the task of the Cabinet is simplified by your letter, for it demonstrates that you and your critics are in complete agreement as to the real value of your last proposals. The only certainty about them is that the Exchequer would this year have to find 56 millions – supplementaries included – for the Navy, whilst the reductions promised for 15/16 do not bind either the Board of Admiralty or the First Lord. Therein you and your critics agree. I have been repeatedly told that I was being made a fool of; I declined to believe it. Your candour now forces me to acknowledge the justice of the taunt. You proposed before Christmas to take 50 millions. As a compromise on that you proposed Friday last to take four millions more this year on condition of coming down 1½ millions next year. Not a sumptuous offer at best. Now you qualify that!

I have laboured these last few days – not to favour you or to save myself – but to rescue Liberalism from the greatest tragedy which has yet befallen it. I have a deep and abiding attachment for Liberal causes, and for the old Party, and the prospect of wrecking them afflicts me with deep distress. That is why I have been prepared to risk the confidence of my friends and to face the gibes and sneers from friend and foe alike with which I foresaw the publication of the figures would be greeted. I know too well that every paper would gloat over my humiliation. That I did not mind if the ship and its precious cargo could be saved. You decreed otherwise, and the responsibility is yours and yours alone.

Ever sincerely
DAVID LLOYD GEORGE

Lord Beauchamp and others to H. H. Asquith[1]
(Asquith Papers)

EXTRACT

29 January 1914

Dear Prime Minister,

Every member of the Cabinet must have been deeply impressed by the appeal which you made yesterday for the cultivation of a spirit of mutual accommodation in discussing the Navy Estimates . . . but the question remains whether the figures now put forward by the First Lord, and the plan now tentatively suggested by the Chancellor of the Exchequer for dealing with them, are calculated to make more certain the happy issue of the legislative programme to which you and we stand committed. . . .

We think it best to put before you in writing a summary of the general considerations (apart from any detailed criticism of this figure or that) which seem to us to justify our deep concern & uneasiness.

1. The effect of so enormous an increase in our Naval expenditure upon the German programme & policy is a matter of surmise; but such excuses as may be suggested cannot obscure the main fact – that the total is unprecedented; the increase is unexampled at a time of international calm; and the impression powerfully created that we are leading the way in yet more rapid outlay.

2. If the announcement of our figure were to be followed by further accelerations by Germany, the whole scheme for retrenchment in 1915–16 falls to the ground.

3. These proposals expose us to Parliamentary attack far more serious than the sporadic efforts of a few Liberal 'economists'. The Labour Party will surely be driven to go to any lengths in dissociating itself from such increases; defection by a substantial group on our own benches is likely; Ulstermen who profess that our defeat is the only protection against 'civil war' will hardly resist the temptation offered.

4. The carrying through of Home Rule may vitally depend on the avoidance of disaster at bye-elections in the meantime. How are our prospects in this regard affected by such proposals?

5. Heavy taxation this year will be represented as the breakdown of Free Trade. . . .

If the difficulties which press upon us appear to you to be of weight, we ask that you should present them with all your authority to those who are disposed to favour a course of high expenditure and new taxation. From first

---

[1] This letter was in Sir John Simon's handwriting.

to last our single desire is to promote absolute unity under your leadership, with a view of giving Home Rule the best possible chance under your guidance.

Yours most truly
BEAUCHAMP
C. HOBHOUSE
R. McKENNA
WALTER RUNCIMAN
JOHN SIMON

H. H. Asquith to the King
(*Royal Archives*)

29 January 1914   10 Downing Street

The main topic of discussion at the Cabinet meeting was the Navy Estimates. Some points which were left outstanding in December were settled without difficulty. It was agreed that the Supplementary Estimate for the current year should be raised to $2\frac{1}{2}$ millions, and in view of the pledges given by Ministers in the past, that the Estimates for 1914–15 should provide for the Construction of 4 (not 2) Capital ships. The total expenditure for 1913–14 will thus be £48,800,000; and Churchill's revised figures show for 1914–15 a total of £52,800,000, and for 1915–16 £49,500,000.

Strong protests were made by the Chancellor of the Exchequer, Lord Beauchamp, Sir J. Simon, Herbert Samuel and others, against this scale of expenditure, the criticism being directed not so much to the programme of new construction, as to the growing cost of maintenance, which has risen no less than 25 per cent in 3 years. It was agreed that large economies might be, & ought to be, made under this law.

The Chancellor of the Exchequer pressed especially for a definite pledge of substantial reduction in 1915–16. He pointed out that according to his present forecast the Revenue in 1914–15 would show an increase of about $3\frac{1}{2}$ millions, while the Expenditure (putting the Navy at 52,800,000) would grow by over 12 millions, leaving an adverse balance of about 9 millions which must be met by new taxation. He had no hope of being able to commend such taxation to the House of Commons, unless he could assure them that in the following year (1915–16) the bulk of the proceeds could be devoted to Education & the relief of local rates.

After a prolonged discussion, in which all the principal items in the Estimates were exhaustively reviewed, the Prime Minister, after warning his colleagues of the disastrous consequences of a split on such an issue, suggested that the First Lord should examine again the chief [items] of the charge for maintenance; and the final consideration of the [Estimates] was postponed until next Tuesday.

Sir John Simon to H. H. Asquith
(*Asquith Papers*)

[January 1914]

1. Dissolution now, if we were beaten, means that Parliament Act is utterly destroyed; House of Lords reconstructed on Tory Lines which only a revolution can alter; Home Rule and Welsh Disestablishment lost.

2. The probability of losing Gen Election is great, *not* because Country is against Home Rule or in favour of Admiralty Extravaganza, but because our *keenest* supporters will think we have given up causes to which we are pledged.

3. The loss of WC, though regrettable, is *not* by any means a splitting of party – indeed large Admiralty estimates may be capable of being carried *only* because WC has gone.

4. The party wd feel itself strengthened in its Radical element & among the Economists; the feeling that the Cabinet *fights for economy* but pursues Home Rule inflinchingly is just what is wanted.

5. A majority of the Cabinet certainly takes this view.

H. H. Asquith to WSC

1 February 1914   Alderley Park
                                          Cheshire

Confidential

My dear Winston,
Very largely in deference to my appeal, the critical pack (who know well that they have behind them a large body of party opinion) have slackened their pursuit.

I think that you on your side, should (without 'Confiteors' or 'Peccavis' or the white sheet) show a corresponding disposition, and throw a baby or two out of the sledge.

Ever yours
H.H.A.

WSC to H. H. Asquith

2 February 1914   [Admiralty]

Private

Copy

My dear P Minister,

For the last 4 or 5 months I have been striving by every means in my power to reduce the cost of the maintenance votes. They have been searched and scrubbed by Macnamara & his Finance Committee as they have never been before. I am circulating today papers on the 3 points – Fuel, Practice – ammunition, & minor repairs – wh were specifically raised at the Cabinet. These will I believe be found conclusive. If other points are mentioned they will be loyally and simply examined. But there is no part of my admin of this office wh has not throughout been conducted with severe economy; & this can be proved by reference not only to facts but to my minutes & directions at every stage. I see absolutely no hope of further reductions in the cost of maintenance & upkeep. The number of ships in commission is not I am sure susceptible of appreciable reduction – but each vessel & squadron can be discussed in detail at the Cabinet. The prognosis of 1915–16 is bad. The volume of shipbuilding shows practically no diminution (under existing contracts & the reduced new programme 1914–15) & there is the inevitable rise due to numbers, & automatic charges. Knowing all I do abt the position I am certain that to produce in these circs 1914–15 Estimates at 'under 50 m.' wd be a prodigy; & no man in this country wd be able to do better. I can only promise to do my best. Everything possible has been done already for 1914–15.

Air has been reduced to £400,000, the [tear in text] programme (subject to Bd agreement) £1,750,000, 36 oil-burning destroyers have been laid up as the result of Cabinet discussions. These follow & accompany a long series of Deptal contractions, postponements, & excisions.

I do not love this naval expenditure & am grieved to be found in the position of taskmaster. But I am myself the slave of facts & forces wh are uncontrollable unless naval efficiency is frankly abandoned. The result of all this pressure & controversy leaves me anxious chiefly lest the necessary services have been cut too low.

Please read my pp today.

The sledge is bare of babies, & though the pack may crunch the driver's bones, the winter will not be ended.

Yours always
W

Memorandum by WSC

2 February 1914   [Admiralty]

In response to proposals that the number of ships in full commission should be reduced, I have reviewed the Fleets and Squadrons at Home and Abroad in detail with the First Sea Lord and the Chief-of-State.

In 1914-15 the German Third Squadron, which already consists of 4 super-Dreadnoughts, will be completed. A newspaper report, however, states that the Second Squadron will be reduced temporarily from 8 to 5 'Deutschlands' through manning stringency. On this basis the Germans will maintain 22 battleships in full commission concentrated in close proximity to our shores. Against this we propose to maintain in full commission 25 battleships at Home and 4 at Gibraltar. (The completion of the 4th Battle Squadron being delayed until the completion of the 3 German Squadrons is effected.) The Germans will also maintain in Home Waters (ex *Goeben*) 4 battle cruisers, against which we think it necessary to provide in Home Waters 4 battle cruisers and 8 armoured cruisers in full commission. We are also maintaining in full commission 4 light cruisers, rising to 12 as the 'Arethusas' are delivered, against the German 8, and 80 destroyers of the First Fleet against 77 German destroyers maintained in commission.

The Mediterranean Fleet has been publicly fixed at 4 battle cruisers and 4 armoured cruisers till the end of the year 1915. This has been announced in the Canadian memorandum and also to Parliament, and no reduction is possible without a deliberate change of policy.

The British Fleet maintained in China is practically equal to the German Fleet in those waters. We are pledged under Treaty with Japan to maintain the strongest Fleet of any European Power in those waters. There are a considerable number of River Gunboats and small craft in Chinese waters which are engaged in Foreign Office duties. The demands upon these are continual and increasing.

The New Zealand Division consists of 3 old cruisers and the notorious *Torch*. The New Zealand Government are extremely dissatisfied with the vessels provided and complain repeatedly that the agreement of 1909 has been broken.

There are 3 old ships at the Cape, all of which are told off to watch individual German vessels on the East and West Coast of Africa on the outbreak of war and to protect the trade routes.

On the South-East Coast of America the *Glasgow* (a small modern cruiser) is covering a German vessel of approximately equal strength.

The *Algerine* and *Shearwater* are the only representatives of the British Flag along the whole 9,000 miles of the West Coast of America.

The 4th Cruiser Squadron (4 ships) and the *Hermione* have been detached from the Home Fleet for the North American Station. Here it is fully occupied with the troubles in Mexico and upon its strategic station rendered the more important by the opening of the Panama Canal to guard the North Atlantic trade route. The *Hermione* keeps order in the West Indies and discharges duties for the Colonial Office.

There are 4 ships in the East Indies, one of which (the *Swiftsure*) is required to cover the heavily armed Dutch Coast defence vessel and cruiser near the Straits of Malacca. The other two in war protect the trade route from India to Aden.

The India Office require the maintenance of 4 gunboats of little military value to keep order in the Persian Gulf.

These, with the 2 Cadet Training Ships (*Cornwall* and *Cumberland*), the 6 mine-sweeping gunboats, surveying vessels, and a limited number of miscellaneous auxiliary craft, comprise the whole of our vessels proposed to be kept in full commission during the year 1914–15.

All the rest of our ships are kept either in the Second Fleet with nucleus crews (which forms our one great makeweight as against Germany in Home Waters) or in the Third Fleet with skeleton crews. The patrol flotillas have been reduced by 36 oil burning destroyers laid up, and by 10 coal burning destroyers attached to the Battle Squadrons of the First Fleet for subsidiary purposes in the First Fleet Flotillas.

The proportion of the British Fleet maintained permanently in full commission is substantially less than the proportion of the German Fleet so maintained; and I am satisfied that there is no opportunity of any further reduction in the numbers of ships kept in full commission, and that a further denudation of the small numbers we will keep on foreign stations could not be justified in peace and would produce grave inconvenience in war.

In order to maintain the narrow limits specified above at a period when so many new ships of all classes are joining the Fleet, a steady and general movement of older ships to a lower grade of commission, to the reserve or to the sale list must be maintained. In pursuance of this policy, during the next few years the 8 'King Edwards' will descend into nucleus crews: the 5 'Duncans' have already been absorbed as gunnery ships: 6 of the 8 'Formid-

ables' will pass into Third Fleet (with care and maintenance parties only):
and the 6 'Canopuses' are to go almost immediately on to the sale list. By
1915 the whole of the 'Duke of Edinburgh' (excepting only 4 maintained in
the Mediterranean) 'Devonshire' and 'Monmouth' classes of cruisers (17 in
number) will pass out of full commission into the Second Fleet, the Third
Fleet, or the Training Squadron. The 4 'Drakes' and the *Terrible* are to go
to the Training Squadron at Queenstown releasing the 9 'Edgars' for
transference to the Material Reserve and the sale list. The 6 'Cressys' will
pass into Material Reserve. The 6 'Diadems' will either have been sold,
employed as training hulks, or maintained in the Material Reserve without
crews. In light cruisers, practically everything earlier than the *Challenger*
now found on page 270e of the Navy List will have passed (except when
required as Depot Ships) to the Material Reserve or the sale list.

Even with these wholesale clearances and degradations the manning
stringency caused by the continuous arrival of new, larger and more complicated ships will be continuous, and unless the provision of manning for
1914–15 is maintained at the level asked for an appreciable shortage is
inevitable.

Cabinet memorandum by WSC

6 February 1914   Admiralty

Secret

During the whole of 1916 Italy will have in the Mediterranean 6 Dreadnoughts and Austria 4 Dreadnoughts and 3 Radetskys. The least number
of British Dreadnoughts which will be required, apart from older vessels, to
maintain the one-Power standard adopted by the Cabinet in July 1912, is 6.
The decision of the Cabinet in June 1913 to accelerate the construction of
three of the 1913–14 battleships secures the position till the end of the first
quarter of 1916. Thereafter, unless measures are taken *now*, the number of
British Dreadnoughts (including Lord Nelsons and the *Malaya*), available
for the Mediterranean, after maintaining the 50 per cent. superiority in
Home waters, will be as follows: –

1916 –					
Second quarter	..	..	..	4	⎫
Third quarter	..	..	..	4	⎪
Fourth quarter	..	..	..	4	⎬ Deficit 2
1917 –					⎪
First quarter	..	..	..	4	⎭

after which, *in the absence of any fresh Austrian or Italian building*, the position will be restored for a time by the arrival of the 4 ships of the programme of 1914–15. The Cabinet was duly informed of this situation in my Memorandum of the 29th November, 1912.

Three courses are open to the Cabinet –

1. To begin two ships of the 1914–15 programme early enough to have them ready by the second quarter of 1916. This is the course the Admiralty recommend.

2. To repudiate the 50 per cent. standard (3 to 2) in Home waters. This would be a grave step.

3. To rescind the decision to maintain a one-Power standard in the Mediterranean. If this is decided on, the emergency to meet which the Canadian ships were required is of course removed. It would be necessary that Parliament and Canada should be officially informed of the reversal of policy.

The Admiralty is bound by Cabinet decisions in questions of policy, and these form the basis of their calculations. If the standards are changed the Admiralty calculations can be adjusted. But the Government, and not the Admiralty, must take the responsiblity for changing the standards; and the Government would no doubt require to be supported by responsible professional advice. In view of the great care with which the Mediterranean question was examined by the Committee of Imperial Defence and the Cabinet in 1912, such advice would be difficult to obtain.

In the existing circumstances, the Admiralty consider that it is necessary to lay down 2 ships of the 1914–15 programme as early as possible, so that they may be ready by the end of the second quarter of 1916. No visit by Mr Borden can be any substitute for these ships. If they were ordered almost immediately, the resulting increase to our general margins of battleship strength in the second, third, and fourth quarters of 1916 would be such as to justify a later beginning of the destroyer and light cruiser programme of the year 1914–15, and a slight retardation of the second 2 battleships of that year, which would practically enable the acceleration of the first 2 battleships to be made without any increase in the first instalment of the 1914–15 new programme. On the other hand, if the 2 ships in question are not accelerated, there would be no military justification for not entering upon the cruiser and destroyer programme at the regular dates originally proposed (before the Canadian default became certain). No financial saving, therefore, would be involved in a decision to restrain the Admiralty from laying down the 2 first battleships of the 1914–15 programme at the dates which are necessary.

Since the Estimates were first prepared, a proposal has been made in the

Cabinet to reduce the number of light cruisers from 8 to 4. This proposal has not yet received the agreement of the Sea Lords, and, in view of the great reduction in the destroyer programme, the decision to make such a reduction would be serious. If it were adopted, the relief in either case would be the same.

The course which the Admiralty advise of beginning 2 ships of the 1914–15 programme before it is too late, has many advantages, and causes no extra charge to the taxpayer. Not to take this course would involve a departure from the standards under which we are now working or a reversal of the Cabinet decision about the Mediterranean. It would destroy the whole basis on which Mr Borden has hitherto acted, and in all probability lose at once and altogether the 3 ships which the Canadian Government are seeking to provide to meet the emergency which they have been assured exists. It would stultify the Admiralty memorandum to which the Cabinet and the Board of Admiralty are equally committed. It would stultify directly the decision of the Cabinet of June last to accelerate three ships of the 1913–14 programme, and would deprive the Government of any Parliamentary defence for the expenditure of 450,000*l* for which a supplementary estimate has now to be presented.

I do not here dwell upon the accusations of breaking pledges and breaking faith which would certainly be capable of being strongly maintained in the House of Commons. If the Opposition were to take this view, they would have no difficulty in justifying a solid vote against the naval estimates as a whole, even if those estimates were presented by the present Board of Admiralty.

I most earnestly urge my colleagues to weigh the issues with the attention that their vital importance deserves.

By adopting the course which the Admiralty recommend, the Mediterranean position will be secured until the end of the first quarter of 1917. Twelve months will be given to Mr Borden in which to renew his proposals – he has stated that he is confident he can do so within that period. If he does so and succeeds, the great resulting addition to British naval strength would, in the absence of fresh developments elsewhere, justify a retardation of the battleships of the 1915–16 programme at least equivalent to the accelerations of the two previous years. If he does not do so, or tries and fails, the Mediterranean position after the first quarter of 1917 could, in the absence of fresh Austrian or Italian building, be safeguarded for another twelve months by the acceleration of one ship of the 1915–16 programme. It is also possible that by that time the progress of naval science, particularly in regard to submarine construction, may enable a new view to be taken of the naval situation as a whole. The Cabinet, therefore, would not be committed by taking the Admiralty advice on the present occasion to the construction of three additional units in the programme of 1914–15 should Canada again make default.

I am deeply sensible of the heavy cost which an unusual combination of circumstances throws upon the coming year, and have endeavoured to reduce it by every means other than those which would merely transfer an equal burden to 1915–16. The following arrangements are proposed as the result of my final survey.

It must, however, be distinctly understood that they, as well as the other technical measures I have at various times indicated to the Cabinet, can only be adopted with the concurrence of the Board of Admiralty as a whole.

If a decision is taken to acquire control of the Anglo-Persian oilfields it would be justifiable, in view of Admiral Slade's report, to review the whole question of oil reserves so as to attain the full reserve at a somewhat later date than was previously thought necessary. This would enable *inter alia* the purchase of 114,000 tons of oil now included in the estimates of 1914–15 to be postponed, and those estimates to be relieved by 450,000*l.* without a consequential addition to the charges of 1915–16.

I have already undertaken, in conjunction with the Secretary of State for War, to reduce the estimate for the Naval Air Service by a further 120,000*l.*

It may be found possible, as a result of fresh scientific enquiries into the life of the boilers, to reduce the expenditure on large refits in 1914–15 by 150,000*l.*

By retarding the provision of shrapnel shell and anti-aircraft guns, Vote 9 could, if the Board assented, be reduced by a further 100,000*l.*

By reducing the number of the patrol flotillas, by restricting their movements, and by reducing and partially immobilising their depôt ships, it may be found possible to save another 100,000*l.* on maintenance under various headings.

The total reduction from all these causes would, if they became effective, amount to 920,000*l.* The Estimates of 1914–15 could then be presented at 51,580,000*l.*, without the prospect of 1915–16 being further impaired.

WSC

T. Vansittart Bowater[1] to WSC

9 February 1914 The Mansion House

Dear Mr Churchill,

I am desired to send you a copy of a resolution unanimously carried at a meeting of the City of London held today at Guildhall, under my presidency, on the subject of the Navy, *viz:* –

'That this Meeting of the Citizens of London begs to assure the Prime Minister and His Majesty's Government of the support of the Commercial Community in any measures – financial or other – that may be necessary to ensure the continued supremacy of the Navy and the adequate protection of the Trade routes of the Empire.'

I venture to hope that the Government may welcome this assurance by the Citizens of the Capital of all political parties.

Believe me, Dear Mr Churchill, Yours very truly

T. VANSITTART BOWATER

Memorandum by WSC

9 February 1914 Admiralty

I circulate to the Cabinet the enclosed memorandum on Manning, which has been prepared by Sir John Jellicoe. It is quite true that the depot ships of the flotillas are a large and increasing cause of expense, which could be avoided to great public advantage in efficiency and economy by the provision of proper shore bases. But the capital charge involved having to be met out of annual estimates, and the difficulty of obtaining the necessary funds, have deterred each Board of Admiralty year after year and have forced them to continue more costly makeshifts, the burden of which falls annually and not all at once. I shall submit proposals later in the year for remedying this evil.

Note at top of page:
Not circulated.

[1] Thomas Vansittart Bowater (1862–1938), Lord Mayor of London 1913–14. His family has since provided two other Lord Mayors of London: his brother Sir Frank Henry Bowater, Lord Mayor 1938–9; and Sir Frank's eldest son, Sir Noel Vansittart Bowater, Lord Mayor 1953–4.

Sir John Jellicoe to WSC

7 February 1914   Admiralty

Secret

It appears probable that a comparison between the total personnel of the British and German Fleets may be made by those who are not fully acquainted with all the facts, and, taking the figures for 1913–14, it may be asked why Great Britain requires a personnel of 146,000 as compared to the German total of 73,000 when our Fleet is not double the size of the German Fleet? I have been looking at the matter lately from this point of view, and the following facts which bear on the subject have been brought into prominence and should be borne in mind when considering the question.

I will first of all take the very considerable excess in numbers which we are compelled to maintain on foreign stations as compared to Germany. The British total personnel outside the North Sea is 22,961; that of Germany 8,591. For the purpose of this comparison I have included in the German total one battle cruiser and one light cruiser temporarily attached to the Mediterranean, thus swelling the German figures (perhaps incorrectly) by 1,383, and I have naturally excluded from the German figures the two battleships and the one light cruiser which are temporarily absent on a world-wide cruise. Under the British figures I have excluded every vessel that does not properly speaking belong to a foreign station. I have therefore excluded even the Fourth Battle Squadron. So far as this comparison goes, therefore, the difference shown between the British and the German figures is really less than under normal conditions.

I will now compare the numbers of men and boys who are not available on mobilisation, being under training as recruits. The figures are: —

        For Germany   1,150
        For Great Britain   7,000

the large difference being, of course, due to the fact that practically the whole of our seamen class are entered as boys at a tender age, whereas the number of boys entered for the German Navy bears a very small proportion to the total seaman requirements.

Further, our system of training seamen as boys, and of entering a proportion of our engine-room artificers as boys, necessitates establishments which absorb 1,797 ratings in peace time, a large proportion of which are petty officers who are to some extent redundant on mobilisation, but the whole of whom are a peace requirement, and as such add to our manning difficulties as pointed out by Sir Edward Grey's Committee, a point which will be referred to later.

There is no corresponding demand on German personnel, the staff required for training the small proportion entered as boys being balanced by our requirements for training youths.

Next I will take the numbers of active service ratings that are employed in war in connection with the war-signal stations. The total for Great Britain, 876; Germany, o.

I will now turn to yet another source which swallows up quite a considerable personnel, and which has no counterpart in the German Navy. I allude to the depôt ships for torpedo-boat destroyers and submarines. Excluding the *Hazard* and the *Hebe,* which vessels would be required in any case to act as target-ships for the training of submarine crews, the total peace personnel of the destroyer and submarine depôt ships is 3,544; this number would be increased in war. There is absolutely no counterpart to this requirement in the German Navy, because the German flotillas are based at Kiel and Wilhelmshaven in what may be termed a regular destroyer and submarine dockyard. The crews live in barracks in this miniature dockyard when not embarked. The stores for the destroyers are housed at these bases, and the whole of the casual and annual repairs for the destroyers and submarines and their large refits are carried out at these dockyard bases *and by dockyard workmen.* These small bases are also provided with docks, floating or otherwise, and in fact they are fully equipped with every requirement for the upkeep, maintenance and repair of the destroyers and submarines. In addition to the bases at Kiel and Wilhelmshaven (a second one is being constructed at Kiel) there is a fortified advanced base at Heligoland, which is also completely equipped for dealing with repairs to torpedo-boat destroyers and submarines and which also contains storehouses. The torpedo-boat destroyer harbour itself accommodates twenty-four vessels and affords a perfect 'rest' place for the crews. As against this minute and perfect German organisation we have to depend for all minor repairs and upkeep upon the depôt ships. The same vessels have to take the place of the German storehouses for housing the reserve torpedoes and stores of the vessels, and since we have absolutely no Government repair establishments at this moment in the vicinity of the war stations of our destroyers and submarines, the depôt ships have to be capable of going to sea in order that they may be at the war bases when wanted. The system is obviously a very wasteful one. For annual refits the destroyers have to depend upon the main dockyards, and their requirements are sandwiched in with the refits of larger vessels.

Taking all the figures which I have given up to date, the British total is 36,178 against the German 9,741. The difference between this total is 26,437, which figure should be deducted from the total of Vote (A) for

1913–14 in order to make the British and German personnel comparable. The British total therefore becomes 119,563, as compared with the German total of 73,000, or a superiority of 63 per cent., which would be little more than sufficient to provide crews for a British superiority of 60 per cent. *in all classes of vessels.* Our standard of superiority in numbers far exceeds this figure.

But there are still further considerations which cannot be omitted when dealing with this matter. One which immediately presents itself to the mind is the fact that the coast defence of the British Islands is very largely entrusted to the Navy, the patrol flotillas and a large proportion of our submarines being practically allocated to this service in the absence of fortifications and mine defences. The total personnel thus engaged is 8,734, leaving entirely out of consideration all the crews of torpedo-boats and other vessels allocated to the ordinary port defences, examination services, boom defences, &c., &c. Against this total it would be proper to put the German Seaman Artillery, manning the coast defences, included in their personnel, and totalling 4,102 men. But if this is done a total of 336 Marines should also be added to the British total, as this number of men is engaged in manning the Cromarty Defences.

It is hardly possible to deal with any question of personnel without a consideration of the Reserves. The comparative figures with regard to Reserves are as follows: –

Great Britain has 36,636 Reservists who have served a term in the Navy, with an addition of 16,667 RNR men; a total of 53,303. The RNR men cannot be said to be comparable in efficiency to the remainder, and only a small proportion of them are available on mobilisation.

Germany has a total of between 68,000 and 80,000 Reservists, all immediately available, and all of whom have been trained in the fleet for three years. The former figure is in accordance with information in the Intelligence Department, but the latter figure was stated by Admiral von Tirpitz in 1913 to be the number of Reservists that would be available on mobilisation.

The efficiency of Reservists must naturally depend upon two factors: –

(*a.*) The length of their previous training in the Fleet;

(*b.*) The time that has elapsed since they left the Fleet.

In regard to (*a*), the advantage lies, of course, with Great Britain on account of our long-service system, but Germany has a considerable advantage under the heading (*b*). A comparison, for instance, of the number of Reservists who joined the Reserve in 1912 shows the German figures as being –

6,800 seamen,
4,800 stokers;

whilst the British figures were –
  2,656 seamen and Marines and
  2,460 stokers.
This means that Germany, in comparison with this country, has about three times as many seamen and twice as many stokers who have only recently left the sea for the Reserve.

Before leaving the subject of Reservists it is as well to note the facility with which Germany can, at any moment, increase the personnel of her Fleet without issuing any proclamation or taking any steps which would indicate to foreign countries the fact that the Reserves are being drawn upon. In October of last year, when the freshly-joined stoker recruits were called up for service in the High Sea Fleet, they were actually replaced in these ships during the period of about five weeks in which they were undergoing their infantry training ashore, before being drafted, by Reserve men specially called in. These men were called up for service by the authorities of the Naval Depôts making a demand for their services upon the Army Corps District Authorities direct. The Secretary of State for the Navy decides annually the number of Reserve men that he desires shall be called in during the year to perform their obligatory drills. Our small 'Immediate Reserve' is the only force which we can draw upon in an emergency.

As showing further that the British Fleet is not in any way manned on an extravagant basis as compared to the German Fleet, a comparison is now given between the complements of certain ships of approximately the same date of construction belonging to each country: –

British	Tonnage	Complement	German	Tonnage	Complement
King George V ..	23,000	774	*Kaiserin* ..	24,310	1,079
Benbow	25,000	882	*Konig* ..	26,500	1,110
Tiger	28,500	1,102	*Seydlitz* ..	24,610	1,108

A further matter of interest in connection with manning requirements of the Fleet is the question as to whether the numbers for Vote (A) should be based upon peace or war requirements. In many cases, more particularly in the seaman class, the peace requirements are very much greater than the war requirements, on account of the absolute necessity of providing a sufficient numbers of boys under training to produce the future trained seamen required in the Fleet. Until quite recently the practice at the Admiralty has been to base our numbers upon the war requirements. The result has been that an insufficient number of boys has been entered in past years to produce the trained seamen required to man the Fleet of 1914–15, 1915–16, and

1916–17. That is one of the principal reasons why it is now necessary to make up for the lost time by entering boys up to our full training facilities. This point was urged very strongly by Sir Edward Grey's Committee in 1902, although no attention was paid to their recommendations in this respect. In paragraph 48 of their report, the Committee state that they 'are of opinion that efficiency and economy both demand that full active service numbers for peace needs should be maintained.' In paragraph 222 of their report they lay further emphasis on this point by saying that they 'wish to emphasise the fact that it is the number of men required for the peace needs of the navy which makes it impossible to recommend a reduction of the active service vote. By the phrase 'peace needs of the navy' is meant, speaking generally, the manning of the proportion of ships commissioned in time of peace and their relief crews, the care and maintenance of the ships in reserve, without which they would rapidly deteriorate, and the instruction of men and boys under training. No amount of increase of reserve men can appreciably affect the performance of these duties.'

What was true in 1902 is equally true at this moment.

JRJ

WSC to Lady Randolph

EXTRACT

10 February 1914   Admiralty

Dearest Mama,

I think the naval estimates are now past the danger point & if so the situation will be satisfactory. But it has been a long and wearing business wh has caused me at times vy gt perplexity. . . .

WSC to Prince Louis of Battenberg

13 February 1914   Admiralty

Confidential

Copy

My dear Prince Louis,

I hope that an agreement will be reached this morning at the Board on the outstanding points. The position is that the Cabinet have decided that the Cruiser programme should not exceed 4 vessels and have expressed a wish that the increase of men should be reduced from 5,000 to 4,000. I have not given my final adhesion to either proposal but, having some information on these subjects, I am bound to say that I consider both propositions reasonable. So far as manning is concerned I am not and have not for some time been satisfied that a sufficient effort has been made to reduce requirements which are of small military consequence or to maintain a proper flow of older vessels to the Third Fleet and to the Material Reserve. This subject will require detailed examination during the next few months. If you or your naval colleagues are not contented with the Estimates for which the Government propose to ask Parliament, I should be willing – though I should regret the change – to relieve the Board of the duty of signing them and to present them to the House of Commons as the Army Estimates are presented upon the sole responsibility of the Minister. This is a step which has been very strongly pressed upon me during the last 2 years, and I have on several occasions resisted it with difficulty.

I could not help being disappointed by the reception which was given to the great and successful exertions I have made on behalf of the Navy and to the immense and unexampled provisions which the Government have determined to make for the service of the year. As one of my predecessors said 'I represent the Board of Admiralty to Parliament and I represent Parliament to the Board of Admiralty.' I hope indeed that I may continue to enjoy your aid and support in both duties.

Yours very sincerely

[WINSTON S. CHURCHILL]

Cabinet Notes
(*Lloyd George Papers*)

1 July 1914   10 Downing Street

LLOYD GEORGE: Philip Snowden in his weekly letter today says that had there been any other Chancellor of the Exchequer your Naval Bill would have been cut by millions.

WSC: There would also have been another First Lord of the Admiralty! And who can say – if such gaps were opened – that there would not have been another Government – which does not necessarily mean lower estimates.

24

Air

(See Main Volume II pp. 687–704)

Report of the CID Sub-Committee on Aerial Navigation
(Asquith Papers)

25 February 1909

Mr C. S. Rolls[1] had purchased a 'Wright' aeroplane, and hoped that the Government would give him facilities for experimenting with it on Government ground. He also offered his services to the Govt in the event of their wishing to benefit by the experience that he gained.
[Esher & Haldane agreed to this.]
Mr Churchill thought that there was a danger of these proposals being considered too amateurish. The problem of the use of aeroplanes was a most important one, and we should place ourselves in communication with Mr Wright[2] himself, and avail ourselves of his knowledge.

Sir Charles Ottley to WSC

3 November 1911   Committee of Imperial Defence

Dear Mr Churchill,

I have now seen Sir R. Chalmers of the Treasury, who is of the opinion that a combined (Naval & Military) School of aviation would be better than two distinct schools, one naval, the other military. I have told Sir

---

[1] Charles Stewart Rolls (1877–1910), pioneer motorist, airman, balloonist, and racing car driver. Drove motor cars before the abolition of the 'red flag' regulation. Technical Managing Director of Rolls-Royce Limited. Killed in a landing accident at the Bournemouth Aviation Meeting 1910.

[2] Orville Wright (1871–1948), pioneer aviator who, with his brother Wilbur, was the first to fly a heavier-than-air machine. This flight took place at Kittyhawk, North Carolina, on 17 December 1903.

Robert that a sub ctee was to [be] assembled shortly to discuss the details of this scheme, and he will be very glad to be the Treasury Representative.

> Yours very sincerely
> C. L. OTTLEY

Lord Fisher to WSC
EXTRACT

10 November 1911

... *Aviation* supersedes small cruisers & Intelligence vessels. You told me you would push *aviation* – you are right – but don't take away our splendid young Naval Officers who have been suckled on Gunnery and sea fighting to do what civilians can do better. The civilian air-man can always carry an expert for observing.

Jack Seely to WSC

17 April 1912   House of Commons

My dear Winston,
    You wrote me a private note asking that Naval Officers should be taught the initial stages (as well as the later stages) of flying at the Central Flying School.
    We will certainly arrange for this to be done.

> Yours sincerely
> J. SEELY

Sir Edward Grey to WSC

26 July 1912   Foreign Office

Dear Churchill,
    The CID have produced a most alarming report of a Sub-Committee on Aerial Navigation. I suppose it has been brought to your notice and I only send this note '*ex abundante cautela*'[1] (I know you like Latin).

> Yours sincerely
> E. GREY

WSC to Sir Robert Chalmers

24 August 1912

My dear Chalmers,
    I am much surprised to get a third refusal from the Treasury on the subject of the Air Department at the Admiralty.

---

[1] 'Out of abundance of caution'.

I had rather hoped from our talk the other day that your objections were removed. I could not be responsible for the conduct of Admiralty business unless this most vital subject of naval aeronautics received the attention and study it requires.

The organisation proposed is absolutely necessary and is already in being. It is most modest in scale and I should certainly not agree to its being broken up. I am very much distressed by these repeated refusals of the Treasury, which are injurious to the public service.

Memorandum by WSC

EXTRACT

1 September 1912

Magazines. I visited Crombie yesterday and am wholly dissatisfied with the arrangements for securing the magazines from overhead attack. It appears to me that it would be quite easy in the course of the next few years for an Aeroplane Depot Ship to come within a certain distance of our coasts and launch a number of aircraft which could easily drop bombs capable of detonating on enormous stores of cordite to be assembled at these magazines. There may be arguments against converting old magazines so as to protect them from aerial attack, but there can be none against building new magazines with such protection.

No further progress is to be made or more money spent on the existing pattern, except in regard to the magazines already definitely commenced. I am told that 2 have not yet been commenced of the old lot, and that 3 new ones have been sanctioned. All these 5 are to be protected against aerial attack.

A small technical committee should be appointed at once to advise what structural methods should be employed. It is clear that two methods should be employed simultaneously. First, actual protection by means either of excavations or of earth and concrete roofs of sufficient strength together perhaps with wire netting at a suitable height, and secondly concealment and deception; concealment by means of trees, shrubs, and rapidly growing creepers; deception by means of a certain number of make-believe canvas houses like magazines which could be folded up and stored away until a period of war begins and which could then be brought out and erected in such a way as to mislead an aerial attack. There should be no difficulty about this and the cost should be small.

Aerial guns are also to be planted in good positions where they can command the magazines against overhead attacks.

Hugh Watson to Edward Marsh

EXTRACT

6 December 1912   British Embassy
                                                          Berlin

Dear Marsh,

These airships are becoming a habit in Germany. Yesterday I saw over the Golf Links, first the new Naval Zeppelin going at a fine pace (weather perfect). As she was turning I could not estimate speed well, she was making a tremendous noise but I fancy they were forcing her. Ten minutes after her one of the newer Parsevals appeared, seeming to follow hard on the Zeppelin's tracks, it looked as if they were having a point-to-point Race. The Parseval was slipping along too.

Half an hour after, the Passenger Zeppelin *Hansa* came over from Potsdam, she was moving more steadily than the naval Zeppelin I thought, not so fast, but less noise.

She, I see by the papers this morning, practised sitting on the Wannsee this morning. We did it last year in the Zeppelin I went up in.

The weather is splendid, and it looks as if it would be like last year, lots of flying done by airships near Berlin about this time.

It seems to me it would be almost worth our airships experts' while running over here now to spend a week in Berlin and watch these 3 ships flying, and book another passenger flight in the Zeppelin passenger Ship.

If the Zeppelins and Parsevals only did their flights in fine weather their danger wd not be great; but the more I hear from practical and previously scornful German naval officers of the Zeppelin *Victoria Luise*'s flight over the Fleet at the Emperor's last Sept Review near Heligoland, when the ship got out of its shed at Hamburg and flew to the Fleet in the teeth of a strong NW wind of force 6, the more I am impressed by their powers.

I suppose we are getting on as fast as we can, but we have lost a lot of ground I fear, and the attitude of the Germans is certainly triumphant.

Where Germany has scored her lead is not so much in the Government's development of the subject, as in the patriotic action of big firms and individuals in doing experimental work, of course in the hopes of reward later – governmentally probably, not commercially, and so provoking competition; also what has helped greatly is the Royal and governmental support of such patriotic action of [sic] the movement towards getting a National Fund for Zeppelins and later towards a Fund for the general development of aircraft. Now talk is of an 'Air Fleet Law'.

It's the old old story, German's desire for '*Verein*'s etc versus England's individual efforts; too many cooks with us, & combined enterprise with the Germans.

As regards other Naval matters, affairs are very quiet and likely to remain so until after Christmas, and we get the Est^es Debates coming on. You can't disturb Germany preparing for its Christmas! . . .

> Yours sincerely
> HUGH WATSON

Hugh Watson to Edward Marsh

16 December 1912   British Embassy
                                                         Berlin

Dear Marsh,

Various Press articles inveighing against the sale of a German airship to England, emanating of course from Pan-German sources, have appeared in the last few days.

My Chief here agrees it wd be well you at home shd know this, in case the negotiations are not absolutely completed, before such articles may have any effect in Germany.

Am writing official letter next Bag, but in view of approach of Christmas send you this note first to avoid delay of waiting for Bag etc.

> Yours sincerely
> HUGH WATSON

Note by WSC
DAD
What is the actual position about the purchase?   WSC
                                                                   19.12

Captain Murray F. Sueter[1] to WSC

20 December 1912   Admiralty

1st Lord
   Submitted

The Parseval airship was ordered in middle of last month. The Firm will deliver her by March 31st 1913. The order was placed through Messrs Vickers. There are no outstanding points with Vickers or Parseval Co.

As material is delivered it will be inspected, but as yet no answer has been received giving the German Governments permission for our Inspecting Officers to visit Germany to watch progress of construction, attend trials &c.

Nothing is being delayed, but we must get permission soon.

MURRAY F. SUETER

WSC to ?

26 February 1913

Copy

I want you to write a short note to the Prime Minister and tell him the serious view you take about the air. I am sure it would do a lot of good. It is all the more important as you are not, I fear, going to be in England for the Estimates, when you would naturally have made some public reference. Although I have not been refused anything that I have asked for, and although the proposals we are making for the year amount very possibly to all the money we should be able wisely to spend in the year, yet it makes a tremendous difference to have a good atmosphere on such a subject. You know how the Prime Minister or the Chancellor of the Exchequer has to be sceptical of all the alarmist projects of the military departments; and I could see that Sir Arthur Wilson's stubborn and well-argued disparagement of airship's capacities made a great impression on them at the Committee of Imperial Defence.

---

[1] Murray Fraser Sueter (1872–1960), Director of Air Department 1911–15; pioneer aviator; created Royal Naval Air Service and anti-aircraft Corps for London; one of developers of armoured tank; of torpedo airplanes; of Empire air-mail service; Conservative MP for Hertford 1921–45; Rear Admiral 1920; knighted 1934.

Lord Northcliffe to WSC

10 March 1913   Hotel Majestic
                                                            Paris

My dear WSC,

Would you kindly read these hasty notes of the opinion of a man who is probably the best living expert on the subject, and show them to Colonel Seely? They entirely confirm what I myself learned in Germany on my last visit and completely accord with my own views. Incidentally Orville Wright used almost your own words. He said, 'provided a sufficient number of dirigibles were employed, they might cause annoyance and perhaps some little damage.'

This week I am seeing Santos-Dumont[1] and the Comte de Lambert,[2] the inventor of the hydro-aeroplane.

                                                        Yrs vy sincy
                                                        NORTHCLIFFE

Duke of Marlborough to WSC

12 March 1913   15 Great College Street

EXTRACT

My dear Winston,

I do not suppose that I shall get the chance of writing you many more letters if you continue your journeys in the Air. Really I consider that you owe it to your wife family and friends to desist from a practise or pastime – whichever you call it – which is fraught with so much danger to life. It is really wrong of you. . . .

Note by WSC:

I want to see him. Will he lunch?

[1] Alberto Santos-Dumont (1873–1932), Brazilian aircraft designer; developed a navigable balloon.
[2] Comte Charles de Lambert (1865–   ), pioneer aviator. In 1909 flew from Juvisy to Paris, around the Eiffel Tower and back, in Wright airplane in 49 minutes.

WSC to H. H. Asquith

12 June 1913

Copy

Prime Minister,

I am becoming increasingly anxious about the delay in reaching a decision on the new Air Programme. We are already so far behind other countries, that we cannot afford to allow more time to slip away. We must begin the construction of at least two Zeppelins in this country so that the art of making them at any rate is not wholly unknown to us. We must further acquire several more smaller airships of the non-rigid type in order to train and develop a personnel which can handle airships, and enable us to form a true opinion of their use and value. These measures will not, it is true, give us an air fleet comparable to those possessed by France and Germany: all they will do is to put us in a position next year to make a substantial advance in this new service if the changed conditions and developments warrant or require it. If we do not begin now, we shall next year find ourselves in a helpless position, hopelessly behind everyone else, and with a long period of experimental and preparatory work between us and any effective power in this new arm. I would therefore ask that either on Tuesday or on Thursday next I may be permitted to raise this subject in the Committee of Imperial Defence now dealing with Invasion; and that for this purpose, if you assent, Sir John Jellicoe may be allowed to attend on the day selected by you.

WSC to Sir John Jellicoe

14 August 1913

I am convinced that it is necessary to authorise and organise the direct entry of civilian flyers to the Naval Air Wing. The maximum age should, I think, be higher than 22. I apprehend that the numbers will not be forthcoming unless the age is raised to, say, 24. It is necessary to offer to a man who will give you ten years flying either (*a*) a pension or a lump sum or (*b*) permanent employment. I cannot doubt that a competent naval flyer who has lived for eight or ten years with naval officers in continual contact with machinery could at the end of his flying period be usefully fitted into some part or branch of the varied and complicated establishments under the Admiralty directions. It is not thought that the numbers would be very large, but every man expects, and has a right to expect, at the end of ten years of risk, or perhaps even at the end of five years, to see his way clear to permanent professional employment. I would reserve specially for this class of naval airman a share of certain appointments both afloat and ashore. Others should be encouraged to fit themselves for regular transference to the regular Navy, like the RNR Lieutenant. Your proposals are novel, but they are forced upon us in one form or another by the progress of science. I am strongly of opinion that the best and truest method of getting really good young men for this peculiar service would be by the personal exertions of the existing members of the Naval Wing. The officers should be invited to bring up names very much as if it were a club, and these names when recommended by a Committee of the Naval Wing should be submitted for Admiralty approval. We need not worry too much about educational tests. What is wanted for this dangerous service is a young gentleman and a good animal.

WSC to Captain William Pakenham[1]

September 1913

The question of what career is to be offered to officers of the Aeroplane Service should engage your attention. The control of aeroplanes is directly personal, and requires a quickness of hand and mind inseparably associated with athletic youth. It seems unlikely that senior officers will be required for or suited to the work of pilots, and we ought not to expect at present that any officer, however young, will continue to fly an aeroplane for more than from three to five years. Officers of the Aeroplane Service who continue to specialise in aeronautics must therefore look forward to the Airship Service as the second phase in their career. The qualities required for navigating airships are of quite a different character from those for flying aeroplanes. Courage, resolution, experience, seamanship, scientific knowledge, are all required and can all be found in officers in the prime of life, and the transition from the Aeroplane to the Airship Section should be a natural progression. In the near future direct entry of naval officers into the Airship Section should be stopped, and they should begin to draw from the aeroplanes. Aeroplane officers should be encouraged to study regularly everything connected with aeronautics, including airships, and should be trained, even while in the Aeroplane Section, in airship work. Most of the men now engaged in airships have every intention of returning to the sea, and are looking for commands afloat. But many of the aeroplane officers will never return to the ordinary sea service, or have never received the regular training of naval officers which would fit them for naval command.

[1] Fourth Sea Lord.

WSC to Sir John Jellicoe

27 September 1913

The principle to be adopted in regard to seaplanes should be as follows: – The number of machines must be such as to enable the war establishment to be continually maintained intact. If we aim at a war establishment of 100 machines, we should apparently require at least 150 or 160 to realise this. It is not necessary, however, to reach it in the first or second year. Machines should be divided into (a) war establishment and (b) machines available for practice. These machines are of course, interchangeable.

WSC flew in a Naval Hydroplane at Cromarty Firth on 6 October 1913. He was watched by the Prime Minister and Jack Seely. According to the *Daily Sketch* of 7 October 1913, 'He went for quite a long flight.'

WSC to his wife
(*CSC Papers*)

23 October 1913   Sheerness

Darling,

We have had a very jolly day in the air. First we all went over to East-church where we found dozens of aeroplanes, & everyone flew – Ivor, Masterton, Sir Ian, Grigg,[1] Halifax,[2] Greenly & me. I let the military & naval officers fly across the river with me to our other air stations in the Isle of Grain – a delightful trip on wh I was conducted by the redoubtable Samson.[3] Here we found another large flock of sea planes in the highest state of activity. Just as we arrived & landed, the Astra-Torres airship, wh I had sent for from Farnborough, arrived, and the Generals & I went in her for a beautiful cruise at about 1000 feet all round Chatham & the Medway. She is a vy satisfactory vessel, and so easy to manage that they let me steer her for a whole hour myself. Then after luncheon more sea planes, & I have

---

[1] Edward William Macleay Grigg (1879–1955), Editorial staff of *The Times* 1908–13; served with Grenadier Guards in World War One; National Liberal MP, Oldham, 1922–5; Conservative MP, Altrincham 1933–45; Governor and C-in-C, Kenya, 1925–31; Joint Parliamentary Under-Secretary for War 1940–2; Minister Resident in the Middle East 1944–5; knighted 1920; PC 1944; created Baron Altrincham 1945.

[2] Charles Lindley Wood (1839–1934), President of the English Church Union 1869–1919; author of *Lord Halifax's Ghost Book*; succeeded his father as 2nd Viscount Halifax, 1885.

[3] Charles Rumney Samson (1883–1931), Pioneer aviator; took his certificate as Air Pilot 1911; carried out first sea-plane experiments, first cross-country night flights and first ascent from the deck of a warship while steaming; Group Captain RAF 1919; Air Commodore 1922.

finished the day by inspecting Sheerness dockyard. It has been as good as one of those old days in the S. African war, & I have lived entirely in the moment, with no care for all those tiresome party politics & searching newspapers, & awkward by-elections, & sulky orangemen, & obnoxious Cecils & little smugs like Runciman.

For good luck before I started I put your locket on. It has been lying in my desk since it got bent – & as usual worked like a charm.

All the birds are coming to dinner to-night. You may imagine how pleased the others were to have the chance of losing their aethereal virginities!

It is vy satisfactory to find such signs of progress in every branch of the Naval air service. In another year – if I am spared ministerially – there will be a gt development. When I have pumped in another million the whole thing will be alive & on the wing.

The Mr Short who makes the bi-planes has got a deformed head 4 times as big as any other head you have ever seen in the world – outside panto-mime. He is a good man, but terrible to look at. He is married & his children are developing the same disease. Ivor has left me – much pleased with his flight.

How are the chickens! The world will be a vy interesting place for them when they are grown up. Good night my darling, fondest love from your devoted husband

W

WSC to Director of Works

7 November 1913

You are to ascertain and report without delay what internal alterations are necessary to make the Coast-Guard stations at –
    Calshot (Warsash),
    Grain Island,
    Felixstowe,
    Yarmouth,
suitable for accommodating the officers and men of the air stations. Only alterations that are absolutely necessary to be considered. Suitable accommodation for forming a small officers' mess is to be provided.

WSC to Sir John Jellicoe and Captain Murray Sueter[1]

12 November 1913

Although the establishment of seaplane bases along the south and east coasts is necessary on strategic grounds, and their erection must proceed

[1] Director of Air Department.

without hindrance, I do not consider it desirable at present to occupy and man them all. Neither our personnel nor our machines are numerous enough for this, and the scattering of officers and seaplanes by detachments of twos or threes is not beneficial either to discipline or efficiency. The occupation of bases which are in an unfinished condition by officers and men leads to heavy expense to them and to considerable inconvenience. It would appear that not more than four bases (including the experimental bases) for seaplanes should be occupied in the current year. At these all available personnel and machines should be concentrated. The construction and equipment of the others should proceed in the regular way, and no attempt should be made to occupy them till they are completed. At the four occupied bases steps should be taken to house the personnel. There should be a minimum of eight or ten officers at each occupied base. It is desirable that regular messes should be formed at which the officers dine in uniform, and where the tariff does not exceed service standards. The Coast-Guard premises in the neighbourhood of air stations, if not required for wireless purposes, should be appropriated to the air service, the responsibility for dealing with wrecks being accepted by the air detachments. Provision should be made at the established messes for the entertainment of officers arriving on duty. Officers of the Navy and Army arriving at the air bases should sign chits for what they receive and should pay their own mess bills. Civilians arriving from the manufacturers of aeroplanes, from the Central Air Factory, or from abroad, should be entertained according to the regular scale of the mess, the cost being afterwards recovered, in approved cases, from the Admiralty. I have reason to believe that the present system throws a wholly unjustifiable strain on the resources of the commanding officers of several of the stations. The bases on which we should concentrate appear to be: –

1. Fort George, under Lieutenant Longmore,[1] into which the personnel from the Firth of Forth base should be thrown.
2. Harwich and Yarmouth – Harwich preferred – should be thrown together under Lieutenant Gregory.
3. The Isle of Grain; and
4. Calshot.

We have arranged with the Army about Fort George, and at the other three Coast-Guard accommodation is available. I wish to receive proposals for utilising this accommodation and for making it available in the shortest possible time. This is especially the case at Calshot and the Isle of Grain.

[1] Arthur Murray Longmore (b. 1885), entered the RN 1900; with Royal Naval Air Service in France and the RAF in Italy; Director of Equipment, Air Ministry, 1925–9; Air Officer Commanding Inland Area 1933–4; Coastal Command 1934–6; AOC-in-C, Middle East, 1939–41; retired 1942; knighted 1935.

When and if the details of transference are arranged, I am prepared to give special instructions to the Director of Works, which will secure the immediate execution of any alterations which may be required.

As soon as the weather becomes warm, probably at the beginning of May, all the seaplanes and officers of the Naval Wing should be concentrated at the Isle of Grain for two or three months' summer exercises. The advantage to discipline of congregating officers and men of such a service in considerable numbers is obvious. Very valuable experiments and exercises can also be carried out both by aeroplanes from Eastchurch and seaplanes at the Isle of Grain. The Isle of Grain should, it would appear, become our principal seaplane base, and there, during the summer months, practically all the flying officers should be assembled and a regular routine should be observed. Temporary hangars and tents may be required in the first year; but a good mess should be started without delay, and during the concentration for exercises a band should be provided and everything done to foster cohesion, unity, and *esprit de corps* in this new service.

Pray give me your views on these points and indicate what steps you consider desirable.

WSC to Sir John Jellicoe

12 November 1913

Without committing myself to details, I am in full accord with the general scope and scale of the air provision which you seek to make in next year's Estimates. It is, however, necessary, that the case for maintaining the Naval Air Service shall be thoroughly established for the satisfaction of the Cabinet. In your paper written earlier in the year, there are various comparisons between our airship and aeroplane provision, actual and prospective, with those of foreign countries. It would appear that these comparisons and the arguments founded upon them should be brought up to date. Stress should also be laid upon the ease with which Germany, for instance, could utilise the military aircraft, in which she has so great a preponderance, to supplement her naval air service. The other part of the argument which should be developed is the actual need and specific services for which the various aeroplanes and airships built, building, and asked for by the Naval Wing are required. The indispensable need of the Air Stations along the coast, in conjunction with the work of the patrol flotillas and coast defences generally; the protection of naval vulnerable points near the sea, magazines, locks, oil stores, &c., the tactical functions of seaplanes, and airships with the sea-going fleet; should all receive some notice in a form not too technical for ordinary consumption. The actual requirements should be explained first; and secondly the relative provision of foreign countries.

I should be glad if you will either prepare this with your own hand or give directions which will enable others to do it. Four or five printed pages should be the limit so far as length is concerned. I should be glad if this could be put in train before you proceed on leave, as during that week it is quite possible discussions on the Naval Estimates by the Cabinet may begin, and I require to be fully armed.

You will note that on other papers I have communicated that I am prepared to make additional provision either by taking over and adapting the Coast-Guard buildings, or by other means, for the proper housing and accommodation of the officers and men. Provision for this should be included in the Estimate; though as the matter is urgent, it may not be possible to present full details at this stage.

Lord Roberts to WSC

1 December 1913   Englemere
                                                            Berks

Dear Churchill,

I must ask you to forgive my approaching you on a subject which is causing me very great uneasiness of mind and anxiety, *viz*, the report that it is proposed to transfer the Airships with their officers and men from the Army wing of the Royal Flying Corps to the Navy.

I have taken the greatest possible interest in the initiation of and all subsequent improvements in our Air Service, and after careful reflection I have come to the decided opinion that this proposed transfer would be a retrograde step, and one which would seriously damage our military efficiency.

Stated briefly, my reasons for coming to this conclusion are as follows: –

The obvious policy as to the sphere of usefulness of the two wings, naval and military, is for the Navy to be responsible for operations over the sea and the Army for those over the land, and possibly for those in conjunction with land defences, though this latter point may be arguable.

Any justification – so it seems to me – for departing from this broad demarcation of responsibility and for taking airships away from the Army would only seem possible for one of two reasons. Either that Naval personnel can handle airships better than Army personnel, or that airships will not be wanted in connection with land warfare.

Now I do not think that there can be any doubt as to the necessity for our land forces being provided with airships in addition to aeroplanes. To begin with, all the Continental Powers are furnishing themselves with airships for land warfare, and aeroplanes would not suffice to deal with these.

Secondly for purposes of reconnaissances the airship is the necessary complement of the aeroplane. The airship can remain in observation, the aeroplane cannot. The airship is eminently suitable for night work, the aeroplane is equally unsuitable and so forth. If this be granted, we come to the question as to whether the Army or Navy can best handle the airships required for co-operation with land forces. On this point I submit that there can be no doubt. To reach the necessary degree of efficiency and to ensure perfect co-operation, the crews will require never-ceasing military training in peace. Without this they must be so severely handicapped as to be comparatively useless in war. It is not only the question of the difference in terrain and objectives, though these are of the greatest importance, there is the further question of the necessity of perfecting our land organisation and methods of administration in connection with the airship service. If these do not exist in peace, they must be improvised for war, and experience teaches us the bitter results that may be expected from such improvisation.

It may further be urged that if the military authorities are given no opportunity to obtain practice in the employment of airships, they cannot be expected to know how to make the best use of them in war.

In short, differing as the naval airship service must from the military as regards methods of training, observation, organisation and administration, it appears to me to be wholly illogical to merge the two services into one for the sole reason that the same machine is employed by both – it would seem almost equally reasonable to expect a naval and a field gunner to be interchangeable.

In conclusion I would suggest that there are strong moral objections to the proposed transfer. In a short life of strenuous endeavour the military wing of the Flying Corps has already built up a feeling of *esprit de corps* and has achieved notable success. It cannot but have a profoundly discouraging effect at this moment for them to receive this blow, as it will most assuredly be considered.

It is for the above reasons that I urge upon you the necessity for reconsidering the question, which is one of the highest importance and which should transcend considerations of mere financial convenience.

Believe me, Yours sincerely

ROBERTS

WSC to Lord Roberts

4 December 1913

Copy

Confidential

The transference of the Army Airships to the Naval Wing has been decided on and is now practically complete, and it will not now be possible to reconsider it. The objections which are stated by you with so much force were not overlooked when the policy was settled. Most of them have, in my opinion, been met and any balance is more than compensated for by the avoidance of duplication of organisation and experimental work, which the new arrangement will secure. The actual change is less far-reaching than might be supposed, because the Royal Flying Corps is itself one body to the general efficiency and development of which both the War Office and the Admiralty will contribute in the closest co-operation through the Naval and Military Wings. The Admiralty have accepted the obligation of maintaining in a proper state of training and efficiency such airships as are found to be needed for the land service.

*　　*　　*　　*　　*

Captain G. Wildman-Lushington RN[1] to Miss Airlie Hynes
(Airlie Madden Papers)

EXTRACT

30 November 1913　　　　　　　　　　　　　　RN Flying School
　　　　　　　　　　　　　　　　　　　　　　　Eastchurch

Darling loved one,

Yesterday turned out to be quite a strenuous day for us, the First Lord and his coterie arrived about noon. We had 17 machines out & besides that there were three private machines, the Dunne, Mr Ogilvy's & Professor Huntingdon's, the air seemed absolutely thick and congested. I started Winston off on his instruction about 12.15 & he got so bitten with it, I could hardly get him out of the machine, in fact except for about ¾ hour for lunch we were in the machine till about 3.30. He showed great promise, & is coming down again for further instruction & practice. I think I did myself quite a lot of good.

---

[1] Gilbert Wildman-Lushington (?–1913), Captain in the Royal Marines who began teaching WSC to fly in 1913. He was killed on 2 December 1913 when his plane crashed while coming in to land. Miss Airlie Hynes was his fiancée – she married Major J. G. Madden in 1918.

I went & dined on board the *Enchantress* last night and sat on the right of
WC. He was absolutely full out and talked hard about what he was going to
do. Before lunch he came up to my cabin to wash his hands & took a great
interest in the photos I have there, he asked me when it was coming off, & I
said when I'd saved some money. We sent a machine over to Whitstable for
oysters for lunch, but they didn't arrive till too late, so I took them on board
as a birthday present from the mess for WC, who is 39 to-day. I've never
had such a day in my life. I was quite tired when we did eventually get back
to bed last night. Courtney,[1] Davis[2] & Clark-Hall[3] also were dining on board.
I hardly expected a letter from you. . . .

WSC to Captain G. Wildman-Lushington
(*Airlie Madden Papers*)

30 November 1913   Admiralty

Dear Captain Lushington,
    I wish you would clear up the question of the steering control and let me
know what was the real difficulty I had in making the rudder act. Probably
the explanation is that I was pushing against myself, though I am not quite
sure about this. It may be that they are very stiff and hard to work. Certainly
the feeling I had was that I was being repeatedly over-ridden, and I thought
you were controlling the steering almost the whole time. Could you not go up
with another flying officer and, sitting yourself in the back seat, see whether
there is great stiffness and difficulty in steering, or whether it was all my
clumsiness.

Yours sincerely
WINSTON S. CHURCHILL

WSC to Captain Murray Sueter

2 December 1913

    I should be glad if one of the Sopwith biplanes at Eastchurch could be
fitted with dual controls of exact equality (*ie* without over-riding power),

[1] Christopher Lloyd Courtney (b. 1890), Flying Officer in RNAS 1912–18; transferred to
RAF 1918; served between the wars in Middle East; Member of Air Council 1940–5; Air
Chief Marshal 1945; knighted 1939.
[2] Edward Derek Davis (b. 1895), served in Royal Armoured Car Division and RNAS
during First World War; commissioned in RAF 1919; air armament expert Air Ministry,
Armament Research and Development 1936–9; Command Armament Officer, Bomber
Command 1940–1; on Ordnance Board 1941–2. Air Vice-Marshal 1946.
[3] Robert Hamilton Clark-Hall (1883–1964), Commander Royal Naval Air Station 1914;
Experimental Air Armament Staff of RNAS 1913–14; Fleet Aviation Officer, Grand Fleet,
1918–19; Air Marshal 1933; knighted 1934.

and if the engine switches, gauges, &c, were duplicated too. This machine would be useful for long distance flying and enable one pilot to relieve the other.

Pray let me have an estimate of the time the work would take to execute and the cost involved.

Captain G. Wildman-Lushington to WSC
(*Airlie Madden Papers*)

2 December 1913   RN Flying School
Eastchurch

Dear Mr Churchill,

In reply to yours of November 30th I have, as you suggested, flown No 2 from the passenger seat. The rudders being unbalanced are slightly heavy, but this is usually considered a good fault for a purely instructional machine, as the pupil is not so likely to get into difficulties. This natural heaviness is not however sufficient to cause the great difficulty you found in steering. I believe you fell into a very common error of beginners, & even of experienced pilots too, of pushing against yourself. I ought to have warned you of the possibility of your doing so, before taking you up. These little faults rectify themselves in time, and as you continue with your instruction, other little errors will continually be arising which you will find out for yourself. Mistakes like this in flying are really all part of the instruction, as a pupil thereby rectifies his own faults. As an instructor, I prefer the pupil to find out these difficulties himself.

Yours sincerely
G. WILDMAN-LUSHINGTON

WSC to Miss Airlie Hynes
(*Airlie Madden Papers*)

7 December 1913   Admiralty

Private

Dear Miss Hynes,

This letter was written to me by Captain Wildman-Lushington on the morning of the second of December. Before it reached me he was dead.

I think you ought to have it; and may I ask you also to accept my deepest sympathy in the blow wh has fallen upon you.

To be killed instantly without pain or fear in the necessary service of the country when one is quite happy and life is full of success & hope, cannot be reckoned the worst of fortune. But to some who are left behind the loss is terrible.

Yours vy tly
WINSTON S. CHURCHILL

Manchester Guardian

3 December 1913

The death of Captain Lushington at Eastchurch yesterday is the first fatal accident in flight which has befallen the Naval Air Service . . .

The accident overshadows the interest of the First Lord of the Admiralty's trip yesterday. It has always been Mr Churchill's way to be in the forefront of adventure, and we need not be surprised at his desire to become a qualified airman, though it ought to be remembered that the duty of the civil, as of the military, head of a fighting force is not to take unnecessary risks. It would surprise no one interested in aviation if Mr Churchill were to become not only a certificated pilot but – what is a very different thing – an airman of great skill and a big reputation. The qualities which make for success in this newest and most difficult form of sport and adventure differ only in degree from those which give eminence in other kinds. Those who read Mr Churchill's speeches or hear him on the platform are apt to forget that he has also made himself eminent in battle, on the polo ground, and in the hunting field. The gifts of coolness, courage and quickness of resource which help to make the successful soldier and war correspondent, polo player, and rider to the hounds are precisely those which tell in the air. Mr Churchill has already been using them, apparently, while the country thought he was merely exercising the privilege of a First Lord to go as a passenger in every kind of naval craft. After the deplorable accident to the man who taught him yesterday we hope he will add to the physical courage which is so strikingly his characteristic the moral courage to take no needless risks.

East Anglian Daily Times

3 December 1913

Captain Wildman-Lushington, Flight Commander of the Naval Wing of the Royal Flying Corps, who was killed while flying at Eastchurch to-day, was one of the most skilful, and at the same time most courageous, aviators in the Navy. Hitherto the Naval Wing has suffered less than the Army Wing of the Flying Corps in the matter of fatal accidents. The death of Captain Lushington is a blow to the Navy. It will be a great grief to Mr Winston Churchill, the First Lord of the Admiralty. It was only on Saturday that

Captain Lushington piloted Mr Winston Churchill in the self-same machine which to-day led to his destruction.

It is a very sad and curious significance that Captain Lushington should meet with a fatal accident to-day. Only this afternoon the *Westminster Gazette*, a paper which is very fond of adopting the paternal roll, protests against the First Lord's flights as 'ill-advised and mischievous'. 'They serve no useful purpose,' the paper adds, 'and from at least one point of view are decidedly harmful.' That point of view apparently is that they set an example to other Ministers to imperil their lives. It must be consoling to Ministers to know that their followers attach so much value to their lives; but it should be borne in mind that there is a great difference between the positions of the First Lord of the Admiralty and the Secretary of State for War and, say, the Home Secretary and the Minister for Agriculture. The science of aviation comes within the scope of the departments of the first two Ministers. They do not pretend to set an example to their colleagues in the Cabinet when they fly, but they do show to the young officers in the great services of which they are the Parliamentary heads that they take a keen interest in a new and important 'fighting arm'. Mr Churchill, it is said, by reason of his flight with Captain Lushington on Saturday, has qualified for an aviator's certificate.

F. E. Smith to WSC

6 December 1913   Carlton Club

Dear Winston,

Why do you do such a foolish thing as fly repeatedly? Surely it is unfair to your family, your career & your friends.

Yrs ever
F E

Mrs D. E. Wildman-Lushington to WSC

8 December 1913   Berkshire

Dear Mr Churchill,

Forgive me for not having written sooner to thank you for the very beautiful wreath & inscription you sent for my dear boy's funeral – I am most grateful to you and to everyone else concerned for the Great Honour done to my son's memory & the many tributes of affectionate regard evidenced towards him – not only by his comrades – but by the large crowd who waited on the procession on Friday.

I cannot express how beautiful & reverent I thought everything was, & what a comfort the heartfelt sympathy of that great public crowd – & of his comrades & officers was to us all & how it helped to alleviate my grief – & that of the dear little girl to whom he was engaged.

The floral tributes were some of the most beautiful I have ever seen & it makes me so grateful to think that they were *all* tributes of both *honour* & *affection combined,* & not just empty acknowledgements as such things so often are. I do feel proud to have been the mother of such a son, who has won his way quietly & unassumingly to such a position at so early an age.

Since then we have suffered another terrible grief in the sudden death on Saturday night of my daughter's little baby boy. He was healthy and well in every way – & had been laughing and playing with us & comforting us up to 6 pm at 7, my daughter saw him in bed smiling & happy. At 9.30 he woke apparently frightened & at 9.40 he was dead. We are laying him to rest to-day. My son-in-law Mr Gordon Fraser returned from Ireland last night.

I have the honour to be, Yours most gratefully

D. E. Wildman-Lushington

PS I should like before closing this to say a word to you about my son's *very high* opinion of & affection for Commander Samson. He may perhaps have told you personally. He thought him deserving of the very highest position. As an aviator in fact he considered there was no one else with the same knowledge and talent. And as his Commander he had a great feeling of affection & respect for him, & thought him a fine straight gentleman with a warm heart though perhaps an abrupt & cold appearance.

After the tragic accident to Mr Berne[1] at Eastchurch in which my son was so unhappily concerned – he told me he felt he could never bring himself to return to Eastchurch again. He was so terribly broken with the shock & sorrow for his friend.

Captain Samson wrote him such an exceedingly nice letter – & it was owing to that letter, that Gilbert braced himself to return, as he felt it would be so hard upon Captain Samson to be deserted by another, when he had just lost such a brilliant officer in Mr Berne. Had it not been for his affection for Commander Samson he could not have done this – as he was in that state when a man is willing to throw up his whole career if he can escape from the horror that is present with him, and he felt that if he returned to Eastchurch, he would always see Mr Berne as he had last seen him & feel the horrible despair of having killed his dear friend.

I thought he would like you to know, if you do not already, of his very high esteem for Commander Samson – & that he considered him, in the aviation world as 2nd to none.

D. E. W. Lushington

---

[1] Berne, a Naval colleague of Lushington's, had been killed by the propeller of a plane which Lushington was about to take up. Lushington thought that Berne was clear when he turned over the engine. The accident took place about six months earlier.

Miss Airlie Hynes to WSC

9 December 1913   Southsea

Dear Mr Churchill,

I want to thank you very much for sending me Gilbert Lushington's last letter, it was kind of you & I am so glad to have it. In his last to me he mentioned that he was writing to you & I wondered if he had. Thank you also for the lovely wreath you sent. I felt so proud when I saw that it was laurel, & most of all I would like to thank you for helping to make Gilbert's last days absolutely happy. He was so pleased at having given you your first instruction and his last letters were all about it and he was so happy. I certainly can't grudge him the splendid end he had, it was a death any man would wish & I am only proud to think that I always encouraged him to fly. I was just as keen on aviation as he was himself & in the future I shall like to think that I have helped to give something towards it. Life seems a blank just now but it is a great comfort to have a perfect past to look back on. With very sincere thanks for being so kind.

Yours very truly
AIRLIE HYNES

Mrs Airlie Madden to Martin Gilbert
(RSC Papers)

6 January 1963   Alverstoke

Dear Mr Gilbert,

It seems very strange to resurrect the past in these letters. December 3rd 1963 will be 50 years since my beloved fiancé's death, though it seems no time at all. His vivid personality does not fade. I am sure some of those he instructed contributed to victory in 1918. I enclose the only letter I have describing Sir Winston's flight, also the others I have kept all these years. You have taken great trouble to locate me!

I married in 1918 Major J. G. Madden DSO. We lost two sons in the last war, one of whom gained the MC. Excuse all this personal reminiscence, of no interest to you. Pride is a great help in old age. I can also boast of having flown several times with G.W.L. in 1913. Return these at your leisure.

Yours sincerely
AIRLIE MADDEN

What a mercy for England that Sir W's flight was not the fatal one.

*   *   *   *   *

WSC to Captain William Pakenham

5 December 1913

1. Directions have been given to the Secretary to transfer the whole work of the Naval Air Service, including appointments and disciplinary questions affecting the personnel, to your general superintendence as a member of the Board. I wish to be consulted in regard to new entries and cases of serious misconduct, and to have appointments and promotions above and including the rank of Squadron Commander submitted for my approval.

2. The time is not ripe for an Inspecting Flag Officer. An Inspecting Captain will be required in the near future. He should ultimately be an officer of extensive flying experience and knowledge of aeronautics; but as no such officer of suitable rank is yet available, it will be necessary to choose a good captain for his personality and general qualities and let him be the first holder of this appointment. During the next three months you should take occasion to suggest several names to me, and I will also look around. Meanwhile, Commander Scarlett[1] should temporarily discharge the necessary office work.

3. I have dealt in other papers with the paying off of *Hermes*.

4. The conference which you propose to summon is a matter entirely for your discretion. I should suggest, however, that Lieutenant Seddon be added; he is one of the cleverest. I shall await with interest your reports, after this conference has sat, on the four important points mentioned in your minute. The provision of a Naval Air Service Order Book, and a Naval Air Service Manual of Training, are urgently needed.

5. The Air Committee at the Admiralty which I propose to set up is a temporary Standing Committee like the Cromarty Committee, intended only for use in the early days of the service, and to enable me to keep myself fully informed of general progress. In these circumstances I prefer that the composition should be as prescribed in my minute. The junior officers attending need not necessarily be the same on each occasion.

6. I fully approve in principle that part of your minute which deals with the Coast-Guard.

WSC to Jack Seely

6 December 1913

There are so many different questions connected with the watching of the East Coast, so much intermingling of naval and military functions, and such

[1] Francis Rowland Scarlett (1875–1934), Captain RN 1914; Wing Captain RNAS 1915; Brig.-Gen. RAF 1918; Air Commodore 1919; Air Vice-Marshal 1924; Commander, Coastal Area, 1928; Commander, RAF in the Middle East, 1929–31; retired 1931.

a growth of petty interests and anomalies that nothing less than the highest authority in the two Departments can frame the outlines of a good and thorough scheme. We are anxious that our naval seaplane stations and the Air Service generally shall gradually replace, as far as possible, the existing Coast-Guards, occupy their premises where required, and discharge their duties. This transition, which offers a prospect of large economies in expenditure, has to be fitted in with the disjointed claims of the Board of Trade, the Customs, and the Life Boats. Next there is the case of the Wireless and War Signalling Stations as distinguished from that of the ordinary Coast-Guard Stations along the strategic front; how the latter are to be manned in the precautionary period or on mobilisation when the Coast-Guards now in them will be swiftly withdrawn, and how these latter stations thus newly manned are to be brought into harmonious relation with the Seaplane, Wireless, and War Signalling Stations; at what moment should the military authorities take them over – as soon as possible during the precautionary period, or on mobilisation? Also the relation of all these to the patrol flotillas moored in various harbours along the coast; the general service of information for the naval and military forces co-operating, and how it is to be made to work smoothly and effectively for both. Then to all these add the existing chaotic telephonic arrangements, their improvement, and the provision of effective peace and war circuits. And, lastly, the division of responsibility for certain batteries and defences as fixed by the treaty of peace, and a proper harmonising of the divided functions.

　　I have come to the conclusion that it will be useless to delegate this work, in the first instance at any rate, to any committee of subordinates, and I propose to you that it shall form the subject of a regular and special enquiry on the high level bridge at which you and I, Sir John French, and Prince Louis, with Hankey as recorder, shall personally deal with it. Any officers that we require can be in attendance for information and advice, and representatives from the other Departments can be asked to come and give their views. Special enquiries into the various spheres of details which will soon be opened up can be undertaken by sub-committees appointed *ad hoc*. The meetings could be held alternately in each Department. Half-a-dozen of two hours each in quick succession would probably block in the whole plan on sound principles and enable details to be worked out by subordinates.

　　If you agree, let us begin next week. What do you say?

WSC to Sir Graham Greene, Captain William Pakenham,
Captain Murray Sueter and others concerned

12 December 1913

Let a list be prepared of steamboats likely to be useful for the Air Service possessed by Third Fleet ships or otherwise.

WSC to Captain William Pakenham and Captain Murray Sueter

21 December 1913

With a view to compression in the Air Service Vote, consider the following: –

1. Postpone for the present year the Elswick Zeppelin.

2. Make a contract with Armstrong's for the three 'Forlaninis' at 50,000*l.* apiece. Make arrangements that the third 'Forlanini' will not be begun during the currency of 1914–15.

3. Suspend altogether during 1914–15 all projects connected with Wolverhampton.

4. Move the army airships and plant to Kingsnorth so as to concentrate, in the first instance, at this centre.

5. Make no progress with the Cromer Airship Station beyond providing the land and erecting one shed, only half the cost of the shed to fall in 1914–15.

6. Concentrate the seaplanes and naval aeroplanes at Calshot, Isle of Grain, Eastchurch, Yarmouth or Harwich, and one Scottish station, presumably Dundee; these to be completed and fully equipped and progress on all the others to be reduced to a minimum.

Take over from the Army the plans and all work done on the [blank space], but incur no further expenditure on that vessel in 1914–15.

8. Limit the amount taken for the new programme of airships for 1914–15 to 10,000*l.* for two. We shall thus have built, and to be maintained and complete, or building in 1914–15: –

(*a*) The army airships.
(*b*) The small naval airships.
(*c*) The 'Astra Torres' and 'Parsival.'
(*d*) The second 'Astra Torres' now under order.
(*e*) The Vickers' 'Zeppelin,' the three Vickers' 'Parsivals,' and the two Elswick.

It will only be necessary to keep inflated and manned half of these simultaneously during the currency of 1914–15, and expense of maintenance in personnel, hydrogen, fuel, &c., on this branch of the service should be reduced accordingly.

9. Give Armstrong's a substantial order for aeroplanes or seaplanes in consolation for the abandonment of the 'Zeppelin.'

10. It appears to me that Eastchurch cannot continue to be only a flying school, and that it should certainly support a squadron of naval aeroplanes which shall have a definite value for war in connection with coast defence. The naval wing must have a proper proportion of good land fighting machines, as it will be impossible for our officers to compete with Army officers if they are relegated exclusively to the seaplane.

Please report to me more fully on these points as early as possible in January. Also please prepare detailed sketch estimates for 1915–16 on the above assumptions, so far as they are found practicable.

WSC to Captain William Pakenham and Captain Murray Sueter

21 December 1913

All the seaplanes of the 1914–15 programme, and as many others as can conveniently be adjusted, should have sufficient uniformity in their design to enable a standard wireless to be quickly and easily fitted or removed as a complete unit.

2. The above principle should be applied so far as possible to engines which should be interchangeable and capable of being removed or fitted in a few minutes.

3. More care and attention should be paid to the seating accommodation. At present, caprice of the makers appears largely to govern this. Proper consideration for the comfort of the pilot and observer, combined with an attempt to arrive at good principles in this field, would conduce to greater efficiency.

WSC to Captain Murray Sueter

21 December 1913

Please let me have the Air Estimates for this year in two distinct sections – airships and aeroplanes – and show me how the sum now approved will be divided under all heads between the two branches of the service.

WSC to Captain Murray Sueter

21 December 1913

Let me have a short report on the results of the conferences held on the specifications and machines of seaplanes and naval aeroplanes for the 1914–15 programme. What types have been decided on? What is to be the general distribution of the orders, and when can deliveries be expected? Remember that we can pay at the very beginning of the new financial year for all machines included in the programme, if desired.

I reserve my opinion on the single-seater fighting machine question.

WSC to Captain Murray Sueter

21 December 1913

One of the twelve school machines approved for this year should also be capable of being used for special reconnaissance at high speed. It should be fitted to carry two pilots side by side with complete dual control, no third person being carried as a passenger. The seating should be comfortable and the pilots well sheltered, special care being taken about this. The type should be a Sopwith tractor biplane, with either a 100-h.p. mono-soupape or a 100-h.p. 9-cylinder Gnome; in the case of the latter a Lalage carburetter should be fitted. Some easy starting gear should be fitted to allow the engine to be started from the pilot's seat, and a release gear on the tail. Four hours' petrol will be sufficient. She should be fitted with the following instruments: Elliot revolution counter; Short maximum barograph; Trip dashboard clock; Ogelvy or Clift air-speed indicator; Negretti and Zambra liquid cyclonometer; map case; and safety belts. This machine would be available for instructional work for advanced pupils, and also for experimental services. It should be ordered at once, for delivery, if possible, in the first week in February. Please telegraph to me that this is being done. I have explained my wishes in detail to Lieutenant Grey,[1] and he should supervise the execution of the minor arrangements on his return to England while the machine is under construction.

WSC to Captain William Pakenham

25 December 1913

My minute of the 21st December, about compressing the Airship Service for 1914–15, should be taken by you as a guide and not as a rule. These are

[1] Spenser Douglas Adair Grey (1889–1937), Lieutenant RN; frequently gave WSC flying lessons during 1912; DSO 1914.

suggestions which I want examined and reported on, so that we may consider together what their full effect would be, and not in any sense decisions. Review the whole situation in your mind. Show me the effect of my proposals in each case and suggest alternatives where you disagree.

2. I am prepared, if you and DAD concur, to settle with Armstrongs for three 'Forlaninis,' the third of which is not to fall upon the Votes of 1914–15, and is to be kept back to catch all the improvements suggested by the experience of the first. This matter must now be very urgent, and if you wish to decide to close, you have only to telegraph to me to obtain full authority.

3. I am increasingly unhappy about moving the army airship sheds. If possible, I would like to leave them where they are during the whole of the financial year 1914–15. To move them at all is to waste 23,000l. To put them at Kingsnorth is to involve personal difficulties which we had hoped had been avoided. We are not ready for them at Wolverhampton and cannot get ready for many months, even if we decide upon establishing a station there. Will you consider a plan on this basis? – Let the naval people come away from Farnborough to Kingsnorth as soon as it is ready, and leave the military airships there during the whole of 1914–15. What arrangements would you make about personnel on this basis, and how could the ships be repaired and maintained in a good condition? Colonel Seely will be very averse to any arrangement of this kind, and before proposing it to him I should have to have a thoroughly good plan worked out in all main details.

Let me have your views.

WSC to Captain William Pakenham and Captain Murray Sueter

1 January 1914

I presume that no time is being lost in proceeding with the surrender by the Coast Guards of the Yarmouth, Isle of Grain, and Calshot premises, and that these are being fitted up as rapidly as possible for the reception of the seaplane squadrons requiring them.

WSC to J. Masterton Smith

1 January 1914

I did not and do not understand how the £210,000 is made up for Aircraft. Please let me have a full explanation of it. I should be very sorry to see the stream of criticism directed on the new construction of aeroplanes and hydro-aeroplanes. I do not think they are at all included in this Vote. It seems to me probable that the £210,000 is simply the cost of the two large airships, and that the other two which I added later were never included in the Third Sea Lord's figure. Now let us have it cleared up.

WSC to Captain William Pakenham

3 January 1914

I am in full agreement with the policy you indicate in your letter on the Air Service, and am very glad that Armstrongs have proved so complaisant in the matter of their big rigid. Parliament has not yet been informed of the supplementary programme embarked upon last year, but a Supplementary Estimate will have to be presented in February. This being so, the whole subject must be reviewed so that the case for the expenditure may be complete and up-to-date. We are entitled, I think, to treat after-thoughts and revisions of judgment as if they were part of our original plans.

WSC to Sir James Caird

5 January 1914

Copy

My dear Sir James Caird,

I thank you very much for your kind letter of the 23rd December and for the good wishes which you sent to me and my wife. You may be sure I will run no risks in flying that are not necessary for the discharge of my present duties as I conceive them. You are quite correct in thinking that my wife shares your views on this subject. She begs me to tell you that her mother is now recovering from the effects of the operation, which were however very severe and out of all proportion to any beneficial result achieved.

WSC to Captain William Pakenham

7 January 1914

1. I know nothing of the Army Council going in for seaplane work. They have a station at Montrose, where they had some empty barracks and where there is good flying country. They have an experimental station at Albor-

ough, where they are going to try their fighting machines. I have heard of
nothing else, and I do not see any objection to this.

A clear definition of the relative spheres of duty as between the Army and
the Navy is to be found in the report of what is called the High Level Conference with the War Office, which took place about two months ago. My
private office can obtain it for you.

2. The arrangements about seniority in the Naval Wing have been prescribed by me in the greatest detail in various minutes which you have with
you. I could never agree to naval seniority superseding flying seniority
within the flying service. The whole of this matter has been discussed exhaustively, and I have reached final conclusions upon it in full agreement
with the Secretary of State for War.

3. There is surely a mistake in Table 'A' of your paper, attached. 'Accommodation approved to 31.3.14' seems in conflict with the entry under
Fort George 'not completed by 31.3.13.'

There appears to be no reference to the developments and contemplations
in 1914–15, which are of course essential to an effective survey of the subject.

As at present advised, I approve in principle the 'proposed distribution of
machines due for delivery by 31.3.14,' viz: –

Cromarty	4
Dundee	14
Yarmouth	8
Felixstowe	8
Calshot	16
Eastchurch	20
Grain Island	25

It will not be possible to provide funds for any developments at Port
Seaton, Blyth, the Humber, or Dover, in the Estimates of 1914–15. If
necessary to accommodate machines, extra sheds must be erected at the
existing stations. Your proposed re-distribution of the personnel on this
basis is approved. Let me have a list of the Squadron and Flight Commanders who are to be given charge of these various places.

4. It appears to me necessary that the Eastchurch Flying School should
acquire a definite military value as well as being merely an instructional
establishment. Proposals should be put forward for establishing there, in
addition to the instructional machines, a squadron of war aeroplanes which
should be maintained at an effective strength of at least twelve.

In this connection it should be remembered that a seaplane can reconnoitre at least 5 miles inland and that landplanes at least 5 miles to seaward
by rising 5,000 or 6,000 feet, and that in clear weather land aeroplanes can
watch an enormous area seaward while keeping within gliding distance of

her shore. For much of the work in connection with the patrol flotillas and the coastal watch, aeroplanes will be more effective than seaplanes.

5. I agree with you fully that the money supplied for the Coast-Guard service must be reduced by every inroad upon its duties by the seaplane stations, and I shall be glad to receive proposals in that sense.

WSC to Captain William Pakenham and Captain Murray Sueter

12 January 1914

Your proposals (1) and (2) on page 2 of the attached minute cannot be reconciled with the conclusions I have reached.

Proposal (1) makes a demand on behalf of the flying officers beyond anything previously contemplated, *viz*, that a very young and junior officer in the Navy advanced to be a Squadron Commander in the flying service shall have substantive rank and executive authority over officers of the regular naval service four, five, and six years his senior. This I am sure would not be assented to by the Second Sea Lord, and would be much disliked in the service afloat.

Your proposal (2) goes equally far in the opposite direction. It condemns an officer of junior naval rank to remain permanently at the bottom of his flying grade, and no matter how long he has been flying or how high his qualifications are he will be automatically superseded by officers of senior naval rank in the same flying grade, no matter how temporary their connection with the flying service may be. It composes an absolute and fatal barrier to the civilian entry, for since they have no service rank they are condemned for all time to a position of inferiority in every grade.

The two proposals (1) and (2) appear in fact contradictory. In the one case flying officers advanced in flying grade for flying service would be given executive control outside the flying service over naval officers in naval duties for which the flying officers' special qualifications afford no basis. On the other hand, within the flying service mere gold lace is to supersede flying experience and attainments and long periods of dangerous service. The second proposal is as unfair to flying officers in the flying service as the first would be to naval officers in the naval service. Why, because an officer is advanced to a higher flying grade, should he have greater naval qualifications and authority? Why, on the other hand, if an officer possesses superior naval rank should he be a better or more experienced flyer?

Paragraph 4 in my minute of 10.12 is perfectly clear. The views I have formed have been reached after much consideration and discussion. The matter is one of principle and not of detail, and on the principle I have no doubts. Someone has to decide questions of this character, and I am the person who for the time has the responsibility. My decision is contained textually and exactly in paragraph 4.

Page 2, paragraph (3) of your proposals. This is a matter of convenient administration. Seniority when combined with flying qualifications is of course an additional factor where selection for promotion in flying grade is concerned.

Paragraph (4) should read as follows: –

'All promotions and appointments in the Flying Corps will be by selection.'

Paragraph (5). I cannot judge this apart from concrete cases. Let me have the actual facts.

Paragraph (6). There is a great distinction between airship and aeroplane work, and I cannot admit the principle that the treatment of the two branches should be uniform. The navigation of an airship requires great skill and serious responsibility, but neither the skill nor the responsibility go beyond what are involved upon the Captains of great ships of war in difficult circumstances of weather or navigation. The work of the subordinate officers in an airship does not involve special difficulty or great responsibility. They are in the position of officers and men in a submarine who have certain definite mechanical functions to discharge and whose safety is entirely in the hands of the Captain. In the case of flights of aeroplanes, on the other hand, every pilot, whatever his rank, does by his skill and address keep the machine from capsizing from minute to minute. It is not intended by these remarks in any way to depreciate the quality and the risk attaching to the airship service, but there are so many differences between it and the aeroplane service that it cannot be assumed that exact similarity of arrangements in regard to pay, rank, &c., will in all cases be appropriate to both. The airship service lies also much closer to the navy in the conditions and character of its work than the aeroplane service, and naval officers would be much less affected in their professional careers through separation by serving in the airship than in the aeroplane section.

Paragraph (7). I approve.

Paragraph (8). I approve.

Let me see circular letter 22 when redrafted.

Obtain the requisite Order in Council.

Page 3, paragraph (1) 'c.' It is not intended to reduce the pay of these officers.

Paragraph (2) of AG's minute. I do not approve of the principle of payments to observers for separate flights. There should be a distinction between persons whose duties take them regularly, and those whose duties take them occasionally, into the air. The occasional allowance should be quite small, but persons drawing it would be liable to be employed in the air whenever the convenience of the service required it. We must not get into the mood of attaching any significance to occasional flights in the air as observers, or mechanics, or regard them as worthy of some special remuneration on each occasion. A small annual allowance is quite sufficient, and if an officer or a man is not satisfied he can revert to his regular duties.

Paragraph (3) of AG's minute. I see no reason to depart from my original proposal. It is not desired to encourage the entry of senior officers in the Flying Corps. In any case the money paid while a man is learning must be regarded as subsistence rather than service pay. He is no use to us until he has learned.

Paragraphs (4) and (5). I agree that no special regulations appear called for in regard to half-pay and accidents, but I think an insurance system should certainly be started, and that the Government should enter into negotiations with some of the big insurance companies on the subject. ACL should be addressed on this.

I am impressed generally with the AG's views on the details of the pay proposed, and I will have a meeting in my room on the subject shortly.

WSC to Captain William Pakenham and Captain Murray Sueter

14 January 1914

1. Naval Air Service Training Manual. The proofs of the War Office and Admiralty Manuals should be considered together, and inter-departmental arrangements made to secure uniformity and co-ordination between and to prevent repetition.

2. Consider whether Captain Paine[1] would not be the best man to preside over this small committee.

3. What are the army arrangements about the number of machines in flights and squadrons?

4. I should like to see the proposals on this head.

5. See my minutes on other papers on the need of making Eastchurch the centre of a war aeroplane squadron with definite military value. Its maintenance as a training and experimental establishment alone could not be justified in view of the development of the Central Flying School.

6. Let me see Lieutenant Longmore's scheme when completed.

---

[1] Godfrey Marshall Paine (1871–1932), Commandant Central Flying School 1912–15; Inspector-General RAF 1919. Rear Admiral 1917; knighted 1918.

WSC to Sir Ian Hamilton

14 January 1914

[Draft]

My dear General,

I have for some time been impressed with the favourable prospects open to aeroplanes and airships in the Mediterranean and the strategic and tactical advantages which might be obtained from their use. I am providing in the Estimates of this year money for starting Air Stations both at Malta and at Gibraltar, and I hope before the end of the financial year we shall have a flight of aeroplanes or seaplanes at each. The question of establishing an airship base is also being examined. The radius of action of such a vessel would enable her to reconnoitre the mouth of the Adriatic, the Gulf of Otranto, and the Straits of Messina effectually. I do not think that Usborne,[1] who has just been promoted Commander, can be spared for such a voyage of enquiry. He is wanted to command the main airship station at Kingsnorth.

All good wishes to you in your inquisitorial peregrination. I hope we shall be able to have another flight when you come back.

WSC to Sir James Caird

28 January 1914

Copy

Dear Sir James Caird,

Some time ago you spoke to me of your wish to do something for the Navy, and you suggested the establishment of some institute or sailors' home or club at Rosyth. After reflection I advised you on the whole against such action, but now another opportunity has occurred and appears to me to be in many ways suitable and appropriate for your benevolence. A new flying station is to be established at Dundee. The Tay Commissioners have leased to the Admiralty land at very advantageous terms, and one of the largest hydro-aeroplane bases will soon be established on the banks of the Tay. A small club or institute, where officers and men could meet and have recreation by means of bowls or squash racquets, would not be a very expensive matter but would be a most gracious and timely gift. It would

---

[1] Cecil Vivian Usborne (1880–1951), Naval officer 1903–33, 1941–5; Captained HMS *Colossus* 1913, *Dragon* 1921, *Malaya* 1927, *Resolution* 1928. Director of Naval Intelligence Division 1930–2; returned to active service for special duties in Admiralty 1941–5; Vice-Admiral 1945.

be a kind of welcome extended by you and through you by the City to the establishment within its bounds of so important a branch of this new and dangerous service. These officers and men run such risks in the discharge of their duties that they deserve to be specially well looked after in their hours of relaxation.

If you like the idea at its first view, I will put a more detailed scheme before you. You will understand that I am thinking of something which would be rather more comfortable and pleasant than anything we should be justified in supplying out of public funds, so that what you would be giving would be in addition to and not in substitution for ordinary naval expenditure.

WSC to Captain William Pakenham and Captain Murray Sueter

10 February 1914

Colonel Seely spoke to me of his desire that we should provide 150,000*l* instead of 120,000*l* out of the 300,000*l* reduction which the Cabinet have decided should be made on army and navy air services generally. Have we not taken 24,000*l* in the estimates of the present year for the removal of the Farnborough airship sheds? If this is so, I should suggest that this 24,000*l* might be conceded to the War Office on the understanding that the sheds are not moved from Farnborough during the financial year 1914–15.

On general grounds I am inclined to think that the War Office are in danger of going a little beyond what public opinion will support in regard to the land air service. The objectives of land aeroplanes can never be so definite or important as the objectives of seaplanes, which, when they carry torpedoes, may prove capable of playing a decisive part in operations against capital ships. The facilities of reconnaissance at sea, where hostile vessels can be sighted at enormous distances while the seaplane remains out of possible range, offer a far wider prospect even in the domain of information to seaplanes than to land aeroplanes, which would be continually brought under rifle and artillery fire from concealed positions on the ground, among trees, behind hedges, &c. Yet, in spite of these tendencies the army is seeking to spend nearly 1,000,000*l* this year on the aeroplane service, as against 400,000*l* provided for this section (or should one not rather say, 'pinion') of the Naval Flying Wing.

I should like to be more fully informed of the projects at the Central Flying School which lead the War Office to require such a large increase on our contribution.

WSC to Captain Murray Sueter

11 February 1914

I think the word 'canteen' would excite misgivings in strict Scottish bosoms. 'Institute' is a much better word. I should like the building to offer accommodation not only to naval ratings, but to officers. There should be two parts and two entrances. Bathrooms with hot and cold water are indispensable. There is no reason why a canteen should not be established, but this must be an incident and not an object. There should be at least two good rooms on the officers' side and one or two smaller ones. A squash court would be better than the second lawn tennis court. The whole should be described as 'The Naval Flying Service Club and Institute.' You want a garage for motor-car or motor-bicycles. There should be a nice verandah in front. I wonder whether a bowling-alley would not be better than a second billiard table.

Let me have a fresh draft of your proposals, stating also the number of men who will be stationed there or who might arrive there from time to time from Montrose or other flying stations.

WSC to Captain Murray Sueter

26 February 1914

Naval Wing Seniority List.

1. I should like to test this list by a regular system of marks, which might be apportioned under the following heads: –

Flying service	10
Naval or military service	6
Flying proficiency and pioneer work ..	5
Age	4

2. I should also like to see the list made out on its present basis, without waiting for the above test, in three parallel columns –

(*a.*) Airship officers, all ranks and branches;

(*b.*) Aeroplane pilots, all ranks; and

(*c.*) Specialist officers with flying duties other than regular pilots.

WSC to Captain William Pakenham and Captain Murray Sueter

26 February 1914

I wish to have full materials for my general statement on estimates of the progress made by the Naval Wing during the year. If the debate on the

Army Supplementary is studied it will show the kind of information with which I should be provided. The more seaplanes and aeroplanes we can show in our possession on the 31st March of this year the better, and I must, of course, show the progress we anticipate in the new financial year, *i.e.,* to the 31st March, 1915.

WSC to Captain Murray Sueter

3 March 1914

Would it not be a good thing to send your specifications of seaplanes and aeroplanes privately to General Henderson,[1] Colonel Sykes,[2] and Mr O'Gorman[3] for their inspection and criticism? Have you obtained for them the specifications of the machines on which they are now at work? It appears to me important that we should keep in touch.

WSC to Captain William Pakenham and Captain Murray Sueter

3 March 1914

A small Inter-Departmental Committee should be formed to draw up a detailed scheme before any appeal is made to the public. Two officers from each of the Naval and Military Wing, and a War Staff Officer should form the committee, and a military officer of the General Staff with flying experience should preside.

2. The object in the first instance should be to establish certain well-marked flying routes along which at known intervals good landing-places will be available. It ought to be possible, by removing hedges and filling up ditches, cutting down trees in the fences, &c., to secure a succession of good landing places at comparatively small cost.

3. The Ordinance Survey should undertake the preparation of a regular

---

[1] David Henderson (1862–1921), Director-General of Military Aeronautics 1913–18; one of creators of Royal Flying Corps; learned to fly at age of 50; Lieutenant-General; knighted 1914.

[2] Frederick Hugh Sykes (1877–1954), Commander Royal Flying Corps, Military Wing, 1912–14; sometime commanding RFC France 1914–15; Wing Captain RFC, Naval wing, while commanding Royal Naval Air Service in Eastern Mediterranean 1915–16; Deputy Director War Office 1917; Chief of Air Staff 1918–19; First Controller-General of Civil Aviation 1919–22; MP Conservative, Hallam division of Sheffield 1922–8, Nottingham Central 1940–5. Governor of Bombay 1928–33. Major General 1918; knighted 1919; PC 1928; married in 1920 Isabel, daughter of A. Bonar Law.

[3] Mervin O'Gorman (1871–1958), Superintendent of Royal Aircraft Factory 1909–16. Lieutenant-Colonel RDC 1916. Chairman Royal Aeronautical Society 1921–2.

flying map in consultation with the above Committee. This map, which must of course be made in sections, should study the country along these routes from a flying point of view. The routes themselves should be studied in the same way as motor car routes are studied, and descriptions and directions prepared.

4. An official letter should be addressed to the War-Office asking for their assent and co-operation.

WSC to Captain Murray Sueter

5 March 1914

Referring to my note about the provision of landing places, the Committee should also consider how such landing places should be made visible to airmen from aloft. To this end metal signs, coloured and numbered, should be planted in the same way as motor car guides are now fixed on all our roads. Flags or other conspicuous aviation landmarks should be erected along the main aerial routes, like lighthouses at sea, so as to enable navigation to proceed with sureness. It ought to be possible for an airman flying along an aerial route to pick up a succession of points which would enable him to verify his position exactly in relation to each of which well-known landing places exist.

WSC to Prince Louis of Battenberg

6 March 1914

There is no question of the airships being employed in Somaliland before September.

With regard to the remark of the COS about the absence of these ships from this country, our policy was to obtain them for training purposes, and the airship service is admittedly in the experimental stage. They are therefore not counted upon as effective military factors at the present time; and so far as training is concerned, no better opportunities for their employment could be found than on active service. The sweeping opinions expressed by the War Staff do not appear to have been arrived at as the result of a careful study of the facts or with knowledge of the local conditions, or after consultation with the officers and administrators serving in the Protectorate. When the COS suggests that 75,000*l.* might be better spent 'on a military expedition,' he cannot surely be aware that over 3,000,000*l.* was expended without any good result on the operations of 1904. 75,000*l.* would therefore not go very far towards providing the alternative.

Generally the question of whether barbarous populations can be controlled by the operations of aircraft in countries whose size and inaccessibility render military expeditions impossible except at inordinate cost, is an issue of novel interest and of very high importance. The authorities of the Protectorate are unanimous in thinking that the employment of the airships would be most effective from the military point of view and from what they know of the Dervish character and habits.

In these circumstances, we should confine ourselves purely to the technical points involved, and leave the special military and political issues to be decided by others.

Minute by WSC

March 1914

The first thing to find out in these exercises is what the seaplane can see and not what it cannot. In the first instance the clearest water, the smoothest day, and the most favourable conditions should be obtained. The submarine should not dive until the aircraft are actually overhead, and they should be permitted to approach as near as possible, as well as taking a position high overhead so as to see how far and how long a submarine submerged can be held in view. The little airships from Farnborough would be very good for this purpose, as they can go slower than the aeroplanes and could keep pace with the submerged submarine. All the exercises for submarines to dodge aeroplanes could take place after the limitations of seaplane vision have been determined under conventional conditions.

Sir James Caird to WSC

22 March 1914   Dundee

Sunday

Dear Mr Churchill,

Do you think that one Racquet Court & say two Billiard Tables would be enough to provide in the club you proposed for flying men in Dundee?

If so I can prepare a plan & meantime I wait a plan of the 8 acres the Admiralty are to have for – years & authority for part of it to be used for the club.

With kind regards, Yours very truly
JAMES CAIRD

WSC to Captain Murray Sueter

1 April 1914

I notice the Secretary of State for War has a very good arrangement for keeping a check on the aeroplanes which are fit for service. Would you kindly ask to be allowed to see it, and make me proposals for a similar system being established for my benefit.

WSC to Sir Graham Greene, Captain William Pakenham and others

8 April 1914 Admiralty

1. Social precedence of flying officers should be regulated by their substantive naval rank. The principle that special flying seniority and rank counts *only* within the flying service is universal in its application; and here they must be the losers.

2. Uniform. I am anxious that all flying officers should wear the same uniform, and that, the executive naval uniforms. Therefore all should have the naval lace and curl of their flying rank. The flying badge however (which must always be worn) excludes them from all executive command outside the RF Service. The flying badge should be the same for all commissioned ranks. It does not denote their rank. It denotes their branch; and under the guise of a distinction imposes the limitations which are necessary in command.

3. Full dress uniform. Paymasters, Surgeons, Engineers, who are members of the Flying Corps, should wear the full dress which they now have *plus* their additional lace (if any) for flying rank, *plus* the flying badge which limits the effectiveness of their flying rank. Naval flying officers should wear their regular uniform with the above additions. The civilian entry will wear the full dress of the naval rank conceded to them *plus* the flying badge. Full dress will not be purchased by these officers during their year of probation.

4. Courts martial. Joining the Flying Corps ought not to deprive a naval, marine, or military officer of any *status* or competence which he enjoys in virtue of his regular commission. The civilian entry cannot without legislation obtain this status; but that should not deprive others of what they are already on other grounds entitled to.

5. When embarked on a ship of war, all flying officers should be treated as ward room officers.

I trust these principles, which are in full harmony with the scheme as a whole, may commend themselves to you for the solution of the various small questions which are outstanding.

WSC

Memorandum by WSC

22 April 1914

The WO give temporary military rank effective for all purposes, even outside the Flying Corps to military flying officers proportioned to their flying grades, involving in most cases an advance of a distinct grade. Thus an Army Captain who is promoted Squadron Commander in the Flying Corps is made an Army *Major for all purposes* on the day of his promotion in the Flying Corps, and so on.

My proposal for the navy is far more modest. I do not make the higher rank effective outside the Flying Service. But I cannot agree that the Naval Flying Service should be denied the honourable treatment, in respect of naval uniform, which has been so freely accorded by the sister service to their own people.

The army uniform must be regarded as not less honourable than that of naval officers; and it would be a slur upon the whole Naval Flying Service if they were definitely treated in a matter of this kind with a marked inferiority of consideration.

The proposals I have made are the result of long consideration, and of many attempts to meet the special difficulties which exist; and the principle of paragraph 2 is one to which I attach the greatest importance. It is indeed *vital* to the success and prestige of the Naval Wing.

Memorandum by WSC

1 May 1914

The conclusion I have reached is as follows: –
The uniform of the Naval Air Service to be –
Naval uniform with an eagle instead of an anchor on buttons, cap badges, epaulettes, and sword belt clasps, and an eagle over the curl on the sleeve.

Squadron Commanders to be given the acting rank for all purposes of Lieutenant Commanders. This will only affect six officers.

All the other ranks correspond normally.

WSC to Captain Murray Sueter

1 May 1914

I examined the Willows airship some weeks ago, and should think it would be a very good type for practice purposes. I am told that a two-seater

25,000 cubic feet 45-hp ship would cost only 1,000*l.*, and that the first could be delivered in three months, and one every month afterwards. Please examine the proposal to purchase three or four of these for training and experimental purposes.

Memorandum by WSC

7 May 1914

I am very glad that mutual concessions in opinion have enabled us to reach a virtual agreement on this question where settlement is urgent.

It will not, I fear, be possible to draw the distinction suggested at (2) between different squadron commanders. The whole scheme of relative rank, as well as the table of seniority in the flying service, would be upset thereby simply for the sake of temporarily excluding three officers from the list. (1) is, however, fully concurred in, and the regulations have been framed to give full effect to it.

WSC to Sir Graham Greene

14 May 1914

The Cabinet have approved in principle the employment of these airships in Somaliland.

A Conference should be arranged between the Admiralty, Colonial Office, and Treasury, to settle the apportionment of expense between the Admiralty and Colonial Office, and to satisfy the Treasury that the minimum claim is being made. Mr Murray[1] should be one of the Admiralty representatives. I do not attach great importance to the allocation of the expense; there are different departments but only one taxpayer.

Memorandum by WSC

18 May 1914

1. The following changes in the appointments of the Naval Wing appear desirable: –

Captain Sueter to be Inspecting Captain of the Naval Wing as well as DAD.

He should have under him two Assistant or Deputy Inspecting Captains

[1] Oswyn Alexander Ruthven Murray (1873–1936), Assistant Secretary Admiralty 1911–1917; Assistant Private Secretary to First Lord of the Admiralty 1899–1902; Private Secretary to the Financial Secretary 1902–4; Director of Victualling 1905–11; Permanent Secretary Admiralty from 1917; knighted 1917.

or Inspecting Commanders in Commander Scarlett and Commander Samson.

Commander Scarlett should command the seaplane ship, in addition to managing the Central Office.

Commander Samson should work with him and under him in the Central Office, in addition to his duties as Commander of the Eastchurch Naval Flying School and of the Eastchurch War Squadron.

Usually the seaplane ship will be at Sheerness, when the work will go forward as at present. When she is cruising, Commander Samson will carry on the work of the Central Office, with which he will be fully acquainted. He will thus obtain knowledge and experience of administration without having to give up the flying duties and command for which his qualifications are pre-eminent.

I am sure this will be found to be a good practicable working arrangement. It will conduce to close and harmonious co-operation; it will not throw undue strain upon either of the officers concerned.

Commander Schwann[1] should stay at the Admiralty, where his technical knowledge and administrative abilities are at present indispensable.

I am anxious to find a semi-administrative post for Major Gerrard,[2] who has been long enough at the Central Flying School, but before deciding on this I wish to know more precisely the character of the training establishment which it is proposed to institute for probationary flying officers and newly joined air ratings and its relation to the Central Office and to the Naval Flying School.

2. It is important that a war squadron of ten fighting aeroplanes should be created at Eastchurch as quickly as possible, in order to assign a definite military value to the personnel assembled there, and so provide to some extent for the aerial defence of the Chatham Dockyard, the Chattenden magazines, and the oil-fuel tanks. So vital are these points that in the near future we must contemplate a large increase in the numbers of this squadron.

In the first instance the squadron should consist of two flights of four machines each, with one in reserve. The design of these aeroplanes should be reconsidered in the light of the latest experience. They should all be identical in pattern, should all come from one maker, and should have all their parts interchangeable. The engines should be capable of being exchanged in not more than half an hour, and two spare engines should be ordered with each flight. These machines should be kept quite separate

[1] Oliver Schwann (1878–1948), Royal Navy 1891; Admiralty 1912; commanded HMS *Compania*, aircraft carrier, 1915–17; RAF 1919; Air Vice-Marshal; KCB 1924.
[2] Eugene Louis Gerrard (b. 1881), Royal Marines. Air Commodore 1923. DSO 1916; CMG 1919.

from the practice and school machines, and eight of the ten should always be ready to fly.

3. The arrangements for the training and instruction of the civilian entries require considerable development. It is essential that all persons joining the naval wing should receive the groundings of a good military training. Flying should only form a portion of their work, and periods of flying should alternate with other forms of instruction. For the present I must regard the Central Flying School as the best means of weeding those who are not likely to make good flying officers. But thereafter, during their first year of training, the probationers should be at least three months at marine headquarters, and three months either attached to the Nore Defence destroyer flotillas or in larger ships, as may be found convenient. Ample accommodation exists at Sheerness in connection with the War College and the Gunnery School to enable the sea-military instruction of these officers to be developed during their periods of flying service apart from their training afloat or at marine headquarters. A course of instruction should be devised and lecturers and instructors provided. The new War Training Division of the War Staff, which is about to be formed, should exercise a general supervision. All flying officers who have not received a military education in either the Army or the Navy should be required to receive this instruction, and flying must be regarded as a privilege rather than as their main duty. It is most undesirable that these young gentlemen should become a mere mixture of pilot and mechanic, and should be incorporated in the Naval Air Service while remaining quite ignorant of the profession of arms.

I wish to receive comprehensive and detailed proposals for dealing with this aspect. These proposals should also include facilities for the study of tactical, strategical, and War Staff problems by the Flight and Squadron Commanders. Later on several must be selected for the regular War Staff course, special arrangements being made to enable them to maintain their flying proficiency. In the first instance something of the nature of a senior class should be organised at Sheerness.

4. The untrustworthiness of the 160-h.p. Gnome cannot be doubted, and I notice with regret that three new machines are being constructed by Messrs Shortt into which this futile engine is being placed. Please advise how this evil can be limited.

WSC to Captain William Pakenham and Captain Murray Sueter

19 May 1914

Before finally deciding on the uniform question I should like to discuss it with the leading Squadron Commanders who are within easy reach of London. Which ones could you assemble at the Admiralty at 6 o'clock tomorrow evening?

WSC to Captain Murray Sueter

19 May 1914

Attention should be paid to the importance of standardising so far as possible all parts and fittings used in aeroplanes and seaplanes of the Naval Wing, even when made by different makers. A small committee should be set up to examine and report on this aspect. I notice at present an extraordinary variety. The principles governing each fitting should be the subject of careful individual consideration, and efforts should be made to get the makers to conform to them. Strength is of much more importance than lightness in regard to the small fittings.

Perhaps you will take an opportunity of speaking to me about this.

Memorandum by WSC

20 May 1914

These amendments do not meet my views in certain respects.

1. *Page 4, paragraph 5.* – I propose to the First Sea Lord, to meet his views, that the words 'if in command' should be inserted after the words 'Squadron Commander,' and that the officer should then rank with Lieutenant RN. I should agree to the amendment in red ink as an alternative regulating the seniority of Squadron Commanders in command.

2. *Uniform.* – The first paragraph of this section seems to indicate that an Engineer Lieutenant or an Assistant Paymaster would still continue to wear the distinguishing marks of their branch, although they are flying officers. This mars the uniformity of the scheme and tends to introduce distinction between officers doing exactly the same work. There can be no ground for refusing to officers long and honourably associated with the engineering and paymaster branches of the Royal Navy the same uniform which it is agreed shall be conceded to a civilian entry. The numbers concerned are very few.

I cannot agree to an option being given to individual Marine officers to retain the uniform of their corps. Any decision of this kind must be taken once and for all with regard to all Marine officers serving in the Naval Wing. I agree that they should retain their full dress Marine uniform and, if desired, their mess kit.

The paragraph relating to special working dress marked 'B' goes more into detail than is necessary at this stage. I have not had time to give full consideration to the details there proposed, though they are important. I prefer that this matter shall stand over for the present, and not be included in the first publication.

3. *Reserve Regulations.* – It should be made clear that civilians belonging to the Reserve will not be compulsorily called out to the detriment of their private business or profession except in a case of war or national emergency sufficient to justify the calling out of the Reserves of the Army or Navy or both.

In order to prevent delay a further provisional reprint of the letter should be made at once. I hope a clean proof can be shown me to-morrow.

WSC to Sir Graham Greene

21 May 1914

I have again carefully considered this question on which I have reached the following decision, which so far as I am concerned is final.

The uniform of the Naval Wing to be as set out in paragraphs 1 and 2 of the print attached and already agreed to. This is to apply to the few pay-master and engineer officers now serving. The marine uniform to conform as stated in paragraph 4. Marine officers to keep their military titles notwithstanding. Moustaches to be optional. A small allowance may be made to cover the cost of the changes.

Reprint the memo accordingly, and let the necessary action be taken without further delay. Paragraph 3 may be omitted as it requires further consideration in detail.

WSC to Captain Murray Sueter

23 May 1914

1. It will cause great hardship to a married officer if he is sent for a couple of months to sea every year and his pay drops down to half. My view is that we have a right to make them fly as often as we like, and if in the interests of

the Service we employ them otherwise, their rates of pay should not be affected. If a man has got a household running on a certain scale and you halve his pay for certain parts of the year, it is certain to cause all kinds of financial embarrassments.

2. A paragraph should be inserted about marriage. Officers of the Naval Wing who marry without first obtaining permission may be reverted to general service. Pray consider this and its wording.

WSC to his wife

EXTRACT

29 May 1914   Portsmouth

My darling one,

I have been at the Central Flying School for a couple of days – flying a little in good & careful hands & under perfect conditions. So I did not write you from there as I know you wd be vexed. But now that I am back on board & am off to Portland, I hasten to tell you how much & how often you & the babies were in my thoughts during these happy & interesting days. I was delighted to get your telegram altho' I read it with an uneasy conscience: but I wd not answer from such an address! – fearing it wd make you anxious – where there was vy little occasion.

We had the false hopes of Hamel's[1] safe arrival and the sombre dispersal of them with the morning newspapers. What a cruel brute the man must have been who invented that plausible lie! I did not wholly accept it; but it seems to have caused an immense wave of interest everywhere; & Masterton tells me that the people in the streets formed little crowds round the newspaper boys in their haste to get the special editions.

I went (by air) over to see the Yeomanry in their camp eleven miles away and found them delighted to see me. We had a gt reception – the men all running out in a mob, as if they had never seen an aeroplane before. I saw also Cecil Grenfell in command of the Bucks & his young Rothschild officers etc. Today I came on here: & find Masterton & Hood and a good deal of work. As I have been up at 4 am each morning I am a little short of sleep, & have been picking some up this afternoon. Goonie & Jack have just arrived on board with A. Sinclair[2] – & that is all our party. . . .

[1] Gustav Hamel (1889–1914), a British airman of French extraction who disappeared while crossing the Channel. He won the Aerial Derby around London in 1913.

[2] Archibald Henry Macdonald Sinclair (born 1890), 4th baronet; entered Army 1910; adjutant to WSC 1916; Private Secretary to WSC at the War Office 1919–21 and Colonial Office 1922; Secretary of State for Air 1940–5; Leader of the Liberal Party 1935–45.

WSC to Captain Murray Sueter

1 June 1914

One of the most important points in the organisation of Air Stations should be the assignment of particular mechanics to particular machines. How far is this principle carried out? The personal interest of the mechanic in his engine is greatly stimulated when he knows that he is made definitely responsible for it. This conduces to safety and efficiency. I should be willing to consider a system of prizes or other rewards for care of engines by mechanics to whom they are entrusted.

WSC to Captain Murray Sueter

4 June 1914

The engine controls of the new Maurice Farman are a good example of what to avoid in this class of work. They are awkward, flimsy, inconveniently shaped, and ill-secured to the fuselage. The switch is also cheap and common in the last degree. No one would put such fittings into a motor car costing 1,000*l.* It is the falsest economy, both in money and in weight, to have these appliances of the jimcrack order. Five or six pounds in weight laid out in making good, solidly-attached controls, would be wise economy. When you open or close the throttle you ought to have a sensation like winding a watch, and there should be no question of any bending movement of the lever from side to side, but only a direct slide fore and aft. All these small fittings require thought and study to reach the best disposition, and a reasonable proportion both of money and weight should be expended upon them, since they are vital to the safety of the machine.

WSC to his wife

6 June 1914   HMS *Enchantress*

My darling one,

I will not fly any more until at any rate you have recovered from your kitten: & by then or perhaps later the risks may have been greatly reduced.

This is a wrench, because I was on the verge of taking my pilot's certificate. It only needed a couple of calm mornings; & I am confident of my ability to achieve it vy respectably. I shd greatly have liked to reach this point wh wd have made a suitable moment for breaking off. But I must admit that the numerous fatalities of this year wd justify you in complaining if I continued to share the risks – as I am proud to do – of these good fellows. So I give it up decidedly for many months & perhaps for ever. This is a gift – so stupidly am I made – wh costs me more than anything wh cd be bought with money. So I am vy glad to lay it at your feet, because I know it will rejoice & relieve your heart.

Anyhow I can feel I know a good deal about this fascinating new art. I can manage a machine with ease in the air, even with high winds, & only a little more practice in landings wd have enabled me to go up with reasonable safety alone. I have been up nearly 140 times, with many pilots, & all kinds of machines, so I know the difficulties the dangers & the joys of the air – well enough to appreciate them, & to understand all the questions of policy wh will arise in the near future.

It is curious that while I have been lucky, accidents have happened to others who have flown with me out of the natural proportion. This poor Lieutenant whose loss has disturbed your anxieties again, took me up only last week in this vy machine!

You will give me some kisses and forgive me for past distresses – I am sure. Though I had no need & perhaps no right to do it – it was an important part of my life during the last 7 months, & I am sure my nerve, my spirits & my virtue were all improved by it. But at your expense my poor pussy cat! I am so sorry.

I thought of coming for you at Dieppe, but on second thoughts it is better not to repeat that voyage. If you telegraph to me I will meet you in the yacht at Newhaven & take you to Portsmouth. Then we can go up together the next day.

Always your loving & devoted
WINSTON

WSC to Captain Murray Sueter

7 June 1914

The wooden shed at Kingsnorth would be a fine quarry for the suffragettes, and it appears to me that it should be watched. The existing watchman informs me that he watches all night long, and on Saturdays from 12 noon till 7 o'clock next morning. This means that he probably walks round once or twice and goes to sleep for the rest of the time. The matter should have your attention, and a regular watch established pending the time when the men enter.

2. What is the position about the airship shed at Cromer? How much money is taken for it this year? What progress has been made, and how far are we committed?

Memorandum by WSC

9 June 1914

Only five naval air stations instead of eight will be developed this year, the money and personnel assigned to the whole being concentrated on the five.

2. As a first instalment this year, the engagement of 200 civilian entries may be approved at the expense of other ratings of Vote A. This will be fully met by economies in personnel in other directions now in contemplation. The engagement of the civilian entries should be begun at once; the matter is most urgent, as lack of proper staff for keeping the large numbers of flying machines now being delivered in good order, may easily be productive of loss of life. I wish to receive a weekly report of the numbers engaged.

3. I do not approve of the engagement of twenty-six additional seamen ratings for Coast-Guard work at the Isle of Grain, Yarmouth, Warsash, and Calshot. This is contrary to the principle by which the Air Service should take over the duties of the Coast-Guard at these particular points. The Air Service are to discharge all these duties as far as they can, and for the rest these duties, which are of no great consequence, must suffer in the early stages of the service. There is no objection to a few of the displaced Coast-Guards, if unmarried, being incorporated in the Air Service for general air duties if otherwise suited, and doing Coast-Guard work in their spare time. But I cannot sanction any specific appropriation of men for Coast-Guard duties at these stations. It was the essence of the Fourth Sea Lord's scheme that the duties should be discharged by the Air Service. If any men of the Coast-Guard turn over to the Air Service, the numbers of the Air Service must be reduced by a like amount.

4. The remaining eighty ratings at these stations are approved as proposed; and I should be glad if they can be supplied with the least possible delay.

WSC to Captain Murray Sueter

1 July 1914

Let me have a return of all officers and men of all ranks and ratings and all machines of every class, stating the conditions, at the Isle of Grain; also the number of sheds, with the number of machines each shed will hold.

WSC to Rear-Admiral Henry Oliver

10 July 1914

Please send for Lieutenant-Commander Clark-Hall, if possible on Monday, and find out what his real objection is. As it has been decided to promote Acting-Commander Samson to Commander in the next 2 or 3 months, Commander Samson will be senior to him both in the Navy List and in the Flying Service. The proposal to appoint Lieutenant-Commander Clark-Hall as first Lieutenant at Eastchurch was intended to be a mark of confidence in him and was also in the interests of the Eastchurch Flying Station. If, however, he does not wish to undertake the work, other arrangements can easily be made.

WSC to Captain William Pakenham

10 December 1914

I have now studied and considered the proposals for revising the pay of the Naval Wing, and I find them from almost every point of view unsuitable and out of harmony with the general principles on which the Royal Flying Corps was founded and should be maintained.

The first of these is the unity of the Royal Flying Corps and the close co-operation and assimilation of its Naval and Military Wings.

The second is a due recognition in all our arrangements of flying seniority within the Flying Corps and the exclusion or temporary suspension of ordinary naval or army seniority within that corps. Seniority in the Flying Corps should be based in each rank upon flying seniority. Promotion from one rank to the other is governed strictly by selection. Officers of comparatively senior rank entering the Flying Corps may be more suited to advancement than junior flying officers who have been there longer; and this is a matter which should be taken into consideration when any particular case for promotion arises. But on promotion to a higher flying rank, an officer enters that rank at the bottom of the list, whatever his naval or army seniority may be. Flying rank confers its equivalent rank in the navy or army according to the table in the DAD's minute (subject to amendment in detail). But this equivalent rank carries with it no executive command outside the flying service. Where the navy or army rank of the officer is higher than the equivalent rank which would be conferred upon him by his Flying Corps rank, it should prevail outside the flying service, and such substantive navy or army rank would, of course, carry with it the regular executive authority.

The pay of the different ranks in the flying service should be consolidated flying pay. It should be the same for the navy and army, and have no reference to the age, origin, or substantive seniority of the officers. D.A.D. has by my instructions worked out a table of flying pay on these lines for officers. I should like to see the financial cost on present rates so far as the Naval Wing is concerned, and similarly for the Military Wing. I also wish to see a scheme of pay for the non-commissioned ratings drawn up on similar lines for consideration.

Will you also let me have your views on the whole subject, which I will then discuss with you.

WSC

25
Oil

(See Main Volume II, pp. 60–79)

———

Sir Marcus Samuel to Sir John Fisher

24 November 1911

Townhill Park
Nr Southampton

Dear Lord Fisher,

How right you have been & how right you are now!

The development of the internal Combustion engine is the greatest the world has ever seen for so surely as I write these lines it will supersede steam & that too with almost tragic rapidity. Enormous strides in its evolution have been made in the last few months, the experience gained in *our* boat the *Vulcanus* leading to discoveries of great importance & once again we have been the pioneers. I am as heartsick as I know you are at the machinations of the permanent officials at the Admiralty & it will require a strong & very able man to put right the injury they have inflicted so far.

If Winston Churchill *is* that man I will help him heart and soul – no one knows better than you what I have done & can do.

We require now nothing whatever from the Government but as loyal Englishmen (in spite of wanton lies to the contrary) will be only too glad to help them *as we have in the past.*

With kindest regards & hoping soon to meet you,

I am, Yours very truly
M. SAMUEL

Please always address me to the Mote, Maidstone.

Lord Fisher to WSC

10 December 1911

Dear Winston,

Old Marcus Samuel writes me gratified at your having seen him and so am I. He is not good at exposition but he began as a pedlar selling 'sea'

shells! (hence the name of his Company) and now has six millions sterling
of his own private money. 'He's a good teapot though he may be a bad
pourer'! – All I wanted you to do was to satisfy yourself that in this one
oil Company alone (and there are heaps of others) we have always on the
Ocean *over two hundred thousand tons of oil*! it's prodigious! And remember oil
like coal don't deteriorate and you can accumulate vast stores of it in submerged tanks so as to be free from destruction by fire or bombardment or
incendiaries *and east of Suez oil is cheaper than coal*! but you wont get your
experts to plunge for it! So I say no more . . . Old Marcus is always offering
me to be a Director but nothing could ever induce me to join any public
Company of any sort whatever. I'm a pauper and I am deuced glad of it!
but if I wanted to be rich I would go in for oil! When a cargo steamer can
save 78 per cent in fuel and gain 30 per cent in cargo space by the adoption
of internal combustion propulsion and practically get rid of stokers and
engineers – it is obvious what a prodigious change is at our doors with oil!

They will talk twaddle to you about coal being a protection! You cant
burn it and have it as armour at the same time! Your old women will have
a nice time of it when the new American Battleships are at sea burning oil
alone and a German Motor Battleship is cocking a snook at our 'Tor-
toises'! *'Oil, Chauffeurs & Wireless!'* That's the Battle Cry! and '30 *Knots &
the Big Gun'!* and *'D—n Armour'* 'except for vitals',

Yours always
F.

'Size and Subdivision'! and *'Submerged War'!*
Mind I dont want you to answer.
Napier[1] *Captain of the 'Bellerophon' ought to be your Private Secretary!* Dont fail
to have him! You will like him!

WSC to Lord Fisher
(Lennoxlove Papers)

25 May 1912   HMS *Enchantress*

My dear Fisher,
    You had much better come with us for a couple of days to Reggio. There
are lots of things to talk over and we shall all like it so much. Nothing will
make me believe that you cannot get back comfortably. Do have all your kit
sent on board tonight and give the necessary orders to the barge.

Yours ever
WINSTON S. CHURCHILL

[1] Trevelyan Dacres Willes Napier (1867–1920), Captain HMS *Bellerophon* 1910–12;
commanded the 2nd Light Cruiser Squadron 1913; Naval ADC to King George V 1913;
commanded Light Cruiser Squadrons 1914–1917; Vice-Admiral 1917. KCB 1919;

WSC to Lord Fisher
(*Lennoxlove Papers*)

26 May 1912   Admiralty

My dear Fisher,

Many thanks for your letter & the papers wh I will in due course return.

It was well worth coming all this way to have a good talk with you. I value greatly your friendship as you feel & act as your instinct tells you. There is work for all in sustaining a national policy for the Navy during years of strain & menace and I am counting on you to take your share. Find us oil in sufficient quantities and at a reasonable price in peace, & without interruption in war, make us feel that we can count on it & swim on it: guarantee its supplies & reserves & you will have added another to those silent victories of peace of wh I spoke last night, & for wh I respect you so highly.

Yours very sincerely
WINSTON S. CHURCHILL

P.S. Hopwood will write to you. Take up your pen & beat out *personnel* with him.

Sir Francis Hopwood to WSC

1 June 1912

My dear Churchill,

Our wild & volatile friend has written me two letters (enclosed), from the second you will see that he now declines the chair of the Oil Commission! He did not even wait for my letter written on the day I received yours. That letter would at any rate have assured him as to personnel.

I don't know the ins and outs of his plan to you to enlarge the terms of reference but it appears to me impracticable to give a Royal Commission the duty of designing ships. Also, at the moment science is struggling with the problems of enlarged Diesel & similar engines on her own account, experiments are in progress in all sorts of places, but no effective warfare has been devised. If Sir P. Watts was asked to design a battle cruiser to be propelled by oil only he would say 'There ain't no such thing.'

If you write to Fisher don't let on that I sent you his second letter as he tries to negative my doing so – which is absurd. Unless anything unforseen happens I go to Rosyth next week end.

You appear to be having a first rate cruise.

Yrs ever
FRANCIS S. HOPWOOD

I took leave of the Comptroller yesterday.

11 June 1912

Copy

My dear Fisher,

We are too good friends (I hope) & the matters wh we are concerned are too serious (I'm sure) for anything but plain language.

This liquid fuel problem has got to be solved, & the natural, inherent, unavoidable difficulties are such that they require the drive & enthusiasm of a big man. I want you for this, *viz* to crack the nut. No one else can do it so well. Perhaps no one else can do it at all. I will put you in a position where you can crack the nut, if indeed it is crackable. But this means that you will have to give yr life & strength, & I don't know what I have to give in exchange or in return. You have got to find the oil: to show how it can be stored cheaply: how it can be purchased regularly & cheaply in peace, and with absolute certainty in war. Then by all means develop its applicn in the best possible way to existing & prospective ships. But on the other hand yr R. Commission will be advisory & not executive. It will assemble facts & state conclusions. It cannot touch *policy* or action. That wd not be fair to those on whom I must now rely. Nor wd you wish it. Its report must be secret from the public, & its work separate from the Admy. I cannot have Moore's position eclipsed by a kind of Committee of Public Safety on Designs. The field of practical policy must be reserved for the immediately responsible officers. Research however authoritative lies outside. All this I know you will concur in.

Then as to *personnel*. I do not care a damn whom you choose to assist you, so long as 1) the represve character of the Ctee is maintained & 2) the old controversies are not needlessly revived. Let us then go into names specifically. Further – 'step by step' is a valuable precept. When you have solved the riddle, you will find a vy hushed attentive audience. But the riddle will not be solved unless you are willing – for the glory of God – to expend yourself upon its toils.

I recognise it is little enough I can offer you. But yr gifts, your force, yr hopes, belong to the Navy, with or without return; & as yr most sincere admirer, & as the head of the naval service, I claim them now – knowing full well you will not grudge them. You need a plough to draw. Yr propellers are racing in air.

Yrs ever in warm regard
W

Lord Cowdray[1] to WSC

14 June 1912   47 Parliament Street

Dear Mr Winston,

Mexican Oil Supply and the Admiralty

I should very much like to have a few minutes chat with you upon the above matter at your earliest convenience. Privately, I may say that we are being pressed to sell the control of the Mexican Eagle Oil Company, Limited to one of the big existing Oil Companies. Should we do so the fuel oil supplies suitable for Admiralty purposes would thereby become controlled by a foreign Company, and it is this position that I should like to discuss with you.

The Mexican Eagle Oil Company unquestionably owns the finest deposits of crude oil suitable for fuel purposes that today are controlled by any one Company.

Yours sincerely
COWDRAY

Note at top of page by Edward Marsh:
ACL says papers are coming on about this & you should not answer till you have seen them. EM

Sir Francis Hopwood to WSC

18 June 1912

First Lord,

Please don't see Cowdray about Mexican Oil without giving me an opportunity of speaking to you about dredging at Rosyth & Dover. My opinion is concreting in favour of contract dredging but it is, as you will agree, uncommonly difficult to come to a sound conclusion without expert advice. The 'works' are for doing it themselves, as you know, & so can hardly give an unbiased opinion.

Cowdray is big enough & independent enough to advise without expecting a contract.

F.S.H.

[1] Weetman Dickinson Pearson (1856–1927), Liberal MP for Colchester 1895–1910; President of the Air Board 1917; Head of the firm of S. Pearson and Son Limited. Created Baron Cowdray 1910; Viscount 1916.

WSC to Lord Fisher
(*Lennoxlove Papers*)

29 July 1912   Admiralty

My dear Fisher,

I have enquired helpfully about the oil-tankers. The names of the Commission will be announced at once. I am delighted you are making such good progress.

I am pleased with the general result of the debates. Beresford was personal, pointless, and futile. Something had evidently stung him. I wonder if it could have been the announcement of a recent Royal Commission!

Yours ever
WINSTON S. CHURCHILL

WSC to Lord Fisher
(*Lennoxlove Papers*)

1 September 1912   Admiralty

My dear Fisher,

I am most interested in the information you sent me this morning. That would no doubt solve the problem, and a Dukedom or an Archbishopric or the Garter on both legs would not be extravagant rewards.

It is such a comfort to me to feel that you are driving ahead and butting into this gigantic question. Pray approach it from every side. Find the oil or its substitute: find out how to store it cheaply and how to get it certainly: how to protect it from aerial attack: where to place it to best advantage; and how to use it in every form of ship. Do not neglect the storage part of the question which deserves your attention for many reasons.

What induced you to think that we are building tankers with steam boilers in them? Every tanker ordered or purchased by the Admiralty will be driven by internal combustion alone, and Hopwood will take care that no more new boilers of any kind are used in the Dockyards.

There are several important matters about which I want to talk to you, but they do not lend themselves much to letters: they are better dealt with verbally. We shall, I am afraid, not return by the East Coast but go round to the West. I pick up the Chancellor of the Exchequer at Criccieth on the 21st September, and if you could come over for a few days after that, it would give me great pleasure and we will go and see Vickers' works at Barrow. Vickers have under construction several experimental 1,000 h.p. cylinders for internal combustion which ought very soon to be reaching an advanced stage of completion. I ordered them more than 10 months ago.

Do you think Lionel Yexley would like to go into Parliament as a Liberal Candidate? I find him a very straightforward man. Will it not be shocking if he displaced Beresford?

I want to talk to you also about pay. The schemes are far advanced, and I am very pleased with them. They include the Officers as well as the Warrant Officers, Petty Officers and Men. I shall have a hard battle to fight before I get the thing settled, as I know the Treasury will simply try to smother it by saying 'what about the Army'. However, I have good hopes and shall put the stable money on.

With all good wishes

WINSTON S. CHURCHILL

WSC to David Lloyd George

5 November 1912   [Admiralty]

Copy

My dear C of E,

I have just learnt that the Treasury are blocking the constrn of the oil tank steamers' sanction for wh was requested in Admy letter of [blank]. This wd be a vy serious step to take. The no. of vessels built & building for the Navy wh will be dependent on oil fuel is already considerable, & will increase & is increasing rapidly. We shall only just succeed in obtaining for them the oil on wh they depend by the time they are completed. Any interruption of this process may produce a complete administration breakdown in regard to matters wh intimately affect the margin of naval strength.

I trust this matter may receive yr personal attention.

Y. vy s.
WSC

WSC to Prince Louis of Battenberg

8 January 1913   Admiralty

Confidential

Oil Fuel Reserve.

The War Staff, acting under your directions, must be the prime authority for prescribing the reserve of oil fuel required for oil burning vessels. This is a question of principle which is governed solely by military considerations. A paper should be prepared as soon as possible setting this forth in a reasoned form. In this connection due weight should be given to the following points: –

(a) The War Staff need not concern themselves with questions of price or market 'corners' or other commercial aspects. It may be assumed that for a purpose so vital as the supply of oil to the Fleet in time of war the British Government could afford to pay a price which, so far as commercial considerations go, would command a market. It is obvious that oil for all other purposes except for those of war would find its most profitable market with the British Government, and this fact would, apart from forcible interception, draw oil from every part of the world, would divert it from every other competitive purpose, and would stimulate to the utmost the production from all existing sources. War prices would rule the market, and these would no doubt be high. But, having regard to the amount of oil produced in the world, to the necessities of the oil producers to maintain a regular flow of their business and to the comparatively small proportion of the world's oil supply which would be required by the belligerent Fleets, it should not be assumed that the prices would rise to unreasonable levels. If they rose beyond a certain point, they would immediately bring all ordinary commercial enterprises conducted by oil fuel machinery to a standstill by destroying the margin of profit for which such enterprises are conducted. There is therefore no danger in peace or war of oil prices being pushed beyond what the consumer can stand, and the British Government as consumer can of course pay prices beyond the maximum which could be exacted from commercial enterprises or neutral powers.

(b) The basis of our whole defensive policy is the command of the sea. It is not understood why if we retain command of the sea there should be any more difficulty in bringing the necessary oil ships to British ports safely than the much more numerous vessels containing other equally necessary supplies of food and raw material; but the War Staff should carefully examine this question, having special regard to the routes traversed by oil vessels and our power to control them in connection with the possibilities of convoy and methods of commerce protection generally. This part of the subject will naturally concern itself not merely with the present situation, but with that which may be reasonably expected to develop between now and, say, 1916–17.

(c) An estimate should be formed of the amount of oil which would be required by the Fleet during the first year of a war in each of the years up to 1916–17. From this should be deducted the approved reserves on which we are at present working, the yearly balance constituting the amount of oil it would be necessary to import, and these amounts having been ascertained should be considered in relation to the sources of supply and the tankers available year by year, as far as can now be forecasted. An estimate should if possible be formed of the number of voyages it would be necessary for oil ships to make in each of these years in order to maintain the supply, and the military problem of bringing these ships safe to shore examined definitely. The basis throughout should be that the producers of oil will be most anxious to supply us at the high prices prevailing, and that the enemy will do his utmost by force to prevent the supplies reaching us.

(d) What is the reasonable consumption of fuel expected to take place during an average 12 months of naval war by the British Fleet? The experience of the Russo-Japanese War is almost the only available guide. Undue importance should not be attached to the fact that the War Orders prescribe that all vessels should have steam for full speed at an hour's notice. This is a very good general rule for the first few days of a war, but it is absurd and impossible for the whole period, or as governing during the whole period all vessels irrespective of their proximity to the enemy or to the war theatre. The present war plans should of course be a guide. Due weight should be assigned to the reasonable expectation we have always held of being in far more complete command of the sea after the first few months of war than at the beginning, and to the gradual extirpation of isolated commerce destroyers which may be found at large on an immediate outbreak.

(e) The great utility and convenience of oil fuel and the desirability of our having the benefits of it, if they can be obtained without throwing burdens on the Estimates disproportionate even to such great advantages should be borne in mind. The only consequence of prescribing impossible standards like those proposed by the Royal Commission will be to arrest the adoption of oil in the British Fleet with consequent loss.

(f) It would appear that in proportion as the Fleet becomes completely dependent upon oil the scale of the reserve should rise because the magnitude of the stake would increase. There would appear facie prima to be no objection to an ascending scale of reserve reaching its maximum with the disappearance from the First and Second Fleets of the last coal burning vessel.

WSC

Lord Fisher to WSC

18 January 1913   Royal Commission on Fuel and Engines
                                        21 St James's Square

Secret & Private

Dear Winston,
    '*Litera scripta manet*'. That's why I write these few lines. You know as well
as I do that oil wants the oil engine (*Any bloody fool knows that!*). You only
want one quarter of the oil that you require for a steam engine.
    Force Oram[1] and d'Eyncourt[2] by telling them *now at once* that in your coal
battleships you want a central oil engine installation. Yarrow[3] has produced
it for the Japanese Government in a Destroyer and increases the radius of
action 3-fold. They can take Yarrow's plan just as it is and drop it into these
battleships and have Parsons[4] new geared superheated Turbine on each side
which will do $22\frac{1}{2}$ knots easy. *Burn this.*
                                                                Yours
                                                                F
    Please be careful in wording of any memorandum about Cabinet Enquiry
for remember all my colleagues are (bar *one*) *very great* men! Just see what
Redwood[5] says spontaneously about our First Report herewith.
    Read the newspaper extracts.[6]
    Burn all this at once.

Lord Fisher to WSC

27 January 1913   Royal Commission on Fuel and Engines

    Dear Winston,
    Please read Beilby's masterpiece herewith.[7] Northcliffe is booming Alcohol.
He has written to me twice. I've told him its fumes are prohibitive for
sailors.

    [1] Henry John Oram (1858–1939), Engineer-in-Chief of the Fleet 1907–17; member of
Royal Commission on Oil Fuel and Engines; Vice-Admiral 1907; knighted 1910.
    [2] Eustace Henry William Tennyson-d'Eyncourt (1868–1951), Director of Naval Con-
struction 1912–23; one of developers of tank; knighted 1917; created Baronet 1930.
    [3] Alfred Fernandez Yarrow (1842–1932), Shipbuilder and Engineer; inventor of the
Yarrow boiler used in many warships; created Baronet 1916.
    [4] Parsons Marine Turbine Company.
    [5] Boverton Redwood (1846–1919), Engineer; a member of the Royal Commission on Oil
Fuel and Engines; knighted 1905; created Baronet 1911.
    [6] *Shipbuilding Industry at Kiel* and *Use of Oil Motors.*
    [7] Memo by a Dr G. T. Beilby on *Alcohol as Fuel.*

I asked Marsh to put Sir Reginald Henderson[1] before you vice Jellicoe. All your Sea Lords worship Henderson. Henderson ought to have been made a G.C.B. for his scheme of Australian Naval Defence which holds the field, but dear A. K. Wilson crabbed it. A.K.W. is a great man in some ways but as an Administrator he would have ruined the Roman Empire.
Pass the Plural Voting Bill.

Yours
F

P.S. I hope you have ordered Percy Scott to take no notice of Bottomley and Beresford!

Lord Fisher to WSC

7 March 1913   Bellevue Lodge
                                                    Richmond

Dear Winston,
   I told you at the time ('Ad nauseam'!) that you were making a d—d mess of it in not obeying your original impulse for swifter 'Swifts'! Read the enclosed.[2]

Yours till hell freezes
FISHER

Lord Fisher to WSC

10 March 1913

Dear Winston,
   Kindly excuse me bombarding you with my hobbies but as I have ever been a firm believer in the Channel Tunnel I venture to send enclosed[3] in case it has missed your eye. I am thinking of getting our oil in war as well as food.

Yours
F

Note at bottom of letter by WSC
I am in favour of it too

WSC

[1] Reginald Friend Hannam Henderson (1846–1932), visited Australia, 1910–11, at invitation of Commonwealth Govt and presented a report giving his advice on the establishment of an Australian Navy; member of 1912 Royal Commission on Oil Fuel and Oil Engines for the Navy; knighted 1907.
[2] Newspaper article on supremacy in speed, and conversion from coal to oil, undated.
[3] Undated letter in *The Times* entitled *A Channel Tunnel*.

Lord Fisher to WSC

31 March 1913 Royal Commission on Fuel and Engines

Dear Winston,

Excuse advice! but I beg you earnestly not to go in for 'Veiled Conscription', which is what 'Compulsory Service' truly is. *It will ruin you.* Seely (like Caiphas on a greater occasion!) did not realise what he was prophesying when he said 'The fewer men you mobilise in war the stronger you are.' *There's an immense truth at the back of that!*

Yours always
FISHER

The masses of our countrymen are dead against any form of compulsion in any degree whatever! *Vox populi vox Dei!* Remember what Abraham Lincoln said!

'You can fool *all* the people *part* of the time.
You can fool *part* of the people *all* the time
But you can't fool *all* the people *all* the time!'

Lord Fisher to WSC[1]

31 March 1913 Royal Commission on Fuel and Engines

My beloved Winston,

You probably never made a better speech in your life than on the Navy Estimates, and it was sad that the despicable Tory trick deprived you of a big audience. But n'importe! it has gone all over the country! I don't agree with you about the small cruisers who will all be gobbled up by 'Goebens' like the Armadillo gobbles up ants and the bigger the ant the more placid the digestive smile – this I've told you ad nauseam, but of course you can't resist your professional advisers. *Neither have you allowed half enough money for submarines. Believe me, they are the coming force!* (However I am preparing an upheaval for you on that point, so no more!)

Please read enclosed by Yexley on that 'hell on earth' the *Lion* as regards coaling and Beresford's German Tramps! But I don't want to put you off stowing guns on board merchant steamers! *It comforts and soothes* and it's a good way of getting rid of redundant obsolete guns, and Trade is timorous – *so go on!*

---

[1] A newspaper clipping was attached to the letter, stating in part, 'The Navy has never in its long history had a more persuasive spokesman in Parliament than the present Minister.' *Note by Lord Fisher: 'Hear Hear!!!' Daily Telegraph*

You will see by enclosed extracts, which kindly send me back, that the Standard Oil Company have made a big bid for China oil. I hope our Foreign Office will be active. The Royal Commission wrote officially in the very strongest manner – go get English concessions of oil preferably near the Yangtse.

I send you second volume on oil with a suggestion for your consideration. *There's no hurry.*

Yours till charcoal sprouts

F

I said to Oram the other day before the Commission. How many hours is prudent to warm up the engines before going full speed? He said about 8 hours but it could be less. With the oil engines you start full speed at once – *see the fighting advantage!!* and yet there are bloody fools who like Canute want to stem the tide of internal combustion!

Lord Fisher to Edward Marsh

11 April 1913   Admiralty

Dear Eddie,

I trust Winston got a telephone in good time that I was unavoidably prevented coming to lunch. Please make sure he got my excuses.

When he has leisure ask him to read enclosed[1] which I am going to put before my colleagues at next meeting.

I fear he wishes to keep on the Royal Commission and of course I will do anything he thinks will be of service. I am his facile dupe!

Yours in violent haste

F

Don't let enclosed get lying about, but either return or burn.

Lord Fisher to WSC

20 April 1913   Langham House
                                                     Ham Common

My dear Winston,

Yesterday a friend sent me enclosed penny weekly paper called the *London Mail*.[2] Please see the marked passage as to a 'Sea Lord' and oil. I presume this is an echo of what you heard I believe some time ago. I am

---

[1] Draft Résumé of Work of Royal Commission on Fuel and Engines. Not found in Chartwell Papers.

in your hands entirely as to any action to be taken, and my Banker's book at your disposal to show I sold out what oil shares I had when the Royal Commission was appointed at no doubt a great prospective loss, as the Shell Company's shares are bound to go up. I was supposed to have bought up all the land round Rosyth and Osborne and sold it to a syndicate! I have never taken notice of libels, acting on Archbishop Whatley's[1] advice –

'Never fight a chimney sweep
You may knock him senseless
but some of the soot comes off on you'.
However, I will now and always act as you think proper.

Yours truly
FISHER

Lord Fisher to WSC

24 April 1913

Dear Winston,

We were so engrossed with the Pomeranian Grenadier yesterday that the object of my visit completely failed, which was to say more forcibly in words than I can by the pen how pressing is the necessity to complete the Californian oil bargain. A million tons of oil *a year* offered to you (c.i.f. – that is delivered free in England) at 53 shillings a ton is a miraculous opportunity and a contract for 10 (ten) years *or more!*

Black[2] no doubt is doing his best writing long state papers, but I fear it is only to get a puny forty thousand tons a year! Remember Californian oil is burnt by the ships on the Pacific Coast as it emerges from the earth without refining, which is an immense advantage.

I also intended to tell you that my colleagues quite shared my views yesterday that the Royal Commission had fulfilled its purpose and should be dissolved, and I will send you the shorthand notes of their views; but you wish us to go on so I say no more.

I am very unhappy at your pessimistic attitude about Invasion. It means ruin to the Navy and a Flemish Army.

Yours
F

Build more submarines – that's the Remedy! Not more Lobsters!!

---

[1] Richard Whatley (1787–1863) was Archbishop of Dublin from 1831 to 1863.
[2] Frederick William Black (1863–1930), Director of Naval Contracts; served in Colonial Office, Admiralty and Ministry of Munitions 1880–1919; Managing Director Anglo-Persian Oil Company 1919–23, of Steaua Romana Oil Companies; knighted 1913.

Lord Fisher to Edward Marsh
(Longleat Papers)

EXTRACT

29 April 1913   Langham House

. . . I don't want to make Winston's blood boil but really the procrastination in coming to terms about oil with the Californian man is *quite damnable!* . . .

WSC to Lord Crewe

1 May 1913

Most Private

My dear Crewe,

To-day Sir Hugh Barnes[1] asked to see me on Anglo-Persian oil. I was enchanted, as I regarded him as one of your right-hand men, and we are eagerly seeking the co-operation of the India Office. It was not until Hopwood and I had unfolded our views from the Government standpoint about the possible contract with the Company that he told us that he was a director of the Company and came on their behalf. All this oil business will be full of opportunities for suspicion and misrepresentation; and I must say that the dual position which Sir H. occupies might easily become a fertile breeding ground for trouble. We are of course anxious to drive a hard bargain with the Company, as well as to get the utmost help from the IO and make them a party to the contract. You will see the bearings of all this, and perhaps you will take some opportunity of talking to me about it.

I don't want to get B into a scrape, but I very nearly gave him a document relating to the contract which no one connected with the Company had any business to see. He mentioned, however, when I told him that in view of his interest I could not let him see it, that it would very probably come before him officially through the P. W. Department. This only shows his complete innocence of the wicked ways of this wicked world.

Yours very sincerely
WSC

[1] Hugh Shakespear Barnes (1853–1940), joined Indian Civil Service, 1874; Foreign Secretary to the Government of India 1900–3; Lieutenant-Governor, Burma, 1903–5; Member of the Council of India 1905–13; Director Anglo-Persian Oil Company and Imperial Bank of Persia; knighted 1903.

WSC to Prince Louis of Battenberg

[Copy]
8 May [1913]   Admiralty

You should take an opportunity with or without your naval colleagues as you may decide, of considering in technical detail the estimates of war consumption of oil proposed by the COS. You should have alternative estimates worked out if you think it worth while, showing different allowances for day's steaming at various speeds, making in the end the most probable and least challengeable basis. So far as possible a reason should be supplied for the adoption of every factor in the calculation. It is most important that no unnecessary demand should be put forward. I do not think sufficient allowance has been made for casualties and repairs of all kinds. While it is impossible to say of any particular ship that she will not be required to have to steam at an hour's notice continuously, it is certain that all the ships taken together will not in fact be so maintained during the whole period of 6 months. I should have thought that steam at an hour's notice for the whole fleet for two-thirds of the period would have been a reasonable calculation.

Again, the use you propose to make of the flotillas has been somewhat changed since the C.O.S.'s original calculations were made; and if they are to be massed for offensive action instead of employed on continuous patrolling, it would appear that the present estimates are on the generous side. I doubt if it is reasonable to assume that all the battleships of the British fleet will steam at full speed for 18 nights and days during the first 6 months of a war. It is likely that when the episode of 2 or 3 days of fast steaming begins, it will be succeeded by some notable change in the situation which will powerfully affect subsequent fuel consumption. Annual manoeuvres are much more a test of the consumption during the climax of a war than they are a representative section of so long a period as 6 months. On the other hand, losses by sabotage and aerial attack appear to present serious dangers.

The question of under-water storage should be examined. There should be no difficulty in constructing under-water tanks which would be completely concealed. The question of utilising the moats at Portland should be considered. I am not satisfied with the seriousness with which the Director of Works has approached this important and urgent branch of the subject. It may be desirable to set up a special technical committee to advise on methods of storage and to make experiments.

The War Staff should make a detailed report on the placing and distribution of the tanks and on all methods of distribution between the tanks and the fleet. There ought surely to be a big oiling depot on the West Coast where the fleet may have to lie for long periods? Land should be very cheap there and capable of being secretly acquired by private persons in our interests.

The Third Sea Lord's Department or D.I.D. who would be accurately informed, should supply C.O.S. with the exact dates at which all new oil-using vessels now building are at present expected to complete, together with their emergency dates Quarter by Quarter as far as can be calculated. The amount of extra oil required for ships commissioned at emergency dates should also be shown separately Quarter by Quarter, in order that we may form a judgment of how far it is fair to set these amounts off against what will probably be found the much more serious factor of casualties and repairs.

The Director of Contracts should make a scheme for supplying the necessary quantities arrived at by the above calculations, so as to have the approved reserves in hand as speedily as possible without undue strain on our finances. In making this scheme he should even expense out as far as possible, bearing in mind the great burden which will fall on 1914–15 from other causes.

I hope it may be possible to enforce a further economy during the next 12 months in the current consumption of oil, every ton of which saved will go to reserve. You should for this purpose consult with the Commodore (T) and make him feel how important the matter is.

The Fourth Sea Lord in conjunction with the Director of Stores should prepare a scheme of tankage in conformity with the requirements of the oil reserve as worked out by the Director of Contracts for each particular Quarter. This must be kept at a minimum during the first two years, though I agree that a margin over and above the existing reserve should be provided as soon as the financial strain becomes less severe.

WSC

[Attached to Letter]

Absolute minimum Per month

Battle ships
- 24 hours full speed
- 4 days at 4/5ths power
- 5 days at 15 knots
- 6 days at 10 knots
- 13 days steam for 12 knots at 1 hours notice
- 1 day fires out

Battle cruisers and cruisers and light cruisers
- 24 hours full speed
- 4 days at 4/5ths power
- 12 days at 15 knots
- 4 days at 10 knots
- 8 days steam at 1 hours notice 12 knots
- 1 day fires out

TBD's $\left\{\begin{array}{l} \text{2 days full speed} \\ \text{8 days 4/5ths power} \\ \text{8 days 15 knots} \\ \text{10 days steam for 15 knots at 1 hours notice} \\ \text{2 days fires out} \end{array}\right.$

Note: When ships are *at sea* fires to be always lit under 90% of the boilers whether required for the speed ordered or not.

J.G.J.

Sir Francis Hopwood to WSC

EXTRACT

29 May 1913

... Thank you for the memorandum on oil. It is being put into final form, and a copy shall be in print by the time you return.

I am making efforts sub rosa to induce the Shell Company to offer us another substantial contract. Fisher has taken fright at the paragraph in *The Times* hinting at 'scandals' with regard to a Mexican oil contract, and is now suggesting that we ought to do without it. On the other hand he does not tell us how we are going to make up the deficit. Lambert wants the Anglo-Persian and Mexican contracts in detail put before the Oil Commission. It is the point we discussed and the action we took. But Lambert would like the Commission to approve the proposals in detail. If they did so, it is true that the blessing of an independent expert tribunal would help you with the House of Commons and perhaps stave off pressure for reference to a House of Commons Committee. I fear however that the Commission who shirked it before would again funk a bald approval.

Sir Edward Clarke[1] – the eminent Lawyer – who is Master of the Shipwrights' Company called yesterday to ask me to press you to attend the Shipwrights' Dinner at Fishmongers' Hall on Friday the 6th. He said that it would be a very representative gathering of people connected with and interested in the Navy, and that he hoped you would make a speech. He suggested that if you did not go I should do so and talk to them about the arming of merchant vessels! But I firmly declined on the ground that that was a subject much better not discussed in public. Would you instruct one of your 'bull dogs' to let me know whether you are disposed to attend the dinner as Clarke is coming back here on Monday for an answer.

---

[1] Edward George Clarke (1841–1931), Barrister and politician; Conservative MP Plymouth 1880–1900; knighted 1886.

You have no doubt collected some interesting material from the Mediterranean which could be made the subject of an attractive after dinner speech.

Ever yours sincerely
FRANCIS S. HOPWOOD

A campaign is already afoot to urge us to 'put down' the three battleships.

WSC to Sir Frederick Black and Sir Francis Hopwood

25 June [1913]   [Admiralty]

Copy

I am very anxious not to add the £413,000 required for the 100,000 tons of oil to this year's Estimates until we know what our underspending or overspending is going to be. Please, if possible, make a plan to order this 100,000 tons at once but to pay for it on delivery in the first month of the new financial year and not in the last month of this. Such an arrangement would avoid any further trouble with the Treasury at the moment, and I am pressing them so hard on other matters that I greatly desire not to have this extra complication on my hands. Provision can be made in the regular course when the estimates for 1914–15 are prepared.

Lord Fisher to WSC

[? 2 July 1913]   Royal Commission on Fuel and Engines

Dear Winston,

I enclose uncorrected proof of Mr Frazer's evidence which may necessitate modification of what you are proposing to say in House of Commons as he says all the Scotch Shale is leased already. Anyhow I suggest your reading Frazer's Evidence closely. We are under the most solemn obligations not to disclose the Evidence of the witnesses before our Royal Commission. So I beg you not to quote the Royal Commission in any way. Your speech is administrative and executive in which the Royal Commission has no part whatever. I fear if *in any way* you quote the Royal Commission you may be forced into producing their thousand pages of print!

You should also study Mr Lane's evidence and I enclose replica of Deterding's[1] evidence to refresh your memory.

Yours vy truly
FISHER

Postscript:
The printers have not sent the Evidence as expected I will post it directly it arrives but I send this on in advance.

I will call and see you at *noon* next Friday July 11th in case you are then free for an hour.

Memorandum by WSC

4 July 1913   Admiralty

Secret

The Admiralty have addressed a letter to the India Office (18th June, 1913, C.P. 20100) urging the desirability of India and Admiralty acting jointly in this matter.

2. The offer of contracts on favourable terms to the Admiralty and to the Indian Government, for naval and railway purposes respectively, is dependent upon the Anglo-Persian Company retaining its independence and not being absorbed by the 'Shell' group of companies. Neither India nor Admiralty will obtain as favourable terms if the company is absorbed by the 'Shell.'

3. The Anglo-Persian Company and the Burma Oil Company are very closely allied, and if the independence of the one is sacrificed, that of the other may be jeopardised.

4. This would in all probability have the effect of disturbing the present arrangement between the Burma Company and the 'Shell' in respect of their shares of the Indian market for kerosene, and would probably lead to the upsetting to the serious detriment of the Indian consumer of the present understanding which sets a maximum on the selling price of kerosene in the Indian market.

5. The desire of the Indian Government, fully shared by the Admiralty,

---

[1] Henri Wilhelm August Deterding (1866–1939), Director-General of the Royal Dutch Petroleum Company; a Director of the Shell Transport and Trading Company Limited; knighted 1920.

that these two companies should remain independent for the development of the Baluchistan and the adjacent oil-fields, would fail of realisation.

6. There are also considerable political interests at stake in the Gulf region, and if the Anglo-Persian sacrifices its independence, it must not only enter into combination with the 'Shell' group, which brings in Dutch influence, but in respect of the Mesopotamian fields, alliance with German interests through the Deutsche Bank and Bagdad Railway interest, is inevitable. In any arrangement for a composite company to work Mesopotamian oil concessions it is important to preserve such British influence and control as, coupled with the proposed action in regard to the Anglo-Persian Company in respect of supplies from Persia, will leave that company in a position to maintain its independence and fulfil contracts to Admiralty and India.

7. It is agreed that in respect of oil, the Admiralty interest in the matter is the more urgent, as the Indian Government, with cheap coal available for its railways, is not under immediate and pressing necessity to make a change from the one fuel to the other.

8. If, however, the Admiralty enters into a large contract with the Anglo-Persian Company now and takes the full onus of the financial advances proposed, it will undoubtedly be serving important Indian interests as well, and there would be a strong case for joint action irrespective of possible oil fuel requirements for Indian railways.

9. The advantage of Indian railways coming in now is that the oil company can immediately and more completely and economically prepare for the necessary outlay on pipe lines, refinery, &c, to produce the maximum required.

10. It is stated by the Indian Government in a recent telegraphic despatch that preliminary calculations on the basis of the price now quoted by the Anglo-Persian Company for supplies of oil to Karachi are favourable. Engineering experience in the running of oil-driven locomotives in America, Russia, and elsewhere is known to be favourable to that fuel, and conversion to coal in any case of temporary suspension of oil supplies is a common practice both in railway locomotives and oil-driven steamships, and not attended with any material difficulty, provided the contingency is kept in mind. The Indian Government estimate that about 200,000 tons of oil annually would be taken. The Admiralty would require from 200,000 to 300,000 tons from that source. The managing director of the Anglo-Persian Oil Company states that he has information to the effect that in the experimental oil-driven locomotive in use on the Grand Peninsula Railway of India the quantity of oil consumed is about one-half that of coal. He therefore urges that the tests which the Indian railway authorities have decided

to make in the next twelve months would appear necessary only for the purpose of determining details as to the best types of burners, &c, and need not delay decision in principle as to adoption of oil. This would undoubtedly aid in prompt solution of this matter, as all interests could be provided for comprehensively and at once.

It is therefore suggested that the procedure should be for an Indian Government guarantee of interest at 4 per cent on 2,000,000*l* to be given for ten years – a total contingent liability of 800,000*l*. If this guarantee be given by India, the Admiralty would undertake to make good to Indian revenues any actual payment that might prove not to be recoverable from the company, *pro rata*, to the quantities of oil actually drawn by the Admiralty. The aggregate financial risk is much lighter than if the Admiralty undertook the full onus of advances amounting in all to 2,000,000*l* during a contract period of twenty years. The difference is that between India *guaranteeing* 80,000*l* a-year for ten years, and the Admiralty *paying* 100,000*l* a-year for twenty years.

11. Moreover, if the guarantee is given by India the situation is relieved in other ways. It is necessary to keep as confidential as possible from foreign countries as well as from competing oil companies the detailed allocation of Admiralty contracts for this important munition of war. We must necessarily, however, permit publication of that portion of the proposed contract with the Anglo-Persian Company relating to the annual advances, as the investing public will require those details. A refusal to disclose the remainder of the contract is thus obviously made more difficult, as public pressure for full details will almost certainly be exerted. If the guarantee is entirely a distinct matter, on lines that will necessarily and properly be made public, as in the case of guarantees of interest on Indian railways, the details of the quantity contract can in this case, as in all others, be treated in the public interests as confidential, and only the general fact of the existence of such a contract will then require to be made known.

12. In a matter where so many complex issues are involved, the general interest points strongly to the Home and Indian Governments acting together and with the least possible delay.

WSC

WSC to Sir Edward Grey

9 July 1913   [Admiralty]

Copy

The Admiralty are proposing to make a contract with the Anglo-Persian for the supply of a large quantity of oil in consideration of an advanced payment on account of the oil by the Admiralty of £100,000 a year for 20 years. The Treasury have already been addressed on this subject and are considering the proposal, which as you will see embodies several features unusual in Government contracts. The Admiralty regard the development of the Anglo-Persian oil supplies as indispensable to the solution of the liquid fuel problem, and the Board have unanimously decided in that sense.

Simultaneously with these negotiations, efforts are being made to induce India to come forward with an alternative proposition by guaranteeing the interest at 4% on the capital of two millions required to develop the Anglo-Persian oilfield. This alternative is in every way preferable to the former. India would guarantee £80,000 a year for 10 years instead of the Admiralty *paying* £100,000 a year for 20. It is hoped that India will come to our assistance. If she does not, we must go forward alone by the more expensive and unsatisfactory method. It appears to me that there can be no doubt that the Anglo-Persian Oil Company will receive substantial financial aid in one form or another from the British or Indian Governments.

Lord Fisher to WSC

Sunday   Langham House
13 July 1913

Very Secret

Dear Winston,

Sir Marcus Samuel urgently pressed me to see him yesterday. I did. I have not seen him since he gave his evidence before the Royal Commission. I've sent Hopwood a resumé of Sir Marcus Samuel's words. I hardly spoke. *Please read them.* I sent them to Hopwood direct as I had taken Sir Boverton Redwood to see him (Hopwood) on Friday to recount what Mr Lane had said to him (Redwood).

All oil magnates are liars! but Sir Marcus told me that Beresford is chortling! thinking he has got you on toast! He had seen Beresford. He said Beresford was working the *Morning Post* as against you. Sir Marcus swore to me that his brother Samuel Samuel MP,[1] was absolutely innocent as regards the *Globe* attacks. As I never asked him and knew nothing of it, I don't know why he told me except that I should pass it on to you!

The greatest mistake you will ever have made (*except not coming to the Admiralty when I exhorted you in Bruton Street!*) will be to quarrel with Deterding. He is Napoleon and Cromwell rolled into one. *He is the greatest man I have met!* Placate him, don't threaten him! Make a contract with him for his fleet of 64 oil tankers in case of war. Don't abuse the Shell Company or any other oil company. *You want to get oil from everyone everywhere.* Abuse Beresford, that will pay!

Yours for evermore
FISHER

No one counts except Deterding!
PS Sir William Mather[2] is coming to see me this afternoon, I hope to get him to put a million into the Junker Engine.

Lord Fisher to WSC

18 July 1913   Langham House

Private

My dear Winston,
Just a line of thanks for your kindness in dealing with Mr Gretton[3] so effectively as regards oil shares. What a pack of slanderers! But you had Archer Shee[4] and Terrell[5] on the trip! and Beresford's gleanings from disloyal Naval Officers fell flat and mostly unreported. You will be too busy to read more!

Yours
FISHER

[1] Samuel Samuel (1855–1934), Unionist MP Wandsworth 1913–19, Putney 1919–34; a founder and director of Shell Transport and Trading Company.
[2] William Mather (1838–1920), Chairman of Mather and Platt Limited, Manchester. Liberal MP Salford 1885–6, Gorton 1889–95, Rossendale 1900–4; knighted 1902.
[3] John Gretton (1867–1947), Conservative MP S. Derbyshire 1895–1906, Rutland 1907–18, Burton Div of Staffs 1918–43; PC 1926; created Baron Gretton of Stapleford 1944.
[4] Martin Archer-Shee (1873–1935), Unionist MP Finsbury 1910–23; knighted 1923.
[5] Henry Terrell (1856–1944), Unionist MP for Gloucester 1910–18; County Court Judge 1920–9.

P.S. Queen Alexandra and her sister[1] and Princess Victoria[2] came here yesterday, and I am confirmed in my opinions often told you, but more when we meet.

WSC to Lord Fisher
(Lennoxlove Papers)

29 July 1913   Admiralty

Private

My dear Fisher,
    A line to tell you that Jellicoe has done wonders & fully justified all your confidence in him.

Yours ever
W.

Lord Fisher to WSC

30 July 1913   Langham House

Dear Winston,
    Your praise of Jellicoe is joy to me! Years and years he was with me when I was Captain of *Excellent* and Director of Naval Ordnance. He never failed me. The sacred fire of originality burns in him. He has the 4 Nelsonic attributes!

Yours
F

Get a lien on Deterding's 64 Oil Tankers for War. Reward! Make Deterding a Knight! Don't forget!

Lord Fisher to Edward Marsh
EXTRACT

6 August 1913

Dear Eddie,
    By this same post I've sent an important express letter to Winston. Please be sure he reads it and that he keeps an appointment at 4 pm today Wednes-

---

[1] Either Marie Sophie Frederica Dagmar (1847–1928), wife of Tsar Alexander III of Russia; or Thyra Amelia Caroline Charlotte Anne (1853–1933), wife of Ernest Augustus, 3rd Duke of Cumberland and Teviotdale, *de jure* King of Hanover.

[2] Victoria Alexandra Olga Mary (1868–1935), second daughter of King Edward VII. Died unmarried.

day with Mr Deterding the Napoleon of Oil and mind he don't hurry and Winston will double his oil! . . .

Lord Fisher to WSC

6 August 1913   Royal Commission on Fuel and Engines

Dear Winston,

In association with the Dutchman conniving in your commandeering of his Oil Fleet, he will put up vast tankage at Alexandria, Colombo, The Cape, &c. Get this from him at first hand. These Tankers would then bring oil from these British depots when foreign sources banned by embargo. Throw your fly this day I beg you and act while Deterding's enthusiasm is red hot. 75 per cent of his oil fleet fly the English flag – let the other 25 per cent be gradually transferred also. I gather he has 60–70 Tankers. He has a son at Rugby or Eton and has bought a big property in Norfolk and building a castle! Bind him to the land of his adoption! 'They can conquer who believe they can' said Virgil. *That's your motto!* Get today a pledge from Deterding to be confirmed later by a sealed secret compact known only to you, the Prime Minister and the Chancellor of the Exchequer. Otherwise Deterding will be on the flat of his back if other oil people hear of it. *Secrecy, Secrecy, Secrecy!* He has just bought up Sir Robert Balfour[1] and all his vast store of Californian Oil. He isolated him and then swallowed him! Napoleonic in his audacity: Cromwellian in his thoroughness! Get Oliver to the Admiralty. You want his jaw there!

Yours for evermore

FISHER

350 vessels go manoeuvring without a hitch or defect! What's wrong with the Navy! *Rub that in!*

WSC to Lord Fisher

13 August 1913   Admiralty

Private & Confidential

My dear Fisher,

I have re-read the first interim report of the Royal Commission, and I agree with you that in view of the secret character of this enquiry and the confidential terms on which the evidence has been given it is undesirable that

---

[1] Robert Balfour (1844–1929), Liberal MP Partick division of Glasgow 1906–22; member of firm of Balfour, Williamson & Company; created Baronet 1911.

any publication should be made to Parliament. On the other hand it is important to safeguard the Admiralty against the suggestion which has been and will increasingly be made that we are proceeding in opposition to the recommendations of the Royal Commission. There is no reason in the immediate future for any further reference to the subject, but I desire to be in a position when Parliament meets to state that the general purport of the recommendations of the Royal Commission is as follows: –

First, that the advantages to be derived from the use of oil fuel are set out by the Commission in the first portion of their interim report.

Secondly, that the Commission are of opinion that the oil resources of the world are amply sufficient, if suitable measures are taken, for the requirements of the Fleet.

Thirdly, that large reserves, based upon peace requirements should be accumulated in this country.

Will you consider at your leisure and let me know whether you agree with such a statement as representing a fair summary of your report.

I must point out in this connection that the responsibility for fixing the standard of reserves rests of course wholly with the Board of Admiralty, who have lately given the closest attention to the subject, and that the Royal Commissioners are not committed to any responsibility beyond that of making the recommendations contained in their report. I do not propose to say specifically what those recommendations were.

Lord Fisher to WSC

EXTRACT

[? August 1913]

. . . We had 3 solid hours of Lord Cowdray before the Royal Commission yesterday. He guarantees a million tons yearly of fuel oil for 15 years if the Admiralty like to make such a contract at 28 shillings a ton, and as we could bring it in our own oil tankers at eight shillings per ton (those with internal combustion engines) the price would be 36 shillings a ton (and as it has been demonstrated beyond question that one ton of oil is equal to 4 tons of coal with internal combustion) *this price is equal to coal at 9 shillings a ton!!!* And oil improves by keeping whilst coal rapidly deteriorates! and then (beyond all this) is the diminution of the personnel with enormous ramifications of economy consequent thereon. *Daily we see the desirability of increasing storage accommodation.*

Lord Fisher to WSC

19 August 1913   Marienbad

Private & Confidential

My dear Winston,

Your excellent letter of Aug 13 has just reached me here, and I have no doubt at all that all my colleagues will join with me in fully assenting to your three statements as to the general purport of the recommendations of the Royal Commission. We are to have plenary meetings of the Royal Commission on the last Tuesday and Wednesday in October, when I will get their assent and write to you officially for public quotation. I shall also put in my official letter that it has been ever present to the Royal Commissioners that the responsibility for fixing the standard of reserves rests solely and wholly with the Board of Admiralty and that the only reason for the Royal Commissioners mentioning in their Report that large reserves based upon peace requirements should be accumulated in the country was not the doubt as to there ever being an insufficiency of oil, but the peculiar circumstances of the oil industry rendering it dependent upon the vagaries which no oil expert has yet fathomed as to the output of oil areas. As Mr Deterding (the greatest of Oil Kings) said in his delicious evidence (he has just swallowed Sir Robert Balfour and the Californian Oil Fields!)

'There is not anybody who can be certain of his oil supply: oil fields in my experience which at the time yielded 18,000 barrels a day within five days went down to 3,000 barrels without the slightest warning.'

In that print I sent you in April 1913, '*Memorandum on Oil and its fighting attributes*' I ended in large capitals – italics!

'*Build reservoirs and store oil*

Keep on building reservoirs and buy oil at favourable rates when they offer!'

Did you have a satisfactory interview with our mutual friend at 4 pm the day after I saw you? Send me one line 'Yes' or 'No' at 21 St James's Square and it will reach me safely.

I see Lord Brassey[1] and others are advocating more ships on foreign stations and so frittering our strength! When Bismark was attacked in the German Parliament for having no soldiers in Africa and asked what defence from an attack from the French Congo – he replied '*A sortie from Metz!*'

Yours
FISHER

[1] Thomas Brassey (1836–1918), served in Admiralty in various political capacities 1880–1885; Liberal MP 1865, 1868–85; Governor of Victoria 1895–1900; Founder and First Editor *Naval Annual*. Knighted 1881; Created Baron Brassey 1886; Earl 1911.

*WSC to Prince **Louis** of Battenberg*

15 September 1913   [Admiralty]

Copy

Please see the attached estimate for the consumption of oil by the flotillas next year. You will see how very serious it is. The Third Sea Lord tells me that with oil burning turbine driven destroyers there is not the same necessity for running high speed trials as in the days of coal using reciprocating engines.

During a year when we are making every effort to accumulate rapidly our oil fuel reserve, and when in consequence the expense is at its highest, special efforts are needed to reduce by every possible means the great consumption of oil by flotillas.

Please consider this in connection with my minute about the organisation of the German flotillas and the proposals for introducing a 'rest' period next year. You have already at an earlier period in the year given much attention to this subject, and I am of opinion that it should be further examined, not merely from the point of view of the amount of oil necessary for the existing programme of exercises but as to the possibilities of restricting movements. The financial problem with which I am confronted in 1914–15 is so grave that I am sure I may count on your aid in every legitimate measure of relief.

I have been wondering whether a committee on the programme of destroyer exercises would be of any value; but I feel that nothing would be so effective as your personal authority. It may be necessary to omit the manoeuvres altogether next year, as was proposed by the Second Sea Lord as an economy for this year, or in any case to leave the oil burning vessels out of them.

It ought to be possible to make at least 50,000 tons reduction without injury to efficiency.

Lord Fisher to WSC

[? October 1913]   Langham House

Secret & Private

My dear Winston,

A few lines to welcome you home and report progress *re Oil*. We have been *hustling* the *blending* and *chemical* to such an extent that I hope to send you report of Committee next Monday 4 weeks which I think will be a record!

Mr Lane has given us big (*very big*) evidence before the Royal Commission. This week he has bought 10 million barrels of Californian oil for himself. He thought he might do the same for Admiralty, so I begged Hopwood to see him *at once*. I don't know the result. *Californian oil is perfect as fuel oil.* What benzine there is in it the producers will take off without charge if you give them the resulting benzine. *The oil is then suitable for our use.*

I am taking a spell off now for a bit while Beilby & Co are hard at the chemical tests. If you send for Oram he will tell you what is going on about Krupps big oil engine of 2,700 horse-power per unit and also about Krupps submarine engine. *I advise you to see Oram at once.*

I had a chance of urging Sir E. Grey and Lord Crewe to push on decision about Persian Oil and the Mesopotamian oil concession. Otherwise Deterding will have it.

Whatever you do don't go in for steam for a submarine! Simply fatal! You can have *at least* 20 big enough oil engine submarines for one Dreadnought!

Yours
F

PS Remember that the submarine is now the dominating sea fighting factor and you are not building enough of them.

Lord Fisher to WSC

18 October 1913

Dear Winston,

Yesterday I handed in at the Admiralty the report of the technical and scientific committee on the blending and mixing of oils. I hope it won't be buried. You had best send for it at once or it may be. I cannot praise my colleagues too highly – they are *splendid!* Like Montaigne I can say 'I have culled a garland of flowers, mine only is the string that binds them'!

In about a fortnight I will send you the Parliamentary statement for you to make use of as necessary as to there being no antagonism between the Admiralty and the Royal Commission. At the same time in another letter I shall present to the Admiralty the third volume of the Royal Commission with a brief recapitulation in my letter of what the Royal Commission has done and suggesting that we terminate our existence on Dec 31st next with a final report. I know there is a strong feeling that the Royal Commission should continue as a powerful body capable of dealing with promptitude and authority with any difficulty suddenly arising and without doubt our close and cordial relationship with very eminent engineers and oil magnates is to be parted from with reluctance. Still I think the arguments are in favour of our decease (Wait and see!)

Secret & Private. I have pressed Oram to put forward a proposal to order 3 cylinders from Vickers at once and work them in shop trials with the view and hope of anticipating the German Admiralty in their intention of an early installation of the oil engine in a battleship.

He agreed with me yesterday that such an installation is clearly in view as practicable with a possible speed of 16 knots – without ever touching your turbines or your coal which remain intact for battle with a speed of 25 knots. This ship so engined could go round the world without re-fuelling! *Push on with this.* He will put it forward shortly. *Please consider all this private. Everything revolves round the oil engine! Nothing can stop it* – but 200 *billions* sterling are fighting against its adoption! So it's a big fight. *It's the same with coal.* But Beilby is going to conquer and turn it into Oil for the Navy. Cheap fuel for the poor man (50 *per cent less!*) Manure for the farmer and a smokeless England!

Yours
FISHER

Your ally Custance and his clique want a job! I see they are writing in *The Times* for a new Committee on Designs! The writer of these articles is highly employed so mind you put Admiral H. H. Campbell[1] on it also! and that d—d old woman and newspaper hack Bridge who has never done a thing for the Navy in his life casts a stone at the Dreadnought type! Isn't it funny that every nation on earth followed our lead! They waited 18 months – *paralyzed!* Wasn't that a gain for us? and then the Germans spent 15 millions in building a new Kiel Canal and another 4 millions in dredging their shallow approaches, so that our 33 pre-Dreadnoughts could go into their guts and hit them! Wasn't that Machiavellian! But what's the good of talking to d—d fools! the only thing is to kick them as Bacon did Custance on Alan Burgoyne's paper at the Naval Architects!

Herewith read it again please if you feel weak-kneed! I am perfectly sick of fools and I want to leave England for good, as I've been invited to settle in America!

---

[1] Henry Hervey Campbell (1865–1933), Assistant Director of Naval Intelligence 1906–9; put on half-pay October 1909 for indiscreet handling of official papers (see Marder: *Fear God and Dread Nought*, II, p. 254); first Governor to Prince of Wales in HMS *Hindustan* 1911; Rear-Admiral Home Fleets at the Nore 1914–17; KCVO 1930.

If you don't pass Plural Voting as I entreated 3 of your distinguished
Cabinet colleagues 3 years ago you'll make a d—d mess of it!

F

WSC to Lord Fisher
(*Lennoxlove Papers*)

21 October 1913   Admiralty

My dear Fisher,

I have asked for the report on the blending and mixing of oils to be sent
to me at once, and I look forward to receiving the Parliamentary statement
which you say will be ready in a fortnight.

Do not let us decide on dissolving the commission until we have had a talk.
The oil situation is so difficult and important that the continuance of an
advisory body of the authority and experience of your Commission to whom
special questions can be referred would be a great advantage.

I am speaking to Moore about the 3 cylinders. He is very keen on the oil
engine and wanted some time ago to have a section made in Germany. I am
afraid the oil engine will not come to affect the 1914–15 ships.

In common with my naval colleagues, I have been much annoyed to read
the stupid articles in *The Times* about naval design. It is an ill service to the
Navy to throw doubt upon the policy which successive Boards have pursued
at a moment when heavy estimates are in progress and the Canadian ships
hang in the balance. Do you know who the author is?

Yours ever
W

Lord Fisher to WSC

11 November 1913   Langham House

My dear Winston,

Your kind reference to me re Submarines at the Guildhall is more than
pleasant, because from 1904 to 1910 I was so vehemently and even malig-
nantly assailed in being really their sole upholder *and they are the weapon of the
strong!*

You made an eloquent speech – Even the 'pole-cats of the Press' are dumb!

In a few days now I send you the memorandum for Parliament and my
Colleagues wish to terminate the Royal Commission with two more volumes
on oil and the oil engine. If you persist in keeping the Commission alive after

reading this letter then we must continue. My colleagues are all patriots and I confess I think we are a powerful engine, though all *I* do is to oil the machinery and now and again chuck a barrel of petroleum into the fire to give a 'burst'!

Yours always
F

I am collecting some interesting financial facts that may be useful to you about the *economy* of the Dreadnought era, as Beresford and Hirst[1] (strange colleagues!!) are preparing an attack:
'And the same day Pilate and Herod were made friends together; for before they were at enmity between themselves'!
My postscript is always the same:
'Stick to Jellicoe'!!!

Lord Fisher to WSC

13 November 1913   Royal Commission on Fuel and Engines

Private

Dear Winston,
I slunk out of the back door below your window but **I am quite ready to come out in the open** if you want me, but I think it a trivial business (Forgive me!) and of course as you rightly said if you had been provided with a Troubridge 'to pay tithe of mint and anise and cummin' while you yourself attended 'to the weightier matters of the law' – all would have been well!

I'm not sure that I would not have him back! He is well down the list and put in some time afloat. I hardly think the one you named would do, because you want the 'Suaviter in modo' as well as the 'fortiter in re'. *Anyhow I entreat you 'to go slow'* and let the First Sea Lord finish off the business, as is his duty and should be his inclination.

As for yourself, may I recommend to you the motto I stuck up in front of my table as First Sea Lord: –
'Reculer pour mieux sauter'
Nevertheless if you are in for a fight I am with you to the last ditch!

Yours always
F

Taken altogether your present colleagues on the Board are the *crème de la crème! non-pareil!* stick to them!

[1] Francis W. Hirst (1873-1953), editor of *The Economist* 1907-16; Governor of the London School of Economics.

Lord Fisher to WSC

16 November 1913   Langham House

My dear Winston,

It was kind of you to let me know at once that all was settled, as it lifted a load off my mind and it never should recur if you are properly served. I hope you will agree to the Royal Commission terminating on Dec 31 as suggested in that letter I left with you, which please now date and deal with. No doubt you will kindly frame some nice words for my illustrious colleagues. They are all '300 *guineas*' men and have given their services bountifully and gratuitously (Lord Mersey (and his colleagues) gets put on a Titanic Enquiry and gets thousands of guineas!!)

Don't trouble to answer. Heaven bless you.

Yours
FISHER

Lord Fisher to WSC

18 November 1913   Langham House

My dear Winston,

It was kind of you to remember that I wanted to see Keyham and the *Highflyer*, but I cannot get away. Can't you nip down here some afternoon? It only takes 35 minutes from your door to this door. Come through Richmond Park to *Ham Gate*. But come before Nov 26 if you do come, and bring Mrs Winston and she will see in our garden a Cedar of Lebanon planted by Abraham, and in this house Maria Edgeworth wrote her novels! But I would like to say some words to you, always so impossible at the Admiralty – you are too engrossed and too interrupted!

Yours
FISHER

I want you to free me to be off abroad at the end of the month if circumstances permit it, but I *must* get clear of that d—d Commission or my mind won't be at rest!

Lord Fisher to WSC

[? 10 December 1913]   Royal Commission on Fuel and Engines

Secret

My dear Winston,

Jellicoe has sent me a nice letter which I will brood over about Chatham. I used to say to Selborne 'Everybody wants everything and *they can't have it'!!!* Unless you have Navy Estimates of £100,000,000!

I would guarantee to save four millions sterling on your next year's Estimates if I were First Sea Lord, but then I must be there as First Sea Lord to do it. The First Lord *can't* do it. (Not even *you!*) It wants the *sea* responsibility and the *fighting* responsibility of your chief naval adviser to see a job of that sort through under the aegis of the First Lord's political responsibility.

There never was such a strong report backed by such eminent witnesses as proposed spending 19½ millions sterling on Dockyard Extension in 1903. *We never spent a penny of it! but please don't rake up this. I don't want to cast stones at Selborne and Pretyman and others who are great friends of mine still!*

As every new ship finishes her trials an old ship ought to be scrapped. You haven't scrapped a dinghy! Neither will you build Super-Swifts instead of those rotten useless oil cruisers. *You are all mad, mad, mad!*

Yours
F

Lord Fisher to WSC

13 December 1913   Royal Commission on Fuel and Engines

My dear Winston,

Thank you for your letter. I say no more about Chatham. 'Let us pray'! for Tirpitz will be a d—d fool if he doesn't 'Jellicoe' the Nore with submarines before war is declared! – when there ought not to be a single British armoured vessel of any sort between Scapa Flow and Dover (I forget how many deep draught ships you can get down in one tide from Chatham to the Nore!)

I note by examining the Navy List there have been no less than 21 removals of Submarines since I was First Sea Lord and only *12* additions. *Do you think this is satisfactory?* and the remainder of 'A' and 'B' classes are now approaching 10 years of age and there are 19 of them which figure in our totals. *We are falling behind Germany in large submarines.* The real issue is always obscured by dealing in *total* numbers – the Germans have a larger proportion of modern sea-going vessels, and by what one reads they have a larger actual number building and projected.

Are you please going to let the Royal Commission die on Dec. 31, as requested in letter I sent you? I enclose a printed copy. *I hope you will acquiesce.*

Yours always
FISHER

Note by WSC:
Say – No. The R.C. must continue for the present

WSC

WSC to J. Masterton-Smith

3 January 1914   [Admiralty]
Copy

Send the poisonous article about Oil Fuel in the *Morning Post* to-day to Lord Fisher. Say it is clearly Beresford's influence which is at work and that I am very glad to think that in the publishable minute of the Royal Commission I have such a complete and decisive answer.

WSC to Sir Frederick Black

3 March 1914   [Admiralty]
Copy

Is Mr Deterding in England? I should like to see him. I wish to propose to him that we take delivery during the year 1914–15 of as much oil of his 1915–16 contract as he can send us within the limits of our freight engagements, and that we have an option to pay for this excess oil either in 1914–15 or in 1915–16.

Memorandum by WSC

11 May 1914   Admiralty

Confidential

We have now settled with the Law Officers and the Anglo-Persian Oil Company the terms (except as to a few minor details) of an Agreement, under which His Majesty's Government will subscribe (if Parliament provides the necessary funds) capital in shares and debentures amounting to 2,200,000*l.* for development by the Company to enable supplies of oil fuel to be furnished to the Admiralty under a separate supply contract.

2. It is now proposed that this Agreement be signed as well as the supply contract, and authority for that action is now sought.

3. It is proposed to present to Parliament a White Paper containing the documents annexed hereto, viz.: –

(1) A Memorandum explaining the terms of the Agreement and the considerations which have led to its being entered into.

(2) The final Report on the Persian Oilfields by Admiral Slade's Commission.

(3) A reprint of extracts from speeches in Parliament by the First Lord of the Admiralty explaining the advantages and present extent of the use of oil fuel in His Majesty's Navy, and summarising the opinions of the Royal Commission on Oil Fuel and Engines under Lord Fisher.

4. A proof of the Parliamentary Paper containing those documents is attached, and also proof copies of the draft Parliamentary Bill and Financial Resolution. It is proposed to lay the White Paper immediately before the Resolution is moved.

5. A proof copy of a letter which it is proposed to issue from the Treasury to the Company explanatory of the manner in which the veto of the two *ex officio* directors will be exercised is also attached. As the important part of this letter is summarised in paragraph 4 of the Memorandum (1) above referred to, it is not proposed to print the letter *in extenso* for publication.

6. The Company will issue a circular to their shareholders convening the necessary meeting to approve the increase of capital and the alterations in the Articles of Association. This circular will be sent out at the same time as information is given to Parliament, in order that the present shareholders and Parliament may receive authoritative information as nearly as practicable simultaneously.

7. The Company have stated that they have no doubt of their ability to

obtain the necessary Resolutions of shareholders, without waiting to make use of the voting power to be acquired by Government. The Law Officers regard this as a point of much importance.

8. The Agreement to be signed will be binding upon both parties, and as the Bill is a Money Bill it will be dealt with in Committee of the whole House. Prompt action will be necessary, and in all preliminary discussions it has been agreed that there can be no question of allowing a reference to a Select Committee.

9. As the Treasury and Admiralty are proposed as parties to the Agreement, it will be necessary for the two Departments to agree in due course as to the selection of the *ex officio* directors and the instructions to be given to them.

10. A letter has been addressed to the India Office by the Admiralty, and copies have been sent to the Foreign Office and to the Treasury for information, pointing out that His Majesty's Government have undertaken no direct obligation of military defence of the Company's property beyond that which would normally be accorded to a British trading company, but that the Agreement itself and its objects would impose upon His Majesty's Government, as a matter of self-interest, such protective measures as might be necessary to secure the objects for which the Agreement has been made.

11. The Foreign Office, Treasury, and Board of Trade have also been communicated with in regard to the extent of the connection which will exist between the Anglo-Persian Oil Company and the Turkish Petroleum Company, formed to control the exploitation of the adjacent Mesopotamian oilfields.

12. The supply contract is proposed to be treated as a confidential document in the usual manner. It would be for about 6,000,000 tons to be delivered in the course of 20 years. The price will be 30s. per ton, reductions down to 20s. per ton being granted in proportion to the surplus profits of the Company after a certain rate of dividend has been paid. Power is taken to vary the description of oil if necessary. The contract will be for oil only, *i.e.*, exclusive of freight. The Admiralty propose to carry the oil in their own or chartered tank-vessels.

13. The Admiralty are not providing in the supply contract for any other quantities beyond those required for naval purposes, but we reserve the power to sell for Indian or other services, if required, any temporary surplus arising, *e.g.*, from accidents to tank-vessels. The India Office informed the Admiralty in May 1913 that if the practical experiments then about to be undertaken in the use of oil on Indian railways proved successful, the preliminary comparisons of relative cost of oil and coal on the basis of an offer

of the Anglo-Persian Company for delivery at Karachi at 28 rupees 12 annas (38*s*. 4*d*.) per ton were favourable to the use of oil. A recent communication from the India Office indicates that the experiments are still in hand. It will undoubtedly be advantageous from all points of view if the Government of India eventually find it to their interest to make use of oil supplied by the Anglo-Persian Oil Company. Preliminary discussion of various possible mutual arrangements as to reserve stocks, &c., took place at Delhi between Admiral Slade and officers of the Indian Government.

14. The books of the Company have been examined by Messrs. Peat and Co. on behalf of the Admiralty, and the title and commitments of the Company have been considered by the legal advisers of the Crown.

WSC

Sir Edward Grey to WSC

28 May 1914
Stones Abbas
Hants

Dear Churchill,

I will say something as to the position in S. Persia.

Is it not the case that some of the oil wells of importance are in the British sphere in Persia? And as to the rest in the Neutral Sphere what distance are they from the coast? Perhaps Admiral Slade would send me a memo of these facts.

Yrs. sincerely
E. GREY

The real point is that S. Persia near the coast is more controllable by us than other centres of oil production in the world, which are entirely out of our reach.

E.G.

WSC to P. H. Illingworth

1 July 1914

Copy

My dear Illingworth,

I have to stay in bed today with bronchitis, and I shall be very much obliged if you will get me a pair.

The Treasury will not pay over the money necessary to enable us to take up shares in the Anglo-Persian Oil Company and thus acquire control until the resolution lately passed in Committee has been confirmed on report to the House. It is therefore important that an early opportunity should be found for this. I am afraid that Friday the 9th is impossible to me, as I have promised to wait on the King on his visit to Dundee on that day, and secondly the Cabinet yesterday were inclined to doubt whether this business could not be disposed of after 11 o'clock. I think myself it is treating the subject with too much importance to consume a whole Friday on the report stage. The resolution has already been discussed very fully, and the whole subject was further referred to in the debate on the Foreign Office Vote. Could you not put it down after 11 o'clock on Monday or Tuesday of next week? I do not apprehend any serious difficulty.

Lord Fisher to WSC

31 July 1914   Langham House
Private

My dear Winston,
I have just received a most patriotic letter from Deterding to say he means you shan't want for oil or tankers in case of war – *Good old Deterding!* How these Dutchmen do hate the Germans! Knight him when you get the chance as well as Yarrow & Gracie – *All 3 deserve it!* I enjoyed seeing you immensely & those devilled whitebait were delicious!
                                                        Yours till a cinder!
                                                        FISHER
Private
Arthur Balfour rushed into my arms as I walked out of the Admiralty and he thanked God that you were First Lord! *This was absolutely spontaneous on his part!* Dont you think it was nice of him? He was going to Gastein in Austria tomorrow but had just cancelled going! *How History repeats itself!* Lord Spencer as First Lord of the Admiralty went against Naval opinion & sent Nelson over the head of Sir John Olde & others to the Mediterranean hence *we got the battle of the Nile!* (*The biggest Battle ever fought!*) Also note Togo[1] superseded a splendid man because as Yamamoto said 'Togo was just a little better'!
The German Ambassador has sent me a *laisser-passer* for Marienbad so 'Wilhelm' will think I'm his facile dupe!

[1] Count Heihachiro Togo (1847–1934), Japanese Admiral who commanded the Japanese Fleet in the Russo-Japanese War of 1904–5. Admiral Gombei Yamamoto was Japanese Navy Minister 1898–1906 and Prime Minister 1913–14, 1923–4.

26

Admiralty 1914

(See Main Volume II, pp. 705–22)

1 January 1914 [Admiralty]

Copy

My Dear General,

I think it would be a gracious act on your part to write a line to the Secretary of State saying that your appointment as Colonel-in-Chief of the 18th has given you pleasure. Seely has a great respect for you and is always very proud to have served in your Brigade in South Africa. I know he would be very pleased to have a personal note from you.

I am very glad to say that Lady Blanche is now out of danger. There were 3 or 4 very critical days, and it looked as if she would not rally from the operation, but the doctors all seem to think that the corner has now been turned. Unhappily no great results are expected from this severe operation.

Clemmie and I heartily reciprocate your good wishes for the New Year.

I am delighted to see that you write from a hunting country. Here we chase the wild boar, which is most exciting.

Lord Fisher to WSC

16 January 1914 Langham House

My dear Winston,

Only a line to say I hope you are keeping your spirits up as you've no cause to be anxious, for the PM is much too wise to go back on his oft repeated 'unassailable supremacy'! I've heard from a friend in Germany that Tirpitz is ordering submarines on the quiet and 'submarines are booming'. It's a weak point in your armour that there are fewer submarines now than 4 years ago!

Did you ever read the report of the Committee on the Dreadnought Design and Selborne's official letter to me thereon? It might be useful to you. Masterton Smith is sure to have it amongst 'Fisher's Collected Works'!

Yours till death
F

WSC to Sir W. Graham Greene

2 February 1914   [Admiralty]

Copy

Importance is attached to the revival of singing in the Fleet. A good song-book should be prepared and issued, together with leaflets of the words. An officer in each ship should organise the singing and take an interest in it in addition to his other duties. Captains should arrange that there is a ship 'singing' not less than once a month throughout the year. Half the programme should be choruses from the song-book and the other half the music hall turns which are now popular. It is desirable that the men should sing together, and that everyone should join. The Vice-Admirals and Rear-Admirals commanding should take an interest in these 'singings,' and money can be provided for a small prize, say a silver wreath, to be awarded by the Vice-Admiral to the best ship in the squadron or on the station each half-year. Part singing should also be encouraged where possible; but this is much more difficult to organise. The ordinary ship's singing should become a regular part of the routine, and should be carried out as unquestionably as if it were a gunnery or torpedo practise.

I wish to receive constructive proposals.

Sir Douglas Haig to WSC

2 February 1914   Government House
                                        Farnborough

Personal & Confidential

Dear Mr Churchill,

When you sent me the copy of the Report on the organisation & training of the Royal Naval War College, you were good enough to write that you wd be very glad to hear my views which might be suggested by reading it.

I have taken you at your word & now send you some Notes on the Report.

Considerable progress has certainly been made in the establishment of a Naval General Staff, and it is satisfactory to read that the need for higher training is now generally accepted by Naval officers, but the evidence in the Report shows that much still remains to be accomplished; & I very much doubt whether the recommendation of the Committee even if carried out in the most thorough manner will really help you to attain the object in view – *viz* the creation of the body of Naval officers capable of performing efficiently staff duties at the Admiralty & in the fleets. Thanking you for the honour which you have paid me by asking for my views on this most important question, and with heartfelt wishes for your success in your most difficult undertaking.

I am, Yours very truly
DOUGLAS HAIG

H. H. Asquith to Venetia Stanley
(*Montagu Papers*)

EXTRACT

4 February 1914   10 Downing Street

. . . I dined with Cassel and played Bridge with Lady Lewis, Lady Paget and Winston. The 'First Lord' made every conceivable blunder: happily I was not his partner, and came home with a slightly replenished pocket . . . I am dining tonight with the Winstons . . .

H. H. Asquith to Venetia Stanley
(*Montagu Papers*)

EXTRACT

5 February 1914   10 Downing Street

. . . I dined at the Churchills' last night. Winston slept placidly in his armchair while I played Bridge with Clemmie, Sonnie and the Lord Chief Justice being our antagonists. With some feelings of compunction I went home with £3 of poor Sonnie's money in my pocket.

This morning we had another Cabinet which did not come to very much, as Winston's field of discussion is quite inexhaustible. A rather unsatisfactory communication (tho' very well put) from the Leviathan.

WSC to J. J. Virgo[1]

24 February 1914   [Admiralty]

Copy

Dear Sir,

George Robbins was, when he worked for me, an honest hardworking lad who read and studied in his spare time and was apparently ambitious to get on. As he was believed to have a turn for electrical engineering, I used my influence to procure him a situation with Messrs Maple. For this firm he has worked for 4 years. I think the opening he found there was a great disappointment to him and the wages paid him were, even after he became fully proficient at his work, extraordinarily low. He appears to have had a great struggle the whole time to maintain himself, and on several occasions when he visited me I learnt from him of his disappointment and dissatisfaction. I fear that some feeling that he was not being properly treated may have combined with other circumstances to lead to his breakdown.

I know he is a youth who has tried very hard and if he has been beaten and failed so far it is because the circumstances have not been at all favourable. I should be very glad to see him given a fresh start, and shall be much interested to know how he does under your guidance.

J. J. Virgo to WSC

25 February 1914   Young Men's Christian Association
                                             Tottenham Court Road W

Dear Sir,

I am in receipt of your esteemed reply of the 24th inst., in reference to George Robbins. I am very glad to have your testimony of the young fellow, and shall be keen to do anything I can in his behalf.

Though we have tried, we have so far not found anyone willing to engage him without a clean testimonial, but we are resolved to continue our efforts to help him.

It is possible that, in the course of a week or two, there may be a junior position here at this building; this, unfortunately, is only worth 17/6 per week, and that of course would hardly be enough to keep him. It would, however, give Robbins the opportunity to redeem his past somewhat.

Again thanking you for the courtesy of your reply.

I am, Yours very truly
J. J. VIRGO

[1] General Secretary of the London Central YMCA.

P.S.: – It occurs to me that you have never visited this Building; we should regard it as a great honour if you could come and look over this, the latest development of Young Men's Christian Association work. The whole proposition has cost a quarter of million pounds sterling, and, from that point alone, the premises are worthy of an inspection. It would be a very great pleasure to me to personally conduct you over the rooms and indicate what we are attempting in this place for the young men of the Metropolis.

J.J.V.

J. J. Virgo to WSC

27 February 1914   Young Men's Christian Association

Dear Sir,

I have to acknowledge your letter of the 26th inst, with cheque value £2 which you desire to be handed out from time to time to Robbins; it will be a great pleasure to me to do this.

After giving the matter some further consideration I have decided to make a position here for him (though it will, for a month, be work that a boy could do) and my intention is to offer a salary of ten shillings a week and to dole out another 10/– for the next four weeks from the £2 you so kindly send in your letter. After this, I shall have another vacancy which he can fill and for this I can offer him £1 a week – this will not be for another month, however, when one of our juniors leaves us to go out to Australia.

I have impressed upon Robbins the absolute necessity for him to make good; even though he cannot earn more than twenty shillings weekly, this will enable him to get a start and provide the opportunity to win back confidence.

It occurs to me to suggest that Robbins may be feeling that he can for ever depend on your kind backing, and, if this is so, he will perhaps be a little easy as to what position he takes up. May I venture to point out that it would be to the young fellow's advantage if you would put through us anything you might wish to give in the way of financial help. I would always keep you posted as to what steps we take.

I intend to take him on as from Monday next, and I hope that the plans outlined may meet with your approval.

Assuring you of my interest in him,

Believe me, Yours very truly
J. J. VIRGO

Cabinet Memorandum by WSC

26 February 1914　　　　　　　　　　　　　Admiralty

The Admiralty consider it indispensable that a Channel Tunnel should be capable of being flooded or otherwise effectually cut at any time by the Navy through the gunfire or other action of warships without military assistance, even though both ends of the tunnel are in the hands of the enemy. It is for the promoters of the scheme and their engineers to satisfy this vital condition. If they are able to do so, the project offers various important strategic advantages, including a greater assistance for our food supply. If they cannot do so, the Admiralty would be compelled to oppose the scheme.

WSC to Sir John Jellicoe

7 March 1914　　　　　　　　　　　　　Admiralty

Second Sea Lord.

I should have thought that a three months' cruise of this character would involve a great interruption in the studies of these Cadets. It must, of course, bring their engineering work entirely to a close. The time available for their professional and military instruction is short enough as it is. It would no doubt be desirable to break the routine of work at Devonport by a short cruise in the *Highflyer* for a few days at a time; but there is not much to be learned from these 'globe-trotting' expeditions, and the Cadets will have plenty of cruising when they enter the Navy. No estimate has been furnished me of the expense involved in such a cruise. I wish to have further information on both these aspects before approving the proposal.

WSC to Cornelia, Lady Wimborne
(Satinoff Papers)

11 March 1914　　　　　　　　　　　　　Admiralty

My dear Aunt Cornelia,

I have thought much about your sorrow in these last days.[1] The final link wh held so long has broken, & of the noontime of your life only the memory remains. Still I feel that the pain & shadow had been so spread over the long succession of years, that nothing in the nature of a shock fell on you.

[1] The first Lord Wimborne died on 22 February 1914.

I am much occupied here, but wd come to lunch with you on Friday, unless, wh wd suit me better, you feel equal to lunching *alone* with us.

Yours affectionately
WINSTON S C

WSC to Sir John Jellicoe

26 March 1914   Admiralty

Second Sea Lord.

There are three points which require to be specially studied: –

1. Widow's pension and marriage allowance. I do not think the Navy has ever dealt properly with the sailor's wife. The problem has simply been thrust outside service consideration; yet it is of high moral and social consequence that the men of the Navy should have a reasonable prospect of marrying and of keeping and leaving their wives and families in decent comfort. The steady development of a naval caste, whose children return regularly to the service which their fathers have taught them to regard as good and fair, is a vital factor in the maintenance over long periods in the future of British naval strength. I do not agree with the Second Sea Lord in thinking that the extension of the late increases of pay to the younger men should take precedence of these claims. I would far rather see the introduction of widows' pensions for sailors dying in the service and the institution of the Army system of 'marriage on the strength' under such conditions as would admit of proper regulation and gradual extension. To take good care of the people who do you good service and their dependants, and to give them a feeling of certainty and security is the true foundation of the well-being of the service. Not to do so is only to squander the human capital of the race.

After the great efforts which were needed to carry the pay scheme of 1912, I cannot expect this year to embark on any new large departure. But I wish this aspect to be examined in all its bearings, and to be considered by those concerned in questions of personnel, and I shall be glad to receive schemes and reports, of course with estimates of cost, for the purpose of giving effect as soon as favourable opportunity offers to this great and needed reform.

2. The second big question is how to encourage men to serve after twelve years. I have called for proposals in this direction. The principle would be that after completing his first engagement the sailor who had not become a petty officer should nevertheless receive distinctive treatment – a substantial increase of pay, possibly with increment, and a recognised status and privileges. The cost of these changes should be balanced against the cost of training an equal number of boys for the ratings required. It is easy to see that 'marriage on the strength' might be one of the privileges of the re-engaged man.

3. In my statement to Parliament in 1913 I referred to the great expense for railway travelling thrown upon the men by the system of leave while in home waters. Nothing has I fear been done. All the papers on the subject should be collected with any further material and forwarded to me. The Additional Civil Lord has promised to negotiate with the railway companies. I should be prepared to take a hand in this myself.

Lord Fisher to WSC

1 April 1914   Langham House
Private & Secret

My dear Winston,
    While the thought is with me may I suggest to you either Jerram or Bethell as second Sea Lord as you told me in confidence (*which I have not broken*) that Jellicoe was going for a rest-cure in the summer prior to succeeding Callaghan and the more I think of it the more I like your idea of sending him to Borden. I am *sure* either Jerram or Bethell would do *admirably* & you would have the prestige attaching to both of them of having commanded a Foreign Station. In the case of Bethell you would relieve him of the unpleasantness of Sturdee a junior officer having been put over his head & commanding him! So much for that! I hope you will have no mercy about the Zealandia. It's damnable that men should be so treated! *What about the London case?* which I hear is moving. Don't trouble to answer. I hope you will soon give out the notice about Jellicoe.

Yours for ever more
FISHER

Wasn't it truly delightful what your Father said of John Morley in 1886!!!
'I have always observed that if there is a thing which it is advisable not

to say he is perfectly sure to say it. He has the most extraordinary talent, one perfectly peculiar to himself, of uttering things absolutely true which are singularly fatal to the cause he is endeavouring to advocate.'

I have a lovely story I can't write of the Cromwellian John Morley succumbing to the aroma of knee breeches & silk stockings!

PPS. I have for the 3rd time read your Bradford speech & again tell you *it's the very best you ever made.*[1]

WSC to Prince Louis of Battenberg

14 April 1914   Madrid

Private

Dear Prince Louis,

Freedom from politics and pouches has enabled me to deal comprehensively with the various Staff questions now pending & I have spent several days on the task. Will you kindly read my memo. & then give it back at once to Masterton Smith for typing. I do not want it to be seen at this stage by anyone except you & the Secretary.

I shall be back on Monday afternoon. The weather, hitherto delicious, has sadly deteriorated.

Yours sincerely
WINSTON S. CHURCHILL

WSC to Admiral David Beatty

15 April 1914   Admiralty

Copy

My dear Beatty,

Many thanks for your letter of the 26th of March and its enclosures. I am afraid the existing Mediterranean dispositions must continue till the end of 1915.

In your enumeration of battle cruiser functions ought you not to include what is to my mind the most formidable and disconcerting of all, *viz* – rupturing an enemy's cruiser line and attacking his cruisers of all kinds wherever found.

---

[1] See Main Volume II, pp. 488–9.

This is what bothers us: and surely we should also make it bother them.

Let us meet soon.

Yours very sincerely
[WINSTON S. CHURCHILL]

WSC to his wife
(*CSC Papers*)

4 May 1914   Admiralty

My darling,

All is well here – though the nurse renews her claims to go to the seaside with the kittens. I rather favour Dieppe: so does Diana, who made a formal *démarche* to me on this subject.

The Budget was calmly received. No one seems to care a rap for the rich. LG's statement was slatternly and obscure, but the design is large & deeply planned. FE did not think that it wd cause ill-feeling likely to affect the Irish settlement. Curtis yesterday bearded the PM at the Wharf, & it is now arranged he meets Bonar Law & Carson tomorrow. This is *Secret*.

My lovely one, I am hoping to receive good accounts of you by telegram & letter. Yesterday was I fear a vy miserable day. I will look after everything here, so you need not worry about anything.

Tender love my sweet cat from your devoted husband
W

WSC to his wife
(*CSC Papers*)

5 May 1914   Admiralty

My darling,

I was vy much relieved to get yr second telegram wh gave some definite information about yr health. I do trust you will not have any more pain or discomfort. So far I do not seem to have contracted the affliction. Keep me informed daily.

Tomorrow night I go to Portsmouth to see that old ship blown up by a torpedo, but I expect to be back here in time for questions on Thursday, so if you are able to come back on that day, I shall be on the spot.

The Budget has been less ill received than I expected, but we have still to hear the squeals of the wealthy. The Tory party do not evidently relish fighting their battle. Bill is indignant on their behalf.

Nellie[1] looked beautiful in her new dress for the Curzons' ball & had a gt success with G. Nathaniel, who made the band play a special dance in her honour at the end.

The PM had a conversation with the Unionist leaders today the results of wh he has not imparted to me, but I learn it was not vy satisfactory. Leonie came to see me before departing for the theatre of war. She was rueful, tearful & trustful. The Tabloids are active & useful.

Fondest love my darling Clemmie from me & from both your kittens.

Ever your devoted husband
W

Lord Fisher to WSC

8 May 1914

Twatley Farm
Malmesbury

My dear Winston,

I am down here trying to get rid of a beastly cold of many weeks duration so cannot attend Defence Committee. I have accordingly written as enclosed to the Prime Minister.

I am still hearing from a reliable source that Tirpitz is 'digging out' with submarines which he is surreptiously building ostensibly for others (I played the same game myself when First Sea Lord!). Myself – I should *secretly* drop a Dreadnought & build 20 submarines in lieu.

Yours always
FISHER

PS Private

What about nominating Jellicoe to succeed Callaghan so as to make sure! You never know what a day may bring forth!

You never did a bigger thing in all your life than your speech at Bradford!

---

[1] Nellie Hozier (1888–1957), sister of CSC and twin sister of Bill Hozier; captured by the Germans in Belgium in 1914 where she was a nurse, but subsequently released; married 1915 Colonel Bertram Romilly; mother of Giles and Esmond Romilly.

WSC to Sir Edward Grey

8 May 1914   [Admiralty]

Secret

My dear Grey,

I told Cassel that Kiel would be impracticable; but asked him to find out whether Tirpitz really wanted to see me and have a talk. He says that he knows this is so, but that he will write to Ballin putting the point precisely. There is no need to consider the matter further till we hear again.

Yours ever
W

Redmond's communiqué is very provocative.

WSC to Prince Louis of Battenberg

13 May 1914   [Admiralty]

Copy

I send you a copy of this paper which I have had prepared for my personal use. The Mediterranean proposals after 1916 are of course purely speculative. You will find the copy useful to keep among your papers. The delivery of 13 capital ships between the fourth Quarter of 1914 and the first Quarter of 1916, as compared with a reinforcement of only 2 to the German navy, is a great military fact altering the whole proportion of battle strength between the fleets. This is one of the strongest justifications for a general review of types. The growth of the Russian fleet must also be considered as a factor of at least equal importance to the Austrian developments.

I should be glad if you would give your attention to the state of the Mediterranean fleet from 1916 onwards, picking out in detail the ships which will be required to match Austria. Although the 'Lord Nelsons' figure in my forecast, it does not by any means follow that they are the best ships to send. I regard the fight over the status of the 'Lord Nelsons' finally settled in the late Cabinet discussions. If it is found more convenient to keep the two 'Lord Nelsons' as flagships of the Second Fleet, we may continue to count them for the 50 per cent standard, even after their date of dropping out in 1917.

Please seek an opportunity of talking with me about this paper, to which at different times I have given a good deal of attention.

WSC to H. H. Asquith and Sir Edward Grey

20 May 1914   [Admiralty]

Copy

In Madrid at Easter Sir Ernest Cassel told me that he had received from Herr Ballin a statement to this effect: 'How I wish that I could get Churchill here during the Kiel Week. Tirpitz will never allow the Chancellor to settle any naval questions, but I know he would like to have a talk with his English colleague on naval matters, and I am sure that if the subject of limiting naval armaments were ever approached in a businesslike way, some agreement would be reached.' On the same day I received a telegram from the Admiralty, saying that the Foreign Office particularly wished a British squadron to visit German ports simultaneously with other naval visits. I thereupon told Cassel that if it were certain that Tirpitz really wanted to see me, I would consult you both. I should personally welcome the opportunity, but of course I must obtain permission. I said that I did not think it would be suitable for me to go on a great liner as Ballin's guest, and that if I were to go at all probably the best opportunity would be for me to turn up in the *Enchantress* at some German port at the time when our squadron was visiting. I told Grey about this when I came back to London and showed him the extract from Ballin's letter. Since then I have heard verbally from Cassel that he knows for a fact through Ballin that Tirpitz would like to see me; but at Grey's wish I have asked that this matter should be made quite clear and I have not yet heard again from Cassel. Personally I should like to meet Tirpitz, and I think a non-committal, friendly conversation, if it arose naturally and freely, might do good, and could not possibly do any harm. Indeed, after all I have said about a Naval Holiday, it would be difficult for me to repulse any genuine desire on his part for such a conversation. The points I wish to discuss are these: –

1st. My own Naval Holiday proposals and to show him, as I can easily do, the good faith and sound reasons on which they are based. I do not expect any agreement on these, but I would like to strip the subject of the misrepresentation and misunderstanding with which it has been surrounded, and put it on a clear basis in case circumstances should ever render it admissible.

2nd. I wish to take up with him the suggestion which he made in his last speech on Naval Estimates, of a limitation in the size of capital ships. Even if numbers could not be touched, a limitation in the size would be a great saving, and is on every ground to be desired. This subject could only be satisfactorily explored by direct personal discussion in the first instance.

3rd. I wish to encourage him to send German ships to foreign stations by showing him how much we wish to do the same, and how readily we shall conform to any dispositions which have the effect of reducing the unwholesome concentration of fleets in Home waters. Quite apart from the diplomatic aspect, it is bad for the discipline and organization of both navies, and the Germans fully recognise this.

4th. I wish to discuss the abandonment of secrecy in regard to the numbers and general characteristics (apart from special inventions) of the ships, built and building, in British and German dockyards. This policy of secrecy was instituted by the British Admiralty a few years ago with the worst results for us, for we have been much less successful in keeping our secrets than the German. I should propose to tell him in principle that we gave the Naval Attachés equal and reciprocal facilities to visit the dockyards and see what was going on just as they used to do in the past. If this could be agreed upon it would go a long way to stopping the espionage on both sides which is a continued cause of suspicion and ill-feeling.

I hope, in view of the very strong feeling there is about naval expenditure and the great difficulties I have to face, my wish to put these points to Admiral Tirpitz if a good opportunity arises, and if it is clear that he would not resent it, may not be dismissed. On the other hand I do not wish to go to Germany for the purpose of initiating such a discussion. I would rather go for some other reason satisfactory in itself and let the discussion of these serious questions come about only if it is clearly appropriate.

Much the best opportunity that could be found would be when our squadron is visiting a German port. I appreciate very fully the importance of doing nothing which would give the visit of the battleships to Kiel any superior significance or éclat to that of the battle cruisers to Kronstadt, and what I propose for your consideration is that I should go in the *Enchantress* to Kronstadt, arriving there with our squadron on the 24th day of June, stay there two days and then go as I can quite easily do in 48 hours, to Kiel, where I should find our other squadron, and where I would also stay a day and a half or two days, thus accepting the German Emperor's invitation and providing the opportunity for my talk with Tirpitz. It seems to me that from a European point of view any special significance that might be attached to one visit would be effectively counterbalanced by the other, while at the same time the opportunity sought for would be secured. It would be necessary if I went away that the First Sea Lord should remain at his post. But Sir John Jellicoe is a personal friend of Tirpitz and has a good deal of cordial correspondence with him on various professional matters. He had in fact been planning to go himself privately on leave to Kiel for the yachting week. I have told him that he could not do this without your sanction. I should propose to take him with me on the yacht both to Kron-stadt and to Kiel.

I think I understand the general position and the naval position well enough to get through without making any mischief.

I do not believe that the Emperor's invitation (which I have not yet received) arose from any plan to make an unfair use of such a visit, but that it came quite naturally out of what he heard from Ballin, though the risk would be fully guarded against by the arrangements I propose.

If you approve, I do not think the matter need be the subject of Cabinet discussion, because that would be lending an undue importance to con-versations which may never take place; and what I suggest is that I should have permission to cruise in the Baltic in the week 24th to 31st June, and visit Kronstadt and Kiel while our two squadrons are there.

The French would certainly have no reason to complain, as I have already visited their fleet at Toulon and have for two days entertained the late French Minister of Marine on board the *Enchantress* at Portland and with the British fleet manoeuvring at sea.

For the present I suggest that nothing should be done until the Emperor's invitation arrives; and, secondly, until we hear what Tirpitz's real wish is.

Sir Edward Grey to H. H. Asquith and WSC

25 May 1914   Admiralty

It is of course very desirable that the points named should be discussed with Tirpitz *if* he is willing to discuss them.

But hitherto all efforts on our part to get naval expenditure discussed have been resented by Tirpitz, even when welcomed by Bethmann Hollweg. When Lichnowsky[1] arrived an invitation was conveyed to me on his behalf that it was hoped in the interest of good relations between the two countries that I should not mention naval expenditure to him.

I think therefore that a visit to Germany with the intention of raising with Tirpitz the points in the memorandum may not only be futile but may cause resentment.

What I think, though I put this forward with diffidence as it is out of my sphere, I should do if I were at the Admiralty would be to send for the German Naval Attaché; tell him of the statement that Ballin has made; give him a memorandum of the points I should like to discuss; say that I was prepared to take them up, if Tirpitz wished, either through the German Naval Attaché here or British Naval Attaché at Berlin, and even to meet

---

[1] Karl Max, Prince Lichnowsky (1860–1928), German Ambassador in London.

Tirpitz to discuss them if it appeared after preliminary discussion through Attachés that this would be profitable. But that while this would remain my attitude I should not press any discussion that was unwelcome to Tirpitz and hoped that he would be quite frank in letting me know direct through Naval Attachés at any time what his desire was about discussion.

As to the personal visits to Kronstadt and Keil, I am most reluctant to stand in the way, but they will make a terrible splash in the European Press and give a significance to the cruise of our squadrons that is out of all proportion to anything that was contemplated when the cruises were planned. The wildest reports will be circulated and we shall be involved in constant explanations to Ambassadors at the Foreign Office and denials in the Press of the things that will be attributed to us.

I hope therefore the Prime Minister and First Lord will agree to a telegram to Goschen on the lines of the following draft –

'Your private telegram of the 18th. I do not gather that the Emperor has actually sent an invitation yet and no formal answer perhaps is required.

'The Emperor's intended invitation is very much appreciated and so is the friendly feeling that has prompted it, but it must have arisen from an impression that Mr Churchill and Prince Louis of Battenberg were going to accompany the cruises of the squadrons; this has never been their intention; it is impossible for them to do so and they will be unable to go to any of the ports that the squadrons will visit.

'The report of the Emperor's intended invitation came therefore as a complete surprise and it is hoped that the inability of Mr Churchill and Prince Louis to come will not be construed in any way as wanting in respect to the Emperor or as due to any want of appreciation of his kindness, which they both feel very much.'

E.G.

WSC to his wife
(*CSC Papers*)

31 May 1914   Portland

My darling,

I have now settled my plans for the cruise. We leave here tonight for Dartmouth tomorrow, Plymouth Tuesday, Cherbourg Wednesday & I hope to put in to Dieppe Wednesday night or Thursday morning to pay you a visit. Then I go back to Sheerness where I shall stay over Sunday.

I am disappointed not to have a letter from you – or at least a telegram. Perhaps tomorrow I shall be luckier.

We had a vy successful dinner last night to half a dozen Captains; & tonight 2 Admirals come. Tomorrow we shall go to the other end of the scale & invite little cadets. But you know this routine so well that I do not need to enlarge on it.

The weather still continues cold, & tends to grey. I do a good deal of work, walking round ships & attending to papers – & the time passes peacefully & pleasantly. I am going to visit the Naval school at Cherbourg if the French authorities will give me the necessary permission.

Goonie is I think happy looking after her Jack. He is much better, but still shows many signs of weakness.

> With fondest love ever your devoted husband,
> W

Really I am hoping to get a letter from you tomorrow.

WSC to his wife
(CSC Papers)

1 June 1914   Dartmouth

My darling,

I was delighted to get your dear telegram at midday. I had been waiting for some message from you, and the posts are slow.

I am planning to reach you during Wednesday on my way from Cherbourg. If the trains are good I shall come overland or perhaps motor. Then in the evening about 10 the yacht will call for me and take me on to Dover & Sheerness.

This has been a day worthy of June: & this beautiful College never looked better. The boys do not seem to be hustled as much as they used to be & my suggestions have all been in the direction of 'easing up'. There is no doubt it is the best education anyone could have.

My business proposals do not go smoothly – for the reason that the insurance companies try to charge excessive premiums on my life – political strain, short-lived parentage & of course flying. I am now proposing a scheme on the following lines. You insure your life against your mother's, & make the £7000 loan a charge on your remaining life interest in her estate. I execute a deed transferring to you from my reversionary estate an amount exactly equivalent to that wh you have mortgaged. I hope they can work out a good plan on these lines – wh will in no respect be detrimental to your particular interests. If not – I shall sell all my shares and pay off everything I can, & try to get along without the loan. I will not be bled by these Insurance Companies. Of course it wd be ever so much better if we cd do without borrowing – at any rate till the vy last minute.

Well good bye my sweet one. I am looking forward so much to seeing you & the kittens – & your Mamma & Nellinita: & hope you will receive me with united welcome.

Goonie is a dear & has been so helpful & easy.

Jack improves.

Ever your loving & devoted

W

WSC to Sir W. Graham Greene and Prince Louis of Battenberg

4 June 1914   Admiralty

Secretary

First Sea Lord

I am greatly concerned at the report in the Foreign Office telegram attached of the proposed purchase by Greece of two of the United States battleships of approximately the 'Formidable' class. An offer like this, if made to us, would enable an enormous improvement of our material to be effected without additional cost. Our strength in older battleships is far beyond what we require. It is incredible that our Naval Mission can have let the Greeks go to the United States without, at any rate, giving us the option. Pray make enquiries and report to me again.

WSC to Sir W. Graham Greene and Sir John Jellicoe

29 June 1914   [Admiralty]

Please let me have a report on the time table for the boy artificers in the *Fisgard*. I visited the establishment on Saturday last, and it seemed to me that the working hours for the boys were too long.

WSC to Sir W. Graham Greene

30 June 1914   [Admiralty]

Let me have attached Section 58 (3) of the Children's Act.

What is the average length of service on board each of these ships of boys committed to them before they pass out to the Navy or into civil life? At what age does the question of their acceptance for the Navy arise? How many boys have been taken from them in the last five years, and generally speaking about how long did those boys serve?

My feeling is that three years' good character from one of these ships ought to be absolutely sufficient to delete all previous records, and I should see no need for application to the police. It is altogether wrong to inflict life disabilities on children. In many cases boys are committed to reformatories and industrial schools for offences like sleeping out, and very often because the magistrates have reason to believe that their homes are such that they will not be properly taken care of there.

*   *   *   *   *

WSC to King Alfonso of Spain

30 May 1914   Portland

Copy

Sir,

The vanity of authors is proverbial and Your Majesty will not I trust be shocked to receive by the Embassy bag *four* books of mine, in the place of the one which I had obtained permission to send. One of them is about House of Commons politics and English party affairs, and it shows I think to some extent how they work – never smoothly, never violently – but within well comprehended limits along the necessary lines of development. The others are about some of the small wars in which I was lucky to serve when a subaltern – not so very many years ago. It would be to me a great pleasure if Your Majesty would accept them even though the daily press of business made it impossible to read them.

I look back with lively feelings to my visit to Madrid and am so glad I came and had the good fortune of such long and interesting talks with Your Majesty. I look forward to a renewal of them in September in case it is found possible to slip in a visit to the fleet with Your Majesty's other plans.

Here the Irish situation becomes increasingly capable of solution; but only the pressure of time and events will force the inevitable accommodation upon parties – and that pressure while it lasts is severe and might become injurious in some circumstances. But I remain confident that matters will arrange themselves satisfactorily before the end of the year.

The King has kindly given me leave to wear the medal of the Cuban War, and I am asking a similar privilege for Colonel Barnes through the War Office.

Let me once more thank Your Majesty for the gracious confidence with which I was treated during my visit to Madrid, and express again my most earnest wish that Your Majesty's statesmanship and courage may long be preserved to the Spanish people.

I am, Sir, Your Majesty's obedient servant
WINSTON S. CHURCHILL

King Alfonso to WSC

1 July 1914   La Granja

Dear Mr Churchill!

I am so grateful for the books you kindly send me. It's always so much more interesting to read a book when one knows the author & he is a friend. We are finishing our stay here & in three or four days I go to the North for the summer. My boats are ready for racing only I think they wont do much this year.

Now I will tell you a great disappointment I have. You very kindly told me that it would be possible for me to see a naval manoeuvre & I assure you I was looking forward & studying all I could to pull the greatest profit; well in Parliament the whole month of May & June has passed discussing what they call the personal power of the King. All my intentions have been misunderstood & although all the loyal people are backing me up I can't deny the fact. You quite understand that I have to be very careful now & not give arms to the enemies. The Government thought that the bill for the second squadron would pass easily & the contrary has happened: now, as the types are English & half of the capital too you quite understand it's better for me not *to see* nor come near anything looking like a man of war I feel convinced they would even say I got a commission. For all these reasons please don't expect me this year for that fire exercise & please postpone it for next year.

Thanking once more I remain very sincerely yours
ALFONSO R.I.

WSC to King Alfonso

9 July 1914   HMS *Enchantress*
at Sea

Copy

Sir,

I am very sorry that YM will not be able to come this year, as I had hoped, to see a Fleet firing, but I followed with concern the debates in the Cortes &

can appreciate the reasons wh: make it undesirable at the present time. I hope however that I shall have the honour of seeing YM during yr visit in Sept in the seclusion of the polo world. We have all greatly rejoiced at the victory & we recognise how much it was due to the generous aid YM gave to our players & to their practice at Madrid. The Irish question now moves steadily forward to its culminating point, & I am more than ever hopeful – tho' everyone lies under the stroke of chance – that a good settlement will be effected.

At the Admy we are vy busy with the mobilisation of the Fleet wh takes place next week & is a considerable affair. The King himself is coming to inspect the Fleet & afterwards will lead it to sea – 53 Battleships & nearly 400 pennants of all classes. Then there will be 3 or 4 days of exercises, tactical & strategic, wh I am looking forward vy much to following.

I learn with gt interest that YM's new ships are to be armed with the 15" gun. All our results with that weapon are so far excellent.

With sincere wishes for YM's health & prosperity,

I remain, Sir, YM's humble servant
WSC

*   *   *   *   *

WSC to Prince Louis of Battenberg

11 July 1914   Admiralty

Copy

Not Sent

My dear Prince Louis,

As you will be proceeding on leave early in August, it is necessary to take in the next fortnight the serious decisions which are outstanding about the new construction programme. In this connection it will be necessary to forecast the programme of next year, for the two must be considered together, and also the fresh advice which we should give to the Canadian Government. Mr Borden has welcomed the visit from Sir John Jellicoe and I hope this will take place when you return early in September. By that time all our plans must be complete in every detail and we must have a thoroughly watertight argument for our Canadian friends. We have discussed these issues together so often and have prepared our minds for them over such a long period that, although I do not under-rate their immense importance, I do not think we ought to find any difficulty coming to a decision.

I propose that at the Board Meeting next Wednesday we should simply deal with the *Polyphemus* on her merits and settle whether the design is or is not a good one without reference to any substitution. No doubt we shall have to refer to the possibility of substitution, but I do not wish to take any decision on the subject then.

WSC to his wife
(*CSC Papers*)

13 July 1914　　　　　　　　　　　　　　　　　　　　Admiralty

My darling,

We made a good passage in spite of fog threatening to Sheerness. Freddie arrived in his motor car & after Venetia & he had both had a flutter we all three returned to London in the motor – a hot but pretty drive.

The PM is vy keen to come on Monday to the yacht, & Venetia also wants to come. You must try & make the effort. I am sure it will repay the exertion. I will make a really good plan for you: and all fog or bores will be forbidden.

It was quite forlorn leaving you last night. I don't know why a departure to the sea seems so much more significant, than going off by train. We watched your figures slowly climbing up the zigzag & slowly fading in the dusk: and I felt as if I were going to the other end of the world.

The kittens were vy dear & caressing. They get more loveable every day. Altogether Peartree [Cottage] is a vy happy, sunlit picture in my mind's eye. Tender love my dearest – I must try to get you a little country house 'for always'.

The autumn session business has been settled on the basis that we work till the end of August, & then begin a new session in December. Tis the best that could be done in the circumstances.

Your ever loving & devoted husband
W

WSC to his wife
(*CSC Papers*)

24 July 1914　　　　　　　　　　　　　　　　　　　　Admiralty

My darling one,

I have managed to put off my naval conference and am coming to you & the kittens tomorrow by the 1 o'clock train.

I will tell you all the news then. Europe is trembling on the verge of a general war. The Austrian ultimatum to Servia being the most insolent document of its kind ever devised. Side by side with this the Provincial Govt in Ulster wh is now imminent appears comparatively a humdrum affair.

We are to go ahead with the Amending Bill, abolishing the time limit & letting any Ulster county vote itself out if it chooses. The Irish acquiesced in this reluctantly.

We must judge further events in Ulster when they occur. No one seems much alarmed.

Tender & fondest love
W

PS I dine with Cassel to meet Ballin.

WSC to Admiral Sir Berkeley Milne

27 July 1914   Admiralty

Secret. European political situation makes war between Triple Alliance and Triple Entente Powers by no means impossible. This is *not* the Warning Telegram, but be prepared to shadow possible hostile men-of-war. Return to Malta as arranged at ordinary speed and remain there with all your ships completing with coal and stores. Warn *Defence* to be ready to join with despatch.

Measure is purely precautionary. The utmost secrecy is to be observed, and no unnecessary person is to be informed.

WSC to the King
(Royal Archives)

28 July 1914   Admiralty

Secret

Sir,

During the last few days the Navy has been placed upon a preparatory & precautionary basis. The First Fleet will sail secretly tomorrow for its preliminary Northern station. The second Fleet will assemble at Portland as soon as its men return in the ordinary course from leave on Friday. The Patrol flotillas have been raised to full strength and are moving in succession to their war stations. The two Irish blockades have been abandoned and all vessels engaged in them will conform to the general dispositions. The aircraft are collected at and around the estuary of the Thames to guard against airship attack. All vulnerable points such as oil tanks & magazines were last night guarded by the army against aerial attack (the air guns being manned)

& against *sabotage*. It is possible that all East coast lights & guns will be manned tomorrow.

The reserves of oil & the coal arrangements are satisfactory. The reserves of ammunition show large surpluses. The torpedo reserve is complete. There will be no deficiency of officers on a complete mobilisation & we shall have at least 20,000 Reservists for whom no room can be found in any ship fit to send to sea.

A variety of other precautions & measures have been taken with wh I will not trouble Your Majesty.

It is needless to emphasize that these measures in no way prejudge an intervention or take for granted that the peace of the great powers will not be preserved.

I understand from Prince Louis that Your Majesty will desire to hear from me, & with my humble duty remain

Your Majesty's faithful & devoted servant
WINSTON S. CHURCHILL

WSC to his wife
(*CSC Papers*)

28 July 1914   Admiralty

Midnight

My darling one & beautiful,

Everything tends towards catastrophe & collapse. I am interested, geared up & happy. Is it not horrible to be built like that? The preparations have a hideous fascination for me. I pray to God to forgive me for such fearful moods of levity. Yet I wd do my best for peace, & nothing wd induce me wrongfully to strike the blow. I cannot feel that we in this island are in any serious degree responsible for the wave of madness wh has swept the mind of Christendom. No one can measure the consequences. I wondered whether those stupid Kings & Emperors cd not assemble together & revivify kingship by saving the nations from hell but we all drift on in a kind of dull cataleptic trance. As if it was somebody else's operation!

The two black swans on St James's Park lake have a darling cygnet – grey, fluffy, precious & unique. I watched them this evening for some time as a relief from all the plans & schemes. We are putting the whole Navy into fighting trim (bar the reserve). And all seems quite sound & thorough. The sailors are thrilled and confident. Every supply is up to the prescribed standard. Everything is ready as it has never been before. And we are awake to the tips of our fingers. But war is the Unknown & the Unexpected!

God guard us and our long accumulated inheritance. You know how will-ingly & proudly I wd risk – or give – if need be – my period of existence to keep this country great & famous & prosperous & free. But the problems are vy difficult. One has to try to measure the indefinite & weigh the imponderable.

I feel sure however that if war comes we shall give them a good drubbing.

My darling one – this is a vy good plan of ours on the telephone. You remember the Grand Guignol play! Ring me up at fixed times. But talk in parables – for they all listen.

Kiss those kittens & be loved for ever only by me
Your own
W

F. E. Smith to WSC

31 July 1914   Wargrave Hall
                                                    Berks

Secret

Dear Winston,

I have spoken to my friends [Bonar Law][1] of whom you know and I have no doubt that on the facts as we understand them – & more particularly on the assumption (which we understand to be certain) that Germany con-templates a violation of Belgian neutrality – the Government can rely upon the support of the Unionist party in whatever manner that support can be most effectively given.

I shall be in London on Monday.

Yours sincerely
F. E. SMITH

Arthur Ponsonby[2] to WSC

31 July 1914   House of Commons

Dear Churchill,

I think you ought to know of the very strong feeling in the party with regard to the present European crisis. We have had two meetings and we

---

[1] This, including brackets, was written by another hand.

[2] Arthur Augustus William Harry Ponsonby (1871–1949), Liberal MP Stirling Burghs 1908–18; Labour MP Brightside Div., Sheffield 1922–30; Principal private secretary to Sir H. Campbell-Bannerman 1906–8; held office during the Labour Governments of 1924 and 1929; created Baron Ponsonby of Shulbrede 1930; his political writings include *The Decline of Aristocracy*, 1929, *Wars and Treaties 1815–1914*, 1917, *Now is the Time*, 1925.

may decide on a full party meeting, but we have held back so far in our desire not to do anything which might embarrass Grey in the slightest degree.

The most emphatic opinion has been expressed that we should on no account be drawn into war when our interests are not immediately affected and no treaty obligations exist to bind us. I cannot for a moment believe that the Cabinet will decide on our participation but should they do so they will at once lose the support of a very large number of their followers in the House. There is no doubt about this.

You are probably living at the moment in an atmosphere of expert strategists and of naval and military men some of whom may hold the view that 'this is our moment to strike'. It is important therefore that you should know how very widespread the opposite view is so that you may use all your influence towards moderation.

Yours sincerely
ARTHUR PONSONBY

WSC to Arthur Ponsonby
(*Ponsonby Papers*)

31 July 1914   Admiralty

Private

My dear Ponsonby,

So long as no treaty obligation or true British interest is involved I am of your opinion that we shd remain neutral. Balkan quarrels are no vital concern of ours. We have done our best to keep the peace & shall continue so to do to the end. But the march of events is sinister. The extension of the conflict by a German attack upon France or Belgium wd raise other issues than those which now exist, and it wd be wrong at this moment to pronounce finally one way or the other as to our duty or our interests.

I think you have shown much discretion & I quite understand your feelings & views.

Yours sincerely
WINSTON S. CHURCHILL

WSC to the King
(*Royal Archives*)

31 July 1914   Admiralty

12.30 a.m.

Secret

Sir,

Your Majesty is informed of the diplomatic, so I confine myself to the military, aspect.

The first fleet is now in the open seas. The second Fleet will assemble tomorrow at Portland. All 'precautionary measures' have been taken. The newspapers have (so far) behaved magnificently. The four old battleships will reach the Humber tomorrow. All the flotillas have reached their stations. Guns and ammunition are being supplied to fast merchant ships wh will be taken up & commissioned. I have taken the responsibility of forbidding the departure of the Turkish battleship Osman (late Rio) with the Prime Minister's approval. If war comes she will be called – and shd Your Majesty approve – the *Agincourt* & will convey Sir Henry Jackson to reinforce, & at the regular date assume command of, the Mediterranean.

Shd war come I shall have to submit to Your Majesty the name of Sir John Jellicoe for the supreme command. I have reached with regret the conclusion that Sir George Callaghan is not equal to the strains wh it wd entail upon the C. in C. These are not times when personal feelings can be considered unduly. We must have a younger man. Your Majesty knows well the purely physical exertion wh the command of a gt fleet demands. This however can remain in suspense till the situation becomes definite.

Arrangements are being made for some form of National indemnity for British traders at sea, & I shall bring proposals before the Cabinet tomorrow morning.

With my humble duty I remain

Your Majesty's faithful & devoted servant & subject

WINSTON S. CHURCHILL

WSC to his wife
(CSC Papers)

31 July 1914   Admiralty

Secret

Not to be left about but locked up or burned.

My darling,

There is still hope although the clouds are blacker & blacker. Germany is realising I think how great are the forces against her & is trying tardily to restrain her idiot ally. We are working to soothe Russia. But everybody is preparing swiftly for war and at any moment now the stroke may fall. We are ready.

I cd not tell you all the things I have done & the responsibilities I have taken in the last few days: but all is working well: & everyone has responded. The newspapers have observed an admirable reticence. The Baron de Forest was startled to receive a telegram that his yacht had been ordered out of Dover Harbour. He hurriedly left for Dover. As he journeyed down the line he found every bridge & tunnel guarded & became increasingly terrified. He telegraphed frantically clamouring for debates & questions in Parliament. But not a man moved – not a question nor so far any mention in the papers. The country will be united when the issue is joined. Be sure of it.

Germany has sent a proposal to us to be neutral if she promises not to take French territory nor to invade Holland. She must take French colonies & she cannot promise not to invade Belgium – wh she is by treaty bound not merely to respect but to defend. Grey has replied that these proposals are impossible & disgraceful. Everything points therefore to a collision on these issues. Still hope is not dead.

The city has simply broken into chaos. The world's credit system is virtually suspended. You cannot sell stocks & shares. You cannot borrow. Quite soon it will not perhaps be possible to cash a cheque. Prices of goods are rising to panic levels.

Scores of poor people are made bankrupts. These nice Derenburgs have been reduced from affluence to bankruptcy. Nelke has lost half his fortune.

But I expect the apprehension of war hurts these interests more or as much as war itself. I look for victory if it comes.

I have resolved to remove Callaghan & place Jellicoe in supreme command as soon as it becomes certain that war will be declared.

I dined last night again with the PM. Serene as ever. But he backs me well in all the necessary measures.

All the *Enchantress* officers on mobilisation go *en bloc* to *Invincible*. I am forcibly detaining the 2 Turkish Dreadnoughts wh are ready. Ireland I think is going to be settled.

I am perturbed at the expense for this month being £175. Please send me the bills both for Pear Tree [Cottage] & Admiralty separately. Rigorous measures will have to be taken. I will pay the bills direct myself, & Jack can check the housekeeping here in your absence.

I am sending you the cheque for Pear Tree. I am so glad you find rest & contentment there.

Fondest love my darling one – your devoted husband
W

WSC to the King
(Royal Archives)

1 August 1914   Admiralty

Secret

Mr Churchill with his humble duty submits to Your Majesty that the present situation renders a change in the supreme command of the Fleet imperative. Sir John Jellicoe has now arrived at Scapa, and Mr Churchill proposes, either tomorrow or the next day to relieve Sir George Callaghan & to appoint Sir John Jellicoe, with the acting rank of Admiral, to be Commander in Chief. Mr Churchill would respectfully and most earnestly ask Your Majesty's approval to the course proposed.

Mr Churchill last night found it necessary to send out summonses to the Reservists for a complete mobilisation of the Fleet, and it is expected that a proclamation regularizing and enforcing these summonses will, after submission to Your Majesty in the course of today, be made public soon after the meeting of Parliament tomorrow afternoon.

Mr Churchill has authorized the First Sea Lord & the Chief of the War Staff to confer with the French Naval Attaché on the naval measures which should be taken in common, should the Cabinet & Parliament decide that France and England are to be allies in the present war.

The general position and strength of the British Fleets, Squadrons & Flotillas is regarded as satisfactory by the Board of Admiralty.

WINSTON S. CHURCHILL

WSC to Sir W. Graham Greene and Prince Louis of Battenberg

1 August 1914   [Admiralty]

Telegrams herewith.

It seems certain to me that the order to mobilise will be issued after Cabinet this morning. Have everything in readiness.

Examination service should be put in force simultaneously.

Lord Robert Cecil to WSC

1 August 1914   Hatfield

Dear Churchill,

I think it well to inform you that I am confident that if the Government decide to take action whether by the despatch of an expeditionary force or otherwise they may count on the support of the whole Unionist Party. I gather from Linkey that he has had some correspondence with you which may have produced a false impression on this point on your mind. Whatever his personal views may be, I am sure that he would take no public action inconsistent with this view.

Yours very truly
ROBERT CECIL

WSC to Lord Robert Cecil
(Cecil Papers)

1 August 1914   Admiralty

Copy

Dear Cecil,

I thought you would not mind my sending yr letter to the Prime Minister.

The news tonight opens again hope. There seems to be a prospect of Austria & Russia resuming negotiations on a formula wh Germany has proposed: and every exertion will be made to that end.

But a collision between the armies may arise at any moment out of an incident or an accident. And I hold that in all the circumstances if we allowed Belgian neutrality to be trampled down by Germany without exerting ourselves to aid France we shd be in a very melancholy position both in regard to our interests & our honour.

I am grateful to you for your letter.

Yours sincerely
WINSTON S. CHURCHILL

Cabinet Notes
(Lloyd George Papers)

David Lloyd George to WSC

[1 August 1914]

Would you *commit* yourself in public *now* (Monday) to war if Belgium is invaded whether Belgium asks for our protection or not.

WSC to David Lloyd George

No.

David Lloyd George to WSC

If patience prevails & you do not press us too hard tonight we [personally] might come together.

WSC to David Lloyd George

Please God – It is our whole future – comrades – or opponents. The march of events will be dominating.

David Lloyd George to WSC

What is your policy?

WSC to David Lloyd George

At the present moment I would act in such a way as to impress Germany with our intention to preserve the neutrality of Belgium. So much is still unknown as to the definite purpose of Germany that I would not go beyond this. Moreover public opinion might veer round at any moment if Belgium is invaded & we must be ready to meet this opinion.

WSC to David Lloyd George

I am most profoundly anxious that our long cooperation may not be severed. Remember your part at Agadir. I implore you to come and bring your mighty aid to the discharge of our duty. Afterwards by participating in the peace we can regulate the settlement & prevent a renewal of 1870 conditions.

WSC to David Lloyd George

All the rest of our lives we shall be opposed. I am deeply attached to you & have followed your instinct & guidance for nearly 10 years.

WSC to David Lloyd George

Together we can carry a wide social policy – *on the conference basis* your idea – wh you taught me. The naval war will be cheap – not more than 25 millions a year.

You *alone* can take the measures wh will assure food being kept abundant & cheap to the people.

WSC to Lord Robert Cecil
(Cecil Papers)

2 August 1914   Admiralty

Copy

Dear Cecil,

I am sorry to say that since I wrote to you we have learned officially that Germany has declared war on Russia. I cannot think that the rupture with France can be long delayed. And the course of events is likely to be very serious as regards Belgium.

Yours sincerely
WINSTON S. CHURCHILL

WSC to his wife
(CSC Papers)

2 August 1914   Admiralty

1 a.m.

Cat-dear,

It is all up. Germany has quenched the last hopes of peace by declaring war on Russia, & the declaration against France is momentarily expected.

I profoundly understand your views. But the world is gone mad – & we must look after ourselves – & our friends. It wd be good of you to come for a day or two next week. I miss you much – & your influence when guiding & not contrary is of the utmost use to me.

Sweet Kat – my tender love –

Your devoted
W

Kiss the kittens.

Admiralty to Commander-in-Chief, Home Fleet. Vice-Admiral, 2nd and 3rd Fleet. Commander-in-Chief, Home Ports

2 August 1914

At 2.20 today, 2nd August, the following note was handed to the French and German Ambassadors: 'The British Government would not allow the passage of German ships through the English Channel or the North Sea in order to attack the coasts or shipping of France.'

Be prepared to meet surprise attacks.

Cabinet Notes
(Lloyd George Papers)

WSC to David Lloyd George

[3 Aug 1914]

The Welsh miners who had gone on their holidays after denouncing the war are returning in full force tomorrow – having apparently satisfied themselves of the justice of the war – and will cut all the coal we need. This relieves a dangerous situation. I want you to send them a strong Welsh message about small nations etc.

WSC to David Lloyd George

Turkish ships not to leave the country pending situation being determined.

David Lloyd George to WSC

He is summing up much too unfavourably to our own friends.

WSC to David Lloyd George

Yes.

WSC to David Lloyd George

Please study the question before you make up your mind. There are all sorts of vital & precise facts – wh you *cannot* have at your fingers' ends.

WSC to David Lloyd George

I am so glad you are turning your mind to the *vital* question of safeguarding the credit & food supply of this country.

* 　 * 　 * 　 * 　 *

Admiralty to all HM ships and Naval
Establishments

4 August 1914　　　　　　　　　　　　　　　　　　Admiralty
11 pm

COMMENCE HOSTILITIES AGAINST GERMANY

Index

Compiled by Roger F. Pemberton, M.A.

Member of the Society of Indexers

Notes

1. Since all the documents in this volume refer directly or indirectly to the subject of the biography, Winston S. Churchill, only those entries which could not be better headed otherwise are grouped under his name.

2. 'WSC' means 'Winston S. Churchill', 'RSC' means 'Randolph S. Churchill' (WSC's son), 's.b.' means 'short biography'.

3. '*bis*', '*ter*', '*quat*' or '*quin*' after a page reference means that the subject is separately mentioned *two, three, four* or *five* times on the page indicated; '*pass.*' or '*passim*' means 'here and there' (scattered references); '*q.v.*' means 'quod vide' (which see).

4. Scottish surnames beginning with 'Mac' or 'Mc' are arranged as if they were all spelt 'Mac'; and they come in strict alphabetical order with other names, *e.g.* Macara, McArthur, Macaulay, McBride, MacDonald.

Admiralty, 1912—*continued*
many's military strength and naval
rivalry with Britain, and hoping for a
satisfactory agreement, 1537–8; to
Asquith on Dominions naval policy,
1538–40; on functions of Yeomanry,
1540–1; to speak on Second Reading
of Home Rule Bill, 1544; reminds
Battenberg that he (WSC) was once
a press correspondent, 1544; and
Fisher's ultimatum, 1547; to Haldane,
on Malta meeting (May 1912), 1548–
9; to his wife, on naval and domestic
matters, 1551; his naval appointments (May 1912), 1551; on the King's
alleged stupidity in naval matters,
1551; studying the torpedo, 1551; to
meet Fisher in Naples (May 1912),
1553; his Memo on naval manœuvres
(mid-summer 1912), 1554–5; on naval
(and marine) honours, 1551, 1557,
1560–3; and a new order (of chivalry)
for Navy, 1551, 1558–9; and the King,
on appointment of his new Principal
Naval ADC, 1559; his Mema on
Naval Situation (June 1912), 1564–78;
his Memo on manning Requirements
for the Navy, 1579; his criticism of
Home Secretary's paper on naval dispositions (June 1912), 1573–8; to the
King, on the same and on his Mema,
1585; his Memo (2 July 1912) on new
German Navy Law, 1585–6 (*see also*
1517–18); draft arrangement with
Kitchener on British naval forces in
Mediterranean, 1586–7; his Memo
forecasting naval situation in Mediterranean and Home Waters in 1915,
1588–91; to his wife, on personal and
naval matters, 1592; his reply to Lord
Roberts on naval and military dispositions in Mediterranean and North
Sea, 1594–5; meeting of CID (11 July
1912) on naval situation, 1595–1607;
his forecast (for Chancellor of Exchequer) of naval expenditure (1912–
17) as determined by German shipbuilding programmes, 1609–14; to
Beauchamp, on use and status of re-

Admiralty, 1912—*continued*
ception rooms at Admiralty House,
1614, 1620; invited by Borden to visit
Canada, 1616–17; Sir Max Aitken
(Beaverbrook) offers to organize the
visit, 1074–5; Morley on this visit,
1617; and Lloyd George's fear of
(national) bankruptcy, 1619; his
Memo on formation of 6th Battle
Squadron, 1621–2; and Garvin: on
Beresford, 1622–3; explains his naval
policy, 1623–5; visiting naval establishments and docks *etc* on East
Coast (Aug 1912), 1625; Northcliffe
urges him to visit Canada, 1625–7; to
Asquith on more recognition of
Liberal journalists by Liberal Party,
1627–8 (*see also* 1625–7); Asquith's
reply, 1629; 'trounced' Bonar
Law, 1629; invites J. A. Spender to
accompany him in *Enchantress*, visiting
Chatham, Shoeburyness, Sheerness
and Harwich, 1629–30; invites Sir Edward Grey to the same for visits
to Scottish ports, 1630; and Morley
for the Tyne and Scottish ports,
also Criccieth and Barrow-in-Furness,
1630–1; and Admiral Limpus as Naval
Adviser to the Turkish Government,
1631; on the entry of naval cadets,
1632–3; on a successor for Admiral
Troubridge as Chief of Admiralty
War Staff, 1633–4; and Botha's
honorary rank in British Army, 1634–5
& n; to Jack Seely, on Service
pensions for widows, 1635; to Lloyd
George on the land question, the
franchise, legislation in hand, political
tactics and WSC's naval pay reforms,
1636; to speak at Dundee (Sep 1912),
1636, 1643, 1644 (*bis*); invites Lloyd
George and family for cruise in *Enchantress*, 1636, 1643–4; wants to see
Fisher, 1637–8; to Grey and Asquith
on French naval policy, the Mediterranean, and defence of France, 1638–
9; on need for recreational facilities on
shore for naval personnel at Harwich,
1639–40; and Sea Scouts (proposed),

Blood, General Sir Bindon, 6 & *n*
on 'Fiscal Controversy' (disinterested),
and on the 'Army in India', 312; on
WSC's speeches and change of party,
392; congratulates WSC on his success
at Belfast, 1390
Blue Ensign, 1775
Blunt, Wilfrid Scawen, 450 & *n*
helps with material for Lord Randolph's biography, 450; praises biography and adds some details of his
experience of Lord Randolph, congratulates WSC on his success at
Manchester, 491; his friendship with
Lord Randolph, 802-3; congratulates
WSC on his promotion and suggests
reform of prison discipline, 1137 & *n*;
his Memorandum on Prison Discipline,
1144-8; suggests WSC meet H. M.
Hyndman, 1159 & *n*; or Redmond
instead, 1159; congratulates WSC on
his conduct at Marconi Inquiry, 1745
Blyth (Northumberland), 1724 (*bis*),
1727, 1728, 1732 (*bis*), 1733 (*bis*),
1903
Boadicea class (of light cruisers), 1767
Board of Agriculture and Fisheries, 155
n, 995
Board (*now* Ministry) of Education, 36,
1038, 1060
Board of Referees for Excess Profits Tax,
190 *n*(5)
Board of Trade: 106, 209, 355, 1133
(*bis*), 1134, 1189, 1208, 1210, 1211,
1212 (*bis*), 1274, 1275, 1308, 1354,
1356, 1506, 1556
WSC as President of *q.v.*, 764; office to
be made equal to a Secretaryship of
State, 765, 1134; Kearley at, 772, 861,
862; H. J. Tennant as Parliamentary
Secretary, 861-2, 862, 870 & *n*;
honours and awards for officials of
(WSC's recommendations), 889-90;
President of (after WSC), 1035; and
London strike (Aug 1911), 1113, 1114;
and Manchester strike (Aug 1911),
1116; and South Wales industrial
crisis, 1164, 1165, 1167, 1171, 1173,
1177, 1178; and unemployment in

Board of Trade—*continued*
building industry, 1253; Conciliation
(industrial) Department of, 1263,
1264, 1266-7; and railway strike (Aug
1911), 1279
Board of Trade Memoranda (by WSC):
on Employment and Trade, *see*
Employment and Trade; on Unemployment Insurance and Labour Exchanges (11 Dec 1908), 851-3; on
Sweated Industries and Trade Boards
(26 Jan 1909), 874-5; WSC's Note on
this (12 Mar 1909), 879-81; WSC's
Note on Memo on Unemployment
Insurance (*above*), 883-5
Board of Trade, WSC as President of
(with a seat in the Cabinet), 764
WSC defeated in by-election in North-
West Manchester (24 Apr 1908), 764,
783; but elected at Dundee (9 May
1908), 764, 794; to John Redmond,
pledging his support for Home Rule
for Ireland, 764-5; asks Sir Edward
Donner to preside over his election
committee at North-West Manchester,
766-7; Donner agrees, 767; requests
E. T. Broadhurst for his support in
coming by-election and explains his
views on the Irish question, the
Licensing Bill and Free Trade, 767-8;
to Killick, hoping for support of Free
Trade League and stating his political
views, 768-9; Killick's reply, 769-70;
to Asquith, on Lloyd George's press
campaign, 772; H. G. Wells's Open
Letter in his support at N.-W. Manchester, 777-81; WSC on the election
campaign, 781-2; defeated at Manchester, 785; on his defeat, and on the
Liberal Party, has been offered eight
or nine safe seats, 787; thanks Sir
Edward Donner for his help at Manchester and comments on the election
result, 788-9; has accepted nomination
for Dundee, 789; taking action for libel
v Manchester Courier on allegation of
breach of parole, 789-92; *Manchester
Courier* apologizes, 793; WSC informed
the King that ship-building strike

Carnarvon Castle, investiture of Prince of Wales at, 1098, 1099 (*bis*) & *n*

Carnarvon, Lord, 859 & *n*

Carnegie, Andrew, 236 & *n*

Carnegie, Mr, 138

Carnock, Baron, *see* Nicholson, Sir Arthur

Carr-Gomm, Hubert William, 124 & *n*, 258

Carrickfergus (Northern Ireland), 1414

Carrington, Charles Robert Wynn-, Baron Carrington, 155 & *n*, 156, 158, 159, 1294

Carruthers, (Sir) Joseph Hector McNeill, 622 & *n*

Carson, Sir Edward, s.b., 1056 & *n*
in House of Commons, 1110; WSC on his tactics, 1394 (*bis*), 1395, 1400; Asquith on, 1400; F. E. Smith on, 1401; to speak in Dundee, 1401; T. P. O'Connor on, 1402 (*bis*), in 'Pogrom' debate (28–29 Apr 1914), 1418 (*bis*), Harcourt on WSC's offer to, 1419; and Redmond, 1423; obstructive, 1423–4; refuses separate treatment for Ulster, 1649; to meet Bonar Law and Asquith (May 1914), 1975; mentioned, 1478

'Carsonism' and 'Carsonites', 1402, 1404

Cartels (or Trusts), *see* Trusts

Cassel, Sir Ernest Joseph, s.b., 35 & *n*
has 'water on the knee', 167; WSC and, 167, 461, 478, 571, 682, 744; 'an excellent host', 175; WSC at his Alpine Villa, 353 (*bis*), 564 (*see also* 887); investing money for WSC, 167, 410; and the rise in 'Unions' on Stock Exchange, 573 (*bis*) & *n*, and Duke of Westminster's loan to George Cornwallis-West, 593; buying stocks and shares at a discount, 687, 690; credits WSC's account with interest on railway bonds, 717; Lady Randolph and, 723; offers WSC his flat in Paris, and proposes a meeting, 740; his movements, 740; meeting WSC in Paris, 744; and a Turkish loan (Nov 1908), 848; invited WSC and wife to his mountain villa, 887; Fisher and, 1299, 1331; WSC thinks it unwise to 'parley'

Cassel, Sir Ernest Joseph—*continued*
with German Emperor (Jan 1912), 1491–2; WSC's visit to Ballin in Berlin (3 Feb 1912) on Anglo-German naval competition, 1515; WSC and German Emperor and Ballin (Apr 1912), 1537–8; WSC discusses his (WSC's) wife's operation, and accompanies him in special train, 1592; invited to *Enchantress*, 1799; WSC finds his proposed visit to Kiel impracticable (May 1914), 1977; WSC and Ballin's wish to get him (WSC) to Kiel, 1978–81

Cassel, Mrs (? Lady Cassell), 176

Cassel's mountain villa, *see* Villa Cassel

Cassell & Company, Ltd (publishers), 468 & *n*, 469 (*bis*), 475

Castell Deudraeth (North Wales), 785

Castlereagh, Charles Stewart Henry Vane-Tempest-Stewart, Viscount, 986 & *n*

'Cat and Mouse' Bill, 1722

Catholic (Roman) Church in politics, 1089

Catholicism, WSC on, xxvii

Catholics, Roman:
and religious education in schools, 299; candidates for parliamentary elections, 322; new Cathedral at Westminster, 1159–63; mentioned, 1060

Causton, Richard Knight (*later* Baron Southwark), 654 & *n*

Cavalry, British, on manœuvres (Aug 1907), 673

Cave, (Sir) George (*later* Viscount Cave), 1041 & *n*, 1071, 1419

Cavendish, Lady (Moyra de Vere Beauclerk), 236 & *n*

Cavendish, Lord Richard Frederick, 236 *n*(1)

Cavendish-Bentinck, William George Frederick, 34 *n*(1)

Cavendish-Bentinck, Mrs W. G. F. (Ruth Mary), 34 & *n*

Cawdor, Frederick Archibald Vaughan Campbell, 3rd Earl of, 1032 & *n*

Cayley, Captain RN (*later* Admiral) George Cuthbert, 1342 & *n*

Chioga (Kyoga), Lake, 712, 735
Chiozza Money, Leo (George), 206
&n
Choate, Joseph H., 173 & n
Choga (Kyioga), Lake, 712, 735
Cholmondeley, Col. Hon Thomas Grenville, 30 n(3)
Cholmondeley, Mrs Thomas G. (Katherine Lucy), 30 & n
Chorley (Lancs), 363
Christie, Gerald (WSC's lecture agent), 28 & n
Christie's, London (auctioneers), 454 n
'Chumbolly, the' (WSC's baby nickname for his son Randolph, q.v.)
'Church as by law established...', omitted from Royal Declaration Bill (1910), 1020
Church of England, xv, xxvi, xxvii, 299
Churchill, Clementine, née Hozier, q.v. (WSC's wife, 'Clemmie', later Lady Churchill and afterwards Baroness Spencer-Churchill; see also Letters): on honeymoon at Blenheim, 819; and Venice, 820; to Stanleys at Alderley, 840; Northcliffe suggests her visiting Canada, 844; her need of rest, 889; WSC on her arrangements at Eccleston (their house), 889; to Stoke Poges, 893; WSC describes 'Goonie's' confinement, and suggests introducing Bourke Cockran to her (CSC), 893–4; her first child (Diana), 902; was to have gone with WSC to German manœuvres, 903; but did not, 911; riding well at Crowborough (Sussex), 916; and WSC at Criccieth with Lloyd George, 1023, 1024; WSC describes 'Peggy' at the Gaiety Theatre, 1069; the King gives her a ticket for his Coronation (1911), 1073; WSC (in camp with Yeomanry) on her progress after giving birth to second child (Randolph), 1087, 1088, 1090; still weak after child-bearing, 1088, 1090; and Maxine Elliott, 1093; at George V's Coronation, 1093; WSC suggests Sir Edward Grey as Godfather to

C II—PT. III—Y

Churchill, Clementine—continued
Randolph, 1094; WSC spends happy Sunday with, and advises no move for a fortnight, 1095; recovering, 1095; her nurserymaid unsatisfactory, 1097; WSC suggests another visit, and sacking the nurserymaid, 1097; WSC (at Penrhos) describes Investiture of Prince of Wales (July 1911), 1099; WSC joining family at Eccleston, 1099; at Garmisch-Partenkirchen, 1106, 1109; WSC on House of Lords crisis, 1106, 1109; at Villa Cassel, 1109; WSC's suggestions for her movements, 1109; at Broadstairs (Kent), 1127; WSC (at Balmoral) on his room and the company (and Dr Laking), 1128; Fisher sends her a gift, 1320; advised not to accompany WSC to Belfast, 1389–90; WSC on his naughty 'Seals' (Sea Lords), 1416; WSC longs for her return, on the welfare of the children, and on family finances, 1416–17, 1417, 1418; coming home (Apr 1914), 1417, 1418; in Paris, 1418; WSC quotes Randolph (aged 3), 1418; her letter to The Times in reply to Sir Almroth Wright's on 'abolishing women', 1483 n; cruising with WSC in Enchantress, 1644, 1739; involved in motor accident, 1714; WSC and furniture at Admiralty House, 1714, 1723; warned by WSC on treatment of suspicious (incendiary ?) parcels, 1715; a week-end with the Asquiths, 1723; entertains Asquith, 1968; WSC on her influence, 1998; mentioned, 840, 851 (bis), 937, 961, 1127, 1132, 1134, 1144, 1294, 1331, 1556, 1631, 1644, 1739, 1902, 1966
Churchill, Lady Cornelia Spencer- (became Lady Cornelia Guest and later Lady Wimborne): her Scrap Books, 167
Churchill, Diana (WSC's eldest daughter, b 1909, nicknamed 'PK' or 'Puppy-kitten'): Christened, 902; WSC and her nurse and bath, 907; 'Clemmie' and, 909;

Games and sports, WSC's:
Bridge, 176, 1968; Golf, 1023, 1027–8, 1042, 1069, 1253 (*bis*), 1778, 1790; Hunting, *see* Hunting; Polo, *see* Polo; Shooting, *see* Shooting; Swimming, 1087, 1107
Gardiner, Alfred George, 864 & *n*
Gardiner, Samuel Rawson, 1668 & *n*, 1670
Garibaldi (Trevelyan), 671
Garnett, Thomas ('Tom'), 337 & *n*
Garrick Club, 214, 368
Garstin, Sir William Edmund, 88 & *n*, 726
Garter, Order of the, 1082–3
Garvin, James Louis (Editor of *The Observer*), 954 & *n*
Sir John Fisher on Dreadnoughts, 954, 956; protests against misrepresentation by Home Rule Council, 1393; supports Bonar Law and Ulster, 1398; on Admiral Beresford, on WSC's naval policy, and on Carlyle (Thomas), 1622–3; WSC's reply, 1623–5
Gastein, Bad (Germany), 220
Gateshead (parliamentary constituency), 283, 302 & *n*
Gaunt, Captain RN (*later* Admiral (Sir)) Ernest Frederick Augustus, 1495 & *n*
Gem class (of light cruisers), 1767
General Elections: (1900), xxviii (*bis*); (Jan/Feb 1910), 963; (Nov 1910), 1027–8
General Post Office, *see* GPO
Genoa (Genova, Italy), 1479
George III (1760–1820), 1218
George IV (1820–1830), 813
George V (1910–36, *formerly* Prince of Wales, *q.v.*):
WSC's draft of his Gracious Message to Parliament on the death of King Edward VII, 1014; will invite Lloyd George to Balmoral, 1021–2; and Mylius, *q.v.*, 1033; 1238 (see also *Liberator* libel case); his Coronation, 1031, 1034, 1216; objects to WSC's references to 'idlers and wastrels at both ends of the social ladder (scale)', 1037;

George V—*continued*
subsequent correspondence on this, 1038–9, 1040, 1044, 1045–6, 1047 (*bis*); gives Mrs Churchill a ticket for Westminster Abbey for his Coronation, 1073; WSC on HM's references to the German Emperor (May 1911), 1079; agrees that 9th Duke of Marlborough (separated from his wife) may attend luncheon in Windsor Castle after Garter ceremony (10 June 1911), 1083; his official birthday (1911), 1085 & *n*; at Carnarvon Castle investiture (July 1911), 1099; and constitutional crisis (1911), 1105; fears that WSC's speech (8 Aug 1911) might give impression that HM would consent to create peers to pass Home Rule Bill, 1111, 1379; WSC's reply and comments to Lord Knollys, 1112 & *n*; and consecration of new RC Cathedral at Westminster, 1159–63; and Shop Hours Bill (1910), 1178, 1188; and riots in South Wales (Nov 1910), 1205, 1207, 1212 (WSC's report, 1205–7); and fighting at Tonypandy, 1213; a baseless slander on HM, 1216–38; his formal (signed) Statement on *Liberator* libel (read in Court after Mylius's trial), 1235, 1236; and foreign criminals, anarchists and the Aliens Act, 1239–40; his speech at unveiling of Victoria Memorial (16 May 1911), 1258–9; and Coal Mines Regulations Bill (1911), 1248; and Liverpool riots (Aug 1911), 1268–9; and railway and docks strikes (Aug 1911), 1274, 1276, 1279, 1280–1, 1282, 1286–90, 1292; on the proper employment of troops in riots, 1274; leaving for India, 1301, 1322; Admiral Fisher and, 1319; and WSC's proposed changes at Admiralty and in naval commands (approves), 1338–40, 1367–8, 1536, 1994; and WSC's proposed names for new ships, 1345 (*bis*), 1524–5, 1664–71 *passim*; approves WSC's proposals for a War Staff at Admiralty, and of Hopwood's appointment

Grenfell, W. H. (*later* Lord Desborough), 29 *n*(4)

Gretton, John, 1949 & *n*

Greville, Sidney Robert, 425 & *n*, 485

Grey, Albert Henry George, 4th Earl, 636 *n*(2), 1364 & *n*

Grey, Sir Edward (*later* Viscount Grey of Fallodon), s.b.

and WSC and Hooligans and Asquith, 78; WSC will answer for, in Commons, 415; his reputation as an administrator, 417; and Portuguese labour in South Africa, 584, 591, 601, 612; and foreign relations and a Colonial Council, 618; and publication of Swettenham papers, 650, 651-2; and Newfoundland, 659 (*bis*); tipped for Prime Minister (by Lady Randolph), 705; refuses to leave Foreign Office, 708; and Radicals, 708; popular, but cannot compete with Asquith for PM, 721-2; WSC's letter to, 'Private' not a State Paper, 748; sending WSC some 'Marlborough Literature', and regrets inability to attend wedding, 818; tells Lloyd George not to discuss naval armaments in Berlin, and WSC not to touch on foreign policy in his speeches in the constituencies, 836; on Asquith, 850, 851; and WSC and his (WSC's) visit to Paris (Jan 1909), and foreign policy, 856-8; congratulates WSC on settling coal dispute (July 1909), 901, 902; and German shipbuilding programme, 938; WSC on naval construction in 1909 and 1910, 954-5; WSC reports on his talk with Metternich (Sep 1909), 958 (Note of talk, 959-61); in Commons (1910) on annexation of Congo by Belgium (1908), 993 & *n*; deputizing for WSC at HO, 1022; on international affairs, 1057, 1058, 1059; WSC on international affairs, 1091-2, 1102-3, 1116-17, 1369-70, 1421; adopts WSC's suggestion of consulting other Powers about recognizing new Portuguese Republic, 1093 (*bis*); suggested by WSC as Godfather, 1094;

Grey, Sir Edward—*continued*
praises WSC, 1094; his defence of Declaration of London, 1096; in Commons, on Insurance Bill (July 1911), 1101-2; asks WSC and wife to visit him, 1109; WSC's advice on Moroccan negotiations, and his reply, 1116-17; wishes to see WSC and Lloyd George, 1117-18; and President Taft (USA), 1121; WSC to visit (Sep 1911), 1125, 1126; Margot Asquith on Asquith, 1134; on a convicted murderer, and on his work at Home Office, 1195-6; WSC on Captain Kell's reports of German espionage in UK, 1342-3; and Germany, 1359; WSC on an arrangement with Turkey, 1369-70; and WSC on Anglo-Turkish relations (Nov 1911), 1370-1 (*see also* WSC's letter, 1369-70); on Ulster, 1405; staying with WSC and health improving, 1417; WSC on Irish question, 1421; and Conciliation Committee for Woman Suffrage, 1430; agrees with Lloyd George on women's suffrage, 1456; and Votes for Women, 1473, 1474, 1476, 1478; and WSC's proposed visits to Germany (1912 & 1914), 1492, 1977, 1979-81; WSC on interchange of naval information with Germany, 1496; WSC reports on Cassel's visit to Berlin, 1503; and Cassel's telegram to Ballin, 1515 *n*; on his talks with Metternich, and on exchange of naval information with Germany, 1537; and a proposed CID meeting in Malta (May 1912), 1552; and German colonies, 1607 (*bis*); WSC invites to sail in *Enchantress*, 1630; WSC on British and French fleets in Mediterranean, 1638-9; WSC sending HM ships to Nauplia (Greek port), 1660-1; Grey objects, 1661; to Lloyd George, on international situation (Dec 1912), *WSC to see*, 1703-4; and Near Eastern crisis (Apr 1913), 1720-1; advises explaining naval expenditure to the public, 1790-1; on France and Germany, and other nations, arming,

Langerman, (Sir) Jan Willem Stuckeris, 601–2 & *n*, 600–3, 619
Langham House, Ham Common (London), 1938, 1940, 1948, 1949, 1950, 1954, 1957, 1959 (*bis*), 1965, 1966, 1973
Langtry, Mrs (Lillie), 138 & *n*
Lansdowne, Henry Charles Keith, 5th Marquess of, 49 & *n*
and WSC's biography of Lord Randolph, 463–4, 472, 474; and House of Lords and Budget Bill (Dec 1908), 860; and hereditary principle, 998; seriously ill, 1070, 1071; his Reform Bill, *see* Reform Bill (1911); his twenty-four 'abstainers', 1106; and Austen Chamberlain on Asquith's Home Rule policy, and on WSC's 'fusionist' policies, 1406–7; mentioned, 720
Lansdowne House, 33
Lardner, James Carrige Rushe, 1430 & *n*
Larkin, Joe (James), 1272 & *n*
Larne, Ulster gun-running at, 1416, 1420 *n*
Laski, Harold J., 354 *n*(1)
Laski, Nathan, 354 & *n*
thanks WSC for his letter on Aliens Bill, 356; congratulates WSC on his vistory for freedom and religious tolerance, and promises support at Manchester, 357; WSC's thanks for wedding-present, 815
Laurier, Sir Wilfrid (Prime Minister of Canada), 610 & *n*
and Australian State Premiers at Colonial Conference (1907), 610, 628, 653; and Bond (of Newfoundland), 719; and the three ships for RN, 1812–14 *passim*; and Canadian independence, 1813
Law, Hugh Alexander, 1430 & *n*
Law Officers of the Crown and the *Liberator* case, 1217–20 *passim*, 1233–6 *passim*
Lawley, Sir Arthur, 512 & *n*
Lawrence, Sir Joseph, 1027–8 & *n*
Laws, Mr, 1177 (*bis*)
Lawton, J. H., 205

Leaders of Public Opinion in Ireland (Lecky), 1374 *n*(7)
League of Ladies (Neil Primrose's), 438
Leasehold Enfranchisement, 405
Lecky, William Edward Hartpole (*books by*), 1374 & *n*
Lecture programme, WSC's (Mar–May 1901), 25 & *ff*
Lecture tour in USA proposed (Dec 1900–Feb 1901), xxviii–xxix
Lee, Arthur Hamilton, 29 & *n*
and dispute between US Government and Governor of Jamaica, 635; 'a snake in the grass' (Fisher), 932; and Army Estimates (1910), 991
Lee, John (of GPO), 1391 & *n*
Leeds (Yorks), 646, 1406
Legge, T. M., 1139
Lehmann, Rudolph Chambers, 644 & *n*
Leicester, 96 & *n*, 380
Leicester Evening News, 380
Leopold II, King of the Belgians, 708
Leslie, Jack (*later* Sir John, 2nd Baronet, WSC's uncle), 34 *n*(1)
Leslie, Sir John (1st Baronet), 22 *n*(1), 34 *n*(3)
Leslie, (Sir) John Randolph Shane, 1135 & *n*
Leslie, Leonie Blanche (*later* Lady Leslie, wife of 'Jack' 2nd Baronet, WSC's aunt):
and Edward Marsh (WSC's private secretary), 421; thanks WSC for book and congratulates him, is glad he and Marsh get on well, 486–7; meets German Emperor, 723; on Clementine Hozier, at a dance at Cowes, 800; mentioned, 22 *n*(1), 176, 1976
Letters to his wife (CSC), WSC's, 886, 887, 889, 893, 907–13, 914–18, 1069, 1087, 1088, 1090, 1093, 1095, 1097, 1099, 1106, 1109, 1127, 1383, 1384, 1416, 1417, 1418, 1422, 1499, 1529 (*bis*), 1542, 1543, 1551, 1592, 1714, 1715, 1722, 1754, 1778, 1780, 1790, 1795, 1883, 1920, 1921, 1975 (*bis*), 1981, 1982, 1987, 1989, 1993, 1997

Letters to the Press by WSC:
On Patriotism (*Westminster Gazette*, 18 Mar 1901), 23-4; on Military Policy (*The Times*, 3 May 1901), 51-2; on the Conduct of War in South Africa (*The Times*, 28 June 1901), 74-5; on Concentration Camps in South Africa (*The Times*, 28 June 1901), 74-5; on Scottish homespuns (*The Times*, 9 Sep 1901), 79-81; on Attacks on Industry in Letters to the Press (*The Times*, 17 Sep 1901), 81; on his Patronage of Church Bazaars (*English Churchman*, Nov 1901), 99-100; on 'J.C.B.' and Harris tweeds (*The Times*, 2 June 1902), 135-6, (*The Times*, 7 June 1902), 139-41, (*The Times*, 14 June 1902), 141-2; on punishments at Sandhurst, (*The Times*, 8, 9 & 11 June 1902), 150-4, 156-8; on Free Trade (*Oldham Chronicle*, Oct 1902), 169; on the political situation (9 Oct 1903), addressed to Travis-Clegg (*The Times*, 12 Oct 1903), 228-31; in *Monthly Review*, 246; on C. Arthur Pearson's purchase of *The Standard* and on Pearson's extensive ownership of newspapers (*The Times*, letters dated 21 & 23 Nov 1904), 377-81; on Joynson-Hicks (teetotaller) and the Licensing Act (*Manchester Guardian*, letter dated 9 Dec 1904), 382
Lettish criminals in London (Dec 1910/Jan 1911), 1238, 1239 (*see also* Sidney Street, 'battle of')
Leveson, Captain, RN (*later* Admiral) Arthur Cavanagh, 1321 & *n*
Levishie, Glenmoriston (Scotland), 1024
Levy-Lawson, Harry Lawson Webster (*later* Viscount Burnham), 487 *n*(2), 488, 490 (*bis*), 1627
Lewis, Lady, 1968
Lewisham by-election (15 Dec 1903), 272 & *n*
Devonshire's letter to, 296
Leyds, Willem Johannes, 116 & *n*
Liberal Imperialists (*see also* Rosebery), 76 *n*(1), 82, 112, 113 (*bis*), 118 *n*(1),

Liberal Imperialists—*continued*
168, 181, 182, 200, 225, 226, 272, 321, 366
Liberal League, 118 *n*(2), 165, 166, 253, 255-6, 284, 390 *n*, 406
Liberal Party (*see also* Liberal Imperialists *and* Liberal Unionist Party):
Lord Rosebery's call to, to 'clean the slate', 103 *n*(3); and Free Trade and 'Capital' and 'Labour', 243-4, 285; and party tactics (and Rosebery), 249; and WSC's proposed candidature at Birmingham, 259-61; terms of alliance for Unionist Free Fooders with, 263; and Unionist Free Traders, 263, 342; at Oldham, 265, 271, 300; Lord Hugh Cecil and WSC and, 267-8; tactics of, 272; and Ludlow election, 273 *n*; Free Trade and Home Rule, 274; WSC attracted to, 275, 279-81; Trevelyan approaches WSC, 279-81; prospects of, 283; in danger from Capital and Labour, 285; WSC 'thanked God for a', 298; in 1887 and 1894, 299; at Preston and Cardiff, 303; in Isle of Wight, 303, 321; and Seely, 321; Eastern Counties candidates at Huntingdon, 321; wish to gain WSC, 331; and electoral reform, 362; WSC (1904) expects 'gigantic victory' at next election for, 367; sweeping victory in General Election (Jan 1906), 426, 427, 492; regarded by Boers as friendly, 560; some Liberals supported Labour at Cockermouth, 574 & *n*; and Chinese slavery, 595 *n*; their achievements when in power, 703-4; and Labour (Nov 1907), 708; seats lost to Conservatives in by-elections (Jan–Sep 1908), 770 *n*; and Labour Party in 1908, 784; *Manchester Guardian* and, 849-50; and Lords' Veto, 1003 (*see also* House of Lords: Veto); and reform of House of Lords, 1078; approves WSC's conduct at Tonypandy, 1215; and undesirable aliens, 1244; and foreign policy (1911/12), 1359; and concessions to Ulstermen, 1419; and Canada, 1627;

Lloyd George, David—*continued*

11–12, 14, 15, 18, 19, 20; Massingham on, 11–12; at Birmingham (18 Dec 1901, 'pro-Boer'), 103, 104; a critic of Chamberlain's policy, 233; and 'A Feast of Pigs', 233, 234; and WSC on political issues, 281–5; and Bishop of St Asaph, 282; and religious education in schools, 282–3; and a 'positive programme', 284; his triple representation, 284; Lord Hugh Cecil's views on his policies, 298–9, 299 (*bis*); and Seely, 321; his 'proposition' (July 1904), 353; and cartoon in *Pall Mall Gazette* (Apr 1905), 390 *& n*; accused by Rosebery of misunderstanding Liberal foreign policy, 391; has some 'jingoism' in him, 392; invites WSC to lunch at Reform Club, 409; and Kearley at BoT, 415; averts a railway strike, 703 *& n*, 716, 722; loses a daughter, 716, 718 *& n*, 722; his 'triumph' (Autumn 1907), 707; Margot Asquith on his Press campaign, 771–2; protests to Asquith about accusation of breach of trust, 773; congratulates WSC on his engagement, and says his (WSC's) Swansea speech was 'tiptop' and pleased the Germans, 812–13; and the armaments race, 814; told not to discuss naval armaments in Berlin, 836; visiting WSC, with Birrell (Oct 1908), 843; Lady Frances Balfour and Margot Asquith on, 851; and Labour Exchanges, 860; and Naval Estimates (1909), 868–9; and his Finance Bill (1909), 869; his parliamentary programme for 1909/10, 869; and Railway Conference (1908–9), 870 *n*; and House of Lords reform, 873; accused by Alfred Lyttelton of betraying Cabinet secrets, 881; advised by WSC on his Development Fund (and plans), 885–6; and Friendly Societies, 894; WSC on counteracting trade depressions, 895–8; and on payment of death duties in land, 904–5; Horsfall on his (LlG's) financial proposals, 905; WSC and (difference in attitude), 917;

Lloyd George, David—*continued*

Fisher and, 931 (*bis*), 932, 933 (*bis*); and naval shipbuilding programme, 934–7 *passim*; going to Cannes, 937; and Dreadnoughts, 938, 954; in House of Commons, 976, 984 (*bis*), 993, 1009 (*bis*), 1015, 1100, 1101, 1104, 1214; and Lords' Veto and Liberal Party, 1003; and Joseph Chamberlain (compared), 1003; and naval expenditure, 1015, 1129; invited by the King to Balmoral, 1021–2; invites WSC and wife to Criccieth, 1023; on political situation of Liberal Party (1910), 1023–4; admires WSC, 1024; advises travel by day-train, 1024; WSC's thanks for hospitality and appreciation of Wales, 1024; WSC on home and foreign politics and Home Rule, 1024–5; and Morley's contemplated 'detachment', 1026; WSC on Cabinet proceedings, 1041–2; on Budget Resolutions (his weak voice), 1049; his financial measures (1911), 1051; and social insurance scheme, 1064; and unemployment insurance, 1069, 1253 (*see also* National Insurance Bill (1911)); and Insurance Bill, 1100; and malingering, 1101; his salary (as Ch of Ex) under discussion, 1079; his speech at Mansion House on Morocco (July 1911), 1106 *n*, 1107, 1109; on 'payment of Members', 1113; 'cool, businesslike and conciliatory', 1116; WSC on a friendly Belgium (Aug 1911), 1118–19, 1120–21; Ottley sends him 'Military Needs of the Empire' (secret), 1119; and European situation, 1121–2; WSC on international situation, 1124–5; and prospect of war, 1125–6; asked by WSC to help in South Wales coal strike and riots, 1210–11; and Pretyman (on Valuation), 1214; and WSC on working conditions in mines, 1247–8; and Carnarvon Castle (Investiture) and golf, 1253–4; and local taxation (rates), 1254; and railway and dock strikes (Aug 1911), 1279, 1287, 1288

Marjoribanks, Edward, *see* Tweedmouth

Markham, Lieut.-General Sir Edwin, 160 & *n*

Marlborough, Charles, 9th Duke of ('Sunny'), s.b.

and Anti-Ritualism, xxviii; received into Church of Rome, xxviii *n*; WSC and his optimism about South African War, 96 *n*; on Leicester meeting, and cost of hunting, 96–7; and Chamberlain 'gone mad', 191–2; and Free Food League, 203; regrets WSC's opposition to Protection, 204–5; and his (WSC's) defection, 205; Under-Secretary of State for the Colonies, 219 & *n*; spoke well in House of Lords, 219; declines hon. membership of Oldham Conservative Club, 301–2; and Lord Hugh Cecil at Blenheim, 326, 327, 331, 345; and Lady Randolph's affairs, 383; and WSC's illness, 408; on WSC's appointment to Colonial Office, 421; WSC suggests as possible Governor-General of Australia, 437; and 'opening fanfaronade' of WSC's biography of Lord Randolph, 477; on *Daily Telegraph's* review of the biography, 487 & *n*; protests to *Daily Telegraph*, and the response, 487–9, 489; proposes a public affront to 'Levi Lawson', 488–9; congratulates WSC on the biography, offers some criticism, and discusses the *Daily Telegraph's* apology and public reactions to the 'fracas', 489–90; and Colonial Office 'statecraft', 557; and Royal Commission on freight charges to South Africa, 568; separated from his wife (Consuelo), 588; Lord Hugh Cecil's comments on this, 588–9; on WSC's letting his house to Sievier, 683; lonely, 706; looking ill, 717; trying to let Blenheim, 723; wants to meet WSC in Paris, 730, 734, 739; invites WSC and his fiancée to Blenheim, 798, 799; spoke at Jack Churchill's wedding breakfast, 800; WSC on his broken marriage (with Consuelo), 800; and Lady Blanche Hozier, 801; congratu-

Marlborough, Charles, 9th Duke of —*continued*

lates WSC on his engagement, will be his Trustee but will not attend the wedding, 809–10; godfather to Diana Churchill, 902; WSC prays the King to allow his cousin (Charles 9th Duke of Marlborough) to be allowed to attend reception at Windsor Castle after Chapter of Order of Garter in St George's Chapel (10 June 1911), 1082–3; HM agrees, 1083; thrice Mayor of Woodstock, 1082; WSC on his abilities, qualities and political prospects, 1082; to speak on Vote of Censure and Parliament Bill, 1109; and Rufus Isaacs, 1224; at Portland naval base, 1529, 1530; his shoulder 'electrified', 1530; in Paris (Nov 1912) recuperating, on international situation, and sending WSC a bath-gown, 1661–2; loses to Asquith at bridge, 1968; mentioned, 83, 199, 463, 587 *n*(1), 605, 670, 678, 679 (*bis*), 682, 912

Marlborough Club (London), 728

Marlborough Conservative Club, East Oldham, 216 (*bis*) & *n*

Marlborough, Duchess of (Consuelo, 1st wife of 9th Duke), xx

and her father's Derby runner to stand in Lord Rosebery's stables, 117; her illness not serious, 331; invites Lady Randolph to Blenheim (Christmas 1905), 409; alone at Blenheim, 456; separated from her husband (Charles), 588, 1082; Lord Hugh Cecil's comments, 588–9; George Cornwallis-West on, 593; to New York, 691; Lady Randolph and, 706; and King of Uganda, 707; to Blagdon, with children, 717, 729; will not meet Lady Randolph, 723, 729; congratulates WSC on his engagement, 807; mentioned, xx, 10, 35, 175, 587

Marlborough, Duchess of (Frances Anne Emily, wife of 7th Duke, 'Duchess Fanny', WSC's grandmother), 490

North Mimms (Herts), 408, 409
North Sea, 1549, 1566–9 *passim*, 1572–5
passim, 1578, 1593 (*bis*), 1616, 1725,
1772, 1773
British and German naval strengths in
(Apr 1914) compared (*according to
Home Secretary's dispositions*), 1575–7;
discussed in CID, 1597 *passim*, 1605,
1606; 3–2 standard in, 1605 (*bis*)
Northampton (parliamentary constituency), 784 (*bis*)
Northbrook, Thomas Baring, 1st Earl of,
33 & *n*, 975, 1367
Northcliffe, Viscount (*formerly* Sir Alfred
Harmsworth, *q.v.*), s.b.
to WSC on his libel action against
Manchester Courier, and WSC's reply,
791–2; congratulates WSC on his engagement, 805; to WSC on Canada
and its Imperial connection, 843–4;
WSC requests *The Times* to report him
at Dundee (3, 4, & 5 Oct 1911), 1127;
has arranged for WSC's Dundee
speeches to be reported in *The Times*
and *Daily Mail*, criticizes WSC's
colleagues, and comments on Germany's bluff and France's recovery
since 1870, and on his newspapers and
Germany, 1127; warns WSC of
imminence of war, 1336–7; on sup-
pression of news of naval (and military)
movements, 1348–9; holding back
news about German naval scheme,
1524; on Ambassadors and Foreign
Ministers and the Press, 1524; urges
WSC to visit Canada, 1626–8; and
treatment of Liberal journalists by
Liberal Party, with WSC's comments,
1628–9; will go in a submarine, 1740,
1747; to WSC on Marconi scandal,
1740, 1741, 1747; and on WSC's
nephew abroad, 1741; WSC on
George Cornwallis-West's transactions
in Marconi shares, 1746–7; to WSC,
on Service aviation, 1880; mentioned,
657, 902
Northcote, Sir Henry Stafford, *Senior*
(*later* 1st Earl of Iddesleigh), 103
n(2), 113 & *n*, 464

Northcote, Sir Henry Stafford, *Junior*
(*later* Baron Northcote *and* 2nd Earl
of Iddesleigh), 437 *n*(3), 613 & *n*
Northern Nigeria, *see* Nigeria
Northumberland, 6th Duke of, 159 *n*(2)
Northumberland, Henry George Percy,
7th Duke of, 76 *n*, 96 *n*, 159 &
n(2)
Norway, coast of, 1652
Norway, Queen of, 698 & *n*
Norwich (parliamentary constituency),
283 (*bis*)
by-election (15 Jan 1904) and result,
293, 302 & *n*; WSC's comments, 303
Norwich, Dean of, 1216
Nottingham, 25, 27, 30, 38
Nottingham, HMS, 1345
Nova Scotia Committee (for Joseph
Chamberlain's proposed visit), 1074,
1617
'Novelle', *see* German Navy Laws
Nuneham Park, Oxford, 798, 799, 800,
1511
Nuremberg (Nürnberg), 911

OFS, *see* Orange Free State
ORC, *see* Orange River Colony
Oakfield Lodge, Ashtead (Surrey), 834
Oban (Scotland), 1555, 1732, 1733
O'Brien, William, 974 & *n*, 999, 1004,
1009, 1402
O'Connell, Daniel, 1398 *n*
O'Connor, Judge: his separate report to
Local Taxation Commission, 369
O'Connor, Thomas Power, 989 &*n*
and Commission on Liverpool riots
(1911), 1287; will speak in Dundee
after Carson, 1401–2; suggests Nation-
alists would rather postpone Home
Rule than agree to partition, 1402;
and the Four Counties and Carsonism,
1405
Oedipus Rex (Sophocles), 1499
Offenders, petty and habitual, 1199–
1202
Officers, naval, *see* Naval
Ogilvy, Mr (an early aviator), 1889
O'Gorman, Mervin, 1910 & *n*
O'Grady, (Sir) James, 1036 & *n*

Oil (as fuel for the Fleet), 1926–65:
advantages of oil-burning ships, 1822;
Sir Marcus Samuel and Fisher on
internal-combustion engines, 1926–7;
WSC on need for oil, 1928; Royal
Commission on, *see* Royal Commission;
Diesel engines for ships, 1928, 1931;
WSC to Fisher, seeking his help, 1929;
sources of oil, 1927, 1930, 1938, 1939,
1940, 1943–4, 1945–7, 1948, 1951–5
passim, 1962–4; oil-tankers, 1931–2;
Oil Fuel Reserve, *q.v.*, 1932–4; 'Oil
demands oil-engines' (Fisher), 1935;
Californian, 1939 (*bis*), 1951, 1953,
1955; WSC on war consumption of
oil in HM ships, 1941–3; 100,000 tons
to be ordered (June 1913), payment to
be deferred, 1944; WSC's Memo (4
July 1913) on proposed arrangement
with A-POC for supply of fuel oil, and
Indian Government, 1945–7; WSC to
Grey on buying oil from A-POC, 1948;
Fisher's advice, 1949; and Deterding,
see Deterding; WSC to Fisher, on first
interim report of Royal Commission,
1951–2; improves by keeping, 1952;
responsibility for fixing standard of oil
reserves, 1952, 1953; uncertainty of
yield of oilfields, 1953; WSC on excessive consumption of oil by destroyers
(Sep 1913), 1954; WSC to Fisher, on
Report of Royal Commission and on
prolonging its life, 1957, 1961; on
Moore and oil-engines, 1957; *Morning
Post* article on Oil Fuel to be sent to
Fisher, 1961; and Beresford's influence, 1961; WSC to Sir Frederick
Black, on earlier delivery of Deterding's
oil, 1961; WSC's Memo on proposed
Agreement with A-POC (11 May
1914), 1962–4; Sir Edward Grey
on Persia as a source of oil, 1964;
WSC on Treasury and A-POC,
1964–5
Oil Fuel Reserve (for the Navy), 1932–4,
1952, 1953
Oil-burning ships, advantages of, 1822
Oilfields, uncertainty of yields of (Deter-
ding), 1953

Old Age Pensions, 184, 186, 721, 821
in Ireland, 998
Old Etonians Memorial Hall (Rosebery's project), 139 & *n*
Olde, Admiral Sir John, 1965
Oldham (Lancashire, WSC's first parliamentary constituency):
by-election (1899), 5 *n*(1); Co-opera-
tive Hall (9 Oct 1901), 38; Mayor's
banquet (9 Nov 1901), 39; Congrega-
tional Church Bazaar (12 Nov 1901),
39; WSC at, 91, 165, 256; and the
(Boer) war, 91, 166; bazaar at, 99–100;
missed, 102; resolution (Radical) on
Corn Tax and Education Bill (1902),
122 & *n*; WSC explains his position,
180–2; Marlborough Conservative
Club (East Oldham), 216 *n*; WSC's
meetings at, 217; Free Traders at, 222;
WSC expounds his views on 'Protection', 228–31; WSC's meeting in
Unity Hall (21 Oct 1903), 235, 237,
238, 239–40, 241–2, 243; Lord Goschen at, 235; position complicated at,
258–9, 261, 272; Press Association and,
279; WSC's candidature at, 305–8
passim, 325, 327, 328; WSC declares
his political position, with suggestions,
261–3; three parties at, 271; WSC
still interested in, 300; WSC to speak
on Education Bill at (Oct 1902), 445;
mentioned, xxviii–xxix, 5, 8, 9, 17
(*bis*), 18, 29 *n*(1), 30 & *n*(7), 31, 33, 34,
68, 70, 82, 83, 123, 124, 161–3 pass.,
165, 173, 221, 224, 232, 244, 246, 247,
256, 257, 265, 268, 269, 270, 283, 285,
287, 288, 289–92 pass., 293–4, 301,
304, 330–1, 337, 344, 906
Oldham Association for the Deaf and
Dumb, 100
Oldham Chronicle, 169
Oldham (Lancs) Conservative Association:
General Meeting (23 Oct 1902), 162;
General Meeting (14 Oct 1903), resolution supporting Balfour's policy,
237–8; WSC declares his political
position, with suggestions, to GP Committee, 261–3; and WSC's Free Trade